CATACLYSM

Also by David Stevenson

The Outbreak of the First World War:
1914 in Perspective

Armaments and the Coming of War:
Europe, 1904–1914

The First World War
and International Politics

French War Aims
against Germany, 1914–1919

CATACLYSM

The First World War as Political Tragedy

D A V I D   S T E V E N S O N

A Member of the Perseus Books Group
New York

Books published by Basic Books are available at special discounts for bulk
purchases in the United States by corporations, institutions, and other
organizations. For more information, please contact the Special Markets
Department at the Perseus Books Group, 11 Cambridge Center,
Cambridge MA 02142, or call (617) 252-5298, (800) 255-1514 or e-mail
special.markets@perseusbooks.com.

Designed by Lisa Kreinbrink

Library of Congress Cataloging-in-Publication Data

Stevenson, D. (David), 1954–
    Cataclysm : the First World War as political tragedy / David Stevenson.
        p.   cm.
    Includes bibliographical references and index.
    ISBN 0-465-08184-3
    1. World War, 1914-1918.   I. Title.
D521.S83 2004
940.3—dc22

                                                                    2003028029

04 05 06 / 10 9 8 7 6 5 4 3 2 1

This book is dedicated with respect and affection to my parents-in-law, Ida and Morris Myers, to my mother, Moira Stevenson, and to the memory of my father, Edward Stevenson.

CONTENTS

Part Three
OUTCOME

Part Four
LEGACY

Maps

ABBREVIATIONS

AC Austen Chamberlain Papers, Birmingham University Library
AEF American Expeditionary Force
AIF Australian Imperial Force
AMTC Allied Maritime Transport Council
AOK Armee Oberkommando (Austro-Hungarian high command)
ASL Auxiliary Service Law
BA-MA Bundesarchiv-Militärarchiv, Freiburg im Breisgau
BDFA British Documents on Foreign Affairs
BEF British Expeditionary Force
CAS Chief of the Admiralty Staff
CCAC Churchill College Archive Centre, Cambridge
CGS Chief of the General Staff
CGT Confédération générale du travail (French trade-union centre)
CGW Comrades of the Great War
CIAMAC Conférence internationale des associations des mutilés et des anciens combattants
CID Committee of Imperial Defence
CIGS Chief of the Imperial General Staff
CPI Committee on Public Information
CUP Committee of Union and Progress
DCG Deputy Commanding General (Germany)
DDP Deutsche Demokratische Partei
DORA Defence of the Realm Act
EEF Egyptian Expeditionary Force
EMA Etat-major de l'armée (French general staff)
EPD Excess Profits Duty
FO Foreign Office
FOCP Foreign Office Confidential Print
FOO Forward Observation Officer

GGS Great General Staff (Grosser Generalstab–Germany)
GHQ General Headquarters
GNP Gross National Product
GQG Grand Quartier général (French high command)
IRA Irish Republican Army
ISB International Socialist Bureau
ISNTUC International Secretariat of National Trade Union Centres
IWC Imperial War Cabinet
IWGC Imperial War Graves Commission
IWM Imperial War Museum
KDL Kyffhäuserbund der deutschen Landeskriegerverbände
KPD Kommunistische Partei Deutschlands
KRA Kriegsrohstoffabteilung
KÜA Kriegsüberwachungsamt
LC Liddle Collection, Leeds University Library
LHCMA Liddell Hart Centre for Military Archives
MFGB Miners' Federation of Great Britain
MRC Military Revolutionary Committee
NAA Northern Arab Army
NADSS National Association of Discharged Soldiers and Sailors
NFDDSS National Federation of Discharged and Demobilized Soldiers and
    Sailors
NLS National Library of Scotland
NNP Net National Product
NOT Netherlands Overseas Trust
N.S. New Style
NUWSS National Union of Women's Suffrage Societies
NWAC National War Aims Committee
OHL Oberste Heeresleitung (German High Command)
O.S. Old Style
PMR Permanent Military Representatives (of SWC)
PRC Parliamentary Recruiting Committee
PSI Partito socialista italiano
RFC Royal Flying Corps
RKK Reichsband der Kriegsbeschädigten und ehemaligen Kriegsteilnehmer
RMO Regimental Medical Officer
SBR Small Box Respirator
SFIO Section française de l'Internationale ouvrière (French socialist party)
SHA Service historique de l'armée de terre, Vincennes
SKL Seekriegsleitung
SPD Sozialdemokratische Partei Deutschlands (German Social Democratic Party)
SRs Socialist Revolutionaries (Russia)
SWC Supreme War Council
TF Territorial Force
TUC Trades Union Congress
UDC Union of Democratic Control

UF Union fédérale

UGACPE Union des grandes associations contre la propagande ennemie

UNC Union nationale des combattants

USPD Unabhängige Sozialdemokratische Partei Deutschlands (German independent socialists)

VDK Volksbund deutscher Kriegsgräberfürsorger

WIB War Industries Board

WO War Office

WSPU Women's Social and Political Union

NOTE ON MILITARY
AND NAVAL TERMINOLOGY

IN 1914 A FULL-STRENGTH *infantry division* in the German army comprised 17,500 officers and men, 72 artillery pieces, and 24 machine guns; in the French army 15,000 officers and men, 36 artillery pieces, and 24 machine guns; in the British army 18,073 officers and men, 76 artillery pieces, and 24 machine guns. These were regulation strengths, and combat strengths after campaigning began were almost invariably lower. During the war most armies reduced regulation strengths while increasing firepower. However, the American divisions deployed to France in 1917 were much larger than the European norm: c. 28,000 officers and men each.

An *army corps* normally comprised two infantry divisions, and an *army* two or more army corps. An *army group* (to be found in the French and German armies after 1914, and the approximate equivalent of the north-western and south-western 'fronts' found in the Russian army) comprised a number of armies, totalling from 500,000 to over 1 million men. Conversely, the normal components of infantry divisions were *brigades* (4–5,000 men), *regiments* (2–3,000), *battalions* (600–1,000), *companies* (1–200), *platoons* (30–50), and *squads* or *sections* (8–11 men).

A *cavalry division* in the German army in 1914 comprised 5,200 officers and men, 5,600 horses, 12 artillery pieces, and 6 machine guns; in the British army 9,269 officers and men, 9,815 horses, 24 artillery pieces, and 24 machine guns.

Artillery pieces (usually referred to in the text as 'guns') were divided into *cannon* (long barrel with a flat/horizontal trajectory for the projectile) and *howitzers* or *mortars* (short barrel and curved/plunging trajectory). They were also categorized by their calibre (the diameter of the barrel bore), although many British guns were named after the weight of their ammunition. Thus the standard light cannon ('field gun') was the 75mm in the French army, the 77mm in the German army, and the 18-pounder in the British army. Medium field howitzers included the German 120mm and 150mm, and (after 1915) the French 155mm and the British 6-inch.

Heavier field cannon were generally over 170mm in calibre; heavier howitzers ranged from 200mm to 400mm. They included the fortress-smashing Austrian 305 mm and the German 420mm.

Machine guns were divided into heavy and light models. All those in use in 1914 were heavy, weighing at least 40–60kg and needing a crew of three to six men to operate them. Light (9–14kg) machine guns were developed during the war, and could be carried by one man or mounted on an aircraft.

The most powerfully armed warships in 1914 are referred to in the text as 'capital ships'. They comprised *battleships* and *battlecruisers*. Battlecruisers carried comparable artillery to battleships, but were faster because they were more lightly armoured. The most modern capital ships were known as 'dreadnought' battleships or battlecruisers (c. 17,000 tons or more in displacement) if they had speed and firepower comparable to or greater than those of HMS *Dreadnought* (1906). However, in 1914 most navies operated both dreadnought and pre-dreadnought capital ships (or hybrid variants). *Cruisers* were divided into heavy (or 'armoured') cruisers (over 10,000 tons), intended to fight as scouting vessels in fleet actions alongside capital ships, and light cruisers (2,000–14,000 tons), less heavily protected and intended to guard trade routes or colonial outposts. *Destroyers* (500–800 tons in 1914) were normally deployed in flotillas and armed with torpedoes as well as light guns.*

---

*Sources: Barnett, *Swordbearers*, p. 363; Pope and Wheal, *Macmillan Dictionary of the First World War*; information from Professor MacGregor Knox.

INTRODUCTION

WHY STILL REMEMBER the eleventh of November? Why commemorate the nearly ten million military dead of 1914–18 when twenty million across the world lost their lives in road accidents between 1898 and 1998 and over thirty million in the influenza pandemic of 1918–19?[1] In part the answer is that the First World War took on characteristics that made it emblematic of other modern wars, extending through the twentieth century and beyond. It visited horrific new experiences on the combatants and forced unprecedented mobilization on their home fronts. As well as being a disaster in its own right it became the precondition for further disasters, including the Second World War, whose casualties numbered millions more. It compelled the creation of new social coping mechanisms in the face of mass death, mutilation, and bereavement, and yet in many regions of the world its legacies fuel bloodshed to this day. Finally, it was a cataclysm of a special kind, a manmade catastrophe produced by political acts, and as such can still a century later both raise powerful emotions and prompt disturbing questions as a portent. Its victims died neither from an unseen virus nor from mechanical failure and individual fallibility. They owed their fate to deliberate state policy, decided on by governments that repeatedly rejected alternatives to violence and commanded not merely acquiescence but also active support from millions of their peoples. Contemporaries on both sides at once hated the slaughter and yet felt unable to disengage from it, embroiled in a tragedy in the classical sense of a conflict between right and right.

When the war descended on a peaceful continent it seemed a reversion to the primitive, an atavistic upsurge of inter-ethnic violence. Yet it engulfed the richest and most technologically advanced societies of the day, transformed by industrialization, democratization, and globalization since the most recent comparable upheaval, the campaigns against Napoleon a century previously. It became the prototype for a new model of conflict. The four years of fighting witnessed a most remarkable military revolution, in which both sides fumbled for – and eventually discovered – far more effective methods of employing modern weapons. Especially after the failure of the pre-prepared plans, contemporaries were intensely aware of the war's novelty and the paucity of historical precedents for it. Many sensed that their statesmen and generals were out of their depth. Yet the struggle did not begin, nor was it prolonged, because of accident or blind fate, and it is misleading to portray it as a sacrificial totem devouring Europe's children which those in authority were powerless to assuage. Even if no government controlled the international system as a whole, each could still decide for its own country between war and peace. As the Prussian military theorist Carl von Clausewitz had concluded from his meditations on the Napoleonic era, warfare contains an inherent impulse towards ever greater destructiveness and yet paradoxically is also a political act, a product both of supercharged emotions and of reason and will.[2]

The 1914–18 war was a colossal upheaval and the literature it has generated is correspondingly massive. Major new syntheses and reinterpretations have appeared in recent years – a symptom of the struggle's enduring fascination – but the outpouring of research and specialist literature still runs ahead of them. Debates apparently resolved and even ossified have been revisited, and events that seemed familiar have regained their freshness and strangeness. Any attempt to write a general history therefore faces the dilemma of what to leave out. The essence of war lies in injury and suffering, in the capture, maiming, and killing of human beings and the destruction of their property, however fertile the English language may be in euphemisms to disguise the fact. Characteristically also, warfare is a reciprocal process, a competition in cruelty, which may turn even the most peaceable of men into killers as well as victims.[3] To cite Clausewitz again, 'War is thus an act of force to compel our enemy to do our will'.[4] In what follows I have tried neither to forget this essence, nor to obviate the conflict's overwhelming impact on the lives of individuals, which other authors have movingly recaptured.[5] None the less, I have sought to represent it as a totality, and therefore emphasized the underlying processes and decisions that equipped millions of men with devastating firepower, set them in mortal combat against each other, and held them in the most appalling conditions for year after year. The four parts of this book concentrate on why the violence started, why it escalated, how it ended, and the nature of its impact. Especially in the second of these sections it employs a thematic treatment in analysing the conflict's underlying dynamics, but it seeks to respect the larger pattern of chronological development. Men and women at the time made history without hindsight, and to unfold the narrative of events is essential both for conveying its extraordinary drama and as a first key to understanding.

Like others who have written about these matters I do so in part because my own family was bound up in them. My grandfather, John Howard Davies, enlisted in November 1914 and served with the Royal Welch Fusiliers and the South Wales Borderers. In 1916 he was wounded by gunshot near Neuve Chapelle and in 1917 by shrapnel near Ypres. He was a phlegmatic man, but sixty years later, with the clarity of recall that accompanies age, the Western Front still occupied his mind on the day before he died. Enid Lea, to whom he became engaged before his active service and whom he married after it, was less reticent: the war was 'awful . . . awful'. My father, Edward Stevenson, who served in the Second World War, awoke my interest in its predecessor by giving me, when I was fourteen, a copy of A. J. P. Taylor's *The First World War: an Illustrated History*. Although in what follows

I have qualified Taylor's interpretations, I remain enormously indebted to him, as well as to the landmark (and recently re-released) BBC television history of *The Great War*. Necessarily, however, a synthesis such as this rests on the work of dozens of other historians, often of outstanding quality. I have deliberately kept the notes to each chapter limited, but they are intended to acknowledge those obligations that it would be invidious to single out here, and to direct the curious towards further reading.

Among the other debts I have incurred are those to the Service historique de l'armée at Vincennes, the Bundesarchiv-Militärarchiv at Freiburg im Breisgau, the Liddle Hart Centre for Military Archives in King's College London, the Liddell Collection in Leeds University Library, the manuscripts section of Birmingham University Library, Churchill College Archive Centre, the Public Record Office (now renamed The National Archives), and the Imperial War Museum. I would also like to thank the students who have taken my course on 'The Great War, 1914–1918' at the London School of Economics and Political Science and my colleagues in the Department of International History, especially Dr Truman Anderson and Professor MacGregor Knox. I am indebted to Professor Roy Bridge, who read the manuscript for errors in its final stages, and to Christine Collins, for commendably thorough copy-editing. To Simon Winder of Penguin Books, who commissioned me to write this book and was unfailingly enthusiastic and constructively critical during its preparation, I am particularly grateful, as to Chip Rossetti of Basic Books for his careful reading and editorial comments. Also very helpful at Penguin were Richard Duguid and Chloe Campbell. Finally, a word of special thanks for their forbearance to the members of my family, and above all to my wife Sue, who has borne with the travails of the writing process for far too long. I hope that everyone who has assisted will share my pleasure at the volume's eventual appearance. Needless to add, for the shortcomings that remain in it I bear sole responsibility.

DAVID STEVENSON
August 2003

MAP 1. Europe in 1914

International frontiers, 1914

FINLAND

St Petersburg

DEN

Stockholm

ESTONIA

LIVONIA

LATVIA

Moscow

COUR-
LAND

Baltic
Sea

LITHUANIA

R U S S I A

EAST
PRUSSIA

Niemen

Tannenberg

WHITE
RUSSIA

Posen

Warsaw

Don

POLAND

Kiev

Kharkov

Vistula

Dnieper

Donets

GALICIA

U K R A I N E

Vienna

AUSTRIA-

Danube

Budapest

Odessa

HUNGARY

CRIMEA

Sebastopol

ROMANIA

Black Sea

BOSNIA

Belgrade

Bucharest

Sarajevo

HERZEGOVINA

SERBIA

BULGARIA

MONTENEGRO

Sofia

Sea

Constantinople

ALBANIA

O T T O M A N

GREECE

Aegean
Sea

E M P I R E

Athens

CYPRUS
(Britain)

LIBYA
(Italy)

EGYPT
(Britain)

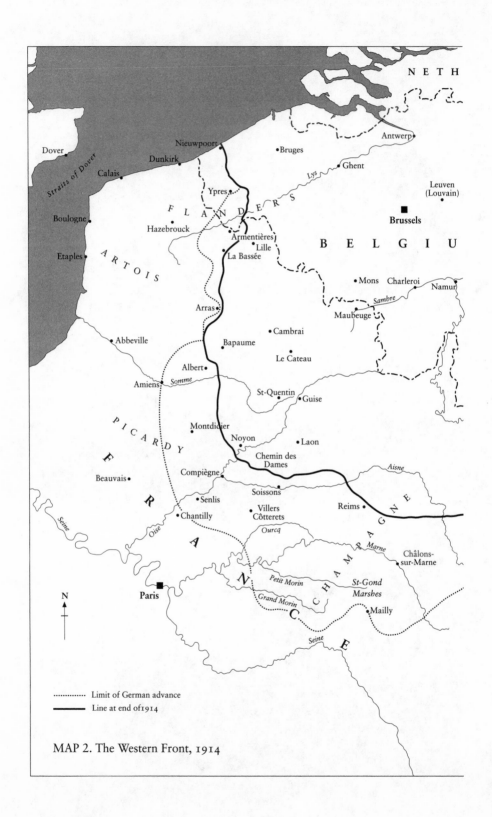

MAP 2. The Western Front, 1914

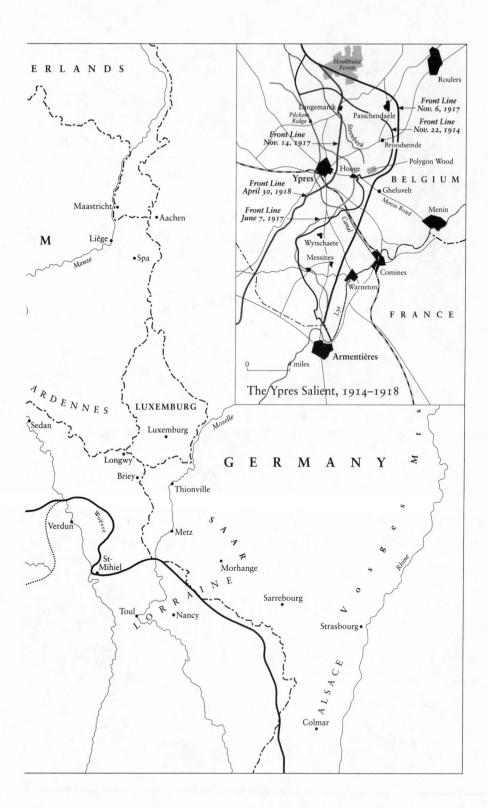

ERLANDS

Maastricht

M

Liège

Spa

Aachen

Meuse

)

ARDENNES

LUXEMBURG

Sedan

Luxemburg

Moselle

Longwy

Briey

Thionville

Verdun

Woëvre

St-
Mihiel

Metz

SAAR

Morhange

Toul

Nancy

LORRAINE

Sarrebourg

Strasbourg

ALSACE

Colmar

GERMANY

Vosges Mts

Rhine

The Ypres Salient, 1914–1918

Houlthulst Forest

Roulers

Langemarck

Pilckem Ridge

Passchendaele

Front Line
Nov. 6, 1917

Front Line
Nov. 22, 1914

Steenbeek

Front Line
Nov. 14, 1917

Broodseinde

Polygon Wood

Ypres

Hooge

BELGIUM

Front Line
April 30, 1918

Gheluvelt

Menin Road

Menin

Front Line
June 7, 1917

Canal

Wytschaete

Messines

Comines

Warneton

Lys

FRANCE

0   miles

Armentières

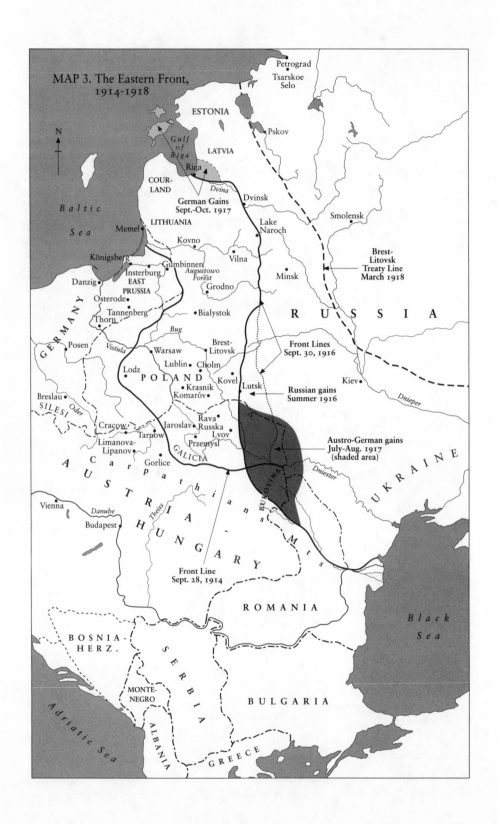

MAP 3. The Eastern Front,
1914-1918

N

Petrograd
Tsarskoe
Selo

ESTONIA

Gulf
of
Riga

Pskov

LATVIA

Riga

COUR-
LAND

Dvina

Dvinsk

Smolensk

German Gains
Sept.-Oct. 1917

Baltic

Sea

LITHUANIA

Lake
Naroch

Memel

Kovno

Vilna

Minsk

Brest-
Litovsk
Treaty Line
March 1918

Königsberg

Gumbinnen

Augustowo
Forest

Insterburg

EAST
PRUSSIA

Danzig

Grodno

Osterode

R U S S I A

Tannenberg

Bialystok

Thorn

GERMANY

Bug

Front Lines
Sept. 30, 1916

Posen

Vistula

Warsaw

Brest-
Litovsk

Lodz

Lublin

Cholm

Russian gains
Summer 1916

Kiev

POLAND

Kovel

Lutsk

Breslau

Krasnik

SILESI

Oder

Komaróv

Dnieper

Cracow

Rava
Russka

Austro-German gains
July-Aug. 1917
(shaded area)

Jaroslav

Tarnow

Lvov

Limanova-
Lipanov

Przemysl

GALICIA

Gorlice

UKRAINE

Vienna

Carpathians

BUKOVINA

Dniester

Danube

Theiss

A U S T R I A

Budapest

H U N G A R Y

Front Line
Sept. 28, 1914

Black

Sea

ROMANIA

BOSNIA-
HERZ.

S
E
R
B
I
A

MONTE-
NEGRO

BULGARIA

Adriatic Sea

ALBANIA

GREECE

MAP 4. The Balkans and the Straits

N

RUSSIA

Vienna

Danube

Budapest

AUSTRIA-
HUNGARY

TRANSYLVANIA

Dniester

BESSARABIA

Pruth

Jassy

Odessa

Sava

CROATIA

Temesvar

Belgrade

Foçsani

Ploesti

Bucharest

ROMANIA

Black
Sea

BOSNIA-
HERZ.

Cer

Kolubara

Morava

Sarajevo

SERBIA

Danube

DOBRUDJA

Constantza

MONTE-
NEGRO

Nish

Cetinje

ALBANIA

Scutari

KOSOVO

Monastir

Vardar

Sofia

BULGARIA

Bosphorus

Constantinople

ITALY

Adriatic Sea

Straits of Otranto

Valona

MACEDONIA

Salonika

Sea of
Marmora

OTTOMAN

EMPIRE

GREECE

Lemnos

Aegean

Sea

Corfu

Athens

Izmir (Smyrna)

Mediterranean Sea

The Dardanelles 1915

Maximum Allied
occupation
August 1915

Aegean Sea

Suvla
Bay

Anzac
Cove

GALLIPOLI

DARDANELLES

Chanak

Achi Baba

•Krithia

Cape
Helles

Salonika Front Line in November 1916

Salonika Front Line at the end of September 1918

MAP 5. The North Sea

N

Shetland Islands

Northern mine
barrage, 1918

NORWAY

Christiania •

Orkney
Islands

Scapa
Flow

SWEDEN

SCOTLAND

Skagerrak

Rosyth

Clyde

Battle of
Jutland,
1916

DENMARK

Copenhagen •

Dogger Bank

Battle of the
Dogger Bank,
1915

Hartlepool
Whitby
Scarborough

North

Battle of
Helgoland
Bight, 1914

Kiel
canal

Kiel

Sea

Lübeck

Liverpool

Terschelling

Wilhelmshaven

Jade
Bay

Hamburg

Texel

Bremen

Elbe

WALES   ENGLAND

HOLLAND

Jade

Harwich

Thames

The Hague

Amsterdam

Ems

Bristol

London

Weser

Zeebrugge

Dover

Ostend   Antwerp

Rhine

Portland

Straits of Dover

FLANDERS

Brussels

English Channel

BELGIUM

Paris •

Marne

LUX.

GERMANY

Seine

Rhine

Loire

FRANCE

AUSTRIA

SWITZERLAND

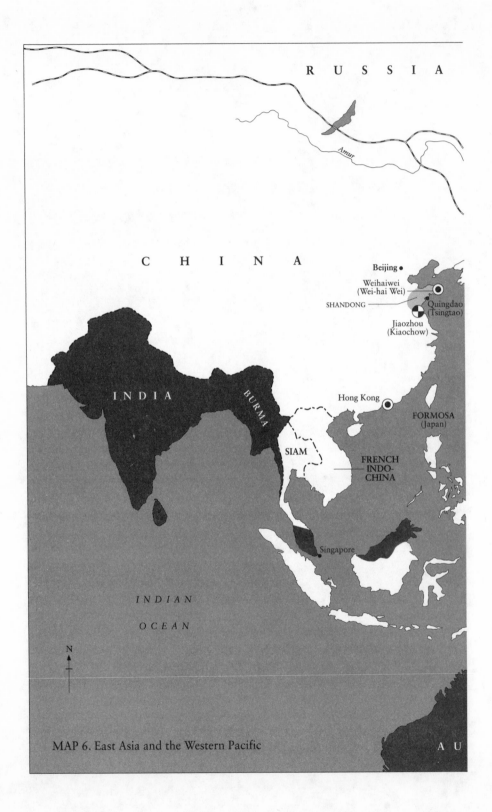

MAP 6. East Asia and the Western Pacific

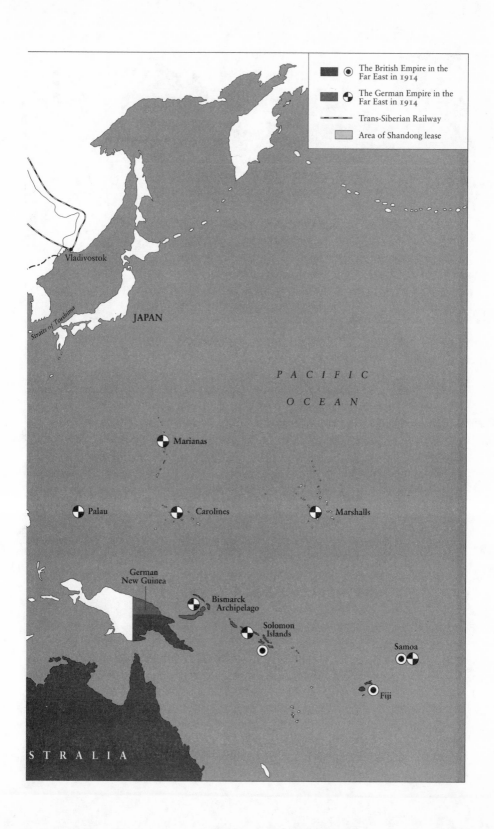

The British Empire in the
Far East in 1914

The German Empire in the
Far East in 1914

Trans-Siberian Railway

Area of Shandong lease

Vladivostok

JAPAN

Straits of Tsushima

P A C I F I C

O C E A N

Marianas

Palau

Carolines

Marshalls

German
New Guinea

Bismarck
Archipelago

Solomon
Islands

Samoa

Fiji

STRALIA

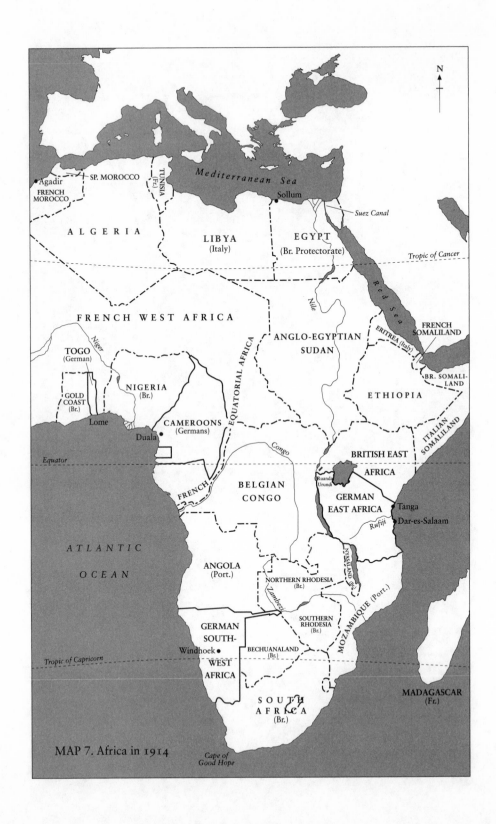

MAP 7. Africa in 1914

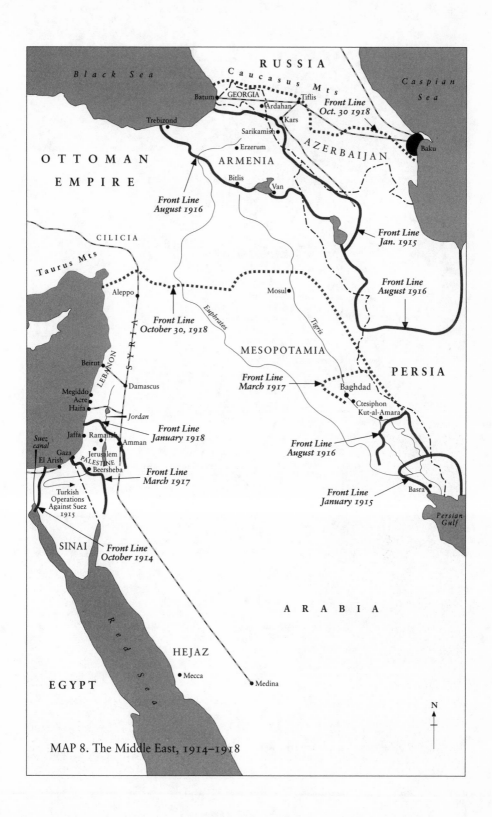

MAP 8. The Middle East, 1914–1918

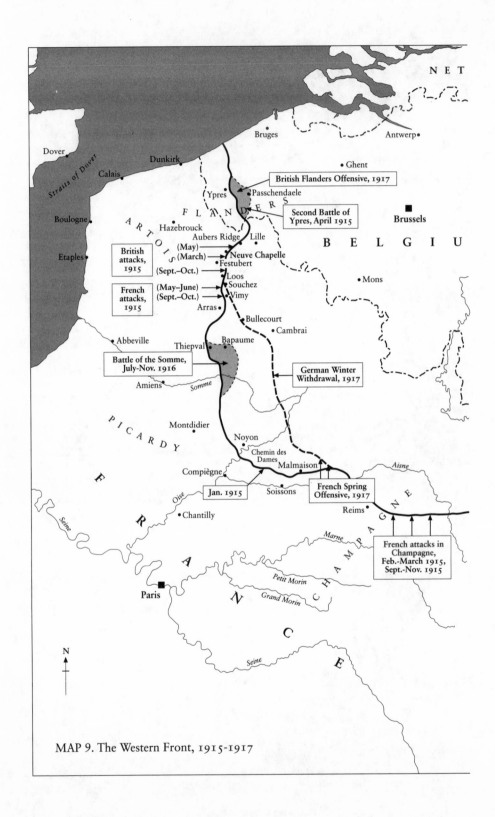

NET

Dover
Straits of Dover
Calais
Dunkirk
Boulogne
Etaples

Bruges
Ghent
Antwerp

ARTOIS
FLANDERS
Ypres
Passchendaele
British Flanders Offensive, 1917
Second Battle of Ypres, April 1915
Brussels

Hazebrouck
Aubers Ridge
Lille
(May)
(March)
Neuve Chapelle
Festubert
(Sept.–Oct.)
Loos
Souchez
Vimy

British attacks, 1915

French attacks, 1915

(May–June)
(Sept.–Oct.)
Arras

BELGIU

Mons

Bullecourt
Cambrai

Abbeville
Thiepval
Bapaume

Battle of the Somme, July–Nov. 1916

Amiens
Somme

German Winter Withdrawal, 1917

PICARDY

Montdidier
Noyon
Chemin des Dames
Malmaison
Compiègne
Soissons

Aisne

Jan. 1915

French Spring Offensive, 1917

FRANCE
Seine
Oise
Chantilly
Reims

CHAMPAGNE

French attacks in Champagne, Feb.–March 1915, Sept.–Nov. 1915

Marne
Petit Morin
Grand Morin

Paris

Seine

N

MAP 9. The Western Front, 1915–1917

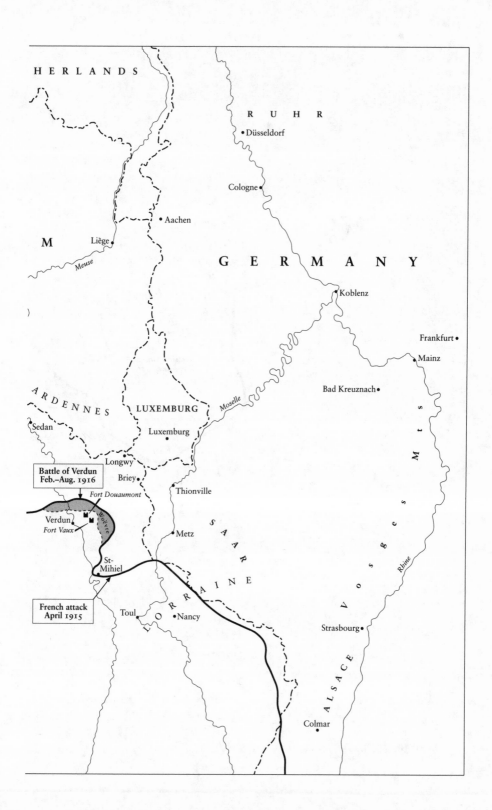

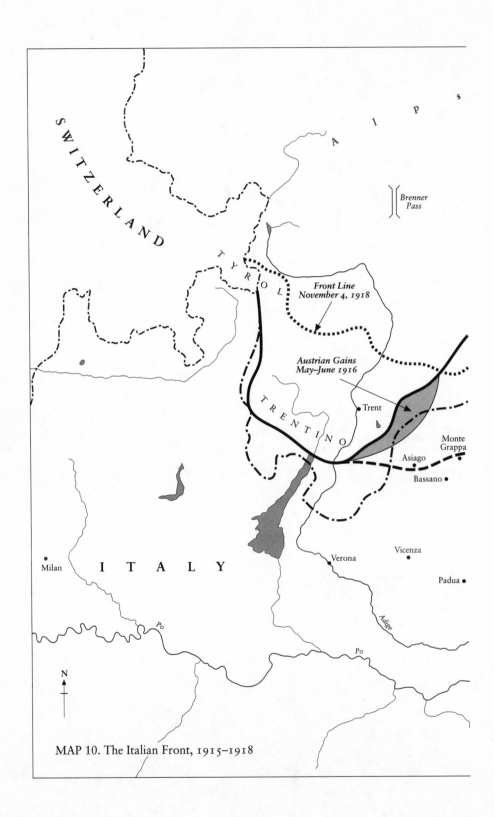

SWITZERLAND

A L P S

Brenner
Pass

TYROL

*Front Line
November 4, 1918*

*Austrian Gains
May–June 1916*

TRENTINO

Trent

Monte
Grappa

Asiago

Bassano

Vicenza

Milan

I T A L Y

Verona

Padua

Po

Adige

Po

N

MAP 10. The Italian Front, 1915–1918

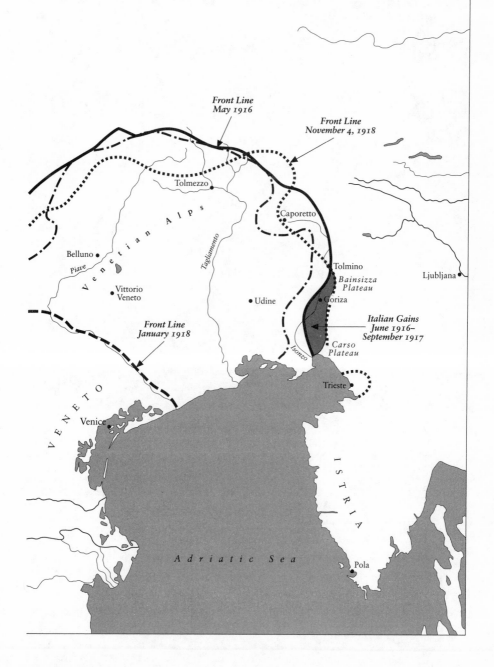

AUSTRIA – HUNGARY

Front Line
May 1916

Front Line
November 4, 1918

Tolmezzo

Caporetto

Venetian Alps

Belluno

Piave

Tagliamento

Tolmino

Bainsizza
Plateau

Ljubljana

Vittorio
Veneto

Udine

Goriza

Italian Gains
June 1916–
September 1917

Front Line
January 1918

Carso
Plateau

Isonzo

VENETO

Trieste

Venice

I S T R I A

Adriatic Sea

Pola

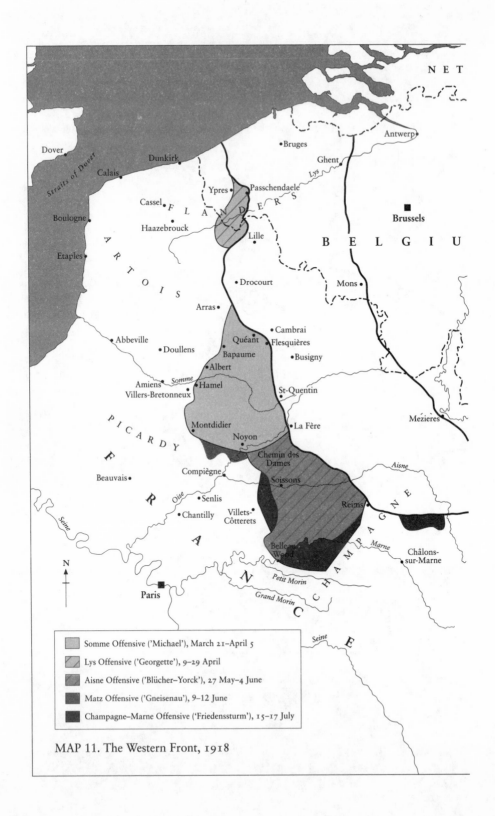

MAP 11. The Western Front, 1918

Somme Offensive ('Michael'), March 21–April 5

Lys Offensive ('Georgette'), 9–29 April

Aisne Offensive ('Blücher–Yorck'), 27 May–4 June

Matz Offensive ('Gneisenau'), 9–12 June

Champagne–Marne Offensive ('Friedenssturm'), 15–17 July

MAP 12. The Central Powers at their Zenith, 1918

Maximum extent of territory controlled
by the Central Powers, 1918

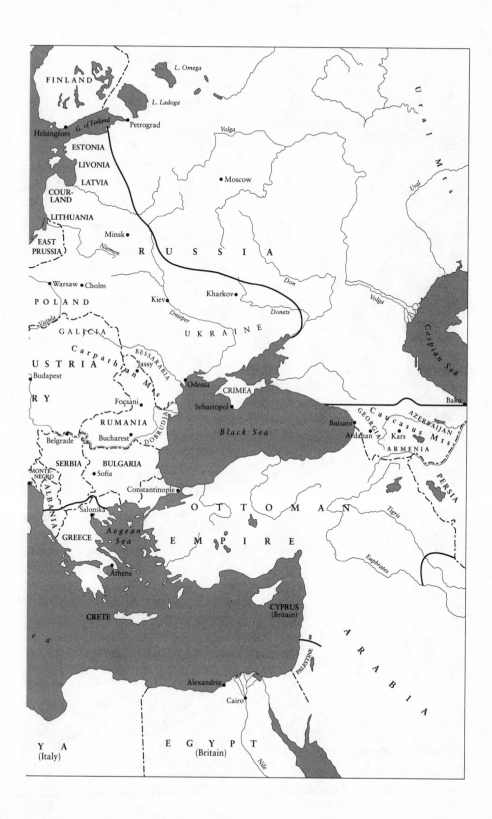

– · – · – International Frontiers, c. 1926	1. Saar Plebiscite Area (under League of Nations, 1919–35)	4. Memel Territory (to Lithuania, 1923)
– – – – International Frontiers, 1914	2. Limit of Rhineland Demilitarized Zone after 1919	5. Klagenfurt Territory (to Austria, 1920)
Rhineland Zone under Allied Occupation after 1919	3. Danzig Free City	6. Burgenland Territory (to Austria, 1921)
		7. Fiume Free State (1920–4)

N

NORWAY

FINLAND

Helsinki

Petrograd

SWEDEN

Oslo

Stockholm

Tallin
ESTONIA

North
Sea

DENMARK

Baltic
Sea

Gulf
of
Riga

Riga
LATVIA

Copenhagen

Memel
LITHUANIA

Niemen

Vilna

Danzig

EAST
PRUSSIA

POLAND

BRITAIN

The
Hague

Elbe

Berlin

Marienwerder

POLISH
CORRIDOR

Vistula

NETHERLANDS

Brussels

Posen

Warsaw

Brest-Litovsk

RUHR

GERMANY

POSEN

POLAND

BELG.

Eupen

Malmédy

LUX.

Weimar

Frankfurt

UPPER
SILESIA

Cracow

Lvov

UKRAINE

Paris

Prague

BOHEMIA

CZECHOSLOVAKIA

GALICIA

Seine

LORRAINE

BAVARIA

Danube

FRANCE

Rhine

Vienna

BUKO-
VINA

BESSARABIA

Berne

AUSTRIA

Budapest

HUNGARY

Theiss

Pruth

SWITZERLAND

SOUTH
TYROL

TRENTINO

TRANSYLVANIA

ROMANIA

Rhône

Po

Trieste

Fiume

KINGDOM OF THE
SERBS, CROATS
AND SLOVENES

Bucharest

DOBRUDJA

ITALY

Adriatic
Sea

DALMATIA

Belgrade

Danube

BULGARIA

Sofia

Mediterranean
Sea

Rome

ALBANIA

THRACE

TURKEY

GREECE

Aegean
Sea

Athens

MAP 13. The European Peace Settlement

Part One

OUTBREAK

THE DESTRUCTION
OF PEACE

TODAY TO JOURNEY almost anywhere in Western Europe is to cross a landscape moulded by prosperity and peace. Between the shopping precincts, motorways, and tower blocks built since 1950 lie the factories, railways, and tenements of nineteenth-century industrialization, and among them linger relics of an older world of churches, cottages, and palaces: a world now long since vanished. Looking out upon this landscape, a traveller might forgivably conceive of Europe's history as a broad and uneventful highway towards modern economic growth and supranational integration. And yet, between its nineteenth- and its later twentieth-century surges of expansion and prosperity the continent underwent three decades of ruin and impoverishment, of industrial stagnation and political cataclysm. That era's traces, too, are etched on the contemporary scene, though discerning them calls for keener scrutiny. Its imprint on the generation who endured it would last for the rest of their lives. It encompassed two great conflicts separated by twenty years, even if as they recede from us they seem to merge as passages in a single upheaval. It began with the war of 1914–18.

The First World War became a global struggle, but originated in Europe. It shattered a century of peace. Since the defeat of the French Revolution and Napoleon in 1792–1815 – the struggle hitherto known in English as the 'Great War'[1] – there had been no general conflict involving all the great powers. European governments and peoples were accustomed to prospective wars of the imagination, in the scenarios of military planners and the best-selling future-gazing literature that proliferated in the pre-1914 decades. They were little better equipped to face the reality than we would be a nuclear strike.[2] Yet the conventions and rituals of warfare were familiar parts of Europe's life, and the memory of previous conflicts integral to its culture. Until the eighteenth century it had known few years in which none of its great powers were engaged in fighting. Only since then had the modern pattern emerged of decades of peace punctuated by successively more total wars. Peace – even in the simple sense of the absence of killing – was a modern phenomenon, and Europe had never known anything comparable to the great peace that ended in 1914.[3]

Yet this peace was fragile. The middle decades of the nineteenth century saw five more limited armed conflicts: the Crimean War of 1854–6, the Italian War of 1859, the Seven Weeks War of 1866, the Franco-Prussian War of 1870–71, and the Russo-Turkish War of 1877–8. The Crimea claimed 400,000 lives, and the Franco-Prussian war involved pitched battles in the Western European heartland and a six-month siege and bombardment of Paris in which thousands of civilians died. Extra-European wars were even bigger. The American Civil War of 1861–5 killed 600,000 and the 1850–64 Taiping rebellion in China killed millions. In the pre-1914 years, moreover, several European powers fought sizeable wars outside the continent: Britain against the South African Boers in 1899–1902, Russia against Japan in 1904–5, and Italy against the Turks in Libya in 1911–12. The Balkan states fought first Turkey and then each other in the Balkan Wars of 1912–13. Nor did the absence of fighting exclude the danger of it, as the newspaper reading public well knew. The pre-war decades were peppered with diplomatic crises, when powers clashed over what they judged their vital interests and statesmen debated over whether to compromise or to fight.[4] Sometimes these crises were isolated incidents; at others they occurred in rapid succession as part of a general upsurge in international tension. They did so in the 1880s and did so again in 1905–14.

Only great powers can wage great wars, and six European states acknowledged each other as such: Britain, France, Russia, Austria-Hungary (divided since 1867 into 'Austrian' and 'Hungarian' halves that shared a common sovereign), Italy (created under Piedmont's leadership in 1861), and Germany (forged under Prussian dominance in 1871). Though unequal in their political influence and military might, all (at least on paper) were stronger than any of their neighbours. All owed their birth in part to violence and all were willing to use it. This willingness proved the Achilles heel of the glittering, if flawed, civilization moulded during centuries of European primacy. True, after Napoleon's defeat his victorious enemies had agreed on regular summit meetings to encourage consensus between them. But this system collapsed within a decade, and by the early twentieth century its vestiges – usually referred to as the 'Concert of Europe' – were shadowy. The Concert had no written rules or permanent institutions. It consisted of an understanding between the great powers that at times of crisis any one of them could propose a conference between their representatives. Its swansong was the London Conference of 1912–13 that convened to discuss the Balkan Wars. But in 1914 itself, though Britain proposed a conference Austria-Hungary and Germany refused. Not for the first time the system buckled under pressure, underlining its weakness. The Concert could function only when the powers agreed: it was a convenient device for saving face, but little more. Europe lacked common political institutions (and outside Europe there was no equivalent even of the Concert), and it possessed only a rudimentary framework of international law. Progressive movements, especially in Britain and America, urged the powers to settle disputes by arbitration and to humanize combat by a framework of rules. But although the

Hague Peace Conference of 1899 indeed established an international court of arbitration, governments resorted to it only when it suited them, which was rarely.[5] Similarly, although by 1914 a body of internationally ratified conventions had evolved to protect combatants and civilians during hostilities,[6] once war broke out these rules would be jettisoned.

International organization therefore did little to restrain the powers. In this respect the European system might seem an anachronistic survival from a previous era. Yet the long peace had witnessed tremendous changes, which – so optimistic commentators supposed – might make war increasingly hypothetical. Technological and economic progress had spurred on what we would now call globalization and democratization. It had also made warfare far more destructive, potentially strengthening deterrence. Yet although these new developments might influence the circumstances and conditions in which governments resorted to force, none precluded them from doing so.

The pre-1914 era was one of globalization, and levels of economic interdependence that were not repeated until well after the Second World War. North-western Europe was the epicentre of this phenomenon, which rested on the Victorian communications revolution – the railway, the telegraph, and the steamship – as well as on massive productivity increases in agriculture and manufacturing. By 1913 exports accounted for between a fifth and a quarter of British, French, and German national output. Worldwide foreign investment (more than three-quarters of it coming from Europe) almost doubled between 1900 and 1914, though whereas the continental countries exported goods and capital to each other, Britain's trade and investment lay mostly outside Europe.[7] The same years saw a tidal wave of emigration, opening up new agricultural frontiers from the pampas to the Rockies and the Australian outback, and placing Europe at the centre of a worldwide chain of economic interconnections.[8] By the decade before 1914 all the European countries had become part of a continent-wide business cycle that extended across the Atlantic.[9] France, Germany, and the Low Countries shared in the creation of an interdependent complex of heavy industries in the Rhine basin, linked by multinational enterprises, migrant workers (Poles in the Ruhr, Italians in Lorraine), and cross-border flows of coal and steel.[10]

Growing economic interdependence might have forced the powers to co-operate, yet in fact its impact was limited.[11] Governments signed international postal, telegraph, and wireless conventions and harmonized cross-border railway timetables, but their most important contribution to the new economy was not to obstruct it. Industrial recession and American grain imports drove up customs tariffs after the 1870s, but still on the eve of the First World War tariffs were lower than they would be again for decades. From the 1890s the European powers (with America and Japan) were linked in a de facto currency union, the international gold standard,[12] by whose unwritten rules their currencies were freely convertible with each other and with gold at a fixed rate. Yet this system too was established by a series of individual decisions rather than by binding multilateral agreements. Occasional ad hoc joint action by central banks sufficed to maintain it. The open world economy, like the Concert of Europe, rested on a minimum of organized co-operation, and in 1914 they perished together. Contrary to the analysis of a pre-war best-seller, Norman Angell's

The Great Illusion, financial interdependence did not make hostilities unthinkable, and the growth of an international bond market would actually facilitate war finance.[13] The admiralty in London calculated that economic warfare would hurt Germany more than Britain; and the general staff in Berlin expected Germany to continue trading with the outside world while smashing its continental enemies.

Pre-1914 globalization was not just economic. It was also cultural and political, imperial expansion being its most conspicuous manifestation. Imperialism projected Europe's rivalries worldwide. Between 1800 and 1914 the proportion of the earth's surface occupied by Europeans, whether in colonies or in former colonies, rose from 35 to 84.4 per cent.[14] If Britain entered a continental war its colonies – including the self-governing dominions – would automatically be implicated. European expansion also impinged on the remaining independent states. After Africa's partition in the 1880s, China at the turn of the century seemed destined to follow, and like the Ottoman Turkish Empire and Persia it was already divided informally into spheres of influence. Admittedly, two extra-European states had also taken on great-power attributes. The USA defeated Spain in 1898, expelling it from Cuba and the Philippines. Japan defeated Russia in 1904–5. But neither country carried much weight in European strategic assessments. Japan's economy remained backward and its armed forces were efficient but remote. America's economy was already the world's strongest, and its navy was large and modern, but Washington was expected to stay neutral in a European conflict and its army was tiny. If the European states fell out, no outside force seemed strong enough to bang their heads together.

Economic development also transformed European domestic politics. In one country after another, faced with sprawling cities and a self-conscious bourgeoisie and working class, monarchies had conceded elected parliaments and civil liberties to win more active consent from the governed. In Britain the 1832 Reform Act tried to rally the middle class behind the constitution; in the German Empire created in 1871 the Prussian monarchy coexisted uneasily with a Reichstag (or lower house of parliament) for which all men could vote; even in Russia, since 1905 the tsar had accepted an elected assembly. By 1914 European adult males were generally free to form trade unions, pressure groups, and political parties, albeit under police surveillance. Most countries had largely uncensored mass media, which essentially meant the press. Newspapers, linked by telegraph cables and news agencies to events around the globe and delivered via railways and steamships at affordable prices, were the principal channel of comment and information. Their numbers reflected it: an advanced city like Berlin had more than fifty titles, and the small and impoverished kingdom of Serbia had twenty-four dailies.[15] War and foreign policy were matters of vigorous debate.[16]

Since the disintegration in the 1990s of the soviet bloc, triumphant western political analysts have insisted that democracies never go to war.[17] This thesis was already common currency among pre-1914 liberals. Yet in fact democratization failed to eradicate armed conflict. This was partly because the process remained incomplete. France's Third Republic, established in 1870, had probably the most progressive constitution in Europe, but even here parliamentary scrutiny over diplomacy and military planning was feeble. In Austria-Hungary, Germany, and

Russia, the ruling Habsburg, Hohenzollern, and Romanov dynasties exercised wide discretionary power over foreign affairs. Moreover, if public opinion did exert an influence it might not be a peaceful one. Most continental countries had socialist parties, which (in common with middle-class progressives) opposed war except in self-defence. Centrist and right-wing parties, however, normally called for firmness in asserting national interests, and most newspapers and a plethora of pressure groups supported them. In 1914 most politicians and military chiefs recognized that a major war needed public support, but neither globalization nor democratization made hostilities unthinkable.

The third consequence of modern industrialization was to transform military technology. It did so in two main phases. The first centred on steam propulsion. From the 1840s warships converted from sail to steam (and from wooden to steel hulls), and railways transported and supplied much larger armies. After the Franco-Prussian War, in which German levies moved by rail outnumbered and overwhelmed French regulars, massive conscript armies and intensive railway building became the norm. The second phase of transformation centred on firepower. In the later nineteenth century chemical high explosives made gunpowder obsolete. Breech-loading (instead of muzzle-loading) guns with rifled barrels (i.e., machined with a spiral groove within the bore to spin the projectile) fired further, faster, and more accurately. Navies equipped their steam-powered warships with telescopic sights and quick-firing guns delivering high-explosive shells. By the early twentieth century they could fight for the first time on the high seas, far away from land, and at ranges of up to five miles.[18] Yet the 1905 Battle of Tsushima, in which Japanese gunfire annihilated a Russian fleet, was not to be a portent of the future, as another clutch of innovations – torpedoes, mines, and submarines – now made battleships more vulnerable and more reluctant to seek action. On land, a comparable firepower revolution similarly enhanced armies' destructive capacity at the price of their freedom of manoeuvre. Muskets were replaced by breech-loading rifles, which infantry could operate lying down and – once magazines and smokeless powder became standard – fire repeatedly without betraying their location. The development from the 1880s of the Maxim heavy machine gun, able to fire 600 rounds a minute, further multiplied defensive firepower. From the 1890s armies introduced the quick-firing field gun, equipped with a hydraulic piston that restrained the recoil of the barrel. It fired up to twenty high-explosive shells a minute without needing repositioning. But the field gun was as useful for the defensive as the offensive, to add to the havoc wrought by machine guns and rifles, whereas modern heavy artillery that could blast out the defenders developed much more slowly. Changes both in naval and in land technology militated against short, cheap, and decisive conflicts.

These developments should have stabilized the balance of power by making the use of force seem less attractive. In practice they did not.[19] European leaders were familiar with the notion that military preparations could deter aggression: for many years after 1870 the Germans believed their army strong enough to do so. It was not yet a commonplace, however, that hostilities would be so destructive that no one would win. The Russian banker, Ivan Bloch, indeed made this suggestion in his book, *The Future of War,* which was widely read. It foresaw a prolonged and ruinous slaughter in which the defence was stronger than the attack and which caused economic and social chaos.[20] All the same, most European armies concluded from their observations of the Russo-Japanese War that infantry could capture trenches protected by barbed wire and machine guns, provided their morale was resilient.[21] General staffs understood that a European war would be extremely bloody and was unlikely to be short, but they concealed their misgivings from their political masters.[22] When they advised against risking one, this was because they saw little chance of winning it, not because they thought technological change had made warfare obsolete. If both sides believed that war was necessary and each believed they could triumph, deterrence might break down. The new factors of globalization, popular involvement, industrialization, and scientific armaments would then make conflict all the more devastating.

Fundamental to calculations of deterrence and strategic advantage were the big alliance blocs. The core partnerships were the Austro-German alliance, signed in 1879, and the Franco-Russian one, negotiated between 1891 and 1894. These alliances were defensive, directed primarily against Russia and Germany respectively. From 1882 Italy was loosely connected with the first bloc and from 1907 Britain still more loosely associated with the second. Such long-term peacetime alignments were new to European politics, in some ways foreshadowing the decades of confrontation after 1945 between the eastern and western blocs. For many years they indeed assisted mutual deterrence, as although their terms were secret, their existence was not. They might also mean, however, that any clash between two powers would trigger a showdown between two coalitions, and they were built into the assumptions of another new phenomenon of the period: institutionalized strategic planning. Here again, the German unification wars of 1866 and 1870 set the standard. They seemed triumphs not only of technology but also of the superior preparation by the Prussian general staff under Helmuth von Moltke the Elder, its chief for a generation. In future military forces would be still larger and more complex, and to control and co-ordinate them more challenging. The other powers therefore imitated, more or less, the Prussian model, which entailed creating an elite body of officers selected by competitive examination. Some staff officers would be assigned to divisional and corps commanders to ensure their decisions reflected a standardized philosophy. Others were rotated through the general staff, where they studied military history, simulated campaigning through war games, manoeuvres, and staff rides, formulated tactical doctrine, and drew up the plans. Planning required information about potential enemies, and intelligence gathering (much of it overseen by staff officers posted abroad as military attachés) became routine. Prepared as contingency arrangements rather than necessarily being intended for application, the strategic plans might have become historical curiosities like their Cold War counterparts for nuclear exchanges across the Elbe. But their underlying assumption was that if deterrence failed it would be perfectly appropriate to use them. And in fact between 1905 and 1914 the bases of deterrence crumbled as the two great alliances moved closer to military equality while armaments competition between them intensified and political antagonism – fuelled through a succession of diplomatic crises round the Mediterranean and in the Balkans – mounted. Although neither side saw war as inevitable, both were increasingly willing to contemplate it. By 1914 Austria-Hungary felt encircled and endangered in south-eastern Europe and Germany felt similarly about the European balance as a whole. Regional conflict and general European tension came to a head together. From the interaction between them the Great War was born.

The spark came from an act of terror at Europe's storm centre.[23] On 28 June 1914 in Sarajevo, the capital of the Austro-Hungarian province of Bosnia, a nineteen-year-old Bosnian Serb, Gavrilo Princip, shot and killed the Archduke Franz Ferdinand, the heir to the Austrian throne, and the Archduke's wife, the Duchess of Hohenberg. Franz Ferdinand was an unattractive man, authoritarian, choleric, and xenophobic, but he was devoted to the Duchess, whom he had married against the wishes of the Emperor Franz Joseph, her aristocratic pedigree falling short of Habsburg requirements. Visiting Sarajevo, and the army's annual manoeuvres, would be a rare occasion when she could ride in public with him. Yet this act of kindness courted disaster. A date heavy with symbolism, 28 June was the anniversary of the Battle of Kosovo in 1389, a catastrophe for the medieval kingdom of Serbia in whose aftermath a Serb had assassinated the Turkish sultan.[24] Despite the emergence of a terrorist movement that targeted Habsburg officials, security arrangements for the state visit were extraordinarily lax. On the fateful day, despite a bomb attempt against the motor-car procession by another member of Princip's group, the Archduke continued his tour, making an unscheduled change of itinerary to console an injured victim. It brought his vehicle right by Princip, who did not miss his chance.

These details matter because although in summer 1914 international tension was acute, a general war was not inevitable and if one had not broken out then it might not have done so at all. It was the Habsburg monarchy's response to Sarajevo that caused a crisis. Initially all it seemed to do was order an investigation. But secretly the Austrians obtained a German promise of support for drastic retaliation. On 23 July they presented an ultimatum to their neighbour, Serbia. Princip and his companions were Bosnians (and therefore Habsburg subjects), but the ultimatum alleged they had conceived their plot in Belgrade, that Serbian officers and officials had supplied them with their weapons, and that Serbian frontier authorities had helped them cross the frontier. It called on Serbia to denounce all separatist activities, ban publications and organizations hostile to Austria-Hungary, and co-operate with Habsburg officials in suppressing subversion and conducting a judicial inquiry. The Belgrade government's reply, delivered just within the forty-eight hour deadline, accepted nearly every demand but consented to Austrian involvement in a judicial inquiry only if that inquiry was subject to Serbia's constitution and to international law. The Austrian leaders in Vienna seized on this pretext to break off relations immediately, and on 28 July declared war.[25] The ultimatum impressed most European governments by its draconian demands, although if Serbian complicity was indeed as alleged the substance of the document was arguably moderate. But the summary time limit gave the game away, as did the peremptory rejection of Belgrade's answer. The ultimatum had been intended to start a showdown, Serbia's skilful reply reinforcing the impression that Vienna rather than Belgrade was guilty of provocation. How far were Austria-Hungary's accusations accurate, and why was it committed to so overbearing a course?

Much of the Austrian sense of grievance was justified.[26] Although the Bosnian terrorist movement was home-grown, it did enjoy Serbian backing. After centuries of Ottoman Turkish rule, Bosnia and the neighbouring territory of Herzegovina had been transferred to Austro-Hungarian administration in 1878. Bosnia was Austria-Hungary's colonial frontier, a wild and mountainous outback to which it brought roads, schools, and a short-lived parliament. None the less, many Bosnian Serbs, who numbered 42.5 per cent of the population (another 22.9 per cent were Croats and 32.2 per cent Muslims), resented Habsburg rule.[27] In 1908–09, despite vehement protests from Serbia and a prolonged international crisis, Austria-Hungary annexed the two provinces. After the crisis Serbia promised not to permit subversive activities on its soil. Yet propaganda bodies such as the Narodna Odbrana (or 'People's Defence') continued to support Serbs outside Serbia, as did the Belgrade press, and the Black Hand ('Union or Death'), founded in 1911, a secret organization committed to unifying all Serbs by violence. The Sarajevo assassins belonged to a group known as 'Young Bosnia', largely composed of school students. They wished to destroy Habsburg authority and unite all South Slavs (including the independent states of Serbia and Montenegro and the Serbs, Croats, and Slovenes within Austria-Hungary) in a new Yugoslav federation. The Austrian ultimatum accused the Narodna Odbrana of aiding them, but the real culprit was the Black Hand, whose head, Colonel Dragutin Dimitrijević, or 'Apis', was the Serbian military intelligence chief.[28]

The Black Hand had provided Princip and his circle with their revolvers and bombs, trained them, and helped them across the border, and the Austrians were right to allege that Serbian officers and officials were parties to the plot, although the cabinet and the prime minister Nikola Pašić appear not to have been. Pašić was a political enemy of Apis, whom his government later tried and executed. The premier was tipped off that armed men had crossed the frontier, but sent the Austrians only an ambiguous warning; nor did his government condemn the assassinations.[29] In fact Serbia's army and intelligence service were out of control. The Serbian military were polarized between supporters and opponents of the conspirators (among whom Apis was a ringleader) who had murdered the previous ruler and brought King Peter Karageorgević to the throne in a coup in 1903. In 1914 Pašić was attempting to restore civilian authority, supported by Crown Prince Alexander, who took over as regent from Peter on 11 June. However, none of the Serbian factions believed the moment opportune for war. Serbia was still recovering from the Balkan Wars, which had doubled its territory and raised its population from 2.9 to 4.4 million but had also incorporated many Albanians whom the Serbs were ethnically cleansing with great savagery.[30] The army lacked rifles and the treasury was empty. But whereas Pašić wanted time to re-arm, Apis feared an Austrian preventive strike and wrongly supposed Franz Ferdinand led the Habsburg war party. In reality the Archduke was the foremost advocate of restraint.

The Serbian evidence confirms that Austria-Hungary had good grounds for rigorous demands. But it also shows that the Belgrade government was anxious for a peaceful exit from the crisis whereas the Austrians meant to use it as the pretext for violence. Austria-Hungary's joint council of ministers decided on 7 July that the ultimatum should be so stringent as to 'make a refusal almost certain, so that the road to a radical solution by means of a military action should be opened'. On 19 July it agreed to partition Serbia with Bulgaria, Albania, and Greece, leaving only a small residual state under Habsburg economic domination.[31] Yet previously Vienna had been less bellicose: the chief of the general staff, Franz Conrad von Hötzendorff, had pressed for war against Serbia since being appointed in 1906, but his appeals had been rejected. The Emperor Franz Joseph was a cautious and vastly experienced ruler who remembered previous defeats. He and his advisers moved to war only because they believed they faced an intolerable problem for which peaceful remedies were exhausted.

Austria-Hungary was by today's standards a strange regime indeed, a conglomeration of diverse territories acquired by the Habsburgs through war and marriage.[32] In contrast to Serbia it was the antithesis of the national principle, containing eleven major ethnic groups. It was only mildly repressive, but it was no Swiss-style pluralist democracy and its leaders did not want it to be. As new nationalities across Europe aspired to self-determination, its destruction seemed foreordained. The two most influential nationalities, the German- and Hungarian-speakers, numbered less than half the total. If the others broke away, they would have little incentive to stay together and the Dual Monarchy would probably disintegrate. It comprised a mosaic of political sub-systems, linked through Franz Joseph's person.

TABLE 1
Ethnic Composition of
Austria-Hungary, 1910, Millions

Germans	12.0
Magyars	10.1
Czechs	6.6
Poles	5.0
Ruthenians	4.0
Croats	3.2
Romanians	2.9
Slovaks	2.0
Serbs	2.0
Slovenes	1.3
Italians	0.7
TOTAL	50.8[33]

The *Ausgleich*, or 'Compromise', reached between Franz Joseph and the Magyars in 1867, set the ground rules. He was emperor of the Austrian lands and king of the Hungarian ones. He and his advisers ran foreign policy and the common army and navy. But the Dual Monarchy's two halves had separate parliaments, governments, budgets, and even armed forces (the latter known as the Landwehr in the Austrian half and the Honvéd in the Hungarian one). The two premiers (and the three common ministers of foreign affairs, war, and finance) met in the joint council of ministers, and representatives of the parliaments deliberated together (though not in the same chamber) as 'the Delegations'. The Reichsrat (or lower house of parliament) in the Austrian half was elected by manhood suffrage, but in 1914 it

was suspended and the government (headed by Count Karl Stürgkh) ruled by decree because it could not form a working majority. In the Hungarian half the government (headed by Stephen Tisza) was more stable but also more authoritarian.
Within the Hungarian kingdom the Croats had their own separate assembly, but
in 1912 it was suspended after a nationalist Serbo-Croat alliance won a majority,
and the legislature in Budapest itself was elected by a rigged voting system that denied representation to anyone except Magyars.

The dualist system had serious implications for foreign policy. The Hungarian
premier had to be consulted before a decision for war. The Hungarians' repression of their two and a half million Romanian-speakers in Transylvania antagonized the Romanian government, which traditionally was Vienna's one reliable
Balkan ally. Moreover, the governments of the two halves decided the common
army's size and budget, and they were parsimonious.[34] Hungarian pressure for
greater use of Magyar as the language of command caused a constitutional crisis
in 1904–06, and postponed an army bill until 1912. Increasingly, such inter-
minable stalemates bred a dangerous fatalism. Many of Franz Joseph's advisers
came to see war as the last chance to force internal reform.[35] Yet in general the political parties representing the different nationalities did not demand independence, though they did want more self-government and equal linguistic rights.
The common army remained loyal, as did the imperial bureaucracy. The Dual
Monarchy had lived with its internal dilemmas for decades, and at times in the
past they had seemed more desperate than they were in 1914.

The South Slav problem, however, was peculiarly intractable, and might set a
precedent for the other subject peoples. The Serbs, Croats, and Slovenes were beginning to co-operate as the Yugoslav enthusiasts intended. By 1914 a terrorist
campaign had started in Croatia as well as Bosnia. But the most exasperating characteristic of the agitation was Serbia's support for it, at any rate after the 1903 coup
that installed King Peter in Belgrade. Previously a secret treaty had given Austria-
Hungary a veto over Serbian foreign policy. Now Serbia became more independent and its stance more nationalist. In the 'pig war' of 1906–11 Austria-Hungary
retaliated by boycotting Serbia's exports of livestock, but the Serbs found alternative markets and turned from Vienna to Paris as their main artillery supplier. Similarly, despite Austrian hopes in 1908 that annexing Bosnia-Herzegovina would
dispel South Slav dreams of unification, covert Serb support for Bosnian separatism persisted. The next upheaval came in 1912–13, when Serbia, Bulgaria,
Greece, and Montenegro defeated Turkey in the First Balkan War before Bulgaria
attacked its former allies and was defeated in its turn in the Second. Austrian pressure limited the Serbs' success by forcing them to evacuate the Adriatic coast
(where they had hoped to win sea access) and by sponsoring the creation of Albania as a new state to counterbalance them. None the less, the wars heightened the
threat on Austria-Hungary's south-eastern borders. Turkey and Bulgaria were
weakened as potential Austrian allies, and in the second war Romania fought
alongside Serbia. From being Austria-Hungary's secret partner, Bucharest became
another enemy, eyeing the Romanian-speakers in Transylvania. Finally, Franz
Joseph's new foreign minister, Leopold Berchtold, concluded from the Balkan
Wars that working with the other powers through the Concert of Europe achieved

little. He got results when in spring 1913 he threatened to use force unless Serbia's ally, Montenegro, transferred the town of Scutari to Albania, and again in October when he demanded that Serbia itself should evacuate Albanian territory. By this stage many Austro-Hungarian leaders agreed with Conrad that only violence could solve the Serbian problem. The main exceptions were Tisza and Franz Ferdinand – and after the Sarajevo assassinations, Tisza alone.

This context helps to explain why the Austrians used the assassinations to force a war they already considered unavoidable. The outrage confirmed Berchtold and Franz Joseph in support of Conrad's views. Tisza was won over by an agreement that Austria-Hungary would not annex more South Slavs, by evidence that Romania would stay neutral, and – above all – by news that Germany encouraged military action. Given Russia's position, this latter was indispensable. Austria-Hungary had long competed with the Russians in south-eastern Europe, but in 1897 the two powers reached an understanding to keep the Balkans 'on ice', and for a decade, while the Russians focused their attention on Asia, they kept to it. Here again, however, the Bosnian annexation crisis, if a short-term triumph, exacerbated Austria-Hungary's plight in the longer term. In 1908 the Russians, still reeling from their defeat by Japan, could do nothing to support their fellow Slavs in Serbia, but they did not forget their humiliation. In 1912, by contrast, they helped to create the Serb–Bulgarian 'Balkan League' that attacked Turkey in the First Balkan War, and they mobilized thousands of troops in order to deter Austria-Hungary from intervening. Although the Russians urged Serbia to compromise in the Scutari and Albanian crises of 1913, they were clearly becoming more assertive. By 1914 almost all the Austro-Hungarian leaders expected war against Serbia to mean a war against Russia as well, and without German encouragement they would not have risked one. And whereas the Austrians were so focused on their Balkan dilemmas that they accepted a general European war without even seriously discussing it, the Germans were much more conscious of what they were doing. It is ultimately in Berlin that we must seek the keys to the destruction of peace.

Before dispatching their ultimatum to Belgrade the Austrians sent the head of Berchtold's private office, Count Hoyos, to Germany. Hoyos conveyed a memorandum from Berchtold and a letter from Franz Joseph, both of which strongly hinted at war with Serbia without being explicit. But when the German Emperor Wilhelm II met Hoyos on 5 July, he responded that Austria-Hungary must 'march into Serbia', with Germany's backing even if war with Russia resulted. The next day the German chancellor (head of government), Theobald von Bethmann Hollweg, reaffirmed the message.[36] Following this secret assurance – usually referred to as the 'blank cheque' – Wilhelm went cruising in the Baltic, while Bethmann and his foreign minister Gottlieb von Jagow urged the Austrians first to send the ultimatum and then to declare war without delay, while advising them to disregard British proposals to refer the crisis to a conference. Only on 28–29 July, after Austria-Hungary had declared war on Serbia, did the Germans urge Vienna to compromise. But once it became clear that Russia was supporting Serbia and had started military preparations the Germans plunged ahead, issuing ultimatums to Russia and its ally, France, on 31 July and declaring war on them on 1 and 3 August respectively. By simultaneously demanding that Belgium should allow free passage for German troops they also brought in Britain, which declared war on Germany on 4 August. Germany willed a local war between Austria-Hungary and Serbia, deliberately risked a continental war against France and Russia, and finally actually started one.

The Berlin leaders' extraordinary conduct in the July crisis became a central issue in the war, their opponents rejecting any return to peace while the authors of aggression went unpunished. Yet historical research into imperial Germany has not exposed a regime committed, like Hitler's, to premeditated plans for aggression and conquest.[37] Unlike the Weimar Republic after 1918, Wilhelm's Germany was not an international pariah and it had a large stake in the *status quo*. In the previous round of wars it had humbled Austria and France and expanded its territory: its economy was one of the fastest growing in Europe. Otto von Bismarck, the first chancellor of united Germany, recognized that it stood to gain nothing from a new war, unless it be to forestall French recovery after 1870; but the French rebuilt their defences and the moment for pre-emption passed. Moltke the Elder, who became the empire's first chief of the general staff, came to doubt whether a war against France and Russia was winnable.[38] In 1888, however, Moltke retired, and in 1890 the newly installed Wilhelm II dismissed Bismarck; no later chancellor had comparable authority. In the decade from 1897 to 1908 Wilhelm intervened frequently in policy-making and he always exerted considerable influence over diplomacy and in military and naval matters.[39] Yet this influence was erratic. Wilhelm was intelligent and open-minded but was also a restless and neurotic poseur who spent much of his reign sailing and hunting, and his officials found ways to work round him. All the same, he was Germany's public face. Although at times of crisis he mostly showed caution, he created the impression that his government was aggressive and militaristic (which normally it was not) and capricious and unpredictable (which it certainly was). His presence for more than a quarter of a century on the throne of such a powerful country grievously undermined European stability.

No less harmful than Wilhelm's blustering was his incapacity for consistent leadership in a fragmented society and political system. Unlike Austria-Hungary, Germany was ethnically homogeneous – the Polish, Danish, and Alsatian minorities formed only about 10 per cent of the population – but national consciousness remained underdeveloped. The empire had no national anthem and even its national flag was rarely used,[40] and religious, class, and regional divisions ran deep. Furthermore, it was a federation, whose member states retained wide powers. Prussia was much the largest – it had enough votes to block constitutional change, its king was also the German Emperor, and its prime minister was usually also the imperial chancellor – yet Bavaria, Baden, Saxony, and Württemberg also kept their own kings, governments, and armies. The imperial (or Reich) government could levy only indirect taxes, and dealt mainly with diplomacy and the armed forces. Army strategy was a matter for the Great General Staff (Grosser Generalstab or GGS), which was independent of the chancellor and reported directly to the emperor, as did the admiralty staff, its naval counterpart. Appointments and promotions in the services were handled by the military and naval cabinets in Wilhelm's personal household. In these circumstances harmonizing foreign and military policy was peculiarly difficult, and as the Reich had no co-ordinating body like the Committee of Imperial Defence in Britain (or the National Security Council in the post–1945 USA), the responsibility rested with Wilhelm, who discharged it incompetently. The consequences included military and naval meddling in diplomacy as well as a habit of addressing political problems with simplistic technical solutions that only worsened Germany's predicament.[41]

The system was neither representative nor coherent. Most Germans could vote for the Reichstag, but the upper house of the imperial legislature, the Bundesrat, represented the state governments, and elections to the Prussian lower house (the Landtag) used a 'three-class' franchise that advantaged the propertied. The chancellor and his ministers were not Reichstag deputies or indeed elected politicians at all, and the Reichstag, unlike the House of Commons or the French Chamber of Deputies, could not overthrow them. They needed its approval, however, for taxation and legislation, including army recruitment and warship construction laws. The Conservative and the National Liberal Parties (which normally the government could rely on) were losing support, mainly because of the rise of the Social Democratic Party (Sozialdemokratische Partei Deutschlands or SPD), which in the 1912 elections became the strongest in Germany. Despite its anti-capitalist rhetoric the SPD was mostly law-abiding and unrevolutionary, but its leaders did want greater democracy, as did those of the left-liberal Progressive Party. The Centre Party, representing the one-third of Germany's population who were Catholics, held the balance, but was pulled between left- and right-wing tendencies. In the years before 1914 there was talk of replacing the constitution with a more authoritarian one, an idea that attracted Wilhelm's heir apparent, the Crown Prince. As the domestic political balancing act became more difficult, the temptation grew for Germany's rulers to unify their country through foreign policy initiatives.

Bismarck had set a precedent: his wars of 1866 and 1870 had been intended to overcome domestic political deadlocks, as had his acquisition of Germany's overseas colonies. The same applied to the new departure undertaken from the late 1890s, known as 'world policy' or *Weltpolitik*. Continental security was now no longer enough, and Wilhelm and his advisers ostentatiously asserted Germany's right to a voice in the Ottoman Empire (where he claimed to be the protector of the Muslims), in China (where Germany took a lease on the port of Jiaozhou), and South Africa (where Wilhelm supported the Afrikaners against British attempts to control them, sending a telegram of support to the president of the Transvaal, Paul Kruger, in 1896). *Weltpolitik*'s most substantial manifestation, however, was the Navy Laws of 1898 and 1900. With Reichstag approval Wilhelm's navy secretary, Alfred von Tirpitz, began building a new fleet of short-range battleships configured for action in the North Sea. Wilhelm, Tirpitz, and Bernhard von Bülow (chancellor from 1900 to 1909) did not intend to fight Britain but rather to apply leverage that would encourage it to come to terms and make concessions in a future crisis. Internally, they hoped the naval programme would rally the right-wing parties, the princely states, and the middle classes in support of monarchical authority.[42]

This reasoning was plausible at the turn of the century, when Britain was at odds with Russia and France and an economic boom swelled tax revenue and made naval expansion affordable. Yet *Weltpolitik*'s eventual impact on Germany's external security and domestic stability – and by extension on European peace – was disastrous. It antagonized London rather than intimidating it, and isolated Germany rather than Britain. The British pulled back warships from more distant waters and stepped up construction. The climactic moment came after 1906, when the Royal Navy launched the *Dreadnought*, a revolutionary battleship equipped with turbine engines and ten 12-inch guns (the pre-dreadnought norm was four), making it faster and more heavily armed than anything afloat. Tirpitz decided Germany must follow suit and with a new Navy Law of 1908 he set a target of four new dreadnought battleships or battlecruisers a year. Alarmed during the 1908–09 winter by fears that he was secretly accelerating even beyond this, and egged on by agitation encouraged by the opposition, the Liberal government in London decided to lay down eight new dreadnoughts in one year, and pushed decisively ahead. After 1912 the Germans' construction dropped back from four to two new dreadnoughts a year and they diverted funds into the army.[43] As for diplomacy, negotiations in 1898–1901 for an Anglo-German alliance were abortive.[44] Instead the British settled their extra-European disputes by agreements with France (the 'Entente Cordiale') in 1904 and with Russia in 1907. In 1904–5 the Germans took advantage of Russia's defeat in the Far East to seek an alliance with Russia and France against Britain, but Russia rejected a deal. In the First Moroccan Crisis (the first big pre-war diplomatic crisis), played out in 1905–6, the Germans tried to separate London and Paris by obstructing France's efforts to establish control over Morocco, which the Entente cordiale had bound Britain to support. The British stood by the French, and the links between them were strengthened. After 1907 London, Paris, and St Petersburg formed a diplomatic alignment (or 'Triple Entente' – though the British disliked the term) against Germany and Austria-Hungary, while the Germans inveighed against 'encirclement'. And at home, far from uniting conservative forces in support of Wilhelm, naval spending pushed the Reich budget into deficit and triggered political infighting over tax increases, which led to Bülow's resignation in 1909 and to his replacement by Bethmann Hollweg. The new chancellor's inheritance was bleak.

At the turn of the century, Germany's external circumstances had been relatively favourable. The empire's internal tensions encouraged the fateful decision for *Weltpolitik*. But under Bethmann the international situation became more threatening, with encirclement as its key characteristic. Germany had long faced potential danger due to its annexation in 1871 of France's provinces of Alsace-Lorraine. No French government was willing to renounce the territory definitively. On the other hand, Paris would not stage a war of revenge while Germany remained militarily stronger,[45] and Bismarck denied it the temptation by keeping France quarantined. This was one reason for his alliance with Austria-Hungary in 1879, to which he added Italy by the Austro-German-Italian Triple Alliance of 1882. During the 1880s he maintained a link with Russia as well, but his successors failed to renew his 'Reinsurance Treaty' with the tsar, who gravitated instead into a French alliance. The consequences were manageable while Paris and St Petersburg were as hostile towards London as they were towards Berlin. They became much graver once Britain settled its differences with France and Russia, while in 1902 Italy and France agreed that in almost no conceivable circumstances would they go to war. France had now escaped from isolation and could consider both Russia and Britain as prospective allies. French diplomacy and financial strength (particularly loans to the Russian government) helped to turn the tables, but the Germans also had themselves to blame. The decade from 1907 to 1917 would witness ever more frantic efforts by Germany to divide its enemies, as it threshed in the tightening net. To begin with, however, Bethmann tried conciliation. In 1910 he agreed with the Russians on zones of economic influence in Turkey and Persia, but the French countered this by tightening military links with St Petersburg and in 1911 secured a secret Russian promise to attack Germany by day fifteen in the event of a war. Bethmann also sought negotiations with Britain, whose Lord Chancellor, Richard Burdon Haldane, visited Berlin in 1912. But the 'Haldane Mission' reached no agreement on the naval race, and the British refused to jeopardize their ententes with France and Russia by pledging unconditional neutrality in a future conflict.[46] Although London and Berlin achieved a *détente* in 1912–14, the underlying pattern of alignments remained intact. Given that Italy was fickle (and weakened itself by its war in Libya in 1911–12), Austria-Hungary was Germany's only dependable great-power ally, and even then only in a war beginning over the Balkans, where Habsburg interests were clearly implicated. Like the Austrians, the Germans felt the structure of alignments was now fundamentally unfavourable to them, and both were loath to use the Concert of Europe machinery if they were a minority within it.

Meanwhile the government's internal difficulties persisted, and the SPD successes in the 1912 Reichstag elections intensified them, though arguments that Germany went to war in order to forestall revolution are unconvincing. For all its divisions, the empire was a prosperous and orderly society, its working class less alienated than in earlier decades, and in June 1914 Bethmann predicted that a war would undermine rather than consolidate the existing order.[47] None the less, domestic and foreign policy were connected via armaments.[48] A further damaging consequence of naval expansion had been to starve the army. Admittedly the war ministry had resisted expanding the latter, believing that it was an adequate deterrent, that money was better invested in updating weaponry, and that if a larger army included more middle-class (rather than aristocratic) officers and more working-class (rather than peasant) troops it would be unreliable for domestic repression. Despite its reputation for being highly militarized,[49] Germany conscripted less of its manpower than France and spent less of its national product on defence than either France or Russia.[50] In the final pre-war years, however, this complacency evaporated. Russia recovered unexpectedly rapidly from its defeat by Japan, aided by a major military reorganization in 1910 that enabled it to move much faster to a war footing and to threaten Germany's eastern border. A second crisis over Morocco in 1911 convinced the German leaders that their ability to deter a newly confident France was weakening. They reassessed their armaments policy and gave the army priority, passing an army expansion law in 1912. Almost at once the Balkan Wars worsened matters still further by making Austria-Hungary more vulnerable. Now Germany might have to bear almost unaided the brunt of a two-front war against Russia and France, and in 1913 it rushed through another army law, the biggest in its peacetime history. But the government passed a capital levy to finance the bill only by co-operating with the SPD, which was willing to support the levy as a wealth redistribution measure. Although Germany's economy could sustain further rearmament the authorities were near the political limits of their capacity to pay for it, and Austria-Hungary's public finances were even more severely stretched.

In contrast, Britain outspent Germany in the naval race. David Lloyd George, as Chancellor of the Exchequer, introduced new progressive taxes in his 1909 'People's Budget' with this goal in mind, and the Liberals did well enough in the January 1910 election to break opposition to the budget from the House of Lords. France and Russia also faced fewer domestic obstacles than did Austria-Hungary and Germany to tax-financed armaments increases. Politically, both were unitary rather than federal states and both retaliated against the German build-up. France passed a law in 1913 to lengthen its term of military service from two years to three, and Russia approved in 1914 a 'Great Programme' to expand its army by 40 per cent over three years. In January 1914, in return for a loan to finance commercial railway construction, the Russians agreed with the French on a programme of strategic railway building in Poland and from the western border to the Russian interior that by 1917–18 would accelerate their military deployment by some 50 per cent.[51] Whereas before 1911 the most dynamic and dangerous armaments race in Europe had been the naval rivalry between Britain and Germany, between 1912 and 1914 a continental land arms race between the Austro-German and Franco-Russian blocs overshadowed it. By spring 1914 the Germans had implemented most of their 1913 law and could scarcely afford another round, whereas France and Russia's retaliatory measures would take effect only in two to three years' time. If a war was coming anyway 1914–15 was the time to have it, as the GGS well understood and impressed on Bethmann and Wilhelm.

The land arms race took on its full significance in the light of the two blocs' war plans.[52] Down to 1912–13 those of France and Russia were generally defensive, reflecting their weaker position. However, France's Plan XVII, approved in spring 1913, reflected the increasing confidence of its general staff by envisaging an immediate offensive, in conjunction with a Russian attack in the east. Correspondingly, Variant 'A', the default version of Russia's Plan 19 Revised of 1912, provided for opening offensives against both Austria-Hungary and Germany. The Austrians likewise envisaged an opening attack, though as they were uncertain whether their main enemy would be Serbia or Russia they too had to devise more than one variant. The Germans' scheme is often referred to as the 'Schlieffen Plan', after Alfred von Schlieffen, chief of the German general staff in 1890–1905, but his successor, Helmuth von Moltke the Younger (the Elder's nephew), amended it so significantly that the 'Schlieffen-Moltke Plan' is a more accurate title. Schlieffen's key innovations were to prescribe that in a two-front war the main attack should be westwards and that in order to outflank France's frontier fortresses Germany's right wing should invade via Belgium and the southernmost tongue of Dutch territory round Maastricht.[53] Moltke, in contrast, strengthened his left wing opposite France and abandoned the idea of going through the Netherlands (in the hope of continuing to trade through Holland if it remained neutral). Hence he kept his options open: but in another respect he closed them off by planning to seize the crucial railway junction at Liège by a standing start attack within the first days of mobilization. For Germany, alone among the powers, mobilization and war thus became almost identical, and the general staff kept the Liège coup secret from the chancellor until 31 July 1914: a glaring example of deficient civil–military liaison. Yet Bethmann, Jagow, and Wilhelm were all well aware of Moltke's analysis of the military balance, and the general provisions of the strategic plan. They knew the time factor was critical, as Germany would face disaster if most of its forces remained in the west while the Russians menaced Berlin. Russia's 1910 army reorganization – and still more the Great Programme and the Franco-Russian railway agreement – meant the plan's days were numbered.

But were such scenarios merely hypothetical? All sides appear to have seen the 1912–14 army bills as measures of deterrence and defence – to dissuade the enemy from invading and to defeat him if he did so – rather than as preparations to initiate hostilities.[54] Yet the German government was increasingly willing to consider the option of starting a war. To understand why it is necessary to add to encirclement and the land arms race a third element in the deteriorating international environment: a succession of diplomatic crises, of which July 1914 was the culmination.[55] Between the 1880s and 1904 such crises mainly started over colonial competition and involved individual powers: for example, Britain and Germany in 1896 over South Africa and Britain and France in 1898 over the Sudan. But in the pre-war decade a new series of crises came closer to home and squared off the two great blocs. In 1905–6 in the First Moroccan Crisis Germany failed to frustrate French attempts (with British support) to establish predominance in Morocco. In 1908–9, in contrast, Austria-Hungary with firm German backing pushed through the annexation of Bosnia. The first of these events consolidated German encirclement and the second deepened antagonism between Austria-Hungary and Germany on the one hand and Serbia and Russia on the other. At the height of the annexation crisis, moreover, in March 1909, Bülow and Moltke promised to support the Austrians if the latter were attacking Serbia and Russia intervened, thus reinterpreting the originally defensive nature of the 1879 Austro-German alliance and setting a precedent that was to be repeated in 1914.

Under Bethmann events moved still faster along a powder trail to catastrophe. In 1911 in the Second Moroccan Crisis Germany bolstered its demand for negotiations with France by dispatching a gunboat, the *Panther*, to the port of Agadir. Undeterred, the French, again with ostentatious British backing, secured a protectorate over Morocco in exchange merely for minor cessions to Germany in the Congo.[56] Not only did disappointment with the outcome precipitate Germany's reappraisal of its armaments policy and switch it back to a land priority: France's absorption of Morocco also prompted Italy to invade Libya, but this in turn distracted the Ottoman Empire and decided the Balkan states to attack it. The Balkan Wars then further intensified the interaction between events in local flashpoints and the rising general tension.[57] The First Balkan War precipitated Germany's 1913 army law, which in turn precipitated France's Three-Year Law and Russia's Great Programme. During the confrontation in 1912 caused by Austro-Hungarian resistance to Serbia's claims to access to the Adriatic, the Russian, Austro-Hungarian, and German governments all held high-level meetings on whether to fight. On Sunday 8 December Wilhelm II, enraged by a warning that Britain would intervene in a European conflict, convened an emergency secret conference at Potsdam with his military and naval advisers. He said that he envisaged fighting in Austria-Hungary's support and Moltke commented that the sooner a European war began the better, but Tirpitz objected that the navy needed another twelve to eighteen months to prepare. This 'War Council' (as the absent Bethmann sarcastically dubbed it) did not in fact decide to start a European conflict, but it did show that the Germans were seriously considering one in order to assist their ally and to break their encirclement.[58] Although during the spring 1913 Scutari dispute they restrained Berchtold, in the October 1913 confrontation over the Albanian borders they fully supported his ultimatum to Serbia, fearing that otherwise Austria-Hungary might lose faith in them.[59] This nightmare of forfeiting their last ally also preyed on them in July 1914.

In winter 1913–14 the Balkan Wars led to a further trial of strength, the Liman von Sanders affair. Liman was a German general sent to head a reinforced military mission to Constantinople and rebuild the Turkish army. Additionally he was to command the Turkish division that guarded the Ottoman capital and the Dardanelles: a neuralgic point for the Russians, who depended on the waterway as the principal outlet for their grain exports. Although after Russian protests Liman lost his command role, the military mission stayed, giving him powerful leverage over the Turkish army and therefore over Turkish politics. Germany and Russia had now clashed directly, instead of at one remove through Germany's support of Austria-Hungary. An ominous press war followed between the two countries, and the German leaders became still more nervous about Russian rearmament. St Petersburg reacted to the affair by signing the strategic railway deal with the French (over which it had previously hesitated) and by reinforcing the Triple Entente, the British agreeing to secret naval conversations with them in June 1914. When an informer in the Russian Embassy in London leaked this information to the Germans (and the British Foreign Secretary dissembled about the conversations in the House of Commons), Germany's encirclement seemed tighter than ever and the new *détente* Bethmann had achieved with Britain appeared a mirage.

By 1914 the crises, the arms race, and Berlin's encirclement phobia had taken on a mutually reinforcing momentum. Both blocs were consolidating and were more likely to hold firm in the next test: Russia and France had rearmed sufficiently to proceed more boldly while Germany and Austria-Hungary foresaw the balance tipping further against them. The recurrent confrontations impelled statesmen to consider fighting as an alternative to endless scares and threats. The crises also (and notably in Germany and France) energized nationalist pressure groups and rallied much of public opinion behind a forceful foreign policy. The chances were against another major clash being resolved peacefully, although this did not mean that any power had taken a premeditated decision to start a general war. In fact Germany's granting of the July 1914 'blank cheque' well illustrates the *ad hoc* nature of its decision-making. Wilhelm convened no Crown Council to deliberate the options with his officials before taking the plunge. Instead he prejudged matters by pledging support to Hoyos before conferring with Bethmann, although the chancellor endorsed his action. Wilhelm had been friendly with Franz Ferdinand and saw the assassinations as an outrage to dynastic authority. His advisers feared that restraining Vienna would alienate it, and appear to have agreed that war was the sole remaining option against Serbia. They wanted and encouraged Austro-Hungarian military action, though they doubted if the Austrians meant business and gave the blank cheque more easily because of uncertainty whether Berchtold would cash it. Further, both Wilhelm and Bethmann reasoned that an Austro-Serb conflict was likely to stay localized. They saw a strong likelihood that Russia would stand aside, and that Britain and France would urge it to do so. But they accepted squarely the prospect of a European conflagration if it did not, their war minister, Erich von Falkenhayn, advising that the army was ready and Moltke having stated repeatedly that it was better to act now than to wait. Privately Moltke acknowledged that France would be hard to defeat, and he and his planners seem to have expected a long struggle, but if war were inevitable at least it should be started at the most opportune moment.[60] Bethmann and Jagow, who were left to manage the crisis while Wilhelm cruised in the Baltic, appear to have seen the optimum outcome as a Balkan Blitzkrieg that would cripple Serbia, prop up Austria-Hungary, and perhaps break up the encircling Franco-Russian alliance, but they were willing to fight a continental war if St Petersburg intervened. They played a two-way bet, as Bismarck had done in 1870.[61] All now depended on Russia's response.

For the Triple Entente, the July 1914 crisis began in earnest with Austria-Hungary's ultimatum. Berchtold delayed it to secure German backing and bring Tisza on board, to allow Conrad's troops to return from harvest leave, and to wait until the French president Raymond Poincaré and prime minister René Viviani had ended a state visit to St Petersburg, in the misplaced calculation that postponement until the two men's return voyage would paralyse the Russo-French reaction. In fact the delay strengthened the impression that Austria-Hungary was not reacting in hot blood but was deliberately exploiting the assassinations to overwhelm Serbia and present the Russians with a *fait accompli*. Yet Tsar Nicholas II and his advisers had no eagerness for a European war, their general staff wanted time to continue rearmament, and they well knew their country needed peace. They focused less on the rights and wrongs of the Austro-Serbian dispute than on broader European power politics.[62]

Russia's internal conflicts were the fiercest on the continent. In February 1914 a prescient memorandum to Nicholas from a former interior minister, Peter Durnovo, foresaw that war would end in defeat and cataclysmic social upheaval.[63] Like Austria-Hungary, the Russian empire was a multinational conglomerate, with Finns, Balts, Poles, White Russians, Ukrainians, and Jews on its western borders and Caucasians and Central Asian Muslims on its southern ones, totalling over half its total population and inhabiting its most valuable provinces. But in addition it faced an urban social revolutionary movement and latent peasant violence. Whereas the German SPD was fundamentally law-abiding and even in Austria-Hungary terrorists like Princip were rare, the tsars had fought an internal war against sections of their intelligentsia for decades. Partly for this reason, they remained wedded to autocracy. Admittedly, after the foreign policy blunders that had led to war with Japan Nicholas II reluctantly accepted an experiment in cabinet government, the council of ministers. In order to defuse nationwide unrest after the defeat, he agreed to a parliament, the Duma, and a set of 'fundamental laws' including limited civil rights. For the next decade Russia enjoyed a more open political system than it would know again until the 1990s. Most political parties were legal, and newspapers were numerous and vociferous. This system was not, however, particularly stable. After 1909 a run of good harvests helped to quieten the countryside and boost tax receipts, much of which funded rearmament.[64] But the government unilaterally restricted the Duma franchise in order to return a more pliable assembly, and even so by 1914 co-operation with the legislature was breaking down. In February 1914 the council of ministers was also weakened, Nicholas replacing its chairman Vladimir Kokovtsov by the ineffectual Ivan Goremykin so that he could deal with ministers individually rather than *en bloc*.[65] As in Germany, civil–military co-ordination was poor, and this move exacerbated the problem. Finally, since 1912 a new strike wave had gathered pace, and in July 1914 a general strike broke out in St Petersburg with barricades in the streets. The internal situation offered excellent reasons for holding back.

Why then did Russia not simply abandon Serbia? No alliance treaty bound it to assist Belgrade. Despite ties of religion and language and a historic tradition of support, the Russians were not motivated by knee-jerk Slavic solidarity. In 1908–9 and 1912–13 they had urged Serbia to show restraint.[66] But in 1914 they advised it that they could not 'remain indifferent' to its fate,[67] possibly encouraging the Serbs not to accept the ultimatum in its entirety, and thus presenting Austria-Hungary with its pretext for war.[68] Although Russia's economic stake in Serbia was negligible, its leaders believed they had vital commercial interests at the Dardanelles, which might be threatened if what Sazonov called the Balkan 'political equilibrium' tilted against them.[69] Serbia was also strategically important, as it could force the Habsburgs to divide their forces in an Austro-Russian war. Furthermore, in 1914 the threat was much more drastic than in 1909 and 1912, when the Austrians had tried to contain Serbia's expansion rather than destroy its independence. So the Balkan issues did matter, but in a crucial meeting of the council of ministers on 24 July Sazonov stressed that behind Austria-Hungary lay Germany. For much of the nineteenth century St Petersburg and Berlin had enjoyed good relations, as adjoining conservative monarchies, both hostile to liberalism and with a common interest in holding down Poland (the last remnants of which they had partitioned in 1815 with Austria). By the twentieth century, however, Germany was backing Austria-Hungary in the Balkans, economic conflicts of interest (for example over Russia's cheap grain exports) had grown, and a popular racist xenophobia had developed in both countries.[70] German backing for Turkey in the Liman von Sanders affair seemed to threaten Russian vital interests, and Germany and Russia were rivals in an arms race. Sazonov and the council of ministers took a dark view of Berlin's intentions and judged that concessions would simply encourage further provocation. They decided it was time for firmness, whatever the risks, in the hope of preventing war while protecting Serbia, and the war and navy ministers supported the common line. This was of questionable wisdom, given that Russia's rearmament efforts would not mature for another three to four years, but the challenge to its interests was felt to be intolerable and rearmament had proceeded far enough for war to be a feasible option, at any rate if France fought alongside.

Crucial to the escalation process was the Russian decision not only to stand by Serbia but also to start the militarization of the crisis. Until 23 July Austria-Hungary and Germany had taken very few military measures, in part to avoid forewarning their adversaries. Even after the ultimatum the Germans remained inactive, hoping thereby to help localize the conflict. But on 26 July the Russians embarked on pre-mobilization measures – their so-called 'period preparatory to war' – along the borders opposite both Austria-Hungary and Germany. Under the conscription systems that all the European powers except Britain had adopted, those young men liable to military service were (typically) called up at the age of twenty to serve for two or three years in the standing army, after which until their late twenties they trained regularly in the reserves. Mobilization meant recalling the reservists to their units and making them mobile, i.e., providing the horses and equipment that they needed to move forward. It trebled or quadrupled the standing army's size. It preceded 'concentration' (the advance of the mobilized units to the frontier – normally by rail) and deployment for combat. Russia's pre-mobilization measures entailed steps such as cancelling leave and clearing the frontier railway lines, so that mobilization proper (which was slower than in the west) could be accelerated. It was therefore bound to alarm the Austrians and Germans when their intelligence services detected it, which they did almost at once.[71] The Russians appear to have seen it as a precaution, but events soon showed that a posture of deterrent diplomacy was unviable. Despite Russian protests, on 28 July the Austrians began a partial mobilization in the Balkans and declared war on Serbia. On the 29th they bombarded Belgrade and on the same day Bethmann warned Russia that even continuing pre-mobilization measures would force Germany to retaliate and probably lead to hostilities. As Sazonov was not prepared to back down and cancel the measures, he and the military chiefs (war minister Vladimir Sukhomlinov and chief of the general staff N. Janushkevich) concluded that war was coming anyway and what mattered now was simply to make ready for it by ordering full mobilization. Sazonov and Nicholas knew the latter was virtually certain to mean a major conflict and, as Nicholas put it, sending hundreds of thousands of men to their deaths. The tsar agonized, first substituting a decree for partial mobilization against Austria-Hungary alone but finally on 30 July authorizing mobilization against both Vienna and Berlin, with effect from the following day. Unless Nicholas and Sazonov were prepared to acquiesce in Austria-Hungary crushing Serbia, they were probably correct to assume a general war was inevitable. As soon as they started general mobilization Germany demanded that they halt it within twelve hours, but they pressed on regardless. In other words, they went forward knowingly to their fate.[72] Neither side would yield over the central issue and if Germany threw down the gauntlet, Russia picked it up. On 31 July the Germans therefore began intensive military preparations and sent a peremptory ultimatum to Russia to cease mobilization. On 1 August both they and the Austrians began their own general mobilizations, and on the same day (although Austria-Hungary waited a few days longer) Germany declared war on Russia. Great-power hostilities had now begun.

Two further factors facilitated the Russian leaders' decisions. The first was the state of public opinion, which seemed supportive. Most of the Duma and the press called for the government to stand by Serbia, Sazonov warning Nicholas that *unless* he supported Serbia he risked 'revolution and the loss of his throne'.[73] The interior minister, though privately filled with foreboding, reported during the crisis that the provinces were quiet and the country would obey the call-up order.[74] Second, there seemed a reasonable chance that Russia and its allies would win. Sazonov was completely uncertain as to whether Britain would support him (and he later argued that firmer British involvement might have deterred Germany). However, the French ambassador, Maurice Paléologue (who seems to have been determined that in a war Russia should aid France quickly),[75] assured him France would stand by the alliance, and for two years the French military had been advising their Russian counterparts that the auspices were favourable. Both St Petersburg and Paris correctly anticipated that in a two-front conflict Germany would attack westwards first, and if the French could hold the Germans Russia could certainly beat the Austrians. At the time of the Bosnian crisis it had been inconceivable for the tsarist army to wage a major war, but five years later, faced with a far more radical challenge to Russian interests, it was not.

Russia's decision cannot then be fully explained without reference to its French ally.[76] It is likely that before Poincaré and Viviani left St Petersburg the French and Russians had an inkling of what was coming, but they discussed only a diplomatic response to it.[77] From 23 to 29 July, however, Poincaré and Viviani were sailing back to France, in imperfect radio contact with Paris, while the Germans tried to jam their communications. Far from their absence inhibiting a forceful Franco-Russian response, it probably encouraged one by allowing Paléologue free rein. When Poincaré and Viviani reached Paris they cabled the Russians to take no action that might encourage German mobilization, but the message came too late to stop Nicholas's mobilization decree. Once the latter was issued, the Germans sent an ultimatum to Paris at the same time as to St Petersburg, demanding French neutrality in a Russo-German war. Poincaré and Viviani refused to abandon an alliance they deemed essential to French interests, even though Russia had mobilized without consulting them. On 3 August, on the basis of trumped-up allegations that French troops had crossed the border and French aircraft had bombed Nuremberg, Germany therefore declared war.

France's contribution to the outbreak of war lay primarily in its actions before July 1914. The Germans had long seen it as their principal military antagonist; only on the very eve of war did Russia alarm them equally.[78] By selling arms to Serbia France undermined Austria-Hungary's position in the Balkans; by lending to Russia in return for strategic railway construction, it intensified Germany's encirclement complex. But in the crisis itself Paris was passive and non-provocative, deliberately keeping one step behind Germany in its military preparations and ordering French troops to stay ten kilometres behind the border. The reasons were partly internal and partly external. Internally, France – uniquely among the European powers – was a republic, its head of state a president chosen by an electoral college. Prime ministers and cabinets depended on majorities in the Chamber of Deputies, elected by all adult males. Given the fragmented party system, they lasted on average only nine months. The army's strategic planners were subordinated to the war minister, the prime minister, and the president. The pre–1914 growth of European tension had polarized opinion, stimulating a 'nationalist reawakening' among Parisian students and intellectuals and on the political right, but also benefiting the socialist party, the SFIO, which opposed the three-year military service law, and in the May-June 1914 parliamentary elections expanded its following. The SFIO and Jean Jaurès, its charismatic leader, would rally only behind a war of self-defence; the main trade-union federation, the CGT, was committed to opposing one in all circumstances. Poincaré had served as prime minister and foreign minister in 1912 and then as president since 1913 with the aims of strengthening the Russian alliance and preparing France militarily and psychologically for a possible conflict, although his philosophy appears to have been one of deterrence rather than provocation.[79] Viviani, in contrast, who had become premier in June 1914, was an independent socialist who had opposed the three-year law, though he had agreed not to tamper with it for the time being. Right up to the top French politics was uneasily balanced, and only when faced with what seemed flagrant and unprovoked aggression did the country fall into line.

The second reason for French leaders' caution was uncertainty about Britain, which until two days before it intervened seemed so likely to stay neutral. That the Germans shared this uncertainty (as indeed did the British themselves), which became evident during the final decision-making round in Berlin between 28 July and 1 August. Since giving the blank cheque Wilhelm and Bethmann had been prepared, if Russia supported Serbia, to fight rather than back down. If the Russians started military preparations, given the hair-trigger nature of the Schlieffen–Moltke Plan, Berlin would have to retaliate immediately. Once the Russians began their pre-mobilization measures, the fate of European peace was therefore virtually sealed. All the same, there were last-minute soul-searchings. First the Kaiser, landing from the Baltic on 28 July, urged that Austria-Hungary should content itself with occupying Belgrade (which lay just across the border) as a surety for the Serbs honouring their promises. On the next day Bethmann too pressed this 'Halt in Belgrade' plan, mainly because of a warning by the British Foreign Secretary, Sir Edward Grey, that Britain would intervene quickly in a European conflict. Until this point British diplomacy had been remarkably mild, Grey seeking co-operation with Berlin in the hope that the latter would restrain Vienna. This was a grave misjudgement, albeit one that Bethmann encouraged. It lulled the Germans into hoping Britain might stay aloof. Consequently, on the 29th Bethmann made a crass bid for British neutrality by promising that in return Germany would take no Belgian territory nor anything from France in Europe – thus admitting his intention to invade Belgium and his designs on French colonies. Grey's warning on the same day (with which the Foreign Secretary was going out on a limb, as the cabinet was unaware of it and still far from committed to intervention) therefore crossed with this remarkable offer. The warning did make Bethmann waver and if delivered earlier it might have caused him and Wilhelm to rein in the Austrians and the military, but now it came too late. Moltke undercut Bethmann's efforts to restrain Vienna by urging Conrad to concentrate his armies against Russia as well as Serbia, and the Austrians rejected the 'Halt in Belgrade' proposal on the grounds that it would merely postpone a solution of their

Serbian problem. By the 30th reports were flooding in not only about Russian military measures but also about French and Belgian ones, and Moltke joined war minister Falkenhayn in insisting that Germany must start its own preparations. Bethmann agreed to wait no longer than noon on the 31st, but in fact on that day news was confirmed of Russian mobilization, thus enabling him to present Germany's own mobilization on 1 August as a response to tsarist aggression. This factor was crucial to maintaining domestic unity, on which both he and Moltke placed a premium, as contacts with the SPD leaders had revealed their attitude would depend on whether the war was one of self-defence against Nicholas II's reactionary regime.[80] Even now further prevarication followed a misleading dispatch on 1 August, which suggested that Britain might keep France neutral and allow Germany to concentrate solely against Russia. Wilhelm ordered a halt in the march to the west, brushing aside Moltke's pleas that he could not improvise an alternative deployment at the last minute. Many commentators have used this episode to highlight the power of the military, but actually it showed that Wilhelm could override them.[81] Once it became clear, however, that the dispatch from London had been misleading, Wilhelm authorized the westward advance to proceed, thereby accepting the likelihood of war not only against France and Russia but also against Britain. Probably the Germans supposed that if France and Russia were beaten Britain could do little, and it was better to accept hostilities with London than give way. When the British demanded that Germany keep out of Belgium, they were ignored.

If the German leaders were willing to accept a war with Britain (and the general staff cared little about the six divisions that Britain could send to the continent), their preference was for a localized Balkan war and, failing that, a continental one against France and Russia alone. Whereas Berlin declared war on Paris and St Petersburg, London declared war on Berlin. From a Balkan and a continental conflict, Britain's intervention began a further massive stage of escalation towards a world war. Almost certainly it prevented Germany from defeating France and Russia in a matter of months. Yet it was undertaken by a progressive Liberal cabinet, most of whose members until 2 August favoured staying out, with the probable support of a majority of Liberal MPs.[82] The Belgian issue was indispensable in causing this turnabout, but provides only part of the explanation.[83]

In the first instance Britain declared war because Germany failed to comply with an ultimatum to respect Belgium's independence and integrity. The great powers had guaranteed Belgium by the London treaty of 1839, soon after the new kingdom was created. In 1870 both France and Prussia had honoured this undertaking. In 1914 the French were willing to do so (indeed Poincaré had ruled out pre-emptive invasion of Belgium, partly with Britain in mind), but sending the right flank of the western advance through Belgium was integral to the Germans' war plan and on 2 August they demanded that Brussels let their forces pass. King Albert I and the government of Charles de Broqueville decided to resist and to appeal for help.[84] As the British prime minister Herbert Asquith put it, Germany's ultimatum 'simplifies matters'.[85] It created a moral issue, a brutal aggression against a small neighbour that Britain was pledged to defend. Belgium provided a point of honour to appease the consciences of Liberal backbenchers and the cabinet sceptics. But it also implicated national security, given that the Belgian coast faced London and the Thames estuary and given the traditional watchword of keeping the Low Countries out of the control of a hostile power. It was for such reasons that Britain had signed the 1839 treaty, albeit at that stage with France as the prospective enemy. Hence Belgium mattered as much for the Unionist opposition* as for the Liberal government (not to mention its significance for Irish Nationalist MPs as a fellow small Catholic nation).

Yet the Belgian issue was not what it seemed. The cabinet decided to resist only a 'substantial violation' of Belgium.[86] If the Germans had merely (as many expected) traversed Belgium's south-eastern tip in the Ardennes, matters might have been different. The cabinet judged that actually Britain was not bound to assist, and a decision to do so would be 'rather . . . of policy than of legal obligation'.[87] If France had invaded Belgium, it is scarcely conceivable that a majority in the cabinet or the Commons would have supported war against it. The vital point was not the invasion, but that Germany was the invader, and the British government and much of the public saw German domination of Western Europe as dangerous. Belgium united the cabinet (only two ministers resigned) and allowed Britain to act promptly (which proved important), but Grey and Asquith already believed that Britain should not let France be overwhelmed, as did Winston Churchill (the First Lord of the Admiralty) and Lloyd George. Although Anglo-German tension had recently eased, the memory of the earlier antagonism weighed with them more heavily.

Anglo-German relations had deteriorated from the 1890s irrespective of whether Liberal or Unionist governments held office.[88] Yet although Germany had a more authoritarian political system, ideological considerations did not inhibit British co-operation with the still more autocratic Russia. Nor were commercial considerations crucial. At the turn of the century Germany challenged British dominance of worldwide trade in manufactures and encroached on Britain's home market. But when British exports revived in the trade boom that preceded 1914 German competition became less contentious. Germany raised its tariffs in 1879 and 1902 (one of the factors that convinced the Unionists to take up protectionism), but the Liberals won the 1906 and 1910 elections and Britain remained a free trading nation. Although Britain ran a deficit with Germany on trade in goods, it ran a surplus in services such as shipping and insurance and the overall economic relationship was more complementary than competitive. More significant, however, was Germany's faster industrial expansion, especially in military-related sectors such as engineering, chemicals, and steel. In 1870 it produced half as much steel as Britain, but by 1914 twice as much. True, Germany's growth was dwarfed by the United States, which by 1914 produced almost as much steel as Britain, France, and Germany combined. But Germany lay not across the Atlantic but across the North Sea, and the uses it made of its expanding resources, at a time of widespread apprehension that Britain had passed its Victorian heyday, seemed ominous. This was where the unpredictability of German policy under Wilhelm really mattered.

The diplomatic aspect of *Weltpolitik* impinged little on British imperial security after the turn of the century. Wilhelm's involvement in southern Africa had

---

*The Conservatives were normally referred to as Unionists in this period, because they opposed a devolved parliament in Dublin as endangering the union between Great Britain and Ireland.

touched a raw nerve because the Cape guarded one of the two great sea routes (with Suez) to India, but by defeating the Boers in 1899–1902 the British established firm control over the region. Thereafter *Weltpolitik* was more a challenge to the French (in Morocco) and to Russia (at the Turkish straits). In 1912–14 Britain and Germany negotiated over spheres of influence in Africa and the Persian Gulf. But the naval challenge was far more significant, and probably did more than anything else to persuade British public opinion that Germany was an enemy, the villain in innumerable invasion scare books and in the 1908–9 dreadnought agitation. The modern British intelligence services originated from a perceived necessity to gather information about German warship-building and the rumoured spy and saboteur networks within Britain.[89] Even so, after 1912 the government knew the naval challenge was slackening, and the Admiralty had never treated the invasion possibility very seriously.[90] This left the question of the balance of power. Although preferring to contain Germany rather than fight it, Grey and his Foreign Office advisers feared that if it did crush France and Russia, Britain would be next on the list. Hence the warnings that Britain would intervene in a European war, delivered during the Adriatic crisis in December 1912 and on 29 July 1914; and hence also a primary reason for Grey's policy of ententes.

The entente policy was controversial at the time and has remained so.[91] Its origins were not specifically anti-German but lay in a reaction against Britain's isolation in the 1890s, when Russia, France, Germany, and the USA all seemed possible enemies. At the turn of the century Britain settled its disputes with America, in 1902 it concluded an alliance with Japan, and the agreements of 1904 and 1907 resolved most of its differences with France and Russia. What turned the ententes from the liquidation of African and Asian disagreements into diplomatic cooperation within Europe, however, was Grey's and his advisers' suspicion (albeit on threadbare evidence) that Germany had ambitions for a 'Napoleonic' hegemony. Britain needed both to deter such ambitions and to encourage Paris and St Petersburg to maintain their independence. On the other hand, as France and Russia should not be made over-confident, and the House of Commons would not ratify alliance treaties with either, Grey aligned himself with them while evading commitment. This meant supporting France over Morocco and Russia in the Balkans, as well as secret contingency planning with the French for military and naval co-operation.[92] In 1911 the two general staffs agreed that a British Expeditionary Force (BEF) of up to six divisions could be sent to the French northern flank; in 1913 the two navies agreed that France would take responsibility for the western Mediterranean and western Channel, and Britain for the eastern Mediterranean and the Dover Straits. None the less, an exchange of letters in 1912 spelled out that if the peace of Europe were threatened the British were bound only to consult with the French and not to activate the joint contingency plans or go to war. In 1914 Grey maintained that Britain had an obligation of honour, but the cabinet did not agree with him. On 1 August he had to tell the French ambassador that Paris must decide for itself on how to respond to Germany's ultimatum, with no assurance of British support.

The crucial day for the cabinet was Sunday, 2 August, during which it met three times and decided to act against a substantial violation of Belgian neutrality and to stop the German fleet from attacking French shipping or the French coast. The latter was as far as it would go in acting on the agreements with Paris, and as the Germans were willing to keep out of the Channel it would not have triggered British intervention.[93] As for Russia, not even Grey would have favoured involvement in a war confined to Eastern Europe. He did fear that if France and Russia won and Britain stayed neutral it would court retaliation from its deserted partners, and India would be vulnerable to tsarist aggression.[94] But such concerns were marginal to the cabinet's decision, which centred on British security against Germany and the impending attack on Belgium. Partisan considerations, however, also played a role. Britain was the only power to debate in parliament the issue of entry into war, and although the Commons did not vote, its support was essential. Since 1910 the Liberals had held a majority only in conjunction with the Labour Party and the Irish Nationalists, and British politics had passed through troubled times. The Liberals had antagonized the Unionists by abolishing the House of Lords' absolute legislative veto, and they had been harried by trade union militancy and by the suffragette agitation for women's enfranchisement. Above all, their Home Rule bill for an autonomous parliament in Dublin had drawn vehement resistance from the Ulster Protestants, who threatened force and received Unionist backing. By 1914 Ulstermen and Irish nationalists alike were drilling and importing arms, and when the government prepared to coerce the Protestants several army officers vowed to resign rather than co-operate. During July 1914, until the Austrian ultimatum, the press and the cabinet focused not on the Balkans but on Ireland. Even so, although Asquith was relieved that all-party support for intervention headed off the threat of civil strife, none of this meant the cabinet opted for war as an antidote to domestic conflict. On the contrary, the government feared it would interrupt food supplies in England and intensify class struggle. Initially it held back two BEF divisions, partly as a precaution against unrest. More significant as a domestic influence was the chasm between the Liberals and the Unionists, many ministers feeling that the latter's extremism had rendered them unfit for office. But on 2 August their leader, Andrew Bonar Law, urged that Britain should come at once to France and Russia's support. Grey threatened to resign if no undertakings were given to France and Belgium, and Asquith was willing to go with him. If the cabinet insisted on neutrality it was therefore likely to split, probably leading to a Unionist coalition with the Liberal interventionists and Britain entering the conflict anyway. Conversely, supporting intervention promised to safeguard party unity and ministers' careers, as well as to protect Liberal principles in wartime. In the absence of a cabinet revolt against Grey and Asquith (Lloyd George's attitude was crucial here), opposition in the party abruptly collapsed.[95]

The government was further assisted by expectations about the kind of war Britain would fight. On 2 August ministers deliberated on the assumption that the BEF would not go to France; the decision to send it after all was taken by a cabinet committee three days later. Britain's contribution would in traditional fashion be naval, colonial, and financial, perhaps with small professional forces on the continent. If the struggle were prolonged the admiralty believed it could maintain command of the seas and damage Germany's economy far more effectively than Germany could damage Britain's.[96] Grey knew both of this appreciation and of that by Henry Wilson, the Director of Military Operations at the War Office, that the BEF's dispatch could tip the balance between France and Germany and it needed to go quickly. Lord Kitchener, the soldier hero who had conquered the Sudan and had helped to crush the Boers, was now brought in as Secretary of State for War and foresaw a conflict that would last two or more years, but his vision was exceptional.[97] Like other powers the British were leaping into darkness, but wishful thinking helped them plunge.

This last point leads to a broader one: the ease with which opposition to entering the war disintegrated across Europe. Governments could destroy peace only because of the weakness of the anti-war political forces and because most of the population acquiesced. In general, opposition to hostilities centred on the trade union and socialist movements. Britain was exceptional in that the Trades Union Congress (TUC) was less politicized than its continental counterparts, while the Labour Party was not yet committed to socialism and the Liberals overshadowed it as the Left's main standard-bearer. Down to 2 August opposition to British involvement was widespread. The City of London panicked at the prospect: Lord Rothschild urged *The Times* to tone down its interventionist leaders (but was rebuffed) and the Governor of the Bank of England pleaded with Lloyd George to keep Britain out. All the Liberal newspapers and some Unionist ones opposed intervention, as did three-quarters of Liberal MPs (according to Asquith) and those attending an imposing rally in Trafalgar Square. Once Germany threatened Belgium and France, however, and the cabinet committed itself, the Commons rapidly acquiesced, leaving the opposition leaderless and with no time to organize. C. P. Scott, the hitherto neutralist editor of the *Manchester Guardian*, felt that now Britain was in, what mattered was to win, even if searching questions would be needed afterwards. Ambivalence about involvement existed from the start and would resurface later, feeding suspicions that the enterprise had all along been tarnished.[98]

On the continent a mechanism existed to concert resistance, in the shape of the socialist Second International, founded in 1889. Its member parties failed to use it, as the governments failed to use the Concert of Europe, and in part for similar reasons.[99] It excluded the non-socialist Left, as well as the trade unions, whose separate grouping, the International Secretariat of National Trade Union Centres (ISNTUC), founded in 1901, included the German central trade union organization but neither the British TUC nor the French CGT.[100] Moreover, the member parties tended to be most radically anti-militarist where they were smallest and most alienated, as in Russia and Serbia. The strongest parties were the French SFIO and the German SPD, both of which were much more moderate, but cooperation between them proved elusive. The French trade unions were ideologically more extreme than the German ones, and numerically weaker. The German unions had close ties with the SPD, but the CGT maintained its independence from the SFIO. Hence it was unlikely that the International's member parties could translate their resolutions into strike action that would paralyse railways and armaments plants. Co-ordinated strikes would hit Germany hardest, because its unions were strongest. But leaving discretion to each national movement might most affect France, whose workers were more likely to down tools. The International attempted to address this issue after the pre-war crises had begun, but it was more agreed on diagnosis than on remedy. The Stuttgart Congress's resolution of 1907 blamed capitalism for generating war, but failed to endorse concerted action if war threatened, largely owing to German resistance. The movement repeatedly postponed a final decision on the issue, and in the meantime the Stuttgart resolution remained authoritative. On 29 July 1914 representatives of the party leaderships gathered in Brussels for an emergency meeting called by the International's secretariat (the 'Bureau'), but they found little common ground and delegated action to a special congress. It never convened.

The International could provide co-ordination only if the national party leaderships wished for it. It was powerless to compel them. In 1914 Jaurès and his German counterparts displayed a certain complacency. The succession of peacefully resolved crises had suggested to some theorists that in modern capitalism war was anachronistic. Moreover, Marx and Engels themselves had approved of wars they judged historically progressive, and for the SFIO a war against Germany – and for the SPD one against Russia – might fit this bill. Nor was ideology the only consideration. Marx and Engels gave little guidance on international questions, and the French and German parties were eclectic in selecting sources for their views. Both accepted that a war of self-defence was justifiable, and the 1914 war appeared to be one, rather than a product of the capitalist imperialism denounced at Stuttgart. From 25 July onwards the SPD organized large but subdued anti-war demonstrations while in secret meetings with ministers its leaders indicated that their attitude would depend on whether the war was defensive or in support of Austrian aggression. Russian mobilization brought them round and undercut the popular movement, and Bethmann's tactic of waiting to put Russia in the wrong proved vindicated, nearly all the SPD's Reichstag deputies voting on 4 August in favour of war credits. Resistance, they calculated, would be unavailing, and if suppressed their organizations would be powerless to protect their members in the trials ahead. In France too, to begin with, the SFIO and CGT organized peace demonstrations, the catalytic event being Jaurès's murder by a royalist fanatic on 31 July. Poincaré set aside peacetime differences and honoured his memory, while the CGT leader, Léon Jouhaux, spoke at his graveside in favour of national unity. The government took care to seem prudent and cautious, and discarded the 'Carnet B', the list of left-wingers scheduled to be arrested. Finally France appeared so plainly the victim of aggression that it is probable that had Jaurès lived he too would have supported the government. All French parties endorsed the 'sacred union' or political truce, although they suspended rather than liquidated their peacetime differences, expected political gain from doing so, and assumed the emergency would be brief.[101]

With the co-option of the socialist parties (all of whom, except in Russia and Serbia, voted for war credits), protest was decapitated. Even so, patriotic and pro-war enthusiasm was largely confined to the big cities and came later than the initial pacifist rallies. Poincaré and Viviani felt buoyed up by the cheers for France and for the army when they returned to Paris on 29 July; two days later the elation of the Berlin crowds humbled Wilhelm and Bethmann. But generally such demonstrations had little influence on governments and were a consequence rather than a cause of the crisis. In Paris, Berlin, and London citizens gathered outside the newspaper offices to await the latest editions, rather than huddling at home round radio sets as in the 1930s or round television sets as during the Cuban missile crisis. From these public gatherings the first patriotic demonstrations in the German cities erupted from 25 July, swelling as events approached their climax. Their scale and inclusiveness were much exaggerated by the Right, who subsequently constructed a myth of transcending national unity when the reality had been much more muted. Certainly many eyewitnesses were impressed by the newfound solidarity. More critical press commentaries on the demonstrations, however, noted that the participants were largely middle-class students and young professional men. Although working-class districts in Berlin flew the Hohenzollern colours for the first time, their mood was serious and anxious.[102] There were runs on savings banks and panic buying sprees in grocery stores. In France reports by prefects and by schoolteachers suggested that shock, consternation, and disbelief were the predominant reactions in the villages to news of mobilization. If the mood became more resolute when the men marched away, this was in reference neither to Alsace-Lorraine nor to revenge for 1870 but to the duty of defence against an unjustified assault by a longstanding aggressor.[103] Even so, the French national consensus probably went deeper than the German one.[104] In Austria-Hungary the German-speaking socialists supported the war (like their SPD counterparts) for anti-Russian reasons, and Vienna too had its patriotic crowds. More surprisingly, Czech politicians were also loyal at first, as were many South Slav ones (particularly Slovenes), although the Croats were divided and the Poles feared being sent against their fellows under Russian rule.[105] Once it became clear that this would be a European and not simply an anti-Serb war, support for it diminished, yet the resolute mood still surprised observers used to the Dual Monarchy's fissiparousness. Finally in Russia the pre-war strike movement died away (possibly because of the arrest of its leaders) and the previously fractious Duma parties mostly supported the war effort, although in the countryside peasant communities reportedly received the news with incomprehension and at best with resignation, at worst with fear and anger.[106]

Across the continent the feeling in the countryside and in small towns – where most units would come from and where most Europeans still lived – was more apprehensive and depressed than in the capital cities. Among intellectuals, although many were exhilarated by manifestations of national unity and welcomed the war as an opportunity for cleansing and regeneration, others viewed it with horror and disgust as a scarcely credible reversion to the primitive.[107] These reactions failed to translate themselves, however, into effective resistance. In Britain the army and the navy were volunteer services and the reservists who had returned to civilian life obeyed the call-up order. Nor did the trade-union movement contemplate disrupting it. On the continent, mobilization depended on millions of conscripts reporting to their units. The Austro-Hungarian authorities expected one in ten to refuse;[108] the French expected a resistance rate of 13 per cent. In the event it turned out to be much lower: in France just 1.5 per cent.[109] Only in Russia was there widespread opposition, mainly in the rural areas. Disturbances erupted in half the districts of the empire and hundreds died, although the eventual response rate was 96 per cent.[110] Nevertheless, even here mobilization and concentration generally proceeded smoothly, and the speed with which they did so surprised Russia's enemies. In Western Europe both the French and Germans deployed on schedule and the BEF detrained in its northern French target zone before the Germans knew it had crossed the Channel. Whatever the foreboding with which Europeans went to war, little force was needed to make them go. The mass conscription and reservist training systems developed over a generation had taught those mobilized what to do, and the spread of literacy, a national press, and festivals such as Bastille Day in France and Sedan Day in Germany had strengthened the sense of national community. When this was absent – among the Poles and Alsatians in Germany, the Slav minorities in Austria-Hungary, or the peasantry in much of Russia – popular support for the war was problematic from the start and later became more so.[111] For the moment, however, it was everywhere sufficient for the fighting to begin.

These were extraordinary events, seen at the time and since as a leap into the unknown and the start of a new era. What made the long peace collapse so quickly? An answer focused on the characteristics of the international system portrays the powers as victims; another stressing decisions by individual governments depicts them rather as perpetrators. Both approaches are illuminating. On the general level, the peace was fragile and had been growing more so. The powers had the capacity, if not necessarily the intention, to wage a great war and given that capacity they were always liable to do it. Neither the Concert of Europe nor the Second International could stop them. The conscription systems and arsenals of weapons built up since 1870 could, after mobilization, cause thousands of casualties within hours. In the pre-1914 decade all the general staffs reoriented their war plans towards immediate offensives, and the arms race placed their troops at higher readiness. The recurrent crises over the Mediterranean and the Balkans accustomed governments to envisaging the contingency of war, and to debating whether to initiate it. These factors helped to spread the view (occurring frequently in military documents of the period) that a showdown between the blocs was inevitable.[112] Not only this, but the successive crises probably weakened the socialists by lulling their leaders into a false sense of security and by encouraging other political parties to rally round their governments. By 1914 opposition to war was losing impetus, leaving statesmen not only with the technical means to launch it but, if they handled the outbreak skilfully, the assurance of public support.

These conditions of more offensive strategies, an arms race, repeated crises, and a growing acclimatization to war resemble those in other periods such as the 1880s, the 1930s, and the peaks of Cold War tension in 1948–53, 1958–62, and 1979–83. Yet this same list shows that such conditions need not end in hostilities. To explain what made this period different we have to revert from the broader characteristics of the international system to the individual powers. The emphasis here has been on governments' initiative, popular support being essential but supplementary. For war to happen governments on both sides had to declare it and to set their military machines in motion. The European peace might have been a house of cards, but someone still had to topple it. It used to be argued that 1914 was a classic instance of a war begun through accident and error: that no statesmen wanted it but all were overborne by events.[113] This view is now untenable. Certainly in late July the frantic telegram traffic became overwhelming, but governments were clear enough about what they were doing. A general conflict was the optimal outcome for none of them, but they preferred it to what seemed worse alternatives. Although Berlin and St Petersburg indeed miscalculated, all sides were willing to risk war rather than back down.[114] The war developed from a Balkan confrontation in which neither Austria-Hungary nor Russia would yield and neither Germany nor France would restrain them. Once conflict spread from eastern to western Europe, Britain too was willing to intervene rather than see Belgium invaded and France beaten. In Vienna, Conrad had long urged war against Serbia, but Franz Joseph, Berchtold, and Tisza moved to military action only gradually, believing alternative choices were bankrupt, and only after considering how force would be used. In contrast they were recklessly insouciant about war with Russia, accepting it was likely but assuming that with German aid they could win. The Germans risked war against Russia and Britain with little idea of how to defeat either (and with what their general staff knew was a defective plan against France). Nor did they consider much how war would solve their political problems, though Wilhelm seems to have envisaged that Russia would lose Poland and Bethmann that France would lose its colonies, even if they were willing (should Britain stay out) to respect the integrity of France in Europe and of Belgium. Like the Austrians the Germans had sought diplomatic solutions to their encirclement problem and found them unavailing, and they perceived a closing time horizon only two or three years hence. Yet whereas for the Austrians the penalties for inaction seemed evident – internal insurrection combined with outside intervention to support the South Slavs – the threats to Germany were much more shadowy. Bethmann talked darkly during the July crisis of a future Russian invasion, but Germany was more cohesive and resilient than the Habsburg monarchy, and its armed forces much more formidable. The danger facing it if it did nothing was less military defeat than an inability to back its wishes by credible military force and therefore loss of great-power status: *Selbstentmannung* ('self-castration') in Bethmann's revealing phrase.[115] Rather than accept this it would risk a European explosion. But the Germans were not alone in viewing the world in these terms. The Russian leaders had painful recent experience of humiliation in a major crisis, and they too feared second-class status unless they stood up to bullying. Indeed the Russians, French, and British were united in their dismal view of German ambitions. Nicholas II and Sazonov would rather risk war than submit, and by the later stages of the crisis they had convinced themselves that war was coming anyway and the imperative was to prepare for it, at whatever risk to peace. By the time the French and British faced their crucial decisions, war in eastern Europe was a fact, and it was up to them to decide how to respond. For Poincaré and probably Viviani it was axiomatic that France could not repudiate the Russian alliance – or else, once again, second-class status, loss of independence, and vulnerability to dictation beckoned. For Asquith, Grey, and Bonar Law, despite their greater remoteness, German domination of the continent likewise appeared menacing, even if such *Realpolitik* considerations would not, without the invasion of Belgium, have secured prompt British intervention. The British were in an unenviable dilemma. They were probably justified in their gloomy reading of German ambitions, but they underestimated – like everyone else – the cost of frustrating them. Once the crisis moved beyond the Balkan level there were only bad choices for everyone involved. The old world that the powers were destroying was a happier environment for all of them than any likely successor created by violence.

Only the Austrians formulated their objectives with much clarity, and even they did so merely for the Balkan arena. The other powers – including Germany – faced the prospect of an imminent general war so suddenly that they lacked time to establish concrete political aims, which they defined only in retrospect. They fought rather to avoid a negative (the loss of great-power status), and had little hesitation in sacrificing their citizens' lives and happiness to that end. In a word, they fought from fear. The questions remain of why statesmen supposed that war could alleviate such fear, and especially why both sides thought it could. The answer lies partly in the pre-war evolution of the arms race to a point where the two blocs were much closer to equality than they had been after Russia's defeat by Japan. By 1914 the French and Russians, although they would have preferred to fight three years later, could contemplate doing so now. Conversely the German general staff (or so it advised its government) believed victory was still attainable – or at least that if fighting were inevitable it was better not to wait. The two sides were approximating towards an equilibrium (and they were indeed evenly matched, as the next three years would show), but an unstable one in which one side was moving up while the other moved down, a point of 'power transition' rather than a stable balance of terror.[116] This very reference to the 'mutually assured destruction' of the Cold War is a reminder that however powerful were the weapons of 1914 their use was not inconceivable. The possibility of war did not yet seem so destructive that all would be losers and 'victory' would mean nothing. Public military parades still harked back to a folkloric view of battles fought with gaudy uniforms and fifes and drums.[117] Governments' points of reference were the mid-nineteenth century European conflicts and more recent clashes such as those of 1899–1902, 1904–5, and 1912–13. These had ended decisively, although the costs incurred were rising. But to extrapolate from such precedents to collisions in Belgium and in Poland between armies of 2 million men required a scarcely attainable leap of the imagination. In the event, once two heavily armed and highly industrialized coalitions of comparable strength engaged each other with modern military technology the outcome, almost at once, would be a prodigiously costly stalemate that propelled the European governments and their hapless peoples into a bleak and cruel new world.

CHAPTER 2

THE FAILURE OF THE WAR OF MOVEMENT, SUMMER–WINTER 1914

T HE INITIAL CAMPAIGNING produced a whole new set of issues to join those already dividing the powers. By Christmas 1914 the belligerent armies had clashed repeatedly, inflicting hundreds of thousands of deaths and injuries. Yet in Eastern Europe they were little distant from their starting points and in Western Europe they were locked into a stalemate that lasted four more years. Although halting the conflict became almost impossible, neither side saw any speedy route to winning it. During these dramatic months, normal politics were suspended. In France, facing massive invasion, the National Assembly on 4 August voted the government war credits and decree powers before dispersing until December.[1] In Britain, parliament similarly approved extraordinary powers under the Defence of the Realm Act (DORA).[2] In Germany, the Reichstag voted decree authority to the Bundesrat (which represented the state governments), responsibility for food supply and law and order passing to the Deputy Commanding Generals (DCGs) in the empire's twenty-four military districts.[3] The Russian Duma agreed to its own suspension, while in Vienna the Reichsrat was suspended already. Governments and high commands were left to conduct operations as they saw fit, though how much the politicians delegated to their generals varied. The French commander-in-chief, Joseph Joffre, had virtually a free hand, whereas in Germany Moltke was constantly looking over his shoulder. Initially, however, money was no impediment. Finance ministries abandoned the domestic gold standard (i.e., paper money was no longer convertible into precious metal) in order to expand the note issue. Most borrowed without difficulty from their citizens, while – more surprisingly – maintaining credit overseas.[4] In the opening battles commanders could concentrate the resources of a bountiful civilization on pursuing victory, whatever the cost. These considerations made the first five months exceptional. Afterwards the war became to some degree normalized.

The Western Front, in northern France and the Low Countries, was decisive for the struggle as a whole. Here the French and German armies, the most formidable in Europe, came face to face. Their war plans have attracted much attention – arguably more than they deserve in view of the remark by Helmuth von Moltke the Elder that no plan survives the first contact with the enemy.[5] They probably influenced the outcome less than did strengths in divisions and in guns. But they did determine where and how the opening battles took place, and their near unremitting failure to accomplish their objectives left the belligerents in uncharted waters. They will be considered with reference first to Germany and then to its opponents.

As the French were too weak to defeat the Germans, the war in the west could end quickly only if the Germans overwhelmed their enemies. The German government had gone to war with this hope in mind, although it appears the German military experts did not share it. In the 1920s, however, former members of the general staff, who were now writing as historians, alleged that Schlieffen, when CGS, had developed a plan that would have won the war outright had Moltke not warped and misapplied it. After the Second World War the 'Schlieffen Plan', in the form of a memorandum written in December 1905, was rediscovered by another historian, Gerhard Ritter, who in contrast saw it as an unrealizable and irresponsible gamble.[6] Most subsequent commentators have agreed with him, concluding that the plan first encouraged Germany to start the war and then proved incapable of delivering victory. It now seems questionable whether Schlieffen's memorandum had much impact.[7] In fact the GGS continuously revised its war plans on an annual cycle (of which few records have survived), and change was incremental. During his tenure from 1890 to 1905 Schlieffen made two fundamental modifications. The first was no longer to adopt a defensive stance in the west with a view to counter-attacking after repelling a French invasion, but instead to attack at once there with most of the army, while maintaining contingency plans for a primarily eastern deployment. Schlieffen reasoned that because the Russians were accelerating their mobilization it would become harder to catch them unprepared, while the French were also becoming more formidable. His second new idea was to invade France via Belgium, thus utilizing the dense Belgian railway system and avoiding the threat of prolonged siege warfare if he assaulted the complex of fortresses along the Franco-German border.[8] His 1905 memorandum envisaged a strong right wing encircling Paris from the west and pinning the French forces from behind against their eastern fortresses. And yet, he warned, if the French escaped or the Germans lost momentum, the campaign would become endless. He acknowledged that the encirclement manoeuvre, which he conducted on paper with much larger forces than Germany actually possessed, exceeded its army's existing capacities. The memorandum was therefore a think-piece rather than an operational plan, and Schlieffen's 1904–5 staff rides suggest he still envisaged the possibility of initially standing first on the defensive.[9]

Schlieffen's successor also kept Germany's options open. Moltke likewise planned his main effort for the west, in 1913 abandoning work on an eastern deployment. He also expected to violate Belgian neutrality, the Kaiser upholding this assumption when the foreign minister questioned it.[10] But Moltke was less self-confident than Schlieffen, and more politically aware. He operated in a more hazardous environment, in which the relative power of France and Russia was increasing while Austria-Hungary's deteriorated, and British intervention seemed probable. He dared not expose south-western Germany to a French invasion. Hence he opted for a right wing three times stronger than his centre, instead of seven times stronger as Schlieffen had recommended. He and his advisers envisaged a lengthy struggle,[11] and he dropped Schlieffen's plans to invade Holland, hoping instead to preserve it as a neutral 'windpipe' through which to circumvent a British blockade. This amendment made it imperative to secure at once the road and rail routes across Belgium by capturing Liège as soon as war was declared.[12] These changes notwithstanding, the staff officers running the western campaign of 1914 still followed Schlieffen in attempting to outflank France by invading Belgium. But in doing so, as he had foreseen, they embarked on an adventure beyond their resources.

Subject to Wilhelm's approval the GGS had untrammelled independence in strategic planning, but the army's size, structure, and equipment were decided by the war ministries of Prussia and the smaller states, which answered to the state and imperial parliaments. The force that resulted was too small. Most continental countries adopted the principle that all adult males were liable to military service, but few applied it. In 1906 France conscripted 0.75 per cent of its citizens (but about three quarters of the relevant age cohorts of able-bodied young men), Austria-Hungary 0.29 per cent, Russia 0.35 per cent, and Germany 0.47 per cent. Despite its smaller population (c. 39 million compared with c. 65 million), France fielded an army almost as big as Germany's in 1914. In the same year, of 10.4 million men aged 20–45 in Germany, 5.4 million lacked proper military training.[13] Although after the 1912 and 1913 army laws the war ministry could call up each year about half the remaining reservoir of untrained men, this increase would take years to feed through into mobilized strength. However, in a long war Germany would have much larger manpower reserves than France, though not than the entente powers combined. Moreover, what the German army lacked in numbers it substantially compensated for in superior competence. The reasons for this superiority included the combination of decentralization with unified purpose provided by the general staff system, which provided greater opportunity than in the more hierarchical entente armies to learn from mistakes.[14] Officer service was probably more prestigious than elsewhere and attracted abler people: it was no longer an aristocratic preserve, nobles falling from 65 per cent to 30 per cent of the Prussian officer corps between 1865 and 1914. The German army had three times more NCOs than the French one,[15] and its equipment was better suited to modern warfare.[16] Entrenching tools were standard issue and soldiers were trained to use them. Infantry units had weapons such as light mortars that their enemies lacked, and were the best equipped in Europe with machine guns. German and entente divisions had twenty-four machine guns each in 1914, but the Germans grouped theirs in batteries to make them more effective.[17] They also had crucial advantages in artillery, which would be the pre-eminent killer in 1914–18. Since the introduction of the French 75mm cannon in 1897–8 all the main armies had re-equipped with quick-firing field guns. The Germans' C-96nA had a lesser range than the 75mm, but they alone complemented their new field guns by also introducing quick-firing 105mm, 150mm, and 210mm field howitzers that were easily transportable by the standard field artillery team of six horses. These weapons fired heavier shells than did the field guns, and at higher angles (up to 45° instead of 16°), inflicting much greater destruction on fortresses and trenches and in the wooded or hilly country where much of the 1914 fighting occurred.[18]

None the less, at the start of the war in the west the Germans were outnumbered, as they would be until 1918. A German field army of some 1.7 million troops faced *c.* 2 million French ones, as well as a Belgian field army of somewhat over 100,000 and a British one of (initially) somewhat under that number.[19] Belgium's and Britain's contributions were therefore secondary. Belgium was a rich country with a sophisticated armaments industry, but in defence it lagged behind its neighbours. Although it passed legislation in 1913 to double its mobilized strength from 180,000 to 340,000, this made no difference before war broke out. Its army, with only a fifteen-month conscription term, had little professionalism or social cachet. In 1914 it mostly comprised hastily recalled reservists.[20] Moreover, Belgium's attachment to its neutrality had inhibited advance planning. Joffre drew up his Plan XVII not knowing whether he could deploy there, and although the British attempted military conversations in 1905–6 and 1911, Brussels broke them off.[21] King Albert and prime minister de Broqueville saw Germany as the primary threat, but some of their military chiefs distrusted Britain and France at least as much. They possessed no prearranged concentration plan and had to improvise.

The British, in contrast, in good measure thanks to Henry Wilson, had prepared in detail to transport an expeditionary force of up to six infantry divisions and one cavalry division to the French army's northern flank near Hirson by day thirteen of mobilization.[22] Unlike the continental armies, the BEF comprised long-service regulars and well trained reservists, many of whom had seen action. They had good modern Lee Enfield rifles and 18-pounder field guns, though they were weak in heavier weapons. But the British army's budget had remained static since 1906 (while the British naval estimates had risen by two thirds) and the French and German field armies were almost twenty times bigger than the BEF.[23] Nor did Joffre assume beforehand that he could use the BEF, which proved to be wise. In August 1914 Kitchener instructed its commander, Sir John French, to 'support and co-operate' with Joffre, but also emphasized that his command was independent, he should consult London before undertaking offensives, and in general he should minimize losses and exercise caution with the only professional troops Britain possessed.[24]

Moltke's opening blow would therefore fall primarily on the French, whose own war plan played into his hands, if to a lesser extent than its critics have contended.[25] French politicians saw the army as a potential threat to the republic because of the officers' royalism and clericalism. At the turn of the century the Dreyfus affair, in which the army wrongfully accused a Jewish staff officer of spying for Germany, had reinforced such suspicions. France had a general staff (the Etat-major de l'armée or EMA), but unlike Schlieffen and Moltke its chiefs were subordinate to the war minister, their terms in office were short, and they would not command the army in battle. When Joffre became CGS in 1911, however, at the height of the Second Moroccan Crisis, he received greater independence and was designated the putative commander in chief, which in 1914 he duly became.

As exemplified by Plan XV of 1903, French strategists proposed an initial defensive posture followed by a counterstroke in Lorraine, where the bulk of the army would concentrate. Plan XVI (of 1909) was similar, but positioned more forces opposite Belgium.[26] By now the French probably knew more about German preparations than the Germans did about theirs. They anticipated that the main enemy assault would come westwards, and through captured documents and their intelligence about German railway building they expected it to come through Belgium.[27] Their prevailing view, however, was that the German army would stay south of the Meuse, as they mistakenly assumed that it was too small to make a wider sweep. This view stemmed from their erroneous belief that the Germans would not use reserve formations in their front line: something that the French themselves resisted doing. Joffre's predecessor had envisaged amending Plan XVI to make greater use of reserve formations in order to meet head-on a German attack coming north of the Meuse, but the idea had been rejected.[28] In Plan XVII, by contrast, which took effect in April 1914, Joffre proposed not a counterstroke but 'to proceed to battle with all my forces'.[29] Probably influenced by advocates of the tactical and strategic offensive such as Ferdinand Foch, who lectured at the Ecole supérieure de guerre, and Loyzeaux de Grandmaison, chief of the operations bureau in the EMA, he wanted an immediate attack, aiming to paralyse the German advance before it gained momentum. Some of Foch's and Grandmaison's language lent itself to caricature as a 'cult of the offensive' in which willpower would prevail over firepower, though in fact Plan XVII emanated partly from an accurate appreciation that the strategic balance was moving to the entente's advantage.[30] Moreover, the plan did not prescribe the direction of the attack, leaving this to the commander at the time. Purely as a concentration plan it had its merits, as French forces would deploy further forward than previously and could strike against a German advance coming either from Lorraine or through Belgium and Luxemburg.[31] Nevertheless, it proved to be a grave error. The government endorsed the principle of an immediate attack, though it rejected (probably for fear of antagonizing Britain) a pre-emptive incursion into Belgium. Yet the alternative of invading Alsace and Lorraine would quickly run into formidable defences against which Joffre would squander his strength.

Despite Plan XVII's drawbacks, the French started with two major advantages. The first was numerical. The 1913 three-year military service law had significantly enlarged the standing army, though only by calling up two cohorts of raw young conscripts in autumn 1913 instead of one. More important was that thanks to decades of intensive recruitment, France possessed a deep well of reservists that allowed its mobilized army almost to equal its rival in total size and to outnumber it in the western theatre. Second, in 1870 French mobilization and concentration had been dilatory and chaotic, whereas now their efficiency matched that of Germany's (admittedly larger) equivalents. The French used over 10,000 trains for mobilization; the Germans 20,800 (moving 2,070,000 men, 11,800 horses, and 400,000 tons of supplies). For concentration, the French used some 11,500 trains, moving six or seven times as many men and horses as in 1870, yet with a maximum delay of two hours. The EMA's organizing ability was partly responsible for this success, but in addition the French had vastly improved their railway network, which would be of capital importance right through the war. By 1890 they equalled the Germans in the numbers of trunk lines running to the common border, and since then they had improved their transverse lines of communication. They could get men quickly to the frontier and could also shift them laterally.[32]

These advantages made it unlikely that France would be trounced again, especially as Russia was committed to strike quickly and Italy's neutrality removed the need to divert French forces to the Alps. Yet serious deficiencies rendered it incapable of the disabling preventive blow that Joffre envisaged. Much of its equipment budget since 1870 had been expended on fortresses. The latter, at least in the major complex round Verdun, had been protected with reinforced concrete and retractable turrets against modern heavy artillery, although many smaller forts remained easy prey.[33] But the consequence (as in 1940) was neglect of the field army. The latter's 75mm field gun was superior to its German counterpart, but French divisions possessed only this one artillery weapon. Because of parliamentary tight-fistedness and war ministry infighting they had no equivalent of the German field howitzers. The heavy artillery service that Joffre knocked together after 1913 comprised only about 300 guns, mostly pre-quick-firing weapons pirated from fortresses, and held at army group rather than at divisional level. The Lebel rifle was serviceable but inferior to the German Mauser. Again, for reasons of parsimony and misplaced conservatism (by parliament rather than the army), the infantry, alone in Europe, had not adopted camouflage and would fight in conspicuous red and blue outfits. Historians have given much attention to the zealots of offensive tactics, who influenced the 1913 infantry field service regulations.[34] Yet they probably did less damage than the basic weaknesses: the French field army was less well trained and equipped than the German one and poorly configured for the task assigned to it.

The argument thus far suggests the stalemate that developed on the Western Front was predictable from the outset. Nevertheless it was not predetermined. Any explanation of the fortunes of war must embrace the roles of chance, leadership, and morale. However efficiently the French mobilized, it would benefit them little unless their troops were able and willing to fight. In the event, the war began with weeks of Allied* disasters before the counter-attack that became famous as the battle of the Marne. The remainder of the 1914 western campaign confirmed that although the Germans were unable to overwhelm their enemies, the latter were also unable to evict the invaders. It is unsurprising that this turning-point has attracted more attention than almost any other moment of the war.

The opening phase of movement was a curious interlude that arguably resembled nineteenth-century warfare more closely than what followed. Mounted troops were essential for reconnaissance and rapid manoeuvre, the Germans deploying 77,000 cavalrymen and even the BEF some 10,000. French cavalry still wore breastplates; British officers carried swords in combat.[35] Yet if aspects of this campaigning recalled magazine caricatures of 1870, the troops and their comman-

---

*The entente powers and their partners will henceforth be referred to as the Allies, although technically they became so only when they signed the Pact of London on 5 September, binding the participants not to make a separate peace.

ders who advanced beyond the railheads were still entering a vast and terrifying unknown. It may seem barely credible now that only ninety years ago Europeans were demolishing frontier posts in order to slaughter each other *en masse*, and the spectacle was scarcely less disturbing at the time.[36] All the same, most men silenced their inward reservations. As early as 4 August German soldiers entered Belgium and the killing – including executions of civilians – began.[37]

Moltke's war plan required his Second Army to seize Liège as soon as mobilization started, before advancing into France along the Meuse corridor. The twelve major forts around the city were built in reinforced concrete and the larger ones had eight or nine turrets.[38] But Germany's Krupp works had not delivered the modern guns ordered from it, and the turrets had not been updated by being made retractable. The forts needed an outer ring of defenders in field fortifications to keep the enemy siege artillery out of range, and to begin with the Liège commandant, General Leman, possessed a reinforced infantry division of some 24,000 men. On 7 August, however, German forces led by Erich Ludendorff, who as Moltke's chief of operations until 1913 had done much to devise the war plan and had now been sent to oversee its execution, stormed the Liège citadel and Leman's infantry withdrew, leaving the fortresses exposed. To bombard them the invaders deployed 305mm Skoda heavy howitzers lent by the Austrians as well as secretly developed 420mm Krupp howitzers that they assembled on site. Direct hits on the turrets smashed the defending artillery, sometimes detonating internal explosions that wrecked the forts completely. Before the last one surrendered German troops were streaming beyond Liège, and from 18 August, with the concentration complete, they embarked on the great advance to the west.[39]

Moltke stationed one reserve corps in Schleswig-Holstein against a possible British landing, and nine infantry divisions and twelve brigades of Landwehr (garrison units composed of men too old or untrained for the field army) in East Prussia, but he committed seventy-eight infantry divisions and ten cavalry divisions, grouped in seven armies, to the western theatre. The Thionville–Metz fortification complex in Lorraine served as a pivot: fifty-two divisions deployed north of it advanced through Luxemburg and Belgium, while those south of it initially stayed put.[40] On the right von Kluck's First Army of 320,000 men, von Bülow's Second of 260,000, and von Hausen's Third of 180,000 would have furthest to march and faced much weaker forces: the Belgians, the BEF, and Lanrezac's Fifth French Army numbering 254,000.[41] Avoiding Holland, and wheeling at furthest only through Brussels rather than reaching the sea, the Germans none the less began with a powerful outflanking movement, although exactly what Moltke intended it to lead to remains unclear.

At first the Germans met little resistance, in good measure due to lack of Allied co-ordination. King Albert appealed for help as soon as he received the German ultimatum, but during August Franco-Belgian co-operation was conspicuous by its absence. Although he concentrated most of his six-division field army on the river Gette in central Belgium, as the advance unrolled he withdrew into the fortified 'national redoubt' round Antwerp. Kluck detached two reserve divisions to mask the city, but for the next two months the main Belgian force did little, depriving the Allies of their numerical advantage when they most needed it. Albert did assign one division to defend the nine forts of the Namur complex, some thirty miles upstream along the Meuse from Liège, but between 20 and 25 August the Germans used their siege artillery to demolish the Namur defences, avoiding infantry assaults.[42] On the French side Joffre deplored Albert's decision to disengage rather than fight alongside the Allies;[43] but although he authorized Lanrezac's Fifth Army to advance into Belgium as far as the Sambre-Meuse line, it gave Namur little assistance.

Two factors contributed to Joffre's underestimation of the northern danger: his preference for striking in Alsace-Lorraine and his uncertainty about Moltke's intentions. As early as 8 August French troops entered Mulhouse in Alsace, whose inhabitants met them with acclaim but which they soon had to evacuate. Once Joffre had completed his concentration he sent his First and Second Armies into Lorraine, hoping they could reach the Rhine and distract the Germans from his main attack. Although at first this operation went well enough, Joffre's two armies were linked only by sporadic telegraph messages, whereas the opposing German Fourth and Fifth Armies benefited from a single staff, were stronger than he realized, and were falling back by design. At the battle of Morhange-Sarrebourg on 20 August French troops toiling uphill ran into a hail of machine gun bullets and artillery fire directed by aircraft. The Germans counter-attacked and the invaders fell back across the border, losing 150 guns and 20,000 men taken prisoner.[44] But worse was to come, for on 21 August Joffre decided on his principal assault. Plan XVII gave him discretion over when and where to launch it, and he delayed while his intelligence clarified the scale and direction of the enemy onslaught. Even so, he committed himself prematurely. Surprised by the strength of the Germans' left in Lorraine and of their right in Belgium, he mistakenly inferred that their centre must be weak. He ordered his Third and Fourth Armies to attack in the Ardennes, thus threatening Moltke's flanking movement near its pivot, while his Fifth Army conducted a supporting attack on the river Sambre. The result was a multiple disaster. The French forces entering the Ardennes were weaker than the Germans in reconnaissance cavalry, and on the morning of 22 August mist grounded their aircraft. Groping forward in echelon along the few roads through the forest, they blundered not into weaker forces but into twenty-one divisions against their own twenty. Their 75mm field guns were ineffective in the hilly terrain, and poorly linked by telephone with the infantry; they were no answer to the German machine guns and field howitzers, which wreaked havoc. In the battle of Charleroi, fought further to the north-west on the same day, Lanrezac's Fifth Army fared no better. In this encounter both sides were advancing, the Germans meeting an outnumbered French force that had not prepared its position, and French counter-attacks failed with heavy losses.[45] By the 23rd Lanrezac had decided to retreat, abandoning the remaining Namur forts and opening a serious rift (both literal and metaphorical) with the British. At French request, the latter had detrained the BEF round Maubeuge (further forward than previously planned) and ordered it into Belgium, where it deployed behind the Mons–Condé canal. Here on 23 August Kluck's First German Army ran into it. Kluck's cavalry had missed the British (while mist had again blinded the aircraft), and the startled Germans began a poorly organized assault against experienced troops who were shielded by miners' cottages and slag heaps, and whose Lee Enfields fired fifteen rounds a minute. Two British divisions held off six German ones, inflicting casualties three times their own 1,850.[46] By the afternoon, however, the German howitzers were in action and the British would have been hard pressed to hold out longer even had they not been forced to fall back during the night by Lanrezac's retreat, which he authorized without consulting them. Matters were not helped by the French mistakenly supposing that the BEF commander had been instructed to obey Joffre's orders, but in addition Sir John French, though popular with his men, showed himself in 1914 to be unsteady and too readily influenced by personal antagonisms, one of which already divided him from Lanrezac. In any case the BEF's success in delaying the Germans was dwarfed by the comprehensive Allied débâcle in the 'battle of the Frontiers' (as the engagements of 20–24 August are collectively known). By the end of August some 75,000 French soldiers had died already (27,000 of them on the 22nd alone) and their total killed and wounded numbered 260,000, against much lighter German losses.[47] On the 24th Joffre reported to his war minister that the general attack had failed definitively and the Allies must revert to the defensive.[48]

When the Allies began their 'Great Retreat', the Germans appeared closer to victory than they ever would be again. Yet although the invaders had repulsed their opponents, the latter withdrew so rapidly that they avoided encirclement, soon making good their losses. As the Germans advanced, in contrast, the logistical shortcomings inherent in the Schlieffen–Moltke Plan wore them down.[49] Many of these problems were common to all the massive invading armies of 1914. Beyond the frontier railheads the troops had to march with heavy packs and chafing boots in sweltering heat, Kluck's men covering 500 kilometres in a month.[50] Men or horses had to carry the supplies, as the entire German army was disposed of only some 4,000 lorries and before it reached the Marne 60 per cent of them broke down.[51] As the Germans moved deeper into Belgium, they encountered systematic railway sabotage, all the Meuse bridges being destroyed and most of the tunnels. By early September only 3–400 miles of the 2,500-mile Belgian railway network were back in operation, Kluck's army was 80 miles beyond its nearest railhead, and Bülow's 100 miles.[52] Once the lines were reinstated, ammunition had top priority and the right wing received adequate supplies of it, while the troops, marching through a fertile countryside in high summer, fed themselves by requisitioning (except for a notable absence of bread). Their horses, however, whose demands were much greater, could not be sustained by forage: green corn made them sick, and vets were few. As Kluck's 84,000 horses needed 2 million pounds of fodder a day, the roads became strewn with dying animals and the heavy guns lagged behind. Nor could the Germans make good their losses in men, as soldiers dropped from exhaustion as well as wounds. By September many units were down to half their initial strength.[53]

The pell-mell advance also strained communications. Whereas the French could use a dense and intact telegraph system, the Germans suffered – and much more acutely – from the problems that had hobbled the French advance into Lorraine. Moltke advanced his headquarters from Koblenz to Luxemburg on 29 August, but was still too distant to reach his army commanders conveniently by road and until 11 September neither he nor his chief of operations, Gerhard Tappen, visited any of them. The commanders communicated between themselves by dispatch riders or by radio, but few wireless sets were available, they were bulky and difficult to use, and rather than lose time encrypting messages the Germans sent them *en clair*, enabling the French to intercept them. Between September and November the Allies read some fifty German radio messages, which betrayed both the weaknesses of their enemies' command system before the Marne and their intentions during the subsequent 'race to the sea'.[54]

In addition to supply and communication difficulties, command decisions eroded the Germans' superiority. As they advanced they detached troops to guard their supply lines and contain unsubdued resistance. One army corps was released to screen Antwerp and a second to besiege Maubeuge, as well as a brigade to garrison Brussels. Admittedly in Antwerp the Germans masked much larger Belgian forces, but the decision still weakened their right, as did two more actions that retrospectively were fiercely criticized. First, following the victory at Morhange-Sarrebourg, Moltke ordered an offensive by his left flank in Lorraine – much to the surprise of his Sixth Army commander, though pre-war planning had allowed for such a counterstroke. He sent no fewer than sixteen divisions to attack round Nancy, yet failed to inhibit Joffre from transferring units from the east to the north.[55] Apparently Moltke believed he could not have done likewise because the railways were wrecked. In fact he probably could have moved troops from his left to his right fast enough to make a difference before the battle of the Marne, but until 5 September he did not even try to.[56] Moltke's second decision, on 25 August, was to move three army corps (two of which actually went) to counter the Russian invasion of East Prussia, only to find that the Russians were beaten before the men arrived. He admitted afterwards that this had been a serious misjudgement, which seems partly attributable to overconfidence at his headquarters (*Oberste Heeresleitung,* or OHL*)* that the battle in the west was virtually won.[57] Some of the reinforcements came directly from Bülow's Second Army, but Bülow advised that he could spare them, and Moltke trusted his judgement.[58]

Moltke's actions at this juncture suggest he was determined to protect Germany's territory, whether in East Prussia or Alsace, but willing to strike wherever the enemy seemed weak rather than staking everything on his right flank. Indeed his 27 August general instructions envisaged attacking all along the line. His Fourth and Fifth Armies were to advance into French Lorraine while his right wheeled south-westwards, the First Army towards the lower Seine and the Second towards Paris.[59] This was his most ambitious directive and the concept behind it remains obscure, though a follow-up on 2 September made clear his main concern was not to take the capital but to outflank the French army. Thus he now ordered Kluck to advance south-eastwards (and therefore east, rather than west of Paris) to protect Bülow's flank as the latter chased the French, though in fact this directive endorsed a south-eastwards turn that Kluck had already begun. As he supposed his uncle had done in 1870, Moltke cultivated a devolved style of leadership, in part making a virtue of a necessity in view of the slowness of communications with his commanders. He delegated to Kluck and Bülow the responsibility for the pursuit. Until 29 August Kluck came under Bülow's orders but then he was released from them, creating a vacuum on the right where neither Moltke nor any of his subordinates was in charge. This soon proved a recipe for trouble.

While the Germans lost impetus, the Allies recovered. During the Great Retreat two battles forced the invaders to pause. After Mons the retreating BEF split into its two constituent corps to pass on either side of the forest of Mormal. On 26 August the commander of the Second Corps, Horace Smith-Dorrien, stood his ground at the battle of Le Cateau with 55,000 men against 140,000 from Kluck's army. Although he delayed the enemy advance, he was lucky to escape (with French assistance) and his men suffered 7,812 casualties.[60] More significant was the check to Bülow's Second Army inflicted by the French Fifth Army three days later at Guise, Kluck first altering his direction to the south-east in order to respond to a call from Bülow for assistance. But the underlying story of this period was Joffre's conception and implementation of a fall-back plan. On the one hand he was ruthlessly sacking older and less competent generals, and by early September one third of his senior commanders had been replaced because of dismissals and casualties.[61] On the other, as early as 24–25 August he thought of pivoting on Verdun, pulling back his left to win time while he constituted a new force drawn from his right and from the French interior that could outflank the Germans from the west. 'Our principal reason for attempting to last out,' he wrote afterwards, was hope that Moltke would divert forces against the Russians, though not until 31 August did French intelligence report German troop trains rolling eastwards.[62] In the meantime, the French used their transverse railways intensively in order to ferry their own troops to the north-west,[63] where a new Sixth Army under Michael-Joseph Maunoury began to form around Amiens, menacing Kluck's lines of communication.

In carrying through his recovery plans, Joffre faced two principal obstacles. The first was Sir John French, who was used to colonial wars and had been instructed to conserve his army. Shaken by the Le Cateau losses, French refused to take part at Guise. On 30 August he told Joffre that he intended to retire behind the Seine to rest and refit. After Joffre understandably appealed to Henry Wilson, the cabinet sent out Kitchener, who met Sir John on 1 September and insisted that he should stay in line and conform to the French army's movements. Sir John was overridden by a political decision (for which he never forgave Kitchener), but as a result the BEF contributed significantly to the Marne battle.[64] Joffre's second problem was the threat to Paris. He had initially intended to counter-attack well north of the city on the Amiens–Laon–Reims line, but the Germans advanced too rapidly.[65] They seemed to be heading straight for the capital, where a national coalition government was formed on 26 August and the new war minister, Alexandre Millerand, made a rare intervention in strategy. Joffre was primarily concerned with creating a new field force, but Millerand insisted on elements of the Sixth Army being added to the Paris garrison even though the government temporarily abandoned Paris on 2 September for Bordeaux. The imperative of defending the city therefore complicated French strategy, while proximity to it buoyed up the exhausted Germans. None the less, France's army rather than its capital was Kluck's and Moltke's primary objective. Their decision to turn east probably saved Paris from a pitched battle in its suburbs that Joffre would still have been too weak to prevent.

While the Germans drove into a sack between Paris and Verdun, the Allies debated on the timing of the counterstroke against Kluck's exposed western flank.[66] Afterwards French commentators disputed over whether Joffre or General Joseph Gallieni, the Paris military governor, had first seen the opportunity. Probably Gallieni did, when after Allied aircraft reported on 3 September that Kluck was turning east from Paris he instructed Maunoury's Sixth Army to prepare an attack. Joffre, however, received independent confirmation of the German turn from radio intercepts, and incorporated Gallieni's suggestion into a broader order dated 4 September for a general offensive on the 6th. After an emotional meeting with Joffre, Sir John French promised the BEF would take part. Joffre's information was that his troops' losses had been replenished, their morale was high, and they saw no need for further retreat. He planned to attack on both flanks from the directions of Paris and Verdun while holding firm in the centre. But shooting started one day early when units of Kluck's First Army and of Maunoury's Sixth clashed near the river Ourcq, and what has gone down in history as the battle of the Marne (the term was a French coinage) actually consisted of a series of interconnected conflicts along a front of 100 miles in which both sides were on the offensive and much of the fighting favoured the Germans.

In the east the French pincer movement from Verdun achieved little and the Germans tried to isolate the fortress by breaking through the fortifications to its south along the Meuse heights. They failed to do so, with the result that if they did fall back it would have to be north of the Marne, to a line behind the river Aisne.[67] In the central sector of the battle, in the St. Gond marshes, the German Second Army halted an offensive by the newly formed French Ninth Army under Foch, and pushed it back towards the Seine. In the west, along the Ourcq, Kluck's Second Corps commander, von Gronau, held a ridge north of Meaux and repelled Maunoury's attacks while Kluck force-marched two more corps from his eastern flank to join him. Despite the French reinforcements sent out (in a celebrated episode) from Paris in taxicabs, by 8 September the battle here too was going the Germans' way. The only exception to the pattern occurred along the Grand and the Petit Morin, two tributaries of the Marne running south of the river. Here Kluck's transfer of troops towards the Ourcq created a gap between his and Bülow's armies, into which the BEF moved cautiously forward against little resistance. The German right wing had been so eroded that in the western half of the battlefield the Allies, fortified by Joffre's railway movements and his and Kitchener's chivvying of Sir John French, enjoyed a numerical advantage of perhaps thirty divisions to twenty.[68] Further, the French had improved their tactics. They used concealed 75mm guns with aerial guidance to break German attacks and support French ones, though firing off most of their munitions in the process. Thus their reserves of 75mm shells on mobilization stood at 530,000 and on 5 September at 465,000, but ten days later at only 33,000.[69] The German field artillery, meanwhile, was running out of ammunition.[70] Yet even with superior numbers, fresh troops, and massive consumption of munitions, the French were still being forced back. Given a few more days the Germans could probably have seen off Joffre's counterstroke, ensconcing themselves within striking distance of Paris and of the trunk railway between the capital and Lorraine.[71] But to the OHL the picture seemed much grimmer, and on 8–9 September it resolved to break the action off. Moltke did not exactly snatch defeat from the jaws of victory, but almost certainly he could have secured a better situation by persisting.

The German withdrawal owed much to misperception and miscommunication. Kluck and Bülow had contrasting command styles, the former being more optimistic and aggressive. Cable links across the thirty-five miles between them were not established until the afternoon of 9 September, after the crucial decisions had been taken.[72] Neither could give the other orders and they failed to liaise, Kluck saying nothing to Bülow before reinforcing his Ourcq front. Nor did they ask Moltke for guidance. But in any case he was scarcely able to provide it, for he was 150 miles away and out of touch. Between 5 and 9 September OHL issued no orders and between 7 and 9 September Kluck and Bülow sent it no reports.[73] On the 8th a staff conference under Moltke at length decided to send OHL's foreign intelligence chief, Lieut.-Colonel Richard Hentsch, to visit the army commanders. Hentsch's mission became the vehicle by which the pessimists triumphed over the optimists, and it remained controversial for years. An inquiry in 1917 found that Moltke had briefed Hentsch orally that if the right wing had begun retreating (that OHL was unsure of this underscores its remarkable ignorance) he should direct the withdrawal so as to close the gap between Kluck and Bülow. Hentsch discovered that Bülow had indeed decided to fall back behind the Marne and when he visited Kluck's First Army headquarters he ordered it to follow suit. The 1917 investigation concluded he had not exceeded his authority, in this supporting Hentsch against Moltke and Tappen, who claimed he had.[74] Probably Hentsch was right, but as he died in 1918 and Moltke died in 1916 the German official history never got to the bottom of the matter. What seems clear is that on 8 and 9 September Hentsch, who had a high professional reputation but was known for pessimism, saw Bülow, who had similar tendencies. They agreed that the Second Army should retreat if the BEF crossed the Marne (which on the 9th German aviators confirmed it had done), and that if the Second Army withdrew a reluctant First Army must do likewise, Hentsch conveying the decision to Kluck's chief of staff, von Kuhl. After Hentsch returned to OHL Moltke neither reproached nor repudiated him, but after himself visiting the army commanders on 11 September ordered the Third, Fourth, and Fifth Armies to retreat too.[75] Moreover, Moltke was the greatest pessimist of all, a man who had always doubted his abilities, had tinkered with the plan before and during the campaign, and by September fell prey to depression and anxiety that alarmed those around him.[76] The contrast with Joffre, eating heartily and sleeping soundly, exuding an air of monumental calm, communicating with his generals, and intervening frequently, is inescapable. It is true that the German commander facing the BEF felt overstretched and vulnerable, but the fall of Maubeuge on 8 September made available an army corps, which could have plugged the gap until Kluck had defeated Maunoury and turned back to deal with the British. Probably there was no need to retreat – which does not mean that if the Germans had stood firm a French collapse was imminent. The most likely outcome would still have been a stalemate, though for Paris and Verdun a more dangerous one.

On the other hand if the Germans had stayed put they would not have occupied so commanding a natural position as the chalk ridge rising 500 feet above the river

Aisne to which they retreated between 9 and 14 September. Moltke had already mentioned this to Hentsch as a defence line, and he now ordered his troops to fortify it. The German infantry had spades and field engineers, and for years when on manoeuvres had practised digging trenches protected by barbed wire.[77] The Seventh Reserve Corps from Maubeuge filled the space between Kluck and Bülow, soon followed by two more corps from Belgium.[78] Meanwhile the Allies moved forward in cold and wet (the weather broke on 10 September), and were short of horses and shells. When they reached the Aisne the rain inhibited air reconnaissance. They crossed it on 12 September, but were forced back. Two days later Joffre ordered a frontal attack, which almost everywhere failed. He argued in retrospect that a faster advance might have dislodged the Germans before they were reinforced, which may have been true but disregarded his troops' exhaustion.[79] Although fighting continued for another fortnight the Aisne appears in retrospect as the first of the paradigmatic Western Front battles, characterized by repeated fruitless assaults against entrenched defenders. The Germans' success casts further doubt on whether they had really been defeated, as opposed to falling victim to their own disorganization. Once they rallied, they halted their enemies with ease. Certainly the Marne brought the Allies important gains – the portion of France under occupation fell from 7.5 per cent to 4 per cent[80] and historic towns and railway centres such as Reims and Amiens were liberated, though not the northern industrial area and the Lorraine iron ore field. Yet dismaying for the German troops though the withdrawal was, OHL did not see it as excluding early victory but rather as a manoeuvre that would shorten the line and make possible a second attempt.[81] Once trench lines extended from Switzerland to the Channel it seemed a more significant turning point. But even before the Marne this process was well under way. Trenches appeared in the eastern sector of the theatre during August and by the Marne they already ran from Switzerland to Verdun; by 9 September they ran on to the Camp de Mailly, and the Aisne retreat extended them 100 kilometres more.[82] Both sides furiously improvised the logistical systems needed to sustain hundreds of thousands of combatants in open country. A tactical stalemate began to develop on the Western Front within the opening weeks, was virtually complete within three months, and then lasted until 1918. After the Allies eventually found out how to break it, the Germans almost immediately surrendered. All of this underlines the probability that the Marne and the Aisne merely settled the timing of the eclipse of a war of movement that was virtually bound to end anyway.

At this point we must turn to the Eastern Front. It has been much less closely studied than the Western one. Of the three powers that did the greater part of the fighting, the Germans stationed at most a third of their army there,[83] Austria-Hungary broke up in 1918, and Soviet Russia preferred to forget what Lenin denounced as an imperialist conflict. Yet for much of the period from 1914 to 1917 as many men were serving in the east as in France and Belgium and here too casualties were enormous, even if relatively more were caused by disease and fewer by combat wounds. Although the war would be won or lost in the west, the east repeatedly had a critical impact on the conflict as a whole, starting with the two army corps that Moltke diverted there at the expense of his right flank on the Marne.

The imperial Russian army was the largest of the contending forces. In August 1914 it committed twenty-one infantry divisions against Germany (whose divisions in the theatre numbered thirteen) and some fifty-three against Austria-Hungary, which fielded thirty-seven smaller infantry divisions against Russia.[84] The total number of divisions was about three quarters that in the west, and Russia outnumbered both Central Powers. Yet the tsarist empire's mobilized strength was not much more than that of France or Germany with their much smaller populations. Traditionally Russia maintained a large standing army, to garrison its extended frontiers and for internal repression;[85] furthermore, its high command believed a longer training period was needed than in the west to break in conscripts of rudimentary education and uncertain reliability. The 1874 military service law provided for generous exemptions among the educated, and from those who remained the army selected what it needed by lot. Much of the budget went on supplying the standing forces, within a total capped by Russia's poverty and by nearly a decade of economic stagnation and fiscal crisis between 1900 and 1909. Thereafter a spectacular boom allowed the authorities to spend more, but they called up barely one quarter of the available manpower each year, with the result that the first-class trained reserve numbered only about 2.8 million, to be added to a standing army of some 1.4 million.[86] Nor were the conscripts particularly well equipped. One reason was that by 1914 Russia was actually outspending Germany on its navy, though as the Russian yards took some six years (compared with three in the west) to build a battleship, it had little to show for the money. Further, Russia spent heavily on fortifications rather than on the field army, a matter causing much pre-war dissension but resolved when the war minister, Sukhomlinov, ruled that some Polish fortresses should be declassified but a dozen others modernized.[87] Sukhomlinov was a controversial figure, who in 1915 was imprisoned for corruption and after the Revolution was convicted of treason. Although on balance he was a reforming influence, the officer corps was split between his protégés and his enemies. He knew the fortresses were vulnerable and would have preferred to abandon them, but was obliged to compromise. In 1914 they had 2,813 modern guns, whereas the field army had only 240 mobile heavy weapons.[88] Like the French, therefore, the Russians had too little of the heavy artillery that would be critical to successful attacks. They had adequate numbers of a good quick-firing field gun but only 1,000 shells available for each, compared with 1,400–2,000 in France and 3,000 in Germany.[89] Similarly their 4.5 million rifles (the 7.2mm Mosin M.91) were enough for the initial mobilization but little more. And although all observers agreed on the courage and endurance of ordinary Russian soldiers, they had too few officers and NCOs. In 1903 Germany had twelve re-enlisted NCOs per company, France six, and Russia two.[90] The 'Great Programme', approved in 1914, would have raised the annual recruitment quota from 455,000 to 580,000 and reinforced the artillery, but the outbreak of war forestalled both this project and the 1914 Franco-Russian railway agreement. In their absence the army went to war with many of the weaknesses of the French forces but without the compensation of a first-class railway network. In particular Russian Poland, a salient hedged in by East Prussia to the north and the Austrian provinces of Galicia and the Bukovina to the south, had deliberately been starved of road and rail links, the authorities seeing it as an invasion corridor into the Russian interior rather than a springboard for advance to the west.[91] By 1914 Russian rearmament had made considerable progress, but it still had a long way to go.

None the less, the Russians would now deliver simultaneous blows against both their enemies. Their adoption of an offensive war plan was recent. The Russian army's greatest days lay in the eighteenth and early nineteenth centuries. Since then its technological lag behind the west had widened. After the defeat by Japan the high command had advised that Russia must avoid a European war. The 1910 military reform had speeded up mobilization, but Russia's 1910 war plan, Plan 19, was the most cautious for many years. Mainly due to Yuri Danilov, the chief operational planner in the general staff, it foresaw an opening German invasion, against which Russia must deploy its main forces defensively and along the eastern edge of the Polish salient, assigning smaller contingents against the Austrians. Yet by 1914 this emphasis had been reversed. One reason was pressure from the French for an early attack, given that they expected the main German offensive to go westwards (as the Russians' own intelligence verified). Russia needed to prevent France from going under, and in 1911 its CGS promised an early invasion of Germany. But alliance pressure was not the only factor at work. Within the Russian army a faction led by Mikhail Alekseyev, the chief of staff of the Warsaw Military District, were increasingly confident about the prospects, objected to abandoning Poland, and wanted to attack Austria-Hungary, both because they doubted whether an invasion of East Prussia would succeed and because of their hostility to the traditional Habsburg antagonist. In 1912 Russia therefore adopted a radically revised scheme, Plan 19 Altered. Variant 'G' still provided for a defensive stance if Germany attacked eastwards, but Variant 'A' assumed it would go westwards and envisaged offensives against both East Prussia and Austrian Galicia with the larger forces directed against the latter. By 1914 a new plan, Plan 20, envisaging a still earlier and stronger dual offensive, was scheduled for adoption from September and closely resembled what was implemented in August.[92] In the event, Russia launched two needlessly weak offensives, whereas almost certainly it would have done better to sit tight on one front while attacking on the other.

Fortunately for the Russians their principal adversary would also attempt a dual offensive, and from an even weaker position. Russia's army budget was more than double that of the Austro-Hungarian common army, and although the Dual Monarchy's population exceeded that of France its army's war strength was less than half the French figure. A lower proportion of the Monarchy's young men were called up than in any other great power, and many did very short periods of service.[93] Whereas Russians were the majority ethnic group in the tsarist army, the Habsburg army's officer corps was three quarters Austrian-German,[94] but its rank and file accurately reflected Austria-Hungary's multinational composition. It included some good units such as the Tyrolean mountain fighters, but even before the war the reliability of its Czechs and South Slavs was uncertain. Moreover, a common army division had only 42 field guns (and a Landwehr or Honvéd division 24) compared with 48 in a Russian division and 72 light and medium pieces in a German one.[95] Unlike the Germans the Austrians had no quick-firing field howitzers. They had smaller shell stocks per gun than the Russians, and fewer NCOs per regiment. In the 1880s they had built a network of concentration railways through the Carpathian mountains, which formed a natural bulwark against Russian invasion, and the Galician plain to the north was guarded by a chain of fortresses, notably Lemberg (Lwów), Przemysl, and Cracow. But since the turn of the century they had concentrated on preparing their south-western frontier against Italy and the Russians had overtaken them. By 1914 the Austro-Hungarian general staff estimated that Russia could run 260 trains a day into the concentration zone, against Austria-Hungary's 153.[96] By almost any measure the Habsburg forces were quantitatively and qualitatively disadvantaged.

Austria-Hungary was further handicapped by having many possible antagonists. Although the Russians faced Japan, China, Turkey, and Sweden, they judged correctly that they could focus mainly on their western borders. The Austrians had to consider not only Russia but also Serbia and Montenegro. They had long considered Italy a potential enemy, and in 1914 Romania seemed about to join the Russian camp. Hence the Vienna general staff had devised contingency plans for 'Case I' (Italy), 'B' (Balkans), and 'R' (Russia). Even Conrad doubted he could fight on all three fronts, but he did plan for hostilities against both Russia and Serbia and against Serbia alone, his problem being that he did not know whether or when Russia would intervene in a Balkan conflict. To address it he sought operational flexibility and attempted to clarify German plans. Thus his mobilized forces would fall into three groups. *A-Staffel* ('A-Contingent') would defend the frontier in Galicia, *Minimalgruppe Balkan* ('Balkan Minimal Group') would do likewise against Serbia, and *B-Staffel* would attack Serbia in a localized Balkan war, or go north in a war against Russia or in one against both countries. In a two-front war he therefore wisely envisaged standing on the defensive against the less dangerous Serbs and sending most of the army to Galicia. More problematic, however, would be an Austro-Serb conflict in which Russia intervened. Conrad could wait for a week before sending *B-Staffel* south or north, but if Russia entered after he had committed it to the Balkans disengagement would be slow and difficult. In early 1909, as the Bosnian annexation crisis approached its climax, he had therefore sounded out Moltke. The latter had responded that if Austria-Hungary invaded Serbia in response to provocation and Russia intervened militarily, Germany would see grounds for war against the Russo-French alliance. But Conrad still feared being drawn into an offensive against Russia while simultaneously fighting in the Balkans. He warned that he would advance from Galicia only if Germany simultaneously attacked from East Prussia, trapping Russian Poland in a pincer movement. Moltke assured him that Germany's Eighth Army would indeed launch such an attack, and in 1914 Conrad seems to have assumed that this assurance still held good. In March he was working on a new plan whereby in recognition of Russia's growing strength Austrian troops would deploy well behind the border and abandon eastern Galicia, but his commitment to an offensive remained.[97]

In the event the Germans deployed in East Prussia only second-rate contingents. The Eighth Army comprised thirteen infantry divisions and one cavalry division with 774 guns: about one tenth of their total forces.[98] Three of the six infantry divisions in the field army were reserve divisions, receiving their officers and NCOs only on mobilization. Contrary to the 1909 undertakings, Moltke instructed the commander, Max von Prittwitz, not to take the offensive but to defend East Prussia while 'supporting' the Austrian advance by drawing Russian strength on to him. He gave Prittwitz discretion to retreat to the Vistula *in extremis*, though warned that doing so would be disastrous.[99] Strategically, the Russians would have been prudent to stay on the defensive against Austria-Hungary and focus on Germany, in order to threaten Berlin and co-ordinate pressure with the French. But politically they felt compelled to assist Serbia. They committed less than half their army against East Prussia and further harmed their prospects by subdividing their forces. Probably their best course of action would have been to advance with their entire strength from the east against the provincial capital, Königsberg. Instead they attempted a pincer operation, partly because of East Prussia's refractory geography. The province was infertile and sparsely inhabited, much of it covered by forests and water. A fifty-mile wide lake chain, known as the *Angerapp Stellung* or 'Angerapp position', formed a barrier in its centre. The Russian First Army, under Paul von Rennenkampf (men of German origin were common in the tsarist elite), invaded to the north-east of the lakes and the Second Army, under Alexander Samsonov, to the south-west. Rennenkampf had six-and-a-half infantry and five-and-a-half cavalry divisions and 492 guns, so was weaker than the German defenders; Samsonov had fourteen-and-a-half infantry and four cavalry divisions and 1,160 guns, so outnumbered them, but not by much. Hence the danger that the Germans would use the Insterburg–Osterode lateral railway to defeat the two forces separately. In contrast to the Schlieffen–Moltke Plan, however, which was inherently highly risky, the Russians had such superiority that they ought to have been able to herd the Germans into Königsberg or towards the Vistula. That they did not was in good measure due to incompetence. [100]

It is true that there were technological problems. Like other invading forces and unlike the defenders, the Russians lacked access to the local railway, telegraph, and telephone networks. The Second Army had only twenty-five telephones anyway. Nor was wireless a substitute. Even the Germans had only forty wireless stations for their entire army; the Russians had still fewer.[101] Encrypting and decrypting wireless messages was complex and time-consuming and the Russian armies lost each other's codes, therefore sending messages *en clair*, which the Germans read (though the Germans did the same, albeit with less unhappy results).[102] Internal communication even within the Second Army soon broke down, let alone between the two headquarters. These difficulties were compounded by the Russian command structure, or lack of one. Nicholas appointed his uncle, Grand Duke Nicholas, as commander in chief, and Janushkevich as his chief of staff, though the most important figure at the Russian general headquarters (or Stavka) was the quartermaster-general, Danilov. After the Stavka's decision to invade East Prussia (where it expected to face only four German divisions) it became even more marginal than Moltke was in the west. It was remote from the front and communications were difficult; it had insufficient staff officers to work out plans and few reserves at its disposal. Nor did the deficient Polish rail network help matters, no trunk line running between the East Prussian and Galician theatres. The Russians did employ 'front' commands to co-ordinate the armies operating against each of their enemies (after the opening campaigns most First World War armies would adopt a similar 'army group' system), but the endemic faction fighting in the officer corps undermined them. Yahou Zhilinski was the commander of the north-west front (i.e., for East Prussia): he and Samsonov were in the Sukhomlinovite faction, but Rennenkampf was not, and neither Zhilinski and Rennenkampf, nor Rennenkampf and Samsonov, co-operated with each other in a professional manner.[103] If things went wrong, they would be ill placed to improvise.

None the less the campaign did not open badly, and it was the Germans who first experienced a command crisis. Russian mobilization against East Prussia was largely complete by 11 August, and hostilities began little later than in Belgium. Rennenkampf was first over the border, though his progress was slow. When the Germans intercepted a radio message that he would halt on 20 August, General Hermann von François, commander of Prittwitz's First Corps, decided to attack. For most of those involved the resulting battle of Gumbinnen was their first combat experience and it revealed no great German qualitative advantage, the Eighth Army attacking straight from marching and without adequate prior bombardment. On the two flanks the Germans drove the Russians back, but those advancing in the centre against Russian infantry sheltered in farms and villages made no headway. After suffering 8,000 casualties in a few hours (out of a force of some 30,000), they fled.[104] Meanwhile radio intercepts and German aircraft revealed that Samsonov was invading in Prittwitz's rear and moving further west than expected, endangering his line of retreat. In a gloomy telephone conversation Prittwitz told Moltke that he wanted to regroup on the Vistula, with the result that on 22 August Moltke (who intervened here much more readily than in the west) ordered his replacement by Paul von Hindenburg, and that of Prittwitz's chief of staff, Georg von Waldersee, by Ludendorff. In the usual German fashion the latter was the key appointment, Ludendorff being a high-profile figure since his role at Liège. Hindenburg, who was called out of retirement, was steadier, if less imaginative and energetic.[105] Actually the Eighth Army's staff had already seen how to salvage the situation and Prittwitz might well have endorsed their proposals had he remained.[106] These were not to retreat but to use the lateral railway to convey most of the Eighth Army south-westwards against Samsonov, a manoeuvre already envisaged in pre-1914 staff rides. The Eighth Army's chief of operations, Max Hoffmann, knew about the antagonism between Rennenkampf and Samsonov but the manoeuvre was not just his idea, although his claim to intellectual authorship would be widely accepted. Moltke's reshuffle may therefore have been superfluous, and his subsequent dispatch of two extra corps certainly was, as Ludendorff advised at the time. Moltke's reading of the war in the east as one of civilization versus barbarism may have played a part here, though in fact the Russians treated German civilians reasonably correctly. He and his advisers were buoyed up by the 'Battle of the Frontiers' and probably aspired to a victory without Habsburg assistance. In other words this decision, which would cost them dear, stemmed less from anxiety than from over-confidence.[107]

Moltke's interventions hampered Germany's larger progress but at least he did not impede his local commanders. Zhilinski, by contrast, based 200 miles behind the First and Second Armies, directed Rennenkampf on 26 August to blockade Königsberg instead of helping Samsonov. Even after he amended his orders, his instructions to help were neither urgent nor specific. Moreover, he broadcast them uncoded and the Germans intercepted them,[108] confirming their impression from aerial reconnaissance that after Gumbinnen Rennenkampf (who had used up much of his ammunition and whose supplies were chaotic) would not give chase. Instead he marked time while Samsonov's army advanced towards its fate. Like the Germans on the Marne Samsonov was far beyond his nearest railhead, which was fifty kilometres behind the border and reachable only over unmetalled roads. At the Stavka's insistence he lengthened his march by advancing north-westwards instead of northwards, probably in order to cut off Prittwitz's retreat. Disengaging from Rennenkampf's army after 20 August, the Germans made contact with Samsonov's four days later. Although the ensuing battle of Tannenberg (the collective name for a series of actions between 24 and 31 August) became the greatest encirclement operation of the war, this was not part of Ludendorff's initial expectation. François, who had attacked Rennenkampf before Gumbinnen in defiance of Prittwitz, now defied Ludendorff, who wanted a precipitate flank attack before François's troops had finished detraining. When François attacked Samsonov's left flank in strength on the 27th, he aimed to cut off the Russians from their lines of retreat and essentially he succeeded, although Ludendorff also contributed to the encirclement by moving forces against the Russians' right. Perhaps the biggest responsibility for the débâcle, however, lay with Samsonov himself, who had been pursuing the German Twentieth Corps and was slow to realize his danger. On 28 August he ordered an advance that drove his forces deeper into the developing trap, instead of breaking out of it. Demoralized and with their rations and ammunition running out, the Russians began to surrender, Samsonov abandoning his staff and killing himself. By the end his force had lost 92,000 prisoners, 500 guns, and perhaps 50,000 dead and wounded, against German casualties of 10–15,000.[109]

The Germans had kept their troops better supplied, had been better informed, and had seized opportunities faster: their decentralized command systems, which functioned poorly on the Marne, had allowed the formation of a recovery plan and enabled François to take the initiative in executing it.[110] Yet the spectacular outcome owed much to Russian blunders, and Tannenberg took on a mythic significance that exceeded its strategic one. This began with the battle's name, borrowed from the nearby village where the Poles and Lithuanians had defeated the Teutonic Knights in 1410. Now publicists could claim that that humiliation had been avenged, the Asiatic hordes repelled, and Berlin delivered. The victory also, not altogether deservedly, launched Hindenburg and Ludendorff on a career trajectory that made even Wilhelm II reluctant to challenge them and gave them mastery over German grand strategy in the second half of the war. Yet the Russians quickly replaced their losses and Tannenberg did not, in fact, eliminate the threat to German soil. Nor was it followed up by a comparable triumph against Rennenkampf. In the battle of the Masurian Lakes, fought from 5 to 13 September, Ludendorff shuttled back his troops against the Russian First Army, which had taken up position east of the lake region. He had now received the two army corps released by Moltke, and began with a numerical advantage. François again broke through the Russians' left flank and worked his way behind them, but although the Germans took 30,000 prisoners Ludendorff failed to complete another encirclement by breaking the enemy centre and Rennenkampf retreated in good time. Once the victors gave pursuit across the border they suffered from the usual problems of invading armies, including exhaustion and outrunning their supplies. On 25 September the Russians counter-attacked, driving the Germans back to the Angerapp line. The September fighting cost the Eighth Army some 100,000 casualties, and despite inflicting still greater damage on the Russians it ended in deadlock.[111] Tannenberg was a major victory, but far from decisive.

Although the East Prussian campaign is better known, the August battles in Galicia involved larger forces on both sides and arguably had greater consequences: given the East Prussian stalemate, a combination of failure for Germany in the west with disaster for Austria-Hungary in the east augured ominously for the Central Powers. This disaster was predictable, given the Austrians' inferiority in numbers and equipment, though German bad faith and avoidable Austrian errors contributed to it. On mobilization the Archduke Friedrich became the titular Austro-Hungarian commander in chief, but in practice Conrad and his advisers (now constituted as the Army High Command or *Armee Oberkommando*: AOK) directed the Galician operations. During the July crisis Conrad found himself in the situation he had long dreaded, of imminent war against Serbia while Russia remained uncommitted. Yet he knew Russian intervention was virtually certain, which makes his behaviour all the more puzzling. After Belgrade rejected the ultimatum, he authorized partial mobilization of *Minimalgruppe Balkan* and *B-Staffel* but not *A-Staffel*: out of consideration for the Russians, who he maintained might be bluffing. On 31 July, however, in the light of Moltke's urgings, he opted for 'Case R'. General mobilization was ordered for the following day, and Conrad inquired whether *B-Staffel* could be redirected from the Balkans to Galicia. His chief railway planner, von Straub, was horrified and said no, and AOK decided to transport part of *B-Staffel* first south to the Serbian border and then north against the Russians while delaying *A-Staffel*'s mobilization in order to free the necessary rolling stock. Probably the railway experts could have improvised more energetically, but the principal blame for this fiasco appears to lie with Conrad's insistence (possibly for political reasons) on precipitating a shooting war against Serbia. The effect was to postpone his concentration in Galicia until 19–23 August, by which time Moltke had warned that he would attack from East Prussia only if Russia were passive against Germany. This development came as a complete and unwelcome surprise to Conrad, yet he persisted with his planned offensive, expecting German help within six weeks because of over-optimistic expectations about how quickly France could be beaten.[112] He also decided, however, to detrain his soldiers well behind the frontier, in the deployment that his staff, foreseeing the need for caution in view of Russian superiority, had investigated in March. From here they would have to march towards the fighting zone, thus arriving tired and further eroding their slim lead in mobilization times.[113] Nevertheless, by late August his forces in Galicia numbered 500,000 men in thirty-one divisions, rising to thirty-seven when three *B-Staffel* corps arrived on 4 September. The First, Second, Fourth, and Third Armies were grouped in that order from west to east, running from south of Lublin to the river Dniester. Conrad knew the principal Russian concentration was further east, and he intended to push northwards along a 175-mile front, with the main tasks assigned to the armies on his left wing. These forces were to fan out, cut the Polish railways, and hit the rear of the Russian advance into East Prussia, thus indirectly assisting Germany's march on Paris while demonstrating Austria-Hungary's ability to win a major campaign unaided.[114]

The Austrians were already outnumbered. By the end of August the Russians had deployed forty-five infantry divisions and over eighteen cavalry divisions against them, and had another eight-and-a-half infantry divisions forming. As Russian units were bigger than Austrian ones (each Russian infantry division had 60–70 per cent more men, 30 per cent more heavy artillery, and eight times as many machine guns),[115] they were committing some 750,000 men in four armies (from west to east the Fourth, Fifth, Third, and Eighth). Overall direction was provided by the south-west front, commanded by Nikolai Ivanov and his chief of staff Alekseyev: a much abler team than in the north-west, though here too feuding in the officer corps hampered operations. The south-west front wanted to attack from the north towards the fortress and railway hub at Cracow; the Stavka favoured a more indirect approach from the east advancing parallel to the Carpathians. The Russians adopted the characteristic compromise of doing both, attempting a 'double envelopment' of their enemies, but the attack from the east did the damage. In the north, where the two sides had about equal numbers, the Austrians were successful in the first clashes at Krasnik on 23–24 and Komarów on 26–31 August. But by early September they were outrunning their supply lines, the Polish population failed to give them the expected support, and a new Russian Ninth Army was marching towards them. Meanwhile the Russians closed in from the east, General Alexei Brusilov's Eighth Army defeating the Austrian Third Army at the battle of Gnila Lipa (26–30 August), and on 3 September taking Lemberg. Conrad attempted an unsuccessful counterstroke against the Russians' flank at the battle of Rawa Russka on 8–10 September, but was obliged to order a general retreat to the Carpathian line in the south and to the Dunajec river east of Cracow, where in late September the front stabilized. By this stage Conrad's northern armies had also been defeated. But now the Russians in their turn were the invaders, struggling with waterlogged roads, inadequate railways of a narrower gauge than their own, and an enemy who could read their radio messages, and they were blocked by the great stronghold of Przemysl, garrisoned by 100,000 troops and ringed by fifty kilometres of trenches.[116] It might seem that as elsewhere stalemate had established itself, but the Russians had hurt the Austrians more grievously than the Germans had hurt the Russians or the French. In fact Danilov's attack on Conrad's eastern flank was the only August 1914 offensive that substantially achieved its objectives. The Austrians lost the Bukovina and much of eastern Galicia, including oil, rich arable land, the fortresses of Lemberg and Jaroslav, and a jumping-off point on the southern flank of Russian Poland. They suffered perhaps 100,000 dead, 222,000 wounded, and 100,000 taken prisoner, as well as the loss of 216 guns, 1,000 locomotives, and very heavy casualties among their officers and NCOs.[117] It is difficult now to visualize these battles, much less well documented than those in France, in which Habsburg troops advanced in blazing heat across featureless plains with little effective cavalry reconnaissance on either side, blundering into superior Russian forces whose artillery took a terrible toll. Their losses were caused in part by their infantry's suicidally brave frontal attacks, sanctioned by pre-1914 tactical doctrine. The Russians also suffered about 250,000 casualties (including 40,000 prisoners), but these were smaller losses in a bigger army. The large numbers of prisoners on both sides partly reflected the campaign's mobile character, but they also betrayed shaky morale. This applied especially in the Habsburg army, whose Czech, Serb, and Italian units were already proving unreliable, and the loss of so many of its best troops and officers would exacerbate the problem.[118] Austria-Hungary was already close to being unable to fight the Russians without German help, and would remain so for the rest of the war. Conrad soon regretted having attacked on his own and made many appeals for assistance, afterwards blaming Germany for the calamity and contemplating a separate peace. But the more the Germans had to prop up their ally on the Eastern Front, the harder they would find it to assemble overwhelming strength in the west.

The final failed offensive in August 1914 was Austria-Hungary's first attack on Serbia. The Austrians did what their pre-war planning had rejected, launching weak offensives in both Poland and the Balkans and prevailing in neither. They were humiliated by a country that was not even a great power, and in many ways poorly equipped to fight. It is true that Serbia's army was large. With a population less than a tenth of Austria-Hungary's, it mobilized more of its male population than any other country in Europe:[119] c. 350,000 men, 185,000 of whom were front-line combat troops, grouped in eleven infantry divisions and one cavalry division, and making up three armies. It had able commanders with (unlike most others in Europe) recent experience from 1912–13, including the chief of the supreme command, Vojvoda Radomir Putnik, who had been in Budapest during the July crisis but whom Franz Joseph, in a chivalrous gesture of dubious wisdom, had allowed to return home. Unusually among 1914 commanders, Putnik concentrated his main forces defensively in the centre of the country, ready for a counterstroke against an invasion. But in other respects the Serbs were more vulnerable. Their ally, Montenegro, was of little value. Its king, Nikita, was near bankruptcy. He mobilized a militia force of 35–40,000 men, whom the Serbs supplied with 100 guns.[120] Serbia's own army had been re-equipped in the pre-war decade but in 1912–13 had lost some 36,000 dead from combat and disease, with 55,000 seriously wounded. It gained few recruits from its new territories and had to garrison them against Albanian insurgents and the threat of Bulgarian revenge. The treasury remained solvent only because of a French loan. Thus although the army had modern French quick-firing field guns, it was short of the basics. It was just beginning to replenish the shell stocks used up in the Balkan Wars. It lacked shoes for its recruits, many of whom turned up barefoot, and most particularly rifles, which Serbia could neither manufacture at home nor import. The Russians delivered 120,000 in late August 1914, but these were too few to give each soldier a modern weapon. In contrast Austro-Hungarian units all had modern rifles, twice as many machine guns, and field guns with more generous munitions stocks, as well as a much better transport and industrial infrastructure behind them.[121]

None the less, Austria-Hungary's initial invasion of Serbia ended in another débâcle. Given the Serbs' defensive deployment the wiser course would have been to do nothing in the Balkans and focus on Russia. But the circumstances in which war had broken out made this politically difficult. Moreover, the Habsburg Fifth and Sixth Armies (the pre-war *Minimalgruppe Balkan*), stationed on Serbia's northern and north-western frontiers, came under the command of General Oskar Potiorek, a rival of Conrad who reported directly to Franz Joseph and was independent of AOK.[122] Potiorek was eager to attack. His two armies totalled 140,000 men, smaller than the Serb forces, but the Second Army, the portion of *B-Staffel* that was sent to the Balkans before being moved on to Galicia, was deployed on the Serb border until 18 August, thus providing a brief diversion while Potiorek launched the other two armies on a converging attack from starting points 100 kilometres distant, advancing slowly through mountainous country with few roads. Once Putnik realized that the main danger lay in the west, he rapidly turned his forces through ninety degrees, attacked the Fifth Army's flank in a night engagement and broke through its centre in the battle of Cer Mountain on 16–19 August. Potiorek ordered his troops to fall back and by the 24th Serbian soil was clear. Serb casualties approached 17,000: Austrian ones were nearly 24,000, including 4,500 prisoners of war. The Austrian armies were too far apart to support each other, and in the hand-to-hand night fighting the Serbs showed their superiority in experience and morale over the invaders (40 per cent of whom were fellow South Slavs), though the Serbs used up much of their ammunition: some 6.5 million cartridges and 36,000 shells.[123] The battle reproduced in miniature what was happening over much of Europe. Determined defenders and a hail of munitions defeated a hasty attack plan executed with inadequate forces. The Serbs benefited from the invaders' lack of co-ordination but they failed to cut off their retreat, thus inviting a renewed incursion.

By mid-September the initial invasion bids had everywhere failed, although the Russians had overrun valuable Austrian territory and the Germans held much of northern France and Belgium. All the attacking forces found themselves severely disadvantaged, both tactically (against the defenders' rifles, machine guns, and quick-firing artillery) and operationally (losing access to secure transport and communications, as well as lacking reliable reconnaissance, once they crossed the borders). They needed massive numerical superiority – which only the Russians in eastern Galicia possessed – to achieve their objectives. In every theatre these accumulating difficulties sooner or later halted the offensives, though only after stunning casualty rates that in the remainder of the war would rarely be equalled. The two sides were far from resigned, however, to static warfare or to stalemate. For the rest of the campaigning season they tried to salvage their position in a series of ferocious battles, establishing patterns of fighting that would endure for the next three years.

Until November the Germans maintained their Western Front priority. They kept Conrad in the dark about the Marne, and their terse press communiqués minimized the setback.[124] Nor did they disclose that on the evening of 14 September Moltke had suffered a nervous breakdown. Falkenhayn replaced him at once as acting CGS (officially from 3 November), thus doubling as CGS and war minister.[125] His appointment was not widely popular, as he was seen as having owed his rise to court connections, and his arrogance and sarcasm had made him many enemies. Moreover, a point of substance soon divided him from Hindenburg and

Ludendorff, who hoped after Tannenberg to finish off the Russians in a second encirclement battle, whereas Falkenhayn preferred to renew the offensive in France. OHL saw the Marne defeat as serious but not irreparable, Falkenhayn briefing Bethmann and Jagow that it had delayed victory rather than prevented it. Tappen (who continued as chief of operations) urged the need to hold the conquered territory, both for its industrial resources and to protect the Ruhr and Germany's western border.[126] In addition, Falkenhayn aimed to capture strongpoints such as Verdun and Antwerp and consolidate control of the lateral railway running from Belgium through Reims to the Argonne. Thus on 19–20 September, only ten days after the retreat, he launched new offensives east and west of Verdun. That to the east advanced nearly forty miles to carve out the so-called St-Mihiel salient, ensconcing the Germans on the Meuse and reducing French communications into Verdun to one light railway. That to the west cut the Verdun–Toul line and brought the Paris–Nancy one within artillery range.[127] His main ambition, however, was to outflank the Allies on their left. Since Joffre, conversely, hoped to expel the Germans by outflanking them on their right,[128] the heaviest autumn fighting flared along the open flank between the Marne and the Channel. A series of confused actions, usually (if misleadingly) known as the 'Race to the Sea', spread through the provinces of Picardy and Artois into Flanders. On 17 September the French Sixth Army tried to manoeuvre round the Germans along the river Oise; on the 27th French and German forces clashed in the Somme region round Albert; on 2 October three German corps attacked near Arras. Quiet towns that would soon become notorious came under the spotlight as both sides dug in and the front's new geography crystallized.

Both sides laboured under serious disadvantages. Falkenhayn has been criticized for not further reinforcing his right, but most of the railways behind his front remained out of action. The French, despite operating round the outside of an arc, had access both to undamaged track and to intercepted wireless messages. Unfortunately they lost about ten days in moving northwards because they had to share the railways with the BEF, which during October was transported from the Aisne to Belgium. This was Kitchener's idea (though Sir John French also wanted to be close to the Channel ports) and Joffre would have preferred to delay it, subsequently blaming it for the loss of Lille.[129] Further, the French now faced a problem that would soon hit every army: that of shell shortage. During the Marne they had fired off much of their initial stock, and (in contrast to the Germans) their resupply facilities were makeshift. On 24 September Joffre warned that at present consumption rates the army would soon be unable to fight. Each 75mm field gun was limited to 200 rounds,[130] and nineteenth-century pre-quick-firers were pressed back into service. Meanwhile, half the workforce of France's largest private arms manufacturer, Schneider-Creusot, had been called up, and the state arsenals' daily output of 75mm shells totalled only 8–10,000, though some batteries had been firing off 1,000 per day. Joffre protested to the war minister, Millerand, who held an emergency conference with French industrialists on 20 September and promised to aim for 30,000 per day within a month, but failed to achieve the figure.[131] Until well into 1915 the French would lack shells, and especially high explosive shells, while the Germans consolidated their defences.

By October the emerging stalemate extended as far as Armentières, close to the northern French border, and Belgium again became the storm centre. It was now the last remaining open flank, and Falkenhayn decided on a great offensive in Flanders. Before it began the Germans occupied Bruges and Ghent and reached the coast near Nieupoort. In addition, from 28 September they began their assault on Antwerp. Their forces were too few to seal off the city's massive concentric fortifications, and reinforcements got in, notably a contingent of British marines sent on the initiative of Winston Churchill (who accompanied them), though it is unlikely that his action much delayed the outcome.[132] Once again the German guns demolished the forts, while Joffre, probably correctly, had already written off Antwerp as a lost cause. He had few troops with which to assist and he held a low opinion of the Belgian army, which he wanted to evacuate the city.

Fortunately, the incompleteness of the siege enabled Albert and most of his troops to leave, before being transported to the line of the river Yser further down the coast. The remainder (including many of the British) were interned by the Dutch or captured when Antwerp surrendered on 9 October. But Antwerp's fall also released three German divisions, and simultaneously four brand new army corps became available to Falkenhayn, composed mainly of civilians who had been training since the start of the war. Three quarters of them were student volunteers from university and school.[133] Despite the war ministry's well-founded doubts that they were ready, Falkenhayn threw them into the offensive that he began on 20 October with the aims of ousting the Allies from Flanders and taking the Channel ports. By this means he hoped to halt the British troop build-up on the continent, capture bases for air and sea attacks against the British Isles, protect his newly acquired conquests,[134] and possibly turn the tide decisively in his favour. But Joffre was equally determined to halt the new advance,[135] and German and Allied attacks now ran headlong into each other.

The struggle for Flanders went through several phases. South of Ypres, round Armentières and La Bassée, British troops pushed back the German Sixth Army and crossed the river Lys, but made no further progress. North of Ypres the German Fourth Army, composed of the four new corps, advanced along the coast to the Yser, where the Belgians halted them by opening the sluice gates of the drainage system and creating an artificial flood plain extending five miles inland. With the two flanks thus fixed, the fighting became concentrated round Ypres itself. The first battle of Ypres began as an attack by both sides against each other, but increasingly the Allies were on the defensive. As extra German troops arrived, Sir John considered disengaging and retreating to Boulogne. But Joffre overruled him and he decided to hold what was emerging as the infamous 'Ypres salient', curving east of the city, although it would probably have been wiser to stand on the shorter and straighter canal line to the west.[136] The British too were running short of shells, Sir John seeking to ration his 18-pounders to a mere ten rounds a day. For most of the battle the Germans had greater firepower as well as numbers, and many of their casualties came from BEF small arms fire when they attacked in dense masses. The Allies sheltered behind streams and farmhouses, and increasingly dug trenches, though at first these were shallow and were only intermittently protected by wire. Alternatively they used breastworks, raised above the surface, because the high water table of the Flanders clay made trenches liable to flood. After more dispersed attacks from 21 to 30 October the Germans concentrated their assault on Ypres between 31 October and 2 November, pushing the British off the Messines ridge to the south and nearly breaking their lines. The successful resistance enhanced the reputation of the commander of Sir John's First Corps, Sir Douglas Haig. After another big general assault failed on 11 November, German attacks became more sporadic and Falkenhayn finally resolved to break off, because of lack of progress and enormous losses but also because his heavy artillery shells were exhausted.[137] Although the Germans had made major gains, the Allies still held the Channel ports as well as Ypres itself, a fine medieval cloth town that bombardment had reduced to rubble but now a hero city whose possession had become a matter of prestige. The Allies also held the salient, a dubious asset that exposed its defenders to constant bombardment from German artillery on the overlooking ridges. For these results they paid a heavy price: in the battle of the Yser the Belgians suffered 20,000 casualties, or 35 per cent of their remaining army; the French (who held the line running north from the salient to the inundations and whose role in saving Ypres has been neglected) lost 50,000 and the BEF 58,000, against German casualties of 130,000. Casualty rates in the first battle of Ypres were comparable (given the shorter period of time) to those in the terrible third battle, fought with much heavier weaponry three years later. In Britain it would be remembered for the destruction of the old BEF; in Germany for the *Kindermord*, or 'massacre of the innocents', i.e., the student volunteers, notably in an attack at Langemarck on 22 October that took on mythic status.[138] Losses in the student divisions (some 25,000 of whose members now lie in the Langemarck cemetery) reached up to 60 per cent. The end of the battle, when Wilhelm accepted Falkenhayn's advice to switch attention to the east, would prove a major turning point. It set the mould of the war in 1915, as Falkenhayn now ordered his western forces to extend and deepen the improvised trenches they had dug since the battle of the Aisne, creating a continuous system of two or more lines.[139] He still saw this as a temporary expedient, to save lives and release troops for mobile operations elsewhere, but Joffre knew that without much greater resources in artillery, munitions, and men the French would be hard pressed to dislodge their enemies from the immense redoubt that they were building.[140] All the same, the decision reached on the Marne had not been overturned.

While Falkenhayn focused on Flanders he could not significantly reinforce the east. In his first discussions during September with Hindenburg and Ludendorff the latter, backed by Conrad, wanted to attack from East Prussia to encircle the Russian armies while the latter pursued the Austrians.[141] Falkenhayn rejected this proposal because he did not want to release the men, but also because the autumn rains would impede mobility and he wished to help the Austrians more directly. Hence he took three corps from the Eighth Army to form a new Ninth Army, of which Hindenburg was appointed commander, Ludendorff chief of staff, and Hoffmann chief of operations. Using 750 trains he moved this force south to fight alongside Conrad on the Austrians' left flank, where it deployed near Cracow. In this position it could parry either a Russian thrust across the Carpathians into Bohemia or a threat to Silesia, whose coal and industry Falkenhayn deemed essential to Germany's war effort.[142] He also consented, however, to a limited offensive designed to protect these territories and buy time for his western plans. In late September the Ninth Army and the Austrians therefore began advancing north-eastwards towards the Vistula and Warsaw. At this point the Russians still fielded 98 infantry divisions in Europe against 70 to 80 German and Austrian ones.[143] They too were conducting a strategy debate, which ended in another compromise between the Stavka and the commanders at the front in favour of two offensives. General Ruszki, who had replaced Zhilinski as commander of the north-west front, was allowed to invade East Prussia again after the battle of the Masurian Lakes, but was halted at the battle of the Augustowo Forest (29 September–5 October). Meanwhile Grand Duke Nicholas, partly to relieve the pressure on the French, moved up troops from southern Poland to concentrate them round Warsaw, and as the Germans and Austrians neared the city in mid-October he delivered a surprise attack. Conrad authorized his First Army commander, General Dankl, to let the Russians cross the Vistula at Ivangorod in the hope of striking them in the flank, but the manoeuvre went wrong and the Central Powers were forced to retreat, resulting in recriminations from Hindenburg and Ludendorff against their allies. The withdrawal was orderly and ended when the Russians ran ahead of their railheads: indeed, they too were now suffering their first serious shortages of shells, cartridges, and rifles, to say nothing of winter clothing.[144] None the less, the Germans suffered 100,000 casualties (of whom 36,000 were killed), while on the Austrian side Dankl's army alone lost 40–50,000. The Central Powers gained nothing from the battle of Warsaw and finished back on their starting line.

One last campaign followed in the eastern theatre before the end of the season, in which the pattern set at Warsaw to some extent repeated itself. When Falkenhayn met Ludendorff in Berlin on 30 October he agreed to Hindenburg and Ludendorff taking over *Ober Ost*, a new supreme command of the German armies in the east (General August von Mackensen replacing Hindenburg in charge of the Ninth Army), but he still refused their requests for troops or to approve more than another limited offensive.[145] Meanwhile the Russians were preparing yet another attack on East Prussia and a drive into Germany from western Poland. The Germans, however, still held two of the advantages they had enjoyed before Tannenberg. From reading the Russians' wireless messages, they knew their planned axis of attack. In addition they had an intact railway running parallel to the eastern border, along which Ludendorff transported the Ninth Army northwards from Silesia to Thorn in his third use of a lateral rail movement to protect German territory. He planned to hit the flank of the projected Russian advance by attacking south-eastwards from Thorn towards Lodz across terrain that was now being hardened by frost. At first the operation went well: when the Ninth Army attacked on 11 November it surprised and routed a Siberian corps, and the Germans had taken 136,000 prisoners by the time they neared Lodz a week later. The Russians called off their invasion of East Prussia and fell back on the city, against which Ludendorff ordered a frontal assault. But from this point the usual dynamics of the Eastern Front asserted themselves: the Ninth Army was short of munitions, whereas Lodz was a supply depot and the defenders recovered their powers of resistance. In one of the most dramatic actions of the war, fought in snow and ice, the Germans at first seemed ready to encircle the Russians, but then barely escaped encirclement themselves, their Twenty-fifth Reserve Corps fighting its way out of a cordon on 18–25 November before retreating, taking 25,000 prisoners with it. Although they had a 2:1 numerical advantage the Russians again ran out of rifles and of shells, limiting their artillery to ten rounds a day.[146] In early December, aided by the arrival of four corps released from Flanders after Falkenhayn broke off at Ypres, the Germans finally took Lodz. Shortly afterwards a new offensive by the Russian Third Army, intended to take Cracow and threaten Silesia, was halted by the Austrians, in one of their few successful independent operations, at the battle of Limanova-Lipanow. The Russians fell back to the rivers Nida and Sunajec, and in central Poland settled down in entrenched positions west of Warsaw, although these trenches were less sophisticated than in the west and the density of forces manning them was lower. In the complex fighting since Tannenberg neither side had achieved a clear advantage and at the battle of Warsaw the first of the Central Powers' limited offensives had failed. In contrast, despite narrowly escaping disaster at Lodz, their second offensive had driven the Russians well back from the German border, while at Limanova Conrad had repulsed them from Cracow. The tsarist armies would never again push so deeply into Habsburg territory, or so threaten East Prussia and Silesia. Their supply crisis would cripple them for months and leave them helpless when in the following spring Falkenhayn finally authorized a major attack. The eastern war of movement was not yet over, but the Russians had passed their peak.

At Tannenberg and Warsaw the Russians twice attacked to relieve the pressure on the French. Similarly their relentless pressure on Austria-Hungary impeded it from subduing Serbia. Following their success in August the Serbs (at Russian and French urging) took the war into enemy territory, raiding into Hungary, invading Bosnia, and reaching a point only twenty miles distant from Sarajevo. But the uprising they hoped to touch off failed to materialize: further evidence that the Austrians' anxieties about their South Slav subjects had been exaggerated. Moreover, the Serbian army was low on ammunition and being depleted by desertion when in November Potiorek launched a second invasion, much bigger than the first. Again his forces advanced from the north and west, but they also crossed the Danube and captured Belgrade. By early December, however, his troops in the west had been on the march for weeks and were dispersed along a long, curving front 100 kilometres beyond their supply bases. Prisoner interrogations revealed to the Serbs that the Habsburg infantry were weary and depressed. Meanwhile Putnik took stern measures to restore discipline, stripped the north of troops in order to attack westwards, and was reinforced by student levies and a consignment of French shells. His forces struck the Austrians' flanks in a series of operations known as the battle of the Kolubara (3–15 December), before recapturing Belgrade. Potiorek lost his command and his army once more retreated to its starting point, having lost 28,000 dead, 120,000 wounded, and 76,500 taken prisoner. Yet the Serbian losses of 22,000 dead, 92,000 wounded, and 19,000 captured or missing were comparable and were sustained by a smaller force. Serbia was now too weak to threaten Habsburg territory and in 1915 the Austrians could strip their Balkan frontier troops, which in view of Italy's intervention against them was fortunate.[147] In the Balkans as in Poland, winter 1914 proved to be an Allied high-water mark.

Concentration on the details of these campaigns can obscure the bigger picture. Time and again in west and east, offensives by both sides lost momentum and were halted with terrible casualties. Attacking forces in enemy territory everywhere encountered similar problems. They advanced beyond their telephone and cable networks and relied on wireless messages that their opponents could intercept; they left behind them the railways needed to provide their weapons with munitions and their men and horses with food, clothing, and medical care. Campaigning in 1914 conditions posed unprecedented challenges for generalship, both to interpret the profusion of incoming intelligence and to manoeuvre in response to it with armies that were far more unwieldy (being both larger and more logistically voracious) than in Napoleon's day.[148] All supreme commanders had difficulty in directing their subordinates, and strategy – for example in the Russian army – might be the compromise outcome of bureaucratic infighting. Commanders had some control over where and when their men opened fire, but not much beyond that, and modern firepower exacted appalling sacrifices from troops in the open who were all too often ill-prepared by training or by doctrine to dig in or to attack in dispersed order. Many considerations therefore benefited the defenders over the attackers, quite apart from the fundamental factors of approximate numerical equality between the two sides on the Western, Eastern, and Balkan Fronts and of untapped reserves of manpower with which to make good losses. They offset the most important outcome of the land campaigning, which was the failure of the Germans' bid for speedy victory in the west, first on the Marne and then in Flanders. For despite this failure the Germans had consolidated themselves in territory where neither France nor Britain could let them stay without admitting defeat. Hence they could stand on the defensive while their enemies wore themselves out attacking their prepared positions, which for most of the next three years was what they did. They had failed to win outright, but the possibility of prevailing through Allied exhaustion remained real. This was the more so as the Russian army had repeatedly failed to capture German territory even while the maximum German forces were in the west. It had occupied Austrian territory, but the latter had less significance. On the other hand, a long war might disadvantage Germany because of the Allies' greater opportunities to mobilize resources from the outside world, both through their colonial empires and via their trading connections with the neutrals. To achieve this mobilization the Allies needed control of the oceans, and this, in the first months of the war, they established, while Germany missed its best chance of challenging it. The decisive clash expected by public opinion (though not the navies) on the two sides failed to materialize and at sea as on land the year ended in stalemate. The Allies' global command of the seas and the naval balance in European waters must now be taken in turn.

Outside Europe the Allies – and more particularly the British – started with tremendous advantages. They owned far more of the world's merchant tonnage, and much of what the Central Powers did possess was impounded in neutral harbours. The Allies cut the Germans' overseas telegraph lines when war broke out, forcing reliance for diplomatic, naval, and military communications on coded telegrams via neutral cables or on wireless messages, on both of which the Allies could eavesdrop and both of which they learned how to decrypt. Austria-Hungary's navy was stationed entirely in the Adriatic; Germany had a worldwide network of harbours and coaling stations, but only Qingdao (in China) was equipped to service modern warships,[149] and British Empire, French, and Japanese forces soon overran most of the Reich's overseas possessions.* Although the German navy before the war had envisaged cruiser raiding against British commerce it had no detailed plans for doing so and did little during the July crisis to send out warships or pre-position supply vessels.[150] Hence the cruisers already beyond home waters in peacetime represented the main threat to British shipping outside Europe, and this threat was manageable. This was fortunate as the Admiralty had done very little to prepare for it, believing the Royal Navy must concentrate its forces against the main enemy fleet, that it could not patrol every sea lane, and that if merchant ships dispersed and avoided their usual routes the inevitable losses would remain bearable.[151] The most formidable German ship outside home waters was the battlecruiser *Goeben*, which with the light cruiser *Breslau* constituted the Mediterranean squadron under Admiral Wilhelm Souchon. On 3 August the German government, which had just concluded a secret alliance with Turkey, ordered the squadron to head for the Dardanelles, where it arrived a week later. A British detachment of four armoured cruisers in the Ionian Sea could have intercepted it, but the *Goeben's* guns were heavier and longer-range, and the commander, Rear Admiral Ernest Troubridge, took a cautious interpretation of his orders not to engage a superior force and turned away, leaving Souchon with a clear run. Troubridge was court-martialled, but acquitted. The two ships' escape later contributed to Turkey's entry into the war, and tied down British forces by shadowing them in the Aegean, but at least they no longer menaced Allied Mediterranean shipping or the troopships carrying French soldiers from North Africa to Europe.

The remaining German warships overseas numbered barely a dozen scattered vessels. The *Karlsruhe*, in the Caribbean when war broke out, operated off Brazil, sinking fifteen merchantmen before mysteriously blowing up. The *Königsberg*, off East Africa, sank an old British cruiser but was crippled by lack of coal. It holed up in the delta of the river Rufiji, where in 1915 a British expedition destroyed it. The *Leipzig* briefly paralysed Allied shipping off California, but both it and the *Dresden* joined up with much the most dangerous of the extra-European challenges to the Allies, Vice-Admiral Maximilian Graf von Spee's East Asiatic Cruiser Squadron. Spee also had two crack modern armoured cruisers, the *Scharnhorst* and the *Gneisenau*, and the light cruisers *Emden* and *Nuremberg*. When war broke out his ships were dispersed, mostly away from their base at Qingdao. The British had not modernized their cruiser fleet as they had their battleships, and their cruisers in the vicinity were too slow or lightly armed to deal with him.[152] Hence Spee's most immediate problem was fuel. He gathered his ships in the Mariana Islands and decided to operate off the Pacific coast of the Americas, where coal might be

*See ch. 4.

purchased, but he dispatched the *Emden* to the Indian Ocean. There it caused havoc, shelling Madras and Penang and sinking a Russian cruiser, a French destroyer, and sixteen British merchant steamers before the Australian cruiser *Sydney* ran it aground in the Cocos Islands on 9 November. In all these episodes the Allies benefited from a good deal of luck rather than foresight: they were fortunate to find the *Königsberg* and the *Emden* and that the *Karlsruhe* exploded, and luck would also help them against Spee, though not before a preliminary disaster.

The disaster was the battle of Coronel off the Chilean coast on 1 November 1914, when Spee encountered a British squadron led by Rear Admiral Christopher Cradock, comprising two ageing cruisers, the *Good Hope* and the *Monmouth*, a light cruiser, the *Glasgow*, and an armed merchant ship, the *Otranto*, manned by inexperienced scratch crews. The *Good Hope* and the *Monmouth* went down with all hands, including Cradock himself, inflicting scarcely any harm on their enemies. Cradock should not have given battle against ships that were faster and more heavily gunned[153] and it is unclear why he did, though Troubridge's example may have weighed on his mind. The Admiralty had ordered him to concentrate against Spee's force but was equivocal about whether he should try to destroy it. It asked him not to engage without the antiquated battleship *Canopus*, but it was so slow that when Cradock advanced from the South Atlantic into the Pacific he left it behind. When the Admiralty finally ordered him to wait, it sent the signal two days after the battle.[154] Once the Royal Navy had suffered its first defeat in a naval engagement for more a century, however, Sir John Fisher, the newly appointed First Sea Lord, saw Coronel not only as a humiliation but also as threatening the Allies throughout the South and even the North Atlantic, as it was uncertain where Spee would appear next. Despite Britain's slim margin over the Germans in the North Sea, the Admiralty sent two battlecruisers to the South Atlantic (the *Invincible* and the *Inflexible*) under Vice-Admiral Sir Doveton Sturdee, and a third to Nova Scotia, as well as concentrating cruiser squadrons off the Cape of Good Hope and West Africa and using Japanese warships as escorts in the Pacific. The emergency might have tied up first-class Allied naval resources for a long time had not Spee left the Pacific to make for home; however, on 8 December he paused at Port Stanley in the Falkland Islands to attack its wireless station and coal stocks. When he arrived in the early morning, expecting to find the settlement undefended, he discovered Sturdee's vessels coaling at anchor. Spee had had no idea that the battlecruisers were in the vicinity, and both sides were surprised. If he had attacked at once he might have inflicted serious damage, but instead he turned away, possibly because of a shot fired by the *Canopus*, which the Admiralty had stationed in the islands. Sturdee gave chase, and as his battlecruisers could manage twenty-six knots against the Germans' eighteen (and it was an unusually fine, clear day in the southern summer) he caught up with the Germans in the afternoon and shelled them with three times their weight of broadside from a longer range than they could match.[155] In contrast to North Sea conditions, neither mines nor torpedoes played a part: this was a traditional battle decided by gunnery, in which the British were not particularly accurate but landed enough hits to destroy the German vessels with almost as little damage to the superior force as the British had inflicted at Coronel. Spee divided his squadron in the hope that his smaller ships could escape, but while the *Invincible* and the *Inflexible* sank the *Scharnhorst* and the *Gneisenau* Sturdee's cruisers sank the *Leipzig* and the *Nuremberg*. The *Dresden* escaped, but was scuttled after two British cruisers found it in Chilean waters in March 1915. Once again good fortune had enabled the British to locate their enemy in the expanses of the southern oceans, but Sturdee deserved credit for seizing his opportunity coolly, as did Fisher and his superior, Churchill, for sending Sturdee out. Moreover, the British battlecruisers at the Falklands vindicated Fisher's original conception of them, during his earlier tenure as First Sea Lord between 1904 and 1910, as an imperial interception force, more lightly armoured than dreadnought battleships but as heavily gunned and faster.[156] The battle of the Falkland Islands virtually eliminated the German cruiser menace that had disrupted Allied shipping and naval dispositions to an extent quite disproportionate to its size. Because of the threat, Australian and New Zealand troops delayed their departure to Europe from September to November 1914.[157] In all the German cruisers sank over fifty British ships, accounting for about 2 per cent of British tonnage, though this should be contrasted with the 133 German vessels that the British captured in the first three weeks of the war.[158] None the less, by early 1915, apart from occasional forays by armed German merchantmen, the Allies enjoyed almost complete command of the sea except in the Baltic and the Adriatic. Whereas on land the Germans controlled territory from which it was imperative for the Allies to dislodge them, at sea – before the advent of the U-boat menace – the map of war favoured their enemies.

The Central Powers' nearly landlocked location gave the British advantages that they had lacked in earlier wars against France and Spain. The British Isles have been compared to a gigantic breakwater, positioned to debar German access to the Atlantic via the North Sea and the Channel.[159] But most of Germany's inappropriately named High Seas Fleet (and especially its capital ships) was built as a short-radius force. The Germans had seventy-four light cruisers in 1914 and would probably have done better to use more of them overseas, but even a German victory over the British Grand Fleet might have caused little damage to Britain's colonies because few German ships could reach them. However, it would have made it difficult to protect shipping round the British Isles, including cross-Channel troopships. It would also have made it difficult for the Allies to blockade their enemies, and would have exposed the United Kingdom to bombardments, raids, and possible invasion. Because the Allies commanded most of the high seas already, the destruction of the German navy would have had much less impact on the overall balance of forces in the first phase of the war (though later on, after German submarine warfare began in earnest, it would have released additional Allied warships for commerce protection). For the British (and by extension the French and Russians because of Britain's indispensability to them) it was vital to avoid defeat at sea; for the Central Powers it was not.

In the event, for the first two years the two main capital fleets never came within range of each other's guns. This was a surprise for public opinion in Britain and Germany, which – sensitized by the naval race – had expected an early clash. The pre-war plans and dispositions suggest it was less of a surprise to the naval commanders. The German navy's operational caution contrasted remarkably with the army's boldness and with Tirpitz's aggressive building programmes. In principle strategic planning rested not with Tirpitz's Imperial Navy Office but with the Chief of the Admiralty Staff (CAS). In practice the CAS lacked the authority of the CGS in the army, and unlike the latter the CAS would not be the *de facto* commander in wartime. Tirpitz had considerable influence on strategy, and his decisions about the shape and size of the fleet limited what was feasible anyway. In 1914 Hugo von Pohl, the CAS, and Friedrich von Ingenohl, the fleet commander, were both his protégés, and Wilhelm ruled that the staff should co-ordinate their advice with him. Yet Tirpitz's pronouncements about the fleet's mission had always been ambiguous and the admirals had failed to formulate an agreed operational plan against Britain.[160] Once war broke out, the navy secretary was increasingly a marginal figure. Wilhelm was losing confidence in him, and was less willing to delegate direction of the war at sea than on land. He refused to consolidate control of the naval war in Tirpitz's hands as the latter had hoped, and once hostilities began the admiralty staff and fleet commander gained in influence.[161] This mattered because the most opportune moment for the High Seas Fleet to seek a decision was early in the war. So Tirpitz urged, at the time and in retrospect.[162] His was not, however, the prevailing view. In December 1912 Wilhelm had directed that in a war the fleet should damage the blockading forces as much as possible, and give battle with all its forces if the circumstances were favourable.[163] But in August 1914 he ordered it to stay in harbour and not to seek out the Royal Navy or attack the BEF troopships. The fleet's general instructions set as its first task to damage the Royal Navy by mining, submarine raids, and attacks on its ships in the Helgoland Bight. Only after attaining parity should it seek battle in favourable conditions.[164] The army wanted the navy to deter coastal landings, and Bethmann maintained that it must be 'saved' as a card for the peace negotiations; Wilhelm agreed and shared Pohl's opinion that it was too early to risk an all-out engagement. Despite Tirpitz's objections, Ingenohl was urged to preserve the fleet; he was not to risk action unless victory was probable.[165]

In part the German navy's leaders were cautious because they knew their fleet was outnumbered, and although it enjoyed certain qualitative advantages they could not compensate for numerical weakness. When war broke out Britain had 22 dreadnought battleships in service and 13 building against Germany's 15 and 5; it had 9 battlecruisers in service and 1 building against Germany's 5 and 3. It had 40 pre-dreadnought battleships against Germany's 22, 121 cruisers in all categories against 40, 221 destroyers against 90, and 73 submarines against 31. Admittedly, due to the greater dispersal of British forces, the North Sea ratios were much more even: 21:13 dreadnought battleships, 4:3 battlecruisers, 8:8 predreadnoughts; 11:7 light cruisers, and 42:90 destroyers.[166] Moreover, Germany had more reliable mines, torpedoes, and shells, and its ships had thicker armour that covered them more completely as well as a broader beam that gave them greater stability if damaged.[167] Yet many of these strengths would become apparent only in action and they were counterbalanced by weaknesses such as Tirpitz's decision to set a 13.5-in. gun calibre for the latest German battlecruisers, which meant they would be outmatched by Britain's new 15-in. *Queen Elizabeth* class battleships. Furthermore, by 1914 the Germans knew the Royal Navy was unlikely to mount a close (inshore) blockade of their harbours. If they wished to bring the

British to battle they might have to do so well away from their own coastline, which argued in favour of a defensive posture, as did the geography of Germany's North Sea estuaries. Its most modern battleships and battlecruisers were moored in the mouth of the Jade, pre-dreadnoughts in that of the Elbe, and a cruiser and torpedo boat force in the most forward estuary, the Ems. Minefields and shoals protected them well, but impeded exit except at high tide and might lead to the fleet being trapped at sea.[168] A major battle was unlikely unless British capital ships ventured to the mouth of their enemy's lair.

But British strategic dispositions also made for stalemate. As First Sea Lord in 1904–10 Fisher had revolutionized the Royal Navy's deployment and construction programmes but disparaged strategic planning. An Admiralty war staff was created only in 1912, after Winston Churchill began his 1911–15 tenure as First Lord of the Admiralty. In 1914 the navy had no strategy for aggressive destruction of the German fleet: sensibly, as it turned out. War plans drafted in 1906–8 had envisaged close blockade, coastal raids, and seizure of offshore islands in order to force the Germans to give battle; but the army objected to providing troops, seeing such operations as a distraction from helping the French. At a meeting of the cabinet subcommittee known as the Committee of Imperial Defence (CID), on 23 August 1911, the CIGS denounced the navy's ideas as 'madness'. Asquith ruled that it must concentrate on escorting the BEF to France quickly.[169] After 1912, moreover, impressed by the threat from mines and torpedoes, the navy abandoned close blockade in favour of an 'observational' blockade (a line of cruisers and destroyers off the Helgoland Bight), and in July 1914 it adopted a 'distant' blockade strategy of guarding the North Sea exits. Britain had too few cruisers and destroyers for an observational blockade, and too few submarines to use them as an alternative instrument for a close blockade. The distant blockade was a default strategy, though it proved effective. The idea was simple – to coop up the Germans in the North Sea and the Baltic by blocking off their escape routes, without exposing British forces to undue risk. At the start of the war Britain constituted its largest and most modern vessels, including twenty dreadnought battleships and four battlecruisers, as the Grand Fleet under the command of Admiral Sir John Jellicoe at the Orkney anchorage of Scapa Flow. He understood his mission as being to maintain the blockade of Germany and command of the seas.[170] He well understood the enemy's superior gunnery and his own vessels' inadequacies, commenting in a memorandum on 14 July that 'it is highly dangerous to consider that our ships as a whole are superior or even equal fighting machines'.[171] The Channel Fleet of eighteen predreadnought battleships and four cruisers was based at Portland. Sizeable forces of cruisers, destroyers, and submarines operated from Harwich and Dover, while the French navy stationed fourteen cruisers with supporting craft in the western Channel. To reach the high seas the Germans had an unenviable choice. They could brave the Straits of Dover and 200 miles of Channel, soon to be guarded by minefields and torpedo-carrying destroyers. Alternatively they could steer round Scotland, entailing a voyage of 1,100 miles to reach the Atlantic shipping lanes, with the Grand Fleet between them and base. The risk was the greater as British capital ships could operate further from port and had longer-range guns, and it would be difficult to take fuel carriers into northern waters.[172]

In the first instance the blockade was directed against the High Seas Fleet, but light forces stationed between Scotland and Norway also halted German merchant shipping. The Admiralty's Naval Intelligence Division had for a decade been investigating an economic blockade and Germany's dependence on overseas supplies, and in 1912 the CID endorsed a report recommending a complete shutdown of German commerce, including limiting imports into Holland and Belgium if they remained neutral. Steps to close down Germany's overseas trade were taken at once in 1914.[173] Distant blockade, with warships at Scapa and Dover available to support interception of merchant ships in the North Sea and the Channel, was sufficient to support this strategy, as it was both to protect the passage of the BEF and to discourage an invasion of Britain, which the Germans never seriously contemplated.[174] Indeed both the British and Germans overestimated the likelihood of armed landings: Moltke kept troops in Schleswig-Holstein and the British held back two BEF divisions partly for fear of it, in 1914 digging three trench systems north-east of London.[175] Yet Scapa Flow was so far from the Channel that it was a curious choice of location for the most powerful British warships, and if the Germans had attacked the BEF troopships the Grand Fleet would have been too remote to forestall them.[176] British strategy worked in part because the Germans deterred themselves.

It was as well this strategy remained untested. The navies' technological environment had changed even more dramatically than that of armies. Since 1900 huge advances had taken place in gunnery, meaning that future battles were likely to be fought at much greater speed and at longer range. They might occur in waters infested by mines and by torpedoes, possibly fired from submarines. In these circumstances sailors might well feel that they were going to war in eggshells, and as battleships took up to three years to build they were much harder to replace than were heavy weapons on land. Moreover, their destructive power had developed faster than their commanders' ability to direct it. British and German battleships had adopted large-calibre, long-range guns without fire-control systems adequate to train them simultaneously and accurately and allow for variations in speed and direction. Few of the shells fired would hit their targets. Furthermore, radio communication was still an emergent technology. In land battles infantry could not use it to call up artillery support. The weight and bulk of early transmitters were no obstacles to placing them in warships, but naval wireless telegraphy could not send voice messages but only ones in Morse, which took ten to fifteen minutes to encode, send, decode, and write up. This was far too slow for use in action and left little alternative to flag signalling as in Nelson's day but at greater distances and faster speeds, amid obscuring clouds of funnel smoke and spray from shell splashes. In sum, the value of the assets at the admirals' command, and the extreme uncertainty they faced, made for caution not only by the British and German navies, the largest, best trained, and most technologically sophisticated of the day, but still more by others, so that the North Sea stalemate reproduced itself elsewhere. Thus Russia's Baltic fleet had five pre-dreadnoughts but no modern battleships. On paper it was no match for the Germans, but the latter kept only small and obsolescent forces facing it, although if necessary they could send reinforcements from the North Sea via the Kiel Canal. Nor did they want losses in what they judged a secondary theatre, as long as their Baltic coastline and Swedish iron ore shipments went unmolested. Nicholas II remembered the destruction of his previous Baltic fleet by the Japanese and he too opposed risks.[177] In the Mediterranean, in contrast, if Italy had joined Austria-Hungary, France and Britain might have been hard pressed to contain their enemies, and even with Italy neutral the Austro-Hungarians had three dreadnought battleships at Pola against France's two and Britain's none. In addition, the French had difficulty sustaining operations in the Adriatic, given that their nearest base was Malta. But the Austrian Admiral Haus, supported by Franz Joseph, preferred not to risk his fleet against the French in case Italy – a much more detested enemy – intervened later.[178] After the flight of the *Goeben* and the *Breslau* the Allies dominated the Mediterranean until German submarines arrived.

Developments in the first six months reinforced both sides' wariness. The French ended their sweeps into the Adriatic after an Austrian submarine torpedoed their flagship, instead maintaining a distant blockade from the Straits of Otranto. The Russians became more adventurous in the Baltic once they realized they faced only second-rank German forces, but after a submarine sank a Russian cruiser they confined themselves to minelaying to protect the Petrograd approaches.* In the North Sea the twists and turns of fortune successively unnerved both sides. Thus the first major action, the battle of the Helgoland Bight on 28 August, alarmed the Germans but suggested to the British that Nelsonian boldness could still pay off. It originated in a plan by the Dover and Harwich commanders, Roger Keyes and Reginald Tyrwhit, to raid the German patrols in the Bight. Fighting began confusedly between British and German destroyers in early morning mist, German cruisers coming out of the Jade to investigate but German capital ships being unable to follow because the tide was low. Consequently when the British destroyers signalled for help and four battlecruisers (under Vice-Admiral David Beatty) with cruisers detached from the Grand Fleet ventured into the mêlée, they quickly sank three light cruisers and escaped before German reinforcements arrived. They were lucky, as their staff work was poor and they nearly lost a cruiser to one of their own submarines. None the less, Wilhelm now insisted that in future the High Seas Fleet must not sail far out of the Bight and its commander must ask his consent before engaging in a fleet action.

In the next few weeks, however, events conspired to threaten Britain's margin of superiority. The threat came (as Jellicoe had feared) from submarines and mines. On 22 September the German submarine U9 torpedoed and sank three elderly British cruisers, the *Cressy*, the *Aboukir*, and the *Hogue*, as they patrolled off the Dutch coast, the second two falling victim when they stopped to pick up survivors. Over 1,400 crewmen lost their lives, many of them middle-aged reservists. After U9 sank another cruiser on 9 October the Grand Fleet temporarily abandoned Scapa (which had no anti-submarine defences and which in November U18 got close to entering), taking refuge in Lough Swilly on the northern coast of Ireland. Yet on 27 October one of its newest battleships, the *Audacious*, struck a mine and went down. The British had neglected mine warfare: their mines were fewer

---

*St Petersburg was retitled Petrograd (a slavicized version of the city's name) after war broke out.

and less reliable than Germany's and the Grand Fleet had only six minesweepers. They now brought in fishing trawlers as minelaying auxiliaries, and from 1915 onwards British warships were fitted with the paravane, a device that destroyed mines or cut them from their moorings. But if minesweepers preceded the fleet it would have to steer together more closely, thus creating an easier submarine target, and if it deployed a destroyer screen against U-boats the destroyers had only 1,800 miles' fuel endurance, compared with battleships' 5,000.[179] German superiority in mines and submarines restricted naval operations long before it threatened British merchant shipping, and Jellicoe feared his advantage was being whittled away. He estimated that he had only seventeen battleships and five battlecruisers against Germany's fifteen and four, and whereas new German capital ships were coming into service, mechanical failures had put five British ones out of action. On 30 October he asked the Admiralty for agreement that the Grand Fleet should fight only in the northern North Sea and turn away rather than risk being lured into a mine and torpedo ambush. Despite growing public unease about the navy's inactivity, Churchill and Fisher agreed.[180]

Against this backdrop the decision to send out three battlecruisers to the South Atlantic after the battle of Coronel was audacious indeed, and after the news of the Falklands the Germans knew their enemies were under strength. On 16 December they attempted to provoke them into fighting before Sturdee's squadron returned, Rear Admiral Franz von Hipper's battlecruiser squadron bombarding Scarborough, Whitby, and Hartlepool and killing 122 civilians. Intercepted wireless messages had forewarned the British about the raid but not that the High Seas Fleet would be at sea in Hipper's support. Hence Jellicoe sent out Beatty's battlecruisers and a squadron of six battleships, and had they encountered the main enemy force the Germans might have succeeded in destroying enough British vessels to equalize the numbers. But Ingenohl feared he might be facing the entire Grand Fleet, which Wilhelm had not authorized him to engage. He turned away before the two sides' capital ships came into range. Subsequently Hipper escaped his stalkers due to a combination of poor visibility with confusing signalling and lack of initiative by the British battleship commander – British weaknesses that would recur later. Both sides quite narrowly escaped what could have been disaster, but the Germans had missed their best chance of striking when the British were weakest. After the next battle, that of the Dogger Bank on 24 January 1915, they virtually ceased trying. This time the action began with a reconnaissance by Hipper into the Dogger Bank fishing grounds, where he suspected British surveillance vessels were disguised as trawlers. He took three battlecruisers and an armoured cruiser, the *Blücher*, which was slower and had smaller guns. The British, again forewarned by decrypted wireless messages, sent out Beatty and four battlecruisers, with Jellicoe's battleships in distant support. In a pursuit action lasting three hours Beatty's flagship, the *Lion*, was so battered that he had to abandon it and lost control of operations. Misleading signals from his flag officer caused the British to concentrate their fire on the *Blücher*, which they sank, while Hipper's three battlecruisers got away. The battle was fought at high speed and at an enormous range of 16–20,000 yards: of 1,150 shells fired by the British only six (except for those directed at the disabled *Blücher*) hit their targets. Hence, although the British public was cheered, Beatty was greatly disappointed and British shortcomings were again exposed. The German battle-cruiser *Seydlitz* was hit in the turret and nearly exploded, but the Germans learned from the experience to improve their turret protection. During the following year they carried out major changes to their capital ships, fitting more armour, heavier guns with a higher elevation, and improved fire control, all of which meant they would be better equipped next time.[181] On the other hand, Wilhelm reaffirmed that the fleet must be protected as 'a political instrument', and should not seek battle outside the German Bight. He replaced Ingenohl by Pohl, Vice-Admiral Gustav Bachmann succeeding the latter as CAS. Given Jellicoe's Admiralty approval for not fighting outside the northern North Sea, a clash between the Grand Fleet and the High Seas Fleet had become extremely unlikely. Moreover, intelligence advantages and a major shipbuilding programme were about to reinforce Britain's lead. In the next phase at sea both battle fleets would become less active, but the war against commerce would dramatically escalate.

The heat and cloudless sunshine of the first month of the war in Western Europe broke after the Marne. They gave way to a rain-soaked autumn and one of the coldest winters in living memory.[182] In previous conflicts the armies might have retired to winter quarters, but now the supplies (not least of tinned food) available from industrialized societies enabled them to stay in contact. In Poland, the Carpathians, and the Balkans fighting went on well into December: after First Ypres Joffre launched a new offensive in Champagne that dragged on from December to March and cost 100,000 French casualties for minuscule gains.[183] In the midst of this carnage occurred one of the war's most poignant moments, the 1914 Christmas Truce. On 24 December lighted Christmas trees appeared in the German trenches in Flanders and both sides began to sing carols. On Christmas morning British and German soldiers met in no man's land, chatted, smoked, played football, posed for photographs, and buried their dead. Often the ceasefire lingered for several days until it was ended (with apologies by the units on the ground) at the insistence of the high commands, which ensured that at Christmas in subsequent years it happened much less, if at all.[184] The episode seems to encapsulate the lack of rancour between many front-line solders, who – now the heady opening days had receded – found themselves trapped in a killing machine by pressure from above. Unofficial truces and tacit agreements to moderate the violence would continue to characterize the Western Front during 1915, in the French sector (where the Christmas Truce was less prevalent) as well as the British.[185] Yet the participants all seem to have expected that the truce would be temporary, and by December the political chasm between the two sides was far wider than in August. Not only were the differences that led to war still unresolved, but also a gamut of new obstacles to reconciliation had joined them.

Foremost among these obstacles was the sheer scale of the killing since hostilities began. Open warfare took an even higher toll than the trench campaigning that succeeded it, and the 1914 casualty rates were proportionately among the worst in the war. The French army suffered 528,000 killed, wounded, and missing between August 1914 and January 1915, higher than during its murderous 1915 offensives or the 1916 battle of Verdun.[186] Its total dead numbered 265,000. The Belgian army lost half its combat strength and BEF losses down to 30 November were 89,969.[187] Of the British troops who landed in August, one third were dead, and of eighty-four BEF battalions (originally numbering 1,000 men each) by 1 November only nine had more than 300 effectives.[188] Russia's casualties were 1.8 million, of whom nearly 396,000 were killed and 486,000 captured;[189] Austria-Hungary's were 1.25 million.[190] Only the Germans' losses were lower in 1914 than in the later years of the war, though they too suffered some 800,000 casualties (or close to half their field army), of which 116,000 were deaths and 85,000 of these deaths came on the Western Front.[191] The full dimensions of this calamity were not yet public knowledge, although by September it was already evident in French villages that the losses were far worse than in 1870.[192] And yet the slaughter was only just beginning. Moreover, mobile warfare directly exposed civilians to advancing armies (whereas trench warfare would protect them). Invasion meant destruction: the Russians burned East Prussian farms and the Germans set ablaze the medieval library at Louvain and bombarded the Cloth Hall at Ypres and the Gothic cathedral at Reims, alleging that the French were using the latter as an artillery observation post. It also meant brutality against the occupied. Although in East Prussia the Russians seem mostly to have conducted themselves correctly, in Galicia they robbed and plundered and killed some dozens of civilians, mostly Jews.[193] During the two invasions of Serbia the Austrian forces executed several hundred people. Above all, in Western Europe the evidence of German soldiers' diaries, linked with the findings of the more sober Allied judicial inquiries and the reports of Belgian refugees, suggests the Germans deliberately killed 5,521 Belgian civilians in 1914 (largely during August) and 906 more in France, mostly because of suspicions that they were partisans. German soldiers, who were advancing at great personal danger through hostile terrain and knew of the French guerrilla warfare in 1870, were all too ready to suspect attack, but their suspicions were largely unfounded. Nevertheless they carried out dozens of executions (killing 674 in the town of Dinant alone) and torched thousands of buildings, as well as frequently using civilians as human shields.[194] Belgium's fate loomed so large in Allied propaganda not only because of its heroic resistance but also because of the menace to women and children, Lloyd George alleging for example that the invaders had killed three civilians for every soldier.[195] As this was also the enemy that had bombarded Scarborough (the subject of a celebrated British poster) and bombed Liège (later to be followed by Paris and London) from Zeppelin airships, many in the Allied countries believed they faced a challenge to civilization. The war took on an ideological dimension, as a crusade to uphold liberal and humanitarian values.

This political polarization was the more ominous because as the western trench systems thickened an early military resolution of the conflict seemed increasingly remote. At sea, experience had made all the navies still more risk averse. Outside Europe the Central Powers had been removed decisively at least from the surface of the oceans, but this development would take a long time to influence the war as a whole. On land the opening war plans had failed everywhere except perhaps in Galicia, and further rounds of fighting had confirmed that failure. By December it was clear that the Germans would have to fight a two-front war with an ineffectual ally and would therefore find it difficult to prevail in either east or west, while the

Allies seemed impossibly remote from the Ruhr and Berlin. Yet if military developments presaged no early resolution, neither did diplomacy and politics. Diplomacy failed in the July crisis, and the remainder of the year provided little scope for it. The American president, Woodrow Wilson, offered mediation but was promptly rebuffed;[196] appeals from the Pope and the European neutrals fell on deaf ears. Only after failing at First Ypres did the German leaders seriously consider negotiation, but even then Falkenhayn and Bethmann wanted a separate peace with one of their enemies rather than a general settlement.[197] But no Allied government was willing to consider such a peace, and by the Pact of London of 5 September Russia, France, and Britain pledged that they would neither negotiate nor make peace independently. The Allies had no interest in conversations until they had cleared their territory and the military balance had altered in their favour, which they believed in due course it would. Germany's aggression had bound its antagonists more solidly together and had tightened its encirclement.*

If diplomacy offered meagre prospects, the home fronts seemed unlikely to falter. The mobile campaigning created a period of national emergency, during which every continental belligerent was invaded and even Britain experienced an invasion scare in November,[198] while in late August, when news came in of Allied defeats in France, the London recruiting stations were jammed with volunteers.[199] During this emergency, when politicians and the public (if not the generals) still expected a short war, legislatures were suspended and normal politics was adjourned. The French formed a national coalition; elsewhere all mainstream parties accepted electoral truces and voted war credits. All the belligerents censored their press. In France the military strictly rationed information and the prefects suppressed items seen as likely to divide or demoralize the public. In Germany the DCGs had a similar role. In Britain the government relied more on self-censorship by agreement with newspaper proprietors and editors, though backed up by its DORA powers.[200] It is questionable how far emergency powers were needed, as the opening months of the war saw preternatural calm on the recently so turbulent domestic fronts. Irish nationalists and unionists retreated from the brink of civil strife and men from both communities volunteered in thousands; after mobilization the Russian towns and countryside were quiet, as were Austria-Hungary's South Slavs. Paris did not rebel after the frontier defeats as it had done in 1870, despite the city's economy being dislocated by business closures and rocketing unemployment. In London and Berlin joblessness and production losses were only brief and within weeks households benefited from separation allowances for those whose breadwinners had joined up, while industrial unrest melted away.[201]

In the absence of normal politics governments took on decree powers, and on the continent they delegated extensively to the military. In Germany this meant the DCGs; in France the GQG (*Grand Quartier général*, the French high command) in the 'zone des étapes' (staging zone) behind the front lines; in Austria, the AOK. Statesmen rarely interfered with operations on land (though Winston Churchill and Wilhelm II were more interventionist at sea), though they did act on big issues. Thus Kitchener insisted on Sir John French staying in the Allied line; the French

---

*See ch. 5.

government approved Joffre's recovery strategy after the frontier defeats but required him to leave troops in Paris; Wilhelm replaced Moltke by Falkenhayn and agreed with the latter on calling off First Ypres. With these exceptions, strategy on land was mostly left to the generals, who as yet needed little from the politicians. Although industrial mobilization began in France from late September after Joffre appealed to Millerand for shells, the 1914 campaigns were largely fought with munitions and equipment available at the outset. Governments needed to pay for their armies and purchase military supplies, but once the gold standard was suspended and parliaments voted war credits they could in the short term afford what they needed without contentious tax increases. The other requirement was military manpower, but on the continent conscription already existed. The French called up their 1914 conscript class (young men reaching military age in that year) in August-September and their 1915 class in December;[202] Russia and Austria-Hungary likewise called up new classes.[203] In Britain the War Office was sending territorials and imperial (including Indian) troops across the Channel by December, although the volunteers who had joined since August travelled out only in 1915. On the continent, in contrast, volunteering by younger and exempted men quickly provided a valuable supplement. In Germany their numbers during 1914 may have exceeded 300,000.[204] The Prussian war ministry began as soon as war broke out to train the extra corps (many of them student volunteers) whom Falkenhayn squandered at Langemarck.[205] Enough extra men were available for the fearful losses to be made good, even if they often had little equipment.

The readiness of young men to risk their lives illuminates the deeper forces that sustained the war effort and would continue to do so after the 1914 emergency. Public opinion continued to express itself, for example in the pro-war pronouncements by the Protestant and Catholic clergy and the rival manifestos of German and Allied intellectuals and academics.[206] If French and British publicists spoke of a crusade for civilization, their counterparts rejoined that Germany represented spiritual values of honour, sacrifice, and heroism against the shallow materialism of the west. How much wider resonance these contentions held is questionable, and the Christmas Truce has rightly been seen as throwing doubt on them. But if on the continent volunteers were commonly men from school or university background, in Britain they came from all sections of the population,[207] and their story underlines that willingness to fight (if not necessarily hatred for the enemy) was not simply a phenomenon of the elite. In their resolve to see the struggle through to victory the belligerent governments still faced negligible unrest and opposition, and saw many signs of strong and widespread support. So far from subsiding because of operational stalemate, the conflict at the end of 1914 was poised for further escalation and for evolution into something historically unprecedented, a new form of total war.

Part Two

ESCALATION

CHAPTER 3

MAKING A NEW WORLD,
SPRING 1915–SPRING 1917

F ROM NOW ON, the drama would unfold without a script. The war plans had been tried and failed, with hundreds of thousands of killed and wounded as the consequence. This fact alone virtually precluded a negotiated return to the *status quo*, with its implication that the dead had died in vain. The Germans had been unable to capture Paris, annihilate the French army, or occupy the Channel ports. The French and British had neither liberated northern France and Belgium nor reconquered Alsace-Lorraine, and the defences against them continued to strengthen. Whether measured by the numbers of troops and heavy weapons or by the scale of casualties the Western Front remained the principal theatre, and the congealing of its trench lines signalled a new phase in the war as a whole. But in other respects too, the 1914–15 winter was a turning point. Both sides now tooled up their industries and raised extra manpower for a prolonged struggle. Both sought additional partners, and Ottoman Turkey's adhesion to the Central Powers in October opened the whole of the Near East as a new arena of hostilities. At sea, in spring 1915 Germany experimented with unrestricted submarine warfare and the Allies with a total blockade of their enemies. In this middle period of the war, between late 1914 and the next major turning point in spring 1917, the powers created a style of combat that in retrospect seemed to encapsulate the conflict as a whole. Its key features were escalation and stalemate, both sides applying rising levels of violence yet failing to terminate the impasse. The war became more nearly total and more global, and from these characteristics much of its enduring impact followed. Yet the seeming equilibrium was not static but dynamic, the initiative passing back and forth as each side strove to pre-empt or thwart the other's gambits and attempted new expedients to catch its adversary off balance.

For six months after the Marne the advantage lay mostly with the Allies. During the winter the French kept up the pressure, attacking in Champagne and the

Woëvre. The Russians repelled a Turkish attack in the Caucasus and the British repelled one on the Suez Canal, while in February Allied warships began an attempt to penetrate the Dardanelles. The gravest danger to the Central Powers, however, was the military emergency facing Austria-Hungary, with Przemysl encircled and Russia pressing into the Carpathians at the same time as Italy and more Balkan states seemed poised to join the Allies. But after Przemysl fell in March the Germans baled the Austrians out, and the big story of 1915 was the Central Powers' advance in the east. Between May and September they regained most of the Austro-Hungarian territory previously lost and drove the Russians out of Poland and Lithuania. They then turned south and (with the assistance of a new partner, Bulgaria) overran Serbia and Montenegro. In the west they confined themselves to a limited attack with poison gas in the second battle of Ypres, which covered the transfer of troops for the breakthrough against Russia. In contrast the Allies' initiatives generally failed miserably. French and British offensives in Artois and Champagne in spring and autumn 1915 provided no relief to the Russians, and smaller German forces arrested them, causing heavy loss. After Italy joined the Allies in May its troops flung themselves unavailingly against the Austrian defences on the river Isonzo. Nor did the establishment of an Allied base at Salonika in October assist the Serbs except as a haven for their routed army. Operations against the Ottomans fared even worse. An expedition from India reached the outskirts of Baghdad by November 1915, but the Turks forced it to surrender at Kut-al-Amara in the following April. After the British and French navies gave up trying to force the Turkish Straits, Allied troops landed on the Gallipoli peninsula in April and August 1915, only to find themselves in another trench deadlock. Before being evacuated they suffered over 250,000 casualties. Whereas Serbia's defeat opened a land bridge connecting Berlin and Vienna with Constantinople the western Allies failed to establish a sea route via the Straits to Russia: if at the beginning of 1915 Austria-Hungary was the most hard-pressed belligerent, by the end of the year Russia had taken its place. Nor did developments at sea provide much comfort. American protests did more than Allied countermeasures to contain Germany's first unrestricted submarine campaign, while the blockade of the Central Powers was very slow to take effect. In short, the Allied record in 1915 was of almost unrelieved disappointment.

This appearance was misleading, because despite the Germans' greater tactical and operational effectiveness the Allies were gradually mobilizing their resources and enhancing their co-ordination. The Russian army staged a remarkable recovery, entering 1916 both larger and better equipped than before its retreat. The Italian army also increased its weapons and numbers. The British Grand Fleet widened its lead over the German High Seas Fleet, and the BEF benefited from the arrival *en masse* of volunteer divisions and of shells. At Chantilly in December the Allies planned a synchronized assault for the following summer. In 1915 there had been Allied offensives in the spring and Austro-German counterstrokes in the summer and autumn; in 1916 the pattern was reversed. Austria-Hungary attacked the Italians in the Trentino (May-June), submarines launched a second campaign against Allied shipping, the German fleet mauled the British at the battle of Jutland, and Falkenhayn tried to cripple the French army in months of savage fighting around Verdun between February and July. Yet none of these efforts achieved their objectives. The Turks' success against the British at Kut was more than outweighed by their loss of most of Armenia to the Russians. The Italians checked the Trentino offensive; the American president again compelled the U-boats to suspend their sinkings; Jutland actually confirmed Britain's naval advantage; and Verdun left the French army dreadfully damaged but still effective and able to retaliate.

Although the Central Powers' spring attacks blunted the Allies' summer offensives by obliging them to start earlier and in reduced strength, the offensives none the less foiled Austria-Hungary's and Germany's plans and for the first time in a year restored the initiative to their enemies. The advance launched by the Russian General Brusilov in June forced Austria-Hungary to move troops from the Trentino and Germany to switch reserves from the west; the Somme offensive in July caused Germany to wind down operations at Verdun (where two French attacks in the autumn recaptured almost all of Falkenhayn's earlier gains). Brusilov's successes prompted Romania to intervene in August and invade Transylvania, while the Italians were freed for another Isonzo attack and the Allies at Salonika probed inland. With Austria-Hungary again at bay the Central Powers faced their worst emergency since spring 1915. Admittedly the new team of Hindenburg and Ludendorff, who took over the high command from Falkenhayn in August, responded energetically. German reinforcements halted Brusilov; troops from all four Central Powers overwhelmed the Romanians and occupied two thirds of their territory; Franco-British progress on the Somme was limited to six miles; and although the Italians captured Gorizia and the Salonika army took Monastir the Allies once more ended the year having gained less territory than their enemies. But the balance now seemed to be moving emphatically against the Central Powers, and in the bitter winter of 1916–17 starvation loomed in Berlin and Vienna. It was in a mood of calculated desperation that the Germans decided to renew unrestricted submarine warfare from February, reckoning that even if America (as they expected) declared war, the impact would be nullified if the U-boat attacks forced Britain to negotiate.

Allied plans for the new year, outlined at another Chantilly conference in November 1916, were to renew their synchronized offensives but to start earlier, because they were better prepared than in the previous campaigning season and because they feared once again being forestalled. They were forestalled, all the same. In February the Germans withdrew from their most advanced positions in France to the newly constructed Hindenburg Line, disrupting the preparations of the new French commander in chief, Robert Nivelle. Still more disruptive were the outbreak of revolution in Petrograd and the abdication of Nicholas II in March, which indefinitely postponed Russia's contribution to the Allied assault. The industrial build-up that enabled Russia to re-equip its army after 1915 so strained its social fabric that it now disintegrated, hobbling the Allies at the moment when they planned a decisive blow. The western Allies attacked regardless in April and May and the British had some successes in the battle of Arras, but the French offensive on the Chemin des Dames delivered mortifyingly less than Nivelle had promised. Against the Turks, meanwhile, although a new British expedition took Baghdad in March 1917, two attempts to break into Palestine through the Ottoman lines at Gaza misfired, and the revolt by the Hejaz Arabs against the Ottomans that began in June 1916 gave the Allies little assistance. After ten months of attacking in all theatres the Allies had lost impetus. They now faced their most difficult moment of the war. With the Russian Revolution, French mutinies after the Nivelle offensive, and the climax of the U-boat assault on shipping, even American intervention in April 1917 might be too late to save them. At all events, the upheavals of spring and summer 1917 marked the entry of the conflict into its third and final phase.

The war's middle period must be viewed in relation to its predecessor and its successor. The 'short-war illusion' that had helped to cause the conflict did not end in 1914. On the contrary, both soldiers and civilians, deprived of the luxury of hindsight, were sustained in part by faith that one more determined heave would bring triumph. The parity of strength between the opposing coalitions that had contributed to causing the war also prolonged and intensified it once it had begun. For the moment the Allies were unable to knock out even so vulnerable an opponent as Turkey, and their operational ineffectiveness has rightly been identified as a major reason for the stalemate of 1915 and 1916.[1] Yet the underlying tectonic shift against the Central Powers that had been under way since 1909 continued to operate despite ever more violent efforts to counteract it. In this respect too the apparent deadlock between winter 1914 and spring 1917 was misleading, for during these months the bases were laid for the subsequent collapse of both Austria-Hungary and Germany (to say nothing of tsarist Russia), although the precise extent to which the Allies' efforts in this phase contributed to their eventual victory remains debatable.

It is therefore inadequate to characterize the middle period of the war as simply one of deadlock. True, until the Germans withdrew to the Hindenburg Line neither side managed to move the Western Front by more than a few thousand yards. The North Sea battle fleets only once made contact, and neither the Allied blockade nor the Central Powers' submarine campaign came close to success. The Italian and Salonika fronts were scarcely less rigid than the Western one, and although the Eastern Front was more fluid it shifted much less (apart from being extended through Romania) after September 1915. Smaller states like Serbia, Montenegro, and Romania might be overrun (though none surrendered), but the great powers remained on their feet. Yet although the map of the fronts suggested little had changed, precisely because the balance was so even each side sought both to extend the conflict, by bringing in new partners and venturing into new geographical areas, and to intensify it, by introducing new weapons technologies and applying existing ones more destructively. Fighting spread from northern Europe into the Balkans, the Mediterranean, Africa, and the Middle East. Combat was no longer two-dimensional but stretched into the skies and beneath the waves. Neither side resisted the temptations to violate the internationally agreed restrictions on the scope of armed conflict and to strike at civilians as well as men in uniform. If Germany generally took the initiative in these respects, its enemies were ready enough to retaliate. Poison gas and flame-throwers on the battlefronts were accompanied by sea and air bombardment of defenceless cities, by torpedoing of merchant ships and liners, by an Allied blockade of all kinds of supplies to the Central Powers, including food and medicine, and by the Turkish massacres of the Armenians. But the war also broke new records in the weight of heavy artillery bombardment with high explosive (the cause of far more deaths than either poison gas or flame-throwers) in battles that by 1916 lasted for months on end. At sea, Jutland was the biggest naval action yet seen, fought with a far heavier quantity of metal than Trafalgar, though with not much higher casualties.[2] On land, the French and Germans at Verdun fired some 23 million shells between February and July 1916, an average of more than 100 per minute, and on the Somme the figures were even higher.[3] Nothing ever seen before compared with such massive concentrations of firepower and of human suffering in such confined spaces over such long periods, and with such meagre results. As the scale of casualties became open knowledge, contemporaries could take a melancholy pride in having entered new realms of experience, and that their own 'Great War' exceeded in its frightfulness any conflict previously known.

The massacre could not continue without an equally unprecedented mobilization on the home fronts. Even at the height of the pre-1914 arms race, defence expenditure had not exceeded 5 per cent of the powers' gross national products.[4] In contrast, military spending by most belligerents was probably more than half of GNP by 1916 and comparable with the levels reached in the Second World War.[5] In Germany, for example, public spending (mostly on the war) rose between 1914 and 1917 from 18 to 76 per cent of GNP.[6] So dramatic a reallocation of resources required a radical reorganization of the labour market and challenged traditional hierarchies in the workplace, including the prerogatives of skilled labour and the advantages enjoyed by men over women. It was paid for through inflationary financing that endangered the living standards of everyone not engaged in weapons production. To prepare their societies to accept such sacrifices, governments and leaders of opinion encouraged psychological mobilization by controlling the flow of information and by the use of propaganda to bolster morale and confidence. Beneath the fraying political truce a contest developed between the underpinnings of patriotic consensus and the pressures that would fracture military discipline and social cohesion in one belligerent after another in 1917–18.

To analyse this stalemate period, and its accompanying dynamic of escalation, a chronological approach is not the most illuminating method. It will therefore be examined here thematically, under eight main heads. The first problem to investigate is the widening of the war: the expansion of the conflict through the entry of new belligerents, the campaigns fought outside Europe against the Ottoman Empire and the German colonies, and the broader impact of extra-European factors. The energy devoted by the Allies to African and Asian campaigning partially offset the benefits provided by their empires for the war effort, although these benefits were probably still an indispensable advantage. The second is the evolution of the two sides' war aims, the objectives for which governments and their publics supposed they were fighting, and the obstacles to a compromise peace. In diplomacy too, an escalation process was at work, and by 1917 the two sides were even more deeply divided than at the outset. The third – and central – topic is that of the strategies adopted for the principal fronts on land: the roads towards the Central Powers' offensives in Poland and at Verdun and the Allies' co-ordinated counter-attacks in summer 1916 and spring 1917. The fourth is that of the tactical, technological, and logistical considerations that frustrated these strategies and produced the great battles of attrition, while the fifth is that of how the belligerents recruited their armies and navies and what enabled soldiers to endure things that to a later generation seem intolerable. The sixth is that of how economies were mobilized for war production and how that production was financed, and the Allies' failure fully to exploit their apparent advantages. The discussion then turns from developments on land to those at sea. By early 1915 the Allies had established command of the oceans and they spent the rest of the war resisting efforts by German surface ships and submarines to deprive them of it. Yet their efforts to exploit their naval superiority were very slow to bite. The final section considers the resilience of political unity and of civilian morale on the home fronts, and the part played by repression as opposed to genuine consensus. It also reunites the strands of the analysis, exploring the interconnections between the factors driving on the conflict and considering which were critical in explaining the catastrophe to which the 1914 generation fell victim.

✦ CHAPTER 4 ✦

THE WIDENING OF THE WAR

In Britain at the time, if not simply called 'the war', the conflict was referred to as 'the great war', evoking the earlier struggle against Napoleon; in France '*la guerre*' or '*la grande guerre*' was the usual description. 'World war' and '*guerre mondiale*' became prevalent only from the 1930s. In Germany, in contrast, '*Weltkrieg*' was the preferred description from the start, the Berlin leaders understanding that they were fighting for world-power status and that their enemies were concentrating the resources of their empires against them. Americans too referred to the conflict generally as 'the world war' (rather than 'the European war') after being drawn in, and by 1917 almost all the biggest and strongest countries across the globe had indeed become belligerents.[1] From much earlier, however, men and resources from other continents were funnelled into the Western Front, and the deadlock in the central theatres drove both sides to seek new partners and fresh battlegrounds. Major operations unfolded in the Middle East, Africa, and Asia. Yet although the extra-European fighting tied down many more Allied than Austro-German troops, the Allies had much freer access to the world at large. The war's extra-European dimension contributed not only to the 1915–17 stalemate but also to the eventual Allied breakthrough. This section will examine that dimension from three perspectives: the intervention of new belligerents, the campaigns in the Middle East, and the war as a collision between colonial powers.

The Germans accurately perceived that Britain's entry was the first and crucial step to transforming the war from an essentially European into a global phenomenon. In 1914 the British Empire embraced 9 million square miles and some 348 million people; the inhabitants of a self-governing dominion such as Australia were officially part of the 'British nation' and entitled to British passports, they did not constitute a sovereign state, and they were automatically involved in hostilities when the British monarch declared them. These circumstances might have created an issue of democratic legitimacy, but in fact they did not. The one exception to the pattern was South Africa, where Britain had suppressed the independent Afrikaner republics of the Orange Free State and the Transvaal barely a decade before, absorbing them into a new union with the British-dominated Natal and Cape Colony. In October 1914 Afrikaners rebelled against conscription for operations against the German colony of South-West Africa, and although the Union government led by the Afrikaner Louis Botha crushed the movement, South Africa's contribution to the war effort remained relatively limited and guarded.[2] In Australia, on the other hand, during the July crisis the Canberra government placed its navy under British command and offered to send an expeditionary force, and politicians and newspapers of all persuasions vied with each other in affirming support for the mother country.[3] The mood in New Zealand was similar. In Canada support came not only from English-speakers and the Conservative prime minister, Robert Borden (who promised to send troops without even recalling parliament), but also from Sir Wilfred Laurier, head of the opposition Liberals and the leading politician in Quebec. Likewise in Delhi Indian politicians on the Legislative Council expressed enthusiastic loyalty and approved military assistance, as did Mohandas Gandhi.[4] In recent decades telegraph communication and intensified investment and emigration had reinforced British links with the Dominions: indeed, many of the Australian leaders were British-born. Away from the political and intellectual elites, support for the war was probably more lukewarm, and once it became prolonged and costly some cracks in the façade of unity appeared overseas as they did in Europe. None the less, to begin with involvement in it was accepted with remarkably little dissension, and in the more authoritarian French and Russian empires still more so.

Apart from the automatic participation of the colonial empires, the war was also globalized by the decisions of independent states to intervene. Several of those that entered (most notably in Latin America) did so largely as a gesture. The main late entrants to have a real impact were Japan and the Ottoman Empire in August and October 1914 respectively, Italy and Bulgaria in May and October 1915, Portugal and Romania in March and August 1916, and the USA, Greece, and China in April, July, and August 1917. The discussion here will take events down to Romania's entry, tracing the extension of the fighting into the Balkans and the Adriatic as well as into East Asia and the Levant. If the original belligerents had justification for not foreseeing what the war would be like, the later arrivals had less excuse. Yet they shared in the 'short-war illusion': the Italians, for example, supposing that they would fight for only a few months.[5] Particularly in eastern Europe the conflict appeared a ding-dong struggle in which the advantage oscillated between the two sides. The difficulties of foresight in such circumstances help explain why Turkey and Bulgaria chose the losers and Italy and Romania underestimated the cost of joining the winners. As in the July crisis pre-existing alliances influenced decisions for war much less than did considerations of national interest. But unlike in 1914 the later entrants had time to define their requirements and to negotiate with the two sides. Although this more leisured timetable should have permitted greater public debate, in fact most of the interventions were driven through by authoritarian governments not only to advance their external interests but also to outmanoeuvre rivals at home.

Unusually among the late entrants, Japan was strong enough and remote enough from Europe to remain secure whoever won. The prime instigator of its intervention, foreign minister Kato Takoaki, told the cabinet that Britain would triumph but if it lost Japan would suffer little.[6] Nor did the terms of Japan's 1902 alliance with Britain require it to go to war, as Germany did not threaten Britain's colonies in Asia. But in August 1914 the Admiralty, fearing Spee's cruisers would wreak havoc in the Pacific, urged Grey to request Japanese naval assistance. Grey's appeal assisted Kato by broadening support for involvement among ministers and the *genro*, a group of elder statesmen who advised the emperor and held a veto over foreign policy. But although Kato could claim to be showing solidarity with Britain, his real purpose was expansion. His guiding concerns were three. First, he wanted Germany's North Pacific islands and its territory of Qingdao, held on a long lease from China, which comprised the Jiaozhou naval base and a railway into the mineral-rich interior. Second, he was alarmed by the Chinese revolution of 1911–12 which had overthrown the Manchu dynasty in favour of a new president, the anti-Japanese General Yuan Shih-kai. In 1913 he had warned Grey that at the right 'psychological moment' he would act to safeguard Japan's Manchurian railway leases against the Chinese.[7] Third, Russia's recovery from defeat in 1904–5 (and its completion of the Trans-Siberian Railway) also worried the Japanese. Their armed forces had been neglected, but attempts in 1912–13 to expand them encountered fierce resistance and brought down two governments. Kato hoped war entry would facilitate rearmament. Grey was wary of Japan's ulterior motives and even attempted to revoke his request for help in view of his concern about them, but Kato assured him that Tokyo would keep out of the South Pacific and sought no aggrandisement in China. Additionally, before taking the plunge Kato learned that if he limited his ambitions the United States was unlikely to act against him. None the less, Japan's ultimatum on 15 August 1914 required Germany to hand over Qingdao at once, with its possible restoration to the Chinese coming only later. After declaring war on the 23rd Kato's officials began work on the draconian 'Twenty-one Demands' that they presented to Beijing in January 1915, and when the Diet continued to resist rearmament the government dissolved it and won new elections. Although early popular enthusiasm for the war soon dissipated, Japan's belligerency propelled it in a nationalist and autocratic direction.[8]

The same applied to Ottoman Turkey. Unlike Japan it was not a unified nation state but a sprawling multi-ethnic conglomerate. Because of its chronic indebtedness and its defeats in earlier wars, as well as its mistreatment of its subject peoples, the European powers supervised its public finances and reserved the right to intervene in order to protect the Armenian and Lebanese Christians. Since the 'Young Turk' revolution of 1908 the empire had tried to modernize its political institutions and armed forces, but it lost Libya to Italy in 1911–12 and most of its European territory in the First Balkan War of 1912–13. The partition of its Asian lands was widely predicted to follow, and on the eve of war the powers were negotiating provisional agreements on their slices of the cake, although none wanted a carve-up yet. In reaction to the defeats, a coup in 1913 brought the leaders of the Young Turks – a conspiratorial nationalist movement known as the CUP or Committee of Union and Progress – to key ministerial positions. The Grand Vizier, Said Halim, the approximate equivalent of a prime minister and the official whom Allied diplomats met most frequently, could be by-passed by the CUP triumvirate of Djemal Pasha (navy), Talat Pasha (interior), and Enver Pasha (war).[9]

Before the war the Turks were not firmly anchored to either camp. Germany was probably the power they least suspected of annexationist designs on them, and since 1913 an influential German military mission had been headed by General Liman von Sanders, who was appointed inspector-general of the Turkish army. But although Enver and his associates signed a secret alliance with Germany on 2 August 1914 – characteristically not informing their cabinet colleagues – they initially stayed neutral because they remained divided among themselves and the country was unready to fight. Before crossing the Rubicon they continued talking to the Allies, but the latter did little to woo them. The British seem to have doubted whether anything would make Turkey sincerely pro-Allied and to have underestimated its military prowess, the cabinet in London being mainly concerned that Constantinople rather than the Allies should be seen to make the break. Moreover, the power the Turks feared most was their hereditary enemy, Russia, against whom they wanted an Anglo-French guarantee – which London and Paris could not give. The most they would offer was to guarantee the empire's integrity on the condition it remained strictly neutral, but the Turks feared this would enable Russia to import all the armaments it needed through the Straits and become stronger than ever. To prevent such a danger they closed the Straits at the end of September to foreign shipping, an overtly anti-Allied act.[10]

A precipitant was still needed to bring Turkey in. Already in early August the British had decided to withhold delivery of two battleships that the Turks had ordered from British shipyards but which the Royal Navy now wanted for itself. The ships would have given the Ottomans the edge over Russia's Black Sea Fleet, and had been paid for by public subscription. The outraged Turks had therefore been receptive when the German warships *Goeben* and *Breslau* eluded their British pursuers in the Mediterranean and reached the Dardanelles. Constantinople agreed to 'purchase' them but they retained their German crews and their commander, Souchon, became the Turkish navy's commander in chief. As such his connections with Enver Pasha gave the Ottoman war party a crucial advantage. It was Souchon's ships that triggered hostilities when on 29 October they led a Turkish flotilla into the Black Sea, attacking Russian shipping and bombarding Odessa, to which the Allies responded by declaring war. The Sultan proclaimed a holy war against them. Yet the Germans had insisted that Souchon would sail only with Turkish authorization, and by providing the necessary orders Enver served as the prime mover in Constantinople as Kato did in Tokyo. If Kato was an anglophile and ex-ambassador in London, Enver had been military attaché in Berlin, admired the German army, and kept a portrait of Frederick the Great above his desk. Insisting that Germany would win, he wanted Turkey to join her, link up with the Muslims ruled by Russia in the Caucasus, and even try to regain the former Ottoman territories in North Africa. His less impetuous CUP colleagues hesitated after the Marne, but Germany's successes against Russia in Poland steeled them to take the plunge once they had strengthened the Dardanelles defences and Berlin delivered a payment worth 2 million Turkish lire to finance their rearmament. Having previously restrained Enver, they now gave him his head. Although the Grand Vizier denounced the Odessa raid, in the face of a majority of the CUP leadership the government accepted the *fait accompli*, and its more liberal and moderate elements were marginalized.[11]

The remaining great-power entrant in the first half of the war was Italy, whose secret Treaty of London with the Allies signed on 26 April 1915 bound it to join them within one month.[12] Unlike Turkey and Japan it appeared to be changing sides. Yet the 1882 Triple Alliance between Italy, Germany, and Austria-Hungary did not bind the Italians to participate in an attack on Serbia, especially as in 1914 their partners did not consult them beforehand. From Rome's perspective Austria-Hungary was actually the principal enemy, and for a decade these two supposed allies had been fortifying their mutual frontier and building rival navies in the Adriatic. They competed for influence in the Balkans, and *Italia irredenta* ('unredeemed Italy') – the *c.* 800,000 Italian-speakers under Habsburg rule in the Trentino and round Trieste – were the top priority for Italian nationalists. Because the Italians were too weak to attack Austria-Hungary and they regarded Germany's army as the best in Europe, the Triple Alliance made sense for them in peacetime, but once Germany was fighting France and Russia Italy had no interest in joining the Central Powers unless they were going to win. Given Italy's vulnerability to the British Navy, which could bombard its coastal cities and railways and prevent its imports of wheat and coal, neutrality was the obvious choice in 1914 and had general public support.

The crucial Italian leaders were prime minister Antonio Salandra and his foreign minister from October 1914, Sidney Sonnino, who kept the cabinet in the dark and could count on support from King Victor Emmanuel III. During the neutrality period negotiations continued with Germany and Austria-Hungary, but in bad faith on both sides. Despite pressure from Berlin, the Austrians would promise Italy only part of the Trentino. They refused to transfer it immediately rather than after the war, fearing to set a precedent for other predators. The Allies, aware that they were in a bidding match, reluctantly conceded most of the demands that Salandra and Sonnino set out in March 1915. The Italians wanted colonial gains in Africa and Asia Minor, but their principal requirements were for defensible frontiers on the Alps (up to the line of the Brenner Pass) and in Istria, and for the islands and coastline of Dalmatia so that they could dominate the Adriatic. Their purpose was not only to complete Italy's ethnic unity but also to achieve military and naval security and to limit Slav expansion, by establishing new frontiers that would include a quarter of a million German-speakers in the South Tyrol and some 700,000 Slovenes and Croats. Rather than breaking up Austria-Hungary, they envisaged maintaining it as a balance to Serbia, while the latter, backed by Russia, opposed Italy's claims.

At each stage along the road to Italian intervention the changing battlefield fortunes were critical. The Marne convinced Salandra that the Allies would win and Italy's interest was to join them. The start of the attack on the Dardanelles (which he expected to succeed and to bring in the Balkan states) encouraged him to negotiate seriously. Salandra, Sonnino, and the CGS, Luigi Cadorna, expected an early peace. Requesting only a modest Allied loan, they hastened to enter while doing so would give them political leverage, even though their army was unready. Finally, the stalling of the Russians' progress on the Eastern Front in April undermined Petrograd's power of veto and persuaded it to value Italian entry more highly at Serbia's expense, making possible a compromise whereby in addition to promises of colonial compensation, the Trentino, the South Tyrol, Trieste, and Istria, Italy would annex the northern Dalmatian coastline and the southern portion would be neutralized. With the Gallipoli invaders now stuck fast on their beachheads, however, and the Russians being routed, in the month after concluding the

Treaty of London in April the Italian leaders would be hard pressed to win parliamentary approval for their commitment.

Italy's entry into the war was unique in being preceded by a domestic crisis, touched off by a public offer by Germany and Austria-Hungary to cede the Trentino and make Trieste a free city. If (and it was a large if) Berlin and Vienna could be trusted, Italy was being granted virtually everything it could justify on grounds of self-determination. If it went to war regardless it would do so for imperialist objectives and against domestic opposition. Most of the press favoured joining the Allies, as did conservative politicians, the Italian Nationalist Association, and patriotic socialists such as Benito Mussolini, but officials in the provinces reported that most of the public was indifferent or hostile. The Catholic church opposed intervention, as did the main socialist party, the PSI, which saw no overwhelming case (such as that which had rallied its French and German counterparts) for national solidarity against a reactionary aggressor. Moreover, Giovanni Giolitti, Salandra's more progressive political rival and his predecessor as premier, asserted that 'quite a lot' might be obtained while staying neutral and war should be avoided unless absolutely necessary. When a majority of deputies indicated their support for Giolitti, Salandra resigned. His action triggered the so-called 'radiant May' of interventionist demonstrations in the major cities, mostly orderly bourgeois affairs, although in Rome the crowds invaded the parliament building and intimidated Giolitti's followers. In any case the anti-war camp was leaderless. Because Giolitti recognized that Vienna had offered so much only because it had been threatened, he refused to form a government, and so did two other candidates. When the king recalled Salandra the opposition collapsed and the government secured big majorities, even the PSI deciding only to oppose rather than sabotage the war effort. Thus although Italy's entry was achieved by constitutional means it signified defeat for the left and centre. The government envisaged a brief and limited operation against Austria-Hungary alone and did not declare war against Germany. It gravely underestimated the price of belligerency, and intervened without general support. The result would be to undermine the political and social order that Salandra hoped to consolidate.

Of the other late entrants, Germany declared war on Portugal in March 1916 after Lisbon agreed to a British request to seize the German vessels detained in its ports. Subsequently Portugal sent a small expedition to the Western Front. Its policy was influenced by concerns to differentiate itself from neutral Spain and ensure Allied support for preserving its empire in Africa.[13] As for the last two countries to be considered, Bulgaria and Romania, they were to some extent mirror images of one another. Bulgaria's option for the Central Powers served it well at first but poorly later; Romania's for the Allies was for most of the war calamitous but in the end turned out better, though probably – like Italy – it could have achieved the same result more cheaply by waiting. In Bulgaria the sovereign mattered: King Ferdinand ran foreign policy in conjunction with his premier, Vasil Radoslovav, whose government prorogued parliament and muzzled the press in order to silence the more pro-Russian opposition. In contrast, Romania's king (another Ferdinand, who succeeded to the stronger-willed Carol soon after war broke out) deferred to prime minister Dmitri Bratianu, who benefited from a consensus in favour of the Allies. Alignments in the region had been much influenced by the Second Balkan War, which left Bulgaria defeated and antagonistic to Serbia, Romania, Turkey, and Greece, whereas Romania had taken territory from Bulgaria and hoped for more from Austria-Hungary. As Bulgaria's priority was Serb-occupied Macedonia and Romania's was Hungarian-ruled Transylvania, the Central Powers operated at an automatic advantage in Sofia and the Allies in Bucharest. Although both countries negotiated with both sides, they did so largely to bid up the offers from the partners they preferred and whom they deemed more likely to deliver.

The Allies promised Bulgaria gains from Turkey, but nothing definite from Greece and Romania, both of whom they wanted to join them. They badgered Serbia into offering some of Macedonia, but on numerous conditions. The Central Powers offered Bulgaria all the Serbian land it wanted, as well as Greek territory if Athens joined the Allies. The Turks, who desperately needed a supply route through the Balkans from Germany, grudgingly conceded to Bulgaria a strip of land along the river Maritsa, though the transfer remained a sore point. Even so, Serbia's early victories and Italy's entry made Radoslavov and Ferdinand hesitate. Only Russia's military collapse in summer 1915 made them resolve to act. They signed an agreement with the Central Powers on 6 September, and entered the war a few weeks later.[14]

Romania's situation resembled Italy's. Its secret alliance of 1883 with Austria-Hungary and Germany did not apply in the circumstances of 1914 and was out-weighed by its designs on the Romanian-speakers in Transylvania. In August 1915 the Allies agreed to support Bratianu's demands not only for Transylvania but also for two more Austro-Hungarian territories: the Bukovina (which ethnically was part Ukrainian) and the Banat of Temesvar (which ethnically was part Serbian and would extend Romania almost to the gates of Belgrade). The Allies' defeats then made Bratianu waver, while the Russians discouraged Romanian entry, see-ing it as a potential strategic liability. After the success of the Brusilov offensive in June 1916, however, the Stavka changed its mind and wanted Romania in quickly to finish Austria-Hungary off. Bratianu also wished to grasp the opportunity, but he lost two months in haggling for extra territory and aid. By the time he signed up to an alliance on 17 August the Central Powers were recovering. None the less, he committed his country to what he foresaw might be disaster, fearing he would lose all credibility with the Allies if he delayed still longer.[15]

Progress in the territorial negotiations and fluctuations in military fortunes de-cided when the late entrants intervened, but pre-1914 aspirations determined which side they favoured. Their intervention created a series of parallel wars, as each pur-sued their individual agendas, complicating the task of strategic co-ordination. Japan, against British wishes, expanded in China; Italy declared war initially only against Austria-Hungary, hoping to limit its involvement; Romania struck into Transylvania. Similarly, Bulgaria's contribution to Serbia's defeat in 1915 was to overrun Macedonia, profiting from an Austro-German offensive against Serbia proper. All the same, both sides incorporated the Balkan and Italian fronts into their general European strategies by 1916.* This was much less true in the Middle East, however, where Ottoman entry effectively created an entirely new war.

---

*See ch. 6.

Turkey proved a more formidable antagonist than expected. It distracted larger Allied resources than Italy and Romania did Austrian ones, and except for the United States it had more impact than any other new belligerent on the overall course of the conflict. Lloyd George and Ludendorff estimated (probably excessively) in retrospect that its intervention had lengthened the war by two years.[16] Yet it had many weaknesses. Despite its imposing extent the empire's population was only somewhat over 20 million and much of it was not Turkish, although most ethnic minorities remained loyal. It could manufacture only basic weapons and its railway network was rudimentary, providing no continuous link from Constantinople either to the Russian border or to Syria and Palestine. Government finances had long been precarious: the national debt tripled during the war and even compared with other belligerents the authorities were reckless in expanding the money supply. Prices rose five times by 1917 and twenty-six times by the armistice. Nevertheless, the government recruited a total of 3 million soldiers (even though half deserted) and some 325,000 were killed or died of wounds. The army rose from thirty-six (admittedly small) divisions in 1914 to seventy. The troops were weaker than European forces in artillery but were quite well supplied with machine guns and were willing to dig in. Aided by German advisers, and by such German materiel as Romania allowed through, they defended the empire well for more than a year.[17] Turkey's war down to 1917 can be divided into three phases: initial Ottoman assaults against the British and Russians and their own Armenian citizens; unsuccessful failed Allied offensives at the Dardanelles and in Mesopotamia; and finally more successful Allied advances in the Caucasus and against Baghdad that showed Turkish resistance was failing.

The Ottomans began by taking the offensive. They declared their intention of uniting 'all branches of our race', and the Sultan proclaimed a *jihad*, or holy war. Aided by pontoons assembled by German engineers, a Turkish force of 22,000 tried in February 1915 to cross the Suez Canal, but a larger British army supported by warships easily repelled it, although the British reinforced their Egyptian garrison as a consequence. But the main effort came in the Caucasus, where Enver ordered 150,000 men to advance in December 1914. The Russians were outnumbered and were defending a remote frontier among mostly Muslim populations whom they had conquered during the previous century. But Enver was operating in mountainous terrain 250 miles from the nearest railhead and in temperatures way below zero. More of his troops succumbed to disease and cold than to the Russians, but after the latter counter-attacked in the battle of Sarikamish in late December 1914 and early January 1915 the Turks retreated and fewer than a quarter of the men they committed to the offensive survived it.[18] The repercussions were far-reaching. An appeal for assistance from Grand Duke Nicholas began the process that led to the Allied campaign to seize the Dardanelles, and the Armenian genocide of 1915 began when the Ottoman Empire faced emergency, its principal army routed and its capital under threat.

Between 1.5 and 2 million Armenians lived under Ottoman rule, almost half on the Armenian plateau in the north-east.[19] When war broke out their leaders were publicly loyal and asked their people to obey the call-up order, which about 100,000 did. However, they refused to summon their fellows across the frontier to rise against tsarist overlordship, and the latter enlisted in the Russian army. Yet although the Turkish government claimed to be retaliating against disloyalty and preparations for insurrection, the Ottoman Armenians appear to have been guilty of neither until the action against them began, after Sarikamish, in late February 1915. First the Armenians in the army were segregated, disarmed, and either murdered or forced to work until they dropped. Those who had not enlisted were searched in their villages for arms, tortured, and killed. With the able-bodied men removed, the second phase from April to August centred on deportations of the remaining Armenians on long forced marches towards detention camps in northern Mesopotamia, where they died in thousands if they had not already lost their lives *en route*. It is true that Zeitan, the first town to be attacked, was violently resisting conscription, but when the Armenians in the city of Van rebelled (and for a time were relieved by the Russians) in April–May, they were clearly doing so in order to avoid their compatriots' fate. None the less, the Van uprising brought matters to a climax. Hundreds of Armenians in Constantinople itself were arrested and murdered, the remainder of the Armenian plateau was cleared, and the Allies warned that they would hold the Turkish government to account and the officials concerned personally liable. As for the Germans, although their advisers deplored the massacres as deeply as did neutral missionaries and diplomats, the Berlin foreign ministry hesitated to press the matter for fear of jeopardizing the alliance. In all, probably over a million people died in what was certainly a centrally planned campaign, inspired by the CUP leaders and implemented by 'Special Organizations' coming under the party and the war ministry. Who took the decision and why remains uncertain, and the relevant documents have been destroyed or withheld. In particular, it is unclear whether a security operation to protect the Caucasus border escalated because of Armenian resistance and the Special Organizations' indiscipline, or whether the aim from the start was to wipe the Armenians out. Some of the statements of the Young Turk leaders give credence to the latter possibility, and in its implementation the policy was indeed genocidal.

The massacres were the most appalling of many signs in 1915 that this would be a war of hitherto unknown intensity, and that nineteenth-century restraints on the conduct of hostilities were collapsing. They happened when the Young Turks' gamble on intervention appeared to have gone disastrously wrong, though this is no plea in mitigation. In contrast, however, in the second phase in the Middle East the Allies took the offensive but the Turks successfully struck back, containing the Russians' summer 1915 attacks in the Caucasus and repelling both an advance by Indian forces on Baghdad and a determined Anglo-French attempt to capture Constantinople.

During the Dardanelles operations from February 1915 to January 1916 the Straits replaced the Caucasus as the principal theatre.[20] At the height of the fighting 350,000 Ottoman troops were concentrated in the Dardanelles region, against only 150,000 in the north-east. By the end of the campaign 410,000 British Empire and 79,000 French troops had passed through it, of whom 205,000 and 47,000 respectively had become casualties. The British estimated the Turkish losses at 251,000, but the real total may have been substantially higher.[21] In Australia and New Zealand, which lost about 8,000 and over 2,000 dead respectively, the campaign took on tragic and lasting significance for its awakening of a sense of national distinctiveness by comparison with a class-bound and incompetent British leadership, the first Anzac Day being commemorated in Australia as early as 1916.[22] In its length and cost, the fighting foreshadowed the great Western Front battles of 1916–17. Yet if the Ottoman soldiers (many of them Arabic-speaking) were successfully defending their capital against an infidel intruder, the Allied losses seem to have contributed nothing to the larger goal of winning the war.

All the same, it was as a war-winning venture that the campaign was conceived. In the first instance it was a response to Grand Duke Nicholas's request for help before Sarikamish, but it evolved out of a pre-existing debate, many in the British government (and particularly Winston Churchill as First Lord of the Admiralty) having already concluded that a breakthrough on the Western Front was improbable and therefore begun seeking more promising alternatives. Churchill envisaged a landing on the North Sea island of Borkum prior to operations in the Baltic, but his advisers rightly considered that German mines and shore defences would make this impracticable; however, they acquiesced (without enthusiasm) in a naval assault on the Straits.[23] If warships reached the Sea of Marmara they could disrupt Constantinople's food supply or bombard the city, though it was hoped their mere presence would cause a coup against the CUP or browbeat the Turks into surrender. If Turkey dropped out both Suez and Britain's oilfields in Persia would be secure, as would Russia's Caucasus frontier, and the only ice-free sea route to Russia would reopen. Italy and the Balkan states might join the Allies, enabling a concerted assault against Austria-Hungary. All this might be accomplished with pre-dreadnought battleships that were useless in the North Sea anyway, while the French were also willing to participate if only to prevent a single-handed British victory in a region where they had financial and prestige interests.[24] Such considerations, powerfully urged by Churchill, won over the Asquith government's War Council, and on 19 February the assembled Anglo-French armada began bombarding the Dardanelles forts.

Almost certainly this strategic conception was fundamentally flawed. Encouraged by news of secret contacts between Djemal Pasha and their agents, the British underestimated both the CUP leaders' determination and how securely they were in the saddle. Even if the naval force had reached Constantinople it had no landing parties and the Turks were not willing to evacuate the city. It seems unlikely the regime that ordered the Armenian deportations would have quailed before offshore warships. If the Turks kept their nerve, the battleships would have to withdraw. In any case the western Allies, in the throes of a munitions famine of their own, had few shells available for Russia. It is less implausible that a success would have brought in Greece and kept Bulgaria neutral, although Bratianu was so cautious that it is far from certain that Romania would have come in. For most Balkan states, Russia's military fortunes in Poland mattered far more than events at the Dardanelles. The one Allied prognostication to be vindicated was that the campaign encouraged the Italians to negotiate seriously, although they might well have done so anyway.[25]

At the operational level too, Churchill underestimated the difficulties. Flat-trajectory naval guns were less effective against Turkey's forts than German and Austrian howitzers had been against Belgium's. Nor could they silence the mobile artillery batteries that guarded the Dardanelles minefields, whose fire inhibited the converted trawlers manned by volunteer fishermen – the only minesweeping vessels initially available – from completing their task. The 15-inch guns of the super-dreadnought

Queen Elizabeth, which the Admiralty yielded most reluctantly for the venture, were inaccurate without spotter aircraft, of which the British had too few. When the main assault took place with sixteen battleships on 18 March, three were sunk and three more were disabled, mainly because the fleet ran into a newly laid minefield on its return journey, yet most of the mines remained unswept and the shore batteries undamaged. The ships were old but the loss of life was heavy (over 600 men on the French battleship *Bouvet* alone), and the Turkish guns had plenty of ammunition. Hence even though specially equipped destroyers were arriving to clear the mines, the defenders could probably still have kept them at bay.[26] But after 18 March the War Council left it to the local commander, Admiral John de Robeck, to decide whether to proceed, and in conference with the leader of the designated land force, Sir Ian Hamilton, he resolved the army must go ashore to overwhelm the defences.

Another of the attractions of the naval campaign had been the supposition that it could, if necessary, be painlessly broken off. This supposition too proved illusory. Grey believed military success was vital to his Balkan diplomacy, and ministers feared humiliation by the Turks would imperil the British Empire's authority over its Muslim subjects.[27] London accepted the decision of the men on the spot. Although Hamilton's Mediterranean Expeditionary Force had been assembled on the understanding that it was unlikely to be used, on Sunday 25 April 30,000 British, Indian, Australian, New Zealand, and French troops landed on five beaches round Cape Helles at the southern tip of the Gallipoli peninsula and at what came to be known as Anzac Cove (after the Australian and New Zealand Army Corps) on the western coast. Some landings were unopposed, but the Lancashire Fusiliers on 'W' beach and the Munster Fusiliers and the Hampshire Regiment on 'V' beach ran into a hail of small arms fire and sustained over 2,000 casualties. Once the Helles beachheads were joined up the invaders moved inland, but little more than two miles from the cape, on the slopes of Achi Baba hill and round the village of Krythia, their repeated frontal assaults over the next few months made negligible progress. Both sides dug trench systems almost as elaborate as those in France, if shallower and with the front lines closer together, and much the same happened in the hills above Anzac Cove. The Allied landing zones had narrow beaches, steep overlooking slopes, and an absence of ground water and of areas for relaxation outside artillery range; the defenders had both water and rest camps.[28] Regardless, on 6–7 August, after London had released three fresh divisions, Hamilton tried a further co-ordinated assault. Its centrepiece was a reckless night attack uphill from Anzac Cove, supported by a diversionary assault from Helles and a new landing further north at Suvla Bay. Initially the latter was almost unopposed, but its leaders moved inland too slowly and like the earlier landings it failed to gain the crests of the heights that formed the peninsula's rocky spine. After a final offensive at the end of August the government rejected Hamilton's requests for further men, giving priority to the September Western Front offensive and to the expeditionary force sent in October to Salonika. After overrunning Serbia in the same month the Central Powers could transport heavy guns overland to the Turks, and the Allies risked being blasted out of their narrow beachheads. The rough autumn seas impeded further operations or even the resupply of existing positions, and having been racked during the summer by heat, thirst, flies, and dysentery, the troops now endured torrential rain, blizzards, and frostbite. Churchill defended his brainchild until he lost office in the autumn, and the government of India feared a prestige disaster if the enterprise were aborted, but in October Hamilton was replaced by Sir Charles Monro, who recommended withdrawing, and London gave the authorization. Remarkably, Suvla and Anzac were evacuated bloodlessly in December and Helles in January, the Turks making no effort to impede the invaders' exit.

By this time any chance for a quick and easy alternative to defeating Germany on the Western Front had long been lost, and the débâcle discredited advocates of such alternative strategies. What had gone wrong?[29] The Allies landed without surprise and gave the Turks plenty of time to prepare. Kitchener, fearing a German attack in the west or even an invasion of Britain, was slow to release the 29th Division, the one contingent of regulars in the Expeditionary Force. More time was lost when Hamilton ordered his supply ships back to Egypt because their cargoes had been loaded in the wrong order. Meanwhile, after the start of the naval bombardment the Turks fortified and reinforced the peninsula. If the operation had been a combined one from the start, the naval attack being delayed and the landing preparations brought forward, it might have had greater success. However, the Allies could scarcely have concealed their massive preparations in Alexandria and at Mudros Bay on the Greek island of Lemnos, and it seems unlikely that surprise was attainable. Events after the landings also cast doubt on whether an easy victory was within reach. Hamilton never got near to disabling the shore batteries in the Straits. On 25 April he attacked six defending divisions with five of his own, most of his troops being novices and equipped for a colonial expedition rather than for a Western Front in miniature. They rapidly used up most of their shells,[30] and they gained almost no territory in months of frontal attacks. The arrival of German submarines forced the battleships to leave the offshore waters after May (when two were sunk), but anyway naval guns were too inaccurate to damage the Turkish trenches, and the Allied artillery failed to silence the Turkish field guns and machine guns concealed in the hills above that repeatedly halted the infantry attacks. Shell shortages were a less critical reason for this failure than the more basic point that at Gallipoli, as in France, the British gunners had still to evolve the tactics needed to silence such defences.[31] For all of this, Turkish and German memoirs suggest that both at Anzac Cove in April and at Suvla Bay in August the defenders were caught off balance and were saved by energetic local commanders: notably the leader of the post-war Turkish Republic, Mustafa Kemal. In contrast Allied leadership was defective. Hamilton's subordinates showed both prevarication and unthinking aggression. He himself, cruising offshore without direct communication with his units on land, was properly reluctant to step in, but especially at Suvla, where there was indescribable confusion and incompetence in the first few hours, his fastidiousness had tragic consequences. It remains dubious, however, whether what evaded the British was more than a local success, and even if the army had cleared the south of the peninsula the fleet would still have had to reach Constantinople and the Turks then to submit: eventualities that seem improbable.[32] Short of fighting overland to Constantinople with far larger resources than the Allies could spare, it is hard to see how the campaign could have achieved what was hoped for it.

Failure at Gallipoli helped to precipitate Britain into a second disaster, in Mesopotamia. The government of India in Delhi had dispatched 'Force D' (comprising one mediocre division) to the Persian Gulf even before Turkey declared war, and in November 1914 it occupied Basra. At Churchill's behest the British government had recently bought a controlling interest in the Anglo-Persian Oil Company, which supplied oil for the fleet from Abadan in Persia, but the main purpose of the expedition was less to protect oil supplies than to strengthen Delhi's hand in contacts with the local Arab rulers, many of whom were restive against the Ottomans, and to safeguard British interests if the Gulf descended into disorder.[33] It fended off a Turkish attack (which encouraged the British to underestimate resistance in Gallipoli), and after a new and more thrusting chief, Sir John Nixon, took command in Mesopotamia in April 1915, Delhi and London approved successive advances up the river Tigris to Kut-al-Amara.

In October the cabinet deliberated on whether to accede to Nixon's wish for Force D to go on to Baghdad, aware that it was tired, diseased, and under-strength, faced Turkish units massing ahead of it, and had too little river transport to sustain its 200-mile supply line. Force D's commander (and Nixon's subordinate), Sir Charles Townshend, needed more than 200 tons of supplies daily, but was receiving only 150. Yet Lord Hardinge, the Viceroy of India, who wanted to control Mesopotamia permanently as an imperial granary and outlet for Indian emigration, predicted an 'immense impression' elsewhere in Asia if Baghdad fell, offsetting the blows to British prestige at Gallipoli. The cabinet left the decision to him, and he authorized the advance. South of Baghdad at the battle of Ctesiphon in November, Townshend failed to break through Turkish positions manned by more numerous and better armed troops than British intelligence had predicted. He fell back on Kut, where after months of siege he surrendered in April 1916 with some 13,000 men; vain attempts by the British to break the encirclement incurred nearly 23,000 casualties. Of those who fell into Turkish captivity almost a third perished before the war ended.[34]

Gallipoli and Kut caused not just disappointment in Britain but outrage. In 1916 the Asquith government accepted commissions of inquiry into both episodes, which did much to destroy its faltering reputation for competence. Yet Kut marked the nadir, and in 1916–17 Allied fortunes against the Turks revived, albeit at the price of a much greater commitment. Even at Gallipoli, in the last stages the Turkish infantry were losing their keenness, but the Russians delivered the heaviest blow. Between November 1915 and March 1917 they inflicted three quarters of the Ottomans' casualties.[35] In a campaign commanded by General Nicolai Yudenich they overran most of Armenia in spring 1916 before the Turks could move back troops from the Dardanelles. When eight divisions released by the Gallipoli evacuation eventually reached the Caucasus, the Russians beat them off. Erzerum fell in February, Bitlis in March, and an amphibious assault took the Black Sea port of Trebizond in April. In contrast only two Gallipoli divisions went to Mesopotamia, where during 1916 the War Office took over responsibility from the government of India and built up a force of 150,000 troops (two-thirds of them Indian). In the cooler weather of December Sir Stanley Maude began a new advance with generous artillery and a big numerical preponderance, not to mention 446 tugs and steam launches, 774 barges, and 414 motorboats, in contrast to the six steamers and eight tugs available to Townshend.[36] A methodical, cautious soldier, Maude retook Kut in February 1917 and entered Baghdad in March. Another methodical man, Sir Archibald Murray, took command of the Egyptian Expeditionary Force in March 1916. Since the Turks' attack on the Suez Canal the British had kept immense forces in Egypt, which after the Dardanelles evacuation reached 300,000. Murray was authorized to cross the Sinai peninsula to El Arish, which he reached in December, building a railway and pipeline as he went and defeating a Turkish counter-attack. When a new British government headed by David Lloyd George approved an advance into Palestine, however, two frontal attacks in March and April 1917 against the machine gun and barbed wire defences at Gaza were repulsed, and Murray lost his command. Yet Gaza was the last of the Ottomans' defensive successes. By 1917 both their economy and their armies were beginning to atrophy. The Lloyd George government was wedded to Middle East expansion in order to restore imperial prestige and uplift morale at home, but also with a view to staying in Palestine and Mesopotamia permanently. British and Indian troops numbering 890,000 were deployed in Mesopotamia during the war, against Ottoman forces half the size.[37] The Turks were no longer strong enough to repel invasion, though they remained invaluable to the other Central Powers for diverting Allied resources.

Compared with the Dardanelles and the Caucasus the other extra-European theatres were small.[38] In the Pacific the New Zealanders took German Samoa in August 1914 and the Australians overran German New Guinea, with its wireless station at Rabaul, in September. The Japanese occupied the Marianas, the Caroline, and the Marshall islands in the following month, and in September–November a Japanese force of 50,000 supported by warships and over 100 heavy guns and howitzers besieged and stormed the defences of Qingdao. Of Germany's African colonies, Togoland, whose wireless station co-ordinated the movements of German ships in local waters, was overrun by French and British forces in August 1914, while (after the suppression of the 1914 Afrikaner rebellion), 50,000 mainly South African troops conquered German South-West Africa between January and July 1915. The remaining two campaigns, however, were longer and more difficult, and in both of them the Germans went onto the offensive. From the Cameroons, a huge expanse of steamy jungles and hills, the German garrison of 1,000 European and 3,000 African soldiers raided into Nigeria and repulsed an initial British invasion, but although the Allies captured the port of Duala in September 1914 it was February 1916 before they overcame the last resistance in the interior. In German East Africa, the most valuable of the Kaiser's colonies, equal in area to France and Germany combined, the local commander, Paul von Lettow-Vorbeck, followed a preconceived strategy of carrying the fighting aggressively into enemy territory and threatening the British Uganda railway, in order to tie down the maximum number of opposing forces. In November 1914 he defeated an assault by British Indian troops on the port of Tanga, and most of German East Africa was conquered (again mainly by South African troops, under the command of Jan Christian Smuts) only in 1916, Belgian forces from the Congo occupying the territories of Ruanda and Urundi on the western fringe of the German colony. Even now Lettow-Vorbeck continued operations in Mozambique and then in Northern Rhodesia, where he finally surrendered, two weeks after the armistice in Europe, in November 1918.[39] In the Cameroons and East Africa, the campaigning devastated large tracts of territory, and its impact was much greater than the relatively small troop numbers involved might suggest. Because much of it took place in disease-infested heartlands without railways, navigable waterways, or roads, both sides depended on African bearers who were pressed into service and forced to carry everything needed, often for months, without adequate rations or medical aid. In the Cameroons some 7,000 French and 11,000 British troops (nearly all African) operated with tens of thousands of carriers. In East Africa Lettow-Vorbeck's fighting forces peaked at some 3,000 Europeans and 12,100 African soldiers (askaris) with 45,000 bearers, while the Allies committed over 130,000 combatants. The British alone contributed more than 50,000 askaris and more than a million bearers, disease (especially dysentery) and wounds killing over 10,000 of the former and perhaps 100,000 of the latter. These casualty lists in a forgotten theatre measured up to those in the great European bloodbaths.[40]

Operations against the Turks and the German colonies involved hundreds of thousands of Allied troops, though probably the Japanese and askari forces engaged (and most of the British Indian ones) would not have gone to the Western Front anyway. Efforts at imperial subversion sucked in further resources. It is true that both sides could use this weapon, the British making alliances in 1914 with Ibn Saud and the Idrisi of Asir in the Arabian peninsula, who were nominally Ottoman subjects but agreed to stay neutral.[41] Furthermore, secret negotiations with the Sharif Hussein of Mecca and his sons led in June 1916 to the outbreak of the misnamed 'Arab Revolt'. In fact this uprising involved 10–15,000 poorly disciplined tribesmen, who secured most of the Hejaz and the Red Sea ports against weak Turkish resistance but failed to spread rebellion into the remainder of the Arab lands or the Arabic-speaking contingents of the Ottoman army, and kept going only with British supplies of arms and cash and offshore naval assistance.[42] But conversely, in an outburst on 31 July 1914 Wilhelm declared that England's intervention must cost it India, and the Germans and Turks had much more territory to target. Berlin and Constantinople appealed to nationalism and Islam, and at first sight the Allied empires were vulnerable. In a population of some 300 million, British India contained in peacetime some 1,200 white officials in the Indian Civil Service, 700 white police officers, and 77,000 British soldiers, alongside 173,000 Indian troops. Similarly, a few hundred British administrators and 4–5,000 white soldiers, with 13,000 indigenous ones, governed 12.5 million Egyptians. Such structures of authority required not just mass acquiescence but also active collaboration by thousands of officials and community leaders from the native population, and the British leaders knew that their eastern empire, in the words of the cabinet secretary Maurice Hankey, 'depends on prestige and bluff'.[43] Yet at one point in the war the British troops in India fell to 15,000; in the Gold Coast the military establishment was cut by one third; and Paris ordered the governor of Morocco, Hubert Lyautey, to send every soldier he could and give up the interior (though in practice he did not).[44] In most colonies war conditions meant inflation, shortages of European investment, and imports from the metropolis cut back for lack of shipping, as well as mass conscription for military or carrier service, and requisitioning of food and other goods. Indeed conscription was one of the targets of the Chilembwe Rising in Nyasaland in 1915 and of revolts in French West Africa in 1915–17, though these movements were easily put down.[45] The combination of European strife with economic hardship created fertile soil for anti-colonial movements.

None the less, German subversive activity was striking in its failure. Nor did the *jihad* proclaimed by Turkey have the impact that the British feared. The Indian Muslims – strongly represented in the Indian army – mostly stayed loyal when British forces menaced Constantinople, the home of the Caliphate;[46] the Gallipoli and Kut defeats provoked no significant unrest. The main Indian nationalist movement, the Indian National Congress, became more radical and broadened its support after 1916, but this development owed nothing to Germany. German agents failed to persuade Afghanistan to attack India's north-west frontier, despite the latter being denuded of troops; German diplomats in America bought arms for Indian revolutionaries but were unable to ship them to Asia. British intelligence broke up a ring of Bengali revolutionaries to which the Germans had sent money, and tipped off the government of Thailand about Sikh revolutionaries whom Germans were training on the Burmese border.[47] From Spain the Germans sent money, rifles, and propaganda to the rebels against French rule in Morocco, but the French broke the code between the Madrid embassy and Berlin and interrupted much of the material before delivery.[48] The *jihad* call may have encouraged the rebellion by the Senussi religious fraternity in North Africa, who with Ottoman aid confined the Italians to the coastline of Libya and in November 1915 captured the Egyptian port of Sollum. Elsewhere its effects were slight. South of the Sahara, scattered revolts against conscription took place in much of French West Africa and parts of British Africa. Yet the French and British empires turned out to be more robust than the Germans and Turks expected and their rulers feared. British and French counter-intelligence and Germany's geographical remoteness and lack of seapower were partly responsible. So were displays of force. The Senussi were expelled from Sollum and 35,000 troops deployed to guard Egypt against them; the French sealed off the frontiers of their North African colonies and in September 1915 sent a 15,000-strong cavalry force into the Sahara.[49] In short, the Allies deployed very substantial resources to secure their overseas possessions in addition to destroying Germany's and invading Ottoman territory. Moreover, concerns of imperial prestige skewed British strategy in favour of the Gallipoli landings and sending Force D towards Baghdad. For their part the British and French colonies supplied generous quantities of manpower, commodities, and manufactures to the mother countries.* On balance – and increasingly as the war went on – the second factor outweighed the first. That the Allies, as long as they commanded the seas, could concentrate in Europe resources from other parts of the world gave them an indispensable edge, not sufficient to explain their victory but probably a precondition for it. It took a very long time, however, for their superior global resources to prevail over the Central Powers' advantages on the battlegrounds in Europe, and it is to the dynamics of that central conflict that we must now turn.

---

*Discussed further in chs. 8 and 9.

CHAPTER 5

WAR AIMS AND PEACE NEGOTIATIONS

A BASIC REASON for the stalemate and escalation of the middle period of the war was the two sides' inability to negotiate. This inability resulted from the incompatibility between the opposing governments' political objectives – or war aims. Such an approach represents only one possible interpretation of the dynamics of the struggle and it addresses many questions only obliquely: in particular why a conflict fought for more modest goals than that of 1939–45 was pursued with such intensity. None the less, to ask why governments persisted with an undertaking that proved quite different from their initial expectations is probably the best way in to the labyrinthine question of what the war was all about.

'War aims' was a term used in the belligerent countries at the time. 'My war aim', said Georges Clemenceau, French premier in 1917–19, 'is to win.'[1] Yet victory in itself was not a war aim but its precondition; war aims were the terms (territorial cessions, indemnities, disarmament) to be imposed after victory. Some aims might be absolute (France's demand for the return of Alsace-Lorraine or Britain's for Belgian independence are good examples), no compromise on them being possible short of complete defeat; others were bonuses to be included if success permitted. They might be moderated if one opposing power deserted its allies and negotiated separately, enabling harsher terms to be imposed on its former partners. But down to 1917 no government sued for peace and no unofficial soundings led to substantive negotiations. Neutral attempts to mediate were invariably rebuffed, and when in December 1916 the Central Powers publicly offered conversations, the Allies indignantly refused them. Detailed study of the powers' objectives shows little scope for compromise (or 'bargaining space'),[2] and neither side desired serious discussions until it had won decisively with its alliance bloc intact. No peace initiative in this period came close to success.

War aims and strategy were interconnected. The two sides' perceptions of the military balance and their campaigning prospects were vitally important, though more for deciding priorities among objectives than for determining the objectives themselves. But public opinion and domestic political considerations also played powerful roles. War aims and peace negotiations should therefore not be seen in isolation, and the two sides' objectives were in continuous flux. For the sake of clarity, however, the Central Powers will here be taken first, before attention is turned to their enemies.[3]

Although Germany's aims carried far more weight among the Central Powers than those of any single member state among the Allies, Berlin's partners must not be neglected. Before it intervened Bulgaria defined its terms, which were essentially to reverse the Second Balkan War. It received a strip of territory from Turkey, together with Serbia's share of Macedonia, which it occupied from 1915 onwards. Its claims provoked a major clash in 1918 when Turkey threatened to walk out of the alliance. The Turks themselves had ambitions to expel the European powers from North Africa and drive back the Russians in Central Asia, but they were fighting to protect their existing empire as well as to expand. They scored a major success in 1916 when they agreed with Germany that neither would make peace while the other's territory remained under enemy occupation. Thus Berlin was committed to fighting until Allied armies left Ottoman soil and was prevented from settling with Petrograd by selling out Constantinople, though it had virtually ruled out such an option anyway.[4]

Austria-Hungary's objectives were much more central to German concerns. The Dual Monarchy put out a feeler to the Russians during its military crisis in spring 1915, which they ignored as it offered far too little, but while Franz Joseph lived the Germans had little cause to fear their ally would desert them. Once its situation improved, moreover, it developed territorial ambitions. Against Italy, despite the unusual unanimity of Austro-Hungarian public opinion in condemning a treacherous former ally, the Dual Monarchy wanted little except minor frontier changes. As the campaigning in the Alps and Dolomites soon demonstrated, the existing frontier provided so formidable a barrier that extending it was pointless, and would merely bring more Italians under Habsburg rule. But in the Balkans the Austrians had agreed in July 1914 that Serbia should be partitioned, and after the victories of autumn 1915 the Joint Council of Ministers in Vienna decided that Serbia should lose more than half its population and that Montenegro's coastline should be annexed, thus hemming in what remained of the two South Slav kingdoms between Austria-Hungary and a Habsburg 'protectorate' in Albania. As Italy had joined the Allies and Germany had few interests in the western Balkans, Vienna for a time had a free hand to dominate the region.[5] This was not true, however, in its third area of interest, Poland, which it claimed for Habsburg sovereignty after the Russians were driven out. Here the Germans had decided interests of their own, and Poland's future became a bone of contention for the rest of the war.

Although Berlin did not generally ride roughshod over its allies' demands, it was the powerhouse of its coalition and if it had sued for peace its partners would have had to do likewise. The basis for all subsequent research on its objectives has been Fritz Fischer's study of *Germany's Aims in the First World War*, published in 1961.* Fis-

---

*Discussed further in ch. 21.

cher interpreted German aims as an ambitious and aggressive bid to stabilize the Hohenzollern monarchy and consolidate German 'world-power status'; these aims enjoyed consensus support in official circles and from non-official elites, and showed continuity throughout the war.[6] The central exhibit in his prosecution case was the 'September Programme' of war aims approved by Bethmann Hollweg on 9 September 1914, which, Fischer argued, set the mould for war aims for the next four years. At that stage the battle of the Marne was still in progress and victory seemed probable, even imminent. Bethmann's programme – initialled by the chancellor but drafted by his private secretary, Kurt Riezler – started from the premiss that 'the general aim of the war' was 'security for the German Reich in west and east for all imaginable time' and that for this purpose 'Russia must be thrust back as far as possible from the German eastern frontier, and her domination over the non-Russian vassal peoples broken' while France 'must be so weakened as to make her revival as a great power impossible for all time'. Yet Bethmann was concerned to achieve these aims while minimizing the number of non-Germans absorbed into the Reich. Overseas he wanted a continuous belt of colonial territory from coast to coast in Central Africa, but the annexations he envisaged in western Europe were limited, if strategically significant: Luxemburg, Liège, and Antwerp, France's Briey iron ore field, the western Vosges mountains, and possibly the Channel coast round Dunkirk and Boulogne. Rather than annexation, Germany's economic strength – in which Riezler placed remarkable confidence – would be the main instrument of political control. France would be weakened by a crippling indemnity and by a commercial treaty that would make it 'economically dependent on Germany'. Belgium would become a 'vassal state', under military occupation and 'economically a German province', while a 'central European customs association', including France and Scandinavia, would 'stabilize Germany's economic dominance' over its members.[7] Yet despite the programme's ruthless language, the chancellor probably saw it as a moderate alternative to the more extreme annexationism of the military and the circles around Wilhelm, and Fischer exaggerated the document's significance. For example, Fischer particularly emphasized the project for a Central European customs association (or *Mitteleuropa*), which indeed remained a German objective for the rest of the conflict but originated as a politicians' plan and never enjoyed great support from business or much economic logic, given that most of Germany's export markets lay outside the area it enclosed. Although preceded by extensive consultations among the German leaders, the programme was not an authoritative policy statement (and was not, for example, signed by the emperor).[8] Modestly described as a 'provisional sketch' for a western European peace, it said nothing about Germany's demands on Britain, and its demands on Russia appeared only in outline. Nor was it a public commitment: it remained a secret for over forty years. For all these reasons its significance must be qualified. Yet it remains an essential guide to Bethmann's thinking. Similar (if less sweeping) proposals for western Europe appeared in war aims documents for the rest of the conflict, and planning for the customs union and the Belgian 'vassal state' began without delay. The programme remained relevant, though after the withdrawal from the Marne events overtook it.

Thus on 18 November 1914 Bethmann and Falkenhayn discussed Germany's situation in much less favourable circumstances. By now it was clear there would be no quick victory, and the two men agreed that if Russia, France, and Britain remained together Germany could not defeat them. The only chance of an 'acceptable' peace, Falkenhayn considered, was to offer generous terms to Petrograd, in the hope that first Russia and then France would settle, isolating Germany's archenemy: Britain. Bethmann endorsed much of this analysis, though he was more sceptical about whether Russia would negotiate, and even if it did, whether Germany could count on a western victory. But he agreed to sound out Russia first, and to offer a peace based on the *status quo ante*, which given that the Central Powers had so far conquered little Russian territory and had lost more of their own was not much of a sacrifice. In the light of this reappraisal the high hopes of the September Programme seem an aberration: two months afterwards the Germans were back in the old predicament of facing a cohesive encircling alliance with greater reserves of strength. They returned to their pre-war policy of trying to split it, but now they combined diplomacy with violence.[9]

It soon became clear that this more modest approach would not extricate the Germans from the danger of exhaustion in a prolonged struggle against a superior foe. In fact they were torn between the September Programme policy and their concern to split their enemies, as became evident in dealings with both Belgium and Russia. King Albert was now in exile on the northern French coast at La Panne. Without consulting his ministers he allowed his emissary, Professor Waxweiler, to meet the German envoy, Count Törring, in the winter of 1915–16. Törring demanded a pro-German alignment in foreign policy (which Albert was willing to consider), but he also wanted a host of guarantees, including Belgian disarmament, German occupation and transit rights, a coastal naval base, and a German majority shareholding in the Belgian railways, as well as a closer customs union. Even if Albert had accepted these conditions, his government would not have done.[10] The affair showed that the Germans were not, in fact, prepared to reduce their claims on Belgium in the interests of a separate peace, despite their hopes that a deal with Albert would embarrass Britain and discourage it from continuing. Falkenhayn was determined Belgium should remain under German dominance, and the foreign and interior ministers envisaged that Germany would control its external relations, occupy its coasts and fortresses, tie it into monetary and customs union with the Reich, and merge the two railway systems. In October 1915 Wilhelm approved the navy's claims to occupy indefinitely the Ostend–Zeebrugge–Bruges triangle, the base for short-range U-boat attacks against British shipping. By encouraging a separate administration and education in their own language for the Flemings, moreover, the Germans hoped to weaken Belgian unity and the authority of the country's francophone governing elite. The consensus among Germany's leaders was more or less as the September Programme envisaged: that Belgium should not be annexed, but its sovereignty should be restored in name only.[11]

The big disappointment, however, was the fate of the feelers to Petrograd. These were extended primarily through a Danish intermediary, Andersen, although the Germans also made contact with the former Russian finance minister Count Witte, who was known to oppose the war. But they had little luck, for Witte died in March and the tsar and his advisers remained loyal to the Allies, refusing, unlike Albert, even to talk. Bethmann and Jagow indicated that they would seek only a favourable trade treaty and small frontier gains, but they were never willing to settle for nothing at all.[12] Bethmann had been impressed before the war by Russia's growing strength; in contrast to Falkenhayn he considered it at least as much of a long-term danger as Britain. He supported the project under secret discussion in the Berlin bureaucracy to annex a 'frontier strip' on Russian Poland's northern and western borders, from which the Jewish and Polish population would be deported and replaced by German settlers. A ministerial meeting in July 1915 approved this plan, which if Germany had won the war would probably have been implemented.[13] The Germans deliberately limited their 1915 advance eastwards to make it easier for Russia to negotiate, but by August after months of rejection they were more inclined to write off Petrograd and move towards an expansionist policy. During the summer and autumn German and Austrian troops overran the whole of Russian Poland and advanced up the Baltic coast. Peace with Russia now would entail sacrificing territory for which thousands of soldiers had died, and (just as Bethmann and Falkenhayn had feared) the advance of the Central Powers' armies crystallized their war aims and reduced their negotiating flexibility in the east.

Poland was the crucial issue. Before 1914 its western and northern districts had been ruled by Germany, Galicia in the south by Austria-Hungary, and Warsaw and the centre and east by Russia. Much of it was an open plain, and it mattered to all three empires as an invasion route as well as for its industry and mineral resources. If in the nineteenth century they shared an interest in keeping Poland divided, the breakdown of relations between them opened a bidding match for Polish support. Wilhelm commented during the July crisis that whatever else happened Russia must lose Poland; the Russians in August 1914 publicly pledged to reunite the German and Austrian portions with the Russian one as a self-governing province within their empire. The conquest of Poland forced the Central Powers to consider what they wanted for it, the Austrians fearing unrest among their Galician Poles if it remained partitioned or fell under German dominance. Therefore in August 1915 they proposed uniting Galicia with Russian Poland in an autonomous kingdom under Habsburg sovereignty – the so-called 'Austrian solution' to the Polish question. That autumn, moreover, as German armies overran the Balkans and overland trains ran again from Berlin to Constantinople, the idea of a *Mitteleuropa* or Central European bloc fired the imagination of the German public and took on a new prominence in German policy.[14] Falkenhayn, disappointed by the lack of response from Russia and fearing the Allies would pursue a 'war of exhaustion', hoped a long-term alliance and economic agreement between Germany and Austria-Hungary would demoralize their enemies.[15] Bethmann feared an Austro-Hungarian-Polish Triple Monarchy would be a less reliable ally than the dual one, but preferred this option to bringing millions of Poles and Jews under Germany's own rule.

In November the chancellor therefore agreed in principle to the 'Austrian solution', but on the conditions of a frontier strip, German economic interests in Poland being safeguarded, an Austro-German mutual territorial guarantee, and a thirty-year Austro-German economic agreement for mutual tariff reductions and an eventual customs union. As envisaged in the September Programme, economic integration would consolidate Germany's control over its neighbours. But for the same reason the package was suspect to the Austrian and Hungarian governments, who agreed to talk but then dragged their feet. Both feared losing political independence, and (except among the German-speaking Austrians) *Mitteleuropa* had little popular support. However, Bethmann himself soon changed his mind. Worried that the Austrian solution would increase Slavic influence in the Habsburg monarchy, he came round instead to a Belgian model: a nominally autonomous Poland linked to Germany by military and economic ties. At this point military developments again impinged on war aims discussions. The success of Russia's June 1916 'Brusilov offensive' demonstrated that Austria-Hungary was an unreliable guardian of Germany's eastern marches and forced it to seek German help, thus weakening its bargaining position. The Vienna agreements in August therefore met Bethmann's wish for a nominally independent buffer state in the former Russian Poland, with no independent foreign policy, Germany commanding its armies, and its railways under the Central Powers' control. The military crisis of the summer had a further consequence, in that when Hindenburg and Ludendorff replaced Falkenhayn in August they recognized a crying need for extra manpower. They responded with a succession of poorly considered initiatives that included deporting industrial workers from Belgium and introducing the Patriotic Auxiliary Service law in Germany.* In Poland, with its history of anti-Russian resentment, they thought they saw a reservoir of military volunteers. Under pressure from the generals, Bethmann agreed on 5 November 1916 to issue with Austria-Hungary a joint proclamation promising a future independent Polish kingdom. It cut little ice with the Poles, producing only a dribble of volunteers. But it was a public and explicit commitment that could not be retracted, and created yet another obstacle to a Russo-German separate peace.[16]

By autumn 1916 German aims were hardening into a more definite pattern. Belgium and Russian Poland would be buffer states, losing Liège, possibly Antwerp, and the 'frontier strip', and would be tied to Germany in foreign policy and defence as well as through economic integration. Similar arrangements were planned for Lithuania and Courland, with their German-speaking urban minorities and landed aristocracy, which Germany occupied in autumn 1915. Bethmann pledged that these provinces would not return to Russia and it was planned to make them nominally autonomous but linked to Germany by the usual railway, military, and tariff arrangements.[17] Regarding France, however, soundings from the German minister in Switzerland, Romberg, made contact only with a few disgruntled journalists and minor opposition politicians. The battle of Verdun in the spring of 1916 failed to deliver the French collapse in morale or willingness to negotiate that Falkenhayn had hoped for. The central German demands remained for the Briey basin (the most important source of France's iron ore and the location of much of its steel industry) and a heavy indemnity, but more severe terms were envisaged if Paris refused a separate peace. Beyond that, *Mitteleuropa* was still desired if Austria-Hungary would agree to it, though by 1916 much of German

---

*See ch. 9.

business was turning decisively against the idea if it meant that Allied retaliation barred Germany from its overseas markets.[18] Finally the colonial ministry claimed the mineral-rich territory of Central Africa, and the navy wanted the Flanders ports as well as a chain of bases in the Mediterranean, the Atlantic, and the Indian Ocean. If implemented, these demands would have safeguarded Germany's eastern and western borders, protected its supplies of food and raw materials, weakened France and Russia in Europe, and menaced Britain's worldwide sea communications. They were not non-negotiable, but it seemed that no one on the other side wanted to talk.

Fischer was broadly right to depict a consensus among the German leaders, at least down to the end of 1916, although soon afterwards Bethmann and the Hindenburg–Ludendorff team drifted apart. Falkenhayn differed from Bethmann over how to handle Russia, but these disagreements were essentially of nuance and in general he deferred to the chancellor over war aims. The chancellery and foreign ministry were the chief sources of policy-making, Wilhelm intervening only sporadically. Before war broke out Bethmann had already contemplated Central African expansion at the expense of Portugal's and Belgium's colonies, and he had been preoccupied with splitting the Entente. But early in 1914 the government had rejected a change in tariff policy, suggesting that at this stage a Central European customs union was not its objective. Hence despite some continuities with pre-war policy, it appears that the German leaders first declared war and then determined what they were fighting for. Basically their objective was security, to be achieved through a network of border buffer states and by weakening France and Russia, although Bethmann foresaw that enforcing such arrangements might overtax Germany's strength and reduce its internal cohesion. It would need to maintain, far into the future, large armed forces and occupation garrisons beyond its borders, and unless its navy expanded still further its overseas bases and colonies would be hostages to British retaliation. Nor was economic domination the panacea that the September Programme envisaged, as the Allies controlled so much of the world's food, minerals, and markets that a permanent confrontation between opposing economic blocs might leave Germany more impoverished than in the relatively liberal and open pre-war world economy. Germany's war aims offered a questionable solution to its problems of encirclement and vulnerability to its enemies, as some of its leaders were aware.

The Central Powers' war aims were not, however, drafted only with external circumstances in mind. The Austro-Hungarian leaders wanted to eliminate the South Slav threat for reasons of internal security, but to avoid absorbing more Serbs. On their northern border, in contrast, the solution arrived at in the Vienna Agreements was highly unattractive to them because they feared it would antagonize their own Polish subjects. They accepted it only under the pressure of military emergency. The Germans too were anxious to avoid extensive annexations of unwilling subjects, and had turned to the Belgian 'vassal state' and Polish frontier strip plans as alternatives. More fundamentally, the German leaders felt a victorious settlement was essential to domestic political stability and, much more frequently than their Allied counterparts, they said so. In November 1914 Bethmann opposed a general peace because its terms 'would appear to the people as absolutely insufficient rewards for such terrible sacrifices'. His deputy, Clemens von

Delbrück, hoped that after the war the increase in Germany's power would make it possible to 'satisfy all parties and thus resolve all political problems'.[19] Similarly, Jagow was mindful of the 'very serious domestic financial difficulties' that would follow a compromise general settlement (which might mean, for example, that the subscribers to government war loans could not be repaid).[20] Germany's war aims were certainly intended to improve its international situation, but they can also be seen as another in a string of expedients dating back through naval construction in the 1890s and colonial acquisitions in the 1880s that were designed to stabilize the Hohenzollern autocracy through expansion.

Sweeping gains were demanded not only within Germany's bureaucracy but still more by lobbyists outside, although Bethmann tried to head off what he feared would be a divisive public debate by censoring press discussion of war aims until 1916.[21] Broadly, as in other European countries, the issue polarized left against right. The SPD leaders opposed annexations, saying that they supported only a defensive war and advising Bethmann that in return they expected internal democratization. But they found it hard to hold this middle line. A breakaway section of the parliamentary party formed in 1916 opposed the war altogether, while another section sympathized with the Reichstag's annexationist majority. Apart from the SPD, all the parliamentary parties backed a 1915 declaration that in the peace negotiations 'Germany's military, economic, financial, and political interests must be . . . guaranteed to their full extent and by all means, including the necessary territorial acquisitions'. Annexations in east and west were also supported by the princes represented in the upper chamber (the Bundesrat)[22] by a 'Petition of the Intellectuals' with 1,347 signatories (including 352 university professors) in July 1915, and by the 'Petition of the Six Economic Associations' of May 1915, representing the leading employers' organizations and the main landowners' group. It is questionable how far the 'economic associations' represented their member firms, many of which seem to have been indifferent or moderate;[23] and both petitions, apart from being gifts to Allied propaganda, testified to the lobbying ability of the extreme nationalists of the Pan-German League. Naturally Allied propaganda conflated them with the views of the government – with some exaggeration but not altogether unjustly. Despite Bethmann's preference for minimizing annexations, as the expansionist 'war aims movement' in the Reichstag and in the country grew in 1915–16 he changed the tone of his speeches, committing Germany to seeking 'securities' at the peace and pledging that neither in the east nor in Belgium would the *status quo ante* be restored.[24]

Both unofficial opinion and governmental planning were becoming harsher. The military emergency of summer 1916 might have been expected to cause a reconsideration, as had defeat on the Marne, but in fact German aims became more draconian than ever. Although the Central Powers' peace note of 12 December 1916 appeared to be an olive branch, the Allies were justified in rejecting it as insincere. Timed to follow the Central Powers' victory in Romania, it was arrogant in tone and simply proposed peace discussions without specifying terms. Whereas the Austro-Hungarian foreign minister, Stephen Burián, had wanted to set out conditions, Bethmann overrode him, preferring not to tie his hands. The chancellor doubted the initiative would succeed and his main purpose was to impress on the socialists that the war was defensive, while undermining the Allies' domestic unity. He expected to be forced soon into a confrontation with the United States over submarine warfare, and hoped a pacific gesture would make Washington less likely to join Germany's enemies. In all these objectives he had little success: the German home front fragmented during the winter and a breach with America came closer. But in any case, under the influence of Hindenburg and Ludendorff Bethmann had been obliged to toughen up the government's war aims, which already in discussions during November 1916 had been set out more systematically than ever before. Luxemburg was to be annexed; Belgium should cede Liège and its economy and railways be placed under German control; France must cede Briey; Poland, like Belgium, should be subordinated and should cede two frontier strips; and Russia should also give up Lithuania and Courland. After the Allies rejected the note Hindenburg called for further annexations and the navy demanded control of the Baltic and Belgian coasts and a worldwide chain of bases. Bethmann resisted and stood by the November 1916 terms, forwarding a summary of them to the American president as a guide to Germany's objectives. The chancellor still controlled German diplomacy, though over the Polish declaration and the November 1916 programme he accepted harsher terms and greater restrictions on his freedom of action than he deemed prudent. However, with Germany's armies under unprecedented pressure and the economy beginning a downward spiral, Hindenburg and Ludendorff sought more sweeping annexationist claims, not fewer, at the same time mobilizing the country for total victory. There was therefore no simple correlation between the military position and German war aims, but with both separate and general negotiations apparently ruled out there seemed little alternative to fighting on in the hope that U-boat warfare would enable Germany to impose much more severe terms.*

The growing annexationist pressure from German public opinion and the military was a major obstacle to Bethmann's hopes for achieving peace by dividing the Allies. But even more formidable was the Allies' refusal to be divided, which was central to their war aims policy and their response to peace initiatives. They embodied their refusal in the September 1914 Pact of London, proposed by Russia and readily accepted by Britain and France, which bound each of them to make no separate peace or offer conditions without the others' prior agreement. As no one of the Allies was as dominant as Germany on the other side, to understand why they stuck to this commitment each country must be considered in turn.

Russia is the best place to begin, as the primary target of German feelers in 1915, and the country whose battlefield setbacks might have made it most susceptible to them. In fact the Russians, like the Germans and unlike the French and British, were quick to define their objectives. Having done so in the relatively favourable circumstances of the winter of 1914–15, they stood by them with little deviation through the greater difficulties that followed. Despite some soul-searching, the Russian elite stayed loyal to the Pact of London until revolution swept it away.[25]

Russia's main territorial quarrel with the Central Powers lay in Poland. However, its August 1914 proclamation, calling for the Poles to be 'united under the

---

sceptre of the Russian Emperor . . . free in faith, language, and self-government' was not all it seemed. Sazonov, its driving force, wanted support from the Poles and from western public opinion;[26] other ministers feared concessions would make the Poles demand more, and set a precedent for the empire's other minorities. Hence it was issued by Grand Duke Nicholas rather than the tsar, and 'self-government' was substituted for 'autonomy'.[27] In March 1915 the council of ministers decided that Poland's foreign policy, armed forces, public finance, and transport would remain under Russian control, and when in July 1916 Sazonov pressed for a more binding commitment in the shape of a constitutional charter, he was replaced.[28] Furthermore, although the proclamation clearly implied expansion at Germany and Austria-Hungary's expense, the government never defined how far this expansion should go. For all these reasons, the Polish proclamation should be seen as largely propagandist.

None the less, in the mood of optimism caused by Russia's conquest of Galicia and its successes in the battles of autumn 1914, the government disclosed a comprehensive war aims programme to Britain and France, in the shape of Sazonov's 'Thirteen Points' of mid-September and of statements made on 21 November by Nicholas to the French ambassador, Paléologue. Although there were discrepancies between the two manifestos (the tsar being more ambitious), the similarities outweighed them. The Russian civilian leaders were in substantial agreement about what they wanted, arguably more so than their German counterparts. They were more annexationist than Bethmann. For Russia itself Sazonov wanted to take the lower river Niemen from Germany and eastern Galicia from Austria-Hungary, and for Poland he and Nicholas wanted eastern Posen and southern Silesia from Germany and western Galicia from the Dual Monarchy. The Stavka wanted the whole of East Prussia up to the Vistula, but the tsar distanced himself from this demand. Germany would remain united, but it would lose territory in east and west and would pay reparations. For Sazonov, 'the principal objective . . . should be to strike at German power and its pretensions to military and political domination', and for Nicholas it was 'the destruction of German militarism, the end of the nightmare from which Germany has made us suffer for more than forty years', and to prevent any war of revenge.[29] Austria-Hungary was to be treated still more harshly: Sazonov proposed it should lose its Poles, Ukrainians, and South Slavs, and on 17 September a proclamation to the 'Peoples of Austria-Hungary' promised 'freedom and the realization of your national strivings'. Yet the Russians were reluctant to come out unequivocally in favour of national self-determination and the break-up of the Habsburg monarchy, both because they feared that Germany would absorb the Austrian Germans and because of the dangerous precedent for their own multi-national empire. In particular, they did not publicly commit themselves to independence for the Czechs, which would make the difference between a diminished but still viable Austria-Hungary and its disappearance from the map. Nicholas privately expected that disappearance, but it was not his government's policy to encourage it.[30]

Turkey's intervention added a further element to Russian aims and for a while made the war more widely popular. Fighting alongside the liberal west against the conservative Central Powers had been problematic for some on the Russian right, but a crusade against the hereditary Muslim enemy was more acceptable. In the opening months few political parties except the Bolsheviks opposed the war, and Sazonov felt pressured by the military, the Duma, and the press to demand more than he thought wise.[31] Resentment against Ottoman aggression focused on Constantinople – the religious centre that Russian Orthodox nationalists had long aspired to control – and the Straits, the waterway whose closure jeopardized Russia's overseas supplies and its economic equilibrium.[32] Even before the Turks came in Sazonov told his allies that he wanted an international administration of the Straits; in November 1914 Grey and King George V promised British acquiescence in whatever Russia decided. Sazonov now knew his partners were unlikely to make difficulties, and his moment came with the Allied naval bombardment of the Dardanelles. Fearing the British and French would occupy the waterway, or – still worse – that they would land Greek troops, he demanded that if the war ended successfully Britain and France should agree to Russian annexation of Constantinople and the European shore of the Straits as well as the Asiatic shore of the Bosphorus. This demand went beyond the needs of maritime security and violated self-determination, as well as laying the basis for a Russian naval presence in the Mediterranean. None the less, with Sazonov hinting that refusal might jeopardize the alliance, in March 1915 the British and French accepted, though demanding in return that Russia should support their own territorial demands. Hence while the Germans extended their feelers to Petrograd, Russia's partners were promising it almost everything it wanted.[33]

The Straits agreement was only one of the reasons why the Russians rejected a separate peace, despite their shattering defeats in 1915. In addition, the tsarist government seems to have remained confident the Allies would win, as their long-term build-up would give them the edge. The Russians were contemptuous of Austria-Hungary and Turkey and wanted to see themselves and their protégés expand at the expense of Vienna and Constantinople. When in spring 1915 Austria-Hungary made what appears to have been its only major peace approach under Franz Joseph, Petrograd rebutted it; and it vehemently objected to Paris and London putting out feelers.[34] Above all, the Russians wanted to weaken Germany drastically and permanently, not only territorially but also by penalizing German business interests on Russian soil. With so much evidence of their country's military inferiority, they believed they could ensure security only by maintaining the anti-German alliance after the war; this objective was a major concern of their diplomacy just as alliance imperatives repeatedly influenced their strategy. Such considerations also militated against a separate peace. Finally, although Russia was the most autocratic of the powers and during the war became more so, there is evidence that the tsar and his ministers believed they must satisfy a patriotic public opinion and feared (like the Germans) that a humiliating peace would shake the foundations of their regime.[35] Hence during the dark days of the 1915 retreat, facing panic in Petrograd and Moscow and a storm of domestic criticism, Nicholas and his advisers repeatedly rejected German approaches, despite Bethmann's warnings that they stood to lose Poland definitively and suffer much worse terms.

In spite of the military disappointments of 1916, in this year too the tsarist leaders generally held to the aims set at the start of the war. In some ways they expanded them. After the Russian spring offensive that expelled the Turks from much of Armenia, in April 1916 Britain and France acknowledged Russia's right to annex the newly conquered Erzerum and Trebizond and to gain a sphere of influence in Kurdistan. Sazonov also wanted predominance in western Armenia and access to the Mediterranean, though here he yielded to resistance from the French, who had registered their claim to the area as their quid pro quo for the Straits agreement. But by now Sazonov was coming to doubt whether Russia would ever get Constantinople, and in November Nicholas despondently told the British ambassador that Russia would probably settle for its pre-1914 European frontiers, as it would cost too many lives to extend them. The Allied ambassadors were becoming more worried about Russia's loyalty, especially after Boris Stürmer, a suspected Germanophile, replaced Sazonov as foreign minister in July. Yet although Nicholas had become more willing to let his agents listen to German soundings, he continued to reject them. In the autumn Stürmer was dropped, and the government, backed by most of the Russian press, joined the other Allies in rejecting the peace notes issued by the Central Powers and by the American president in December. At Christmas Nicholas reaffirmed his commitment to uniting Poland, and in February–March 1917 the Russians reached a secret deal with the French, the 'Doumergue agreement', whereby they promised support for French buffer states in the Rhineland in exchange for French support for expanding Poland's borders westwards. None of this suggests that the ambitions of 1914 – to hobble the Central Powers by defeating them, depriving them of territory, and maintaining the alliance against them – had been abandoned. As events after March 1917 would demonstrate, however, if the Russian elites remained wedded to the old objectives, they carried less and less of the country with them.[36]

Despite repeated setbacks and enormous casualties, the French leaders were even more unanimous than the Russians in rejecting a separate or a compromise peace, and by 1917 they had developed a war aims programme comparable with those of Bethmann and Sazonov. Yet in July 1914 they had only vague ideas about their goals. Their immediate concern was to prevent Germany from defeating Russia and becoming the strongest power in Europe, and this remained a leading objective. Security preoccupied government and public alike, and French statesmen believed they could not achieve that security alone, given Germany's superior resources and its record, as they saw it, of provocation. Like the Russians they expected the wartime alliance still to be necessary after the peace, and they refused even to listen to enemy emissaries. They also opposed all efforts to mediate. Only a decisive victory, they asserted, would ensure the job did not have to be done again. At no point down to 1917 did they think the moment for negotiation had arrived.[37]

While being emphatic that victory was necessary, French governments were slow to define that victory's objectives. They were under less internal pressure than their German counterparts to define their aims, and feared that doing so would cause controversy and undermine the domestic political truce; hence they censored press discussion of war aims until 1916. As they did not want negotiations until they had improved their position, defining terms was a hypothetical exercise while the emergency created by invasion forced many other claims on their attention. During Viviani's premiership public information about French aims remained sparse. He told parliament in December 1914 that France would seek the restoration of Belgian independence, 'indemnities' for its devastated regions, and to break 'Prussian militarism'. It would not make peace without regaining Alsace-Lorraine; and this insistence, given that Germany was willing to cede only a few frontier villages, in itself ruled out a compromise. Behind the scenes, in contrast, Viviani's foreign minister, Théophile Delcassé, extracted a quid pro quo for the Straits agreement of Russian support for any French demands against the Ottoman Empire 'and elsewhere' – by which Nicholas II made clear he meant the Rhineland. Once the French possessed this assurance, however, they had still less incentive to clarify their objectives.[38]

Aristide Briand's tenure as premier and foreign minister from November 1915 to March 1917 was more eventful. Compared with Delcassé and with Poincaré (who remained president throughout the war), Briand was more mercurial and opportunistic and less consistently anti-German, but at this stage he was committed to pursuing the struggle more vigorously and to co-ordinating Allied efforts. Outside Europe the French responded to British initiatives but inside they set the pace. By the time Briand departed the result was an impressive edifice of inter-Allied accords.

In Africa, Britain and France had already agreed on provisional boundaries in Togoland in August 1914, and an understanding in February 1916 gave France control over most of the Cameroons, making it likely that it would keep these territories permanently. The Middle East, however, was much more important to most French ministers and officials, many of whom belonged to colonialist pressure groups whose small size belied their disproportionate influence. A good example was François Georges-Picot, the former consul general at Beirut, whom Briand selected as his representative in the negotiations with Britain over the future of the Ottoman Empire that led to the Sykes–Picot agreement, initialled in January 1916 and finalized in May. Following the impetus given by the Straits agreement, the Allies had decided it was time to settle the terms of a partition of Turkey-in-Asia. Picot demanded the whole of Syria (where France had missionaries and railway and port investments), Palestine, and the oil-bearing Mosul district in northern Mesopotamia. The British, represented by Sir Mark Sykes, agreed to French 'direct or indirect administration or control' in a 'blue area' covering Cilicia and the Syrian and Lebanese coasts, while a similar British 'red area' covered central and southern Mesopotamia and Acre and Haifa in Palestine. The 'brown area' in the rest of the Holy Land would come under an 'international administration', and the interior between the red and blue areas would ostensibly come under independent Arab rule, but be divided into a northern area 'A' and a southern area 'B', in which France and Britain respectively would have sole rights to appoint advisers and would enjoy preference in extending loans and applying for contracts. The Sykes–Picot agreement was extended by the April 1916 understanding with Russia over Armenia and laid the basis for a system of colonies and protectorates spanning the Arab Middle East. Although the French had dropped their claim to Palestine they gained most of Syria, and Mosul came under their influence as part of area 'A'. Despite their military weakness in the region, they secured most of their objectives. Middle Eastern expansion, however, was a valuable potential extra rather than a central reason for continuing the war.[39]

But in Europe too Briand's ministry marked a turning point. When he decided to push towards decisions, moreover, pools of ideas already existed on which to draw. During 1915 discussion of France's aims had already begun in the press (as far as censorship permitted), in the army, in parliament, in business circles, and in various official and semi-official investigatory committees.[40] Some of these discussions concerned the industrial imbalance between France and Germany; others concerned territory, although the issues were interconnected. Most reached the conclusion that simply retaking Alsace-Lorraine with its pre-1870 frontier, although giving France almost all the Lorraine–Luxemburg iron ore field, would be inadequate, as it would provide only a partial frontier on the Rhine and leave the country more dependent on imported coal. Starting from these premisses, logic pointed to adding the Saar coalfield and even to controlling the entire left bank of the Rhine.

Briand brought to office the energetic commerce minister, Etienne Clémentel, who dominated French economic planning in 1915–18. Clémentel wanted an answer to the *Mitteleuropa* customs union project. He also wanted to end France's pre-war dependence on Germany for products such as chemicals for explosives, and ensure it had the raw materials needed for reconstruction. Briand therefore proposed, and the other Allies consented to, an economic conference that met in Paris in June 1916. It agreed to apply discriminatory tariffs against the Central Powers after the war, to assure the Allies first claim on each other's natural resources, and to eliminate dependence on the enemy for strategic manufactures and raw materials. The Paris resolutions seemed a triumph for French diplomacy and went much further than any economic plans agreed to by the Central Powers, who were greatly alarmed by them. But neither Russia nor Italy wanted to risk their postwar exports to Germany, and the United States fiercely protested against a trading bloc from which it stood to be excluded. The resolutions were never given teeth by implementation agreements.[41]

Economic safeguards were needed for France's future, but were less fundamental than protection against another invasion. Briand and Poincaré both called publicly for 'guarantees' of French security, echoing Bethmann's coded language in Germany. Only in summer 1916, however, did the French council of ministers turn to consider in detail what those guarantees should be. Debate in the country at large (facilitated by relaxation of press censorship) was one reason for this change, but external developments were more important. On the one hand, the recent sudden improvement in Allied military fortunes suggested victory might be within reach; on the other Paléologue was warning that Stürmer's Russia might make peace unless locked in by new war aims accords, while the British too were reported to want a discussion. Briefed by memoranda from the foreign ministry and the high command, ministers decided in October to demand a free hand from their allies to decide the future of the left bank of the Rhine. Russia had already promised this in 1915, and the 'Cambon letter' sent confidentially with the council of ministers' approval in January 1917 to the ambassador in London, Paul Cambon, demanded the 'preponderant voice' for France in settling the issue. It insisted that German sovereignty over the left bank must end (though otherwise left the region's future open), and that France should regain Alsace-Lorraine with its frontier of 1790, therefore incorporating much of the Saar. Cambon did not show the document to the British until July, by which time circumstances had so changed that it had become an embarrassment. But the colonial minister, Gaston Doumergue, did use it as a basis for discussion when he visited Petrograd in February, though reaching a more ambitious and precise understanding. According to the secret Doumergue agreement France would receive 'at the very least' the entire Saar, and the left bank would be divided into nominally independent buffer states under its control, while Russia was promised 'complete liberty' to fix its western frontiers. Briand endorsed the understanding, but he did not consult the council of ministers, in which a majority would probably have opposed the pact as too expansionist. As the premier fell from office shortly afterwards, the Cambon letter is more authoritative as a statement of French war aims. The ministers approved the letter at a moment when the Allies still had reason to expect major successes in their spring offensives. It foreshadowed the demands the French brought forward at the 1919 peace conference, yet it suggested that the French rulers shared the Germans' reluctance to undertake massive annexations of unwilling subjects, preferring to rely on indirect safeguards through military occupation and through economic provisions. All the same, given the simultaneous hardening of German war aims at the end of 1916, it held out little prospect of any early end to the conflict.[42]

British thinking followed a similar evolution, though in London no agreed programme for the European settlement ever emerged. Although Falkenhayn identified Britain as Germany's most implacable enemy, the evidence does not bear him out. British ministers were as hostile as French and Russian ones to a compromise peace (which they argued would be only a stopgap) and they opposed separate negotiations, though with their tradition of detachment from European diplomacy they were less committed to an anti-German bloc in the longer term. Public support for territorial expansion was weaker than in the continental countries, and pacifist and internationalist pressure from the left was stronger, though British leaders, like their French and German counterparts, preferred to keep their public statements on war aims vague for the sake of domestic harmony.[43] The British also differed in that European territorial arrangements were not their central preoccupation. They combined vagueness about the continent with precision about their extra-European objectives.

Liberal and Unionist ministers seem to have taken for granted that Germany would lose its navy after the war, if the ships escaped from being sunk during it. Germany must forfeit its colonies too, especially after the unexpected efforts needed to conquer them. Events had demonstrated that as wireless and coaling stations they could support submarine and cruiser assaults against Britain's trade and overseas possessions, and they could also serve as reservoirs for recruiting 'black armies' that might threaten their neighbours. Britain itself was most interested in German East Africa, for which it fought longest and hardest and which was seen as threatening its control of the Indian Ocean, but although the British alone might have been willing to return some colonies the demands of the Dominions and of France and Japan for shares of the spoils meant everything had to go.[44]

Considerations of appeasing others also influenced the British in the Middle East, but here too they had their own strategic imperatives. Both the Suez Canal and the Persian Gulf were regarded as essential interests.[45] Once the Ottoman Empire became an enemy the British decided it should no longer be preserved and that it was time to stake out claims, safeguarding British interests through partition. The Straits, unlike Suez, were no longer strategically vital, and worth abandoning in order to help keep Russia friendly and distract it from expansion nearer to India (for example in Persia). The Sykes–Picot agreement protected Suez by keeping France out of Palestine: Britain would keep the parts of Mesopotamia it conquered (and thus shield the Gulf), while a French-dominated buffer zone would separate Mesopotamia from the Russians. A longer-term problem with Sykes–Picot, which remains controversial, was its questionable compatibility with the 'McMahon–Hussein correspondence' that preceded the Arab Revolt.[46] Hussein, the Sharif or local ruler of Mecca, governed nominally under Ottoman suzerainty but in practice was autonomous, though he feared the Turks intended to re-establish control over him. In July 1915 he offered the British an alliance in return for helping him to replace the Turkish Sultan as Caliph of the Sunni Muslims and to win independence for almost all the Arab-inhabited portions of the Ottoman Empire. Initially sceptical, the British administration in Cairo (which handled the negotiations under notably lax supervision from the Foreign Office) panicked when it received a misleading report that the Turks and Germans had conceded all the demands of the nationalist groups that had formed among the Arab officers serving in the Ottoman army in Syria (with whom Hussein claimed to have links). The crucial letter was sent by Sir Henry McMahon (the British High Commissioner in Egypt) on 24 October. It promised to 'recognise and support' Arab independence in the areas Hussein had specified, but excluded Cilicia, western Syria and generally the localities where France had an interest as well as a zone of 'special administrative arrangements' (i.e., British rule) in southern and central Mesopotamia. The quid pro quo would be an Anglo-Arab alliance, directed to expelling the Turks from the Arab lands.[47]

This letter was hastily and clumsily drafted, and sent without proper consultation. It included numerous ambiguities, which the remainder of the correspondence failed to dispel. McMahon was calculatedly liberal with promises in order to get the Arabs to commit themselves. None the less, he probably intended to exclude Palestine from the independent Arab region, and the Sykes-Picot negotiations built on this exclusion.[48] Yet Hussein rebelled without receiving the promised clarification of French claims and still in ignorance of the complexities of the British position, which after Lloyd George became prime minister grew even more complex. In spring 1917 a report by a committee under Lord Curzon to the Imperial War Cabinet (IWC), composed of senior British ministers and the Dominion premiers, recommended that both Mesopotamia and Palestine should remain 'under British control' after the war, i.e., that the latter should be neither Arab nor international. The IWC accepted the report as a non-binding statement of priorities for the eventual peace conference. Lloyd George's detestation of the Turks and his determination to destroy what he regarded as their corrupt and vicious rule had married with the concerns of the imperialists around him. The Ottomans were seen as a tool for German influence and a menace to the Suez Canal, the Persian Gulf, and ultimately India. Palestine was a potential Mediterranean terminus for oil pipelines and lay in close proximity to the canal; it needed to be British-dominated. Partly to mollify its allies and bring in Hussein, partly in order to assure its own imperial interests, Britain by 1917 had adopted Middle Eastern war aims that left little possibility of a negotiated peace.[49]

As regarded Germany itself, the economic strand in British war aims was less important than for France. Britain's financial position was much stronger, it had not been invaded and devastated, and Germany had been its second-best pre-war export market.[50] London took steps to protect its strategic industries, it signed up to the Paris Economic Conference resolutions in 1916, and it discussed with the Dominions greater imperial self-sufficiency, but the idea of a common external tariff for the empire made no headway. Nor was it British policy (any more indeed than it was French) to seek high cash reparations after the war. On the contrary, the Board of Trade doubted the practicality of trying to reclaim the cost of the conflict and even whether the 'permanent crushing' of Germany was desirable. British thinking (without reaching definite conclusions) inclined more to reintegrating Germany than to isolating it or holding it down.[51]

The same broadly applied to European territorial issues, on which likewise there was no such fixity of purpose as in Paris. The exception was Belgium, British ministers pledging themselves from the start to restore its independence and integrity. The Germans' use of Belgium as a corridor into France and as a U-boat base underlined the need to wrest it from them. The Allied governments knew of Albert's contacts with the Germans, which was one reason why they issued the 'Declaration of Sainte Adresse' in February 1916, promising to fight on until Belgium had been compensated for the damage it had suffered and had regained its independence. Even this most fundamental of British European aims, however, was less simple than it seemed. The French wanted future military co-operation and a customs union with Belgium, and the Belgians themselves, while hoping to annex Luxemburg and to take territory from the Netherlands, hoped for British support against French claims. The British, however, stuck to a commitment to restore the pre-war *status quo*, rather than see Belgium either expanded or realigned as a French satellite.[52]

Beyond this, Britain's position remained vague. In the first half of the war it made no commitment to restore Alsace-Lorraine to France, for example, or to liberate Poland, although at the end of 1916 Britain and France did try to outbid the Central Powers by publicly endorsing the tsar's promise of Polish autonomy. This implied no pledge to fight for any particular dispensation in Poland, any more than elsewhere in central and eastern Europe. In August 1916, however, more or less simultaneously with Briand's efforts to define French war aims, Asquith invited memoranda on Britain's objectives, which were duly submitted by the Foreign Office, the Admiralty, the Board of Trade, and the Chief of the Imperial General Staff, Sir William Robertson. The motives seem to have been confidence (as in France) that because of the summer offensives a decisive victory might be imminent, fear that the French might already be formulating their objectives, and expectation of American mediation. In fact no cabinet discussion resulted, but the memoranda provided a snapshot of Whitehall thinking. They revealed (especially in the Foreign Office) a cautious preference for applying the self-determination principle to territorial disputes on the continent, which would favour France in Alsace-Lorraine but otherwise imply a moderate treatment of Germany in Europe, while destroying it as a naval and colonial rival. Robertson put explicitly what others no doubt thought: Britain's interest was not to crush Germany so completely that it ceased to balance France and Russia.[53] This would be a difficult circle to square: but the Curzon Committee's report to the IWC in the following spring reached similar conclusions. It recommended that Serbia and Belgium should be restored, and Alsace-Lorraine and Poland settled in accordance with the wishes of their peoples and the interests of a lasting peace. Lloyd George's statement to the IWC on 20 March put the emphasis on democratizing Germany and proving to it that aggression did not pay.[54] Probably most British politicians hoped to eliminate Germany as a rival overseas and to force it to renounce attempts to dominate the continent, but not to weaken it excessively in Europe.

In the meantime ministers agreed that the essential was to continue until victory and to honour the Pact of London obligations to the Allies. They had to balance this commitment, however, against Britain's growing dependence on America and the Wilson administration's ambitions to mediate. The most remarkable example was the secret 'House–Grey Memorandum' of 22 February 1916, embodied in an exchange of letters between the British Foreign Secretary and Colonel Edward House (Wilson's adviser and personal emissary) during one of the latter's visits to explore the mediation prospects. According to the memorandum House favoured as peace terms Belgian independence, restoring Alsace-Lorraine to France (with compensation for Germany outside Europe), and a sea outlet for Russia (possibly at the Straits). These terms (which Grey had first suggested) would meet several basic Allied objectives and none of the Central Powers' goals, and the memorandum envisaged that at a moment of France's and Britain's choosing Wilson would call a peace conference and would 'probably' declare war if Germany refused to attend or if the conference broke down because Berlin was 'unreasonable'. Wilson endorsed the understanding without consulting his cabinet or Congress, but it is doubtful if he had the domestic authority to deliver on it. Probably fortunately for him, the French had no interest in an American-brokered peace, and nor really had the British. Asquith's cabinet agonized about the cost of the war but in the end decided to gamble on a victory in the battle of the Somme rather than to play the American card.[55]

After failing to mediate in co-operation with London, Wilson took up a much less pro-Allied posture, and his next major initiative, a note of 18 December 1916 calling on both sides to declare their war aims, was preceded by financial pressure on Britain from the Federal Reserve Board.* Although following within a week of the December peace note from the Central Powers, Wilson's message was sent independently and was rushed off to keep open the possibility of negotiations before the Allies spurned their enemies' gesture. Moreover, he wanted to be even-handed, and by suggesting that both sides' aims seemed the same he infuriated the Allies. The French wanted a defiant reply that specified nothing, and it was at British insistence that the Allies replied on 10 January 1917 with a public statement of war

---

*See chs. 9 and 13.

aims – admittedly neither very precise nor corresponding very closely with their real objectives, but still more concrete than anything published before or than the Germans were willing to offer. Hence the Allies won a propaganda victory and re-gained credit with Wilson at a critical moment.[56] Humouring the president, how-ever, implied no reduction in British willingness to carry on. When in November Lord Lansdowne had suggested in a cabinet memorandum that in view of the lack of progress on the Somme Britain should consider settling for war aims of less than twenty shillings in the pound, he found no support, and was vigorously repu-diated by Grey and Robertson with Lloyd George's encouragement.[57] The latter's accession to the premiership if anything made the cabinet more unyielding against Germany as well as Turkey. The British might not know what they would do with victory, but they were determined to win it.

Britain, France, and Russia were the pivotal members of the anti-German coalition and their partners were in some ways fighting wars of their own. Italy intervened to complete its unification and to establish strategic frontiers, and after joining the Allies it more or less stood firm on the 1915 Treaty of London. At St-Jean de Mau-rienne in April 1917 Britain and France promised it additionally a 'green' zone of direct administration and a 'C' zone of indirect influence in southern Asia Minor, although as Russia never ratified this extension of the Sykes–Picot agreement, it re-mained technically a dead letter.[58] Romania was similarly promised Habsburg ter-ritory in return for its entry into the war, and the Allies expressed sympathy for Serbia's aspirations to unite with the South Slavs of Austria-Hungary, though they never bound themselves to accomplish them. In the east, by contrast, Britain did secretly promise in February 1917 to support Japan's claims to Germany's North Pacific islands and rights in Jiaozhou, in return for Japanese warships being sent to escort Allied shipping in the Mediterranean and for Japanese support for British claims to Germany's South Pacific possessions. Fourteen Japanese destroyers duly arrived to protect convoys and troopships, and France and Italy gave similar back-ing to Japan's claims soon afterwards.[59] Germany's colonies, however, were only one of the incentives that had drawn Japan into the war, the other being its desire to profit from the power vacuum in East Asia by advancing its position in China. The result was the notorious Twenty-one Demands, presented to Beijing in Janu-ary 1915 after consultation between the Japanese foreign ministry, business interests, and the nationalist Black Dragon Society. The Japanese had specific concerns – taking over Shandong, extending their port and railway leases in Manchuria, and safeguarding their industrial interests in China against national-ization – but Part V of the Demands went further by asking Beijing to employ Japanese advisers, reducing China to a virtual protectorate. After a crisis that lasted until May the Chinese accepted most of the more specific points but success-fully resisted Part V, the Japanese backing down over the issue mainly because Grey warned that if they persisted they might endanger the Anglo-Japanese al-liance. This impressed the *genro*, and Kato, the main author of the Demands, re-signed as foreign minister.[60] Under his more emollient successor the Japanese mended their fences, joining the Pact of London in October and relaxing the pres-sure on China. Although they made secret contacts with the Germans in 1916, they were unlikely to desert the other Allies, even if they did little to help them. The 1917 agreements reinforced this solidarity.

The details should not obscure the bigger picture. War aims were necessarily hypothetical and transitory sets of options. Few entailed unconditional commitments. The peace terms governments envisaged varied with their military and diplomatic prospects, as well as with their appraisal of domestic opinion. Ultimately their objectives were products of the fear and insecurity that had haunted the great powers before the July crisis and that developments since had intensified, though they were also characteristic expressions of European nationalism and imperialism. What matters most here is their contribution to the stalemate and escalation of 1915–16. The two sides were too divided for peace feelers ever to have much chance. The stumbling blocks were partly disputes over territory – Belgium, Poland, Alsace-Lorraine – and the rival colonial and economic projects. In addition, the Central Powers saw peace feelers primarily as a means of splitting their enemies, while the Allies (who launched few feelers of their own) refused to be split. In fact much of the Allies' strategy and diplomacy was directed to widening their coalition and maintaining it, whether through concessions to Russia at the Straits or through strategic decisions such as Britain's commitment to the Somme offensive, which was decided on partly to keep France in the war. The Allies were quite right that Germany (whose continental gains outweighed its colonial losses) stood to gain more from peace negotiations, at least if these came before the military balance had shifted against it. After conquering Poland and Serbia in 1915 the Central Powers had the territorial advantage in the east as well as the west, and the Germans felt that abandoning Belgium or Poland would be an admission of defeat that might have fatal consequences at home. In 1916–17 the Central Powers expanded their war aims, despite their sense that they were losing; but the Allies also expanded theirs. By spring 1917 the gap between the two sides was wider than ever and the scope for bargaining still less: the escalation on the diplomatic plane therefore kept pace with escalation in other spheres. But examining what divided governments gives only a one-dimensional explanation for the conflict's escalation and prolongation. We must now consider the manner in which the war was fought and why the governments could count on their peoples' acquiescence.

CHAPTER 6

THE LAND WAR
IN EUROPE: STRATEGY

I F WAR AIMS determined what the fighting was for, strategy decided where and when it happened. Yet governments oversaw the commanders' key decisions, and the basic strategic choices made in the war were as much political as technical. Moreover (and this is often overlooked), the two sides' strategies interacted, each reflecting an appraisal of the other's intentions. Both the Allies and the Central Powers committed themselves to mounting levels of violence, culminating in the massive Western and Eastern Front battles of 1916. And when these battles failed to bring decisive results, both approached strategic bankruptcy. Once again the underlying themes here are therefore stalemate and escalation. They will be examined under five main headings: the Central Powers' 1915 drive to the east and the Allies' response, the Central Powers' spring 1916 attacks and their enemies' summer counterstrokes, and finally the Allies' April 1917 offensives.

Until Falkenhayn resigned in August 1916 he remained the leading influence on the strategy of the Central Powers. The Turkish and Bulgarian high commands mostly deferred to him. Conrad did not – and OHL's and AOK's reluctance to cooperate would cause serious difficulty – but Austrian weakness gave Falkenhayn the upper hand. Within the German army his responsibility for allocating resources between west and east made for tension with his commanders in both theatres, and Ludendorff detested him. He also got on poorly with the chancellor, whom he neither respected nor kept well informed. In January 1915 Bethmann Hollweg conspired with Hindenburg and Ludendorff to remove him, following the disappointing outcome at the first battle of Ypres. Wilhelm's staff resolved the resulting crisis – during which Hindenburg threatened to resign – by a compromise whereby Falkenhayn had to relinquish his position as war minister to his deputy, Adolph Wild von Hohenborn. Nevertheless, he remained as CGS. He continued to enjoy support from the emperor and from the imperial entourage, and during 1915 he and the other German leaders agreed that the Eastern Front should take priority, even if they disagreed about the extent.[1]

Falkenhayn reached this view reluctantly, as his preference for the new year would have been another attack against the British. Two circumstances modified his views. The first was the January conspiracy, after which he mollified Hindenburg and Ludendorff by sending extra troops for a new offensive from East Prussia against the Russians. The result – the so-called winter battle of the Masurian Lakes from 7 to 21 February – inflicted 200,000 Russian casualties and finally cleared German soil, but again failed to re-enact the Tannenberg encirclement and caused the Germans themselves heavy losses. The second and more important circumstance was Austria-Hungary's military emergency. From the start the Habsburg army had been small, ill equipped, and badly led. It lost many of its most experienced officers in 1914, its troops were often poorly trained territorials, and its Czechs and Ukrainians soon proved unreliable against their fellow Slavs. In January 1915 Conrad committed it to an offensive in the Carpathians that continued until in sub-zero temperatures a vain attempt was made to lift the siege of Przemysl. Casualties in the Carpathians between January and April (mainly from cold and sickness) reached the staggering figure of nearly 800,000,[2] and in March the fortress and its 117,000 garrison surrendered regardless: news that reduced even the stoical Franz Joseph to weeping. Meanwhile the Russians' counter-attacks had taken the crests of the Carpathian passes and they planned to push on into the Hungarian plain. With Italy and possibly Romania poised to join the Allies, the threat to Austria-Hungary seemed terminal, and Conrad warned it might make a separate peace.[3] After Przemysl fell Falkenhayn therefore decided to send more troops, but he told Conrad nothing until the transport trains had started rolling and he kept the reinforcements under German command in a new Eleventh Army under August von Mackensen. In fact he was beholden neither to the Austrians nor to Hindenburg and Ludendorff, whom he antagonized by rejecting their proposals for a gigantic pincer operation whereby German forces invading Poland from the north would converge with Austrian ones from the south. Not only did he doubt this manoeuvre was feasible, but also he did not want Russia completely overthrown. On the contrary, he believed Germany must extricate itself from the war by splitting its enemies.[4] Profoundly affected by the huge casualties and the failure to break through at First Ypres, Falkenhayn, in contrast to the Ober Ost leaders, doubted if a decisive outcome on the lines of 1870 was possible, remarking that if Germany did not lose the war it would have won.[5] Military pressure was necessary to make the Russians negotiate, but it should neither humiliate them nor conquer territory that might obstruct compromise.

As well as having powerful reasons for turning east, Falkenhayn commanded the resources to do so. Convinced of his troops' superior effectiveness, he created extra units by taking a regiment from each of his Western Front divisions but gave the latter more machine guns to compensate for their diminished manpower. He reduced the Western Front field gun batteries from six to four guns each but left each battery with the same total stock of shells. Whereas Allied shell shortages were acute, in Germany new production was coming on stream and firepower was substituted for men, in what would become a developing trend of the war.[6] In spring

1915 Falkenhayn could therefore transport large forces from west to east. While doing so he attempted to pre-empt an Anglo-French counter-offensive by launching Germany's first Western Front gas attack, at the second battle of Ypres in April–May. His troops forced the British back into a narrower salient that barely covered the ruins of the city, but the attackers lacked the reserves to exploit the breach that the new weapon had opened, and Falkenhayn always intended this operation to be limited.* The real object of his preparations was the blow on 2 May that shattered the Russian front at Gorlice-Tarnow. In the attack sector Germany and Austria-Hungary massed 352,000 troops against 219,000 Russian ones, 1,272 field guns against 675, and 334 heavy guns and 96 mortars against 4 Russian heavy weapons. They delivered the biggest bombardment yet seen in the east, against thinly fortified positions in a quiet zone. Even though the Russians had had warning, their resistance crumbled rapidly and the Germans drove a wedge between two tsarist army corps, advancing eight miles in two days. The Russians could not seal off the breakthrough, and by the end of June the Germans and Austrians had retaken Przemysl and virtually freed Habsburg territory, as well as capturing some 284,000 prisoners and 2,000 guns. Falkenhayn now advanced into enemy territory, authorizing still larger operations that by September had overrun the whole of Russian Poland and Lithuania. The Russians' casualties finally totalled perhaps 1.4 million and their armies retreated some 300 miles, although German and Austrian casualties in the east during the year also exceeded a million.[7]

This advance was the big strategic story of 1915. Yet Falkenhayn still showed restraint and expected the decisive campaign of the war to come later and in the west. At Gorlice-Tarnow he attacked from the centre of the Austro-Hungarian front in order to push the Russians back, rather than further south in order to encircle them. When driving beyond Galicia into Russian Poland he authorized Hindenburg and Ludendorff to advance from the north and meet up with Mackensen coming from the south, thus capturing Warsaw and its surrounding fortresses in July and August, but he rejected Ober Ost's usual pleas for the pincers to reach wider. In September he allowed Hindenburg and Ludendorff to invade Lithuania, but insisted they should not advance beyond a defensible position. He denied that 'annihilating' the Russians was his intention, and he resisted being sucked in too deeply. He was mindful of Napoleon's catastrophic invasion of Russia, of Austro-Hungarian ineffectiveness, of the continuing danger on the Western Front, and of his high valuation of Russian fighting qualities.[8] Almost certainly he was correct. Hindenburg and Ludendorff persistently underestimated the Russians, and inadequate roads and railways impeded rapid manoeuvre, while the autumn rains impeded it still more. The tsarist armies recovered sufficiently to halt the Germans east of Vilna, and an Austro-Hungarian offensive that took Lutsk in August (launched in an effort to assert Conrad's continuing independence) lost it again in September to a counter-attack. The Eastern Front, following the Western one a year before, stabilized along a shortened line.

Falkenhayn admitted that a wider encirclement might have ensnared more Russians, but most of them would probably still have escaped. Such an ambitious operation would have faced even longer odds in Poland in 1915 than it had in France

---

*See further in ch. 7.

in 1914. But Falkenhayn's more modest aspirations also proved unrealizable. His belief that he had destroyed Russian offensive capability, and therefore could now concentrate on the west, was over-optimistic. Moreover, he occupied Russian Poland in part because Petrograd had rejected Bethmann's peace feelers, but victory made the German annexationists eager to detach Poland from Russia permanently, while defeat made Nicholas II no readier to talk. Falkenhayn's continuing pursuit of a separate peace with Russia helps explain why in September 1915 he switched his attention to the Balkans, Bethmann having advised him that while Russia aspired to gain Constantinople it was unlikely to negotiate. Defeating Serbia would help dash such hopes by giving the Central Powers a dependable overland supply route to Turkey, as well as further assisting the Austrians. Indeed Bethmann and the Berlin foreign ministry had wanted such an operation since the spring, but Falkenhayn, impressed by Serb military prowess and the difficulties of the Balkan terrain, waited until he was sure Bulgaria would help.[9] Once Sofia committed itself, however, there was little doubt about the outcome. Since its successes in the previous year the Serbian army had been ravaged by typhus. The German, Austro-Hungarian, and Bulgarian forces outnumbered it by more than two to one. In contrast to Potiorek's 1914 attacks on Serbia's mountainous western border, this time Germany and Austria-Hungary captured Belgrade and advanced down the Morava valley into the heart of the country, before the Bulgarians moved in from the east. The Allies could do little. The Italians launched a supporting offensive on their front, but Russia was in no position to help and the relieving force landed by France and Britain at Salonika in northern Greece was too small and too late to help. The Serbs retreated in a terrible winter march through the Albanian mountains, losing almost half their men before Allied vessels rescued them from the Adriatic coast and shipped them to Salonika, their government taking exile in Corfu. The Austrians conquered Montenegro in early 1916 and occupied northern Albania. With the first through train reaching Constantinople in January the Central Powers dominated the western Balkans, and Germany's goals of relieving Turkey and Austria-Hungary had been triumphantly accomplished. Even so, the more fundamental objective of a separate peace with Russia remained as elusive as ever.

German preponderance among the Central Powers contrasted with diffused authority among their enemies. In the first half of 1915 the Allies dissipated their resources in unco-ordinated campaigns. In the second half, shaken by the disasters in Poland and Serbia, they began improving their liaison, although only in the following year did they start to benefit. In the meantime it was hardly possible to talk of a unified strategy, although all the main Allies were on the offensive. Thus British strategy has traditionally been seen as disputed between 'Westerners' who wanted to concentrate in France and 'Easterners' who favoured operations elsewhere, but in reality it also reflected the ambiguity in British war aims, which were torn between fear of Berlin and distrust of Petrograd and Paris.[10] Strategy was the responsibility first of the Liberal government's War Council and then (in the coalition government formed under Asquith's continuing premiership in May 1915) of the cabinet's Dardanelles Committee, although Kitchener as Secretary of State for

War was the leading adviser to both bodies. Political considerations influenced Kitchener's hope that he could postpone involving British troops in major land offensives in Western Europe. He wanted the Germans to exhaust themselves first in fruitless assaults, an aspiration Falkenhayn had no intention of obliging. Despite entreaties from Sir John French and from Joffre, Kitchener delayed in sending the 'New Armies' – the newly recruited volunteer divisions – to the continent. Foreseeing that the decisive moment might not come until spring 1917, he wanted France and Russia to take the strain, enabling Britain to intervene decisively at the climax and exert pivotal influence at the peace conference. In the meantime, during the winter of 1914–15 the British considered amphibious operations in the Baltic, against the Flanders ports, at Salonika, and in Syria before deciding on the Dardanelles operation, and even when they opted for the latter they hoped it would not require ground troops.

Yet if the British wanted to minimize losses and avoid committing their fighting power prematurely, they also feared their partners would collapse. Kitchener was sceptical about France's military capacities, and foresaw that if the Germans defeated Russia and concentrated their forces in the west they might break through the Allied lines and threaten Britain's home islands. Hence he and the cabinet could not disregard French pressure. They authorized the BEF to attack at the battle of Neuve Chapelle on 10 March 1915, in part to show Joffre that it must be taken seriously. A combination of a heavy bombardment with surprise enabled British and Indian troops to break clean through the German lines (only one deep at this stage), although by the evening enemy reserves had come up and soon halted further progress.[11] Similarly, the next British attacks, at Festubert and Aubers Ridge in May, both of which achieved even less than at Neuve Chapelle, were support operations for a French offensive. None the less, until summer 1915 the British strictly limited their Western Front presence, while also sending too few troops to Gallipoli.[12] Thereafter, Falkenhayn's drive into Poland forced them to reconsider.

Throughout the year, however, France's commitment in the west dwarfed Britain's, whether measured by the length of front, by troop numbers, or by losses. Joffre attacked in Champagne from December 1914 to March 1915 and in the Woëvre in April (as well as in numerous smaller operations) before launching his biggest effort yet in Artois in May–June.[13] The French had several motives for these offensives, which cost them grievously, their total casualties between December 1914 and November 1915 being some 465,000.[14] In the 1914 emergency the politicians had delegated control of strategy to Joffre, and although the legislature reconvened in 1915 his prestige as the victor of the Marne still allowed him great independence, while Millerand shielded him from criticism. Joffre and GQG believed they must keep the initiative and that a passive defensive would sap morale. He wanted to win quickly, while the French army appeared to have contributed most to victory, thus maximizing French leverage in peace negotiations. Politicians and public opinion shared his impatience to see the invaded territories liberated and the war ended before the next winter. Moreover, by the time of the Artois attack it was becoming imperative to help Russia. Nor, given that the enemy trench system was still recent and rudimentary (and the Allies had numerical superiority), did the notion of a breakthrough seem fanciful.[15] Joffre advised the French politicians that he could win in a matter of months, and his GQG persistently overestimated the Germans' casualties and underestimated their manpower reserves.[16] Yet the tactical obstacles proved stubborn. The numbers of heavy guns and howitzers available were far smaller than later in the war. Although unprecedented quantities of artillery and infantry were committed to the Artois operation and on its first day men from General Philippe Pétain's corps reached open country, the French reserves were too far back to exploit the breach before the Germans closed it. A month of follow-up attacks made no difference.[17]

The French and British operations in the spring and summer of 1915 liberated only insignificant parcels of territory, and failed to divert forces from Germany's operations in the east. Similarly, Gallipoli diverted Turkish forces from the Caucasus but did nothing for Russia in Europe. Meanwhile Grand Duke Nicholas reported to his allies in December 1914 that he had virtually run out of rifles and artillery shells, and would need several months to replenish them.[18] This meant a defensive posture against the Germans though not the Austrians, and in spring 1915 the Grand Duke still hoped that by driving through the Carpathians while Italy and Romania assaulted Austria-Hungary's other frontiers he could bring the Habsburgs to their knees.[19] But despite the Austrians' crisis in these months, the Allies failed to press home their advantage. As a result of the haggling that preceded the Treaty of London, Italy delayed its entry until after the battle of Gorlice-Tarnow, thus missing the most opportune moment. Sonnino believed Austria-Hungary's complete disintegration would be against Italy's interests, and he failed to liaise with Romania before intervening. Joffre had hoped to coordinate his May Artois offensive with the start of Italian operations, but Luigi Cadorna, the Italian commander, delayed his first advance until June.[20] Serbia, unwilling to launch a supporting offensive and thereby help Italy to absorb fellow Slavs, remained inactive. Hence the intended vice around four sides of Austria-Hungary failed to tighten. Despite months of preparation and the lessons from the other fronts, the Italian army in 1915 had fewer machine guns, shells, aircraft and heavy artillery pieces than the Austrians,[21] and was very slow to mobilize and deploy. Italy's political objective of seizing Habsburg territory required an offensive strategy, and Cadorna tried to seize what he could of the mountainous Trentino, but his main projected advance was to be north-eastwards across the river Isonzo and towards Ljubljana, thence to combine with the other Allies for an assault on Vienna.[22] In practice, the Italians were barely across the border when they were halted. Four battles of the Isonzo, between 24 May and 30 November 1915, cost them some 62,000 killed and 170,000 sick and wounded.[23] A war against Italy evoked none of the ambivalence felt among the Habsburgs' Slav populations about fighting Russia, and although the Austrians moved some units from Galicia and the Balkans they succeeded with some 0.3 million men in repelling attacking forces three times their strength.

After the Allies passed their high-water mark in May 1915, their strategy became more reactive. The Russians slowed Ludendorff's progress into Poland and Lithuania and drove the Austrians out of Lutsk. But they were too weak to counter-attack against the Germans, and for three months after the Artois offensive Joffre made little response to the Stavka's entreaties, despite warnings from the

British and French ambassadors in Petrograd that Russian public opinion was becoming anti-Allied and pacifist.[24] Joffre needed lengthy preparations for his new plan, which aimed not just to relieve the Russians but also to break through in France before the winter. For this purpose GQG believed an attack on a wider front was needed, so that the troops spearheading the effort would be out of range of German artillery on their flanks.[25] Aided by heavy guns removed from France's fortresses, the opening barrage would be bigger than ever, and a preliminary attack in Artois would draw off enemy reserves from the main assault in Champagne. Thus the Allies would hit both sides of the 'Noyon bulge', the great salient in the German line pointing towards Paris. Joffre seems genuinely to have believed that the operation could break the German defences. His government, more doubtful, agreed to it with Russia in mind and with the stipulation that GQG should break off if there were no speedy success.[26] The British role in the scheme would be to attack near Loos, to the left of the French in Artois, in a sector where the enemy was sheltered by slag heaps and miners' cottages. The BEF commanders disliked the choice, but Kitchener, though sharing their scepticism, ordered them to accept if necessary 'very heavy losses indeed'.[27] For the first time the New Armies would participate, and the battle of Loos would be much bigger than earlier British attacks, but the government reluctantly approved it (now that there was no more hope at Gallipoli) for fear that otherwise France or Russia might sue for peace. This decision marked a transitional stage towards the more wholehearted British commitment to a Western Front offensive strategy in 1916 and underlined once more the importance of political considerations.[28] In the absence of adequate artillery, the British pinned their hopes at Loos on poison gas released from cylinders, but on the first day the air was still and the gas hung suspended in no man's land or even blew back towards the British lines. None the less the right wing of the attack captured the town of Loos and took the German first line. Sir John French had kept his two reserve New Army divisions so far back, however, that when they advanced on the second day with virtually no preliminary bombardment against uncut wire and well prepared machine gunners they suffered thousands of casualties within an hour. Although the muddle over the reserve divisions finished off French's reputation, the inadequacies of the artillery were probably once again the real source of failure.[29] Similarly, the French Artois attack at Souchez captured some strongpoints but never came close to breakthrough. Although the principal assault in Champagne was moderately successful at first and reached the Germans' second line, the arrival of enemy reserves as usual defeated subsequent efforts to widen the breach. Despite causing hundreds of thousands more casualties,[30] the September offensives neither liberated significant French territory nor much helped the Russians, who were saved mainly by their own efforts and by the autumn rains as well as by Falkenhayn's self-imposed limits on his objectives.

Allied efforts to halt the Germans in the Balkans were no more successful. Their centrepiece was the Anglo-French Salonika expedition.[31] Politicians such as Lloyd George in London and Briand in Paris had for some months been considering such a landing as the basis for a Balkan offensive against Austria-Hungary and as an alternative to the Western Front. What made action possible in autumn 1915 was the existence of a Greco-Serb alliance and the willingness of the Greek prime minister, Eleutherios Venizelos, to send 150,000 troops to Serbia's aid if Britain and France would supply a matching contingent. The real driving force behind the expedition, however, was French domestic politics. In July Joffre had dismissed his Third Army commander, Maurice Sarrail, one of the few French generals with left-wing affiliations. Given Joffre's diminishing credibility as a strategist and French deputies' endemic suspicion of GQG, the 'Sarrail affair' caused a furore that threatened both the government's parliamentary majority and the country's pro-war consensus.[32] The Salonika operation offered the government an opportunity to find Sarrail a face-saving command, and they agreed to Venizelos's proposal without consulting the British, who grudgingly went along with the *fait accompli*. The French wanted to send a small expedition quickly; in the end inter-Allied disagreements delayed its departure, but the numbers sent were still too small to be able to intervene effectively in support of the Serbs.[33] Hardly had the troops begun to land, moreover, when Venizelos fell from office and King Constantine (who wished to keep out of the war) appointed a successor who denied that the alliance obligated Greece to help Serbia. Sarrail advanced into Bulgaria but too late to save the Serbs, and his forces therefore fell back into Greece, remaining as an unwelcome presence in a neutral country. In London the military and most of the cabinet wanted the expedition withdrawn but failed to insist, primarily for fear, once again, that if they did so a neutralist or pro-German government would take over in Paris. Briand, after succeeding Viviani as French premier in October, wanted to remain at Salonika, not only to manage the Sarrail problem but also to strengthen Allied diplomacy and French influence in the Near East. Hence the expeditionary force stayed, and by 1917 its strength had risen to nearly half a million. It tied down forces that were needed on the Western Front, as well as diverting scarce shipping. Its chief enemy, apart from malaria, was Bulgarian troops whom their government would not allow to serve elsewhere. Salonika was the best example of a waste of Allied resources on a sideshow that contributed almost nothing, until the last weeks of the war, to Germany's defeat.

For the Central Powers 1915 was the most successful year of the war. No Allied initiative had delivered much, and the Russians and Serbs had been routed. Joffre now took the lead in seeking a concerted response. At a conference at his Chantilly headquarters in December representatives of the Allied high commands agreed to aim for synchronized offensives on the Western, Eastern, and Italian Fronts at some date after March 1916.[34] If on the other hand the Central Powers attacked one ally, the others would assist it. Smaller preliminary attacks would step up the enemy's 'attrition' rate (*usure*), though in view of the impending exhaustion of French manpower these would be a British, Italian, and Russian responsibility. The Stavka too was coming to favour an attrition doctrine,[35] as was the British general staff, which supported most of the Chantilly principles. Despite the subsequent evil reputation of the concept, attrition initially implied economy in casualties,[36] at least during the preliminary phase. For the main assault, an alternative Stavka plan for combined attacks against Austria-Hungary was rejected, the British and French insisting that the mountainous terrain and the logistical difficulties facing their Salonika force would make this approach impossible.[37] The enemy to concentrate on was Germany, and the aim was to prevent the Central Powers from shuttling reserves around their internal lines of communication in order to repel the Allies piecemeal. The war would be won by even more ambitious coordinated offensives than those of September 1915, and a massive increase in casualties and destruction would be the inescapable consequence.

The Chantilly agreements were made between the military chiefs, but the disappointments of 1915 facilitated their approval by the Allied governments. When Briand became French premier he called for stronger inter-Allied liaison, and he believed Chantilly served French interests. He strengthened Joffre by appointing him generalissimo over all the French armies, including Sarrail's troops in Salonika. Meanwhile in Russia the tsar replaced Grand Duke Nicholas in September and took over the supreme command himself. In practice this meant strategy would be directed by the CGS, Mikhail Alekseyev, who proved willing to consult Russia's allies and to help them when in difficulty. Finally in December Sir Douglas Haig replaced French as BEF commander (and generally got on better than French had done with Joffre), while in London Sir William Robertson became CIGS. Robertson insisted on being designated the government's sole strategic adviser and on signing all operational directives to the field commanders, thus marginalizing Kitchener. A blunt and forceful man, he agreed with Haig that to win Britain must beat the German army in western Europe (and that Britain should play the major part in gaining victory). If this meant heavy losses, so be it. He shared Joffre's optimism that the underlying balance was moving in the Allies' favour, given their superior manpower and expanding production.[38] They needed persistence and co-ordination. In the next campaigning season events would seem at first to vindicate this optimism, only to dash it later.

Events in spring 1916 would be dominated not by Joffre but by Falkenhayn. The Germans' Verdun offensive from February to July was their sole major attack in the west between the Marne and 1918. It was a new type of battle. Including the French counter-attacks in October and December it lasted for ten months, and inflicted perhaps 377,000 French casualties and 337,000 German ones (though the ratio of killed and missing has been estimated at about 160,000 to 71,504).[39] It broke previous records for length and concentration of killing and destruction, even if the Somme and Ypres would soon rival it. Although the proving ground for new technologies such as flamethrowers and phosgene gas, it was above all a struggle between artilleries, the infantry being reduced to occupying terrain that was pounded with unprecedented intensity. Yet the maximum German advance was barely five miles.

Falkenhayn shared the Allies' judgement that the long-term balance was moving in their favour. He doubted whether Germany's economy and public morale could endure for more than another year. Further advances eastwards might conquer the Ukraine breadbasket but would also absorb more troops on garrison duty and stretch his lines of communication. He needed stronger medicine.[40] In his 'Christmas Memorial' submitted to Wilhelm in December 1915 (though the authenticity of this document is unproven and it may have been fabricated by Falkenhayn after the war) he rejected an attack on the BEF, which would need too many men and would be impossible until the Flanders clay had dried out after the winter.[41] Instead he would checkmate Britain by submarine attacks and by disabling its French stalwart. No breakthrough like Gorlice-Tarnow seemed feasible in the west, but he planned to inflict such casualties that the French – whose resilience he misjudged – would sue for peace. Verdun suited his purpose because of its historic associations and emotive resonance: a major French fortress since the time of Louis XIV, its fall to the Prussians in 1792 had triggered the first republican revolution in Paris. It had been besieged in 1870, and formed the pivot for Joffre's 1914 retreat. It also had a suitable topography. Fortresses ringed Verdun on the wooded heights east and west of the river Meuse. If the Germans took the heights they could bombard freely both the town and its defenders, who would have to attack uphill to dislodge them. A trunk railway ran behind the German front, facilitating the supply of munitions, whereas French access routes were limited to one road and a narrow-gauge line. Finally, the forests and slopes, combined with winter mists and local air superiority, created the potential for surprise. Until shortly before the attack much of the preparation was concealed, the artillery being hidden in the trees and the assault troops in bunkers. All the same, in terms of means if not of ends Verdun was planned as a limited operation. Falkenhayn intended neither to break through into open country nor – probably – to capture the town itself, although his Fifth Army commander, the Prussian Crown Prince, proclaimed the latter as an objective.[42] With only a small surplus of troops available and aware that he was defending two extended fronts, Falkenhayn allocated just nine divisions for the assault. The aim was to take the heights east of the Meuse, and for the artillery to do the real damage when the French counter-attacked. If the British launched a relief attack they too would be bled white. Mirroring the evolution of strategic thinking on the Allied side, Falkenhayn expected to prevail through an offensive version of attrition administered through massive quantities of heavy artillery and high explosive shells, transported to the sector by 1,300 munitions trains over seven weeks. This bombardment would dwarf even Gorlice-Tarnow, and on 21 February 1916 some 1,220 guns, half of them mortars or heavy artillery pieces, fired 2 million shells in eight hours along an eight-mile front before the infantry rose to attack.

After February GQG came under justified criticism for complacency. Verdun had been a quiet sector, lightly garrisoned and with incomplete trenches, while its fortresses had lost most of their guns for use as field artillery. In January Joffre sent his deputy, Curières de Castelnau, to inspect the sector, and the French received some warning, but they underestimated what was about to befall them. Verdun itself may have been saved by bad weather, which postponed the attack by nine days. The bombardment failed to annihilate the defenders, who did not surrender like the Russians at Gorlice. Despite the Germans' use of sophisticated infiltration tactics – small squads equipped with grenades, flamethrowers, and light mortars preceding the regular infantry and being supported by aerial bombing – resistance continued. None the less, progress in the first few days far exceeded that in the Allies' 1915 offensives, and on 24 February Fort Douaumont, the most powerful east of the Meuse, fell almost undefended to a lucky probing attack. But by the end of the first week the advance had stuck fast without controlling the heights, and five months later the Germans had still failed to do so.

Falkenhayn did succeed, however, in committing the French to an attrition contest. GQG was willing to write off Verdun as a liability, but Briand, believing national morale and his government's survival were at stake, descended on Chantilly in the middle of the night to rouse Joffre and insist that the city must be held.[43] Joffre appointed Philippe Pétain to command the Second Army at Verdun, and Pétain rapidly organized the defences. Along the *voie sacrée* or 'sacred way' – the solitary thoroughfare linking Verdun to the rest of France – lorries passed night and day in both directions every fourteen seconds. French divisions, unlike German ones, were rotated so as not to serve in the front line for more than two weeks continuously, even if this meant that some seventy out of ninety-six French Western Front divisions passed through the inferno (the German total was forty-six and a half).[44] Finally, the remaining forts were rearmed and French guns west of the Meuse enfiladed the Germans east of the river. Falkenhayn, anxious to ration his infantry, had ignored advice to attack on both banks in February, but in March and April he tried to clear the west bank after all, and now without the benefit of surprise – another sign that Verdun was ceasing to be the carefully calibrated operation he had envisaged. Not only did the battle suck in more divisions than he had intended, it also became as detested and demoralizing for the German troops as it was for the French and it further estranged him from his commanders. He considered cancelling the operation, but he would need at least a month to prepare another jumping-off ground elsewhere, and he mistakenly supposed the casualty ratio was running five to two in Germany's favour whereas in fact after the opening phase it was more equal. Given the failure to capture the whole of the Verdun fortress complex, simply inflicting casualties became OHL's primary rationale for the campaign.[45] Moreover, the Germans' own mounting losses were making this a prestige battle for them too. Falkenhayn's men eventually captured the west bank heights of Mort Homme and Côte 304 before turning back to the east, where in May and June they made more progress, taking another major fortress, Fort Vaux, and nearing the edge of the heights. Joffre feared the battle would compromise his entire Chantilly strategy and as in 1914 he was determined to husband resources for a counterstroke. He capped the men and artillery allocated to the sector and moved Pétain up to a supervisory command, transferring the conduct of the battle to the less defensively minded Robert Nivelle. This judgement called for iron nerves, as the French troops' morale was faltering and by 12 June they had only one fresh brigade in reserve. At this critical point, however, Falkenhayn paused and sent three divisions to the east. When the Germans made their supreme effort on 23 June, assisted by the first use of phosgene gas shells, they were too weak to prevail. Events elsewhere had come to France's rescue.

Joffre had quickly realized that Verdun was a German bid to win the war, and appealed for assistance under the Chantilly agreement. The Russians responded on 18 March with an attack at Lake Narotch. They enjoyed a local numerical superiority of almost two to one, and were confident of achieving success while the Germans were distracted. Yet the assault was stopped in its tracks with 100,000 casualties, the Germans committing only three extra divisions against it of which none came from the west.[46] As for the British, Haig refused to wear his troops out in the preliminary attacks envisaged at Chantilly, and Joffre did not press him, thus frustrating Falkenhayn's hopes that the BEF would launch a futile relieving offensive. Yet it was Falkenhayn's failure to liaise with Conrad that eventually derailed German strategy. During 1915, despite personality clashes, the two men had pursued similar objectives. But for 1916 Conrad planned an attack from the Trentino that would push the Italians out of the Alps, or even cut off their Isonzo army and reach Venice. He requested nine German divisions for this *Strafexpedition* ('punishment expedition'), intimating that an Italian collapse would release 250,000 Habsburg troops for service elsewhere. Leaving aside the problem that the German government was not at war with Italy and did not wish to be, however, Falkenhayn doubted whether the operation would make Italy surrender, and even if it did, whether this would help Germany to win. Instead he assigned the requested divisions to Verdun, and told Conrad nothing about the latter operation until just before it started. He did not try to halt the *Strafexpedition*, but he asked Conrad not to weaken the Eastern Front, despite which Conrad moved six of his best divisions from Galicia to the Trentino. Hence the Austrians achieved a small numerical superiority in the attack zone and a 3:1 advantage in heavy guns, which had to be lifted laboriously into position using specially constructed railways and cable cars. As at Verdun, bad weather caused postponement and denied the attackers surprise, but after launching the offensive on 15 May they advanced some twenty kilometres to the edge of the Asiago plateau and caused consternation in Rome. Like Joffre, Cadorna had been complacent, yet he too kept his nerve, moving up reinforcements via his railways (which were superior to the Austrian lines) and in Fiat lorries. On 2 June the Italians counter-attacked, regaining half the lost territory.[47] But in the meantime Cadorna and Victor Emmanuel had appealed with extreme urgency to the Russians to advance their contribution to the Allied combined assault envisaged by the Chantilly agreement. Once again the Russians obliged. And at this point, for the first time in over a year, the Allies recaptured the initiative.

Russia's 'Brusilov offensive' began on 4 June, the Anglo-French attack on the Somme opened on 1 July, Italy launched the sixth battle of the Isonzo on 6 August, Romania joined the Allies on 17 August, and in September Sarrail again advanced inland from Salonika. Despite the Verdun and Asiago battles the Chantilly offensives went ahead, later and less simultaneously than planned, but still applying unprecedented pressure to the Central Powers and contributing to Falkenhayn's overthrow. None the less, by October Austria-Hungary and Germany had contained the emergency and the end of the year found both sides increasingly desperate, the Germans willing to gamble on unrestricted submarine warfare and the Allies on Nivelle's startling assurance that given forty-eight hours he could breach the enemy trenches at will.

The precondition for the Chantilly offensives was an Allied build-up in weaponry and manpower. Italy's armed forces rose from about 1 million in 1915 to about 1.5 million; the BEF grew in the first half of 1916 by a similar number. Russia's front-line troops rose in early 1916 from 1.7 to 2 million, restoring its units to their regulation strength. Russian officers doubled in number from 40,000 in 1915 to 80,000 in 1916, and now all the men had rifles, while 1,000 rounds were available for each field gun.[48] On the other hand, mainly because they were running out of trained manpower, the Russian leaders were convinced that they needed to win soon. They were therefore willing to work with the Chantilly programme; Alekseyev fearing that unless the Allies took the initiative Germany would again make Russia its primary quarry. Although he still needed more heavy artillery he felt he could not wait. He informed Joffre that from May he would be ready to strike.[49]

This left the question of where to deliver the blow. Previously Austria-Hungary had been Russia's chief target, but Ludendorff's 1915 advance along the Baltic directly threatened Petrograd.[50] Yet after the Lake Narotch débâcle Generals Kuropatkin and Evert, who commanded the northern and central army groups facing the Germans, were loath to attack. In contrast, Alexei Brusilov, the new commander of the south-west front opposite Austria-Hungary, was eager to do so, and that he got his way once more highlighted the scope allowed to army group commanders by the decentralized Russian system. A Stavka conference on 14 April, chaired by a bored and passive Nicholas, permitted Brusilov to take the offensive, though he would receive no reinforcements and his operation was to be preliminary to the main assault by Evert.[51] After Italy appealed for help Alekseyev brought forward the starting date, fearing that otherwise Italy would not contribute to the Chantilly attacks and another opportunity for concerted pressure on Austria-Hungary would slip away.[52]

Part of the reason for the other commanders' wariness was the unorthodoxy of Brusilov's proposed tactics. Lacking numerical superiority, he intended to strike with minimal warning at numerous points along his 300-mile front, although the main blows would come at the northern end (to assist Evert) and in the south along the Carpathians (which would encourage Romanian intervention). His forces carried out detailed reconnaissance (including aerial photography) of the Austrian positions, moved up artillery secretly, and dug bunkers (as the Germans had done at Verdun), to conceal the assault troops near their starting points. On the day a brief but intense bombardment with howitzers and gas sufficed to cut the wire and overwhelm the enemy field batteries and machine guns. Many of the best Habsburg units were in Italy, and the Austrian commanders, who had been fortifying their positions since December, underestimated their vulnerability. Two-thirds of their infantry were in the front line and the Czech troops surrendered *en masse*, while the reserves came up too late. Within two days Brusilov had achieved a breach twenty kilometres wide and seventy-five deep.[53]

The sequel to this spectacular start, however, was more disappointment, partly because the Central Powers had a breathing space before the other Chantilly attacks. In the centre of Brusilov's front a German division held firm, limiting the advances to the north and south of it. Along the Carpathians his troops ran ahead of their supplies. The Germans had transferred fifteen divisions to the Eastern Front by 15 September, and though the Stavka reinforced Brusilov from the other army groups what he really wanted was Evert's attack – which, when it was belatedly launched, made no headway. Russian methods now became more orthodox, focused on a series of frontal attacks directed towards the railway town of Kovel. The operations consisted of heavy bombardments and dense infantry assaults, Brusilov's style of elaborate preparations being dispensed with on the grounds that they took too long and were unsuitable for untrained troops, and that what had worked against Austrians would not work against Germans. Hence the Russians undertook their own version of the attrition offensives in the west, and with no greater success, until after October Brusilov turned to helping Romania.[54] All the same, his offensive was the biggest Allied success since the Marne. It advanced the front line by between thirty and sixty miles, though the only major town it captured was Czernowitz. By capturing 400,000 prisoners and inflicting losses of 600,000 killed and wounded it destroyed half the Austro-Hungarian army on the Eastern Front, as well as bringing in Romania, forcing Conrad to abandon his Trentino offensive, and forcing Falkenhayn to suspend Verdun. Once again the Russians might feel they had saved France from defeat, but once again their casualties were enormous: probably over a million killed, wounded, and captured. Unless they could defeat the Germans it seemed they could accomplish little, and by the end of the season many in Petrograd were questioning whether the war was winnable.

All the same, Brusilov delivered more tangible gains than did the battle of the Somme, another hecatomb that between 1 July and 19 November inflicted 420,000 British and 194,000 French casualties. German losses remain disputed but may have been about half a million.[55] The fighting here was even more concentrated than at Verdun, the British and Germans firing a total of some 30 million shells at each other. It rivalled Verdun in the number of deaths per square yard.[56] Yet no major communication lines or industrial complexes lay behind the German lines, and the British found themselves fighting up a long and steep ridge, whose lower slopes were dotted with coppices and fortified villages, against some of the strongest positions on the Western Front. The visitor to the Somme today might well wonder how it was ever selected. In fact it appealed to Joffre as the junction between the British sector and his own, where the BEF could fight alongside him and broaden the attacking front in what he had first conceived of as a predominantly French operation. It probably appealed to the British commander for the same reason, though Haig may have envisaged the Somme merely as a preliminary assault and he simultaneously prepared for an offensive in Flanders that might follow once German reserves had been drawn off.[57] Joffre and Foch (the French northern army group commander) intended this time not a breakthrough effort like that in September 1915 but a Verdun in reverse: a methodical attrition campaign in which repeated limited assaults and the French army's newly reinforced artillery would wear down German cohesion.[58] In February Joffre and Haig agreed to attack jointly on the Somme that summer. In April the Asquith government's War Committee endorsed British participation, in good measure due to fresh warnings that otherwise the French might not carry on. Ministers knew that they were gambling: prolonged fighting and heavy casualties were likely, which might necessitate conscripting married men and jeopardize Britain's capacity to manufacture the exports needed to finance essential purchases from the United States. Yet these risks seemed preferable to the alternatives of leaving Germany unmolested and of endangering the French alliance.[59]

The high commands had agreed on the Somme plan before Verdun began, and Joffre was determined not to let the latter disrupt his schedule. Although he balked when Haig suggested delaying until 5 August, both men appear to have contented themselves with the end of June as the start date. It is not true that the British catastrophe on the first day of the battle resulted from the attack being launched prematurely under French pressure, although Verdun did reduce Joffre's planned contribution from thirty-nine divisions in February to twenty-two by May. As Britain would contribute nineteen the battle would now be an approximately equal effort and less ambitious than in its original conception, though Haig was still ambitious enough. He maintained reserves in Flanders for a follow-up offensive, and he rejected as too cautious the planning of his Fourth Army commander, Sir Henry Rawlinson. Rawlinson envisaged a 'bite and hold' operation: occupying a limited area after clearing out the defenders by artillery fire, so that the Germans would be forced to take casualties in counter-attacks. But Haig insisted the preliminary bombardment must target the enemy's second and third lines as well as the first, one of several indications (including the massing of cavalry) that he wanted to break through and roll up the German front. Whereas Falkenhayn had attacked at Verdun along a sector of eight miles – narrow enough to leave his infantry exposed to enfilading fire – Haig would attack on one of twenty, but once he doubled the target area by adding the rear lines his 1,000 field guns and 400 heavy guns were quite insufficient. Many of the shells they fired were duds, two-thirds were shrapnel rather than high explosive, and accuracy was poor. Nor, after the unhappy experience at Loos, did the BEF use gas, although nothing else could have neutralized dug-outs burrowed into the Picardy chalk to depths of forty feet. On the morning of 1 July most of the German first line opposite the British sector (including its wire, machine guns, field artillery, and garrison) was intact, in contrast with the French sector where the bombardment was twice as heavy. This failure in preparation, exacerbated by the British tactic in many sectors of sending the New Army infantry forward in waves at walking pace, made for a massacre. Of some 120,000 British troops taking part, about 57,000 became casualties, and over 19,000 died: French casualties were 7,000 and German 10–12,000. The French reached and even exceeded most of their first-day objectives; the British, except in their southern sector, made no gains whatever.[60]

After 1 July Haig apparently considered breaking off but Joffre insisted on his continuing and he shelved his preparations in Flanders. Instead he and Rawlinson concentrated on the southern sector, where a dawn attack on 14 July (following a much more intense and surprise bombardment) took most of the German second line. The BEF notably failed, however, to repeat this successful model thereafter. Instead the battle became bogged down, the British suffering another 82,000 casualties in dozens of minor operations between 15 July and 14 September, with the aim of straightening out the line before the next general attack. Meanwhile Falkenhayn insisted that the ground must be held, and during the whole course of the Somme the Germans are estimated to have launched 330 counter-attacks.[61] Prominent in this middle phase were the Dominion contingents, following the example of the 1st Newfoundland Regiment, which had sustained 91 per cent casualties on 1 July. The South African Brigade captured most of Delville Wood and held it against heavy shelling and German assaults; the Australian 1st Division similarly seized the village of Pozières on 23 July but lost 6,800 casualties from bombardment and in further attacks and counter-attacks before being pulled out of the line. The New Zealanders, too, made a successful attack in September.[62] British tactical effectiveness did improve, the artillery becoming more adept at supporting the infantry with creeping barrages (running just ahead of the assault forces) and with counter-battery fire against the enemy field guns.[63] Two general offensives on 15 and 25 September, both using tanks, took most of the Germans' original third line. But by now the Germans had constructed fourth and fifth lines between the battlefield and the town of Bapaume (which had been a target for the first phase), while the French were halted along the Somme river. After September the Germans moved in fresh troops and more artillery, and it became clear there would be no decisive result that year, although at the end of the month the British took Thiepval, the dominating position at the top end of the ridge. Limited attacks continued in worsening weather until the final 'battle of the Ancre' in mid-November, which took the villages of Beaumont Hamel and Beaucourt. Having captured the heights north of the Somme the British were now descending again, still at most seven miles from their starting point, and without even a tactical justification for their continued advance.

Haig went into the Somme with an attritional model of a 'wearing-out fight' that was the unavoidable precondition for a decisive result.[64] He persisted (despite growing doubts in London) in part because this was an agreed contribution to an inter-Allied effort, and in part because of optimism (fed by his intelligence chief, John Charteris) that the Germans were approaching breaking point. At the end of the battle he argued, somewhat lamely, that it had relieved Verdun, fixed German forces on the Western Front, and worn them down.[65] It indeed contributed to the first of these objectives, Falkenhayn ordering a 'strict defensive' at Verdun on 11 July.[66] It did not, however, prevent Germany from sending enough troops eastwards both to contain Brusilov and to crush Romania. As for Haig's third point, testimony by the Germans leaves no doubt that they felt severely strained and were awed by the new weight of Allied firepower, feeble though it was compared with later in the war.[67] The damage to German morale, albeit unquantifiable, was real enough, though Allied morale may have suffered no less severely. Yet the defenders sustained fewer casualties than the attackers, and the losses were easier for the Germans than for the French (though not the British) to make good. As of November 1916, Allied losses appeared quite disproportionate to Allied gains. The more important repercussions of the Somme were longer-term: ultimately it prompted Hindenburg's and Ludendorff's decisions to step up armaments production, intensify Germany's submarine campaign, and shorten their lines in the west.* Only the last of these developments, however, can be seen as a direct consequence of the Anglo-French attacks.

The third shock for the Central Powers in summer 1916 was Romania's entry into the war.[68] It came when Austria-Hungary was beleaguered not only in Poland but also in Italy. In July Cadorna halted his Trentino counter-offensive and rushed his heavy guns to the Isonzo. There in early August his troops achieved surprise and took Gorizia, their first significant conquest, though they were soon held in the hills east of the town and their autumn attacks on the Carso plateau failed dismally. It was Brusilov's successes, however, that triggered the decision in Bucharest. Ro-

---

*See chs. 5, 9, and 10.

mania was resource-rich and had supplied oil and food to the Central Powers, including 30 per cent of Austria-Hungary's grain needs in 1914–15. Its army numbered some 600,000, though it was poorly led and had too little modern equipment and too few shells. Even so, its intervention created a new emergency, as the Hungarian frontier in Transylvania was virtually undefended. In return for German help Austria-Hungary had to abandon much of its strategic independence, a supreme warlordship for all four Central Powers being created in September whose titular head was Wilhelm but which in practice was dominated by OHL. And this was a new OHL, for in Berlin the crisis had even more impact. Verdun, the Brusilov offensive, and the Somme had deprived Falkenhayn of most of his remaining support in the army, and Bethmann was again intriguing to replace him by Hindenburg and Ludendorff, whom he mistakenly hoped would lend their prestige to cover a new peace initiative. Wilhelm, however, felt threatened by Ludendorff and could not stomach him. It was Romanian intervention – which Falkenhayn had predicted only for later, if at all – that panicked Wilhelm into fearing that the war was lost, and broke his resistance. In August Hindenburg became Chief of the General Staff and Ludendorff his principal assistant (but in practice continuing as the driving force of the partnership) as First Quartermaster-General.[69]

Once they had recovered their nerve, the Central Powers soon retrieved the position. Like the Italians before them, the Romanians missed the bus. Bratianu delayed until after Brusilov had been halted, and the Romanians invaded Transylvania rather than attacking Bulgaria as the Russians advised. They met unexpectedly stout resistance from improvised local forces, and at first the Stavka assisted them with only three divisions, reluctance to help carve out a Greater Romania probably being part of the reason. The Serbs advanced from Salonika and took the town of Monastir in September, while Cadorna's attacks prevented Austria-Hungary from moving more than a few brigades from the Italian front. None the less, between August and December Germany and Austria-Hungary committed against Romania some thirty-three infantry and eight cavalry divisions, some transported from Verdun and others from Russia. The Romanians fought bravely, but were qualitatively and quantitatively outmatched. Bulgarian, Turkish, and German forces under Mackensen attacked from the south, while Germans and Austrians under the demoted Falkenhayn repelled the invasion of Transylvania, broke through the Carpathian passes before the autumn snows, and joined up with Mackensen to drive the Romanians back to the river Sereth. In the final stage Russia did provide major assistance, sending thirty-six infantry and eleven cavalry divisions to help stabilize the new line. None the less, three-quarters of Romania was occupied, including Bucharest, the Black Sea port of Constanza, the Ploesti oilfields, and the richest grain-producing areas. As a result of taking over the defence of Romania the Russians lengthened their front and diminished their own strategic reserve. With Romania overwhelmed, the Somme offensive deadlocked, and Italy and Russia exhausted, the Central Powers again ended the year controlling more European territory than at the beginning, and having survived the Chantilly onslaught.

Events during 1916 had wrecked Falkenhayn's grand strategy and called that of the Allies into question. As late as May, Falkenhayn had supposed that he remained on course towards his objectives of rendering Russia harmless and breaking France's will to resist. Brusilov and the Somme overturned these assumptions, and showed that Germany remained far from splitting its enemies. Hindenburg and Ludendorff brought to OHL a new energy and open-mindedness. They closed down Verdun completely, and adopted a more elastic defence at the Somme with a thinner front line, leaving more troops and artillery in reserve for prompt counter-attacks.[70] Yet they were less sensitive than Falkenhayn to the greater risk of overstraining Germany's resources. They set over-ambitious arms production targets, they resisted compromise over war aims, and they backed a new submarine campaign even if it meant war with the United States. While waiting for the U-boats to deliver, however, they planned no new land assaults. Hindenburg refused extra divisions to Conrad, who wanted another Trentino attack in spring 1917. Indeed OHL, correctly foreseeing a new Anglo-French offensive in the west, withdrew in February to a new 300-mile long defensive position, known in the sectors where the greatest withdrawal took place as the *Siegfried Stellung*, though christened the Hindenburg Line by the British. The disengagement shortened the front by thirty miles and released ten divisions. Combined with reorganizations of the infantry and artillery and the early call-up of the 1897 conscript cohort, it enabled the creation of a strategic reserve 1.3 million strong.[71] Yet although the new team responded effectively to the immediate crisis, they seemed to have little idea – unless Germany's submarines could do the trick – of how to win the war as a whole.

The Allied military chiefs concluded from their 1916 experiences that they should try more of the same. A further conference at Chantilly on 15 November agreed to prepare for a new concerted effort in February, to avoid being preempted by another stroke like Verdun. The main effort would be in the west, supported by Russian and Italian attacks. Haig and Joffre agreed to renew operations on the Somme, but with the French contributing larger forces south of the river.[72] Once again, the Allies would attack on a broad front, in order to draw off enemy reserves prior to what they hoped would finally be a decisive result.

This strategy overlooked how much the Allies themselves had been worn down, and turned out to be untenable. In Italy the *Strafexpedition* had shaken Cadorna's reputation and his confidence. Although in 1917 his army grew to 2.2 million,[73] he was mesmerized by the danger of a new Trentino attack. At a conference held in Rome in January Lloyd George proposed that the other Allies should supply heavy artillery for an Italian drive towards Trieste, but Cadorna was unenthusiastic, saying he would also want three or four Anglo-French corps and would expect them to defend the Trentino if the enemy struck first. He refused to start before 1 May, and he would wait until the situation on the Western Front and the enemy's intentions were clarified.[74] As for Russia, the Stavka hoped to reopen the offensive in Brusilov's sector, but the army's morale had been grievously damaged by its 1916 setbacks and its logistical back-up was disintegrating, the soldiers no longer being properly fed. At a further inter-Allied conference held in February in Petrograd, the Russians said they too would not be ready before 1 May, they had fewer reserves than a year before, and the Romania commitment had overextended them.[75] Within a month Nicholas II had abdicated and the new Provisional Government was pleading for time to restore discipline before it could even contemplate a new offensive.[76]

Even in Britain and France the Chantilly strategy was under attack. When Lloyd George became prime minister in December 1916 he was in private deeply critical of the outcome on the Somme, and suspected French generalship was better than British. Many other ministers shared his reservations, and at first his political position was strong enough for him to try to outmanoeuvre Haig and Robertson. His government stepped up British efforts in Mesopotamia and Palestine. At the Rome conference he tried vainly to encourage the Italians to take the casualties. Within weeks, however, the French offered him a new alternative.[77] The 1916 disappointments not only brought down Falkenhayn and Asquith but also shook the Briand ministry and caused Joffre's fall. Joffre was widely suspected of having been caught napping by Verdun, and Romania's defeat discredited him further. By December Briand realized that unless he ditched the generalissimo his government would be in danger. His solution was to make Joffre a Marshal of France and the government's 'technical military adviser', a post from which Joffre resigned when he realized it meant nothing. The command on the Western Front passed to Nivelle, but he did not inherit Joffre's overlordship of French armies everywhere else. A War Committee of ministers would now exercise supreme strategic authority. Greater civilian involvement did not, however, end French commitment to the offensive.[78]

Nivelle owed his promotion to his October–December 1916 attacks at Verdun, which had retaken Forts Vaux and Douaumont and much of the territory east of the Meuse. Tremendous preparatory bombardments using 400mm 'super-heavy' railway guns, as well as efficient counter-battery fire and a creeping barrage, had enabled rapid progress against weary German defenders, thousands of whom had given themselves up, though as their more serious defensive positions lay behind the forts the success was partly illusory.[79] Nivelle had charm, self-confidence, and persuasiveness as well as left-wing political connections. He maintained that with new mobile 155mm guns (in fact still few in number), creeping barrages, and dispersed-order tactics he had discovered how to breach enemy lines, and he offered an alternative to the slow and costly Somme attrition process. His tactics foreshadowed the more mobile campaigning of 1918, although he oversold them. But his proposed strategy resembled that of September 1915: a preliminary Franco-British attack near Arras, followed by a principal stroke delivered by the French against the Chemin des Dames ridge north of the Aisne. He won backing not only from Briand but also from Lloyd George, who at a conference at Calais in February achieved a *fait accompli* against his generals by accepting Nivelle's plan and placing Haig under the latter's command for the duration of the campaign. Actually, as in 1916, Haig and perhaps also the government envisaged combined operations as a prelude to a British-led Flanders offensive. But in the meantime Nivelle's plan meant the French would take the heaviest losses, and a British commander whose competence Lloyd George doubted would come under a French one who spoke fluent English and had won over the cabinet. These were shifting sands on which to base the Allies' first experiment with a single commander-in-chief.[80]

From this point on Nivelle's star faded. The German retreat to the Hindenburg Line was not in itself crippling, as the attack sectors at Arras and on the Aisne were largely unaffected, and although the Germans now held shorter lines, so (as Nivelle pointed out) did the Allies. But revolution in Petrograd dashed hopes of Russian support, Italy remained inactive, and America's imminent intervention cast doubt on whether the Allies really needed to take the risk. In March Briand was replaced as premier by Alexandre Ribot, whose war minister, Paul Painlevé, was openly sceptical about the plan and encouraged Nivelle's subordinates to voice their doubts. Nivelle insisted that not to attack would invite another German onslaught like Verdun, and that France's strength was waning while Ludendorff was restoring Germany's advantage. The risks of doing nothing exceeded those of acting. Finally, and on condition that he called off the operation after two days if it was unsuccessful, the government gave him the go-ahead.[81]

The preliminary British offensive at Arras that began on 9 April suggested that the BEF too had learned from the Somme. The opening bombardment was twice as intense (fewer shells were duds and they were more accurately delivered), new and more sensitive '106' fuses cut the wire, and unprecedented quantities of gas killed the Germans' transport horses and silenced their guns. The assault troops, moved up in tunnels or concealed in cellars in the town, numbered eighteen divisions against seven; the Germans had expected a longer bombardment and held their reserves too far back. In a feat of arms that became as emblematic for their Dominion as Gallipoli was for the Anzacs, Canadian troops stormed the heights of Vimy ridge on the left of the advance, taking 13,000 prisoners and 200 guns. Though the attack of 9 April 1917 was on almost as large a scale as that of 1 July 1916, British casualties in the first three days were fewer than half those in the opening phase on the Somme, and the infantry advanced up to three-and-a-half miles. Arras was not meant as a breakthrough operation, however, and an attempted cavalry follow-up in a snowstorm on the second day was a predictable failure. Once again Haig then prolonged the battle beyond the week that was originally planned. Australian attacks on the right flank of the sector that (unlike the rest of the offensive) ran up against the Hindenburg Line eventually established a foothold in the German positions, but at tremendous cost. Operations continued into May (at the price of 150,000 British losses against 100,000 German ones) mainly in order to support the French, from whose attack on the Chemin des Dames much more had been expected and whose mediocre results were therefore all the more mortifying.[82]

The Chemin des Dames was where the Allies had been halted after the Marne. From the ridge the Germans, aided by air superiority in the sector, could see far below them. Having captured crucial French documents in raids during February they had plenty of warning and time to prepare, concentrating twenty-one divisions in the line and fifteen counter-attack divisions behind it. The French preliminary bombardment of 11 million shells was dispersed over a front of thirty miles; it tailed off towards the end and was simply not intense enough, partly because Nivelle insisted (like Haig in 1916) that it should cover the full depth of the German positions rather than concentrate on the front line. On 16 April the French attacked in a blizzard, placing 10,000 Senegalese in the crucial sector. The colonial troops had no experience of such conditions, and over half became casualties.[83] The German guns set the French Schneider tanks ablaze, and the infantry had to pick their way through fortified zones infested with machine guns mounted in pillboxes. After two weeks Nivelle's troops had captured most of the ridge at a cost of 130,000 killed and wounded, but breakthrough never looked near. In May Painlevé replaced him by Pétain, who halted the operations, but too late to prevent the units involved from mutinying.[84] The débâcle also weakened Lloyd George relative to the British military and ended ignominiously the first experiment with an Allied supreme command. The British reverted to their Flanders priority and for the next few months Allied strategy was hardly better co-ordinated than in 1915. It was back, almost, to square one.

If the great trench systems were the outstanding strategic novelty of 1915, the immense attrition battles fought in 1916 at Verdun, on the Somme, and in the east were even more unprecedented. The two sides had followed contrasting roads in order to arrive at this slaughterhouse. On the Central Powers' side, during 1915 Falkenhayn pursued big but still limited offensives in order to secure Germany's and Austria-Hungary's eastern borders and force Russia to a separate peace, or at least to destroy its offensive capacity. He achieved enough to be able in spring 1916 to strike westward, as he had wanted to do all along, but in an operation with which he intended less to take territory than to mete out casualties until France could stand no more. Yet this enterprise proved almost as damaging to the German army as to the French one, and when the Allies retaliated he was forced back on the ropes. Hindenburg and Ludendorff contained the immediate crisis, but had no remedy, beyond the submarine campaign and an armaments build-up, for the larger strategic conundrum. Germany's enemies were too strong for it.

The Allies, by contrast, lacking a central leadership, pursued a series of parallel wars until the 1915 defeats enabled Joffre (with Briand's backing) to steer them towards the Chantilly plan. The plan might serve French interests but it would also co-ordinate Allied efforts. Refusing to be panicked by Falkenhayn's and Conrad's spring 1916 offensives, the Allies regained the initiative in the summer, and Haig, Foch, Brusilov, and Cadorna followed Falkenhayn in inflicting and incurring enormous losses. Even if the military wished to persist with the Chantilly strategy and with offensive attrition in 1917, however, not one of the Allied governments had the requisite political will for it, and Nivelle's defeat, followed by the French mutinies and the Russian Revolution, left them as bereft as their enemies of a viable strategy. Germany, Austria-Hungary, France, and Russia all faced looming manpower crises for which increasing unit firepower could only partially compensate. Britain and Italy were approaching a similar predicament, raising the question for everyone of whether the war could yet be won, and whether 'winning' any longer had much meaning. One strategic concept after another had foundered on tactical, technological, and logistical realities, and these realities must now be analysed.

CHAPTER 7

TECHNOLOGY, LOGISTICS, AND TACTICS

T HE HISTORY OF the two sides' strategies from 1915 to spring 1917 was one of frustration and failure. To explain why, it is necessary to re-examine how the battles were fought: how the troops and their equipment were deployed, and what weapons were available. An impasse at the level of tactics drove the two sides towards more ruthless strategies: the Allies towards escalating doses of attrition and the Germans towards Verdun and unrestricted submarine warfare. But this was not a static equilibrium, and both attackers and defenders were increasing their tactical sophistication and the number and power of the weapons at their disposal. Developments were in progress that after 1917 would break the stalemate. The emphasis here will be first on the conditions of defence and attack in the west, and then on a consideration of how far these conditions also held good elsewhere.

The Western Front has been likened to the outworks of the Roman Empire and the Iron Curtain that bisected Cold War Europe, but really it was without historical parallel. The trenches at the siege of Petersburg, in the closing stages of the American Civil War, were fifty-three miles long; but both they and those round Mukden in the Russo-Japanese War were eventually outflanked. In contrast the Western Front extended for some 475 miles and could not be outflanked, short of violating Dutch or Swiss neutrality, or by an Allied landing in Flanders.[1] From the end of 1914 until 1918 it moved, with the exception of Germany's voluntary withdrawal to the Hindenburg Line, barely more than five miles in either direction. It was also the most decisive and intractable front, where more troops and guns were concentrated than in any other theatre, and the graveyard not only of Falkenhayn's grand design at Verdun but also of successive Allied initiatives in Champagne, on the Somme, and on the Chemin des Dames.

The ultimate defence was the infantry: German, French, and British Empire soldiers all displaying a stubbornness and resilience that many Russian and

Austro-Hungarian units lacked. As all three armies showed comparable determination in attacking, however, the morale variable mattered less than on other
fronts or in later periods of the war. The Western Front was distinctive not only
for the troops' fighting qualities but also for their numbers. The French and
German armies were several times their size in 1870, and a huge British army
later joined them. Each side mustered some 5,000 troops per mile of front,[2]
enough to garrison it thickly and to hold counter-attack forces in reserve. It
helped that the more rugged and forested southernmost hundred miles was less
suitable for large-scale operations and saw little fighting apart from a series of
French attacks in the Vosges mountains in 1915. Even between Verdun and
Ypres many sectors were quiet and never saw great battles. The most active sectors were in Flanders and on the two flanks of the Noyon bulge in Artois and
Champagne.[3] Although the high force-to-space ratio was an essential reason for
the Western Front's immobility, however, it must be considered in conjunction
with the field fortifications and their supporting infrastructure, the weapons
used to hold them, and defensive tactics.

The Germans took the initiative in creating the trench system. Trenches might
be claustrophobic, verminous, smelly, wet, and cold, but they offered the best protection available against blast and bullets, and they saved lives. Most of the armies
suffered their heaviest proportionate losses during the mobile campaigning of the
first weeks of war. Digging in gave Germany a glacis for its western border while
consolidating its grip on France and almost all of Belgium, either to keep in perpe-
tuity or to trade in. It released forces to attack elsewhere, at Ypres in autumn 1914
or later in Poland and Serbia, and OHL endorsed it as a lesser evil that would at
least halt the Allies' advance.[4]

In January 1915 Falkenhayn directed that the line must be so organized that a
small force could hold it for a long time against superior numbers. A strong first position must be the backbone of resistance, to be held at all costs and at once retaken
if any part of it were captured. Linked to it by communication trenches should be a
second line, to shelter the garrison when the first was bombarded. Further lines to
the rear should be beyond the range of enemy field guns. Falkenhayn wanted to
lessen casualties by keeping the front-line cover thin, but if the main garrison were
too far back the advanced guard would be more likely to surrender and the artillery could not protect them. Some of his commanders opposed a second line in
principle, as making the defence of the first less stubborn. In the light of experience
OHL nevertheless ordered in May that a reserve line must be built 2–3,000 yards
behind the first along the entire front: a colossal undertaking that was completed by
the end of the year.[5] The Germans had the advantage of being able to select higher
and drier ground, with good digging and above the water table, which lent itself to
artillery observation. The great battles in Champagne, on the Somme, and at Arras
therefore consisted of Allied attacks uphill against defences that by 1916–17 were
up to 4–5,000 yards in depth, against the 1,000 yards characteristic of British ones.[6]
Those on the Somme, which followed Falkenhayn's prescriptions closely, lay behind two belts of barbed wire, each three to five feet high and thirty yards deep.
The 'front line' actually comprised three trenches 150 to 200 yards apart, the first
for sentry groups, the second for the main garrison, and the third for support

troops. The Germans' forward trenches (like British ones) were not straight but set in every ten yards or so in a 'traverse', or dog-leg, that protected troops against shell blasts or enfilading fire if the enemy captured a portion of the line. They built deeper dug-outs: six to nine feet down in 1915 and twenty-five to thirty feet on the Somme. A thousand yards behind the first position lay an intermediate line of machine-gun strongpoints; and behind that communication trenches led to the reserve position (the 'second line' of Falkenhayn's memorandum), as heavily wired as the first and out of range of the Allied artillery, which would therefore need to be moved up to support an assault on it. Another 3,000 yards back lay the third position, added after the experience of September 1915, when the French had reached the German second line. Telephone cables laid six or more feet deep linked the artillery in the rear with the front trench. On the Somme the British did not capture most of the third line until late September.[7]

'No man's land' between the front lines might be as narrow as five to ten yards or as wide as 1,000, but it averaged 100 to 400 yards. Beyond it, when the Germans attacked, they encountered trench systems less solid and elaborate than their own, though still adequate. The Belgians held the sector stretching fifteen miles inland from the coast, and the British zone ran south of them for twenty to twenty-five miles at the end of 1914 but over 100 by the start of 1917. None the less, until the Americans arrived the French guarded at least three-quarters of the Allied line. In January 1915 Joffre directed his troops to divide their front between 'active' and 'passive' sectors. Strongpoints in the former would cover the latter, which would be heavily wired but guarded only by sentries. Shellproof shelters behind the strongpoints should accommodate counter-attack companies, and a second line would be dug two miles behind. The entire complex should be garrisoned thinly to economize on manpower and save casualties. In the forested Vosges, and even in the tangled woods around Verdun, there were separate blockhouses rather than a continuous defence.[8] The British approach lay somewhere between that of the French and the Germans. Their front was more thickly garrisoned than most of the French one, and they could yield less ground without surrendering their lateral railways or being driven into the sea. Normally they had three parallel positions: the front, support, and reserve lines. The first line was built up with sandbagged breastworks as well as being dug into the earth: in waterlogged areas the 'trenches' might be mainly above ground. The first line comprised the fire and the command trenches, some twenty yards apart. In the fire trench small forward units occupied the 'bays' between the traverses; the command trench contained strongpoints, dug-outs, and latrines. Communication trenches ran to the support trench, 70 to 100 yards behind, which had more wire and deeper dug-outs; another 4–500 yards back lay the reserve trench, with yet more strongpoints and dug-outs; and behind that, the artillery. In practice the system was far less orderly than laid down in regulations, or than in the mock-up created in Kensington Gardens for the London public. In active sectors trenches were continually blown up by mining and bombardment and the approach to the front became a labyrinth of craters and impasses, to whose complexities newcomers needed seasoned guides.[9]

In their way the trenches were an imposing engineering achievement, the more so if account is taken of the immense infrastructure behind them. It comprised

hospitals, barracks, training camps, ammunition dumps, artillery parks, and telephone networks, as well as military roads and canals, but pre-eminently it meant
railways. The Western Front lay in one of the most densely tracked parts of Europe, and both sides added hundreds more miles of standard- and narrow-gauge
line. In 1914 the Germans took the trunk railway running from Metz to Lille (and
onwards east of Ypres towards the sea); the fighting stabilized between it and the
main lines running behind the Allied front from Nancy via Paris to Amiens. In the
British sector two transverse lines extended northwards from Amiens to Hazebrouck and Dunkirk, and a third, to Arras, was added after the Somme.[10] Both
sides pre-positioned support forces near vulnerable portions of their fronts, but the
railways enabled larger reinforcements. By day two at Neuve Chapelle the German number of defenders had risen from 4,000 to 20,000;[11] the French ran in 832
reinforcement trains to Verdun in the first three weeks of that battle; and in the
first week of the Somme Germany moved up ten divisions in 494 trains.[12] Beyond
the railheads both sides depended heavily on horses and ultimately men to convey
supplies to their artillery and the front lines,[13] but the railways gave the defender a
crucial advantage in funnelling in reinforcements before the attackers could consolidate and expand their footholds.

In addition to the railway network, Western Front defenders benefited from the
panoply of innovations ushered in by the nineteenth-century revolution in military
technology. In trained hands a breech-loading magazine rifle could fire up to fifteen rounds a minute, at a range of half a mile. Using smokeless powder and firing
in a prone position, riflemen were almost invisible, and the kinetic energy of a ro-
tating high-velocity bullet gave it an impact against bones and tissue out of all proportion to its size.[14] But machine-guns and field artillery were the mass killers.
European armies all had versions of the Maxim gun, and were equipped with light
as well as heavy machine-guns as the war progressed. A heavy machine-gun typically weighed 40–60kg, even without its carriage and ammunition belts, and
needed three to six men to operate it; light machine-guns (such as the British
Lewis gun and the German MG 08/15) weighed 9–14kg, and were more suitable
as offensive weapons, as a man could – with difficulty – carry one. In August 1914
a standard German infantry regiment comprised twelve companies of riflemen
and only one of machine-gunners (with six weapons), but in 1915 six more
machine-guns were added and in 1916 the same again, raising the proportion of
machine-guns to rifles from 1:12 to 1:4. By 1917 the ratio in many divisions was
1:2.[15] One heavy machine-gun could fire up to sixty rounds a minute, equivalent
to as many as forty riflemen. Its range was greater, and it could 'beat' (i.e., fill with
flying lead) an ellipse 2,500 yards long and 500 yards wide.[16] As long as its atten-
dants fed in belts of bullets and topped it up with cooling fluid it could continue its
lethal traverses, one at Loos firing 12,500 rounds in an afternoon.[17] At Neuve
Chapelle two machine-gun posts held up the British until reinforcements arrived;
and two guns halted the French at Neuville St-Vaast on the first day of the May
1915 attack.[18] On the second day at Loos German machine-gunners inflicted thousands of casualties on novice BEF divisions for almost no loss to themselves. On 1
July 1916, however, many British casualties were caused by artillery rather than
machine-guns.[19] Both sides kept field guns targeted on no man's land and the op-

posing first line so that they could respond at once with 'SOS fire' if the sentries sent up flares. By September 1915 in Champagne the Germans had perfected the art of siting their field guns on 'reverse slopes', so that as the Allies came over a crest and advanced downhill they were in full view from the German artillery, which the slope had kept invisible from the Allied gunners.[20] At Verdun French artillery west of the Meuse disrupted Falkenhayn's attack plan, while on the Chemin des Dames German guns wreaked havoc on Nivelle's tanks. In this period of the war the combination of trenches, railways, rifles, machine-guns, and artillery was too strong for attacking forces to overwhelm.

The principal weapon available to the attackers was bombardment. Both GHQ and GQG altered their tactical doctrine during 1915 to stress its vital role in destroying enemy positions before the infantry could occupy them.[21] It has been calculated that shellfire caused 58 per cent of the war's military dead.[22] Yet the artillery was a blunt instrument.[23] The quick-firing field gun's flat trajectory made it of little use against entrenchments, especially as in 1914 most field gun shells were not high explosive but shrapnel, scattering fragments that mowed down infantry in the open but lacked the blast effect needed against earthworks. In any case the Allies were short of shells of any description by the first winter of the war. For precisely such reasons the Germans could protect themselves against the French 75mm cannon by digging in. Moreover, French divisions were not equipped like German ones with light field howitzers (whose curved trajectory was much more appropriate against trenches), the whole army possessing only seventy-eight 105mm howitzers in June 1915.[24] Their stock of heavy artillery was small, outdated, and kept under GQG's central control. Matters did improve. In Champagne in September 1915 the French attacked with 1,100 heavy guns, compared with 400 in Artois in May, and after a bombardment lasting not four hours but several days.[25] Similarly, before the Somme the British had in total more than twice as many guns as at Loos, and four times the number of howitzers.[26] But it was still not enough, and not simply because the German defences grew ever more sophisticated. High explosive shells needed a heavy metal casing to stop them disintegrating: the explosives themselves accounted for only 900 tons of the 12,000 tons of munitions fired before the Somme.[27] Even so, many shells failed to detonate or did so in their own guns. Also, artillery fire was highly inaccurate. In the open campaigning of 1914, guns could operate as in previous wars by 'direct fire': the crew could see their target and fire ranging shots until they hit it. But in such conditions they too might be visible, and on the quick-firing battlefield visibility was hazardous. In trench warfare 'indirect fire' from a concealed position against an invisible target became the norm. In a procedure known as 'registering' the gunners adjusted the range, barrel elevation, and explosive charge on advice from a forward observation officer (FOO), ideally telephoning from the front line, or from an observer in an aircraft reporting by wireless.[28] Registering was slow and gave the enemy warning, while the FOO might be blinded by rain or smoke or his telephone line might be severed (and in a battle it often was, making communication dependent on carrier pigeons or runners). The Germans could tap into British telephone conversations within a one-mile radius, though in 1915–16 the British developed more secure communication methods such as the 'Fullerphone' and the 'power buzzer'.[29] Even when a gun had found its target, varying wind speeds and atmospheric temperatures and pressures could alter the fall of the shell, as could wear and tear to the barrel. For all these reasons, artillery preparation repeatedly yielded disappointing results. On the first day at Verdun an unprecedentedly intense German bombardment failed to annihilate a sketchy but cleverly dispersed French defence. When the assault troops advanced they came under heavy fire. On the Somme the British fired over 1.5 million shells in five days but on most of the front neither cut the Germans' wire, nor smashed their dug-outs, nor silenced their guns. British commanders operated by guesswork and failed to calculate (in fact grossly underestimated) the bombardment needed to destroy the enemy front line. They arrived at the correct formula almost by accident at Neuve Chapelle, where they stealthily concentrated almost all the BEF's artillery against a single-line defence, but they did not match this density of shells until Arras two years later.[30] Such quantities were needed against just the first position, however, that it was not feasible to destroy the entire depth of enemy trenches, and by attempting to do so Haig on the Somme and Nivelle on the Chemin des Dames ensured their artillery would be ineffective. Moreover, as the Somme battle developed the Germans left their trenches during barrage and dispersed into the surrounding shellholes, creating such an extended target that no bombardment could destroy it. Enlarging and prolonging the bombardment in the hope of blasting through a passage by weight of explosive and metal was a fruitless quest.

Reliance on artillery preparation also contributed to tactical inflexibility, and made surprise virtually unattainable. Preparing a Western Front offensive was akin to a major civil engineering project. The British used 21,000 black South Africans in labour battalions in Europe: by the end of the war they made up 25 per cent of the labour force on the Western Front.[31] The French imported labourers from China and Vietnam. But the soldiers themselves did most of the work, and an integral part of the trench experience was hard and unremitting manual effort. Preparations on the Somme began in December 1915 in a poorly accessible region that lacked housing, roads, and railways, and even surface water because of the chalky terrain. By July 1916 the British had dumped forward 2.96 million artillery rounds, laid 70,000 miles of telephone cable (7,000 at a depth of more than six feet), and built fifty-five miles of standard gauge railway for a battle expected to require 128 trains a day.[32] The French were at work for two months before the September 1915 offensive and the April 1917 attack – though in the latter case they needed more time than Nivelle's impatience allowed them because the proposed location's drawbacks included very poor transport links.[33] Among the reasons why Falkenhayn persisted at Verdun, Haig on the Somme, and Nivelle on the Chemin des Dames was the scale of the preliminary investment in each battleground and the delay and expense entailed in preparing fresh attacks elsewhere.

Given the limitations of heavy artillery it was unsurprising that both sides sought alternative solutions, mobilizing their scientific and industrial communities for the purpose. To begin with the Germans were not only better trained and equipped than their opponents for trench construction but also better provided with assault weapons. Hand grenades were standard issue in the German army in 1914, as were light mortars. The Mills bomb, which became the main British grenade, caused many accidents when first introduced, and only in 1916 did a safer version follow. The Stokes mortar, designed at private initiative and ordered by Lloyd George as minister of munitions, was similarly in general service only from 1916.[34] The Germans also introduced the flamethrower, first employed on the Western Front in February 1915. Virtually all the flamethrowers in the German army were brought to bear against the fortresses and blockhouses at Verdun, but they were used less frequently in the later stages of the battle as they had only a short range and their operators presented easy targets. The British on the Somme also employed flamethrowers, but despite the horrific injuries and panic they could generate, they were more spectacular than effective.[35] All these weapons, however, were more suited to raids or to clearing enemy trenches than helping troops cross no man's land in an offensive. Three other technologies promised more in this latter respect. The first was tunnelling under the enemy trenches to lay mines, which began in the winter of 1914–15 and was mainly a feature of the Anglo-German front. Mines were exploded on the first day of the Somme, although by being detonated ten minutes before zero hour they gave warning of the assault. Mining was an even slower and a more hazardous activity than preparation with heavy artillery, though if kept secret it could bring the benefit of surprise. It was unsuited, however, to be more than a supplementary attacking device.

The remaining two developments – poison gas and tanks – were much more important in the course of the war. Both were designed to overcome the trench stalemate. The British had experimented with gas before the war and the French fired projectiles from rifles and may have used gas grenades in the winter of 1914–15, but the substances concerned were irritant rather than lethal.[36] Although there are plausible grounds for saying the Allies would have used gas if Germany had not, the Germans are rightly saddled with the opprobrium attached to introducing it, which was to be one of the war crime charges levelled against them at the peace conference. After trying out tear gas against the Russians, on the afternoon of 22 April 1915 they commenced the second battle of Ypres by releasing the cloud of chlorine that began the massive chemical warfare that distinguished the First World War from preceding and from most subsequent armed conflicts. In all, 124,208 tons of gas were used during the war, half of this quantity by Germany. The quantity quadrupled from 1915 to 1916, doubled in 1917, and doubled again in 1918. By 1918 the technology employed about 75,000 civilians in large and dangerous manufacturing operations, as well as thousands of specialized troops. It claimed perhaps half a million casualties on the Western Front (including 25,000 fatalities), in addition to 10,000 in Italy and a large but unrecorded number in Russia. But gas warfare was a microcosm of the conflict as a whole in its combination of escalation with stalemate. The best chance of its becoming a breakthrough technology was when it was first used, but if a moment of opportunity existed here, it was, as usual, lost.

Germany much exceeded Britain and France in its manufacturing and research capacity in chemicals and until the end of the war it mass-produced toxic gases faster and more efficiently. Falkenhayn saw gas as a tactical tool that might facilitate the decisive result he craved in the west and compensate for shortages of shells. The Germans satisfied themselves that they could reconcile their actions with a pedantic reading of the 1899 Hague Convention, and Falkenhayn's technical adviser, Fritz

Haber, told him early retaliation was unlikely. Most of the army commanders were hostile, fearing that if the Allies did reciprocate Germany would be disadvantaged by the prevailing westerly winds over France and Flanders. The commander in the Ypres salient was willing to try, but it became evident that gas had major shortcomings. To save shells it was decided to deliver the chlorine from almost 6,000 pre-positioned cylinders, which were bulky to transport and difficult to conceal (although the Allies ignored the intelligence warnings), as well as being liable to leak and therefore extremely unpopular with the troops. Success depended on a favourable wind, which took weeks to materialize. OHL therefore did not expect spectacular results, but envisaged a limited operation that would disrupt the Allies' spring offensives, distract attention from Germany's troop movements to Russia, and (by capturing Pilckem Ridge), make the Ypres salient indefensible. In the event, when the gas cloud was released at 5 p.m. against Algerians who mostly panicked and fled it opened an 8,000-yard wide breach north of Ypres, but the Germans had few reserves on hand and the troops they sent forward had no masks. The Allies used the night to close the gap, and a second release, against Canadians two days later, had less impact. By June primitive respirators had been issued en masse to the Allied armies, and in September the French used gas in Champagne and the British at Loos. Haig had high hopes for it and was confident it would enable him to break the German line despite his continuing shortage of shells, but on the morning of the attack at Loos the air was still and although the chlorine cloud helped in some sectors it gassed more of his own men than the enemy.[37]

After Loos there was little likelihood or expectation on either side that gas would be a war winning weapon, although both continued to use it (the Germans against the Russians during the summer campaign in Poland in 1915 and on the Western Front a dozen times more down to August 1916). On balance it aided attack over defence. Although both sides introduced better respirators (notably the British Small Box Respirator or SBR) they also introduced more poisonous gases and new methods of delivering them. Phosgene, six times more toxic than chlorine, was brought in by the French at Verdun, fired in shells and therefore less dependent on the wind; the Germans used diophosgene or 'Green Cross' shells before their culminating attack there on 23 June (though they ended the bombardment too soon and French masks were reasonably effective against it).[38] On the first day at Arras the British fired great quantities of phosgene from a new mortar-like device, the Livens projector. The projector was much easier to set up than the cylinders had been, and the Germans greatly feared it because it gave almost no warning. In general the Allies were gaining the edge in the gas war until in July 1917 the Germans attacked the British with mustard gas, opening a major new phase. Although both sides pointed out, with some justice, that gas caused less terrible injuries and fewer fatalities than did high explosive, it continued to evoke peculiar horror, and made conditions for the front-line soldiers even more difficult. Once the gas shell replaced the cylinders its use became much more widespread. Yet it remained an ancillary, harassing weapon that at Second Ypres, Verdun, and Arras facilitated temporary successes but produced no radical results.

Such results were even less likely from tanks, which the British used on the Somme in September 1916 and at Arras, and the French in the Nivelle offensive.

Tanks were initiated independently in Britain and France, the Germans making no move until they saw the Allied weapons in action. In France the visionary behind them was Colonel J. E. Estienne, who secured an audience with Joffre in 1915 and was authorized to work in conjunction with the Schneider armaments firm. However, it was in Britain that the first combat-ready tank, the Mark I, was built by Foster & Co., a Lincoln agricultural machinery company, under the aegis of the Landships Committee at the Admiralty, which Churchill had set up and funded. Churchill in turn had been fired by a memorandum that Hankey had submitted to the cabinet after meeting Estienne's British equivalent, Lt.-Colonel Ernest Swinton. Both Swinton and Estienne had seen the Holt tractor, an American vehicle with caterpillar tracks, and both viewed it as a model for a trench-crossing device. And if Joffre's backing was crucial to Estienne, Swinton (who headed a new Tank Detachment created in February 1916) enjoyed Haig's enthusiastic support once the latter heard about the project. Indeed, Swinton found the enthusiasm excessive: he would have preferred to wait until a mass attack could be unleashed without warning.[39] All the same, neither Haig's use of tanks on the Somme nor his use of gas at Loos suggest that he was blindly resistant to new technologies.

Tanks achieved little at this stage not because of obstruction by the military establishment but because they were far from being the weapons of 1939–45. Even if deployed *en masse*, they could not have restored open warfare. The basic problem was that they were underpowered. The British Mark I to Mark V tanks weighed approximately thirty tons and had engines of up to 100 horsepower; the Shermans and T-34s of the Second World War were of similar weights but had engines of 430 and 500 horsepower respectively.[40] The Mark I had a top speed of three to four miles per hour, and a maximum of eight hours' endurance. It was lightly armed, with machine-guns or two small cannon. It was difficult to drive, hot and full of carbon monoxide fumes, an easy target for artillery, and highly susceptible to breakdown. Despite its weight, the Germans' new armour piercing bullets could penetrate it. It could not negotiate the ruined Somme woods and was vulnerable in villages. Nor could it climb steep slopes and extricate itself from shellholes. Of forty-nine machines fit for duty on 15 September 1916, thirteen failed to reach the start line. The preparatory barrage left 'lanes' along which they could travel over undisturbed ground, but because so many failed to move forward the supporting infantry walked into intact German machine-guns. However, three reached and helped to capture Flers, one mile from the start, and two carried on to the next village before German guns halted them. On day one at Arras sixty were available but again many broke down before the start of the offensive, to which they contributed little. On day two eleven tanks had been detailed to support an Australian attack on the village of Bullecourt, but they failed completely and an unsupported infantry assault was repulsed with 3,000 casualties, creating a legacy of bitterness against the British high command and tank crews.[41] On the Chemin des Dames the heavy French Schneider models suffered even more severely from breakdown, their fuel tanks were located where they were easily ignited, and German gunfire set many ablaze. The state-built St-Chamond machines presented even easier targets.[42] The tanks' debut was patchy, to put it mildly. They seemed best suited to small-scale infantry support, crushing wire, silencing machine-gun posts, boosting the Allied troops' morale, and unnerving their opponents. These accomplishments were enough to convince GHQ that hundreds more should be ordered, while the French responded to the Chemin des Dames debacle by pinning their faith on lighter Renault two-man vehicles. During the central period of the war, however, neither tanks nor gas could restore mobility.

This being the case, the best prospect remained with the infantry and artillery, and better co-ordination between them. Another new technology – that of aircraft – was mainly important precisely for improving artillery effectiveness, both through direct observation (used by the British as early as the September 1914 battle of the Aisne) and especially through aerial photography, which was practised from spring 1915.[43] In 1914 aircraft had had a prominent reconnaissance function – a French plane had observed von Kluck's First Army turning east of Paris and German planes had monitored Russian movements before Tannenberg – but this became less crucial once the fronts stabilized. An independent ground attack role was only just beginning, essentially because the aircraft were under-powered for carrying heavy payloads, although German aircraft dropped bombs in the opening phase at Verdun while British ones bombed five enemy trains during the battle of Loos and strafed German troops and dropped fifty tons of bombs during the Somme.[44] Finally, a strategic bombing role was also in its infancy, and it began not with aircraft but with the German navy's Zeppelin airships, which lay unused because of the High Seas Fleet's inactivity. Initially raiding near the British east coast, they first hit London in May 1915, killing 127 people and injuring 352 during the year. Typically they arrived on fine, moonless nights, and although the British soon learned how to detect their movements by intercepting their wireless messages, at first there was no means of destroying them.[45] In 1916 they ranged more widely, reached the Midlands and Scotland, and forced widespread black-outs. From September 1916 onwards, however, the defenders got the measure of the problem, locating the airships by eavesdropping on their radio messages and then shooting down several with anti-aircraft artillery and with fighter aircraft firing new explosive ammunition. From 1917 Gotha bombers replaced the airships as the main air weapon against Britain. The Zeppelins set a precedent for new forms of attack on civilians and reinforced the British public's sense that its enemies were beyond the pale, but their damage to the Allied war effort was slight.[46]

Assistance to the artillery was therefore the crucial role of the new arm. By 1915 British aircraft were carrying radio and evolving special codes to communicate with their gunners and monitor the effects of their fire, but the task of direct observation was mainly accomplished by tethered balloons, linked by telephone cables to their batteries.[47] The balloons, however, were obvious targets for enemy fighters, and soon aerial combats swirled round them. Aircraft defended the balloonists, and carried out photographic reconnaissance themselves. In general the advantage in these operations lay with the Allies, and especially with the French, who had far more planes and pilots than Britain or Russia in 1914 and owned the world's biggest aircraft industry. The British Royal Flying Corps (RFC) lagged behind France and Germany for the first two years. Yet at first there was barely an air war in the literal sense, as neither side's aircraft had machine-guns mounted, and many more casualties resulted from accidents than from enemy action. Most aircraft had 'pusher' engines situated behind the pilot, even though these provided less power and manoeuvrability than a 'tractor' propeller at the front, the problem with the latter being that a fixed machine-gun might damage the blades. In spring 1915, however, the French aviator Roland Garros equipped his aircraft with a machine-gun that fired through the propeller, which had blades fitted with plates to deflect any bullets that hit them. The Germans downed and captured his machine, and the Fokker firm used the information derived from it to pioneer a synchronization device, enabling them to fit a forward-facing machine-gun that fired through the propeller of a new single-engined monoplane without hitting the blades. For several months in the winter and spring of 1915–16 the 'Fokker scourge' gave the Germans the edge, though more because of the intimidation created by their monopoly of the new technology than because many Allied aircraft were shot down. By concentrating their airpower round Verdun the Germans partially concealed their preparations for the battle, and they enjoyed control of the skies in the first weeks of action. But by May they had lost it, the Allies capturing a Fokker plane as well as devising their own synchronization system and introducing new models with 'pushing' propellers that did not need such equipment and yet still outperformed German aircraft.[48] In the opening phases of the Somme, the RFC commander, Hugh Trenchard, shared with Haig a commitment to a 'relentless and incessant offensive', and to driving the Germans out of their airspace, even if this meant neglecting the defence of British spotter aircraft and accepting punishing casualties among his crews.[49] Beginning the battle with 426 pilots, the RFC lost 308 killed, wounded, and missing, and a further 268 were sent home, to be replaced by cursorily trained novices whose life expectancy by the autumn was barely one month.[50] By September, however, a new generation of German Albatros D.III fighters was helping to redress the balance once again, and in the 'bloody week' of April 1917 the German 'circuses' or fighter groups inflicted unprecedented losses on the RFC at Arras and commanded the sky over the Chemin des Dames, virtually halting French photographic reconnaissance and balloon observation. Only in May and June, with the arrival of a further generation of aircraft, including the British S.E.5 and Sopwith Pup and the French Spad, did the Allies regain the edge.[51] In the skies as on the ground, therefore, the initiative passed backwards and forwards, yet ultimately air combat was still marginal. Crushing air superiority helped the British very little on 1 July 1916, and its loss did not prevent much greater success on the first day at Arras, even if at other times (the first phase at Verdun, the last stage on the Somme, the Chemin des Dames) the Germans' air superiority reinforced their effectiveness on the ground.

Aerial observation and photography contributed, however, to a less glamorous but more significant trend towards greater artillery effectiveness. By 1917 the French and British had more and heavier guns firing larger numbers of more reliable shells, and a greater proportion of high explosive rather than shrapnel. They were also achieving improved accuracy. One manifestation was 'map shooting': the ability to hit a map co-ordinate without giving prior warning to the enemy and disclosing one's own position by registering. This became easier once the BEF had prepared new large-scale maps of the entire British front, and was linked to a second development, which was improved counter-battery fire, the British using new techniques such as flash-spotting and sound-ranging to catch up with the French expertise in detecting enemy guns.[52] These were highly skilled techniques, and it took months or even years for men from civilian life to learn them.[53] The third was the creeping barrage, which was first attempted at Loos and become general in the later stages on the Somme. Infantry followed as closely as possible behind a barrage that advanced as little as twenty yards ahead of them, its purpose being less to destroy than to neutralize the enemy defences by forcing the Germans to take cover until the attackers were almost upon them, denying them the moments after the barrage lifted when they could take up firing positions on the parapet. Its effects were even greater when combined (from Arras onwards) with new '106' fuses that detonated the shells when they hit the soil rather than after burying themselves, thus causing much more damage to barbed wire.[54] In the Allied attacks of 1917 – especially later in the year – more of the German artillery was silenced beforehand and the attacking infantry were better protected.

To some extent also, the infantry's own conduct when attacking had altered. The notorious waves sent walking forward on the first day of the Somme were atypical by this stage in the war. The Germans began in 1915 to experiment with surprise attacks and raids by prototype units for their later stormtroop forces: specially trained and equipped squads moving independently and using flamethrowers, trench mortars, light machine-guns, and grenades. On day one at Verdun pioneer units with wirecutters and explosives cut the French wire, flamethrowers were turned on the strongpoints, and although the main assault came in a wave it followed behind a creeping barrage. When Ludendorff took over at OHL he demanded an assault squad in each army, and issued new instructions on assault tactics.[55] On the French side, Pétain used aerial photography as early as May 1915 to assist his gunners before attacking Vimy ridge, and trained his infantry to advance as soon as the barrage lifted. The French amended their tactical doctrine after the 1915 offensives and Verdun, and at the start of the Somme their infantry dashed forward in small groups that gave each other covering fire to distract the defence. Nivelle's Verdun counterattacks followed a similar model,[56] and the French created their own special assault formations, the *grenadiers d'élite*, in January 1917.[57] These new practices foreshadowed a transformation in doctrine. The French captain André Laffargue's pamphlet on 'The Attack in Trench Warfare', written in the light of his experiences in the Artois offensive of May 1915, has attracted much attention from historians as a pioneering statement of the need for infiltration tactics, though it was neither completely innovative nor the sole source of the doctrinal changes. None the less, it was used as a French army manual and by 1916 had been translated into English and German, influencing both Nivelle and OHL.[58] Even the British, whose commanders appear to have followed their unimaginative tactics on 1 July 1916 because they doubted the New Armies had the skill, experience, or cohesion to behave more independently, reconsidered in the light of the Somme and issued new guidelines early in 1917.[59] In short, Verdun and the Somme were a learning process, although no combination of tactics without massive material superiority was likely to spare attacking forces from slow and difficult progress at high cost.

A final reason for the tactical stalemate was that the defenders too were on a learning curve.[60] Falkenhayn's insistence on holding the first line was increasingly criticized in OHL's Operations Section in 1915–16, its officers foreseeing that as Allied artillery improved, the cost of garrisoning it would rise. Both sides suffered at Verdun from concentrating men in the forward trenches, and in the early stages on the Somme the Germans suffered again. As the battle developed they mounted a more dispersed defence, which Fritz von Lossberg, the Second Army's chief of staff, encouraged by devolving tactical decisions to battalion commanders, recognizing that messages from divisional headquarters took eight to ten hours to reach them. After Hindenburg and Ludendorff closed down operations at Verdun, fresh troops and guns became available while the Germans challenged Allied air superiority, thus succeeding after September 1916 (assisted by the weather) in bringing the Anglo-French advance virtually to a halt and repulsing offensives with counterattacks. In response to the greater weight of enemy artillery they evolved a more flexible system of defence, despite the misgivings of many of their own commanders. Ludendorff wished to fight a more economical defensive battle in the west and had a more open mind than Falkenhayn about how to do it. As well as approving in September 1916 the construction of what became the Hindenburg Line he asked his staff to prepare a new text on defensive doctrine, which was issued – not without criticism – in December 1916. Its authors advocated a thin forward line that would lure the attackers into an extended battle zone where they would be fired on from all sides before being repulsed by counter-attacks from fresh troops stationed beyond artillery range in the rear, and in April 1917 the front lines were indeed less densely garrisoned than in July 1916. At Arras the German Sixth Army was surprised with its counter-attack divisions fifteen miles distant when the British attacked at 5.30 on a snowy April morning, their barrage having lifted earlier than the defenders had anticipated. On the Chemin des Dames, in contrast, where the Germans knew exactly what to expect, they held the front line thinly, and the French infantry who got beyond the first defences found themselves ringed by fire from concrete machine-gun posts. If Arras demonstrated how the methods and technology of attack had moved on, the Chemin des Dames underlined that the defence had evolved too, and still retained the overall advantage.

How far can this analysis be extended to other theatres? The Gallipoli peninsula was a tiny battlefront in which the force-to-space ratios were even greater than in Western Europe. As it had no railways both sides were supplied by sea, the British and French from Mudros and the Turks from Constantinople across the Sea of Marmara. The Allies were less well endowed with munitions and supplies of all kinds than on the Western Front, they had minimal air support, and they lost their backing from naval guns when the U-boat threat prompted the Admiralty to withdraw its battleships. None the less they attempted to fight up more precipitous hills than any in France against a determined enemy equipped with modern rifles and machine-guns. Once the Central Powers could transport heavy artillery by rail to Constantinople the Allies had little alternative to disengagement. In general terms high force-to-space ratios and the firepower revolution operated similarly at Gallipoli and in France.

The same applied to the Italian front, where by 1916 1.5 million Italian troops faced perhaps half that number of Austrians. Although the Austro-Italian border was

some 375 miles long, its two active sectors – the Isonzo and the Trentino – formed
only a small portion of the whole, the Isonzo front being some sixty miles long.[61]
Hence the force-to-space ratios were again high. Along most of the border the Alps
rose like a wall from the north Italian plain, effectively inhibiting the attackers. Conditions here were far worse even than in France: trenches had to be blasted out of
the rock with explosives, or cut into the sides of glaciers. Thousands of soldiers froze
to death, were asphyxiated at high altitudes, or were buried by avalanches. In the
Isonzo sector a narrow gap existed between the Julian Alps and the limestone
plateau known as the Carso, but the river Isonzo itself formed a barrier and the Austrians established fortified positions parallel to it. Stalemate set in almost immediately on the Isonzo and persisted down to 1917, while the 1916 Austrian attack in
the Trentino, though gaining more ground (and in more mountainous terrain) than
the Italians on the Isonzo, had been contained even before Brusilov's offensive distracted Conrad. In 1915 the Austrians were relatively more outnumbered than the
Germans in France, but they had the benefit of topography – arid and rocky
plateaux rising to the east of a fast-flowing watercourse – and they had been improving their railway infrastructure for years. The Italians were less well supplied with
heavy guns and munitions than the French and British, and the Austrians outnumbered them in machine-guns. Halting the attacks proved unexpectedly easily. According to a French observer the Italian artillery, dispersed along too wide a front,
simply failed to destroy the Austrian guns and trenches and the high command
seemed not to know how much preparation was needed.[62] A year later the position
was similar: because the Italians' artillery failed to destroy the Austrian second-line
defences and was poor at counter-battery fire, their infantry ran into accurate defensive barrages and counter-attacks. They took more prisoners and gained more territory than in 1915, but were still only crawling forward.[63] Although Cadorna
increased the troops and guns at his disposal as the war progressed, his army seems
to have learned little from the Western Front, experimenting with the creeping barrage only in spring 1917, and reforming its infantry tactics very slowly.[64] Yet the Austrians themselves were too weak to attack, and the endurance of the ordinary Italian
soldier should not be underestimated. Until the Germans arrived in autumn 1917
neither side could break the impasse.

If at Gallipoli and on the Italian front the tactical dynamics of the fighting resembled those in France and Belgium, elsewhere this was less true. The force-to-
space ratios in the Middle East and Africa were infinitely lower and the logistical
circumstances vastly different. The initial problem might be in locating the enemy,
rather than reconnoitring across no man's land. The Caucasus front, an unknown
theatre with extremes of climate and terrain, is difficult to compare with anything
in Europe, though the mountain warfare of the Carpathians and the Trentino may
offer analogies. On the other hand attacking forces were frustrated by entrenched
defenders with rifles and machine-guns at Tanga in November 1914, at Ctesiphon
a year later, and when the British relieving force failed to break through the Turkish siege positions round Kut. When Murray attacked Gaza in spring 1917, he
launched tank attacks against barbed wire and trench defences, though the Turks
left an open flank to the interior, which the British would later exploit. Despite the
vastly different operational circumstances outside Europe, Western Front tactical

conditions still tended to develop wherever modern weapons and high force-to-space ratios coexisted.

The Eastern and Balkan Fronts fell into a category midway between France, Flanders, the Isonzo, and Gallipoli on the one hand, and Mesopotamia and Africa on the other. Measuring some 1,060 miles at the start of 1915, the Eastern Front was more than twice the length of the Western, though the Russian retreat shortened it to about 620 miles before the Romanian campaign extended it by more than another 250. As the armies fighting there were significantly smaller than in the west, the force-to-space ratios were lower. In the winter of 1915–16 the western Allies were deploying 2,134 men per kilometre of front, but Russia only 1,200.[65] Germany garrisoned with one-and-a-half divisions in the east a sector in which it would have deployed five in France or Belgium, while Austria-Hungary manned its Italian front six times more densely than its Russian one.[66] Machine-gun and artillery densities were also lower in the east and no man's land was wider. Sometimes livestock grazed between the armies. With less risk of bombardment, trench systems were thinner, with more men bunched in the front line and smaller mobile reserves. Yet the east also had fewer railways, making it slower to move up reinforcements. All these factors made breakthrough easier, and both the Germans at Gorlice-Tarnow and Brusilov at Lutsk achieved it, if in significantly differing circumstances. At Gorlice the Russians had stationed their field artillery in earthwork bastions on low hills, from which they commanded the intervening trenches. The sector was strong by Eastern Front standards, though not by Western ones (its barbed wire was rudimentary). The Germans' bombardment was the biggest yet seen in the east, but their artillery superiority was less than France and Britain enjoyed in 1915 or on the Somme and their infantry tactics were not innovative.[67] The assault forces moved up during the previous night and trenches had been dug towards the Russian positions, but on the day the troops advanced in thick skirmishing lines (supported by aerial strafing) and took considerable casualties from rifles and machine-guns. They were fortunate that in most of the sector resistance collapsed quickly, the Russians surrendering or being hastily pulled back because their generals feared encirclement. By 1916, in contrast, the Austrians opposite Brusilov had constructed three fortified lines, each of three trenches, with machine-gun nests, deep dug-outs, and extensive wire, though his aerial reconnaissance established they had few reserves. Brusilov's men achieved surprise by digging trenches up to the enemy lines and unleashing a rapid bombardment, followed by an assault with specially selected and trained units. In other words the defensive positions were more elaborate and the attacking tactics more sophisticated than a year before.[68] Along a shorter and more static front than in 1915, conditions here too increasingly approximated to the Western Front norm. The obstacles to mobility increased on other fronts even while the armies in the west fumbled towards solutions to them. Essential though considerations of tactics, technology, and logistics are in explaining the course of the war, however, if treated in isolation they are insufficient. After Brusilov's triumph the later Russian attacks against the Germans round Kovno, though delivered on a narrow front and with heavier barrages, were unavailing. The Eastern Front still differed from the Western in one major respect. The British, French, and German armies were not equally effective,

and the Germans tended consistently to inflict higher casualties than they suffered.[69] But all three were comparable until 1917 in their willingness to persist in
action even when taking very heavy casualties. In contrast Brusilov overwhelmed
prepared positions that neither side would have abandoned so easily in the west,
and the Germans broke through at Gorlice with far less firepower and tactical skill
than they would have needed in France. Many Austro-Hungarian units were as inferior in cohesion, morale, and equipment to the Russians as the latter tended to
be to the Germans. Developments in arms production were fundamental, too, in
accounting for the contrasts between the theatres and the general pattern of the
fighting. The quality and quantity of military manpower and the successes and
failures of the war economies must now be brought into the equation.

CHAPTER 8

MANPOWER AND MORALE

T HE WAR'S DEMANDS on manpower were voracious. Germany's armed forces averaged 6 to 7 million troops, some 5 million of them in the field army, and during the war it mobilized 13.2 million men: some 85 per cent of its male population aged between seventeen and fifty.[1] Russia mobilized between 14 and 15.5 million;[2] France 8.4 million (7.74 million from metropolitan France and 475,000 from its colonies);[3] the British Isles, 4.9 million for the army and 500,000 for the navy and air force, or a third of the pre-war male labour force.[4] Navies and air forces were big recruiters, and a massive civilian workforce was needed to keep the services supplied and to staff expanding wartime bureaucracies, but armies made the greatest claims on human resources and, overwhelmingly, took the casu-alties. As in other spheres, so in this one the Allies increased their advantage over the Central Powers in the middle period of the war, but by spring 1917 both sides had made their maximum effort. From then on they could fight at the same level of intensity only by substituting firepower for men.

Although no continental power had expected so long and punishing an ordeal, their conscription systems meant that they had mostly registered their able-bodied men in peacetime and possessed the machinery to call them up, and also that many men had had military training. Even so, after the first year it proved harder to find trained officers and soldiers than to produce weapons. Before 1914 France had conscripted some 80 per cent of its men of military age, against Germany's 56 per cent and Russia's 25 per cent.[5] When war broke out, following the lesson from 1870 that everything must be thrown into the first battles, the French called up, in addition to the three (1911–13) conscript classes who were already under arms, twenty-four older classes dating back to 1887.[6] They added the succeeding cohorts as they came of military age or even earlier: the 1914 class (nearly one in three of whom would end as killed or missing) in August–September 1914, the 1915 class in December, the 1916 class in April 1915, the 1917 class in January 1916, the 1918 class in April–May 1917, and the 1919 class in April 1918.[7] By January 1916 87 per cent of all the men France mobilized had been called up,[8] and (as each new cohort averaged 250–300,000) from then on the new recruits barely compensated for the casualties. They were numerous enough, however, despite the enormous losses at Verdun and on the Somme, to keep France in the war. Three quarters of France's total losses had been sustained by the end of the Nivelle offensive. [9] Numbers of French fighting soldiers on the Western Front peaked in July 1916 at 2.234 million men, and by October 1917 had fallen to 1.888 million.[10] A growing proportion of those serving in the army were non-combatants (reflecting a more general trend for support services to expand) and by April 1917 some 550,000 men in the mobilized classes were exempted for munitions work, which many deputies considered violated the Republican principle of equality of sacrifice. The Dalbiez law of August 1915 and the Mourier law of August 1917 were meant to establish that young skilled workers would go to the front and only older men would be retained in the arms factories. But it suited neither the government nor the high command to comply, and both bills were so radically amended as to make them ineffective.[11] The army therefore declined to fill its gaps from the munitions workforce; on the contrary, its commanders wanted more weapons and munitions to compensate for dwindling numbers. Nor did colonial recruits make up the shortfall. During the war France recruited some 607,000 combatants from its empire, mainly in North and West Africa. Of these, 134,000 came to Europe, were frequently used as shock troops (for example on the Chemin des Dames), and 31,000 died there. Yet even at their maximum they numbered little more than 4 per cent of all French combatants on the Western Front, despite big recruitment drives in 1916 and in 1918.[12] After the Nivelle disaster the French army simply could not afford massive casualties in further big offensives, even had its troops been willing to undertake them.

If France was near its limits by spring 1917, Russia was ill placed to take the strain. This may seem surprising, given its far larger population, but for a mixture of financial and policy reasons the Stavka had held down the pre-war conscription rate to well below the levels typical in the west. In July 1914 Russia mobilized some 4.5 million men, adding to the active army (the 1911, 1912, and 1913 classes) about 3.1 million reservists of the first class (those who had done service between 1904 and 1910), most of whom had continued to undergo annual training. But the empire lost nearly half its pre-war trained manpower before the 1915 retreat even began, and by late 1916 casualties totalled 5.5 million.[13] In response to losses that were far higher than expected, the authorities called up the trained reserves of the 1896–1910 classes, and added all the 1914–18 classes (each numbering about 550,000 men) in 1914–15. A special law in December 1915 allowed the 1919 class to be called up as well.[14] In addition to calling up trained reservists and those reaching the age of seventeen and eighteen, the army also conscripted men who had been fortunate in previous ballots and escaped military service, as well as older ones who had passed on from the reserves into the militia (the *ratniki*). In the scramble to make good the losses suffered during the 1915 Great Retreat the government rushed through a law allowing it to call up *ratniki* of the second category, i.e., men who had been exempted mostly because they were the sole breadwinners in families with widowed mothers or many young children. The authorities expected trouble when they drew on this category and they got it:

disturbances broke out all over the empire in the autumn of 1916. None the less, in 1916 they called up further *ratniki* up to the age of forty, as well as making greater use of non-Russians, at the cost of draft riots in Central Asia.[15]

These expedients accentuated the tsarist army's peculiar features. If it continued the trawl beyond the *ratniki* the army would have to call up men of whom it had no administrative record.[16] But to match up to the Germans it needed more than raw backwoods levies. The proportion of urban working-class recruits in its ranks by 1916 was probably only about 2 per cent, or even less than in peacetime, because of casualties and men being withheld for munitions production.[17] Furthermore, NCOs and officers were proportionately much less numerous in the pre-war army than in Western European forces,[18] and during the war educated men could find administrative employment behind the lines relatively easily while an already overstretched officer corps suffered even heavier casualties than did the rank and file. By 1915 some regiments had only half their regular officer establishment,[19] and by the end of 1916 officer casualties numbered 92,500.[20] In this emergency the authorities trained up candidates *en masse* and by spring 1917 all vacancies had been filled, but fewer than one in ten of the officer corps were now regulars.[21] The men who took over (mostly very young school leavers and students) were inducted in crash courses in the military schools that for the infantry lasted only four months, or received still more rudimentary instruction in the so-called ensign schools, whose entrants were mostly of peasant or working-class background with only four years of formal education. These expedients narrowed the social divide between junior officers and the ranks (without necessarily ameliorating the latter's treatment) but widened the gulf between the aristocratic products of the elite military academies in senior command positions and most of the rest of the army. Because of Russia's industrial efforts the army was better equipped by winter 1916–17, but less reliable and cohesive.

If the Russians were poorly placed to take over from the French, in Britain neither volunteers in 1914–15 nor conscripts thereafter satisfied the army's demands. The pattern of British recruitment was quite different from that on the continent. In the first place, the empire was far more important, India alone raising 1,440,037 volunteers. In 1915, 138,000 Indian troops were stationed on the Western Front, where temporarily they filled a major part of the British line; in the Middle East they served in much larger numbers. Canada sent abroad 458,000 men, Newfoundland (at this stage a dominion in its own right) 8,000, Australia 332,000, New Zealand 112,000, and South Africa sent 136,000 whites as combatants as well as enlisting 75,000 non-whites to serve in Europe and Africa in the South African Native Labour Contingent. From the Caribbean 16,000 volunteered, British East Africa raised some 34,000 fighting troops, the British West African colonies 25,000; and the Africans pressed into service as bearers were even more numerous.[22] In general these units were paid for by the governments that sent them – an enormous subsidy to the mother country. Second, Britain made much greater use of volunteering. There were volunteers in France and Germany too – mainly educated young men enlisting before they were called up. But on the opening day of the Somme the great majority of French and Germans present were conscripts whereas all the British, in one way or another, were there by their own free will.[23]

In the home islands, only one eighth of those who served in the army during the war had joined before 1914, though half of those in the navy had. The government had no pre-war contingency plans to raise a mass citizen army or send to the continent more than the six regular divisions of the BEF; even most members of the Territorial Force (TF) had not committed themselves to serve overseas.[24] The volunteer surge after war broke out enabled the Liberal government to project power into Europe and accept heavy casualties without violating its principles or risking political consensus by introducing compulsion. Yet the surge was quite unexpected and by delegating recruiting to bodies such as local authorities and employers the War Office lost control of the phenomenon, far more men enlisting than it could feed, kit, train, or even house. By September, 478,893 men had joined up, the greatest inflow coming during the anxious weeks between Mons and the Marne. Kitchener disliked the TF as a non-professional organization, and although it did greatly expand most of the recruits went into his 'New Armies', a brand-new creation distinct both from the Territorials and from the old regular force.[25]

Like much else in 1914–18, volunteering had little parallel in the rest of British history. During the war, 2.4 million volunteers enlisted (compared with 2.5 million conscripts).[26] They came from all regions of the British Isles; only in the southern English and southern Irish agricultural counties was the phenomenon weaker, and even so over 140,000 Irishmen volunteered during the war and some 35,000 died.[27] All sectors of the economy were represented, as were all social classes, although the volunteers were predominantly younger men and often below the stipulated minimum age of nineteen, sometimes far below.[28] In so far as generalization is possible on the basis of letters, oral testimony, and memoirs (and the motives varied according to social class), travel, adventure, and the opportunity to participate in great events were all widely relevant, as were the all-party propaganda campaign directed by the Parliamentary Recruiting Committee, pressure from social superiors and peers, and the desire to prove oneself as a man. Unemployment played a role, at least during the opening weeks before the labour market tightened. So too did patriotism, if by that is meant responding to an appeal from the state authorities to defend the homeland, and enlistment peaks followed the military crises at Mons, First Ypres, and Loos.[29] In the Dominions the rush to enlist was even more remarkable, given their geographical remoteness: 52,561 Australians, for example, had joined the colours by the end of 1914. One in five of the Australians and two in five of the Canadians who served had been born in Britain, but even less recent immigrants enlisted in their tens of thousands, for reasons that (as in Britain itself) included joblessness, a quest for adventure, and an innocence about modern warfare, though also a genuine desire to help the motherland. In India recruitment came mainly from the traditional northern reservoirs of Nepal and the Punjab, identified by the British as the homelands of the 'martial races', although as the war went on more came from southern India and from lower-status groups.[30] By contrast in South Africa the Afrikaner uprising of October 1914 was partly directed against military service for the empire, and in Canada the French-Canadians numbered 35 per cent of the population but only 5 per cent of the Canadian Expeditionary Force.[31] Everywhere the monthly totals fell off markedly after the initial rush of enthusiasm,[32] and in Britain itself after summer 1915 volunteering consistently failed to meet the army's requirements, opening up a prolonged political crisis over what to do next.

The conscription controversy was the most important political debate in Britain during the year following the formation of Asquith's first coalition government in May 1915. It was widely understood that too few were enlisting, especially after Kitchener at the Calais conference in July 1915 accepted a seventy-division target for the BEF, the New Armies suffered their first heavy losses at Loos, and the government agreed to a major offensive in 1916 as part of the Chantilly strategy. Meanwhile Lloyd George, who had moved under the coalition from the Exchequer to the newly created Ministry of Munitions, was determined to push up shell production and knew his political future depended on succeeding. He became converted to conscription as essential to guarantee the skilled workers he needed by *protecting* them from military service. The debate was therefore never a simple contest between Liberal fastidiousness and the army's need for men, although Asquith's critics demanded conscription partly on symbolic grounds, to root out 'shirkers', using the issue (as Bethmann's critics in Germany did that of submarine warfare) as a touchstone of the government's will to win. It threatened to alienate Labour and the TUC, who feared it would lead on to compulsory civilian labour and would cripple trade union bargaining power. It also threatened to split the Liberal Party and the cabinet and eject Asquith from the premiership: precisely what many Unionists (and probably also Lloyd George) wanted. However, the Unionist leader, Andrew Bonar Law, hesitated to provoke a crisis that might force a divisive general election, acquiescing instead in Asquith's stratagems to delay a decision. Compulsion therefore entered by stealth. The National Registration Act of July 1915 required all men and women aged from sixteen to sixty-five to report their name and occupation. The 'Derby scheme' of October–December, overseen by Lord Derby as Director of Recruiting, invited men of military age to 'attest' their willingness to serve. As the scheme failed – and may well have been intended to fail – to meet its targets, the January 1916 Military Service Act provided for conscription of single men aged eighteen to forty-one, though with numerous exemptions (to be administered by a tribunal system) that included war work, hardship due to family or business commitments or ill health, and conscientious objection. After an uneasy interlude in which monthly enlistments under the new regime ran at half those under the voluntary one, a second Military Service Act in May extended compulsion to married men, though like its predecessor it exempted men from Ireland. The premier probably accepted that conscription was unavoidable, but he wanted it on a basis that kept his party united and himself in Downing Street: he therefore waited until the National Register and the Derby scheme confirmed the existence of a pool of manpower that only compulsion could drain. None the less the conscription of married men was forced on him by demands from Robertson (newly installed as CIGS), backed by Lloyd George and the Unionist leaders as well as much of the press. His authority never recovered, and the imbroglio hastened the decline of the Liberal Party as well as confirming Britain's commitment to a form of total war.[33]

The British decision set a precedent for the Dominions, New Zealand introducing compulsory military service in July 1916. Yet Canada did not follow suit until the last year of the war, and in Australia the government lost two referendums on the issue in October 1916 and December 1917, the first narrowly but the second by a wider margin. Opposition came partly from radicals and socialists but also from a portion of the Irish community and the Catholic hierarchy, antagonized by the suppression of the Easter Rising in Dublin in 1916. Even in Britain itself conscription failed to solve the 'manpower' problem (a term that entered the political lexicon at this time).[34] Fewer soldiers were recruited in 1916 with conscription than in 1915 without it.[35] The provision for conscientious objection on moral and religious grounds, a controversial concession made by Asquith to personal scruple and his Liberal critics, was not the primary reason.[36] Nearly all the 779,936 men exempted between 1 March 1916 and 31 March 1917 escaped not for reasons of conscience but due to poor physical condition or because they were employed in essential industries. Conscription meant that trades such as railways, mining, and armaments were better protected than previously (as volunteering was now abolished), even though military recruiting bit deeper in other sectors, such as commerce.[37] It spelled no bonanza for the army, whose shortfall was exacerbated by the huge Somme losses.[38] Caught between the Front and munitions production, the authorities had too few men for either. Although the BEF grew from 907,000 on 1 December 1915 to 1,379,000 on 1 October 1916 and 1,801,000 on 1 October 1917, in the latter year it peaked and its combat strength began to fall.[39] The Italian army also reached its maximum in 1917, and showed signs of a similar predicament.[40] Britain and Italy lagged behind France and Russia in the cycle but not by much.

The Allies embarked on the Chantilly strategy assuming that the Central Powers' reserves of manpower were near exhaustion.[41] The conference advised that the Allies needed to inflict losses on the Germans of 200,000 a month.[42] In fact the Allies rightly calculated that the Central Powers' reserves were more limited than theirs, but overestimated their own ability to absorb casualties and underestimated enemy – or at any rate German – resilience. Leaving aside Bulgaria, whose role was marginal, the most hard-pressed Central Power was probably the Ottoman Empire, whose Christians and Jews (about one fifth of its population) could exempt themselves from military service by paying a tax, as could the more affluent Muslims. The Kurds were used largely as irregular cavalry; the empire's 6 million Arabs (mainly in Syria and Iraq) were increasingly drawn on as the war continued, but the authorities regarded them as inferior to Turkish troops. The bulk of the recruitment burden therefore fell on the approximately 10 million Turkish peasants of the Anatolian plateau, and even when fully mobilized the army of 800,000 men represented only 4 per cent of the population (whereas in France it was 10 per cent). It lost its best units early on in the Caucasus and Dardanelles campaigns, although its numbers reached their maximum in early 1916. A year later it was down to 400,000 and by March 1918 to 200,000.[43] Austria-Hungary, though richer and with a total population of over 50 million, was another multinational empire that before 1914 had kept its army (and therefore its reserves) small, training only about one in five of each age cohort. One reason for Germany's continuing commitment on the Eastern Front was that the Russians massively outnumbered its ally. In 1914 Austria-Hungary called up 3.5 million men, including almost all its trained reserve as well as untrained territorials, and suffered 1.25 million casualties in the first six months. Despite early enlistment of the 1915 class, one reason for the Habsburg military emergency in spring 1915 was a shortage of men.[44] The army's numerical strength peaked earlier than in the other belligerents, and from 1915 onwards it led a hand-to-mouth existence. For example, 48 per cent of the officer corps were lost or missing by early 1915, compared with 25 per cent in Russia and 16 per cent in Germany.[45] In April 1915 those aged eighteen to twenty were enlisted for Landsturm (territorial) duty, and the field army was kept going in 1916 only by calling up the 1898 class seven months early. Until the class of 1899 became available the military would have to make do.[46]

Germany's position, as an ethnically mostly homogenous bloc of 65 million which before 1914 had called up a proportion of its manpower second only to that called up in France, should have been much more favourable. Yet even here, when Hindenburg and Ludendorff took over a manpower shortage was causing great anxiety. Like the French the Germans had a large trained reserve, which enabled them to maintain a big field army from the outset; unlike the French, they had a strong birth rate and much greater numbers in each conscript class, which they did not hesitate to draw on, calling up two classes (1895 and 1896) in 1915 and two more (1897 and 1898) in 1916.[47] Virtually all men born between 1879 and 1899 did military service, the 1892–95 classes suffering between 35 and 37 per cent deaths. Even so, the field army, though averaging 4.6 million from August 1914 to August 1915, 5.3 million from August 1915 to August 1916, and 5.8 million from August 1916 to August 1917, fell to 4.9 million in the period August 1917 to August 1918. It remained a very big army with deep manpower reserves to sustain it, and Allied attrition efforts in 1916 did not halt its expansion, but in 1917 it too reached its maximum size.[48] Ludendorff applied sticking plaster by calling up the 1898 class early (in September 1916) but also by withdrawing to the Hindenburg Line and forgoing a great offensive in 1917. In addition he and Hindenburg pressed for a new Patriotic Auxiliary Service law, but this (like conscription in Britain) resulted in more men being withheld from the front.* Germany peaked simultaneously with Britain and Italy rather than with Russia and France, but after 1916 it turned like the other belligerents to unit reorganization and to more numerous and powerful weapons to compensate for its dwindling manpower and in order to remain in the ring.

Given the extraordinary casualty rates that the war inflicted from its opening weeks, it may seem strange that the manpower crisis that all the belligerents suffered by 1917 did not set in much earlier. Enough men were found not only to keep the fighting going but also to intensify it in the battles of 1916. One reason, paradoxical as it may seem, was trench warfare. The immediate instinct of troops exposed in the open to bombardment was to dig. The French army lost by far its largest monthly totals killed in action of the entire war in August and September 1914, the next highest peak coming again in another month of relatively open warfare, June 1918.[49] The German army on the Eastern Front suffered worst during

---

*See ch. 9.

the mobile operations of the 1914–15 winter and the summer 1915 offensive. In the first year of the war its unit losses in the east exceeded those in the west by more than a quarter.[50] High though attrition rates were on the Western Front even when no offensive was in progress, without the apparatus of trenches, sandbags, dug-outs, and pillboxes they would have been higher still, and shellfire was surprisingly ineffective against them. It has been estimated that during the Somme it took thirty British shells to kill one German.[51] Admittedly, the argument is double-edged: without trenches the two sides could not have remained in such constant close proximity, especially as they were armed, as the war went on, with an increasingly powerful array of weapons.[52] Trenches, and innovations such as railway supply lines and tinned food, enabled the killing to continue throughout the year instead of the armies retiring in the traditional manner to winter quarters. Moreover, commanders such as Falkenhayn and Joffre intended trenches to release men to join the mobile reserve kept for attacks elsewhere. Digging in reduced casualties between battles and slowed down the rate of attrition. Whether it saved lives over the war as a whole is debatable.

The role of medicine was much more significant. The decades before 1914 had seen spectacular advances in anaesthetics, antiseptic and aseptic surgery, and bacteriology, as well as the rise of the civilian and military medical professions. In 1914 Germany, the best prepared belligerent in this respect, had 33,031 doctors (most of them state employees), 80 per cent of whom were mobilized.[53] Some 18,000 French doctors were called up by October 1915,[54] as, eventually, were half the 22,000 in Britain.[55] It has often been pointed out that the Great War was the first major conflict (apart from the Russo-Japanese War) in which deaths from wounds exceeded those from illness. In the Boer War, for example, two thirds of the British soldiers who died did so from disease.[56] Yet the generalization carries more truth for the Western Front than elsewhere. Seven times as many Turkish troops died from disease as from wounds,[57] disease was the major killer in East Africa, and the Allies in Macedonia lost many more men to malaria than to the Bulgars. Typhus afflicted a quarter of the Serbian army in 1915 and was a major reason for its collapse;[58] and on the Eastern Front over 5 million Russian soldiers were hospitalized on account of disease, mainly scurvy but also typhus, typhoid, cholera, and dysentery.[59] None the less, most of them survived, and over the war as a whole, five times as many soldiers died from combat wounds as from sickness.[60] On the Western Front until the influenza pandemic of 1918 disease was a nuisance rather than a mass killer, which given the squalor of the trenches was a remarkable tribute to the BEF's Regimental Medical Officers (RMOs) and their French and German counterparts. British troops were provided as far as possible with clean water, and baths and laundry facilities once they were out of the line. German troops were deloused in mobile 'louseleums' paid for by public subscription. Smallpox had ravaged the French army in 1870, but was little known in 1914–18.[61] In the BEF in 1914, 32 per cent of the wounded contracted tetanus, but by the end of the war infection rates were down to 0.1 per cent.[62] One in five of the American troops who fought the Spanish in 1898 contracted typhoid, but very few did in 1917–18, and 90 per cent of the BEF were inoculated against the disease by early 1915.[63] None of this is to say that diseases ranging from syphilis to 'trench foot' (a condition similar to frostbite caused by constant immersion) did not threaten armies' fighting strength and efficiency, but thanks to the rise of a professional medical corps before 1914, as well as new developments in preventive medicine, they affected proportionately fewer than in previous wars, and most of those who did fall victim could return to active duty.

Still more remarkable was medicine's success in rehabilitating the wounded: and this more than anything else accounted for the armies' ability to keep fighting despite seemingly prohibitive casualty rolls. Most lists compiled during the war lumped together dead and wounded without indicating that only a minority of the latter were unable ever to serve again. The first hurdle for wounded soldiers on the Western Front was evacuation by stretcher-bearers to receive initial medical attention. But the static nature of the campaigning meant that emergency treatment was usually available within artillery range of the front line, and increasingly in the British army major surgery took place on the fringes of the battle zone in casualty clearing stations. The war witnessed few dramatic surgical breakthroughs, though there were some: notably the treatment of 'gas gangrene' (infection of wounds) by a combination of removing dead tissue ('debridement') and continuous irrigation in a special mild solution. Among the other techniques beginning before the war but improved during it were X-ray diagnosis, team surgery, and (on the Allied side) blood transfusion. Overall mortality (as a per centage of total casualties) has been estimated at 8 per cent, compared with 13.3 per cent in the American Civil War and 20 per cent in the Crimea: machine guns and high explosives inflicted more terrible and complex damage to the human body, but to a considerable extent physicians kept up with them. In the French army the proportion of casualities labelled as 'healed' or 'recuperating' was 54 per cent.[64] In the British army, according to the official history, 82 per cent of the wounded were 'ultimately returned to some form of duty';[65] of 4.3 million German wounded, three quarters returned to service;[66] and at least 1 million Russian soldiers returned to the front after being wounded, despite much worse facilities.[67] British Indian troops in France regarded it as tantamount to a death sentence that even after having been seriously wounded they were still liable to return to the line,[68] but hundreds of thousands of soldiers had to do so. By healing the sick and wounded, calling up eighteen-year olds as they came of age, and pressing men in their forties and even older into garrison and home-front responsibilities, the belligerents maintained and even increased their combatant numbers until their 1917 peak. In this as in so many other respects, European society proved strikingly resourceful.

If medical science was more effective than in previous wars in caring for more terrible physical injuries, it had less success with psychological wounds. This problem had received little pre-war attention, and not only the military authorities but also the newly established psychiatric profession were feeling their way. Post-traumatic stress disorder, to give its modern name to the condition labelled 'shell shock' in the English-speaking countries, had doubtless existed in earlier conflicts, but had not been diagnosed as such. It was exacerbated by the special conditions of static warfare in which soldiers endured repeated bombardments in confined spaces with little control over their fate, and lived day after day in close proximity to their comrades' decomposing remains. In the mobile fighting of 1914 and 1918 its incidence diminished. As early as February 1915 the English physician Charles Myers identified its basic characteristics in an article in the *Lancet*.[69] To begin with the condition – which in the BEF reportedly took the forms of paralysis and mutism among common soldiers and nervous exhaustion among officers – was tentatively attributed to changes in atmospheric pressure under bombardment. Only after the rush of cases during the Somme did the British authorities reluctantly accept that they confronted a disorder that was essentially psychological, triggered by the sights and sounds and stresses of the combat zone. In Britain the methods used to treat it varied from rest and what would now be recognized as counselling to hypnosis and electric shocks; German doctors were less inclined to view it sympathetically and resorted liberally to shock treatment and other procedures akin to physical torture. In both countries such methods might have some success in alleviating the symptoms, though it was probably short-term. Thus 87 per cent of shell-shocked British troops were back on front-line service within a month.[70] Officially the cases recorded – some 200,000 in Germany and 80,000 in Britain – seem surprisingly few in relation to the size of the armies concerned and the conditions they experienced. Yet they probably represented only the tip of an iceberg of trauma and misery, whose full effects were suffered years afterwards.[71]

The shell-shock epidemic serves as a reminder that though the men of 1914 may have been tougher than we are, they were not superhuman and their capacity was finite. The manpower problem was qualitative as well as quantitative. Among the most insistent questions raised by the war are those of how soldiers endured it and why they fought. A spate of inter-war veterans' memoirs provides essential testimony, but mostly from the perspective of junior officers rather than private soldiers, and much of it coloured by retrospective debates over whether military service had been worthy and ennobling or futile and dehumanizing. In Germany in particular, the myth of a heroic venture in which all the combatants had faith became a staple of nationalist orthodoxy during the Weimar Republic and remained difficult to question even after 1945. Only within the last two decades have historians used contemporary sources, such as soldiers' letters, reports by military censors, and 'trench newspapers' produced by fighting units, to recapture attitudes in the line and unveil a more complex picture, confirming neither patriotic nor disenchanted stereotypes. The most important single conclusion from the new research is the diversity of the war experience. Enormous differences existed not only between theatres but also between active and quiet sectors on the same front, and between conditions in the same sector when a battle was and was not in progress. All the same, for fighting to continue not only did governments and commanders have to issue orders, but also officers and soldiers had to obey them, rather than desert, surrender, or observe a truce.

In fact all three of these alternative options were resorted to even in the middle period of the war, before morale and discipline crumbled in one army after another in 1917–18. All was not mere passive suffering and obedience. More than 300,000 Turks had deserted by November 1917;[72] the Russian army lost 1 million prisoners (many after little resistance) during the 1915 retreat[73] and 2.1 million by December 1916.[74] Although after 1914 the two Central Powers maintained forces of comparable size on the Eastern Front, the Russians took about 2 million Austro-Hungarian prisoners during the war, compared with 167,000 Germans, and during the Brusilov offensive over a third of the Habsburg army in the theatre surrendered.[75] On the Western Front, desertion and surrender were comparatively tiny in scale: over the entire war prisoners accounted for 11.6 per cent of French losses, 9 per cent of German ones, and only 6.7 per cent of British[76] (the absolute numbers were 500,000 French prisoners and 180,000 British).[77] Partly this reflected the stalemated nature of the fighting, with little scope for large-scale encirclement or opportunity for men to desert, given that the military police were behind them and both sides knew that captives might be butchered rather than sent to the rear.[78] Instead what took place along extended sections of the front, for weeks or even longer, were tacit truces, and not only in the west but also on the Eastern, Italian, and Balkan fronts. The Christmas 1914 fraternization was part of a much bigger phenomenon, whose full extent remains uncharted. Tacit truces rested on informal, unspoken understandings. They might break up when a new and more aggressive unit entered the line, or continue if the relieving unit took the hint from its predecessor. Typically they entailed keeping firing to a minimum, or at any rate respecting moments such as breakfast, and avoiding shelling rear areas so that supplies could be brought up and the wounded evacuated. On patrol, soldiers deliberately aimed high or contrived to bypass one another. Much of the British front was always active, and became more so after GHQ insisted on more frequent raids as a contribution to the attrition strategy agreed at the 1915 Chantilly conference. Even so, it has been estimated that up to one third of the trench tours of duty by BEF units may have been made easier by some form of a 'live-and-let-live' principle. On the French and Italian fronts, to judge from British troops' findings when they took over sections of them, raiding was less frequent and live-and-let-live more prevalent. Two were needed to play this game, but the British found that Saxon and South German (if not Prussian) troops were often willing to do so, as were Habsburg forces in Poland and the Alps, though not the Turks at Gallipoli.[79]

The trench truces matter here because they help to explain what made the war more bearable (and therefore what prolonged it) and because they suggest the intensity of fighting was to some extent negotiable, the front-line troops and their NCOs and line officers often interpreting leniently their commanders' injunctions to be constantly active and to kill at every opportunity. If this applied in quiet times, it probably applied in battle too. Once Western Front offensives began, especially in the first half of the war, commanders could do little to maintain or even monitor progress after sending the infantry over the top. They relied on individual units, or what was left of them after they crossed no man's land, to advance to the stated objectives. In the vast decentralized confusion of a major offensive, in which tens of thousands of men might be engaged along fronts of many miles, the personal control still possible in Napoleon's day was no longer attainable. Such 'battles' had little in common with Waterloo except the term itself. But this meant in the French army by 1915, for instance, that an order to attack meant in practice doing what the unit judged feasible, which rarely entailed fighting to the last man or advancing if the sole result would be pointless casualties. Governments and high commands created the circumstances in which thousands of troops with merciless weaponry were obliged to kill and maim, but they could not determine the speed and scale of carnage.

This being the case, however, even more depended than in previous wars on the individuals' combat motivation. And it remains true, with all the qualifications so far stated, that from the Marne and Tannenberg to the Somme and the Chemin des Dames citizen soldiers did kill and maim each other, often at rates of several thousand a day for weeks at a stretch. Two overlapping questions arise: what enabled them to endure 'ordinary' front conditions, and what motivated them to give battle, not only risking dying but also inflicting death? As usual we know far more about the Western Front (or at least about the Allied experience there) than any other, but the conclusions drawn from it can to a degree be extended. They fall under four headings: first, the basic conditions in which soldiers served; second, coercion; third, the dynamics of the groups in which men encountered combat; and fourth, larger ideological factors.

Foremost in the first category was that soldiers were not continuously at risk. On the contrary, the usual British rhythm was for a unit to serve three to seven days in the forward trench, the same period in the support trench, and the same again in the reserve trench before spending a week behind the lines.[80] Many accounts stress the tonic value of even a short period of rest. Trench newspapers and letters likewise confirm the preoccupation of serving soldiers with sleep, hot food, and creature comforts, and for veterans a common legacy of the trenches was heightened awareness of bodily needs and delight in their being met.[81] Games – and especially football – were the most immediate form of recreation for even exhausted British troops when they left the line, supplemented by canteens, cafes, clubs such as the 'Toc H' refuge at Poperinghe, and concert parties, thus linking in with Edwardian England's music hall enthusiasms and sporting obsessions.[82] Almost equally important for satisfying emotional needs was contact with home life. A paradox of the Western Front, in contrast with nineteenth-century imperial wars, was that the troops were close to their homelands geographically, even if in other respects they might have inhabited a different planet, and they desperately needed lifelines to their former existence. British officers could read the London magazines in their dug-outs and the *Daily Mail* was sold at the approaches to the trenches.[83] The BEF handled 7,000 mail sacks and 60,000 parcels daily and the soldiers looked forward intensely to their contents;[84] French trooops were equally preoccupied with news about their families and, among the majority who were farmers, with the progress of the agricultural year.[85] Too many dying men cried out for their mothers, for the centrality of home and family, to be disregarded. It was a commonplace of letters and memoirs that combat experience was incommunicable to those who had not known it, and according to writers such as Erich Maria Remarque this incommunicability made home visits almost intolerable.[86] Yet such a view seems to have been atypical. Precisely the infrequency of home visits was a leading complaint in the French mutinies of 1917.

This last point is a reminder, however, that even if many soldiers' needs were simple, they were often not met. In June–July 1917 over 400,000 men in the British army had not been home for over twelve months, to say nothing of the

Australians and Canadians who could not return at all.[87] Nor were troops allowed to recuperate properly when out of the line, often being subjected to a punishing regime of fatigue and physical exertion. Front-line service in France and Flanders often meant sleeplessness, monotonous and calorifically barely adequate food, and exhausting physical labour with minimal protection against the elements in all seasons. It also meant loss of control over one's existence because of subjection to harsh military codes of discipline and to unpredictable orders from superiors who might have little familiarity with the combat zone.[88] In many respects (including food and medical care) French troops were less well looked after (and less well paid) than the British, which contributed to a lingering sense of grievance. Some of these conditions, it has been plausibly argued, were not so different from those of civilian life for South Wales miners, Provençal farmers, or labourers from Berlin or rural Brandenburg. Many soldiers were used to submission and privation, though others, and not only the members of the literate class who wrote the inter-war memoirs, were not. But conditions in the Russian or Italian – let alone the Turkish – armies were much worse than those in the British or French, and material comforts, even where they were provided, were at best palliatives to reconcile men to an existence that few of them would have chosen voluntarily. In any case, other aspects of the front experience went beyond anything to be found in civilian life even at that time, most notably the constant presence of violent death – like inhabiting a garden of exotic and sinister plants, as Ernst Jünger put it[89] – and the knowledge that at any moment a careless act or unexpected projectile might reduce the living to the same condition as the corpses.[90] With time, most soldiers accommodated themselves to the sights and smells of mortality and putrefaction, but the constant fear was harder to cope with. And other experiences were normally too terrible ever to become inured to, most notably those of undergoing bombardment and jumping the parapet for an attack. In the words of Lord Moran, who was a medical officer during the war and later Winston Churchill's doctor, every man had only a limited capital of courage. Once it was spent he was bankrupt.[91]

In explaining why soldiers endured, and also fought, it is important to remember what First World War 'combat' was like. Most of the killing was done at a distance by missile weapons such as mortars, machine guns, rifles, grenades, and (especially) artillery. Face to face encounters with knives, bayonets, or revolvers certainly happened but were comparatively rare, and more typical experiences were of surviving under enemy (or friendly) shelling, occupying terrain under machine gun fire, or clearing trenches the enemy had evacuated.[92] None the less, authority had placed both attackers and defenders in a predicament where they had to kill in order to survive. If the German defenders on 1 July 1916 clambered from their dug-outs and set up their machine guns too slowly they stood to be bombed out while a curtain of artillery fire cut off their retreat. For Haig's infantry, once out in no man's land, their only hope of cover might be to seize the enemy front trench. Behind them, for both sides, were apparatuses of coercion. German troops were sometimes forced into action by officers threatening them with pistols.[93] Each British unit on 1 July had its 'battle police' to round up stragglers, and the Germans had their equivalent.[94] In the BEF the ratio of military police to servicemen rose tenfold from 1:3,306 in 1914 to 1:339 in 1917.[95] In the Italian army, Cadorna believed – probably unjustly – that only the harshest discipline would keep his troops fighting. He terrorized his generals (of whom he sacked 217 in 1915–17) with the aim that they should do the same to their subordinates. Between 1915 and 1918 some 330,000 Italian soldiers (one in seventeen) were charged with military crimes and 61 per cent were found guilty.[96] Capital convictions in the Italian army totalled 4,028 and actual executions around 750. And yet these figures were notably higher than those in the larger British army (3,080 and 346), in the French army (c. 2,000 and 700), and in the much larger German one (150 and 48).[97] German discipline, indeed, was far harsher in the Second World War, when the sceptical opinions tolerated in soldiers' letters in 1914–18 would have incurred a death penalty.[98] The statistics seem to bear out the old adage that the best discipline is self-discipline: if an army's discipline has to be imposed it is already fragile.

Aside from the role of coercion, it is therefore necessary to consider what more positive forces maintained the soldier in combat. All armies contained a significant number who simply enjoyed the life, whether because they had already chosen a military career before the war, or because they relished hunting and destruction. Many air aces seem to have fitted into this category,[99] as did volunteers such as Ernst Jünger in the German army, and (at least until he rebelled in 1917) Siegfried Sassoon in the British. Others, such as artillerymen, who have left few personal testimonies, were shielded by remoteness from the consequences of their actions (even if they themselves suffered from enemy artillery fire), while specialized volunteer arms, such as the German stormtroopers and the machine gun corps in almost every army, seem to have attracted aggressive personalities. Even in the infantry self-consciously elite units were often more active when holding the line as well as during battle, and many writers have stressed the importance of male camaraderie – concern not to lose face or let down one's comrades – in motivating units to act. Indian soldiers' letters stressed above all their desire for *izzat* (standing, prestige, or reputation) and revealed an intense fear of shame.[100] Similarly, according to the French philosopher (and 1914–18 veteran) Alain, 'honour is the real motor of war'.[101] However, the same small-group dynamics could also accelerate mutiny and desertion if morale were lost, and the leadership provided by NCOs and junior officers, rather than the non-combatant staff and higher grades, must be factored in. As junior officer casualties were generally even higher than in the other ranks, few such officers by 1916–17 had been experienced regulars before the war. It is true that in the French army, which did not expand as much as the British one and already possessed a corps of reserve officers, promotion from the ranks happened less.[102] But in the BEF few regular officers served in the New Armies even in 1915, and a notable democratization occurred by 1917–18: at least 40 per cent of officers were estimated to have been working-class or lower middle-class in origin. This process probably benefited relations between officers and men, which contemporary evidence suggests were generally good at least until the Somme.[103] In Austria-Hungary, in contrast, which suffered exceptionally heavy officer casualties, two thirds of the regular corps were German-speaking and most of the rest were Magyar, and the middle-class reservist officers who were brought in to replace them made less effort and had less time to learn their men's languages.[104] Similarly, the Russian army created 170,000 new commissions during the war,[105] and the Italian army created 160,191.[106] Small-group dynamics and effective leadership seem to have been crucial at particular places and times, but they counted for more in some armies than others and casualties took their toll on all such close-knit units as the war went on.

We are driven back to larger considerations. Among them organized religion seems to have been conspicuously absent. Many soldiers were certainly superstitious,[107] denizens as they were of an unfamiliar and hostile landscape and existing in constant proximity to nature and death. In the midst of modern technology, their circumstances resembled those of mediaeval Europeans, before the advent of scientific rationalism and urban-industrial civilization.[108] By and large, however, any religious sentiment expressed itself in recourse to talismans and private imprecations rather than to army chaplains, and the surviving first-hand evidence – naturally with many individual exceptions – makes little reference to the official faiths.[109] Faith in the nation, on the other hand, was much more significant, as became apparent when it was absent. The Habsburg AOK justifiably feared that Czech and Bosnian Serb units would be unreliable, and Czech desertions began early.[110] Despite some spectacular surrenders by Czech units, however, it seems that the ethnic make-up of the Austro-Hungarian prisoner-of-war population resembled that of the Habsburg army as a whole, the huge numbers of captures mostly testifying to the army's general demoralization and inefficiency rather than to national separatism.[111] In the Russian army, the authorities distrusted minorities other than Belorussians and Ukrainians. Jews were excluded from the tsarist officer corps; Poles, Balts, and Central Asians were kept dispersed and not normally allowed to exceed more than 15–20 per cent of a regiment.[112] In the German army the authorities discriminated against Alsatian recruits.[113] In the Ottoman army, nationalist conspiracies developed among officers in the Syrian Arab contingents, though they had little impact. Even within communities supposedly sharing a language, the Italian command believed regiments from southern Italy were less reliable than northerners, and the French GQG viewed its southerners similarly, in both cases probably with some justification. National and patriotic loyalties, in other words, did make a difference to staying power.

This is not to say that overt national feeling played a strong positive part in keeping armies fighting. It would be better to speak in a more general way of soldiers having confidence in their 'cause' – an amalgam of beliefs that included assurance of victory and acceptance that the war's purpose was legitimate, as well as patriotic sentiment. Patriotism was probably most conspicuous in the French army, whose soldiers and officers in letters and trench newspapers referred frequently to the invasion of their country and the need to continue until the enemy had been expelled and the soil for which their comrades had died was liberated. Soldiers did not constitute a race apart, ignorant of domestic politics, and evidence of unity and determination at home fortified them. French troops felt a growing contempt for journalists and politicians who misrepresented the ugly reality of front-line conditions, as well as for profiteers and munitions workers who battened on the conflict while soldiers earned a pittance; yet they also felt a continuing, often heightened, appreciation for home and family life, the defence of which seemed to many the essential justification for persevering in the struggle. To judge from the evidence of letters, trench newspapers, and censors' reports, they remained convinced at least until 1917 that victory would eventually come.[114] Turkish soldiers at Gallipoli were confident in the justice of their cause and the prospects for success, some indeed being convinced that if they died they would go to paradise.[115] Even British troops, although not on their national territory, wrote without irony before the Somme about fighting for king, country, and empire.[116] Writers and memoirists of the BEF focused on a complex of characteristically sportsmanlike values, such as punishing the bully and upholding the rules of fair play against an enemy that unless thrashed might threaten their own islands. Probably most soldiers identified the homeland with their families, streets, and towns or villages, rather than anything more abstract. Even the seemingly more hard-bitten often harboured a stubborn faith in their superiority over other peoples (those from the Dominions still more so), and believed no less firmly than the French in the certainty of victory.[117] Although units from both the French and British armies observed tacit local truces, this did not mean they liked an enemy that was blamed for aggression and atrocities, or that many believed in the existence of a community of front-line soldiers with common interests against capitalists and militarists in the rear.

About the German army we have much less information, and it is possible that many of its troops were a good deal more sceptical, at least to judge from the rough reception they gave to volunteers.[118] Until Verdun they were buoyed up by successive triumphs and the hope that victory would bring peace. On the Somme, facing for the first time an adversary almost as well equipped, more German units seem to have envisaged the war as essentially a defensive struggle, fought to hold the outposts guarding the Rhine and the fatherland.[119] In contrast to the 1915 battles the Somme went on far longer and caused much greater strain, some fifty divisions (or 45 per cent of those on the Western Front) passing through it.[120] Possibly the war became easier to justify once it took a turn for the worse, as it did for Italians at the end of 1917 when Italy was invaded. Even so, patriotism was probably felt and expressed more explicitly by the officers who later dwelt on it in German regimental histories than it was by ordinary soldiers. If professional pride upheld morale, however, German soldiers had good reason (at least until the summer of 1916) to believe in their superiority against all comers.[121]

It has been argued here that the enigma of combat motivation can be approached from four directions: material conditions, coercion, small-group dynamics, and ideological or patriotic affiliation. 'Front propaganda', in the sense of efforts deliberately to undermine the enemy army's morale by leafleting and other devices, was of minor importance in the middle period of the war, though later it would be attempted on a more ambitious scale.[122] In 1915–16 an army's cohesion was determined more by conditions on its own side than by the actions of the enemy, and if these conditions were supportive they could withstand very high casualties indeed. By winter 1916–17, however, there was growing evidence that the factors that had kept the armies fighting with such intensity were losing their grip. Officially, in Haig's estimation and in reports to the cabinet, BEF morale after the Somme was still high. The British Third Army's military censors found from their scrutiny of soldiers' letters no wavering in willingness to see the war through, or much desire for a 'premature' compromise peace.[123] Yet the later stages of the battle, after the weather finally turned in October, seem to have been a gruelling experience that shook the confidence of those involved and began to alienate them from their leaders.[124] In the other Allied armies, the situation was worse. Those found guilty of desertion in the Italian army rose from 10,000 in the period from June 1915 to May 1916, to 28,000 from June 1916 to May 1917.[125] The censors of soldiers' letters in the French army found evidence of faltering morale during the final stages at Verdun,[126] and in the 5th Infantry Division in the winter of 1916–17 desertion ran at unprecedented levels.[127] In the Russian army, similar evidence suggests that many soldiers were convinced by 1915 that they could not beat the Germans, and that by the end of 1916 they were full of despondency and recrimination against the authorities who had sent them into war without the wherewithal to win.[128] The evidence that victory was as remote as ever, despite Brusilov's initial successes and another million casualties, produced a still uglier mood. Soldiers' letters revealed a deep anxiety about the deteriorating quality and quantity of their provisions (the daily bread ration was reduced from three pounds to two, and then to one, during the winter), as well as anger about rocketing inflation and scarcities that endangered their loved ones' welfare. Many wanted to end the war whatever the cost, and over twenty mutinies seem to have occurred in October–December 1916 (the first on this scale in any army during the war), some involving whole regiments, and in each case taking the form of a collective refusal of orders to attack or to prepare to attack.[129] The British, French, and Italian armies were still usable as offensive instruments, though in the latter two cases their soldiers were increasingly resistant; but the Russian army hardly fitted into this category any longer. Yet on the other hand, the Turkish army was sliding into wholesale desertion, and the Austro-Hungarian army had shown its propensity to surrender *en masse*. Except against Italy, it could keep going only with support from its ally. The great flywheel whose momentum sustained the war remained the German army, whose self-confidence had deteriorated during 1916 but whose discipline remained exceptional; it remained very large and formidable in both defence and attack. It was probably no longer strong enough for Hindenburg and Ludendorff to achieve their war aims, but neither were the Allies near to defeating it, and the Romanian campaign had showed that it could still prop up its partners. While this force remained intact, there was little prospect of any early resolution to the conflict.

CHAPTER 9

ARMAMENTS AND ECONOMICS

WAR WAS EXPENSIVE. Every one of the millions of bullets and shells fired off had a price tag. Every soldier had to be paid (however miserably), clothed and fed, transported to and from the front and cared for if wounded or ill. His equipment had to be manufactured and tested, and then transported by trains that needed fuel and maintenance and by animals requiring fodder and stabling. The soldiers' families were allocated separation allowances, and the disabled, widows, and orphans needed sustenance, as did thousands of refugees. Because most people in Western and Central Europe, at least, lived above bare subsistence level, more of national income than in previous wars could be diverted from civilian to military purposes, which was just as well. The conflict's total cost has been estimated at $208,500,000,000 in wartime prices, or $82,400,000,000 in 1913 prices, i.e., before the price level in most countries more than doubled.[1] Economic mobilization levels came close to those of the Second World War. For example, German public spending (most of it on the war) rose from 18 per cent to 76 per cent of NNP between 1914 and 1917;[2] in Britain, military spending in relation to GNP reached 70 per cent in 1917, compared with 20–25 per cent in 1814–15, and 54–57 per cent in 1943; in France, military expenditure may actually have exceeded National Income (due to borrowing) in 1917.[3] Moreover, deadlock cost more than the opening campaigns. Between 1914/15, 1915/16, and 1916/17, Germany's expenditure rose from $2,920 to $5,836 to $5,609 million; France's from $1,994 to $3,827 to $6,277; and Britain's from $2,493 to $7,195 to $10,303.[4] The big jump came between year one and year three.

A further reason for the stalemate and escalation of 1915–16 was that both sides commanded the wherewithal with which to fight, both financially and in real resources of raw materials, labour, and equipment. If the Germans gained an initial advantage in industrial mobilization, by 1916 the Allies had narrowed the gap, though the effort drove Russia to the brink of chaos and Britain into a foreign exchange crisis. By spring 1917 economic constraints were hitting both sides with a vengeance, yet for most of 1915–16 they had been remarkably weak, despite the

prognostications of pre-war commentators such as Ivan Bloch that modern societies could not afford a long conflict.[5] In Italy for the first year Salandra resisted
Cadorna's appeals for resources and tried to contain costs, but after the shock of
the *Strafexpedition* restraint was abandoned. General Alfred Dallolio, the official responsible for munitions production, reiterated that his aim was high production
'cost what it may'.[6] The British Treasury agreed in 1914 to waive its normal right
to vet army and navy purchases. Karl Helfferich, the German finance minister in
1914–16, tried unsuccessfully to challenge the traditional army principle that
'money plays no part', but in the end made the best of things by boasting he had
never refused anything the military thought necessary.[7] In Austria-Hungary and
Russia too, until 1917, the war ministries had a free hand. Legislatures and finance
ministries relaxed their oversight on military spending, initially expecting a short
war, and failed to regain control when it proved to be long. In the colossal Western
Front bombardments the fruits of years of patient capital accumulation went literally up in smoke.

All the belligerents met only a fraction of their spending out of taxes. The reasons were partly technical: tax increases took months to approve and implement,
and many revenue collectors had been mobilized, forcing greater reliance on public goodwill. In addition it was argued that if governments borrowed rather than
taxed the next generation would be made to share the cost of a victory from which
it would derive the benefit. But at least equally important was concern to preserve
the political truces formed in 1914. Even in Britain, which relied most on taxation,
it covered only 26.2 per cent of wartime expenditure. By lowering thresholds from
£160 to £130 per year income tax was levied for the first time on large numbers
of manual workers, and between 1913 and 1918/19 the standard rate rose from
5.8 per cent to 30 per cent. Income tax and the excess profits duty (EPD) introduced in 1915 (a charge on profits that exceeded peacetime norms and a measure
that would be widely imitated) became the mainstays of wartime revenue. None
the less, the Treasury reduced the thresholds only after consulting the trade
unions to determine which sections of the working class could pay most painlessly, and much of the EPD liability could be postponed and was eventually cancelled.[8] Skilled workers and businessmen, the social groups who did best out of
the war, were handled with care.

In Germany taxation probably covered 16.7 per cent of wartime expenditure
by the Reich and state governments together and of that by the Reich alone only
8.2 per cent. Traditionally the Reich ran separate accounts for ordinary expenditure and for 'extraordinary' spending on capital projects. Helfferich treated the
war as an extraordinary item, maintaining that taxes should pay just for routine
civilian spending and to service borrowing; he told the Reichstag he did not wish
to add to the people's burdens and tax increases would be a drop in the ocean anyway. If the government raised indirect taxes it would increase working-class living
costs and jeopardize left-wing support for the war. But to impose direct taxes it
needed support from the states, which (as before 1914) was not forthcoming; as
Bethmann was at odds with the right-wing parties over war aims and U-boat warfare he hesitated to antagonize them further. The Reich did introduce taxes on
turnover and excess profits in 1916, but their yield was small.[9]

In other countries the contribution from taxation tended to be even less. Russia, France, and Italy followed Britain in introducing war profits levies but these were token gestures in the interests of national unity at a time when public clamour against profiteers was everywhere rising.[10] After years of controversy the French legislature had agreed in principle to income tax on the eve of war, but the finance minister, Alexandre Ribot, was unsympathetic to it and delayed until 1916 before implementing it at a nominal rate. For the first two years French government revenue hardly rose at all. Despite socialist protests the tax burden was more regressive than elsewhere and its 15 per cent contribution to total war costs was the lowest in any major belligerent. Indeed this figure was only enough to cover the French state's normal outgoings, rather than any of the cost of military operations.[11] Italy's estimated 23 per cent was higher,[12] as was Russia's 26 per cent, although in the latter case this was partly because Russia dropped out early. The tsarist government began by suppressing the vodka trade (hoping that temperance would improve output), although gross receipts from its monopoly of the trade had accounted for almost a third of its peacetime income.[13] Like France, Russia relied mainly on taxes on consumer goods and on services such as the post and railways, and the government waited until 1916 to introduce income tax. Liberal and autocratic states therefore differed little in their behaviour. Everywhere on the continent tax revenues rose little in real terms until 1916/17, and expenditure left them far behind.

European treasuries were caught between untrammelled military outgoings and the political imperative of not reviving peacetime controversies through tax increases. They tried – and here again the 'short-war illusion' was evident – to cover their deficits by borrowing at home and abroad, and beyond that in effect by 'printing money' if they received central bank credits without collateral. No central bank preserved much independence in wartime conditions: even the Bank of England, supposedly a private corporation, yielded to the Treasury its influence over interest rates and sterling's exchange value. In all the belligerents in 1914 the domestic gold standard was effectively suspended: paper money was no longer convertible on demand or a minimum proportion of gold reserves required to back the currency issue. With the ground thus cleared governments could obtain unlimited cash from the central bank in return for short-term liabilities such as treasury bills, which were typically redeemable in three to six months. In Germany special lending banks (*Darlehenskassen*) performed the same function for the state and local authorities. The consequence was a massive increase in money supply, accelerating as the war went on. From 1913 to 1918 notes in circulation (more sophisticated monetary indicators are lacking) rose by 1,151 per cent in Britain, 1,141 per cent in Germany, 532 per cent in France, and 504 per cent in Italy.[14] Yet monetary growth failed to generate a corresponding rise in prices, the wholesale index in 1913–18 roughly doubling in Britain and Germany (from 100 to 227 and 100 to 217 respectively), tripling in France (100 to 340) and quadrupling in Italy (96 to 409).[15] Part of the reason for the disparity was that the biggest German price increases were registered on the black market and therefore were excluded from official statistics. But in addition, governments absorbed excess liquidity by prevailing on their citizens to lend to them, though with increasing difficulty. States' borrowing power proved to be one of the key phenomena of the war, crucial to their ability to raise the sums they needed without undermining social cohesion through massive tax increases or even faster inflation. It was the more remarkable in view of Germany and Austria-Hungary's dwindling credit in the face of much smaller state deficits before 1914.[16] Hundreds of thousands of institutions and private citizens in the belligerents and the neutrals lent to governments whose outgoings were racing ahead of income and whose repayment capacity would be questionable even if they won. The European middle classes proved willing to gamble with their own prosperity as well as with their children's lives.

There were significant differences between the blocs. The German Reich launched nine war loans (*Kriegsanleihen*) at six-month intervals from September 1914 to September 1918. Issued normally at a generous 5 per cent interest rate and redeemable after ten years, they formed a propaganda focus: banks bought them in blocs and businesses sold them on to employees. 1.2 million people subscribed to the first loan and a peak of 5.2 million to that of March 1916. Over the war as a whole they were much the most significant source of revenue, bringing in about 100,000,000,000 marks, or two thirds of war costs. But whereas up to summer 1916 they more or less kept pace with spending, mopping up short-term treasury bills and containing the growth in the note issue, subscriber numbers began to dwindle with the issue of the fifth loan in September, and the floating debt, the money supply, and the inflation rate increasingly slipped out of control. The adverse turn in Germany's military fortunes also weakened it as a credit risk.[17] In contrast, Austria-Hungary had a much smaller public and although it also relied on German-style war loans and offered higher interest these met only 45 per cent of Austro-Hungarian war costs. The Austro-Hungarian banknote circulation increased by fifteen times during the war, and the currency depreciated much faster.[18]

In France, Ribot felt that in an invaded country he could not expect investors to be as confident as on the other side of the Rhine. He did not offer a war loan until November 1915, and then at the higher interest rate of 5.73 per cent tax-free. Three more loans in October 1916, October 1917, and September 1918 raised the total yield to around 24,000,000,000 francs, but this was less than a third of the revenue from the mainstay of French budgeting: national defence bonds (*bons de la défense nationale*). These treasury bills were redeemed over periods from three to twelve months at an annual equivalent of 5 per cent interest. They were promoted in the press and were widely available in post offices and savings banks. They offered a financially attractive package without the riskier commitment attached to long-term loans. Despite the danger that they would all be cashed in at once, in practice enough could always be sold to keep state debt rolling over.[19] Not only did France levy less tax but more of its debt was short-term than in Germany or Britain. The latter occupied a midway position, issuing large amounts of medium-term debt, relying less on long-term bonds (as Germany) or short-term bills (as France), and borrowing more than any other country from the United States. Italy too was relatively successful in containing currency expansion and inflation by issuing long-term war loans. But in Russia, whose war costs rose from 2,540 million roubles in 1914 to 9,380 in 1915 and 15,267 in 1916, both the money supply and prices quadrupled by January 1917. Although the tsarist government issued war loans, they yielded not much more than 10,000 million roubles and left the largest contribution to be made by treasury bills, mostly taken up by the state bank. In the absence of a large investing public Russia expanded war production impressively but paid for it with a monetary destabilization that went further and faster than elsewhere. And inflation, which impoverished anyone on a fixed income or who held money as wealth, was the most arbitrary tax of all.[20]

The Allies had larger borrowing requirements to satisfy, not least because collectively they spent much more:

TABLE 2.

War Expenditure [21]

$ Current Billion

Britain	43.8
British Empire (excl. Britain)	5.8
France	28.2
Russia	16.3
Italy	14.7
USA	36.2
Others	2.0
Total Allies and US	147.0
Germany	47.0
Austria-Hungary	13.4
Bulgaria and Turkey	1.1
Total Central Powers	61.5
Grand Total	208.5

On the other hand, they had more opportunity to borrow abroad. True the smaller Central Powers could borrow from Germany, which from 1915 granted Austria-Hungary a subsidy of 100 million marks a month and also allowed it to borrow from a banking consortium to finance its purchases (by October 1917 Vienna owed this consortium more than 5,000 million gold marks).[22] Both powers also lent to Sofia and Constantinople; indeed Bulgaria largely met its war costs from foreign borrowing. On the other hand, Germany itself purchased very substantial quantities on credit from the neutral countries on its borders, especially Holland, Switzerland, Denmark, and Sweden – although Allied pressure gradually diminished these deliveries.* By the end of the war it owed Holland alone 1,600 million gold marks, and it sustained the mark's value on the foreign exchanges with considerable success.[23] None of this compared, however, with the webs of interdependence that from 1914 to 1917 developed first among the Allies and then between them and the United States.

This web is best investigated by beginning with the weaker Allies. Part of the Italians' price for intervention was a £50 million loan on the London capital market, though they limited their financial requests so as not to weaken their hand in the territorial negotiations. So far from maintaining the autonomy they had hoped for, however, within months they depended on Britain not only for coal

---

*See ch. 10.

and shipping but also to finance imports from America of wheat and petroleum that had been blocked from Italy's peacetime Romanian and Russian suppliers by the closure of the Dardanelles. By August 1915 the British were subsidizing Italy by £2 million per week, and they insisted (as for France and Russia) on it shipping gold in return as a security. It was probably partly in return for an increased coal allowance that Italy finally declared war on Germany in August 1916.[24] Russia, similarly, borrowed from Britain and France to finance its purchases from them and from the United States. The Commission internationale de ravitaillement (international supply commission) enabled the weaker allies to import from America on financial terms arranged by Britain and France with their superior credit ratings. The tsarist empire commanded little confidence with American investors even before attacks on Jews in Poland during the 1915 retreat earned it more odium. In February 1915 the British and French governments agreed to support Petrograd in raising £100 million in the London and Paris capital markets. An agreement in September provided for British credits of £25 million a month for the next year. Over 70 per cent of American funds lent to Britain and France in the neutrality period were for Russian use.[25]

None the less, the burden of financing their partners, linked to their own increasing needs, dragged France and Britain down. As France's payments deficit widened, its foreign borrowing rose from 2,800 million francs in 1915 to 8,800 million in 1916; between 1914 and 1916 it borrowed 7,800 million from Britain and 3,400 million from the United States. Not only did Britain place and finance all Russia's American purchases from 1915, and increasingly those of Italy, but from May 1916 it also financed all France's American orders, as well as supporting the franc in the foreign exchange markets. The entire Allied war effort would be vulnerable if Britain's American credit-worthiness deteriorated. By October 40 per cent of all the British government's war purchases, for itself and for its allies, were made in North America, and the Treasury was expected to come up with more than $200 million a month.[26] Whereas financing Britain's war effort domestically was relatively easy for the first two years, finding the dollars to afford American purchases became its Achilles heel.

The problem had two interrelated aspects: paying for orders and maintaining the sterling–dollar exchange rate.[27] The normal means of solving the problem would have been through exports. But France's exports, hit by invasion and the priority for armaments, were halved between 1913 and 1915, Russia's had always been tiny and were interrupted with the rest of its commerce, and although Britain ran a balance of payments surplus for most of the war, it suffered from the cabinet's 1915–16 decisions for conscription and a munitions build-up at the expense of traditional exports such as textiles. Conversely, between 1913 and 1915 the volume of British imports from America rose by almost 68 per cent. The British authorities had made a fundamental decision in the crisis of August 1914 to maintain the foreign exchange convertibility of sterling, and the Bank of England actually increased its gold reserves during the war.[28] Nevertheless, the currency began to slide from the pre-war parity of £1=$4.86, causing a scare when in August 1915 it touched $4.70 and only $4 million were available to meet bills of $17 million due in the next week. The sterling–dollar parity was a prestige issue, flagged up in Allied propaganda to contrast with the depreciation of the mark, and intrinsic to British self-perceptions of economic robustness. More practically, letting sterling fall would add millions to the cost of import bills. Of course one possible response was to limit purchases. In January 1915 the British appointed the New York banking house of J. P. Morgan & Co. as their purchasing agent, in order to minimize competition between government departments and to drive harder bargains with suppliers. They used Italy's and Russia's growing dependence to insist on supervisory rights over their procurement. But Britain's own spending departments fought off a Treasury move to restrict their American orders. Other expedients would therefore be called for.

One possibility was to sell assets. Britain, France, and Russia agreed in 1915 to pool their central banks' gold reserves. But gold was much less valuable than the huge European investments built up in America over previous years, the British alone holding more than £835 million of American securities in 1914. After the August 1915 scare the government requested owners of these assets to sell them to the Bank of England, which would dispose of them in New York for dollars. In 1916 it imposed a discriminatory tax on those who failed to comply, though the French were less rigorous. Naturally this disposing of the family silver meant forgoing investment income in the future, thus compromising the Allies' long-term prospects in order to meet short-term need, and by late 1916 the scope for further such financing was nearing exhaustion. But neither was borrowing more than a temporary solution. Again in response to the August 1915 scare, the British and French governments decided to raise an unsecured loan of $500 million, J. P. Morgan leading the consortium of underwriters. They had to offer an interest rate of nearly 6 per cent, more than for their war loans at home. Even so, the purchasers were mainly east coast bankers and manufacturers, many of them beneficiaries from Allied contracts. Otherwise the bond issue met with indifference or hostility, fed by German-American propaganda and by scepticism about whether the Allies would win (the securities would not mature until 1920). Far from the loan reaching the general public as the Allies had hoped, non-institutional investors took up only $33 million. After this disappointment the French government left it to French private companies and municipalities to borrow in America, as their creditworthiness was better than that of the French state. The British government resorted to borrowing on its own account, raising $250 million in August 1916 and $300 million in October that year, but on both occasions it had to pledge collateral by dipping into its dwindling pool of dollar securities.

By autumn 1916 Allied financial relations with the United States were reaching crisis point, and not only for technical reasons. Having initially judged that allowing foreign governments to borrow would be un-neutral, Wilson changed his mind on advice from the United States Treasury and State Department, a major consideration being to secure the export boom. By February 1916 90,000 tons of freight a month were being moved in America on the account of Britain's munitions ministry, and Allied traffic clogged the port of New York. For a year between May 1915 and May 1916 Wilson was embroiled with Germany over U-boat warfare and he downplayed his irritation over the Allied blockade's infringement of American maritime rights. But thereafter the Germans were temporarily quiescent, while friction over the blockade intensified.* Britain's repression of the Easter Rising in Dublin in 1916 antagonized Irish-Americans, as Russia's anti-semitism had alienated Jewish Americans. Probably more fundamental was Wilson's irritation that the Allies were blocking his efforts to mediate. In spring 1916 the British decided not to follow up his offer in the House–Grey memorandum,† gambling that the Somme would deliver a decisive victory before they reached their borrowing limits. By the autumn the offensive had evidently failed to do so, and its cost had made Britain still more vulnerable.[29] In response to rumours that Wilson planned another peace initiative, Lloyd George tried to head him off by reaffirming in a press interview on 28 September that Britain would carry on without outside interference until it had achieved a 'knock-out blow'. The president therefore had no reason to be accommodating when in November Morgan's disclosed to the Federal Reserve Board that Britain planned an emergency issue of Treasury bills. The Board feared American banks would be choked with short-term obligations that Britain could not redeem; in any case it wished to rein in the boom for fear of it getting out of control and causing a post-war slump. With political considerations in mind, Wilson toughened the wording of the Board's announcement on 28 November that warned American citizens and banks to be wary of foreign bills. The statement killed the Allies' new financing plan, placed great pressure on the pound, and forced the British to suspend new orders. By the time the United States entered the war in April 1917 London had enough gold and securities remaining to finance just three more weeks of purchases and only advances from Morgan's enabled the Treasury to meet its obligations in the United States. Although the British could still have covered their dollar requirements without American intervention they would have had enormous difficulty in continuing to bankroll their allies.[30]

The crisis did not mean that the Allied war effort would have collapsed if the Americans had not intervened. As British and Russian munitions production came on stream American contracts were becoming more dispensable. The exchange rate could have fallen from the $4.76 (itself below the pre-war parity) that had prevailed for most of the neutrality period, though by making imports more expensive this too would have choked off supplies. Wilson had previously proved willing to accommodate the Allies financially to assist the American boom, but it was now in America's economic interest to restrain the expansion. Diplomatically, the Foreign Office feared that Britain would be less and less able to resist Washington's pressure to end the war by negotiation. The longer-term outlook might be one of creeping paralysis at the very moment when a co-ordinated strategy and plentiful artillery and munitions at last held out better prospects. Relations with America were not, however, the only point of Allied strain. In Russia by late 1916 inflation was spiralling out of control and impinging on the real economy (including urban food supply), though it is true that a similar process was beginning to show itself in the Central Powers. The belligerents' resilience was not endless, and both sides seemed to be nearing their borrowing limits. Thus far they had financed spectacu-

---

*See ch. 10.
†See ch. 5.

lar increases in war production with only modest increases in taxation and the money supply. In large measure this resulted from the willingness of the minority of their populations with substantial savings to buy bonds that would mature long after the fighting was over. The investing public in Germany and Britain wagered on victory in a desperate and evenly matched conflict. To be sure, there were few alternative financial outlets and governments offered attractive incentives, at the cost of mounting debt service and an albatross round the necks of post-war taxpayers. But the willingness to lend also testified to an innocence derived from pre-war monetary stability as well as to a residuum of patriotism. War finance depended on traditional values and assumptions that the conflict itself was subverting.

Finance mattered because money gave claim to real resources. It could pay for labour, food, and raw materials, and set up machine shops and assembly lines. What counted militarily was not so much general economic potential as capacity to maintain and supply armed forces.[31] It was as well that the Allies could draw on American supplies, for their inherent advantage in real resources was small. True, they had more people: the British Empire, France, Russia, Belgium, and Serbia in 1914 numbered some 656 million to the Central Powers' 144 million. Much of the Allies' population, however, was remote from industrial centres. Britain, France, and Russia accounted for some 27.9 per cent of world manufacturing production, which was less than half as much again as Germany and Austria-Hungary's 19.2 per cent. In the most relevant industries for arms production, the Central Powers had the edge, producing on the eve of war some 20.2 million tons of steel against the Allies' 17.1 million and leading in many branches of chemicals and engineering.[32] After war broke out Germany's industrial output fell by an estimated 23 per cent in 1914–16, but by 1915 the Central Powers controlled most of Belgium, much of northern France, and the Polish industrial areas, and they exploited them mercilessly. On the other hand Italy joined the Allies and Russia's industrial output rose by 17 per cent by 1916, but much of France's heavy industry was lost and in 1914–16 Britain's industrial output fell by 3 per cent, expansion in armaments failing to compensate for the running down of civilian sectors.[33] None the less, the record for armaments production (as opposed to that for economic growth as a whole) suggests that after a disastrous start the industrial contest moved to the Allies' advantage.

How this happened is best studied by considering the French, British, Italian, and Russian examples in turn. France was the most extreme case. Like everyone else the French underestimated the vast munitions consumption of quick-firing field guns that in static warfare could simply shoot at the enemy until shells ran out. Compared with Germany's or even Russia's their army was poorly endowed with heavy guns, which were much harder to manufacture than shells. The occupied regions accounted for 58 per cent of France's steel production, 83 per cent of its iron ore, 49 per cent of its coal output, and major portions of its engineering, chemicals, and textiles industries. Yet France seems to have been more successful than any other belligerent in converting manufacturing potential into arms and munitions deliveries, and it did so to the benefit of other armies besides its own: it exported to Russia and Romania and later provided much of the equipment of the American Expeditionary Force.

The French achievement has some parallels with the Soviet one in 1941–5: previously isolated regions such as the south-west entered into military production. Yet the major centre of arms manufacture was the Paris basin, barely fifty miles from the line.[34] And unlike in Stalin's Russia civilian living standards fell only slightly and the driving force behind industrial transformation was private profit, albeit fuelled and steered by state subsidies and contracts. Before 1914 France, like most European countries, had a mixed arms economy of state ship-yards and arsenals alongside private firms; pre-eminent among the latter being Schneider at Le Creusot. During the war the state sector expanded its capacity and workforce, the government constructing for example a massive new arsenal at Roanne (which turned out to be an expensive failure). But of 1.675 million employees in arms production in 1918 (compared with 50,000 four years earlier), only 0.285 million (18 per cent) worked in state-owned enterprises.[35]

Joffre and GQG decided requirements, initially in consultation with the war ministry. After May 1915 an under-secretariat for artillery and munitions under the socialist deputy Albert Thomas took over procurement, and later became a ministry in its own right. After the Marne the top priority was for 75mm shells, along with machine-guns, rifles, and cartridges; after the 1915 offensives the emphasis switched to heavy guns and munitions.[36] The authorities met regularly with representatives of each industrial sector, starting during the autumn 1914 munitions crisis. Ministers preferred to deal not with individual companies but with committees of leading producers, whom they left to allocate contracts. Thus the metallurgical industry was represented by its trade association, the Comité des Forges, which took responsibility for all metal supplies to factories. In the chemical industry a similar privileged relationship existed with one company, St-Gobain, though the authorities encouraged a broadening of the circle of companies in war production. Generally (as with the other belligerents) state plants and established arms firms concentrated on the more difficult manufacturing tasks such as heavy artillery (Schneider) and machine-guns (Hotchkiss). Simpler work, for instance the turning out and filling of shell cases, went to firms that had converted from civilian production. State loans (probably totalling over 10,000 million francs) and subsidies assisted conversion, for example by the future car giants Citroën and Renault, manufacturers respectively of munitions and tanks. The government offered advantageous prices but lacked powers to verify company accounts. By October 1915 Thomas believed profits were excessive, but when the government tried to force down prices the industrialists threatened to withhold production and the authorities backed off.[37]

In addition to manufacturing plant, the armaments drive needed raw materials and labour. Because of the loss of the northern coalfield, much coal had to be imported (mainly from Britain), as did steel (from Britain and the United States). In addition, France had to expand its output of chemicals, such as sulphuric acid, that it had previously purchased in Germany. By 1916 French foreign exchange and British shipping shortages began to bite and raw material constraints became tighter. British pressure forced the French to introduce wide-ranging controls over raw material supplies and production. But in general labour shortages were more serious, as France conscripted a higher proportion of its manpower than any other belligerent. In August 1915 the Assembly passed the Dalbiez law on labour supply – a key sign that the French were resigning themselves to a long war. Its purpose was partly to comb out civilian 'shirkers' (*embusqués*) for the army, but under its terms some 350,000 soldiers were released to the war industries, where they remained technically mobilized and subject to military discipline. A second major labour source, generally for less skilled work, was women, often older and married and transferring from textiles or domestic service rather than entering employment for the first time. Between January 1916 and January 1918 their numbers in munitions production more than trebled.[38] Finally, the French drew heavily on immigrant labour, either from abroad (particularly Spain and Portugal but also from China)[39] or from their colonies in North Africa and Indochina. In summary, of 1.7 million armaments employees in November 1918, 497,000 were soldiers, 430,000 women, 133,000 juveniles under eighteen, 108,000 foreign, 61,000 colonial, and 40,000 prisoners of war. The government permitted long working hours and worsening health and safety standards, and such a diverse and rapidly expanding labour force was ill placed to resist. None the less, it delivered the goods. Initially quality control was poor: faulty munitions destroyed 1,000 artillery pieces in 1915.[40] But the big expansion came between autumn 1914 and spring 1917. Daily output of 75mm shells rose from 4,000 in October 1914 to 151,000 by June 1916; that of 155mm heavy shells, from 235 to 17,000; that of rifles from 400 to 2,565.[41] In 1917 France produced more shells and artillery pieces per day than Britain and as many aero-engines as Britain and Germany together.[42] By July 1915 the war ministry was well satisfied with 75mm shell production, and by August 1916 GQG was confident it had enough heavy artillery munitions for it to fight on the Somme until winter and continue with even better supplies the next spring.[43]

In comparison Britain had a larger (and uninvaded) industrial base, plentiful domestic coal and iron ore, and virtually unimpeded raw material imports. It also had a bigger skilled labour force, although one much more highly unionized and better organized to defend its own interests. Its state armaments sector was small, but it had large and efficient private manufacturers such as Vickers and Armstrong. On the other hand its greatest strength was in warship construction, and it faced special problems in equipping an expeditionary force that in 1914–16 grew more than tenfold. The response came more slowly than in France, and gave the state a more interventionist role. Lloyd George's *War Memoirs* gave the impression that the crucial change came with the political crisis of May 1915 that led to the replacement of the Liberal cabinet by the first coalition government. It included a new Ministry of Munitions, independent of the War Office, with himself at its head.[44] In fact munitions output expanded nineteen times in the first six months of war and the War Office under Kitchener's leadership was blamed excessively for supply failures. Like everyone else the British took time to invest in new machinery (much of it imported from America), retrain labour, and step up explosives production, for which the denial of German chemicals proved a crucial bottleneck, though one that was eventually overcome by producing acetone (the gelatinizing agent) from maize mash and nitrates from Chilean saltpetre.[45] However, the War Office exacerbated matters by sticking mainly to its list of approved companies and letting them compete with one another for raw materials, workers, and machinery. They contracted for more than they could deliver, and by June 1915 the shortfalls were 12 per cent for rifles, 19 per cent for artillery pieces, 55 per cent for machine-guns, and 92 per cent for high explosive shells.[46] The issue caused great tension between Kitchener, who resented interference, and Lloyd George, who in February 1915 called for the total mobilization of engineering resources. Matters came to a head with the 'shells scandal' that followed the abject failure of the attack at Aubers Ridge in May 1915. Sir John French told *The Times* correspondent, Charles Repington, that the defeat resulted from lack of high explosive shells, which an editorial in the same newspaper blamed on Kitchener. Actually, although the inadequate bombardment was indeed a big contributor, at this stage the artillery would probably not have known how to use more shells even if they had been available.[47] All the same the episode gave Lloyd George his opportunity, with Unionist support and Asquith's acquiescence, to set up the new department and to stake his political future on solving what appeared the key problem of the war.

Although the Ministry of Munitions fell short of its own ambitious targets, there were certainly impressive increases in all production categories before Lloyd George moved on to the War Office in July 1916, and the foundations were laid for even greater ones before British growth, like French, levelled off in the spring of 1917. Shell deliveries rose from 2,278,105 in the six months from January to June 1915 to 13,995,360 in January–June 1916, and 35,407,193 in July–December, though (as in France) higher totals were offset by mediocre quality control. Deliveries of Vickers machine-guns rose from 109 in March 1915 to 1,000 in November 1916, and artillery production also rose substantially for the heavier calibres.[48] Indeed Britain was ahead of France and Germany in shifting its priority from field guns to heavier weapons.[49] Other devices, notably the tank and the invaluable Stokes mortar, might never have entered mass production without the ministry's sponsorship. As raw material bottlenecks were still minor, except in explosives production, the key problems lay in finding plant and labour. As concerned the first, Britain could draw on capacity in its empire. Australia supplied smaller quantities of field gun shells and India delivered rifles and all categories of munitions for Europe and for the Indian troops in Mesopotamia, but the main provider was Canada. Canadian manufacturers could not produce more complex items such as fuses and at first most of them fell behind on their contracts, but by 1917 over 250,000 people in Canada were employed in armaments work under the supervision of a branch of the British Ministry of Munitions, the Imperial Munitions Board, and in that year Canada delivered between a quarter and a third of the artillery munitions used by the British on the Western Front.[50] None the less, the home islands remained the main production base. Lloyd George's new ministry, drawing heavily on seconded executives, brought greater order to procurement. It instigated a census of capacity in some 65,000 factories and divided the country into local areas in each of which business representatives were grouped in boards of management. But in contrast to most continental countries, in Britain the state also became a major manufacturer, expanding its existing arsenals (particularly Woolwich), and building and operating National Shell Factories, National Projectile Factories (for heavier munitions), and National Filling Factories.[51] It directly controlled seventy factories by the end of 1915 and 250 by the armistice.[52] The filling factory at Barnbow, near Leeds, for example, built on a greenfield site in 1915, filled nearly 25 million shell cases and its workforce rose to over 16,000.[53] Running its own plants helped the ministry to assess reasonable production costs, and it was empowered to inspect accounts and to pay only a cost price rather than a market price for its orders; it could also commandeer private establishments, and frequently did so.[54] War profits in the private sector were permitted, but were held down.

The government also intervened to increase the availability and contain the cost of labour.[55] Britain was much slower than France to send its young men to the front, and throughout the war a lower proportion of its manpower was in uniform. But the incidence of volunteer recruitment was haphazard, and often led to the loss of skilled workers in key industries. By mid-1915 the per centage of the male workforce taken by military recruitment was 21.8 per cent in mining, 19.5 per cent in engineering, 16 per cent in small arms manufacturing, and 23.8 per cent in chemicals and explosives. Nor did the War Office prevent the enlistment of skilled men.[56] The munitions ministry did recall soldiers from the front to work under military discipline, but it made much less use than the French of this device, or of foreign and colonial labour. Instead Britain's basic response was 'dilution'; i.e., quickly training up unskilled and semi-skilled workers (notably women) to undertake jobs previously reserved for skilled trade unionists. Dilution therefore required negotiation to persuade the unions to relax their apprenticeship rules. The first experiments began in the winter of 1914–15 but the main dilution programme followed from October 1915 onwards. Government intervention was needed to train the women and insist that state contractors employ them, as well as to regulate their pay rates and working hours and ensure that proper canteens, washrooms, and nurseries were provided. As in France, the main influx of women into factories came in the middle period of the conflict: 382,000 entered employment in the year from July 1914 to July 1915, 563,000 from July 1915 to July 1916, and 511,000 from July 1916 to July 1917.[57] Woolwich Arsenal increased the number of its female employees from 195 in June 1915 to over 25,000 by July 1917.[58] After the trade unions agreed to the principle of dilution in 1915, and resistance from established workers (principally on Clydeside) was broken in 1916, it proceeded rapidly. The vastly expanded munitions workforce of 1917–18 was of a very different composition from that of 1914 and was also more tightly disciplined, the 1915 Munitions of War Act outlawing strikes and lockouts in the industry and instituting compulsory arbitration. Until 1917 it also restricted employees' rights to move from plant to plant, though as a *quid pro quo* it imposed a profits ceiling in 'controlled' establishments.[59] Between them these measures created a huge nationalized or state-regulated munitions sector that did service until the end of the war. Yet the BEF had meanwhile so expanded that the arms effort could barely keep pace with it; only in 1917–18 were the fruits of the production revolution gathered in.

The two remaining Allied powers – Italy and Russia – present a contrast. The Italian government re-equipped slowly during the neutrality period, and even during the 1915 campaigning season it tried to fight a limited liability war.[60] In September, according to the French attaché, Italy was producing fewer than half the number of shells the government had planned. The steel industry was still delivering mainly on civilian contracts, which the government – concerned to uphold normal business conditions – had not overridden. Some skilled workers had been called up, and others were reluctant to assist in a war that the PSI had opposed.[61] Nevertheless, by 1917 Italy's production in some weapons categories became impressive. Although way behind Britain and France in machine-guns and shells, it manufactured 3,681 aircraft, and was close to Britain in artillery and rifles.[62] Yet its 1914 steel output had been only one third of France's in volume and one ninth of Britain's, and nearly all its coal and iron ore were imported.[63] Alfred Dallolio, who became under-secretary in the war ministry for arms and munitions in 1915 and an independent minister in 1917, played an analogous role to those of Lloyd George and Thomas. After the Trentino offensive he was given a free hand to increase production without limiting costs, and expenditure rose sharply; it was perhaps symptomatic of his regime that in 1918 he resigned because of corruption allegations.[64] He created a 'central committee for industrial mobilization' and a network of regional committees, representing the services, business, and labour, which shared out contracts and were responsible for industrial relations in the localities.[65] State production did expand, but the private sector accomplished most of the work and Dallolio wanted its voluntary collaboration if possible. Although the government took powers to requisition factories, it did not use them, permitting large profits that it scarcely taxed. Although Dallolio was sympathetic to wage increases and tried to work with the trade unions, he coerced labour much more freely than he did business. Workers were forbidden to strike or move freely from job to job and many were placed under military discipline: 128,000 by December 1916 and 322,500 by August 1918. By August 1916, 198,000 women had been brought into war production plants, though they were used later and in smaller numbers than in France, and in the plants in southern Italy hardly at all.[66] In general, therefore, Italy's industrial mobilization followed the French model, though it began later and was implemented less drastically, delivering less impressive results.

In contrast the Russians, after a delayed start, made their maximum effort in 1916. Their version of the general early shell shortage was particularly prolonged, also affecting rifles and machine-guns and restricting their operations until the winter of 1915–16. Yet Russia's heavy industry, if small in relation to the country's size and population, was comparable to that of France, and although depending on imports for more sophisticated items Russia produced its own (very successful) 76mm field gun and heavy artillery. It had the usual mixed armaments economy, though the state sector was stronger than elsewhere. In 1914, however, it lost its sea outlets and overland trade with Central Europe. Hence it could import neither German machinery and chemicals nor British coal, which was the main energy source for the arms firms concentrated in Petrograd. Instead the city resorted to the Donets coalfield in the Ukraine, some 800 miles distant and connected by inadequate railways.[67] Government policy added to these handicaps. The tsarist regime confined its interaction with private industry to placing contracts, while skilled workers were being called up and domestic coal and iron ore output was falling. Unlike the French authorities, the Russian ones did not widen the supplying firms beyond the customary peacetime circle,[68] as they feared losing control over quality and prices.[69] A decree required plants to give priority to naval and military orders, but in general the approach was one of *laissez-faire*.[70]

Sukhomlinov doubted Russian industry could produce complex modern equipment to a sufficient standard, and he preferred to go abroad. By the start of 1915, 14 million shells had been ordered from British and American firms, followed by 3.6 million rifles from Winchester, Remington, and Westinghouse. This policy proved to be an expensive mistake, as the foreign suppliers were unreliable. By November 1916, 40.5 million shells had been ordered abroad but just 7.1 million had arrived; only half the rifles ordered from America were delivered by March 1917. Yet the overseas orders were enormously expensive and became more so when by 1916 the rouble had depreciated to half its pre-war value.[71] Even when available they were difficult to transport, given that the Trans-Siberian Railway had very limited capacity, that only an incomplete narrow-gauge track ran to Archangel (which was not ice-free), and that a line to Murmansk was completed only in March 1917. Foreign contracts became a major source of machine tools and raw materials such as copper, but most of Russia's war supplies were manufactured on its own territory.[72]

In summer 1915 the shell shortage caused a political crisis, the government being assailed by Duma deputies, city and provincial authorities, and business representatives. As a result structures for government–industry co-operation were created on the model of those of the other belligerents, notably Germany. Sukhomlinov was replaced as war minister by A. A. Polivanov, for whom business and the Duma had greater respect and who was more willing to spread contracts.[73] The government created a 'special council for defence' representing industrialists, officials, and parliamentarians, with authority over all state agencies and private firms working on defence contracts: it could place arms orders, supervise their distribution and execution, and assist firms to invest in equipment. Special commissions and factory boards in the regions could inspect accounts, dismiss managers, sequestrate factories, and insist on government orders being fulfilled. However, the predominance of representatives of Petrograd industry on the special council caused a revolt by their Moscow counterparts. The main national business organisation called for the formation of local war industry committees (VPKs) and a central committee (TsVPK) in Petrograd. By February 1916 thirty-four district and 192 local VPKs had been created, the initiative coming from local councils and enterprises. Although these were non-governmental organisations the special council worked closely with the TsVPK, delegating to it responsibility for distributing grants, contracts, and raw materials among its members. As a result of these changes, orders for simpler items such as grenades and shells were distributed much more widely among Russian manufacturers, although many of the firms delivered late. Probably more significant was simply the fact that the government was prepared to spend far more in 1916 than in 1915, in response to the invasion of Russian territory and the upsurge of feeling against the occupiers. Re-equipment was generously subsidized, and contracts set with wide profit margins to encourage new firms to tender. By 1916 Russia, exceptionally among the belligerents, was experiencing a regular boom, with rising growth and a bullish stock exchange: coal output was up 30 per cent on 1914, chemicals output doubled, and machinery output trebled.[74] Armaments rode the crest of the wave: new rifle production rose from 132,844 in 1914 to 733,017 in 1915, and 1,301,433 in 1916; 76mm field guns from 354 to 1,349 to 3,721 in these years; 122mm heavy guns from 78 to 361 to 637; and shell production (of all types) from 104,900 to 9,567,888 to 30,974,678.[75] During the war Russia produced 20,000 field guns, against 5,625 imported; and by 1917 it was manufacturing all its howitzers and three quarters of its heavy artillery.[76] Not only was the shell shortage a thing of the past, but by spring 1917 Russia was acquiring an unprecedented superiority in men and *matériel*. The price of this Herculean effort, however, was dislocation of the civilian economy and a crisis in urban food supply. The very achievement that moved the balance in the Allies' favour by summer 1916 contained the seeds of later catastrophe.

It is now necessary to consider the Central Powers' response to the revolution in Allied production. The response was mainly German, though Austria-Hungary's contribution was not negligible. The Dual Monarchy had a small but sophisticated armaments industry that produced advanced dreadnought battleships and the 305mm mortar that hammered the Liège and Verdun fortresses. After war broke out Germany insisted on the Austrians organizing *Zentralen*, or 'centres', for their industries: limited liability companies owned by the firms in each sector, which took over the supply of raw material, provided capital, and allocated quotas under government supervision (although the system was confined to the Austrian half of the Monarchy).[77] Companies such as Skoda, the biggest arms firm, doubled their profits, and output rose sufficiently to meet most of the army's needs, aided by the capture of large numbers of Russian rifles. By September 1915 the AOK was satisfied with shell and rifle provision,[78] and indeed rifle and machine-gun output was not far behind Russia's.[79] The updating of the field artillery showed its benefits in the Trentino campaign; and lack of equipment was not the main reason for the Brusilov disaster. All the same, Austrian industry suffered from serious handicaps. Labour shortages were alleviated by similar measures to those taken elsewhere, though fewer women were recruited than in the Allied countries. Moreover, in the Austrian half the authorities invoked emergency powers to conscript unfit men aged under fifty for the war industries; in factories placed under this regime the workers were under military discipline, wages reduced, and an eighty-hour week was not uncommon.[80] Shortages of raw materials were pressing: Austria-Hungary lost its main oilfield (in Galicia) in 1914, and the wells had been badly damaged when it regained them.[81] It depended partly on Germany for coal, as well as for Swedish iron ore. Germany supplied its ally with gas masks, hand grenades, trench mortars, and aircraft, and in 1916 it produced more than four times Austria's number of shells. Austria-Hungary could more or less equip itself, but gave little help to a German economy that was by far the most important supplier to the Central Powers.[82]

   Germany had the biggest manufacturing potential in Europe, its territories were intact and unoccupied, and it could draw on Belgian, French, and Polish resources. It enjoyed strength in depth in crucial strategic industries. The army made the usual mistake of calling up skilled workers in 1914, but labour shortages were alleviated by a modest increase in the female labour force, achieved mostly by redirecting women out of textiles and domestic service rather than drawing them into paid employment for the first time.[83] The most serious production constraint seemed likely to be scarcity of raw materials, the Allied blockade immediately halting, for example, nitrates and copper from Chile. The nitrate shortage – critical to explosives manufacture – was addressed by the use of the Haber/Bosch process for fixing nitrogen from the atmosphere, though the slow growth of explosives production using this method became the key determinant which for the Berlin war ministry planners regulated the growth rate for everything else. The shortage also led, however, to a major organizational innovation, sold to the authorities in August 1914 by Walther Rathenau, the head of the AEG electrical concern. This was for a 'war raw-material section' (*Kriegsrohstoffabteilung* or KRA) in the ministry, staffed mainly by businessmen. It monitored and controlled raw-material output and encouraged the search for substitutes for commodities that were unavailable. The main branches of each industry set up 'war raw-material companies' (KRGs): joint-stock companies empowered to buy, store, and distribute raw materials to their members under government supervision. Some production controls were delegated to existing cartels or syndicates, such as that for coal.[84] Subsequently the government agreed to deal not with individual firms but with bodies such as the *Kriegsmetall*, the KRG for the metal industry. In all cases it retained a final say over their decisions. Finally, the 'war committee of German industry' (KdI), a special body set up by the leading employers' associations, provided advice to the ministry. The system therefore included a large element of industrial self-government. It was based on private enterprise, and arms firms such as Krupp made large profits. To begin with war contracts were awarded on a cost-plus basis with a guaranteed 5 per cent margin.[85] But in 1915 the war ministry tightened up its cost control and monitoring of accounts, and its labour policy also caused friction with business. Under the Prussian law of siege the DCGs in charge of Germany's military districts were directly responsible to Wilhelm for 'public safety' in their areas, and their extensive decree powers included authority over labour supply. Many DCGs, like the 'exports and exemptions office' (AZS) in the ministry, which issued guidelines to them, wanted good relations with the trade unions. The AZS resisted business demands for more men to be exempted from the army, and advised the DCGs to mediate in labour disputes rather than simply back the employers.

Over questions of both cost control and labour relations the war ministry therefore had poor relations with the business community. The latter's chance to strike back arrived when Germany came under pressure. Although a munitions shortage had impeded operations in autumn 1914, it was overcome quite quickly.[86] The BASF chemical concern, using Fritz Haber's process for 'fixing' nitrogen, produced ammonia, and manufacture of the other key components needed for explosives was also successfully improvised. Despite the loss of imports due to the Allied blockade, the Germans obtained the tungsten, nickel, and aluminium needed for weapons manufacture from their own or from Austrian deposits. Field gun production rose from 100 to 480 monthly in the year after December 1914 and in 1915 output of field gun and light howitzer ammunition substantially exceeded consumption.[87] Admittedly the Germans were helped by their principal 1915 operations being against the Russians in the more mobile conditions of the Eastern Front. But even in the west, when Falkenhayn turned against Verdun he at first enjoyed both artillery and aerial superiority. The summer of 1916, however, partly because of the need to help the Austrians, became a crisis period for Germany in munitions supply as well as in other respects.[88] The war ministry had expanded powder production from 1,200 tons per month in August 1914 to 4,000 in December 1915 and 6,000 by July 1916, and was planning a further rise to 10,000,[89] with commensurate increases in shells and artillery. Yet it still looked vulnerable after the unexpected demands on the Somme, which – however catastrophic its opening might have seemed to the British – greatly impressed the German soldiers who took part in it with the Allies' new strength in *matériel*. Falkenhayn's resignation brought to power an impatient and inexperienced new leadership of OHL, and one of its staff officers, Colonel Max Bauer, who had friendly contacts with Krupp and heavy industry, played a key role in formulating Hindenburg's and Ludendorff's policy. Following hard on a memorandum in which the industrialists assailed the ministry's record, on 31 August Hindenburg wrote to the war minister, Wild von Hohenborn, outlining what would become known as the 'Hindenburg Programme' of armaments expansion.

The programme can be seen both as an attempt by OHL to redress the strategic balance and as one by business to shake off official constraints.[90] Tactically, as Hindenburg put it, it was an effort to keep pace with the Allies in a revolution in warfare, in which machines were replacing horses and men. Output of munitions and trench mortar output, he pleaded, should double by spring 1917; that of machine guns and artillery should treble; and aircraft should also be a priority. Financial obstacles should be disregarded. A supreme Allied effort could be expected in the next year, and more artillery, trench mortar, and machine-gun detachments were needed to hold the front line with fewer men and to reconstitute a mobile reserve. So that more soldiers could be recruited and the production increase achieved, legislation was needed to extend compulsory service (or labour related to the war effort), to all men and women aged between sixteen and fifty, while all non-essential industries should close down.[91] Where earlier the Russians had copied German models, now it was Lloyd George's ministry of munitions and British practice that OHL wished to emulate.

Hindenburg and Ludendorff wanted more weapons, new legislation to discipline the labour force (and restrict women's rights), and to marginalize the war ministry. Following its Allied counterparts, the latter would have its wings clipped. Little of this turned out as its proponents envisaged. Wild von Hohenborn, an associate of Falkenhayn, was replaced by a man the new OHL trusted, Herman von Stein. A new agency for procurement matters, the WUMBA, was created in September. The war ministry's armaments responsibilities, including the KRA, the AZS, and relations with the DCGs, were hived off to another new agency, the war office or Kriegsamt, which was placed under the GGS's former railway chief, Wilhelm Groener. Ludendorff would oust him too in 1917 for being too sympathetic to the unions and too willing to limit profits. But the Kriegsamt was to administer the new ASL, or 'Patriotic Auxiliary Service Law', which was submitted to the Reichstag in November 1916. Because Bethmann Hollweg objected to compulsion for women as excessively harsh and radical,[92] the bill required all men aged seventeen to sixty who were not already in the services or war industries to work for the war effort where needed. In its passage through the Reichstag it underwent numerous modifications in favour of the trade unions, which Groener welcomed, seeing stronger unions as an insurance against revolution in the event of defeat. Local committees comprising military officials, employers, and employees would decide on the labour needs of each trade in a district; the committees would decide whether workers should change their place of employment, and could mediate in disputes over pay and conditions; while in all businesses operating within the system and employing over fifty people, workers' committees would be elected.[93] In short, the law, as passed in December, turned out to be a charter of union rights, and its value for implementing OHL's objectives was small: some consumer goods plants were shut down and 118,000 workers released for redeployment, but the big movement of labour was out of the army and back into industry. Between September 1916 and July 1917 the number of conscripted workers rose from 1.2 to 1.9 million, while combat strength stagnated.[94]

This stagnation made more weapons all the more urgent, but the Hindenburg Programme was slow to deliver them. The Austrians took part in it, but their shell production actually declined.[95] Yet the Germans themselves did little better. The completion date was May 1917 but before then the programme had effectively been suspended with all its targets well short of fulfilment. It may have increased industrial profitability, contracts being once again awarded on a cost-plus-profits basis.[96] But it released men from the army and committed transport and raw materials to a programme of new factory construction that turned out to be unnecessary and unrealizable: much of it was soon abandoned. Its demands, coming on top of those for troop movements to Romania and an exceptionally severe winter, overstrained the railways.[97] Matters were exacerbated by a crisis in the coalfields, where Ruhr production in April fell to two thirds of peacetime levels. In February steel production was not only below target but actually less than it had been six months earlier, while powder production, which had been scheduled to reach 12,000 tons in May, was still only 9,200 in July.[98] The aviation target was 1,000 new aeroplanes a month, but coal and transport shortages reduced the total to 400 in January, and 900 was not regularly exceeded until August.[99] It is true that higher targets were reached in most of the designated sectors by the second half of 1917, but the war ministry's previous plans had intended to do this anyway, without the wasteful excesses that the programme engendered. During 1917 the production ratio between the two sides did move back in the Central Powers' favour, but as much because of the slowdown in Allied production (and collapse in Russia) as Germany's own increase, while Austria-Hungary's output was slipping into absolute decline. In the meantime, the winter economic crisis and the Hindenburg Programme's failure encouraged OHL both to embark on the retreat to the Hindenburg Line and to press for unrestricted submarine warfare, in order to protect Germany's depleted and under-equipped forces against a new Allied assault.

Financial and industrial developments were therefore essential in shaping the evolution of the war in 1915–17, as the initially unprepared Allies moved the munitions balance in their favour and regained the strategic initiative. The cost disastrously overheated the Russian economy and drove Britain into a foreign exchange crisis, and in the spring of 1917 the production increase would peter out. But the Central Powers were hardly better situated. After the measured expansion under Helfferich and Wild, Hindenburg and Ludendorff pushed for more, at the moment when, as will be seen,* harvest failure was about to expose German civilians to dangerous privation. The great upsurge of borrowing since 1914 had temporarily relaxed the material constraints on the belligerents, but now they were coming to be felt again. For this reason among others, the next phase of the struggle would be very different from the all-out battles of 1916.

---

*See ch. 11.

CHAPTER 10

Naval Warfare and Blockade

AN ESSENTIAL precondition for the 1915–17 stalemate was economic mobilization. But a precondition for that mobilization was that neither side could stifle its adversary by cutting off supplies. Hence the need to analyse the Allied blockade of the Central Powers and the U-boat campaign against Allied shipping. In the middle period of the war although both were intensified both remained comparatively ineffective, but in 1917–18 both took a tighter grip. None the less, for the time being the Allies maintained command of the sea over most of the world's oceans and denied it to their adversaries. In conjunction with their world-wide empires and trading connections this command was an incalculable advantage to them, though it took time to yield its benefits.

The war at sea after 1915 resembled that on land in being a stalemate, neither side succeeding in destroying the other's main forces. But this was a stalemate of inactivity punctuated by raids and ambushes rather than one of grinding battles of attrition. The British and German battleship fleets opened fire on each other only for two periods of less than ten minutes each on 31 May 1916; the opposing Adriatic, Baltic, and Black Sea capital ships never even came within range. The admirals' caution owed much to their vessels' vulnerability to mines and to torpedoes fired from submarines, torpedo boats, or destroyers. Battleships that had taken years to build might disappear within minutes. Moreover, in each main theatre one side clearly had the advantage: Britain over Germany in the North Sea; Germany over Russia in the Baltic; France and Italy over Austria-Hungary in the Adriatic; and Russia over Turkey in the Black Sea. The weaker side had little motive to risk annihilation, nor the stronger to risk nullifying its lead. In contrast to the situation on land, however, that at sea disadvantaged the Central Powers. The major challenge to this generalization was the predicament of Russia, whose pre-war outlets via the Dardanelles and Baltic were severed. But elsewhere, once Germany's cruisers had been swept up and its overseas bases captured, the Allies' fleets everywhere dominated. Command of the sea allowed them to use it as a highway for their navies, merchant vessels, and troop ships, and to deny it to their enemies.

Having access to the resources of most of the planet, they could also conduct amphibious operations, and throttle their enemies' seaborne trade. The latter, with exceptions such as Germany's success in shipping in 17 million tons of Swedish iron ore,[1] could not do likewise.

Of these three advantages the most important was probably the first. In 1914 the Allies had 59 per cent of the world's steamer tonnage (and the British Empire alone had 43 per cent) against the Central Powers' 15 per cent.[2] Command of the sea enabled British steamers to ferry over a million Dominion soldiers across the world without loss,[3] and to ship hundreds of thousands of men back and forth across the Channel. During the war British shipping moved over 23.7 million people, 2.24 million animals, and 46.5 million tons of British military stores.[4] Command of the sea allowed the French to bring their troops from Africa and Britain to double its imports from the empire, receiving vast quantities of Australian wool and Canadian wheat and shells.[5] France, with its main coalfield occupied, became newly dependent on British coal; Italy had always been poor in resources and relied on maritime imports of food and raw materials even in peace. By the second half of the war British shipping brought in almost half of French and Italian imports.[6] American seaborne supplies of oil, grain, steel, and arms were still more significant, even before the USA became a belligerent. The Allies' logistical advantage was crucial to the build-up that made their offensives of summer 1916 possible.

In contrast, the Allies made little use of seapower for amphibious operations, and possibly less than they could have done. Admittedly their vessels rescued the retreating Serbs in 1915, the Russians attacked Trebizond from land and sea in 1916, and the Salonika, Mesopotamia, and Gallipoli operations all began with troop landings. But of these latter only the last was opposed, and the scope for similar operations in Northern and Western Europe was limited. Even in the eastern Mediterranean, Salonika was constantly problematic because of submarine attacks, which also drove the Allies' battleships from Gallipoli. Cadorna ruled out using landings in the Adriatic (apart from a brief expedition to Albania from December 1915 to February 1916),[7] and the Germans did not attempt to land behind the Russians during the 1915 Baltic coast advance. Britain sent marines to Antwerp in 1914 but the cabinet rejected plans to disembark in Germany or on its offshore islands, and Haig's plans for amphibious assaults on the U-boat bases in Flanders were shelved in 1916 in favour of the Somme and in 1917 because of the slow progress of his Third Ypres offensive. The obstacles were partly technological, particularly the lack of landing craft and the array of devices developed in the Second World War for overcoming shore defences. Support ships in European waters were highly vulnerable, and a rapid advance from a coastal bridgehead was scarcely more likely than a breach in the inland trench lines. But wartime experience also bore out the pre-1914 contention of the geopolitical thinker Sir Halford Mackinder that land transport, in the form of modern roads and railways, was supplanting the seaways as the most effective channel for moving armies and supplies.[8] On the principal fronts amphibious operations remained might-have-beens.

Blockade was another maritime instrument whose results were disappointing. Technically neither side mounted a blockade in the sense used in the Napoleonic Wars, i.e., a line of ships stationed outside enemy ports to intercept merchant shipping and confiscate contraband (war-related goods). 'Economic warfare' – a term that became current during the conflict – more accurately depicted the two sides' measures. Its use against Russia is often overlooked. The Central Powers halted the tsarist empire's overland trade (which had been its main pre-war source of imports)[9] while Denmark (acting for fear the Germans would do the job, and violate its sovereignty) mined the passages through its territorial waters connecting the Baltic with the North Sea.[10] This action left German vessels free to pass between the two through the Kiel Canal, but debarred the Baltic to outside shipping, apart from submarines. Finally in September 1914 the Turks closed the Straits. Between them these actions greatly impeded Russian contact with the other Allies. Goods sent to Vladivostok had to travel 4,000 miles along the Trans-Siberian Railway; items shipped to the Arctic ports were at the mercy of such inadequate links to the interior that they piled up at the wharves; and material sent across Sweden was used by Stockholm to demand 'compensation' – every transport allowed for the Russians was balanced by one for the Central Powers.[11] Yet transport difficulties did not prevent Petrograd from placing huge orders in America and Britain: and manufacturing difficulties in the west rather than logistical factors were the most serious obstacle to delivering them. Down to 1916 Russia's war economy grew faster than Germany's.

The effect of the Allies' blockade of the Central Powers was also limited for its first two years, despite beginning with major advantages. In 1914 64 per cent of Germany's merchant shipping was interned in neutral ports ,[12] and the British Isles' geographical location allowed the Royal Navy to close off access to Germany's ports by operating a distant blockade. A minefield laid early in the war compelled all vessels in the Straits of Dover to use the narrow passage between the Goodwin Sands and the Kent coast, where they could be halted and searched. The cruisers of the northern patrols watched the seas between Scotland and Norway.[13] They intercepted some 3,000 Allied and neutral ships (mostly Scandinavian) in 1915 and 3,388 in 1916, and very few slipped through the net.[14] Italian and French ships stationed at Otranto and Corfu could monitor shipping in the Adriatic even more closely. The naval aspect of the blockade was close to being hermetic, and Germany's imports shrank to 55 per cent of their pre-war value by 1915[15] and 34 per cent by 1918, which in volume terms meant only one fifth.[16] Yet this contraction, if far more drastic than the Allies were suffering, remained well short of the total suppression of enemy commerce, and Germany's dependence on imports had traditionally been less than Britain's anyway. On a few points, such as the lack of Chilean nitrates (needed for fertilizers and explosives) Germany quickly felt the pinch, but in many cases it found substitutes and it could cope without food imports until its domestic agricultural output began to fall.[17] Austria-Hungary suffered more severely, but in part because the government of the predominantly agrarian Hungarian half of the Dual Monarchy withheld supplies from the cities of the Austrian half. Food riots began in Vienna as early as 1915.[18] In Germany, however, British intelligence detected little discernible fall in civilian living standards until the autumn of 1915, and no serious deterioration until a year later.[19]

The crucial problem for the Allies was less maritime than diplomatic: their relationship with the ring of 'northern neutrals' surrounding Germany (Switzerland, the Netherlands, Denmark, Norway, and Sweden), which was closely connected with their relationship with the greatest neutral, the United States. Except against Switzerland (where France was responsible)[20] Britain took the lead, and its policy became to impose the tightest controls that the Americans would tolerate. Yet Germany ran up big trade deficits with its neighbours, its overall deficit during the war averaging 5.6 per cent of net national product.[21] Imports of Swedish iron ore, Norwegian nickel and copper, and Dutch and Danish food, in large measure financed by credit from the neutral banks, became on a smaller scale the Central Powers' equivalent of American supplies to the Allies. As the Royal Navy could spare only a few submarines for the Baltic and the Russian navy was unwilling to operate beyond the Gulf of Finland, maritime power could do little directly to stop the leakage. If it were to be brought to bear on the problem it would have to be indirectly, through trade restrictions imposed on the neutrals in order to limit their assistance to the enemy.

Acting thus would mean violating international law and therefore risking confrontation with America, though this proved a less serious problem than were the negotiations with the northern neutrals themselves. The law of war governing blockade and contraband had been to some extent consolidated in the Declaration of Paris in 1856 and the Declaration of London in 1909. The latter tried to protect neutrals by dividing merchandise into 'absolute contraband' (war-related goods such as munitions, subject to confiscation in all circumstances); 'conditional contraband' (goods with both military and non-military uses, such as food and fuel); and a 'free list' of goods such as cotton, oil, and rubber that should always be immune from seizure.[22] However, the British House of Lords had refused to ratify the London Declaration, and in 1914 Britain and France undertook to respect it only with such qualifications as to deprive their adherence of much meaning. They quickly eroded the status of conditional contraband by applying to it the 'continuous voyage' doctrine, i.e., detaining food consigned for a neutral port if they suspected the ultimate destination was Germany. Although they used the spurious pretext that all food supplies in Germany were under government control, their real aim was to stop German stockpiling against the possibility of a long war and to satisfy public clamour to throttle the enemy.[23] Furthermore, on 2 November 1914 the British Admiralty proclaimed the entire North Sea a 'war zone' that merchant ships could enter safely only if they followed specified paths. The British tried to justify this step by invoking their right of reprisal against German minelaying, but in doing so they set a precedent for a tit-for-tat that would quickly subvert the framework of law altogether.[24] When the Germans cited Allied illegalities to justify introducing unrestricted submarine warfare in February 1915, Britain and France again cited their right of reprisal in order to retaliate (in a British Order in Council of 11 March) by announcing their intention to prevent all commodity movements in and out of the Central Powers. Neutral as well as enemy harbours were now blockaded and the distinctions in the London Declaration collapsed – the Allies soon declared that cotton was contraband and eventually revoked their adherence to the Declaration's terms. In reality submarine warfare was simply used as a pretext for a policy the British were determined on anyway, in response to the pressure of their own public opinion and the growing evidence that defeating Germany would be long and costly.

The Allies tightened the screws with little American opposition. Overriding advice from his Secretary of State, William Jennings Bryan, to react more forcefully, Wilson was slow to respond to the British measures. In a series of protest notes he maintained that they were illegal and that he reserved the right to claim compensation, but he neither made threats nor demanded that the measures should be revoked, and he implied that much would depend on how they were implemented.[25] He seems to have feared the dispute would escalate into a repeat of the confrontation over neutral rights that had caused the Anglo-American war of 1812. In addition, he regarded an Allied victory as being in America's interest, he hoped to co-operate with London in mediating an end to the war, and he understood the importance of Allied purchases for American prosperity. Nor did he desire simultaneous conflict on two fronts, given that for a year between May 1915 and May 1916; German submarine warfare was his top diplomatic priority. After May 1916 he took up a tougher position, partly because the blockade seemed to be harming United States interests more directly. Two measures in particular aroused the American public: from the end of 1915 the British opened mail (including American mail) on the neutral ships they detained and in July 1916 they published a 'blacklist' of neutral firms (including American companies) that they suspected of dealing with the Central Powers and with whom they forbade British firms to do business, thus denying them access to British coal and shipping.[26] The president's anger (he described the blacklist as 'the last straw') was shared in Congress, which in September 1916 voted him powers to deny Allied shipping access to American ports, as well as a navy bill with which Wilson intended to give America more diplomatic leverage against Britain. None the less, he held back from invoking his new embargo powers, avoided an ultimatum, and ignored a proposal from the European neutrals for joint action.[27] The British made some concessions over the opening of neutral mails, but essentially American protests had no impact.

The blockade machinery looked impressive on paper, but even after the declarations of March 1915 it remained full of holes, and for two more years German trade with the neutrals remained substantial. No inter-Allied agencies existed to oversee the blockade until a 'permanent committee' was set up in Paris in June 1916; it proved to be purely consultative and of minor importance.[28] The French suspected, with some justice, that the British were more lax in their approach than they claimed. Thus British legislation (unlike French) allowed British subjects in neutral countries to continue trading with the enemy. Some Allied financial and business interests militated against too tight a blockade: French plans for pre-emptive purchasing of Dutch meat and Swiss cattle were defeated by the Paris finance ministry's refusal to pay for them[29] and City of London traders successfully opposed restrictions on supplying coffee to Germany via the neutral countries. The Board of Trade and the Treasury, in contrast to the Foreign Office and the armed services, favoured continuing British commerce with the neutrals, both to earn foreign exchange and to safeguard export markets. Moreover, Britain needed Dutch margarine and Swedish pit props, and at one stage 90 per cent of nitrates destined for France and vital for explosives production came from the Norsk Hydro company in Norway.[30] There were also diplomatic reasons for not pushing the neutrals too hard. Quite apart from the Allies' claim to be fighting on behalf of the rights of small nations, Sweden could retaliate by blocking the transit trade to Russia, and Germany might invade its neighbours if their neutrality came to seem one-sided. Although the Allies had cards in their hands, too – they controlled the neutrals' seaborne supplies and the Scandinavian economies depended on British coal – their efforts to tighten the blockade rested on negotiated agreements with the neutral governments, who had to take account of their publics' divided loyalties (though Norway and Denmark were generally pro-Ally) and the need to balance between the two blocs.

Despite these obstacles, the loopholes were gradually eliminated. In the first months Allied exports to the northern neutrals mushroomed, much of the extra food and raw material being passed on to Germany.[31] In a series of negotiations the Allies agreed not to interfere with the neutrals' imports of contraband if the latter promised not to re-export them.[32] The Dutch government approved the creation in January 1915 of the Netherlands Overseas Trust (NOT), a private agency that took over all Dutch imports, the British agreeing not to restrict them if the NOT vouched for their consumption within the country.[33] The British saw the NOT as a major success. It served as a model for the Société suisse de surveillance économique, which fulfilled a similar function for Switzerland, and for agreements with the Danish Merchants' Guild and the Copenhagen Chamber of Manufacturers, which took on comparable responsibilities for Denmark. The Swedes, on the other hand, resisted any such arrangement, while negotiations with Norway broke down when the Danish agreement was criticised in Britain for being too favourable to Germany.[34] This 'consignment' system, as it was known, hindered but did not stop neutrals from re-exporting to the Central Powers and still less did it prevent them from selling their own agricultural surpluses to Germany. In spring 1916 the Netherlands was Germany's largest foreign supplier of food, while until Romania joined the Allies its wheat deliveries were crucial to Austria-Hungary.[35] The Allies responded by limiting the neutrals to such quantities of imports as were deemed essential for their domestic needs. By October 1916 imports of over 230 categories of product into Switzerland were restricted, though the system was much less comprehensive elsewhere.[36] Second, the British made preclusive purchase agreements, notably with the Netherlands in 1916, to buy up a proportion of neutral produce at guaranteed prices. These agreements substantially reduced food imports into Germany, and appear to have contributed to its decision to renew unrestricted submarine warfare in February 1917.[37] By now the blockade had probably been tightened as much as diplomatic constraints permitted (until the United States entered the war), and it was beginning to inflict real damage at a moment when inflation, harvest failure, and over-expenditure on armaments were pushing the German economy into crisis. As with Allied strategy on land, so in the sphere of economic warfare persistence was beginning to yield results.

Germany had two instruments for challenging Allied command of the seas: surface ships and U-boats. It could not make maximum use of both simultaneously, as its capital ships needed submarine accompaniment if they ventured out. Hence a phase of intensified High Seas Fleet activity in 1916 fell between two longer periods dominated by U-boat campaigns. The reasons for the Germans' caution on the surface included weakness in numbers, geographical disadvantages, and an inferiority complex, which the Helgoland and Dogger Bank battles reinforced. Increasingly the German navy's purpose (as before the war) was as a 'fleet in being', maintained for power political purposes against London, rather than for action. Even more emphatically was this true of its Austro-Hungarian counterpart, whose capital ships bombarded Italy's coast on the night the latter declared war but never approached it again, and whose main use was to tie up Allied resources.[38] The High Seas Fleet likewise compelled the British to invest in an enormous infrastructure for supporting the Grand Fleet, whose ships could otherwise have been released for commerce protection and anti-submarine warfare. It helped deter an inshore blockade and raids against the German coast, and protected Germany's iron ore imports from Sweden. But there was little prospect of it wearing the British down to parity by attrition or by isolating and defeating their warships in detail. It is true that after the bombardment of Britain's east coast towns in December 1914 the newly constituted Battlecruiser Fleet, under Beatty's command, was stationed as a forward interception force at Rosyth, while the Battle Fleet, under Jellicoe, remained at Scapa. But when Pohl replaced Ingenohl as High Seas Fleet commander after the Dogger Bank battle he agreed with Wilhelm that he would not risk battle more than one sailing day's distance from port,[39] and during 1915 only the navy's most modern capital ships were kept operational.[40] Nor was there much likelihood of Jellicoe playing into German hands. Thoroughly aware of the unpredictability of a great naval battle fought with modern technology, he set it as his dictum not to gamble when he had the upper hand. In a memorandum to the Admiralty of 12 April 1916 he reiterated his longstanding doctrine that he would not risk losing his own capital ships in order to destroy the enemy's.[41]

While the Germans hesitated, the British emerged from their most vulnerable period in the first months of the war, and benefited from two huge new advantages. The first was their ability to decrypt intercepted German naval wireless messages, an operation based in Room 40 of the Admiralty building in Whitehall.[42] For this they were indebted to the abilities of the Room 40 team but also to remarkable good luck. Three German naval codebooks were retrieved within weeks of the start of the war, from a cruiser boarded by the Russians in the Baltic, a steamer seized by the Australians, and a chest fished up by a British trawler off the island of Texel. From December 1914 Room 40 normally gave advance warning of a German sortie (even if the navy's Operations Division did not always make best use of the information), whereas the Germans never had comparable success in reading British traffic. The British changed their codes more frequently and observed greater wireless discipline, the Admiralty communicating with the Grand Fleet by land line whenever it was in harbour.[43] The second advantage came from naval construction. In 1914 the Royal Navy had twenty-two dreadnought battleships and a far from crushing margin of superiority. By contrast, when the two fleets met in May 1916 at the battle of Jutland the British had twenty-eight dreadnought battleships against sixteen German ones (and nine battlecruisers against five).[44] Because their capital ships had heavier guns, their total broadside weighed twice that of the Germans: 400,000 tons against 200,000.[45] To an extent these developments had pre-war origins. The Germans in 1914 were still benefiting from their peak construction rate between 1908 and 1912, but from late 1915 the arrival of the extra ships built by the British after the scare of 1909–10, including the *Queen Elizabeth* class of fast oil-fired super-dreadnought battleships with 15-inch guns, redressed the balance to their advantage.[46] But in addition, during the war German warship construction times lengthened as submarines took priority. The labour force suffered drastically from army conscription, and the blockade made nickel and copper scarce. Germany completed two battleships in 1916, one battlecruiser in 1915 and another in 1917,[47] but Britain had thirteen battleships under construction in 1914 and added nine battlecruisers during the war, while the fleet received a total of 842 warships and 571 auxiliary vessels. 'Badges' protected skilled men in the shipyards from military recruitment, and the Admiralty held on to its experienced workers; army weapons plants had to recruit many more workers with no former training. The navy took precedence over the ministry of munitions in steel allocations, and warship building took priority over construction of merchant ships. Britain's worsening shortage of commercial tonnage and its inadequate shell provision on the Somme resulted in part from the traditional priority given to the fleet, to an extent that even sympathetic ministers like Churchill found excessive and that may have reflected concern to take advance precautions against American and Japanese rivalry after the war.[48]

It may seem surprising that an encounter between the battlefleets took place at all. In large measure the battle of Jutland resulted from a change in the German naval command, Admiral Reinhard Scheer replacing Pohl in February 1916. Scheer also wanted to avoid an all-out clash of titans, but he did intend (and gained Wilhelm's approval for) submarine and air attacks, raids on British shipping and the east coast, and sorties with his entire fleet, in the hope of luring a portion of the Royal Navy to destruction.[49] From February onwards the High Seas Fleet put out to sea at least once a month, and the British did likewise, carrying out two air raids against the German coast. A clash became increasingly likely. Early on 31 May Scheer and his First Scouting Group of battlecruisers under Hipper began a sweep through the Skagerrak against British patrols and merchantmen. Thanks to a warning from Room 40 Jellicoe and Beatty were already at sea and the fleets steered on converging courses, though neither realized they were doing so. On the contrary, because of a misleading report from the Operations Division the British commanders supposed the High Seas Fleet was still in Wilhelmshaven several hours after it had actually left port. The result was that Jellicoe steamed slowly to conserve fuel and Beatty was dangerously far ahead of him when he ran unexpectedly first into Hipper's battlecruisers and later into Scheer's battleships. He then led Scheer into an equally unexpected clash with Jellicoe's main force, from which Scheer twice turned away before escaping during the night.[50]

In the initial phase of fighting between Beatty and Hipper which began at 3.48 p.m. – known as the 'run to the south' – Beatty's battlecruisers were supported only belatedly by the four new super-dreadnought battleships of Hugh Evan-Thomas's Fifth Battle Squadron, although the latter had been assigned to the Battlecruiser Force since May. Beatty had been cruising with the four battleships too far behind him, and incompetent signalling by his flag lieutenant (as at Helgoland and the Dogger Bank) may have contributed to the delay, though so too may have a lack of initiative by Evan-Thomas. But in addition the British battle-cruisers engaged too late, failing to exploit their superior range. Silhouetted against the horizon they presented better targets, their gunnery was inaccurate, and their armour-piercing shells poorly designed. Above all the flash doors between their magazines and gun turrets had been left open for quicker loading, and the cordite propellant charges for their shells were more poorly protected than in their German counterparts. Probably for these reasons two battlecruisers, the *Indefatigable* and the *Queen Mary*, blew up with the loss of almost all hands. After the surviving British ships were led on to the main German force, however, they turned away soon after 4.30 p.m. and in the ensuing 'run to the north' headed back until at about 6.20 p.m. the pursuing Scheer came under the guns of Jellicoe's dread-noughts. A third British battlecruiser, the *Invincible*, was now lost, but Jellicoe, though inadequately informed by Beatty of the High Seas Fleet's whereabouts, skilfully deployed his battleships in line formation to the east of Scheer, thus en-abling him to rake the latter's vessels and interpose himself between them and their harbours. Scheer turned away almost immediately behind a smoke cloud and a destroyer attack with torpedoes, and Jellicoe did not pursue him closely, but half an hour later Scheer ran into the British battleships again: according to German writers in a deliberate effort to fend off a British pursuit.[51] He took heavy damage before turning away a second time behind the cover of a battlecruiser charge and a destroyer attack, to which Jellicoe responded by turning away as well. This proved to be the last chance to get even for the earlier British losses, as during the night the Germans managed to cross behind Jellicoe as he steamed southwards. They made their way home through a swept channel in the minefields off the German coast, leaving the British on the morning of 1 June on an empty sea.

With some 150 ships involved on the British side and some 100 on the German, Jutland was one of the most dramatic moments of the war. In contrast to the naval actions of the Second World War, aircraft played no part and submarines lit-tle (primarily influencing the battle through Jellicoe's fear of them). It is the leading historical example of an action between steam-powered capital ships, in which long-range gunnery caused most of the damage. The guns of 12-inch or broader calibre fired by the capital ships were bigger than almost anything used on land, and although both sides fought in poor visibility and aiming problems slowed the rate of fire, no 'shell shortage' impeded them. The biggest battleship squadrons were only briefly in contact, but Jutland was destructive enough. In contrast to the land battles of 1916, nearly all the casualties died, many from flash or scalding in-juries unknown in Nelson' s day or entombed in their foundering hulls. Fourteen British ships (totalling 110,000 tons) went down, including the three battlecruisers, and eleven German ships (totalling 62,000 tons), including one battlecruiser and one pre-dreadnought battleship. In a matter of hours the British lost 6,094 dead and the Germans 2,551, out of a total of 110,000 seamen engaged on both sides.[52]

Scheer made several errors, including bringing along a squadron of old and slow pre-dreadnought battleships. But the Germans clearly had the better of the fighting and exposed some serious British weaknesses. Their gunnery was more accurate as a result of better training, superior rangefinders, and more effective armour-piercing shells with delayed-action fuses, while the British ships were less well armoured and had fewer watertight bulkheads. Even though the Grand Fleet was much sooner ready again for action, the Germans gained a public relations victory on account of the number of British ships sunk. The memory of that loss still rankled after the war, Beatty (or at least those round him) alleging that Jellicoe had lost an opportunity to annihilate Scheer's force. Few commentators now question the shrewdness of Jellicoe's initial deployment or his prudence in avoiding night fighting against an enemy that was better equipped and trained for it. However, Jellicoe overestimated the danger from torpedoes and if he had pursued Scheer more vigorously after the latter's first about turn and had not turned away after the second he could probably have destroyed more German ships before night fell, and he could have done more to monitor the German movements after darkness.[53] It is of course easy in retrospect to criticize a commander who operated in circumstances of great confusion and inadequate intelligence, as well as growing exhaustion as the evening wore on. Jellicoe was perfectly justified in insisting that destroying the High Seas Fleet was secondary and the imperative was not to lose the battle,[54] though this raises the question of why he had put to sea at all. The central fact remains that Scheer failed in his strategic aim of annihilating Beatty's battlecruisers and equalizing the balance between the two fleets, thus ending up no better placed than before to attack the British Isles or shipping in the Channel, send out his cruisers as commerce raiders, or break the Allied blockade.

Jutland did not quite mark the end of the most active phase of the surface war. Scheer sallied out again on 18–19 August, Room 40 again warned the British, Jellicoe and Beatty put out to sea, and both fleets missed each other, Jellicoe showing more caution than ever in his fear of submarine ambush. At a conference on 13 September he and Beatty agreed, with Admiralty endorsement, not to venture again into the eastern or southern North Sea unless in exceptional circumstances. When Scheer came out once more on 10 October the Grand Fleet did not steam out to meet him. The British leaders perceived Jutland at the time less as a missed opportunity than a narrow escape from catastrophic danger, to which the appropriate response was greater caution rather than boldness, and when Beatty replaced Jellicoe as Battle Fleet commander in November he made no alteration. But Scheer too felt he had had a narrow escape, reporting to Wilhelm in July – and the latter accepting – that it was not possible by fleet action to eliminate Britain's superiority and force it to terms within a reasonable time.[55] He advised that only unrestricted submarine warfare could achieve these results, and it seems that one source of the U-boat campaign in the following spring was a perception that no decisive result was attainable on the surface. In October his fleet lost its submarine escorts, as well as twenty-four destroyers sent to Zeebrugge to facilitate the U-boats' passage through the Straits of Dover.[56] It did not venture out again until April 1918. As between surface and submarine action, the emphasis was shifting decisively to the latter.

Germany's decision in January 1917 to resume unrestricted submarine warfare from the following month was among the most epochal of the war. It was an indispensable precondition for American intervention and ultimately for Allied victory. For the purposes of the argument here, however, the first question is that of why down to 1917 submarine warfare had such *little* impact – less than that of the Allied blockade of the Central Powers – and therefore helped sustain the stalemate. The second question concerns what lay behind the escalation after that date.

The U-boats were held back before 1917 more by technical considerations than political ones. They were a very new weapon and their numbers were simply too small. Submarines had joined the navies only since the turn of the century and at first most admiralties had little use for them. Before 1914 the German admiralty staff made plans to attack Allied merchant shipping, but with surface raiders. Moreover, Tirpitz's main goal since the 1890s had been a battle fleet able to fight or at least intimidate its British counterpart; he saw a navy directed primarily against commerce as a heretical strategic concept and tried to silence its advocates.[57] In August 1914 Germany had twenty-eight U-boats in service, but many of them were unseaworthy. By the end of 1915 it had fifty-four operational boats and by the end of 1916, 133. Submarines suffered less than surface ships from wartime constraints: the number of shipyards involved was expanded and the labour force mostly protected against call-up. Ocean-going vessels could be completed in about eighteen months while smaller ones suitable for the Channel or coastal waters took six or seven. Much wartime expansion came in the lighter (UB and UC) classes based at Bruges in German-occupied Flanders. Even so, and fortunately for the Allies, building came in stops and starts. There was a big increase in boats ordered in autumn 1914 and spring 1915, but then a year's delay,[58] and few of the submarines ordered from 1916 onwards saw active service. Moreover, the U-boats should more accurately be described as submersibles rather than true submarines: they needed to surface regularly and they travelled with different propulsion systems and at different speeds when on the surface and beneath it. Only in 1915 were they provided with deck guns and explosive charges to sink their quarry, and although the larger models introduced later in the war carried twelve or more torpedoes, the smaller ones current at the start had only four. Finally, at any one time up to two thirds of the ocean-going U-boats were liable to be in port or travelling to and from their hunting grounds rather than on station. The submarine campaign could therefore never be an 'effective' blockade in the sense of an orderly and comprehensive procedure required by maritime law: it was random, indiscriminate, and calculatedly relied on terror. Even when they became more numerous, U-boats could not escort vessels into port, confiscate contraband, or install prize crews. Lacking space to take on goods, or merchant seamen as prisoners, they could only sink the ships they encountered. If they surfaced they could not linger, as in this condition they were most vulnerable. Following 'cruiser rules' meant surfacing, giving notice, and allowing the seamen time to scramble into the boats; 'unrestricted' submarine warfare meant sinking without warning, i.e., by torpedoes while submerged. The Germans began their first unrestricted campaign within months of the outbreak of war.[59]

The German action was a classic instance of the existence of a new weapon creating an incentive to use it. U-boats sank very few Allied merchantmen during 1914, but in September that year U-29 spectacularly torpedoed the *Aboukir*, *Cressy*, and *Hogue*.* Bauer, the U-boats' commander, began to urge a campaign of commerce destruction and insisted he had enough craft to undertake it. The idea was

*See ch. 2.

aired in the press, and publicly endorsed in November by Tirpitz, despite his previous neglect of the new weapon. Pohl, as CAS, doubted whether the results would justify so flagrant a violation of international law, but he allowed himself to be overborne and in January 1915 Wilhelm and Bethmann also submitted to the pressure. Notice was given that all shipping (Allied or neutral) entering a 'war zone' around the British Isles was liable to be sunk without warning. The navy argued (as it would again in the next two winters) that the time to strike was the spring, in order to cut off Argentinian and Australian wheat shipments before Britain's harvest was garnered. Retaliation against London provided one motive, the declaration being justified as a reprisal against British illegalities such as declaring the North Sea a war zone. Anger against the Allied 'hunger blockade' was a second factor, together with the navy's need to justify its existence and its future, given the inactivity of the surface fleet while German soldiers were dying in thousands. Finally, like the use of poison gas a few weeks later, unrestricted submarine warfare can be seen as a reaction against the prospect of a long, stalemated war. Bethmann and the foreign ministry never questioned its legality or morality but only its expediency, and thus far reactions from the neutrals against violations of international law had been slight.[60]

The Allies were totally unprepared for submarine attacks upon their commerce and had no effective answer to them. They destroyed forty-six U-boats in 1914–16, but this was only a third of the replacement rate and contrasts with 132 in 1917–18 (not to mention 785 in the course of the Second World War).[61] Most of the losses were due to mining, despite the lack of an effective anti-submarine mine at this stage. But at least British minelaying in the Channel led to a decision in April 1915 that henceforth U-boats must sail to the western approaches to the British Isles via the north of Scotland, which lengthened their voyages and lessened their hunting time. Surface patrolling achieved much less. Hydrophones were the only means of locating submerged submarines and their range was very short. Destroyers were twice as fast as surfaced submarines, but by 1916 U-boats could dive in forty-five seconds and there were too few destroyers anyway. An effective depth charge had to wait until June 1916 and a depth-charge thrower until July 1917. Of 142 actions between Royal Navy destroyers and U-boats up to the end of March 1917, submarines were destroyed in only six. Nor did the 'Q-ships' or decoys played up in British propaganda cause many losses: their main contribution was to make it riskier for U-boats to stick to cruiser rules, though at first most sinkings of merchantmen were by gunfire rather than torpedoes. The British were fortunate that when the Germans called off their first unrestricted campaign in September 1915 their merchant marine was still only 4 per cent smaller than at the start of the war.[62]

The campaign was suspended not due to Allied countermeasures but because of a shortage of U-boats and above all because of a confrontation with the United States. Bethmann had not foreseen this. Although Wilson immediately used much harsher language about the submarine campaign than about the British blockade and threatened to hold Berlin to 'strict accountability', he responded mildly to the first sinkings and even to American casualties. But on 7 May 1915 U-20's torpedoes sent to the bottom the Cunard liner *Lusitania* off the coast of Ireland with

1,201 dead, many of whom were women and children and 128 were Americans. Although the submarine commander could have had no doubt about the nature of his target, the sinking of the liner (which was in fact carrying munitions) caused no qualms in Germany. Yet it was a major coup for Allied propaganda in the struggle for American sympathy, and it tilted Wilson into a harsher course. Hardly anyone in America – and certainly not the president – favoured war, but Wilson rejected the option of warning his citizens not to sail on belligerent ships, and he demanded that Germany repudiate the sinking and pay compensation. When he failed to gain satisfaction he issued a second note requiring all merchant vessels (belligerent as well as neutral) to be treated according to cruiser rules, which from now on was the cornerstone of his position. He was not obliged to take this stand in defence of international law (which he had not upheld against British violations), but he argued that showing weakness would invite more trouble and danger, and that the damage to America's credibility arising from inaction would jeopardize his ambitions to mediate. He would not take on both sides at once, and he attached greater urgency to Germany's threat to American lives than he did to Britain's to American property, even if his indifference to the starvation of German civilians compromised his impartiality from Berlin's perspective. Bryan saw this point and wanted Wilson to protest against both U-boats and blockade, but after the second *Lusitania* note he resigned and was replaced by the robustly pro-Allied Robert Lansing. Wilson took no further action when the Germans failed to apologize or make reparation, but his prestige was now on the line.[63]

The consequence was twelve months of conflict over submarine warfare, during which the Germans tested the limits of American tolerance before reluctantly giving way. After the *Lusitania* sinking a gap opened between the naval chiefs, who mostly opposed concessions to Wilson, and Bethmann and the foreign ministry, who believed that avoiding American belligerency should take precedence over the submarine campaign. In June 1915 Bethmann secretly ordered that liners must be respected. The issue came to a head in August after the torpedoeing of another British liner, the *Arabic*, again with loss of American life, and the Germans now agreed first to follow cruiser rules for liners and then to call off unrestricted warfare altogether, diverting their boats to easier pickings in the Mediterranean. Because of his intransigence Tirpitz lost his advisory role on naval strategy and his supporter Bachmann was replaced as CAS by Henning von Holtzendorff, a longstanding enemy of Tirpitz and a submarine sceptic.[64] In 1915 the civilians had support from Falkenhayn, who feared that American intervention might bring in Holland and who wanted no distractions at least until he had completed his Balkan campaign. But a fiercer debate followed in spring 1916, once the naval staff had won over Holtzendorff into backing a second attempt to starve out Britain by interrupting its southern hemisphere supplies, and this time Falkenhayn encouraged them, as he believed a submarine offensive would assist his purposes at Verdun.[65] Although Tirpitz finally resigned on the grounds that only unrestricted warfare would suffice, a Crown Council at Charleville approved the compromise of an 'intensified' campaign. Liners and neutrals could be spared, but Allied merchant ships in the war zone would again be sunk without warning, as would all armed merchantmen. On 24 March, however, U-29 sank the French Channel steamer *Sussex*, and Americans

were among the injured. Wilson peremptorily insisted on cruiser rules being applied to merchant ships as well as liners, and threatened to break off diplomatic relations. The Germans acquiesced, and in their '*Sussex* pledge' of 4 May agreed to
follow cruiser rules, although reserving the right to reconsider if Wilson secured no
relaxation of the Allied blockade. It seemed that America had drawn a line in the
ocean and Germany had decided not to cross it.[66]

Wilson's stance was radical, for although he did apply more pressure to the
British in succeeding months he maintained the Germans must respect cruiser
rules whatever the Allies did. In other words, he was telling them not only to respect neutral rights but also how to pursue the war against their enemies, and he
resisted pleas from his party in Congress to be more emollient. Bethmann's response was to pursue the U-boat warfare to the maximum short of American belligerency, which he presciently forecast might bring the Allies financial aid,
armaments, and hundreds of thousands of troops, as well as demoralizing Germany's partners. He believed that the navy had too few submarines to starve
Britain into surrender, and was underestimating London's will to win. To give the
U-boats their head, he argued, would be a 'break-the-bank game' with national
survival, and for the moment he convinced Wilhelm.[67] Germany submitted to demands from an American president who permitted massive loans and arms sales
to the Allies and who acquiesced in their blockade. It did so with resentment but
out of prudence.

This was hardly a stable basis for détente and by the end of 1916 Bethmann's
position had crumbled, partly because of Germany's deteriorating circumstances
and partly due to internal power shifts, though the two developments were mutually reinforcing. Despite the Anglo-American friction during 1916 the Allied blockade was not lifted and instead became more complete, notably through the
preclusive purchasing agreement with Holland. Germany's remaining food imports dwindled at the same time as its home production dropped, following the
failure of the 1916 potato crop. Germany's cities suffered their first real subsistence crisis, and conditions in Austria-Hungary and Turkey were even worse.[68]
These developments, following the reversal of military fortunes and the Allies' co-
ordinated offensives in the summer of 1916, meant that Holtzendorff renewed the
submarine debate after August in a much bleaker climate than in the spring, and
against the prospect of further co-ordinated enemy attacks in the new year. When
Hindenburg and Ludendorff took over OHL they feared initially that an unrestricted campaign might mean hostilities with Denmark and the Netherlands
when the army was already stretched to its limit. They were less concerned about
the United States, whose military power they regarded as low. But after Romania
fell they could take more risks, and a U-boat campaign might, as Hindenburg put
it, protect his troops from a new Somme. As with so many of the duumvirate's
early initiatives, their backing for the navy was a response to the summer 1916
emergency. Their opinions mattered, because whereas Wilhelm II was willing to
override and ultimately dismiss Tirpitz and Falkenhayn, he was frightened of the
public adulation accorded to the Tannenberg victors and feared a showdown with
them. Their arrival also mattered in the Reichstag. A 'U-boat movement' of intellectuals, businessmen, and right-wing parties, overlapping with the campaign for

annexationist war aims, had supported the navy in the press and parliament since 1914, not only to hit back at the Allies and allow Germany's submariners to fight in greater safety, but also because it saw the issue as a good one with which to belabour Bethmann. In spring 1916 the chancellor was still supported by a majority in the Reichstag, where the Conservatives and National Liberals supported U-boat warfare but were outnumbered by the SPD, the Progressives, and part of the Catholic Centre. In October, however, the Centre's deputies passed a resolution that OHL's wishes must be decisive. Bethmann was increasingly isolated both outside the corridors of power and within them, and he had little to offer as an alternative to the navy's gamble beyond continuing attrition in which Germany's enemies were gaining the upper hand. Nor did diplomacy promise much. In December OHL pressure contributed to Jagow's replacement as foreign minister by the more bellicose Arthur Zimmermann. The Allies had not been split, and they rejected the Central Powers' peace note of 12 December, while Wilson's request on the 18th for statements of war aims failed to initiate a general negotiation – which Hindenburg and Ludendorff opposed anyway. The chancellor was at the end of his resources.[69]

While Bethmann's leverage was ebbing, Jutland had buttressed Scheer's position as Tannenberg had Hindenburg's, and the navy leadership – including the previously moderate chief of the naval cabinet and member of Wilhelm's entourage, Georg von Müller – united in support of an unrestricted campaign. Submarine numbers had doubled since a year before, 108 boats being completed in 1916, many of them longer-range and with more torpedoes.[70] In October the navy predicted that twenty-four more large U-boats and ten small ones would become available over the next six months.[71] In the autumn a fresh campaign opened following cruiser rules, in which the new Flanders boats figured prominently and Allied shipping losses rose to nearly 350,000 tons per month, more than double the previous average.[72] Even on a restricted basis the extra craft were making greater inroads on shipping than the Allies could replace, rendering the navy's claims more plausible than in previous rounds of argument. Its final push centred on a 56-page memorandum sent by Holtzendorff to Hindenburg on 22 December.[73] Holtzendorff predicted sinkings of 600,000 tons a month for the first four months and 400,000 thereafter, while 40 per cent of neutral shipping would be frightened off the high seas. The shipping available to Britain would shrink by two fifths, leading to food stocks falling below danger point, economic chaos, and crippling strikes and unrest. If the campaign began promptly in February, the British would have to sue for peace within five months. America's intervention was expected as a consequence, but neither its money nor its troops would arrive in time. The grim alternative was the war ending from 'exhaustion', which would be 'fatal for us'. Yet despite the batteries of statistics that a team of journalists, academics, and businessmen had culled to support the memorandum, its precision was spurious and it was much more a work of intuition than it purported to be. It accurately projected shipping losses, but underestimated Britain's economic and social adaptability, its willingness to contravene *laissez-faire* principles through food rationing and shipping control, its ability to expand its grain production, and the effectiveness of convoys. Privately the fleet command thought the document too optimistic,[74] and probably the admirals only half believed their case, but they chafed under the restrictions placed on them and their crews and they hoped to contribute decisively to a German victory. In fact Ludendorff was not convinced that the navy could win the war so quickly, though he believed that action was better than doing nothing and he hoped the U-boats could ease the situation on the Western Front, where he foresaw enormous pressure in the spring of 1917.[75] In the end the decision was not based on the strength of the arguments. With Romania defeated the trap was sprung. Hindenburg and Ludendorff made clear they would resign unless the navy got its way, Wilhelm caved in at a preliminary meeting before the decisive Pless conference on 9 January, and Bethmann resolved beforehand to go along with the decision rather than to publicize the disagreement by resigning. Helfferich was skilled in rebutting the navy's contentions, but Bethmann did not use a memorandum that his deputy had prepared for him.[76] At Pless, Helfferich made the charge that 'your plan will lead to ruin', but Holtzendorff rejoined, 'You are letting us drift to ruin'.[77] It was agreed to renew unrestricted submarine warfare from 1 February.

Well before the five months of Holtzendorff's estimate had elapsed it was clear that Pless had been a mistake. Had the U-boats continued to follow cruiser rules their rapidly growing numbers would have inflicted not much smaller losses, while Britain ran into financial crisis, Russia into revolution, and France into military mutiny. The choice was not, in fact, one of ruin versus ruin, and it would have been better, as Bethmann foresaw, to delay. The Holtzendorff memorandum resembled Nivelle's strategy in its desperate quest for alternatives to attrition, but it also resembled the Schlieffen Plan as a technical fix to Germany's political dilemmas. As in 1914, Berlin forced the issue and staked all on such a gamble, rather than pause in the hope that the situation would improve. The parallels matter, for it was precisely its willingness to opt for such expedients that made imperial Germany such a menace to its neighbours and ultimately caused its downfall. Pless was tantamount to a second decision for war, and it was no accident that Bethmann felt he was reliving the July crisis.[78] If in 1914 the target was France and Russia, and war against Britain the by-product, now the target was Britain, and war against America was accepted as the price. Whereas in 1914, however, Bethmann had been converted by the military's arguments, in 1917 he went along more passively with a course he knew to be misguided but felt too weak to resist. This time the options were thoroughly debated, but the wrong side prevailed. Like the Japanese before Pearl Harbor, the dominant party in Berlin hoped by rapid military action to present Wilson with a *fait accompli* that he would lack the will to reverse. It underestimated its antagonist but it courted the risk, even likelihood, of war against America with open eyes. Whatever the truth about the outbreak of the war in 1914, its extension in 1917 was no accident.

CHAPTER 11

THE POLITICS
OF THE HOME FRONTS

T HE ASSUMPTION THUS far has been that Europe's ruling elites started
and prolonged the war. They took the decisions that caused its outbreak, and
after it began they mobilized men and weapons, rejected peace feelers, and concentrated resources on the crucial fronts. Their actions would have been impossible, however, without willing co-operation from broad sections of the public, less
from those who cheered in the July crisis than those who subscribed to war loans
and who volunteered to work in armaments industries and to fight. Much of this
response to the emergency was generous and unforced, and given the suffering
that the war inflicted it may seem baffling. Part of the explanation (as with troop
morale) is that the home fronts' solidarity was temporary and provisional: by 1917
it had disintegrated in Russia, and much of the rest of Europe was experiencing
grave discontent. Moreover, resentment had little opportunity to be channelled
into politically effective protest. However weary many civilians became, censorship restricted criticism and all the political parties, except on the extreme left,
were committed to fighting until victory was won. Even so, the First World War
cannot be understood without acknowledging the widespread and continuing acceptance that it was a just, even noble cause. Every belligerent relied on a combination of state compulsion with patriotic support from society, even if the former
was relatively more important in the eastern European countries and the latter in
the western European ones. Between them these forces not only created an initial
political truce in 1914 but also maintained domestic cohesion when the conflict intensified, with a corresponding increase in its demands.

A plethora of surviving official reports have made the French home front among the
easiest to research, and it is full of interest for its insights into how a society notorious
for political divisions succeeded in holding together.[1] France's casualties were higher
relative to its population than those of any other great power, and its economy was

drastically reconverted to a war footing. Yet little challenge to the policy of fighting until victory came either from politicians or from the public. Viviani's centre-left government was broadened on 26 August 1914 to bring in representatives of most of the main parties, including the socialists, as well as parliamentary veterans such as Delcassé as foreign minister, Millerand as war minister, Ribot as finance minister, and Briand as deputy premier. In a further reshuffle in October 1915 Briand and Viviani changed places, and although Delcassé had resigned and Millerand was dropped the ministry's scope was extended by adding Denys Cochin, a leader of the Catholic right. In this form it survived, with smaller further changes, until Ribot replaced Briand as premier and foreign minister in March 1917. Despite parliament being in continuous session from February 1915, the changes of premier were fewer than in peacetime and there was much continuity of personnel between the Viviani, Briand, and Ribot cabinets, which included most of France's senior statesmen. The principal exceptions were Georges Clemenceau (who was thought to be temperamentally incompatible with President Poincaré) and Joseph Caillaux, the sole leading politician to be suspected, probably with reason, of favouring a compromise peace. Compared with Britain and Germany, few issues disturbed this unity. France had no counterpart to Britain's Irish question, and conscription was taken for granted. War aims might have been more divisive, but in January 1917 Briand united his cabinet behind a policy of separating the left bank of the Rhine from Germany without annexing it.* As for strategy, there was only one front on which France could or should seriously fight. The person of the commander-in-chief, however, did become more controversial once Joffre had spent his capital of prestige from the Marne. During 1915 deputies pressed for (and achieved) the right to send inspection missions to the trenches, and concentrated their attacks on Millerand, who was an easier target than Joffre and was seen to be protecting him. A firestorm followed Joffre's sacking of Sarrail, and in 1916 the attacks continued in secret sessions of parliament. Hence in December Briand finally replaced Joffre by Nivelle in order to keep the left on board.† From now on the government insisted on political control over strategy and the high command, and civil-military relations became less contentious.[2]

The unity at the top reflected a broader accommodation within French society. Traditional class and sectional conflicts fell into abeyance. The political parties suspended elections and the trade unions renounced strikes. Jouhaux, head of the CGT, which had previously been committed to a revolutionary general strike in the event of war, sat alongside representatives of the government and the Church in the National Assistance Committee, set up to relieve hardship. The interior ministry under Louis Malvy practised a 'policy of confidence' towards the trade unions, instructing police and prefects not to harass them in the belief that this approach would best secure their co-operation.[3] Insinuations that the Protestant churches sympathized with their German counterparts were unfounded, while the Catholic hierarchy, despite the neutral stance of Pope Benedict XV, emphatically supported the war.[4]

---

*cf. ch. 5.
†cf. ch. 6.

The first and foremost cause of national unity was the legacy of the events of 1914. France seemed to have suffered an unprovoked attack from an aggressive neighbour that had already invaded it a generation before. Its richest provinces were under occupation, and by the end of the year more than a quarter of a million of its young men were dead. An official commission of inquiry into German atrocities was established in the opening weeks of the war, and in January 1915 its first report documented the evidence for enemy brutality against non-combatants.[5] The press debated how to treat the hundreds of births to be expected from women whom the invaders had raped.[6] The threat to family, heritage, and nationhood was patent. Yet given that this time the onslaught had been beaten back and France had allies, it seemed natural to persevere until Germany had been so thoroughly defeated that no future generation need face invasion again. Politicians from Poincaré downward reiterated this message in their speeches, coupled by 1915 with demands for Alsace-Lorraine, for reparation, and for security against any recurrence of the attack. None the less, their basic position was that war had been forced on them. The facts of the situation made it difficult to contest this judgement.

French leaders therefore needed to do little, beyond the speeches and manifestos that were their normal stock in trade, to persuade the public of the legitimacy of their cause: German actions were the most telling of arguments. Briand's private secretary, Philippe Berthelot, organized a *Maison de la presse* (press service) in the foreign ministry, although its propaganda efforts were mainly directed overseas.[7] At home, the education ministry insisted on the message being conveyed to schoolchildren by radically reorganizing the curriculum. In French classes pupils wrote essays on the war, in history lessons they learned about its origins, and in geography they studied maps of the fighting.[8] Among adults, the censorship regime was the government's most important contribution to shaping opinion. The war ministry supplied journalists with anodyne daily bulletins on events at the front, the prefects in the departments monitored local newspapers, and the Paris press was vetted not only for military disclosures but also for attacks on the government and high command. In general, according to instructions issued in late 1914, it should exercise a 'calming' influence.[9] Bad news and casualty totals were suppressed, but losses were not the primary influence on public feeling. Reports from the prefects suggested morale actually went up when a new push was expected, in the belief that at least it might bring victory closer.[10] French civilians had not relinquished hope of an early triumph or the illusion of a short war.

Censorship of the press softened the horror of the image of conflict. Soldiers' letters might have provided an antidote, but they too were liable to vetting. In any case examination of samples that have survived suggests that although less prone than the press to glamorize they broadly shared its confidence in victory.[11] While the troops' morale was good—and mostly it seems it was until at least 1916 – neither their letters nor their visits home would endanger civilian determination. This points towards a more general conclusion. Censorship stifled what the government disliked; it could leave proselytizing to private initiative. The press became notorious – perhaps even more so than in other belligerents – for its *bourrage de crâne* (or 'skull stuffing'). It hyperbolized French audacity and panache and German callousness and blundering.[12] But others produced more sophisticated justifications of the national effort. The clergy widely acknowledged that France was fighting a just and sacred war: indeed, priests younger than the age cohort of 1905 (when church and state had been separated) were called up not only for the medical corps but also as soldiers and officers, and over 4,500 clerics lost their lives.[13] French academics, divided before 1914 between conservative, classical thinkers and 'moderns', more open to progressive and foreign (including German) influences, agreed in interpreting the struggle as a clash of cultures, pitting Latin civilisation against Teutonic barbarism. Historians, philosophers, and men of letters felt impelled to take this line in speeches, books, and pamphlets.[14] As for the major French writers, some, such as Marcel Proust, remained largely silent, but others – notably the conservative nationalist Maurice Barrès, whose war writings filled fourteen printed volumes – argued the pro-war case vociferously. Some of the many younger writers who had seen combat described it with brutal realism, but at least for the first two years few advocated anything short of a victorious peace.

The mobilization of French manpower was therefore paralleled by a mobilization of the emotions and the intellect. In 1914 the clergy reported a religious revival and that the churches were packed.[15] To Germany's actions should be added as a second pillar of home front solidarity the unity of the French elites and the vindications reproduced down to village level by teachers, mayors, and priests. Both factors remained valid after the war began to 'normalize' and settle down into a pattern of offensives alternating with stasis. Until Nivelle's offensive proved one disappointment too many, they sustained morale even when attacks were unsuccessful. None the less, ideological justifications were insufficient without at least tolerable material conditions, and these French civilians still enjoyed. In autumn 1914 mobilization and invasion caused industrial collapse, with bankruptcies, heavy unemployment, and wage cuts, but from 1915 until 1917 the economy experienced an inflationary boom. Civilian death rates appear not to have risen until 1918,[16] which is *prima facie* evidence that living standards were satisfactorily sustained until unrestricted submarine warfare curtailed seaborne supplies. All the same, there were winners and losers. In urban areas the latter included bourgeois dependent on investment income and employees in inessential sectors. Skilled munitions workers' wages, on the other hand, kept pace with price inflation or exceeded it. Soldiers' wives received separation allowances, although less generous ones than in Britain and Germany and available only for women below a certain income.[17] As rents were frozen, food shortages became the main threat to their welfare. The countryside suffered more bereavements, but benefited from the combination of high food prices with separation allowances, enabling families to pay off debts and purchase land. As contemporaries observed, the cemeteries were filled and yet the villages had never been more prosperous.[18] France, wrote one observer, settled down to the war as if into a new home.[19] The conclusion, perhaps a disturbing one, might seem that given reasonable physical comfort hostilities could be endured indefinitely.

In the event, however, even the French political and social truce – among the firmest of any belligerent – could not withstand erosion. All parties concluded the 'sacred union' in the expectation of a brief interruption and an early political payoff.[20] Once the 1914 emergency was over, the normalization of French life included a recrudescence of its peacetime tensions. Left-wing journalists charged that priests were evading military service, and (confusingly) both that the church had wanted the war and that the pope wanted peace.[21] A new press, braving heavy censorship, reacted against *bourrage de crâne*, notably *L'Oeuvre*, which began life in 1916, and the satirical *Canard enchâiné*, which started a year later. Henri Barbusse's *Le Feu: journal d'un escouade* ('Under Fire: the Diary of a Squad'), which presented an uncompromisingly bleak picture of life and death in the trenches and concluded with a plea for French and German soldiers to unite in revolution, was allowed by the censor to appear first serialized and then as a book in 1916, and became a best-seller.[22] Its success reflected a perceptible change in the intellectual climate after Verdun, and in this climate the political truce was first seriously tested when the *minoritaires* ('minoritarians') in the CGT and the SFIO began to challenge the leadership. The war encouraged reformists in the left-wing parties who felt it showed the working class could benefit from cross-class collaboration and state intervention. In France the outstanding example was Albert Thomas, the socialist baker's son who became minister of armaments.[23] Yet conversely, after the initial disorientation caused by the collapse of the Second International in 1914, the conflict also revived hopes of radical social transformation. Most of the *minoritaires* were not revolutionaries, but they did oppose annexations and indemnities, advocated seeking peace through negotiation, and questioned the movement's cooperation with the government. Their nuclei within the CGT were the metalworkers' and schoolteachers' unions; within the socialist party their base was the Limoges region in the rural hinterland, remote from the front and the occupied regions. In the trade unions they were relatively weak, but the division in the SFIO was more serious. In July 1916 they almost attained control of the party's National Council.[24] By the winter coal and food shortages threatened living standards for the first time, although it seems that soldiers and civilians alike still hoped the spring 1917 offensive would bring a breakthrough. After it failed to do so, and in the process almost extinguished the flickering light at the end of the tunnel, the sacred union faced its gravest test.

Britain shared many of the conditions making for unity in France, including protected civilian living standards and a rallying among its elites. Whereas in France a consensus behind a form of total war existed from the outset, however, in Britain one had to be moulded, amid fierce partisan controversy and soul searching over the country's traditions of liberal individualism and antipathy to strategic engagement on the continent. This debate underlay two cabinet crises in May 1915 and December 1916. It was resolved in favour of a major land effort in mainland Europe, and that it was so resolved had a critical impact on the war.

Like France, Britain began under a government of the moderate left. Again as in France, intervention was followed, or so it seemed, by a political truce. The trade unions renounced strikes, and the Labour Party and the Irish Nationalists, as well as the Liberals, the Unionists, and churchmen of all denominations, supported the common effort. Unlike in France, an electoral truce was not at first accompanied by a coalition government, partly because of the bitterness between Liberals and Unionists that lingered from the pre-war struggles over the House of

Lords and Irish Home Rule. The Liberals had avoided a cabinet split in part through their common belief that if a war was necessary they must ensure that it was fought according to their principles. But whereas the challenge for French politicians was to keep on board the radicals and socialists, in Britain Asquith made successive accommodations with the right. Thus the question of who should direct strategy immediately became controversial. Asquith wanted to reinstate Haldane at the War Office, where he had served with distinction from 1905 to 1911, but the press condemned Haldane (unfairly) as Germanophile, and Kitchener was appointed instead. Because of similar and equally spurious allegations Prince Louis of Battenberg was dropped as First Sea Lord and replaced by Sir John Fisher. Difficult though Kitchener's cabinet colleagues found him to work with, his appointment was a successful public relations coup and for some months shielded the Liberals from their critics. By 1915, however, he was as vulnerable to attack over shell shortages as Millerand was across the Channel, and was losing his effectiveness as a lightning conductor.[25]

The pre-1914 Liberal governments had intervened extensively in the workings of the market. If the BEF had too few shells, this was due to slow industrial adjustment and War Office misjudgements rather than to objections on principle to state action.* All the same, the munitions shortage was one precipitant of the May 1915 political crisis that was resolved by Liberals, Unionists, and Labour entering a coalition under Asquith's premiership. The second was Gallipoli, which caused Fisher to resign in protest against more warships being sent from home waters but also in the hope of removing Churchill from the Admiralty and directing the naval war himself. Between them, these circumstances galvanized the Unionist backbenchers into threatening to instigate a Commons debate over munitions and to repudiate Bonar Law's restraint towards Asquith. Rather than go down this road, Bonar Law preferred an arrangement that brought the Unionists into the cabinet, though nearly all the major offices remained in Liberal hands. The exception was the Admiralty, where Arthur Balfour replaced Churchill, who was anathema to the opposition and was demoted. On the other hand the Unionists supported Lloyd George's efforts to profit from the crisis by creating the new Ministry of Munitions with himself as its chief.[26]

The formation of the coalition did not end the Liberals' woes. In fact it was while Asquith remained premier rather than after Lloyd George replaced him in December 1916 that the key decisions to escalate Britain's commitment were taken. The external motor of these decisions was the imperative of defeating a formidable enemy, and the risk that France and Russia would make a separate peace unless Britain did more on land. Hence the logic first of stepping up arms production and then introducing conscription, as adjuncts to a continental strategy. But in the domestic political context, pressure for escalation came from four sources. The first was again the Unionists, and especially their backbenchers organized in the Unionist Business Committee. Second, a 'ginger group' of Liberal MPs with similar views supported Lloyd George, who seemed increasingly the protagonist of victory at all costs. The third element was the press, which in this period was at an

---

*cf. ch. 9.

apogee of influence, especially *The Times* and the *Daily Mail*, both owned by Lord Northcliffe. The newspapers helped to break Battenberg and Haldane, detonate the 'shells scandal', and demolish Asquith's reputation.[27] Finally the fourth factor, unusually in British history, was the army. Civilian control over strategy was discredited by the Gallipoli and Mesopotamia débâcles, and when Robertson became CIGS in December 1915 he insisted on being designated the government's sole authoritative source of strategic advice. Kitchener had little influence as a counterweight even before his death by drowning when HMS *Hampshire*, on which he was sailing in June 1916 on a mission to Russia, hit a mine. With backing from Unionist ministers and the press, Robertson threw his imposing weight behind the decisions for conscription and for an attack on the Somme.* The coalition also introduced protective tariffs, restricted civil liberties, and repressed the Easter rising in Dublin with full-scale military force, shelling the city's buildings and executing most of the leaders. These developments inclined beleaguered Liberals to feel that few of their principles remained intact and that there was little purpose in supporting Asquith, whose decline in powers of leadership became glaring well before the upheaval of December 1916.

The December crisis was triggered by another threat of Unionist revolt against Bonar Law. Underlying it were exasperation with Asquith and doubt that his government could extricate Britain from its deepening crises: lack of manpower, lack of dollars, and failure at the Front. To begin with, Bonar Law and Lloyd George proposed that Asquith should continue as a figurehead premier but transfer direction of the war to an inner cabinet from which he would be excluded. When he refused, Lloyd George and the Unionists resigned. Without backing from Labour and from many Liberals Lloyd George could not have formed an alternative cabinet, and deeply though many Unionists distrusted him they preferred his leadership to governing single-handedly. None the less, the reorganization marked a further shift to the right and over half the Liberal MPs moved to the opposition benches. As Asquith's followers included advocates of a compromise peace, British politics might have polarized between a government fighting a war *à l'outrance* and a negotiation-inclined alternative. This did not happen because Asquith himself did not support the peace movement and he refrained from systematic opposition. Pacifist feeling remained deprived of a rallying-point. On the other hand Lloyd George brought in the imperialist Lords Milner and Curzon as members of a five-man supervisory war cabinet, and recruited businessmen to lead new departments formed to deal with shipping, labour, war pensions, and food. Furthermore, one of the Unionists' key conditions was that there should be no interference with Robertson and Haig. Although a sceptic about the high command's strategy, Lloyd George had therefore made a Faustian bargain. Still, the crisis certainly brought to power a vigorous leader, even if he was more determined to win the war than clear about the method. He had made his name as the man who had solved the munitions problem and championed a decisive victory as the only acceptable outcome. His advent meant that despite mortifying disappointments there would be no going back.[28]

---

*See chs. 6 and 9.

For all the arguments about how to fight the war, the British leaders were as firm as the French about continuing until they won. This elite consensus both reflected and contributed to a similar consensus in society more generally. Although the Defence of the Realm Act provided sweeping powers to intervene by decree, in practice the government made little use of them, and Britain even more than France 'self-mobilized' for war.[29] The obvious example is reliance on voluntary conscription (and the devolved way in which the War Office handled it),* but the system of opinion management confirms the picture. The only official propaganda organization in the first part of the war was the Secret War Propaganda Agency or 'Wellington House', named after its London location. It operated clandestinely, and mainly to promote sympathy for Britain overseas. Other attempts to manage public opinion positively in the first half of the war were largely confined to war loans and recruitment. Thus the Parliamentary Recruiting Committee, fronted by MPs of all parties but spending government funds, led what seemed a prodigious effort, producing between October 1914 and October 1915 more than 5.7 million posters (including several justly celebrated designs) and 14.25 million copies of books and pamphlets. Yet even in this case the volunteering wave peaked in September before the PRC's expenditure began, the quantities of leaflets and posters were comparable to those produced by the political parties in peacetime election campaigns, and its poster budget was exceeded by the expenditure of the Rowntree company in advertising just one brand of chocolate in one year before the war.[30]

The government did contribute, however, to mobilizing the intellectuals. The Director of Wellington House, the Liberal MP Charles Masterman, made contact with leading authors and urged them to write in defence of Britain's case. Writers such as Thomas Hardy, H. G. Wells, Rudyard Kipling, Arnold Bennett, and John Galsworthy were well known and their books were widely read. Like academics, for instance members of the Modern History faculty at Oxford, they claimed that Germany had committed inexcusable crimes and the war was one of civilization against barbarism.[31] The British reading public was also a poetry reading (and writing) public to an extent scarcely conceivable now, as a reading of *The Times*, or of memoirs such as Vera Brittain's, will confirm.[32] Most of the poetry published during the war in Britain, France, and Germany was by civilians, not soldiers, and was patriotic.[33] Its influence was manifest in the 'high diction' characteristic of educated prose discussion of the war, an inflated, euphemistic range of vocabulary that remained prevalent down to 1916–17.[34] High diction emanated from religious as well as secular sources, the Church of England and the nonconformist clergy preaching that the doctrine of an amoral State had led the Germans astray, and (in the words of the Cardinal Bishop of London) the struggle was a 'holy war' to destroy their militarism.[35] As in France, the Germans' own actions hardened the feeling against them. The invasion of Belgium was central to the case made in the press, by the clergy, and by men of letters. Labour leaders who at first were dubious changed their minds once enemy troops stormed through western Europe, trailing atrocities in their wake. A concatenation of developments in winter 1914 and spring 1915 – the shelling of Scarborough, unrestricted submarine warfare,

---

*See ch. 8.

the sinking of the *Lusitania*, the gas cloud at Ypres – confirmed that Germany would neither respect civilians nor hesitate to use the most ruthless new technology. It threatened not only Belgium but also the laws of war and (if this issue seemed abstract) the sanctity of the family.[36] The point was underlined when the Bryce Report into alleged atrocities appeared in May 1915. Some of the picture it painted was accurate, though it accepted exaggerated accounts from refugees too uncritically and without corroboration.[37] At the same price as a daily newspaper (and reproducing prurient details of the violation of Belgian women and the mutilation of their children), it sold sensationally well. The 'rape' of Belgium, as it was habitually referred to, now symbolized a challenge to social and political order, as recruiting posters hastened to stress.[38] In June the Allies warned that the Young Turks would be held to account for their atrocities against the Armenians, and public demand increased for Germans to be tried as war criminals, especially following the execution in Brussels in November 1915 of Nurse Edith Cavell for assisting Allied prisoners of war to escape from custody. A further outcry followed the execution in July 1916 of Charles Fryatt, a sea captain whom the Germans had captured when commanding an unarmed Channel steamer but who was then tried for previously attempting to ram a U-boat. Asquith now announced in the Commons that when the time came the government would bring war criminals to justice, by implication including Wilhelm II himself.[39]

Positive opinion management was accompanied by censorship. The government rationed information from the fighting fronts. It set up a Press Bureau to supply information but at first refused to accredit war correspondents. Eventually five were attached to the BEF in May 1915, though subject to their reports being vetted.[40] The worst horrors were concealed from the public, as Lloyd George himself acknowledged. Yet the system depended on voluntary co-operation and self-censorship by editors and proprietors. The Press Bureau maintained a list of fifty editors to whom it disclosed confidential information, accompanying it with directives called 'D' notices on how to treat the material.[41] The newspapers respected military secrets and concealed information such as casualty lists, which were not published until May 1915. They exaggerated the Allied forces' achievements and downplayed those of their enemies. However, proprietors also resisted ministerial pressure to tighten the regime, and it was not particularly rigorous.[42] Provincial papers, which were less subject to scrutiny than was Fleet Street, not only carried sensitive information but also printed letters from the front that were open about conditions there and about fluctuations in morale.[43] During the Somme, moreover, many papers published the forbidding casualty lists in full, and their impact was magnified by the live recording of the events of 1 July in the best known official war film, *The Battle of the Somme*. By October over 2,000 cinemas had booked it, and several million people probably watched it. Even if some of its sequences were faked, it was remarkable for its gruesome and realistic coverage of casualties, as both press reviews and audience reaction testified.[44] By the end of 1916 much of the civilian population therefore had some inkling of the nature of trench warfare and the cost of the fighting. The Somme, as many commentators have noted, spelt the end of innocence.[45]

Yet still no general mood of anti-war opposition resulted. This was the more surprising as pre-1914 politics had been so embittered, the antagonism between

Unionists and Liberals at Westminster being matched outside it by the suffragette movement for women's emancipation, by the strikes and 'labour unrest' of 1910–12, and by preparations for civil war between Irish unionists and national-ists. For the Irish, for women's leaders, and for trade unionists the political truce of 1914 was a temporary measure, accepted without prejudice to their ultimate objectives. Once the war settled down to a stalemate, their loyalty might be ex-pected to falter.

Irish nationalists were indeed not prepared to wait indefinitely. An uneasy com-promise was struck over Home Rule by placing it on the statute book but postpon-ing its implementation until the war ended. One of the surprises of 1914 was to see the nationalist leader, John Redmond, supporting intervention, and thousands vol-unteering in both north and south. Yet while men in the Protestant counties (as in Wales and Scotland) volunteered in comparable or even greater numbers to those in England,[46] volunteers in the Catholic counties were significantly fewer, and the government exempted Ireland from conscription. Superficially the country was prosperous and quiet in the first two years, but members of the Irish Republican Brotherhood were preparing, with very limited German support, the botched Easter rebellion, whose suppression changed the political landscape forever, under-mining Redmond and fuelling the rise of the independence-minded Sinn Féin. Henceforward Ireland provided one of the clearest examples in Europe of how eth-nic divisions qualified support for the war.

In England, both the militant wing of the women's movement, the Women's So-cial and Political Union (WSPU), and the moderate National Union of Women's Suffrage Societies (NUWSS) suspended their campaigns.[47] Emmeline Pankhurst, the WSPU leader, joined Lloyd George in arguing for women to be able to partic-ipate on equal terms with men in armaments manufacture. Millicent Fawcett, her NUWSS counterpart, calculated that supporting the war would benefit the suf-frage movement in the longer term, and that for the moment agitation should wait. The perception of men as killers may have changed the direction of the younger generation in the British feminist movement, towards accepting a different destiny for the two genders rather than seeking to emulate men in every sphere.[48] To some extent the war can indeed be analysed in gender terms: British women (or some of them) urged British men to defend Belgian women against German men, and sup-plied the weapons for them to do so. The posters of the Parliamentary Recruiting Committee called on women to exhort their men to fight, and some women pre-sented men in civilian clothes with white feathers.[49] Upper-class women created or-ganizations such as the Women's Volunteer Army, at first to resist invasion and then to help the forces as clerks and drivers; thousands served as nurses in the Vol-untary Aid Detachments (VADs).[50] To begin with the women's movement ceased to be a significant opposition force, though feminist and pacifist alternative voices made themselves heard later.

None the less the government's greatest challenge was to retain support from urban workers, who were the dominant element in the British population, as peas-ant farmers were in France. On the whole it succeeded. Manual workers seem to have been almost as likely as those in commerce and the professions to volunteer, and the new BEF that fought on the Somme was predominantly a working-class force.[51] It is true that industrial unrest, if less than in peacetime, was still quite frequent. In 1915, 3 million working days were lost, and 2.5 million in 1916.[52] The South Wales miners (crucial for fuelling the navy) struck in July 1915, but Lloyd George intervened to award them a wage increase.[53] In spring 1916 the Clyde Workers' Committee led a revolt in the shipyards against dilution, although after the authorities deported its leaders to Edinburgh the movement subsided.[54] Yet neither episode was motivated by political opposition to the war, and until 1917 the trade unions contained no significant *minoritaire* movement, TUC and Labour conferences supporting motions to fight on until victory.[55] Prosperity helped. After heavy unemployment in the autumn of 1914 the economy was characterized by a tight labour market and mild inflation. Flat-rate wage increases eroded skilled workers' differentials – though probably not by much[56] – and earnings in war-related industries could keep pace with prices. Nor were there food shortages for the first two years. Separation allowances were more generous than on the continent, and by 1916 cost the government almost as much as the soldiers' wages.[57] In many working-class households nutritional standards and infant mortality rates seem actually to have improved.[58]

In these circumstances it is unsurprising that opposition to the war was marginal, coming mainly from dissident Liberals and the socialist wing of Labour. A notable example was conscientious objection, although the numbers involved were small. Compared with the 2.5 million men conscripted in Britain, only 16,500 applied for exemption, and over 80 per cent of objectors who appeared before tribunals were guaranteed some form of exemption, often working for the war in some non-military capacity. Public attention focused on the 6,000 who refused to appear before a tribunal or rejected its decision, all of whom were deprived of their liberty and some were punished with repeated terms of hard labour, during which some seventy lost their lives. Neither the military nor the government knew what to do with these 'absolutists' (mostly socialists), whose treatment was denounced by civil libertarian writers, clergy, and lawyers, yet whom they felt unable to release, both because of public feeling against them and for fear of setting a precedent. However, the protest peaked in 1916–17 and by 1918 many absolutists had decided it was futile.[59] They had less long-term influence than the radicals in the Union of Democratic Control, which denounced Britain's pre-war balance-of-power diplomacy and demanded democratic control of foreign policy, collective security, national self-determination, and arms limitation. From 5,000 affiliated members in November 1914 it rose to 300,000 in November 1915 and three-quarters of a million by the end of the war.[60] Ramsay MacDonald, the Labour Party chairman in 1914, resigned when war broke out and joined the UDC, but at first lacked support from his colleagues. Generally, however, the Labour and TUC leaders remained loyal to the war effort, focusing on working-class economic interests rather than strategy and war aims. The nucleus of an alternative tendency appeared early, but for the moment it remained contained.

Germany at first displayed a similar unity to that in France and Britain. Public opinion mattered, although the Reich was more autocratic than the two western powers. Chancellors ultimately answered to the emperor and were appointed and dismissed by him, as were commanders-in-chief. Yet the government still needed a parliamentary majority, which (except on the submarine issue) Bethmann generally commanded until 1917. The Reichstag voted war credits at six-monthly intervals, and its sub-committees cross-questioned officials. Moreover, Germany remained remarkably decentralized. Not only did the separate states retain their prerogatives, but also the Prussian law of siege, which came into force in 1914, delegated extensive powers to the DCGs, who took responsibility for public order, transport, censorship, and food supply. As they too answered directly to Wilhelm, who lacked the appetite for administrative detail and spent much of his time away from Berlin, the central government had great difficulty in co-ordinating them. In November 1916 the Prussian war minister gained authority over the DCGs in economic matters, but in other spheres he had only a supervisory role.[61]

Germany's appearance of unanimity was in part imposed from above. Whereas in Britain, despite the government's reserve powers, press censorship largely meant self-censorship by Fleet Street, in Germany the DCGs, the Central Censorship Office (created by OHL in 1914), and the War Press Office (created in 1915 in the Prussian war ministry) provided much more detailed guidance, and the newspapers generally complied with it. The government made the semi-official news agency, the Wolff Telegraph Bureau, the exclusive channel for supplying war news, and required the foreign ministry to vet all items beforehand. The War Press Office supplemented the Wolff material with daily briefings, and any military news gathered independently had to be cleared with the DCGs.[62] The authorities' monopoly of information gave them leverage over the smaller newspapers in particular, many of which were vulnerable because although their circulations increased their paper allocation shrank and their actual size diminished.[63] From 1915 the censorship regulations prescribed both what could and could not be discussed, as well as the appropriate 'tone'. In general they reflected Bethmann's desire to discourage controversy, preserve unity, and keep his hands free over war aims and strategy. Editors were to stress the war's defensive character and make no mention of annexations. But the authorities also wished to conceal that all was not going as planned. Casualty totals were suppressed, together with news of food shortages and peace demonstrations.[64] Operational reports never mentioned a defeat until autumn 1918, the withdrawal from the Marne, for example, being disguised as 'repositioning'.[65] Because of the autonomy of the DCGs, the stringency of the censorship probably varied more from district to district than in France or Britain. It fell most heavily on Berlin and working-class areas like the Ruhr, but its influence generally was pervasive.

The censorship applied not only to the press but also to the other mass media. Through the local police, the DCGs controlled the cinema, theatre, music halls, opera, cabaret, postcards, humorous magazines, and popular fiction. Prior approval was needed for publications and performances. In general the authorities, suspicious of popular culture, opposed material that was scurrilous or unpatriotic. They suppressed items that were boastful, that suggested victory would be easy, or that undermined national unity by attacking other groups. Later they silenced protests about food shortages.[66] Film, as a new and exceptionally powerful medium, was a good case in point. By 1914 Germany had over 7,500 cinemas, and

1.5 million people may have visited them each week. After war broke out all foreign (including American) imports were banned, and the war ministry permitted only patriotic and morale-boosting items. In January 1917 OHL set up its own photographic and film unit and highlighted the Hindenburg Programme's supposed achievements.[67] With ministry approval the Messter-Woche company produced newsreels, but they showed (in contrast to *The Battle of the Somme*) only stirring, sanitized scenes.

In general, however, until 1917 the authorities' efforts to influence opinion positively (as opposed to negatively through censorship) were few and ineffectual. The War Press Office lamented Germany's inability to generate equivalents of French and British slogans and poster images.[68] The official 'White Book' of documentation on Belgium unconvincingly parried atrocity charges by presenting executions of civilians as legitimate reprisals against partisan attacks.[69] The government insisted that it had gone to war in self-defence, and the circumstances of 1914 were sufficiently ambiguous for many to believe it, especially given the preceding years of arms races and encirclement. Initially, unanimity among the politicians was mirrored in religious and intellectual circles, and as in the Allied countries a self-mobilization of opinion-leaders took place. Support for the government from the Lutheran clergy was unsurprising,[70] but German Catholics also welcomed the war as an opportunity to break out of political isolation (as did the Jews, some 10,000 of whom volunteered for military service).[71] Wilhelm declared that the struggle was a God-given duty; the Catholic hierarchy characterized it as a struggle of Christian order against atheism (represented by France) and chaos.[72] Religious attendance revived in 1914,[73] and Protestant pastors identified Britain as the main enemy, driven by greed and hypocritical envy.[74] In this their position reflected that of much of the wider circle of authors and academics. Many felt with Thomas Mann that the spectacle of unity in 1914 revealed that the national community was neither dead nor sapped by alien influences, and this belief stayed with them for the rest of their lives.[75] Secular intellectuals joined with Protestant and Catholic theologians in signing the October 1914 'Declaration of the 93', which eventually attracted some 4,000 names. This document, a gift to Allied propagandists, was intended to rebut the latter's claim to be fighting not the culture of Kant and Beethoven but Prussian militarism. On the contrary, it insisted, 'It is not true that the struggle against our so-called militarism is not a struggle against our culture. . . .. The German army and the German people are one.'[76]

University academics and the intellectual community therefore rejected Allied invitations to repudiate their political chiefs. Many interpreted the war as underlining the Germanic world's distinctiveness from the west. Like their counterparts abroad, they portrayed it as an ideological contest, but one in which Germany stood for the 'ideas of 1914' as against the 'ideas of 1789': for deeper cultural and spiritual values against French rationalism and British materialism.[77] The 'German idea of freedom', in contrast to the hedonism of the country's enemies, meant self-restraint and a balance between liberty and obedience. In another juxtaposition, the sociologist Werner Sombart contrasted British 'merchants' (*Händler*) with German 'heroes' (*Helden*), men who instead of simply pursuing commercial gain unfolded all their human potentialities and who showed a willingness for sacrifice.[78]

Soon after the war began the right came to portray London rather than Paris or
Petrograd as Germany's arch-enemy and as the puppet-master in a plot that had
ensnared the Reich. Perhaps because Britain had supposedly betrayed its racial
kinship and obstructed Germany's pre-war naval and colonial ambitions, attitudes
towards it from Wilhelm downwards took on the intensity characteristic of an inferiority complex. Critics of Bethmann's moderation over war aims and the submarine issue insinuated that he was secretly anglophile.[79]

Neverthless, by the later stages of the war Germany was more politically polarized than its western enemies. Its pre-1914 divisions were partly to blame, but the
struggle exacerbated them by provoking controversy over war aims and inflicting
material hardship. The German economy shrank between 1914 and 1918,[80] and
working-class conditions deteriorated more severely than in France and Britain.[81]
The main decline, however, came in the second half of the conflict. In the armaments centre of Düsseldorf, food prices in 1914–16 approximately doubled, but
metalworkers' average purchasing power fell only slightly.[82] During the same period living costs in Berlin increased at much the same rate as in London and Paris,
but thereafter they climbed much faster.[83] The problem that set in earliest was deficient food supply: rising prices, worsening quality, and an outright lack of basic
commodities. According to reports from the police and the DCGs, nothing did
more to undermine patriotism and unity.[84] Although the war did not bring
famine, it did bring malnutrition-related diseases. For millions of civilians the predominant experience associated with it was going hungry. The biggest cause of
grievance may have been resentment that sacrifices were unequal, but Germany
did have a more serious absolute shortfall than France or Britain.[85] Because of the
blockade (particularly the absence of imported fertilizers) and of manpower being
withdrawn for the army, agricultural production fell by a quarter, and purchases
from the neutrals failed to compensate for the loss of overseas sources (about 25
per cent of Germany's pre-1914 food consumption had been imported). While the
army and the rural areas held on to their shares, the remaining three quarters of
the population scrabbled over half the pre-war production.[86] In these circumstances the authorities could at most have alleviated the problems, but in fact their
actions probably exacerbated them and sharpened the perception of unfairness.
No contingency plans existed for feeding the civilian population, and the division
of control between DCGs and local authorities hampered a concerted response.
At first local authorities set price ceilings on some commodities, as a result of
which farmers switched to others or sold in regions with higher prices. The government rationed bread in spring 1915 (much earlier than in France and Britain)
and most key commodities by summer 1916, while special war corporations representing the leading farmers and dealers purchased the entire supply of key foodstuffs for sale to the public authorities. As the official rations were insufficient to
feed a family, however, city dwellers increasingly resorted to the black market, often breaking with a lifetime of law-abiding habits. In October 1915 'butter riots'
began among women queuing in the Berlin working-class districts. They went on
for days, attracted public sympathy, and began months of unrest.[87] Each year the
greatest difficulties extended through each winter and until the next harvest was
brought in, but the first two war winters were as nothing compared with the third.

With dwindling cereal supplies, consumers became more dependent on the potato, and precisely this crop suffered from the cold, wet autumn of 1916 and the long freeze-up that followed. Almost half the harvest had been lost by the end of the year and *per capita* consumption of the vegetable fell by more than a third, while its availability as a livestock feed also diminished, cutting supplies of eggs, milk, and meat. Shortages were worst in the urban and industrial areas, and especially (apart from Berlin) in the Ruhr, thus dividing west from east as well as city from countryside.[88] Although conditions were never so bad again as in spring 1917, supplies did not regain previous levels.[89]

Germany also differed from the Allies in the centrality of war aims to political controversy. Public debate continued through petitions and pamphleteering, and loopholes in the censorship allowed it to seep into the media. The basic problem was that the 1914 political truce (or *Burgfrieden*)* rested on conflicting expectations. The SPD expected democratization and social reform to flow from their co-operation with the war effort; conservatives hoped that victory would consolidate the existing order. While the socialists and trade unions did not rule out economic and territorial expansion, their war aims were generally less ambitious than those of the Conservatives, the National Liberals, OHL, and Pan-German racist nationalists. As the war dragged on with no early resolution in sight, Bethmann found straddling these extremes increasingly uncomfortable. During 1915 the Pan-Germans orchestrated a campaign in favour of annexationist war aims, notably through the 'Petition of the Six Economic Associations' in May and the 'Petition of the Intellectuals' in July.[90] Their goals went further than Bethmann's, but he feared that his own preference for indirect domination by economic methods was too subtle for his countrymen, and he showed increasing willingness to reject the pre-war territorial *status quo* and to make encroachments on Belgium that were intended to be permanent. He still remained suspect to the right as too emollient over war aims and domestic reform, and his enemies used the agitation over submarine warfare in order to undermine him.[91] Beleaguered, he turned in August 1916 to Hindenburg in the hope of using the general's prestige as a cloak behind which to make a compromise peace.[92] This miscalculation proved one too many.

Bethmann was impressed by the rallying of the labour movement in 1914 and believed that it had compromised more than the right. The trade union leaders renounced industrial action, but as in Britain their loyalty to the government led to more frequent unofficial strikes and greater shop-steward influence.[93] In 1914 the unions agreed to abide by existing wage contracts for the duration of the war, but by 1916 inflation had forced them to renege on this undertaking.[94] As for the SPD leaders, they stood by the *Burgfrieden* until 1917, but only at the price of a socialist schism. At first Karl Liebknecht, who opposed the war and voted against credits for it, was isolated within the party. During 1915, however, he drew increasing support from the SPD's left centre, who did not share his revolutionary anti-capitalism and his opposition to fighting even in self-defence but rightly suspected that the government was becoming more annexationist. Liebknecht's imprisonment for inflammatory statements on May Day 1916 provoked political strikes in protest,

---

*The allusion (revealingly) was to the unity within a besieged city.

and he did much to galvanize the emergence of a German counterpart to the French *minoritaires*, who abstained on or voted against military credits, opposed constraints on civil liberties, and would support only a strictly defensive war effort. At the local level, the SPD began to fragment. In March 1916 the majority expelled the left-wing opposition from the party's Reichstag delegation and after the passage of the auxiliary service law (which the majority accepted but the minority denounced), the opposition was expelled from the party altogether and set up an Independent Social Democratic Party (USPD) at Easter 1917. Germany now had a nationally organized movement that opposed the war or supported it only conditionally.[95] Meanwhile a moderate, pro-Bethmann tendency emerged after 1915 in the German academic community and the clergy, although the extremists outnumbered it.[96] The country was becoming divided between aggressive imperialism and an emerging democratic movement. Despite the darkening economic outlook at the end of 1916, according to the DCGs' reports the public was cheered by Hindenburg's appointment to OHL, by the crushing of Romania, and by the prospect of U-boat successes. If the submarines failed, however, the future was bleak.[97]

Austria-Hungary, Italy, and Russia all tended to be more authoritarian than France, Britain, and Germany, and the forces of social self-mobilization were weaker. In the Dual Monarchy, however, conditions differed in the two halves, those in the Hungarian half more closely resembling Western Europe. The Budapest legislature remained in session, the deputies reaching the usual political truce (known as the *Treuga Dei*) and unanimously voting war credits. The Catholic church supported the government (its primate discerning a sacred duty to act against Serbia), Tisza silenced his doubts about using force, and the normally vociferous parliamentary opposition was more bellicose than he was, offering a coalition if he stood down. He refused, but they co-operated anyway. The government suspended civil liberties and censored the press, placing workers in war industries under military supervision, but in general civilian officials remained in charge and Hungary, unlike Germany and Austria, avoided military rule. In the Croat lands the party leaders co-operated with the authorities partly to avoid being suppressed but also (especially after Italy entered with its designs on Croat-inhabited territory) because the war was relatively popular. Tisza tried at first to be conciliatory to the Croats and Slovaks, and to renew negotiations with the Romanians of Hungary, as he had no wish to antagonize them while Romania's attitude remained uncertain. But the Serb-inhabited areas of Hungary were rightly seen as unreliable and were at once placed under martial law, leading to mass arrests and internments.[98]

The Austrian half differed in fundamental respects. Because of its more varied ethnic composition it was unclear what cause its citizens were fighting for beyond the personality of Franz Joseph.[99] The Reichsrat had been suspended before war broke out, and the premier, Stürgkh, took on further special powers, for example by shutting down the provincial assemblies. Most of the Austrian half, except for its Czech- and German-inhabited areas, became a 'war zone' under martial law. Journalists were assigned to a war press office, remote from Conrad's headquarters at Teschen; they could not visit the fronts freely or do much except embellish the AOK's communiqués. The AOK created a 'war surveillance office' (*Kriegsüberwachungsamt*: KÜA) for the Austrian half and for Bosnia-Herzegovina, responsible for censorship and counter-subversion. It forbade the publication of anything unpatriotic or pacifist, and on the pretext of preserving domestic harmony banned provocatively nationalist, religious, or socialist pronouncements. All post crossing the frontiers was intercepted and checked, as well as a selection of domestic correspondence, and the KÜA gave special attention to letters to and from the growing numbers of prisoners of war.[100]

By these methods the Austrian authorities repressed or at least contained subversion for the first two years, aided by a rallying behind the Habsburgs and against Serbia. This phenomenon was strongest in the German-speaking lands and among the intelligentsia. The Reichsrat's deputies accepted the legislature's continuing suspension.[101] By December 1914 nearly half the university students enrolled in the Austrian half had volunteered for active service, and their teachers lectured and published pamphlets on the justice of the cause.[102] Among the cultural elite, men such as Ludwig Wittgenstein and Oskar Kokoschka also volunteered and fought against Russia.[103] It has to be to said that others were much more loath to serve, and in general the patriotic upsurge was short-lived, although the 1915 victories revived it.

Once hostilities failed to end quickly the authorities faced an uphill struggle to maintain support for an enterprise which it was hard to portray as defensive, proved enormously costly, and in which Habsburg victories were largely due to Germany. The government produced little domestic propaganda, although the war ministry built an exhibition in Vienna's Prater amusement park and the head of the film division at the war press office was the boss of Sascha-Film, a private company that made patriotic newsreels.[104] But on the whole the Austrian leaders could rely on the unofficial media less than elsewhere, and the military's main concern was to keep the lid on discontent. In the German-speaking lands this was relatively easy, the large and moderate Social Democratic Party taking the same line as the German one. Of the other national groups the Poles were the most supportive, their leaders deciding that Russia was the main enemy and Józef Piłsudski recruiting a legion of volunteers. But others were less reliable, and repression further antagonized them. The army went in heavily against the Serbs straightaway, executing many and interning or deporting others. Many Ruthenes welcomed the invading Russians in 1914. Italy's intervention strengthened support from the Slovenes but weakened that from the Italians. All but one of the Italian-language newspapers were suppressed, as were the Italian nationalist groups. The most delicate case, however, was that of the Czechs, whose leaders were divided. Some were loyal to the government, but others such as Tomáš Masaryk and Edvard Beneš went into exile, seeking an Allied commitment to Czech independence; still others, like Karel Kramář, founded an underground organization for sabotage and passive resistance inside Bohemia, known as the 'Mafia'. In spring 1915 Stürgkh submitted to army pressure and cracked down: many thousands were arrested, Kramář was tried and condemned to death (although Franz Joseph commuted the sentence), and much of the Czech press was closed down. None the less, the Mafia remained in being, and kept in contact with the leaders abroad.[105]

Increasingly the Habsburg dynasty forfeited its capital of goodwill and the authorities held down the dissident nationalities by pure repression. In addition economic conditions in the Austrian half deteriorated further and faster than in Germany. The military authorities were anxious to avoid a confrontation with the labour movement, and for the first year strikes were few.[106] But in the spring of 1915 bread rationing was introduced in Austria and in May the first food riots hit Vienna.[107] The Austrian lands had been barely self-sufficient even in peacetime, and in 1914 their Galician and Ruthenian breadbaskets were overrun. During the war the cereal harvest fell from 91 to 49 million quintals in Austria and from 146 to 78 million in Hungary.[108] And although Tisza agreed that Hungary would supply the entire needs of the army, beyond this he would deliver to Austria only grain that was surplus to Hungary's' own requirements, and even that at stiff prices. Hence the Austrian lands began to split up into self-sufficient units, leaving Vienna and the cities high and dry.[109]

The pressures created by economic hardship and discontent among the subject nationalities came to a head after the military emergency created by the Brusilov offensive and Romanian entry into the war. In July 1916 Count Michael Károlyi broke ranks with the rest of the Hungarian opposition by forming a new political party that wanted to conclude a peace without annexations and to reduce the tie with Vienna to a personal union. Although Romanian forces were expelled from Transylvania, they took 80,000 of the local population with them while the Romanian-speakers left behind had Magyar imposed on them in their churches and schools.[110] In October Friedrich Adler (son of the socialist leader Viktor) assassinated Stürgkh in a Vienna restaurant, crying, 'Down with absolutism! We want peace!' The Central Powers' November proclamation of independence for the former Russian Poland dashed Austria-Hungary's hopes of unifying the country under the Habsburg sceptre and left the Poles with little motive to remain loyal. Finally, in the same month Franz Joseph died, to be replaced by the young and inexperienced Emperor Karl. At a moment when the 1916–17 winter was causing terrible privation, Karl intended to gain greater independence from Germany abroad and to experiment with greater civil liberties at home after two years of harsh repression. For the Austro-Hungarian as for the German home front, this was the pivotal moment of the war.

The politics of the Italian home front superficially resembled those of Britain and France, but in reality occupied a half-way position between the Western and the Austrian or Russian models. Italy was unique among the great powers in being a late entrant, whose intervention in the war could not be justified as self-defence and which had been fiercely contested. Moreover, Salandra hoped at first, like Asquith, to carry on business as usual. He hardly broadened his cabinet at all and his ministers relied on the interventionist movement to justify the country's involvement. To some extent this approach paid off. Despite Pope Benedict XV's undisguised regret over Italian belligerency, most Catholics did rally round, and the church hierarchy made patriotic pronouncements.[111] Artistic groups such as the Futurists saw a chance to modernize the country and purge it of teutonic influences: Italy's most eminent philosopher, Benedetto Croce, struggled (like Kant's defenders in France) to reconcile his continuing esteem for Hegelian thinking with his support for the war.[112] After the crisis of June 1916, when the Austrians threatened to break out of the Trentino, Paolo Boselli replaced Salandra at the head of a broader coalition that included both progressive and conservative liberals, radicals, and the reformist socialists Bissolati and Bonomi, as well as a Catholic politician, Meda, and a Giolittian, Colosimo. As economic mobilization was now intensified, Boselli's takeover resembled the formation of Britain's May 1915 coalition as a milestone towards greater commitment. In August the new ministry declared war on Germany and presided over Italy's first substantial victory with the capture of Gorizia. It seemed that the wounds caused by the intervention controversy were healing.

Yet it remained true, much more than in Britain and France, that Italy had been launched into war by aggressive elites with little support from a population whose national consciousness was weakly developed. The bulk of the socialist party remained detached, operating under the maxim 'Neither support nor sabotage' and calling for an early peace. Italy had its *minoritaire* movement ready made. But parliament was rarely convened, except to pass the budget or in a ministerial crisis. Both Salandra and Boselli ruled extensively by decree, restricting freedom of speech and assembly and censoring the press. The military could open letters passing to and from the front through the 'war zone' behind it; elsewhere the prefects did so. Censorship and public order in the war zone became military responsibilities, as did arms production. Under the 'Industrial Mobilization' (Mobilitazione Industriale: MI) created in 1915, factory discipline also came under military control, and in plants subjected to it abandoning the workplace became the equivalent of desertion. By 1916, although the political truce still held at the centre, grass-roots unrest was growing. Living standards fell less than in the Central Powers, but more than in Britain and France, while Italy's separation allowances were very small and for two years were not adjusted for inflation. As the latter accelerated and food shortages emerged during the summer, demonstrations began. In the countryside they were often led by women, initially in response to bread shortages or to delays in the monthly allowances, but they developed into anti-war protests and calls for the men to be returned. Unrest also broke out in the factories, women again being prominent (they began entering industry on a large scale in 1916), abandoning their jobs in protests against fines and unfair dismissals and expanding their action into anti-war opposition. Italy's home front was less obviously in crisis than those of the Central Powers, but the cracks were showing.[113]

The Italian discontent bore more than a passing resemblance to that in Russia. Here too by 1916 a groundswell of popular resistance to war-imposed burdens was stirring. Alongside it emerged a nationalist movement among elite opinion that wanted, like the Italian interventionists, to pursue the war more vigorously, but unlike them found itself in opposition to the government. In this latter respect Russia resembled not so much Italy as Germany, but its social polarization was much more dramatic, and by 1917 the tsarist government faced revolutionary movements directed both at intensifying the war effort and at abandoning it.

Russia kept fighting because Nicholas rejected a separate peace. The Empress Alexandra shared his views, despite allegations that her German origins made her unpatriotic. Indeed, to begin with Russia manifested the usual pro-war consensus, albeit more transiently than elsewhere. In July 1914 most of the Duma parties, including the government's critics, invited it to prorogue the legislature and rule by decree. Only the far left (the Bolsheviks, Mensheviks, and Trudoviks) dissented, walking out or abstaining in the vote on war credits, although its spokesmen said the Russian proletariat would defend their country.[114] Indeed the pre-war strike wave abruptly collapsed, although this may have happened because the police carried out wholesale arrests, banned all trade unions, and closed down left-wing newspapers.[115] The Orthodox church bestowed its blessing, though given its dependence on the Russian state this was unsurprising. The leading intellectuals were mostly sympathetic, without outspokenly championing Russia's fight in the manner of a Kipling, Barrès, or Thomas Mann. Maxim Gorky was among the artists and scholars who signed a manifesto proclaiming a struggle against the 'Germanic yoke', but he later turned against the war, as did the Symbolists, the leading school of Russian poets.[116] None the less, the opening months did witness an upsurge of what historians have called 'patriotic culture'. The state-supported propaganda agency known as the Skobelev Committee produced films and postcards, but private initiatives dwarfed its efforts.[117] Among the latter's characteristic forms were broadsheets known as *lubki*, which were printed in millions, as well as cartoons and posters. The performing arts contributed circus shows, cabaret acts, operettas, and plays. The Russian cinema turned out several dozen patriotic feature films. Much of this material exhibited common themes – a fierce satirical hatred of Germany (focused on caricatures of Wilhelm), enemy atrocities, and terror weapons such as zeppelins and U-boats; and by way of contrast, the heroism of Russia's soldiers and the greatness of its soul.[118] After the 1915 retreat began, however, the boom in all such art forms tapered off, and by 1916 a very different mood prevailed.

The retreat confronted Russia with a national emergency, not least because of a huge movement of refugees: 3.3 million by the end of 1915 according to official figures, and in reality possibly more than 6 million by the beginning of 1917. They came from the Caucasus as well as the western frontiers, and many – notably the Jews – were forcibly deported by the tsarist authorities.[119] Moreover, the Polish disasters began the division of Russian society into pro-war and anti-war movements, both of which were hostile to the tsarist regime. On the one hand the war acted as a catalyst for the liberal opposition, and a confrontation between the court and the Duma politicians dominated high politics in 1915–16. Many liberals favoured expansionist war aims, and in some ways they deserve comparison with Bethmann's nationalist critics in Germany. They supported the war but were acutely discontented with the leadership of Nicholas and his ministers. Their reemergence in response to shell shortages and military disaster reflected the conviction of many educated Russians that institutions on the Western (or German) model could run the war far better than what they condemned as a corrupt and incompetent autocracy with reactionary, even treasonable, ministers. They wanted more widely representative government, though they were far from being a democratic movement for representation of the Russian people as a whole. They were organized both at local and at national level. Russia's elected district councils (zemstvos) and municipalities, which helped to supply the army and provide medical services, formed the Union of Zemstvos and the Union of Towns before merging in a body known as Zemgor. From 1915, businessmen were organized in the national network of war industries committees.* The two movements shared leaders with each other and with the liberal opposition that took shape in the Duma in September 1915 as the 'Progressive Bloc', which included some 300 out of 430 deputies as well as many members of the upper chamber of parliament. The Bloc did not ask to form a government itself, but it did call for a ministry enjoying 'the confidence of the nation', (which in practice meant the confidence of the Bloc) even if the premier continued to be an unelected bureaucrat. It certainly did not mean the Goremykin government that Nicholas continued to back. Disregarding not only the Duma but also many of his ministers, the emperor rejected an accommodation, and he disregarded them again by appointing himself commander-in-chief in place of Grand Duke Nicholas. He offered a few crumbs to the opposition, but he believed his constitutional concessions after the defeat by Japan had destabilized Russia and that if he yielded again fresh demands would follow.[120] Hence the government co-operated with the liberals and with private business in local administration and through the war industries committees but not at the centre, convening the Duma only briefly and at long intervals and proroguing it again when its demands became embarrassing. After Nicholas left for army headquarters, Alexandra and her enigmatic confidant Grigorii Rasputin had greater control over appointments. They changed ministers and provincial governors with bewildering speed and they ousted most of the more liberal ministers, replacing them with others whom the Duma detested. Men such as Stürmer, premier and foreign minister for much of 1916, and A. D. Protopopov, minister of the interior in the winter of 1916–17, were attacked (though probably without foundation) for being in treasonable contact with the enemy. Even in peacetime this situation would have brought the government into disrepute. In wartime it deprived the regime of almost all its defenders and alienated several members even of the Romanov dynasty itself. To an extent the patriotic feeling of 1914–15 was redirected against the enemy within. As Rasputin's murder in December 1916 showed, desperation was driving even politicians of the reactionary right to consider quasi-revolutionary action, if only to head off the genuine popular revolution that they dreaded.

One reason for this fear of popular revolution was that a democratic Russia would be unlikely to intensify the war effort and would most probably rebel against it. Evidence was growing that disenchantment had proceeded much further in Russia than elsewhere. Posters, plays, films, and cabaret shows, in so far as they continued, now dwelt on war's hardships.[121] Since summer 1915 the strike movement had revived with growing intensity after police opened fire on textile workers at Kostroma, killing and wounding scores of victims. In November the elected labour representatives on the Petrograd War Industries Committee, one of the few legal workers' organizations, proclaimed that the government had taken Russia into a war for capitalist markets and called for a democratic peace without annexations and indemnities.[122] 1915 also witnessed mass anti-conscription

---

*cf. ch. 9.

protests in Petrograd and in provincial cities, wives mobbing induction points and demanding that the police should be called up.[123] Dozens of subsistence riots flared across European Russia, some linked to strikes and ending only when troops fired on the crowds. Often these riots too were led by *soldatki* (soldiers' wives), protesting about non-payment of separation allowances or attacking shop-keepers over price increases. By 1916 rioters were increasingly blaming the tsar for their problems and for sending their men to the front.[124] Little now separated the regime from the abyss except the loyalty of its army, but this too was in question even before the mutinies that shook it at the end of the year.* The head of the po-litical police in Petrograd warned that it was clear to all officials concerned with law and order that an 'unavoidable . . . catastrophe' was 'rapidly approaching', but his superiors refused to recognize the peril.[125]

Ironically, in some ways the regime was a victim of its success. It had re-sponded energetically to the 1915 military crisis, to some extent by co-operating with its critics. Industrial output grew rapidly, and many of the army's shortages were overcome. But success was achieved only on an unsustainable basis of gener-ous subsidies and contracts for Russian manufacturing, which the government could not borrow to finance and did not cover by increased taxation. Hence the in-creases in the note issue and in inflation were faster than in any other great power.[126] Russia entered the conflict with a weak popular consensus and a state apparatus that relied heavily on coercion. By 1916 much of the peasantry and ur-ban lower class were involved in violent protests against conscription, shortages, and price rises, and increasingly they blamed their hardships on the Romanovs. Like Austria-Hungary, Russia was vulnerable because of its multi-ethnic composi-tion, and like Italy it had been slow in cultivating a sense of national identity. By the winter of 1916–17 it faced a more acute subsistence crisis than either country. The empire stood on the verge of a revolution triggered by the demands placed on its population by the war.

With the Petrograd revolution of March 1917 the escalation dynamic that had dominated the conflict until then ran into the buffers, and a new phase in its his-tory began. While it had operated, however, the dynamic had had powerful ef-fects. From its origins in Central Europe the war had broadened out to include most of the nations of the world. New technologies, ranging from submarines to zeppelins and poison gas, had been brought to bear. Mass conscription and mass production of armaments galvanized the home fronts. The length, intensity, and cost of the 1916 battles dwarfed anything imagined in 1914. The escalation had been driven by the strategic impasse and the determination of both sides' leaders to intensify their efforts rather than negotiate for less than victory. Some factors contributing to this impasse were permissive: states surprised themselves by their ability to borrow from their citizens and to finance the war by printing money. As-sembly line techniques and women's willingness to enter the manufacturing work-force enabled them to produce enormous quantities of armaments without much diminishing the forces in the field. The achievements of medical science in rehabil-

---

*cf. ch.8.

itating the wounded and fending off disease maintained the armies' strength, as did the courage and endurance of the combatants. All these things were preconditions for the escalation of the war, and by making escalation possible they reduced the pressure on statesmen to back down. On the other hand, the approximate balance of strength between the two sides and the technical factors favouring the defensive made for stalemate on land and at sea. Admirals shrank from risking their dreadnoughts in pitched battles in an environment made hazardous by mines, torpedoes, and submarines. Germany had too few U-boats to cut off Allied commerce, and both the German submarine blockade and the Allied surface one ran foul of neutral resistance. The deficiencies of heavy artillery and the inability of new technologies such as wireless, tanks, poison gas, and aircraft to compensate for them left attacking armies at a basic disadvantage against entrenched defenders behind barbed wire with field guns, machine guns, and rifles, backed by railways and manufacturing hinterlands that could rush in reserve troops and supplies.

With all this said, however, the fundamental driving force behind the war's continuation and escalation (as behind its inception) was political, but political in more than one sense. One element was strategic: the presumption of both sides that they could win, even if they were unsure how. This was not a simple matter of generals dictating to politicians: strategy in every country was decided by military and civilian leaders in consultation, usually increasingly so as time went on. The Allies experimented in 1915 with peripheral operations, hoping the Dardanelles offensive, Italian intervention, and the Salonika expedition would bring in the Balkan countries and disable the Ottomans and Habsburgs. In 1916 they attempted to co-ordinate their efforts in massive and simultaneous sustained offensives, and for spring 1917 they intended more of the same. The Central Powers, who held the initiative from summer 1915 to summer 1916, hoped to bring one or other of their enemies to the conference table, first through the attack on Russia in 1915, then through Verdun, and finally through unrestricted submarine warfare. Strategy was therefore interconnected with a second level of explanation: that of war aims. The Central Powers offered too little to split their enemies diplomatically and the Allies had no intention of being split. On the contrary, in 1916 both sides expanded their objectives and new leaders came to power, notably Lloyd George and Ludendorff, who would be less likely to compromise. As the chasm of fear and hatred between them widened, their demands on each other increased.

It would be facile, however, simply to equate the two sides. The Central Powers had taken the offensive in 1914 and occupied northern France and Belgium. In 1915 they had added Poland and Serbia. The Allied governments felt, with considerable justice, that they were fighting aggression. They acknowledged Germany's superior military efficiency, but believed that with their geographical advantages and larger resources they could impose a decisive defeat on the aggressor and that it was worth suppressing their internal divisions and making the necessary sacrifices until they had done so. The German and Austro-Hungarian rulers felt they had been gravely threatened before 1914, professing (and to an extent sincerely believing) that they too had responded to aggression. Their task was to end the war while holding as much as possible of their gains. These circumstances influenced the politics of the home fronts, the third and in some ways most decisive level of political explanation for the prolongation of the war. On the one hand for the war to continue citizens had to be willing to take up war loans, accept the call-up, and simply go about their daily lives without rebelling. On the other hand conditions on the home fronts provided powerful motives for political and military chiefs to insist on far-reaching war aims and accept immensely costly attritional strategies rather than relinquish them. No more than the outbreak of the war can its escalation be explained by a crude 'social imperialism' thesis: that politicians pursued external expansion to avoid internal revolution.[127] On the contrary, by 1916 it was becoming disturbingly clear in the eastern European empires that the war, so far from consolidating the internal *status quo*, was undermining it. Yet the authorities were caught in an insoluble dilemma: Alexandra warned Nicholas in 1915 that a separate peace with Germany would mean 'revolution' at home; and in February 1917 despite the 'very alarming' internal situation, Nicholas believed that Russia must hang on in the hope of decisive results from the impending spring offensive.[128] Many on the German right, as well as the German leaders themselves, feared revolution in their country too if they settled for compromise.[129] Governments in all the belligerents were under intense domestic pressure not to terminate the conflict without achieving their declared objectives. To an extent they were trapped by their own rhetoric.

Domestic support remained essential for continuing the war, and yet in Italy it was fragile from the start and in Austria-Hungary and Russia it faded fast after the first few months. In Britain, France, and Germany it was more resilient. The evidence from 1914–17 is that casualties alone, even extremely heavy casualties, could not destroy a pro-war consensus if other factors remained favourable. Nor was a drip-feed of regular military successes essential. At least as important were agreement among political and intellectual elites that the war was legitimate and necessary, evidence that it would eventually be won, and tolerable material circumstances for the mass of the population. In Britain and France down to 1917 these conditions were met. In Germany they were to begin with, but the elite consensus slowly fragmented, and material conditions deteriorated sharply after 1916. After a year of military successes the supply of victories dried up and in summer 1916 Germany faced a crisis of morale, though one from which Hindenburg and Ludendorff, unrestricted submarine warfare, and the Russian Revolution were to rescue it. In Italy, in contrast, elite consensus was always deficient, and by 1916 there too material circumstances were deteriorating, though as for the other Allied powers grounds for hope remained that victory might soon be at hand. Finally Austria-Hungary and Russia were the most vulnerable links in the two chains. In Austria-Hungary consensus existed among the Germans, Magyars, and arguably the Croats, but much less so among the other nationalities. By 1916 material circumstances in the Austrian half of the Monarchy were very straitened indeed, and it was hard to see how even with German assistance the war could be won. In Russia, conditions were worse still, the army had tried its best against the Central Powers and failed, and the political elite, though agreed on the necessity of carrying on fighting, was bitterly divided.

This survey raises broader issues, one of which is gender. Many women protested against the costs of war, either through their role in pacifist movements or indirectly by demonstrating against price increases, conscription, factory discipline, and inadequate allowances. Yet other women chivvied men to volunteer, and everywhere in 1915–16 they crowded into munitions plants, to support themselves and their families but also for patriotic motives, arming their own husbands and sons against the husbands and sons of women on the other side. A second issue is propaganda. One of the surprises of 1915–16 is the relatively minor role of official opinion management, in contrast with an immense unofficial effort. However, it was not possible to fool all of the people for all of the time, and propaganda's effectiveness did bear some relationship to the underlying circumstances.[130] Domestic unity was most robust in the two countries – France and Britain – which had the strongest case for claiming they were fighting external aggression that threatened their security. Yet most Germans appear to have accepted their leaders' assertions that they were, too. In contrast the Italian government did not claim to be fighting in self-defence, though both in Russia after 1915 and in Italy in 1916 defeat and invasion made such a case more plausible. In general, consensus was firmer in countries that were ethnically homogeneous, or at least had cultivated a strong national identity. The qualification is important: in the British Isles the Welsh and Scots, to judge from by-elections and volunteering statistics, identified with the war as strongly as the English, but the southern Irish certainly did not. (In the Empire, similarly, Australians of Irish descent led the opposition to conscription, French Canadians volunteered less readily than did their anglophone countrymen, and Afrikaners rebelled against the South African government.) This does not mean in any simple way, however, that the driving force behind the war was nationalism.[131] Only Italy and France, among the great-power belligerents, were fighting for nationalist goals in the strict sense of bringing all co-nationals into one state; and even so their governments wanted more than the Trentino and Alsace-Lorraine. Like the other powers, in fact, they were imperialist. Patriotism, on the other hand, in the sense of a concern to defend an existing territorial state and a way of life within it, was much more fundamental. Even disadvantaged groups, such as French and German socialists and Catholics, threw in their lot with their respective states because they identified their own futures with those states' survival. For all their divisions and disunity each Western European country constituted, in the expressive German term, a *Schicksalsgemeinschaft* – a community of fate. But in Eastern Europe's multi-national empires this perception was much less widely shared, and its collapse in Russia now brought both sides to the watershed of the war.

Part Three

OUTCOME

CHAPTER 12

THE THIRD PHASE, SPRING 1917–AUTUMN 1918

SPRING 1917 MARKED the second turning point in the history of the war. In autumn 1914 the phase of movement had ended in the west; by autumn 1915 it had virtually ended in the east as well. The leading characteristic of the conflict's central period was a stalemate. The intractability of that stalemate led on inexorably to a second feature: escalation in scale and in ferocity. Neither side, however, could sustain the peak of mobilization attained in 1916. The Allies' synchronized offensives and the Germans' efforts to divide their enemies had overtaxed both sides. They needed to pause. At this point the overthrow of Tsar Nicholas in March 1917 and American intervention in April seemed to revolutionize the international political constellation. Yet the shockwaves from these events travelled slowly. The Russian Provisional Government remained loyal to the Allies, rejected a separate peace, and launched a new offensive. At first its army stayed mostly intact. Only from the winter of 1917–18 were the Germans in a position to move massive forces to the west after the Bolsheviks seized power in November, concluded a ceasefire in December, and signed the Brest-Litovsk peace treaty in March 1918. American involvement took even longer to achieve its maximum impact. Certainly, from the spring of 1917 US government loans, destroyers, and merchant ships helped the Allies to survive financial crisis and U-boat attacks. But the slow arrival of the American Expeditionary Force caused bitter disappointment in London and Paris.[1] Only 150,000 of its troops reached France by January 1918,[2] and the task of halting the five German offensives launched between March and July fell mainly on their battle-weary partners. Only in the final months of fighting did the Americans compare with the French and British in the numbers they committed and in the casualties they suffered and inflicted, and by then they faced a beaten enemy. This is not said to belittle the American contribution, which was indispensable to the Allies' victory, but rather to underline that Russia's departure and America's entry did not simply cancel each other out. In

243

1918 the war in the east ended (though it was followed almost immediately by a civil war in which both the Allies and the Central Powers participated), but the war in the west intensified.

Until the final year, however, the escalation mechanism of 1915–16 went into reverse. In 1917 all three main armies on the Western Front began to shrink. Following the Germans' lead, first the French and then the British reduced the number of battalions in each division.[3] Although trying to compensate through increased firepower, one army after another converted from an offensive to a defensive posture in response to changed strategic priorities, shortage of men, and ebbing morale. Hindenburg and Ludendorff decided after the Somme to remain passive in the west during 1917 and let the U-boats make the running; after the Russian Revolution they did so in the east as well, calculating that to attack would rekindle Russian patriotism.[4] After the Austro-Hungarian army's mauling by Brusilov it was incapable of unaided offensives, and until late 1917 Hindenburg and Ludendorff denied it assistance. On the Allied side, after Nicholas fell the Stavka postponed the operations scheduled for the spring, and after staging a belated summer offensive Russia was incapable of more. The French army, shaken by mutiny after the Chemin des Dames disaster, undertook only limited efforts. The Italian army battered away on the Isonzo, but in October an Austro-German counter-attack at Caporetto crippled it for months. These developments left the British alone in maintaining their offensives into late autumn, and soon afterwards even Haig accepted that the transfer of German troops from Russia now obliged him to hunker down.

The fading impetus on the fighting fronts was paralleled behind the lines. Except in America war economies had hit production peaks or were entering decline. French arms output, after vertiginous growth, reached a plateau;[5] German industry fell short of the objectives of the Hindenburg Programme.[6] In all the European belligerents serious challenges arose to pro-war consensus. Only Russia withdrew, but everywhere governments reappraised their war aims, and mostly reduced them. On the Allied side Nivelle's defeat, the upheaval in Petrograd, and delays in American assistance contributed to a radical change of mood. Governments and public alike resigned themselves to fighting into 1919 or even 1920, and a long-war illusion replaced the earlier short-war one, to the extent that many were surprised when the Central Powers capitulated. This lowering of expectations was symptomatic of a deeper transformation of western attitudes towards armed conflict that would be among the war's enduring legacies. It was no accident that the quest for a compromise peace was at its most sustained between spring and autumn 1917.

Yet negotiation failed and in 1918 the fighting flared up more fiercely than ever. Even the Americans, in barely two months of full-scale combat, suffered as many dead as they were to do during their entire involvement in Vietnam years later. Behind this climax at the front lay a regeneration of patriotic faith at home. After months of doubt and dissension, German public unity and confidence revived,[7] and the Allied coalition gained stronger leadership and more effective co-ordination. But whereas the Central Powers held the initiative in the first half of 1918, in the second half fortunes were reversed. To some extent the 1915–16 cycle was repeated. In summer 1917, as in 1915, the Allies launched unconnected and unsuccessful assaults. Between autumn 1917 and summer 1918, as between Gorlice-Tarnow and Verdun, the advantage passed to their enemies. But the second battle of the Marne in July 1918, like at the opening of the Brusilov and Somme offensives in June–July 1916, saw the Allies regain the edge, and in September–October they launched onslaughts in all theatres against opponents who were now much weaker than two years earlier and had run out of expedients and of hope.

The analysis of this complex and crowded period will be structured chronologically rather than by topic, in order to reintegrate the themes that in discussing 1915–16 were treated separately. It falls into five main subdivisions. First, the spring 1917 turning point and the origins of the Russian Revolution and American intervention. Second, the belligerents' moral and political crisis in the ensuing summer and autumn. Third, the Central Powers' revival and their triumph in the east after the Bolshevik Revolution, associated with climactic offensives. Fourth, the Allies' recovery in the summer of 1918 and the sources of their regeneration. Fifth and finally, the road to the armistices of late 1918, marked for the losers not only by defeat but also by revolution. If the underlying problem discussed in Part Two was the war's prolongation and intensification, that in Part Three will be its termination: the Central Powers' triumph on the Eastern Front but defeat on the Western, and therefore overall. The key question is why the Allies won, which even after American entry was far from a foregone conclusion, and did not seem to be one at the time.[8] By autumn 1918 the victors faced demoralized forces, exhausted by strategic errors and the cumulative workings of attrition and blockade. Yet the Allies' triumph was not simply handed to them by dint of superior resources: they had to fight for it. Moreover, for the war to end not only did the defeated have to sue for a ceasefire but also the victors had to grant them one rather than press home their advantage. In the east the Bolsheviks needed peace if their regime was to survive, but it was the Central Powers who decided on the terms and steeled themselves to do business with a regime that despised them. Similarly, in October–November 1918 in the west both sides had to be willing to stop the bloodletting as both had been willing to start it. Finally, a precondition for the last act was a transformation in military operations, as both sides discovered solutions to the previous deadlock. If politically 1918 can be interpreted as foreshadowing 1939, militarily it pointed ahead to 1940. Explaining how the war terminated at the time and in the manner that it did is essential to an understanding of its legacies and impact.

CHAPTER 13

THE FEBRUARY REVOLUTION AND AMERICAN INTERVENTION, SPRING 1917

T HE WAR'S THIRD PHASE began with the two events whose consequences would dominate it. The 'February Revolution' in Russia would bring
the Central Powers victory in the east; America's intervention ultimately spelt
their defeat in the west. Both developments had their origins in the second phase,
and they spotlighted the Allies' and the Central Powers' respective weaknesses.
The February Revolution resulted in part from the strategy of the Chantilly conferences, which its outbreak wrecked. American entry followed from the Pless conference, the latest of the gambles by which the Germans tried to knock out their
opponents individually. With the Chantilly and Pless approaches bankrupt, neither side possessed a formula for victory. Both went through a time of soul-
searching before the Bolshevik seizure of power opened the endgame. Despite the
obvious contrasts, Nicholas II's abdication manifesto and Woodrow Wilson's war
message mirrored each other in their impact on the conflict's subsequent history,
and in their repercussions over the rest of the century.

The February Revolution took place, according to the western calendar, in March.*
It comprised a sequence of interrelated challenges to tsarist authority. The first was
a wave of demonstrations and strikes in the capital, starting on 23 February/
8 March. The second was a mutiny by the Petrograd garrison on 27 February/
12 March, expanding into an insurrection that took over the city. The third was the

---

*One of the first Bolshevik actions was to replace tsarist Russia's Julian calendar by the West's Gre-
gorian one, running thirteen days ahead. Hence the 'October' (i.e., Bolshevik) Revolution took place
by western reckoning in November. Because the 'February' and 'October' titles have stuck they will be
used here. Dates will where necessary be designated O.S. (old style) or N.S. (new style).

formation on 27–28 February/12–13 March of two competing authority centres: the Petrograd Soviet, led by revolutionary socialists, and the Provisional Government of Duma politicians. Fourth and finally, on 2/15 March, under pressure from the Duma and the army, Nicholas stood down and Russia became a republic. The key issues to address here are the contribution of the war to these events and their influence on its course.[1]

The popular movement began on International Women's Day, 23 February O.S., when thousands of women demonstrated against food shortages. The city governor judged stocks were adequate for a week, but during January Petrograd had received only forty-nine wagonloads per day whereas it needed eighty-nine.[2] Rumours of impending rationing caused panic buying, and citizens queued for hours in sub-zero temperatures (the February average was -12.1°C), though only to be disappointed all too often as flour and fuel shortages forced many bakeries to close. The emergency had two fundamental causes, both war-related. One was transport paralysis. Petrograd and Moscow were hundreds of miles from the grain- and coal-producing regions in the Ukraine. Russia's railways were inadequate even in peacetime and during the war the army had commandeered much of their rolling stock to service the front. The locomotives remaining for civilian purposes were poorly maintained, and many had become unusable. The freeze-up added to the chaos.[3] The second cause was a breakdown in grain marketing. The harvest in European Russia (excluding Poland) rose from 4,304 million poods* in 1914 to 4,659 million in 1915 before falling to 3,916 million in 1916 and 3,800 million in 1917. In itself this was hardly a catastrophic reduction, as the same region had exported 640 million poods in 1913–14 but less than 3 million in 1917, a fall that outweighed the increase in army demand from 85 million poods in 1913–14 to 485 million in 1916–17. But the amount of the crop that was actually marketed fell from some 1,200 million poods in 1913–14 to only 794 million in 1916, or *c.* 15 per cent instead of *c.* 25 per cent. Because the troops took priority, deliveries to the towns fell from 390 million poods in 1913–14 to 295 million in 1916–17, while in the same period the urban population rose by a third.[4] Most Russians lived in largely self-sufficient villages, and most of the harvest came not from Chekhovian gentry estates but from peasant smallholdings, where normally most of it stayed. In wartime Russia the countryside (as in other countries) was prosperous. But the very success of rearmament by 1916–17 caused the production of fewer consumer goods that grain could be sold to purchase, and the depreciation of the rouble weakened the incentive to sell for paper that was becoming worthless. Nor did the tsarist government (unlike its Bolshevik successor) compel the growers to disgorge their surpluses, the agriculture ministry being slow to intervene in urban supply arrangements. In June 1916 the government decided to fix wholesale cereal prices, but then deliberated for months over the appropriate figure. In November it introduced a plan for requisitioning, but did not authorize it until the February demonstrations began.[5] Hence a small but vital extra proportion of the harvest remained in the rural areas, to be stored, fed to livestock, or eaten by the peasants themselves, and with dire consequences. Even the Petrograd

---

*1 pood = 36 lbs.

CROWNED HEADS: NICHOLAS II (LEFT) MEETS
WILHELM II (RIGHT) AT SEA
[© BETTMANN/CORBIS]

NAVAL GUN TURRETS IN THE KRUPP WORKS, ESSEN, 1912
[CREDIT: AKG-IMAGES]

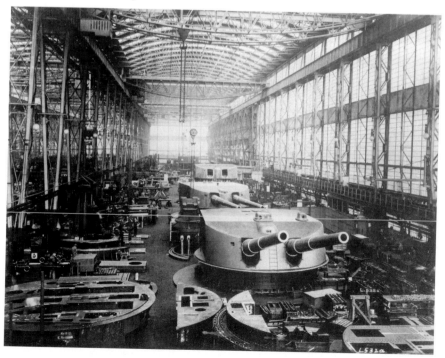

THE WARS BEFORE THE WAR: JAPANESE SOLDIERS MAN A TRENCH IN MANCHURIA, RUSSO-JAPANESE WAR [© CORBIS]

THE WARS BEFORE THE WAR: DEAD ON THE BATTLEFIELD AT ADRIANOPLE, BALKAN WARS [CREDIT: HULTON ARCHIVE]

German reservists, 1914 [© Imperial War Museum]

British troops arrive in France, August 1914
[CREDIT: Hulton Getty]

BETHMANN HOLLWEG IN
MILITARY DRESS (CENTRE)
[© CORBIS]

FALKENHAYN ON THE MARCH
[©BETTMANN/CORBIS]

WILHELM II (CENTRE), FLANKED BY
HINDENBURG (LEFT) AND LUNDENDORFF
(RIGHT) [© CORBIS]

KITCHENER RETURNS FROM THE
GALLIPOLI TRENCHES, NOVEMBER 1915
[© IMPERIAL WAR MUSEUM]

JELLICOE [© IMPERIAL WAR MUSEUM]

BRUSILOV [© IMPERIAL
WAR MUSEUM]

JOFFRE (LEFT) AND PERSHING (RIGHT) MEET
AGAIN, 1922 [© BETTMANN/CORBIS]

FRENCH TRENCH AT VERDUN
[CREDIT: ROGER-VIOLLET/REX FEATURES]

LOADING A LARGE 9.45-INCH TRENCH MORTAR IN A CAPTURED GERMAN TRENCH; PIGEON WOOD NEAR GOMMECOURT, MARCH 1917 [Q. 4923. CROWN COPYRIGHT]

GERMAN UNIT MOVES AN OBSERVATION BALLOON
[CREDIT: ROBERT HUNT LIBRARY]

BRITISH TANK HELD UP IN THE GERMAN SECOND LINE AT
CAMBRAI, NOVEMBER 1917 [© IMPERIAL WAR MUSEUM]

AMERICAN SOLDIERS IN GAS MASKS
[© IMPERIAL WAR MUSEUM]

GERMAN BARBED WIRE, QUÉANT, 1918
[© IMPERIAL WAR MUSEUM]

German Rumpler C-1 on a raid from
Palestine over the Pyramids, Giza, 1915
[© Imperial War Museum]

Turkish cavalry move up in Palestine, April 1917
[CREDIT: Robert Hunt Library]

ARMENIAN
REFUGEES IN
SYRIA, 1915
[CREDIT:
ROBERT HUNT
LIBRARY]

MASS BURIAL OF
LUSITANIA VICTIMS,
MAY 1915
[© HULTON GETTY]

BERLIN CROWD
WAITS FOR SOUP, 1916
[CREDIT: THE
PHOTO LIBRARY-SYDNEY/
HULTON-DEUTSCH]

British women fill shells
[CREDIT: The Art Archive/Imperial
War Museum/The Art Archive]

Annamite munitions workers in France
[CREDIT: roger-Viollet/REX FEATURES]

EMPEROR KARL
[© CORBIS]

KERENSKY IN 1920
[© HULTON-DEUTSCH
COLLECTION/CORBIS]

TROTSKY HARANGUES RUSSIAN TROOPS
[© UNDERWOOD & UNDERWOOD/CORBIS]

Anzacs on the road to the front, December 1916
[© Imperial War Museum]

Canadian machine gunners at Third Ypres, 1917
[CREDIT: The Art Archive]

GERMAN INFANTRY DURING THE 'MICHAEL'
OFFENSIVE, MARCH 1918
[CREDIT: ULSTEIN BILD]

AMERICANS RESTING ON A ROUTE MARCH, MAY 1918
[© IMPERIAL WAR MUSEUM]

GERMAN TROOPS RETURN TO BERLIN AFTER THE ARMISTICE [CREDIT: BILDARCHIVE PREUSSISCHER KULTURBESITZ]

ALLIED LEADERS IN LONDON, DECEMBER 1918 (FROM LEFT TO RIGHT, FOCH, CLEMENCEAU, LLOYD GEORGE, ORLANDO, SONNINO) [© BETTMANN/ CORBIS]

WOODROW WILSON LANDS IN FRANCE, DECEMBER 1918 [CREDIT: HITON-DEUTSCH]

BRITISH SCHOOLCHILDREN VISIT WAR CEMETERY, 1923
[© 2003 TOPFOTO.CO.UK]

metalworkers, the industrial group that had been most successful in maintaining living standards down to 1916, then saw them erode like everyone else's.[6]

The war's effects on Petrograd resembled those on other cities ranging from Paris to Berlin, Turin, Vienna, and even London, but the capital's social tinder was exceptionally combustible. Events in Petrograd dictated to the rest of the country first the fall of the Romanovs and then the triumph of the Bolsheviks. With a 1917 population of 2.4 million Petrograd was by far Russia's greatest urban area and industrial powerhouse. It contained 392,800 factory workers (up from 242,600 since the start of the war), 60.4 per cent of them in metalworking and 70 per cent in plants employing over 1,000 people: a concentration in gigantic establishments unparalleled elsewhere in the world.[7] The wartime boom had sucked women and rural migrants into the factories, exacerbating strains on food and housing. Overcrowding in Petrograd apartments was at twice the level in Paris, Berlin, or Vienna, infant mortality doubled in 1914–16, and by February 1917 women were averaging forty hours a week waiting in queues on top of ten-hour working days.[8] Moreover the influx of new blood failed to swamp the local traditions of radicalism. Many young men escaped conscription because of their munitions work or were allowed to return to their plants. In 1917 more than half the Petrograd working class had been there since before the war.[9] This mattered because its history was exceptionally militant. Between 1895 and 1916 about a quarter of the Russian factory labour force went on strike each year, and in the two strike waves of 1905–6 and 1912–14 an average of three quarters – far more than in Germany, France, or Britain.[10] From summer 1915 a third wave gathered momentum. At first it focused on workplace issues, especially wages, as prices moved ahead of earnings. As the movement expanded, however, its target became the state. The number of industrial workers taking strike action climbed from 539,528 (28 per cent of the workforce) in 1915 to 957,075 (49.8 per cent) in 1916. A total of 676,000 went on strike in the two months of January and February 1917 alone, and of these strikes 86 per cent were political protests.[11]

The war caused the subsistence crisis, but that crisis ignited the protest movement rather than being its driving force. Although the February Days began with demonstrations over bread, they touched off the biggest strike in Petrograd's history, and from the first afternoon slogans and banners also denounced the tsar and the war.[12] Tens of thousands spilled out into the streets, attempting to break police cordons and reach the heart of the city. Whereas the revolutionary district *par excellence* in 1790s Paris, the Faubourg St-Antoine, was a warren of artisans' workshops, the storm centre in 1917 was the 'Vyborg side', a suburb of working-class tenements and metal and armaments plants lying just across the river Neva from Petrograd's central districts. A revolt on this scale required organization, and experienced employees from the larger plants, especially Vyborg side metalworkers, supplied it.[13] Whether the February Days were a planned Bolshevik action, however, is more questionable. Although historians in the former Soviet Union emphasized the role of party members, Western writers until recently stressed the uprising's spontaneity.[14] Probably the truth lies somewhere between these viewpoints, the movement becoming increasingly concerted as it went on. The leadership came, however, not only from Bolsheviks but also from other socialist organizations such as Mensheviks and Socialist Revolutionaries, or from people not belonging to any group. Most of the Bolshevik leadership was in exile abroad or in Siberia, and the left-wing parties did not initiate the protest, though they acted quickly to secure control of it.

The demonstrators could create a revolutionary movement; they could not accomplish a revolution. For that the essential condition, accomplished remarkably rapidly on and after 27 February, was the mutiny of the Petrograd garrison, after which the soldiers collaborated with the strikers in seizing the power centres. At first Petrograd's military commander, General Khobalov, had hoped to ride out the situation by avoiding violence. On the 25th, however, Nicholas, who was away at army headquarters in Mogilev, had telegraphed that the disorders were unacceptable in the face of the enemy and must be suppressed. Khobalov had then outlawed street gatherings and posted troops with authorization to use their rifles. On Sunday 26 February, shootings had followed at several flashpoints, notably Znamenskaya Square, causing a hundred or more casualties. On the morning of Monday, 27 February, the NCOs of the Volynskii regiment led their men in defying their officers and refusing to fire. They spread the mutiny to neighbouring regiments and began to seize arms and occupy public buildings. A parallel action by the Vyborg-side workers, in which Bolshevik leadership was prominent, took control there. Once the two movements joined up they controlled a third of the city and cut off the pro-government forces from weapons and ammunition. By the 28th Khobalov had hardly any loyal troops left, and he reported that he had lost control over the whole of Petrograd.[15]

The authorities had only 3,500 police, who were dwarfed by the crowds and by the garrison, which numbered 180,000 in the city and a further 150,000 in the suburbs.[16] The defection of the garrison was decisive, though little is known about its motives. Troops had already refused to fire on strikers in 1916 and although at the start of the February Days cavalry and Cossacks co-operated with the police this was partly because they did not have to shoot and the crowds avoided provoking them. The tsar's command of 25 February forced them to choose, after they had had three days to develop feelings of solidarity with the demonstrators. The instruction to fire on men, women, and children seems to have triggered the disobedience, and once it began the logic pointed to disarming officers and toppling the regime in order to prevent retaliation.

It is necessary, though, to relate the mutiny to the transformation of the army since 1914. The mutiny spread among supposedly elite guards regiments, personally loyal to the emperor and by origin primarily rural rather than from the industrial areas. But many of the garrison were veterans who had returned to service after being wounded, raw young recruits, and middle-aged *ratniki* who had been called from their villages late in life. Among the most alienated members of a disillusioned force, they were huddled in makeshift barracks near the city centre, where the crucial discussions on the night of 26/7 February took place.[17] That NCOs took the lead was no coincidence, given that they differed little in social standing from their men and in view of the paucity of regular officers, those of the latter who remained being mostly young and inexperienced. Russia's shattering casualties therefore contributed to making discipline so fragile, and so did discontent over inadequate rations, the war's apparent lack of purpose, and the enemy's invincibility.[18] The empire's build-up had given it, on paper, an advantage in numbers of men and heavy weapons,[19] but at the price of a diluted army, a devalued currency, and an insurrectionary workforce. At the moment when the Chantilly strategy called for a decisive blow, Russia (and therefore the Allied coalition as a whole) was too weary to deliver it. That the garrison joined the revolution was due partly to tactical mistakes by the authorities but also to the war's corrosive effects.

So much for the crumbling of the old order. We now come to its successor, or more precisely to the two new sources of authority, the Petrograd Soviet and the Provisional Government. If the first motor of the revolution was the disaffection of the masses as represented by industrial workers and peasant soldiers, the second was the alienation of the intelligentsia and the propertied and educated, a decades-old phenomenon that wartime conditions had brought to a head. The intelligentsia constituted a self-perpetuating opposition to the political system, and within it a powerful element was committed to violent social transformation. However, since the turn of the century the opposition had been organized in political parties, some of which had ceased to be revolutionary after the constitutional reforms of 1905–6. The basic fault line separated liberals such as the Kadets and Octobrists, who formed the backbone of the Progressive Bloc in the Duma, from the socialists, most prominent among whom were the Socialist Revolutionaries (or SRs), the Bolsheviks, and the Mensheviks. The Provisional Government represented the first group, and the Petrograd Soviet the second.

The organizers of the Soviet (or 'Council of Workers' and Soldiers' Deputies') gained a few hours' lead. A similar institution had existed in 1905, and on 27 February the socialists revived it. The initiative came from the Menshevik representatives in the Central Workers' Group on the Central War Industries Committee, an elected body that the Bolsheviks had boycotted. A meeting set up a Provisional Executive Committee (*Ispolkom*), and factories and military units elected Soviet representatives. Most of the *Ispolkom*'s members were Mensheviks, though during March representatives of other socialist parties were added. Increasingly, though, it acted in the Soviet's name without consulting plenary sessions.[20] It had no hesitation in issuing executive orders, and it set up a military commission that assumed responsibility for commanding the garrison and assuring law and order. As most of the soldiers seem to have accepted its authority, it might have taken responsibility for the city's government, but it deliberately refrained from doing so. The reasons stemmed partly from Marxist exegesis (the Mensheviks believing a phase of bourgeois-liberal rule was needed before Russia would be ripe for socialism) but were also severely practical: it lacked administrative experience and feared counter-revolution and civil war if it moved too fast. Hence it preferred cooperation with the emerging Provisional Government, with which on the night of 1/2 March it reached an eight-point agreement, thereby establishing the dual authority (*dvoevlastie*) that would characterize the next few months.

Some historians have argued that Nicholas had lost his last and best chance to save the monarchy when he refused concessions to the Duma in 1915.[21] The evidence points both ways. On the one hand it seems unlikely that the liberals could have done more against the Germans or mobilized the war economy still faster, and if they had succeeded in the latter they would have intensified popular protest. A revolt like that of February would probably have happened anyway. Most likely the main difference would have been stronger resistance from the authorities and perhaps a split in the army, with a heightened risk of civil war. But Nicholas, encouraged by his wife, had stuck by his conviction that he must protect his autocratic powers to pass on to his son, and he had refused compromise. By late 1916 the Progressive Bloc and even the Stavka were in a near revolutionary temper. In a sensational Duma speech in November Pavel Miliukov of the Kadets asked rhetorically whether the government's errors were due to stupidity or treason, while the Octobrist A. I. Guchkov was in contact with senior officers about a possible coup. Yet the liberals were in a cleft stick, dreading a revolt that would sweep away the social elite in its entirety and therefore hesitating to risk revolutionary acts rather than inflammatory words.[22] Besides, the war had increased practical co-operation between liberals in the *zemstvos* and municipalities (and industrialists in the war industries committees) and the bureaucracy. Arguably Nicholas's concessions had given the opposition too much of an interest in the system for them really to rock the boat.[23]

These considerations help explain the Duma's caution when the revolution began. On 27 February the deputies in the Tauride Palace found themselves encircled by insurgents while the Soviet was emerging as a potential rival. They risked physical attack if they sided with the old regime, to which most were vehemently hostile. Yet they wanted to protect public order and the war effort, and they feared reprisals from the autocracy if it crushed the revolt. They set up a provisional committee to 'restore order', under the Duma president, Rodzianko, which began to act as an embryo cabinet. By 2 March they were willing to risk establishing a self-styled Provisional Government, with the Soviet's acquiescence. Under the terms of the agreement between the two authorities, all political prisoners were amnestied, freedom of speech, assembly, association, and to strike would be guaranteed, provincial authorities would be elected as would a militia (to replace the police), and the units that had participated in the uprising would keep their weapons and would not be sent to the front. Hence the Provisional Government would remain at the mercy of the Soviet and the city garrison: it had dismantled the apparatus of coercion and permitted complete political freedom in the midst of a desperate war. Led by Prince Lvov and unenthusiastically supported by *Ispolkom*, it assumed power in circumstances which made effective exercise of that power almost impossible.[24]

The final point to consider is the dethronement of the dynasty. At first Nicholas hoped to suppress the uprising with loyal soldiers from the front, and ordered an expedition under General Ivanov to advance against the capital. Railway workers delayed the train movements, and Ivanov's vanguard fraternized with mutinous units it encountered *en route*, but the main reason why the expedition failed was that Nicholas countermanded it. His decision resulted from an appraisal by the Stavka that the monarchy was not worth saving, which was crucial in persuading him to abdicate. Some members of the Provisional Government, notably foreign minister Miliukov and war minister Guchkov, wanted a constitutional monarchy rather than a republic, but even they were not attached to Nicholas. Among the generals, Brusilov had long favoured a government acceptable to the Duma, as did Ruszkii, the northern sector commander. Nicholas was re-routed to Ruszkii's head-quarters at Pskov after vainly seeking to rejoin his family at the Tsarskoe Selo palace. Here, without Alexandra to fortify his resistance, he faced two rounds of pressure. On 1 March Alekseyev, supported by Brusilov, Ruszkii, and Grand Duke Nicholas, urged him to accept a Duma government. He reluctantly assented. But that evening Rodzianko reported from Petrograd that only abdication would do, and Ruszkii, backed by Alekseyev, Grand Duke Nicholas, and the other front commanders, now urged this course on Nicholas.[25] This proposal he likewise accepted, abdicating in favour of his brother, Grand Duke Michael, who in turn stood down when the Provisional Government warned him that persisting might lead to civil war and it could not guarantee his safety. With the publication of both abdications on 4 March, the Romanovs' three centuries of rule expired with a whimper. Nicholas, who had always been a curious combination of diffidence with callousness, had found himself almost completely isolated and his theoretical abso-lutism crumbled in his hands. Such sovereignty as remained in Russia now passed nominally to the Provisional Government.

Nicholas had maintained his resistance to a government responsible to the Duma until Alekseyev advised him to give way. Similarly, he had abdicated at his comman-ders' behest. Brusilov and Ruszkii supported the Duma before the revolution, but Alekseyev changed his mind only during it, apparently influenced by evidence that the movement was spreading (to the towns round Petrograd, to the fleet at Kron-stadt, and to Moscow) and infecting more and more units. He wanted to contain it while the army was mostly intact, and he respected Rodzianko's advice, probably hoping that Nicholas's departure would lead to a more patriotic and effective succes-sor. Similar considerations weighed with Nicholas himself, and he referred to them in his valedictory proclamation. Once he had surrendered his autocratic powers, giv-ing up the imperial title was comparatively easy and may have been a relief. The Pet-rograd crowds certainly wanted the monarchy to go, and the news that it had done so caused explosive celebrations in the capital and at the front. Across the country statues, double-headed eagles, and other emblems of dynastic rule were smashed. For the high command and Nicholas, however, whose decisions in this relatively bloodless upheaval were crucial, the key concerns were preserving the army and avoiding defeat, which imperatives meant the monarchy must be sacrificed. The war had started the revolution and was central to its culminating act.

Yet the Stavka's and the Provisional Government's hopes of channelling the rev-olutionary impulse soon proved misplaced. They received a body blow even before Nicholas abdicated in the shape of the Petrograd Soviet's 'Army Order No. 1' of 1 March. *Ispolkom* members drafted this command with some military involvement, whether from rank and file soldiers or from hand-picked officers remains unclear.[26] It seems to have been a response to efforts by Duma politicians to gain control over the army and restore respect for officers, *Ispolkom* fearing the military would become the platform for counter-revolution and intending to remove this menace once and for all. Army Order No. 1 asserted that in all political matters the armed forces were subordinate to the Soviet, which could countermand Provisional Government in-structions. It required all units from company up to regimental level to elect soldiers' committees, which would take control of weapons and equipment. The Soviet acted without consulting the Provisional Government, which acquiesced in the order but disliked it, Guchkov lamenting that he could do nothing of which the Soviet disapproved. Nor did it consult the Stavka, and if the high command had foreseen this development it might have hesitated before ditching Nicholas. Army Order No. 1 asserted the Soviet's pretensions rather than actually establishing its control, though the revolution had severely weakened the tsarist officer corps (many of whom were arrested and replaced by more popular substitutes, while at Kronstadt dozens of naval officers were lynched). In most of the army the order became known within days, and officers' memoirs unanimously testify to its disintegrating effect. Most of the army remained in place, desertions running at between 100,000 and 150,000 in March in a force of 7.5 million, but soldiers' committees spread rapidly and shadowed even senior commanders. In mid-March the death penalty was abolished and officers' powers of summary discipline were transferred to elected courts, while soldiers were proclaimed free to engage in political activity.[27] Especially given the army's continuing food shortages, to terminate its leaders' coercive powers invited an accelerating break-up.

Developments in the army were a microcosm of larger processes. By the terms of the agreement with the Soviet the Provisional Government removed the provincial governors, lifted all censorship, and replaced the police. The removal of the dynasty, intended to help contain the revolution, probably did more than anything else to convince the peasantry that they could challenge the social order with impunity. By dismantling the structure of repression the new authorities hoped to neutralize the risk of counter-revolution, but they left themselves exposed to greater radicalization. Although the Stavka and the Provisional Government hoped to maintain and even intensify Russia's contribution to the war, they were losing the capacity to do so. However, the socialists did not yet call for peace, and the petitions sent by soldiers to the Soviet and the Provisional Government in March and April generally did not call for an immediate ceasefire, instead rating democratization and social reform as higher priorities.[28] Nor did the Petrograd garrison demonstrate for an end to the conflict, and its members cold-shouldered agitators who did. February was not therefore initially an anti-war upheaval. Even so, the popular movement was fuelled by opposition to the war's effects, not to mention by opposition to authority of all kinds: to the naval officers who were murdered and to the factory foremen who were ejected in wheelbarrows as much as to Nicholas. In these circumstances the chances of support for the war continuing were small.

While one pro-war consensus fragmented in Russia another crystallized across the Atlantic. This development was sudden. Barely two months before America declared war on Germany on 6 April 1917 there seemed hardly any wish among the public or in Congress for intervention, and no desire by Wilson to propose it. During 1916 American entry alongside the Allies had seemed increasingly unlikely. True, in the year between the *Lusitania* and the *Sussex* sinkings Washington had been in almost continuous confrontation with Berlin over submarine warfare and Wilson's pro-Allied sympathies were at their height. He had allowed the British government to issue bonds on Wall Street, soft-pedalled his opposition to the blockade, and with the House-Grey memorandum had hinted at intervention to achieve Allied war aims. But by summer 1916 Britain and France had set aside the memorandum and the *Sussex* pledge had sidelined the U-boat issue, while Washington was at odds with London over blacklisting and the interception of neutral mails. American exports to the Allies were in question because the latter were nearing the end of their capacity to pay for them. Indeed the American authorities welcomed a slackening of the boom, as the Federal Reserve Board's November 1916 warning against purchasing British Treasury bills demonstrated.* Nor did the presidential elections in the same month demonstrate any desire for belligerency. The Republicans selected Charles Evans Hughes as their candidate rather than Theodore Roosevelt, in part because the latter was one of the few leading politicians who (insisting that Germany was a menace and the Allies' cause was just) openly advocated intervention. Wilson branded Hughes regardless as a warmonger and the Democrats projected the president as 'the man who kept us out of the war'.[29]

Wilson's diplomacy, however, revolved around three interlocking themes: trade and loans, blockade and U-boats, and his urge to mediate. His mediation attempts forced him to elaborate his vision of the peace settlement and whetted his appetite for involvement in it. From early in the conflict he contemplated creating an international collective security organization, and pressure groups lobbied for the same objective. In a speech on May 1916 to the most prominent of them, the League to Enforce Peace, he declared himself in favour of establishing such an organization and of American membership in it. Both he and Hughes reaffirmed this viewpoint in their election platforms. Despite the apparent agreement between Democrats and Republicans on the point, however, Wilson had imbibed his internationalism from socialist and progressive thinking.[30] Hence in addition to the League of Nations he embraced the ideal of a democratic peace, based on the consent of the governed, national self-determination, and freedom of the seas. This 'progressive internationalism' contrasted with the 'conservative internationalism' of the Republican east-coast leaders, who envisaged upholding peace by transatlantic cooperation.[31] Progressive internationalism was probably more easily reconcilable with the Allies' objectives than with those of the Central Powers, but Wilson was suspicious of both sides, and believed both must be restrained in the interests of a lasting settlement. When Bryan's successor as Secretary of State, Robert Lansing, suggested in 1915 that America might declare war on Germany to defeat German militarism but also to restrain Allied imperialism at the peace conference, Wilson replied that this conception ran along the lines of his own thought.[32] The possibility of belligerency was in his mind from the *Lusitania* crisis onwards, but he had little wish to risk it and expected to have little public following if he tried to.

None the less, even while campaigning against Hughes Wilson knew that Berlin was unlikely to respect the *Sussex* pledge much longer and that another submarine crisis was impending. After his re-election he returned to diplomatic activism, increasingly desperate to broker peace before he had to choose between war and humiliation. But he delayed too long, and when the Central Powers

---

*Cf. chs. 5, 9, and 10.

published their peace note on 12 December he felt obliged to issue his own on the 18th in order to forestall an angry Allied rebuttal that would ruin all prospect of compromise. Maintaining that the two sides' aims as so far publicly stated seemed indistinguishable, he appealed to them to specify their objectives.[33] Whereas the Germans politely refused, however, the Allies' reply of 10 January 1917 set out their aims in unprecedented (if misleading) detail. Hence the note brought the parties no closer together but enabled the Allies to begin rebuilding bridges to Washington, Wilson acknowledging their greater candour in his next major initiative (on 22 January), his 'Peace without Victory' speech. In it he committed himself for the first time not only to the League of Nations but also to a larger progressive internationalist agenda. The United States, he said, would join the League only if the peace it guaranteed was one with no resentful loser. The peace must rest on democratic liberties for all peoples, territorial transfers only with the inhabitants' consent, freedom of the seas, and limitation of armaments. As an illustration, he called for a 'united, independent, and autonomous Poland': a formula he expected would be uncontentious but which caused fury in Berlin. His objectives were becoming clearer and he was now tilting back towards the Allies, but American belligerency still remained distant.[34]

Wilson's policy changed largely in response to German actions, notably the resumption of unrestricted submarine warfare on 1 February and the dispatch of the 'Zimmermann Telegram'. Without these events, America would probably have stayed aloof and the war would have ended on terms far more favourable to the Central Powers, with Russia collapsing anyway and Britain and France being too weak to win on their own. But while Wilson was pursuing mediation, the Germans met at Pless and cast the die. Characteristically, Bethmann pursued negotiations until the last minute in the hope of somehow reconciling U-boat warfare with American neutrality. As late as 29 January he persuaded Wilhelm and Hindenburg to agree to send to Washington a confidential outline of Germany's war aims; but this uncompromising document merely underlined the gulf between the two sides,[35] especially as it was communicated on 31 January, simultaneously with the announcement that unrestricted submarine warfare would resume on the following day. Certainly, this timing was hardly calculated to convince the Americans of the chancellor's good faith, but in any case, while both Bethmann and Wilson might have preferred to keep America neutral, their priorities were fundamentally in conflict. Bethmann intended to confine Washington's role to bringing the two sides to the conference table, after which America should withdraw while Germany imposed its demands and return only to help set up international institutions that would guarantee the new *status quo*. Wilson, however, was willing to join a League of Nations only if the peace settlement respected liberal principles. The German leaders were right to suspect he would be biased against them. The escape route of an American-mediated compromise occupied a great deal of attention in Berlin and Washington but was never likely to get anywhere.[36] It was typical of Ludendorff that rather than persist with it he resolved to act.

The German navy wanted the 'war zone' round the British Isles to be established with almost no warning, so as to maximize the shock effect, to prevent the British from stockpiling, and to frighten off neutral ships. Wilson was initially stunned and disoriented by the news, coming at a moment when he thought he was at last making progress in clarifying war aims.[37] The Germans had manifestly violated the *Sussex* pledge (at least in the American interpretation of it), and consistency required him to act on his threat to break off relations. The president was governed, however, by an ethic of self-control, and he refused to let anger move him. He knew that breaking off relations might lead eventually to war. He considered the alternative of acquiescing, but after consulting his cabinet and the Democratic leaders in the Senate he sent the German ambassador his passports. Most of the press applauded his action, but at this stage the voices calling for war were a tiny minority and even if the president had asked Congress to declare it he would still have been unlikely to win its support. The conversion of both president and public to intervention came only in the next two months, and as far as the latter was concerned the Zimmermann Telegram represented the key development.

Arthur Zimmermann (the new German foreign minister) sent the telegram on 16 January to his Washington ambassador, Count Bernstorff, for forwarding to the German minister in Mexico City, Heinrich von Eckardt. If the United States entered the war Eckardt was authorized to offer Mexico an alliance in which the two countries would fight side by side, Germany providing financial aid and consenting to Mexico's regaining the territory it had lost to the United States after the war of 1846–8. Eckardt was also to encourage the Mexican president, Venustiano Carranza, to invite Japan to change sides. The document was transmitted in the German diplomatic code and by three different routes. The first was via a wireless message from Germany to a receiving station on Long Island that the Americans had permitted to stay open. The second was via the 'Swedish roundabout', i.e., the Stockholm foreign ministry, which allowed German telegrams to be sent along its cable to its representatives in the Americas. The third was via the Americans' own diplomatic cable service between their Berlin embassy and the State Department, a special facility made available to the Germans by Wilson when he was trying to mediate, though hardly for the purpose of organizing a coalition against him. Naval intelligence in London intercepted the message on all three routes, as the Swedish and the American cables touched land in Britain. Further, the British possessed the relevant codebook, which they had apparently captured in 1915 in the baggage of Wassmuss, a German agent in Persia. Finally one of their agents managed to steal a copy in Mexico, so that if necessary they could vouch for the text's authenticity without admitting they had intercepted neutral cable traffic. In short the saga testified to the formidable global reach of British intelligence. Finally the Director of Naval Intelligence, Reginald Hall, arranged with the American embassy in London that Balfour, an ex-prime minister who was now Lloyd George's foreign secretary and a man whom the Americans could be expected to trust, would present the document personally to the American ambassador. All this took time, and it was 24 February before the text of the telegram reached Wilson. In fact he seems never to have doubted its authenticity and soon decided that it should be published. It was released to the press on 1 March, the American government vouched for it, and on the 3rd Zimmermann confirmed that it was genuine.[38]

The story seems bizarre. It is necessary to delve further. Since 1910 one of the twentieth century's great revolutionary civil wars had been unfolding in Mexico,

and American troops had twice intervened. First, in 1914–15 Wilson stationed
troops at Veracruz as part of a successful bid to oust Victoriano Huerta, who had
seized power from the elected reforming premier Francisco Madero. Second, Carranza and his 'Constitutionalist' supporters had established control over most of the
country before in March 1916 troops under the northern rebel (and anti-Carranza)
leader Pancho Villa attacked the American border town of Columbus, New Mexico, and an American expedition under General John Pershing entered Mexico in
pursuit. Supposedly this expedition had Carranza's consent, but as Pershing pushed
south he clashed with Constitutionalist forces and an American–Mexican war
seemed on the cards. Eventually Wilson withdrew Pershing's troops in January and
February 1917, a decision he would probably have taken anyway, even had there
been no risk of a new clash with Germany.[39] In November 1916, however, during
the confrontation with Washington, Carranza had offered Germany a political understanding and a cable station in return for help in rebuilding his army and fleet.[40]
The Germans responded only after taking their submarine decision, and even then
Zimmermann instructed Eckardt not to approach Carranza until war against the
United States was inevitable – though in a follow-up telegram of 5 February (also
decoded by the British) he asked Eckardt to act at once. The Germans had long-
established business interests in Mexico, they had sold arms there, and had tried
since early in the war to tie down the Americans in a conflict with their southern
neighbour. They had no means of seriously helping Carranza, but Zimmermann
hoped to encourage a Mexican attack on America if Wilson entered the war. As for
the Tokyo dimension, in 1916 the German and Japanese representatives in Stockholm had held secret talks about a possible Russo-Japanese separate peace, though
the contacts had been abortive. All of these considerations help to explain Zimmermann's original initiative, which was a high-level enterprise undertaken with the approval of Wilhelm and of OHL, though possibly not Bethmann. The foreign
minister's subsequent admission that the telegram was genuine is more of a mys-
tery, but perhaps he hoped to intimidate Washington, underestimated the American
reaction, and feared being exposed as a liar if he tried to bluff his way through.[41]

The origins of the telegram matter less than its effects. Wilson, once again, was
shaken and angered, not least at the use made of a cable that he had placed at
Berlin's disposal. The episode reinforced his conviction that he could not trust the
existing German rulers. But the telegram's main significance was that after its publication large sections of the American press called for the first time for war. After
the *Lusitania* sinking Wilson had observed that Americans had a 'double wish': to
see their national interests defended and yet take no steps that might lead to hostilities.[42] Neither the *Sussex* crisis nor the resumption of unrestricted submarine
warfare had greatly changed this picture. Nor had the two sides' propaganda. It is
true that German propaganda was ham-fisted and incompetent, and handicapped
by the invasion of Belgium, by U-boat atrocities, and by attempts to sabotage
American munitions production.[43] The British effort (orchestrated by Wellington
House) was both much larger and more subtle.[44] But no amount of Allied public-
ity could create an interventionist mood until German actions abetted it.

American opinion was divided on ethnic, partisan, and geographical lines. Pro-
Allied sympathies and feeling about the trade and submarine issues were strongest

on the east coast. Support for neutrality was strongest in the interior and especially the Middle West, where the German Americans were concentrated, of whom only an insignificant minority favoured intervention on the side of the Central Powers.[45] Of a US population in 1910 of 92 million, 2.5 million had been born in Germany and 5.78 million had one or two German-born parents. In 1917, 522 German-language newspapers and journals were published in the United States, and German Americans were the largest ethnic group in Baltimore, Pittsburgh, Chicago, Detroit, Los Angeles, and San Francisco. Yet they lacked influence proportionate to their numbers and wealth. They were poorly represented in the two main political parties, many were sensitive about appearing un-American, and they were divided between Catholic, Protestant, and secular tendencies as well as on generational and party lines.[46] The anti-British mood among many Irish Americans and the anti-Russian feelings among Jewish-Americans did not offset these weaknesses, and at least as measured in newspaper editorials pro-Allied sympathies were always in the majority. More important obstacles to entry into the war were isolationism in the heartland and ideological opposition from the Left, meaning not just the socialist party (which at this stage in America's history was sizeable), but also the progressive wings of the Republicans and Democrats. The Zimmermann Telegram, however, made a German security threat seem palpable not only in the east but also in the south-west and west. Even though the Mexicans disregarded Zimmermann's offer and the Japanese repudiated it, a psychological barrier had been crossed. The Atlanticist papers on the eastern seaboard demanded war, important sections of opinion in the rest of the country followed their lead, and most of the German-American press and leaders fell silent.[47] Yet vigorous left-wing efforts to stem the tide continued into March, and the feelings of outrage aroused by Zimmermann began to subside. To bring over the progressives and complete the interventionist consensus, the man who had given the Democrats two election victories had to give a lead. It now came.

Wilson had been far from converted by the resumption of U-boat warfare. He remembered the nineteen United States servicemen (and many more Mexicans) killed at Veracruz, and wanted no more blood on his hands. He had believed what he had said in the 'Peace without Victory' speech about a draw being the best outcome for both Europe and America. Nor did he want to act, or believe he could act, without majority support. He had no wish to give Berlin grounds for alleging provocation, and during February he took no special military or mobilization measures. Moreover, he had retreated from his earlier insistence that the U-boats must respect cruiser rules. When he broke off relations he bought himself time by declaring he could not believe the Germans would do what they threatened, and he would wait for 'overt acts'. The first torpedoings of Allied merchantmen did not modify his stance or much affect the public, even when Americans were on board.[48] But as it became evident that the Germans meant business, this position became untenable. The threat was not simply to Americans travelling on belligerent vessels but to all shipping, Allied or neutral, entering the designated 'war zone'. American merchantmen hesitated to put to sea, goods piled up on Atlantic wharves, and food riots broke out in the eastern cities. By mid-February, even before the news of the Zimmermann Telegram, Wilson had decided to seek

Congressional authorization to place navy guns and personnel on US merchant ships, a course he knew was virtually certain to lead to a shooting war on the high seas. He would probably have got a majority anyway, but the telegram made the majority in the House of Representatives a massive one. In the Senate it might well have been comparable had not four isolationists, to the president's fury, filibustered the measure out. He judged he could go ahead and arm the ships regardless. Soon afterwards the 'overt acts' began: on 16 March the American vessel *Vigilancia* was sunk without warning and fifteen lost their lives. Other ships soon followed her. Berlin and Washington were now on a collision course.

Wilson's decision for war came at about this time. He had definitely made it by 21 March when he asked that Congress should be reconvened early for what became his 2 April war message. On the 20th he had consulted his cabinet, which unanimously recommended in favour. Yet on the previous day when he saw Lansing he had still seemed hesitant. His motives remain mysterious, although we know how his advisers counselled him.[49] He had ignored House and Lansing in the past, but this time he seems to have heeded them, even if the decision itself was characteristically solitary and he composed his war message in conjunction with House alone. He could have given armed neutrality a longer trial, but he knew that *de facto* hostilities were coming anyway unless he submitted to flagrant trampling on American rights, a course he considered but consistently rejected. Nor, experience suggested, was there much chance of an agreement with Germany – at any rate of an agreement that would stick. Moreover, armed neutrality, as Lansing pointed out and Wilson reiterated in his war message, would not bring representation at the peace conference. Such representation had become a personal ambition for the president, and would be crucial for carrying progressive intellectuals and the idealists in his party with him.[50] Finally, he knew by March – for the first time – that if he recommended war, Congress and the people were likely to follow him. In the end the majorities in both houses were crushing.

This does not mean that Wilson was forced into war by public opinion, any more than by his officials. On the contrary, his own commitment did more than anything else to subdue the remaining opposition. If he had decided to oppose intervention he would have faced a divided Congress but would probably have prevailed. Nor did he take any pleasure in war, in contrast to his arch-critic Theodore Roosevelt. Unlike the European leaders in 1914, the president had the evidence before his eyes of what modern conflict could mean. He agonized for nights on end and acknowledged that he was sending men to their deaths. Nor, although he saw it as part of his duty to promote national prosperity, does he seem to have been concerned about the export trade and the loans to the belligerents. On the contrary, he and his advisers expected the Allies to win, though American aid could accelerate the process.[51] He was unaware of the depth of Britain's financial difficulties and the brittleness of French morale, while at first the February Revolution, news of which reached Washington on 15 March, was expected to strengthen Russia's war effort. In turn this means that the strategic argument (that a German victory would imperil the western hemisphere), though it weighed with the Republicans and with Lansing and House, was also not critical for Wilson. Like the press, he welcomed the overthrow of the tsar for making it more plausible that assisting the Allies would promote self-determination, and he considered that to 'hasten and fix' democratization in Germany and Russia was an additional reason to go in.[52] But his starting point was that given the challenge to neutral rights he saw no alternative to belligerency. Unrestricted submarine warfare was an essential cause of American entry and not simply a pretext for it. Even so, the key attraction of belligerency over armed neutrality would be in giving Wilson leverage over both sides at a peace conference.

Wilson's belief that the Allies held the advantage is crucial to understanding what he was doing, which was not simply joining them to crush Germany in disregard of the 'Peace without Victory' principle. Events had convinced him that the Hohenzollern autocracy must be humbled, but he remained committed to a peace on liberal principles, which the Allies might oppose as strongly as their enemies. This notwithstanding, he authorized assistance to them even before declaring war. The Federal Reserve Board annulled its warning of November 1916 and encouraged private credits to Britain, while the State Department suspended its protests against the blockade.[53] But Wilson's war message envisaged substantial rather than all-out assistance: the United States would deliver supplies, extend loans, build up its navy, and call up half a million conscripts. The implicit calculation – that America's partners would do the heavy fighting – resembled Kitchener's in 1914. Unlike Britain, moreover, America declared war only on Germany rather than on the other Central Powers, and it stayed outside the Pact of London. It intervened as an 'associated' power, jealous of its independence and reserving the right to conclude a separate peace. It entered not to save the Allies from defeat but to help clip Germany's wings and moderate the eventual treaty. Yet Wilson and his officials, like the British before them, had underestimated Germany and overestimated Russia and France. America too would be sucked in deeper than it had anticipated, until in the autumn of 1918 the Central Powers eventually crumbled and Wilson could revert to his original plan. Though the Russian Revolution was only a secondary factor influencing US intervention, its implications would overshadow the history of the next twelve months. Summer 1917 would be a season of Allied crisis and in spring 1918 the Central Powers would reach their zenith. These events must be considered before returning to the outpouring of American resources that finally allowed the Allies none the less to prevail.

CHAPTER 14

TOWARDS EXHAUSTION, SUMMER–AUTUMN 1917

THE YEAR 1917 saw the end of the short-war illusion. Even after military deadlock had set in, the hope that one more heave might yet bring victory had lured both sides on. But unrestricted submarine warfare failed to break the British, and the February Revolution wrecked Allied plans for a new round of synchronized offensives. American power would need at least a year to take full effect, and in the meantime Allied co-operation withered. Weapons output peaked, armies diminished, home-front consensus and troop morale faltered, both sides explored less costly strategies, and both moderated their war aims. Yet although the struggle seemed to be losing impetus, this appearance was deceptive. This chapter will examine why, by tracing four interlocking themes. First, both sides faced strategic stalemate but neither gave up hope of winning. Second, domestic political consensus was under strain across Europe, but nowhere outside Russia did it collapse. Third, 1917 saw repeated efforts to negotiate peace, but none came near to success. Fourth – and essential to understanding the remaining pieces of the puzzle – American policy was set against a compromise.

Hindenburg and Ludendorff refused to moderate German objectives, and planned to reconfigure the Central Powers' war effort in pursuit of total victory. They aimed to step up arms production and comb out civilian manpower, re-work battlefield tactics, and improve co-ordination with their partners. But they accepted that on land Germany must stay on the defensive against the expected Allied spring onslaught, and Austria-Hungary had no choice but to do likewise. The centrepiece of their western strategy was withdrawal to the Hindenburg Line; in the east, after Nicholas II abdicated, they remained passive for fear of reviving Russian resistance, and even redirected some troops towards the Western Front and Italy.[1] In the air and at sea, in contrast, they took the offensive against Britain.

Although the Zeppelin raids had done little damage,* in May 1917 bombing of London and south-eastern England resumed with 80 m.p.h. twin-engined Gotha bombers that carried a 1,000-pound payload. The first raid missed the capital because of cloud cover, but killed ninety-five people in Folkestone; the second hit Liverpool Street station, causing 162 deaths. The British improvised a defence system of observation posts, sirens, balloons, and anti-aircraft fire, as well as fighters repatriated from France. The Gothas turned to night attacks, but these too were countered with blackouts, searchlights, and night fighters, and continuing losses persuaded the Germans to call off the campaign in May 1918.[2] By this stage twenty-four Gothas had been destroyed and another thirty-seven lost through accidents in a total of 397 sorties over England, though they tied up over 300 defending aircraft. Between them, Zeppelins and Gothas killed 1,413 civilians in Britain during the war (and another 267 in Paris).[3] The raids caused panic and disruption in London, where up to 300,000 people took nightly refuge in underground stations, and they occupied much of the cabinet's time.[4] Even so they were a minor threat compared with that from the U-boats, which in spring 1917 were Germany's best hope of success.

From 1 February the waters round the British Isles were proclaimed by Germany a *Sperrgebiet*, or prohibited area, which any shipping entered at its own risk. Most of the Mediterranean (and the seas round Russia's Arctic ports) were likewise designated. At first the U-boats not only frightened many neutral vessels into keeping port, but also attained and even exceeded Holtzendorff's projections for sinkings.

TABLE 3.
Gross Tonnage of Merchant Shipping Lost,
January–December 1917[5]

	British	World Total
January	153,666	368,201
February	313,486	540,006
March	353,478	593,841
April	545,282	881,207
May	353,289	596,629
June	417,925	687,505
July	364,858	557,988
August	329,810	511,730
September	196,212	351,748
October	276,132	458,558
November	173,560	289,212
December	253,087	399,111
Total	3,729,785	6,235,878

Most of the losses occurred in the western and south-western approaches to the British Isles, where the merchantmen (after remaining dispersed while crossing the Atlantic) were funnelled in towards the Clyde, Liverpool, Bristol, and the English

*See ch. 7.

Channel.[6] In the 'black fortnight' of 17–30 April nearly 400,000 tons of British shipping went down. The numbers of British, Allied, and neutral ships sunk rose from 234 in February to 281 in March, to 373 in April, and to 287, 290, and 227 in May, June, and July.[7] The chances of an ocean-going steamer leaving the United Kingdom and returning safely fell to one in four, the losses far exceeded replacement building, and if they had continued at this rate Britain would indeed have had to sue for peace before the year ended.[8] So confident was the German admiralty that it placed no major orders for new submarines until June,[9] whereas its British counterpart was close to panic. Meanwhile Allied counter-measures achieved little. The total of operational U-boats actually rose from 105 on 1 February to 129 on 1 June; from February to April only nine were destroyed (mostly by mines).[10] Sweeps by surface ships – such as 'Operation BB' by forty-nine destroyers over 111 days off the Scottish coast – were complete failures.[11]

The Allies' salvation was the convoy system. Though adopted gradually and as one element in a package of measures, it was their most decisive single step. Convoy meant dispatching merchant ships in an organized group with a warship escort. This strategy had been successful in the Napoleonic Wars. During the nineteenth century the Admiralty had abandoned it, and in 1914–17 merchant ships sailed independently along recommended routes while the navy conducted offensive anti-submarine operations such as patrolling and mining. The Admiralty's Operations Division (supported by the shipping companies) rebuffed advocates of the convoy system. Merchant ships, it insisted, could not be disciplined to a uniform speed and would have to sail at the pace of the slowest; unloading them *en masse* would overwhelm the ports; if the U-boats located a convoy they might massacre it; and the navy had too few escort vessels. These arguments betrayed the 'offensive bias' characteristic of the era. Though plausible, they were mistaken. Five factors overrode them. The first was convoy's success on a limited basis. Troopships were escorted throughout the war, and none went down. Regular convoys to the Netherlands began in July 1916 and of colliers to France in February 1917, both with strikingly low losses. Because of the new U-boat campaign, Norwegian convoys followed. These experiments strengthened the case for an Atlantic trial, and the second factor, American entry, made more escorts available. Admiral William Sims, sent in April as the US naval liaison officer in London, found a far graver crisis than Washington imagined. He successfully lobbied an American navy that shared its British counterpart's scepticism. It sent six destroyers to Queenstown in Ireland in May, and thirty-five by September. The third development was that Commander Reginald Henderson computed from shipping ministry figures that about twenty ocean-going vessels left and twenty reached British ports each day, in contrast to the Admiralty's previous assumption of 300 leaving and 300 arriving in all categories and nationalities. Given that a convoy averaged twenty merchantmen, it was entirely feasible to introduce the system for ocean-going shipping. With the technical arguments against convoy weakening, the fourth factor was the 'black fortnight': faced by such an emergency, Jellicoe (now moved from the command of the Grand Fleet to become First Sea Lord) and his officers were forced to recognize that convoy could scarcely be more disastrous than the *status quo*. But finally, Henderson apparently revealed his figures to the cabinet secretary, Hankey, a longstanding convoy advocate, and through him to Lloyd George. The prime minister reacted slowly, although he subsequently claimed responsibility for the convoy decision.[12] Actually Jellicoe knew that unless he acted soon the cabinet would probably force convoy on him anyway,[13] and he had already approved the principle before the theatrical stroke on 30 April when Lloyd George descended on the Admiralty and took the chair.

The first outward-bound North Atlantic convoy sailed on 10 May. From June a regular system began of eight every eight days, and regular homebound convoys started in August. The Admiralty erred on the side of prudence, making the convoys smaller than necessary, and insisting on a fast speed and numerous escorts.[14] The results were still spectacular. Of 5,090 merchant ships convoyed during 1917, only 63 were lost.[15] As convoy proved itself it was extended to the Mediterranean and the South Atlantic. The key reason why it worked seems to be simply that it emptied the seas, a convoy being scarcely easier to find than a solitary vessel. The sharpest fall in sinkings occurred in the principal killing grounds.[16] Moreover, after Room 40 was placed under the Director of Naval Intelligence in May, the Admiralty could direct convoys away from U-boats whose radio messages it had intercepted. Vessels in convoy were far less likely to be attacked, but if they were targeted destroyers were on hand and other vessels might pick up the crews. By the autumn the U-boats were therefore redeploying into coastal waters, where convoying had yet to be organized.

The new system took months to complete, and the climax of danger reached in April initially subsided for other reasons. One was that the U-boats were over-extended. In the first weeks of the campaign the maximum possible numbers were at sea, and between April and May those on station fell from fifty to forty, though in June they rose again.[17] In addition, Holtzendorff's planners miscalculated other aspects of the Allied response.[18] The British forced neutral merchantmen back into service by threatening them with internment. German vessels held in the USA since 1914 (and in the Latin American countries that followed Washington into declaring war) were placed at the Allies' disposal. Lloyd George's cabinet acted resolutely to safeguard supplies until the harvest. Munitions output was lowered, to release labour for shipbuilding and to reduce imports. (Even so, shell stockpiles were huge and 75 per cent more guns were produced in 1917 than 1916.) Shipping was concentrated on the crucial North Atlantic run, and the capacity saved was used to build up reserves, Britain's wheat stocks falling from twelve and a quarter weeks' worth in February to less than seven in May but recovering to thirteen in August. From July shipbuilding expanded, though this measure would take longer to have an effect.[19] Between September and December the U-boats' monthly losses crept up to ten, six, eight, and eight,[20] or roughly equivalent to their construction rate, mainly because of the wider deployment of better mines. But attacking the submarines was secondary. What mattered most was stopping shipping losses. Britain had turned the most perilous corner before convoys had become general, but they were essential to its safety in the longer run. The U-boats were Germany's answer to the checkmating of its surface fleet, but convoying checkmated them in their turn.

If Germany could not win at sea, however, new opportunities might yet arise on land. As the failure of Holtzendorff's gamble became apparent, the Central Powers pinned their hopes on the east. In summer 1917 the Allies consumed their strength in isolated operations, among which the Russian 'Kerensky offensive' was arguably the most disastrous. It undermined the Provisional Government and prepared the way for Bolshevism. Yet after the February Revolution the Russian commanders had wanted an early attack, fearing that otherwise the Germans would attack them[21] but also hoping to compel the government to tackle indiscipline.[22] Soldiers' committees had appeared in most units after the Petrograd Soviet's Army Order No. 1, and officers had to coexist with them or risk arrest. At first the committees passed resolutions in favour of defending the country, but after the Soviet published a decree in favour of peace without annexations and indemnities they became more hostile to the war. Germany and Austria-Hungary responded with intensive propaganda at the front, the prototype for later such efforts by both sides.[23] Over Easter (a traditional season for fraternization) they encouraged their soldiers to mingle with the enemy. For several weeks hostilities virtually ceased and German and Austrian intelligence officers circulated behind Russian lines, addressing the soldiers' committees and stressing their wish for peace. Yet this tactic was risky, especially for the Austrians, to whose troops the Russians preached socialism and separatism. In May the Central Powers lost patience and called off the initiative. Instead they put out feelers to the Russian military and political chiefs, but with no greater success.

For by this time a change of government had taken place in Petrograd. On 5 May (O.S.) Lvov broadened his cabinet to include Socialist Revolutionaries (SRs) and Mensheviks from the Soviet while Alexander Kerensky, a man of Napoleonic ambitions and remarkable talent as an orator, if little else, became war minister and replaced Alekseyev by Brusilov. The new government urgently desired an end to the war, but it refused to negotiate separately. In order to achieve a general peace it believed it must persuade its allies to reduce their war aims, and that as a precondition it must restore its credibility by proving to them that Russia was indispensable.[24] For these reasons it resolved on an offensive. Attacking for peace was a difficult concept to communicate, but government spokesmen – notably Kerensky himself – toured the front haranguing the troops to fight for a free Russia, and temporarily won them over. Kerensky also tried to re-establish discipline, reviving officers' rights to impose corporal punishment and appointing commissars to mediate between them and the soldiers' committees. But the committees, by supporting the government, jeopardized their authority over the men and created an opening for the Bolsheviks, the one party that uncompromisingly opposed the war. During May 'trench Bolshevism' grew rapidly, and the party paper, *Soldatskaia Pravda*, achieved a 50–60,000 print run.[25] As preparations for the offensive proceeded during June major mutinies broke out, regiments in the designated sector refusing to move up until they were assured that the Soviet approved the operation. Most units were soon prevailed on to obey, or were disbanded and the men moved elsewhere, though in one case the rebels were surrounded and shelled. None the less, when finally launched the offensive broke the army.

The main assault was scheduled for 18 June/1 July against the Austro-Hungarians on the south-west front. The Stavka estimated its local superiority at 84:53 divisions, the bombardment was the heaviest yet in the east, and again Czech units surrendered *en masse*; but although the Russians advanced up to thirty kilometres their troops in the rear refused to move up to exploit the success. Follow-up attacks against the Germans were crippled when troops refused to jump the parapet, or fled. Five days later the Central Powers began a long planned counter-offensive. Although Ludendorff limited its scale by holding troops back in France, it achieved surprise and progressed up to 160 kilometres, completely freeing Habsburg territory from occupation by recapturing not only the latest Russian gains but also those made by Brusilov in 1916. The Russians eventually rallied and even counter-attacked in their turn in conjunction with the Romanians, but as an offensive force they were finished. In September Ludendorff pressed home his advantage by reopening campaigning at the northern end of the front, releasing reserves for an attack on Riga.* Like the Galician counter-offensive, this was a limited operation, but the Germans calculated, correctly, that it would intensify Russia's internal dissensions by threatening Petrograd. Both battles underlined how the eastern balance was shifting. The Central Powers had remained on the defensive since 1915, while the Germans had been preoccupied in the west. But after the February Revolution Germany and Austria-Hungary targeted Russia's will to continue, by combining propaganda at the front with peace feelers and – increasingly – with military action. By the autumn Ludendorff was losing patience and wanted to hasten the end in preparation for an attack in the west in 1918. Little, except paucity of men and transport, now hindered him.

Ever since the start of the war troops and their line officers had curtailed operations by refusing to sacrifice themselves to the last man. By 1915–16 French troops were becoming less willing to press attacks, and many Austrian and Russian contingents surrendered without resistance. During 1917 units in almost every army refused to attack at all, or even to enter the front line. It may seem surprising that the self-preservation instinct had hitherto been so muted. Repression by military police and by courts martial was part of the explanation, along with lack of opportunity on static fronts remote from home to run away or desert to the enemy. Discipline had never depended simply on intimidation, however, and by 1917 other elements in the combination that cemented the belligerent forces were falling away. Grievances over inadequate food, rest, and leave usually became prominent once mutinies started, but they rarely triggered them. Probably more significant were impatience for the war to end and lack of evidence that it would do so. Although there was unprecedented unrest on all sides, the Allies suffered more because they were predominantly on the offensive, and unsuccessful offensives repeatedly catalysed discontent. Thus the Austro-Hungarian army, which faced growing food shortages but launched few major attacks, suffered from increasing desertion rather than collective indiscipline.[26] In general this also applied to its ally, although some German units experienced disturbances during the summer. Saxon and Württemberg

---

*See ch. 15.

troops were particularly affected, in incidents along the Western Front.[27] French military intelligence detected the unrest, but it seems to have ended quickly. More is known about the mutinies that took place in the High Seas Fleet, on five battleships and a cruiser at Wilhelmshaven in August 1917. Tedium and inactivity contributed, but resentment focused on the rarity of leave, on a diet of turnips and dehydrated vegetables, and on officers' privileges and bullying. When some commanders refused to implement a government decision to establish food commissions on the warships, several hundred sailors marched ashore. The authorities soon regained control; five mutineers were convicted of treason and two of them were executed, but the men's grievances were not redressed and their resentment continued to fester until the much graver revolt of October 1918.[28]

The Allies' difficulties were more serious. Many Russian officers survived on sufferance after March, and training and trench maintenance deteriorated, while the order for the Kerensky offensive provoked mass disobedience and flights to the rear. Similarly, the Nivelle offensive – or more precisely the decision to persist with it – precipitated the French mutinies of May and June. Scattered refusals to move forward began immediately after the first day. The unrest grew after Pétain replaced Nivelle on 15 May and ordered further piecemeal assaults (partly to make the conquered ground more defensible). Incidents now affected whole regiments, and in early June the crisis reached its climax, marked by increasing violence and an attempt to march on Paris. Statisticians counted 119 outbreaks in almost two thirds of the army's divisions, and around 30,000 to 40,000 troops were deeply involved. After mid-June the unrest subsided, though it revived in August (significantly round Verdun where Pétain was preparing a new attack) and not until January 1918 did it completely die away.[29]

Since the final stages at Verdun in 1916, GQG had noticed that the spirit of the troops was faltering. Joffre and Nivelle blamed pacifist propaganda, and accused the government of laxity. Some of the anti-war opposition's ideas did indeed reach the men, but the court martial records provide little evidence that the mutineers came from the left. Those sentenced were distinctive neither by social class nor by region of origin nor even by age. Much more striking was that most of the unrest occurred in Champagne, behind the sector of the April and May attacks. Involvement in or designation for the latter was the common factor, and soldiers' letters and officers' reports confirmed the mortifying impact when the hopes invested in it were dashed. Analysis by the postal censors suggested that the troops were willing to fight defensively, demanding a settlement without annexations and indemnities but rarely challenging the French Third Republic's legitimacy. Unlike many of their Russian counterparts they still felt part of a national community. The fundamental characteristic of the discontent was a refusal to attack, although the mutineers expressed other complaints, for example over food and over leave, of which a backlog had built up and permission for which was erratic. Although some chanted pacifist and revolutionary slogans and elected soviets, the incidents were mostly over within days and officers were treated respectfully; indeed it was persuasion by officers that normally ended the incidents. The mutinies have been likened to industrial action: most men still held the line but they wanted better treatment and they refused to allow their lives to be thrown away.[30]

Pétain restored discipline in part by repression, mainly after the soldiers had returned to their posts. Some 2,873 were sentenced, 629 to death, of whom, as the government commuted most of the capital penalties, some forty-three were executed – perhaps 0.1 per cent of the total. The figure may seem small, but the victims were singled out arbitrarily and their fate was meant to create an example.[31] Pétain tried to counteract pacifism by ordering officers to lecture their men on the disastrous consequences of an immediate peace. Yet he also made major concessions. Leave was extended from seven days in every four months to ten, and backlogs were made good. Soldiers were allowed a period of complete rest after leaving the line, and their food and barracks were improved.[32] Above all, in his Directive No. 1 of 19 May Pétain accepted that for the moment a breakthrough was impossible. He was supported by Foch, formerly an apostle of the offensive who now became the CGS, and by the war minister Paul Painlevé, who declared in parliament that during 1917 France would launch no more great offensives.[33] Instead Pétain proposed limited, surprise attacks, following quickly one on another in different sectors after maximum artillery preparation. The first was the Houlthulst Forest operation on the left flank of the British Flanders offensive that began on 31 July. Units unaffected by the mutiny were used, with unprecedented aircraft and artillery protection, and they reached their objectives quickly and at low cost.[34] The second was an attack at Verdun from 20–25 August, which took 10,000 prisoners and advanced two to three kilometres. The third and largest, in late October, was at La Malmaison on the Chemin des Dames itself, the infantry taking 15,000 prisoners and advancing with sixty tanks and up to three times the artillery density achieved under Nivelle. Evidently Pétain wished to lay the ghost of April and restore his army as an attacking force that could underpin French political influence. But a full-scale effort must wait until his men were better equipped and the Americans had arrived in strength.[35] In the meantime, in contrast to Joffre and Nivelle's attempts to pinch out the Noyon bulge and drive to the north, he planned in 1918 to strike eastwards and overrun Alsace, thus strengthening France's position if it came to peace negotiations. He suspected that Haig, with his concentration on Belgium, was following such a strategy already. But for each partner to pursue its territorial objectives independently was a startling deviation from the Chantilly philosophy, and underlined the depth of Allied strategic discord.[36]

With Russia and France disabled, only Italy and Britain pursued sustained offensives through the summer and autumn. They too ended up exhausted with their troops despondent, or worse. Italy attacked twice on the Isonzo and once in the Trentino. To begin with morale was reportedly good. There had been a pause in major operations between November 1916 and May 1917, the 1897 conscript cohort provided fresh recruits, and the army was larger and better equipped than ever. Rather than synchronize the tenth battle of the Isonzo with Nivelle, Cadorna postponed it until 20–26 May and launched it with thirty-eight divisions against fourteen. None the less it was an abject failure, with the loss of 127,840 Italian dead and wounded (Italy's highest monthly total of the war) against 75,000 Austrian casualties. Whereas the Austrians had previously fought purely defensively, now – reinforced by transfers from Russia – they struck back. They did so again after Cadorna unsuccessfully attacked in the Trentino on 10–25 June. In the eleventh battle of the Isonzo (from 17 August to around 20 September), preceded by the biggest preparations yet, the Italians advanced seven to eight kilometres and took part of the Bainsizza plateau, but lost another 100,000 men – again almost twice as many as the Austrians – and ended up with a less defensible front. By now the Italian army was showing alarming symptoms. Observers reported that the tenth battle of the Isonzo had had a disastrous effect, the infantry going forward weeping. Military tribunals issued many more sentences for indiscipline and insubordination, and in November Cadorna claimed (though with exaggeration) that 100,000 deserters were at large. Soldiers fired from military trains, abusing railway workers and carabinieri as shirkers. In March the troops of the Ravenna brigade, worn out by a long tour of duty and hearing that leave had been cancelled, refused to move up again. Although their officers prevailed on them to do so, several men were subsequently picked out and shot. In July two regiments of the Cattanzaro brigade rebelled when carabinieri infiltrated them and uncovered a mutiny plot. Loyal forces encircled them and the revolt collapsed, twenty-eight men being summarily executed. Once again the trouble had followed a long tour at the front and suspension of leave. However, the unrest was localized and does not seem to have contributed to the army's lack of progress. On the contrary, before the eleventh battle of the Isonzo, observers reported optimism and belief that the war must be nearly over. Surprisingly, even after these hopes were disappointed, officers signalled that the army's mood was calmer and gave little cause for concern. This tranquillity, however, arose partly from an assumption that operations had closed down for the winter, which proved gravely mistaken.[37]

If the land stalemate was to be broken in 1917 it seemed that only the British army might accomplish it. It was now increasingly a conscript army, chastened by the Somme, whose infantry no longer sang while marching up.[38] But it was bigger, had more weapons, and was more skilled in using them. The production aspect of the projectile shortage had been cracked: in 1916 the ministry of munitions tightened quality controls and in 1917 output reached new heights.[39] In so far as the problem was distribution, in the winter of 1916–17 Sir Eric Geddes reorganized the BEF's railway system, dramatically improving the flow of supplies.[40] During the Somme the artillery improved its counter-battery work and introduced creeping barrages for infantry support, and at Arras it added Livens projectors and 106 fuses to its panoply as well as achieving much denser fire than in July 1916, and with more reliable munitions.* Some dozens of tanks were now available, but greater artillery effectiveness was the key to the BEF's 1917 successes, supplemented by a new generation of fighter aircraft delivered in much greater numbers – the S.E.5, Sopwith Camel, and Sopwith Pup – that enabled it by the summer to regain and to keep air superiority.[41] The British (like the French) were becoming more adept at breaking into fortified positions. Yet the Germans were still improving their defence measures, and the return of a war of movement was as remote as ever.

Not that Haig and GHQ were daunted. During 1917 the BEF launched major attacks in April–May at Arras, in June at Messines, from July to November at

Ypres, and again in November at Cambrai. The cost was commensurate and the contrast, for a second season, between unprecedented casualties and exiguous gains seared British life for decades. Strategic responsibility lay with GHQ, although the cabinet could, with difficulty, have exercised a veto. The military and political aspects should be taken in turn.

Haig's commitment to the offensive derived from his Staff College training, as did his understanding that victory came through a 'wearing out fight' before breakout and exploitation.[42] After the spring offensive he ceased to be subordinated to GQG and no longer needed to defer to his ally. For Haig this meant liberty to undertake a major Flanders offensive, which he had long desired and had ordered to be prepared from early in the year, as he expected Nivelle to fail.[43] He may have been attached to Ypres for personal reasons, given its importance in 1914 in establishing his reputation. But respectable strategic considerations favoured Flanders, indeed, stronger ones than had pointed to the Somme. The Ypres salient was overlooked by the encircling Messines–Menin–Passchendaele ridges and pounded by German guns concealed on the reverse slopes. British casualties there ran into thousands each month.[44] Five miles east of the ridges lay the junction of Roulers on the key trunk railway running laterally behind the Germans' front. Haig therefore assumed that they would have to stand their ground. Moreover, Flanders was the base for the Gothas attacking London, and beyond Roulers beckoned the Belgian coast. The light submarines stationed near Bruges and putting to sea from Zeebrugge and Ostend formed about a third of the U-boat fleet; German destroyers harboured there raided the Dover Straits in the winter of 1916–17 and could threaten Channel troopships. Haig envisaged that once the ridges had fallen a second force would advance along the seaboard towards Nieupoort, and a third would land near Ostend. By clearing the coast he would assist the navy at a critical moment, at long last outflank the Germans, and force them back against the Dutch border or out of the Low Countries altogether.[45] The concept was bold and imaginative.

Haig had hoped to start before Ludendorff moved in reinforcements, but his first obstacle lay in London.[46] Here he enjoyed Robertson's vigorous (if privately sceptical) assistance. The CIGS generally shared Haig's opposition to diverting troops from the Western Front, and also wished to stay on the offensive, if only to deny the Germans the initiative. But he was much less optimistic than Haig about Russia, feared the BEF would be worn out, and foresaw that the usual tactical obstacles would inhibit progress.[47] He backed the Flanders plan for lack of an alternative, but warned Haig not to oversell it and advised the cabinet that the rationale should be to keep up pressure on the Germans and grind them down rather than achieve a breakthrough. At times these differences caused friction between the two men, but on the whole they presented a united front.[48] The civilians did not. The 'great argument' about the offensive was not a simple confrontation between soldiers committed to attrition and politicians looking elsewhere.[49] Lloyd George was the principal doubter, but he lacked support, even from cabinet colleagues such as Curzon and Smuts who wanted to pursue imperial interests outside Europe rather than concentrate everything on the Western Front. Not usually lacking in self-confidence, the premier hesitated to override the professionals, and had damaged himself by backing Nivelle. Given that his colleagues and a Commons majority thought him indispensable, he could probably have overruled Haig,[50] and his failure to do so troubled him for the rest of his career. But as ever the military's arguments seemed plausible, and Lloyd George lacked a credible alternative. Earlier he had supported the Salonika expedition, but now he was losing faith in it. True, in June King Constantine submitted to an Allied demand for his abdication, and Venizelos, who had already formed a provisional government under Allied protection, returned as premier and took Greece into the war. But German U-boats operating from Austria-Hungary's Adriatic coastline hampered supplies to the Balkan front, and in May the biggest Allied offensive yet undertaken there made no impact on the Bulgarians and cost 14,000 casualties.[51] Instead Lloyd George turned to Italy. In the cabinet's War Policy Committee, which met sixteen times between 11 June and 18 July, he proposed sending heavy guns to Cadorna. If the Italians could advance the eight miles to Trieste, Austria-Hungary might make a separate peace, ceding the city itself as a token but keeping the other territories promised to Italy in the Treaty of London. His colleagues feared, however, that Germany would help the Austrians and doubted both that the Italians could reach Trieste and that Vienna would negotiate if they did. They were probably correct on all counts. The prime minister's remaining alternative was to advance into Palestine, but he neglected this option until after the Flanders offensive began. He wanted to conserve manpower, so that Britain could contribute strongly in the war's closing stages, and to cheer the home front with cheap successes. He hoped to isolate Germany by knocking away its partners, but he underestimated not only the logistical difficulties of operating outside northern Europe but also Austrian and Turkish determination.

In any case, two considerations ruled out doing nothing in the west. One was evidence that the Americans might not field a substantial army for two years, which meant that waiting for them might delay a war-winning offensive until 1919. The second was anxiety about France. Foch and Pétain welcomed a British offensive, but not the Flanders project: Foch doubted it would work, and Pétain suspected it had ulterior motives. Nor did they request assistance because of the mutinies. On the contrary, Pétain concealed them, and although GHQ had a good sense of what was happening it held back information from the cabinet. But the War Policy Committee knew more about the political situation across the Channel, where strikes and ministerial instability had revived the spectre of a separate peace. As before Loos and the Somme it convinced them that the BEF must be seen to act.[52] Some ministers also heeded Jellicoe's warnings that if the U-boats held on to their Flanders bases Britain risked defeat by Christmas, and that it would be disastrous if Germany controlled the Belgian coast after the peace. When the cabinet eventually bestowed its 'wholehearted support' on the offensive, however, this blessing was neither sincere (Lloyd George had abandoned none of his reservations) nor unqualified, as it reserved the right to review and halt operations if the battle became another long and costly undertaking with inconclusive results.[53] The French had approved the Nivelle offensive on similar terms, and both governments were determined to avoid a repetition of the Somme. Yet such a repetition, more or less, was what the campaign proved to be.

It is true that the preliminary battle of Messines was a success. On the morning of 7 June, in their second major attack (following Arras) of 1917, the British detonated twenty-one mines sixty feet below the surface of the German forward positions on the Messines–Wytschaete ridge south of Ypres, nineteen of which went off. They had been under preparation since 1915 and the huge explosion was discernible in London, but it was only the climax of a seventeen-day bombardment with 3 million shells.[54] The first two German lines fell within hours; it was Haig's characteristic order to push down the far side of the ridge that prolonged the fighting by a week and cost some 25,000 British casualties, as well (unusually) as higher German ones. Messines cleared the opposing forces off high ground from which they could observe the preparations in the Ypres salient, but it warned them that a larger offensive was in the offing. German sources indicate that an immediate British follow-up attack might have taken the crucial Gheluvelt plateau north of the ridge, but in the event it was the Germans who followed Messines by cramming men into the salient and strengthening their defences during six weeks of mostly fine weather. The War Policy Committee's deliberations were not the primary cause of delay. One problem was that the British had to transport their heavy guns to the new direction of attack, and needed time to win artillery superiority; but even more important was Haig's decision to switch responsibility for the offensive from Sir Herbert Plumer's Second Army (which had carried out the Messines operation) to Sir Hubert Gough's Fifth. Haig had considered plans from Plumer and from Rawlinson, the Fourth Army commander at the Somme, but seems to have preferred Gough because he believed he would aim higher. The result was a compromise in some ways resembling the plan for 1 July 1916. Gough did not explicitly make breakthrough the objective, but he set a very ambitious target for the first day's infantry advance of 4–5,000 yards that would take the attackers beyond the range of artillery protection. In the event on the opening day of the third battle of Ypres on 31 July nine British divisions (c. 100,000 men) gained some eighteen square miles for 27,000 casualties, compared with 3.5 square miles for twice the losses on the first day of the Somme. Even so, they fell far short of the day's objectives, despite advancing on a shorter front than in the previous year with air superiority and forty-eight tanks, and after firing four times as many shells. The subsequent course of the battle confirmed that the BEF's tactical improvements could still not overwhelm the defence. What had gone wrong?

The British were attacking one of the strongest sections of the German front, precisely because OHL as well as GHQ understood its significance. Third Ypres was fought on a clay coastal plain with a high water table, where lines of concrete pillboxes formed the core of the defence system, supported by converging artillery on the Gheluvelt plateau and Passchendaele ridge. After Messines Ludendorff appointed Lossberg, his most experienced defence specialist, as chief of staff of the Fourth Army in Flanders. The Germans had already prepared three lines, but Lossberg ordered two more and prescribed new tactics, similar to those first used in the counter-attack against the Kerensky offensive. The British should be held as far forward as possible, at first by outposts occupying shellholes, supported by machine guns and by field guns supplied by light railways. Further back counter-attack (*Eingreif*) divisions waited, armed with new Mark 08/15 light machine guns and organized round squads (*Gruppen*) of light machine gunners and combat rifle-men who were to infiltrate the enemy forces.[55] The Germans had an additional new weapon in the mustard-gas shell, which the British took another year to de-velop. Mustard gas was less lethal than chlorine, but it caused intensely painful blistering and temporary blindness, and enormously encumbered the attackers' progress.[56] But the Germans' final advantage was rain, which hampered visibility during the preliminary barrage and fell heavily on the first afternoon, the 127mm during August being almost double the norm.[57] Against such formidable defences the British saw no alternative to an exceptionally thorough bombardment, but their shellfire destroyed the intricate local drainage system and the unremitting downpour turned brooks such as the Steenbeek, which ran athwart the main axis of advance, into morasses. The consequences were dire. Aircraft could not ob-serve; tanks made no progress and even sank completely; rifles and machine guns jammed; guns could not be brought forward; and only with the greatest difficulty could shells be transported and the wounded evacuated. Gough captured the out-lier known as Pilckem Ridge but failed to overrun the Gheluvelt plateau, and the Germans successfully counter-attacked. The weather then forced Gough to sus-pend operations until 16 August, when he tried another general offensive. It took the village of Langemarck on his left, but elsewhere counter-attacks nullified all the initial gains. At the end of the month Haig transferred the Gheluvelt plateau to the Second Army front and once more entrusted Plumer with principal responsibility for operations. The latter, a prudent soldier with a competent staff, took three weeks to prepare, during which time the terrain greatly improved as September was abnormally dry. He planned limited advances supported by an even greater weight of fire than under Gough. In the three battles of the Menin Road (20 Sep-tember), Polygon Wood (26 September), and Broodseinde (4 October) he largely attained relatively unambitious targets and beat off counter-attacks, while at Broodseinde, where the defenders concentrated more troops in the first lines, Ger-man losses were very heavy indeed and included 5,000 of their men taken pris-oner: an unmistakable sign of demoralization. This change in tactics betrayed OHL's nervousness, and indeed it had no answer to Plumer's methods. Haig sup-posed the Channel ports might yet be reached, and even that the war might end that year. But Plumer had actually taken less ground than Gough for heavier casu-alties, and he too succumbed to impatience. He left shorter intervals between each assault, and less time to relocate his guns. In October heavy rain returned and two attacks towards the Passchendaele ridge on the 9th and 12th were expensive fail-ures, the Germans reverting to their previous tactics while the British barrages failed, for the first time in the campaign, to cut the enemy wire. At this point, all commentators agree, Haig should have halted. But he insisted on carrying on, even when Gough wanted to stop.[58] In the final phase he limited the objective, in effect, to the ridge.[59] During this phase the Canadian Corps under Sir Arthur Cur-rie took the leading role, and insisted on longer intervals and more thorough bom-bardments before each attack. In successive bounds on 26 and 30 October and 6 and 10 November the Canadians took Passchendaele but suffered at least 12,000 casualties. By this stage the battlefield had become the wilderness of brimming shellholes, perilous duckboards, shattered forests, and obliterated villages that were reproduced in photographs and paintings by British war artists to become emblematic of the Western Front as a whole. Even the Somme, Guy Chapman was told when his unit moved up, was by comparison a 'picnic'.[60]

By December Haig was preparing for a defensive battle in 1918, and the offensive had left him worse placed to fight it. The capture of Passchendaele left the British less exposed to German gunfire and in command of most of the ridge, but the salient was deeper and more angular than in July and Haig admitted to Robertson that it would be untenable.[61] The BEF had come nowhere near Roulers, still less the coast. Although the French had gained a breathing space, their chief protection was that the Germans never divined the extent of the mutinies and in any case did not intend a big offensive. Nor is it plausible, as it may be for the Somme, to argue that at least the British had learned something and improved their tactics. The BEF's effectiveness improved considerably during 1917, but not at Ypres. Three weeks after the battle ended fresh enemy forces repulsed the British offensive at Cambrai, and the evidence regarding both casualties and morale suggests that the much larger German army was less damaged than the British. 'Attrition' was not an official objective of the battle, but 'wearing out' the enemy had certainly been one of Haig's intentions. In fact he inflicted far smaller losses than his intelligence chief, Charteris, thought necessary to defeat the Central Powers by Christmas; and although Broodseinde shook OHL, during October it diverted troops from the Western Front to Italy. The British official history put German losses at 400,000 but modern estimates suggest a figure somewhat over half that number: less than the British though not by much. The BEF's own killed and wounded at Messines and Third Ypres were fewer than on the Somme but may still have totalled 275,000. Its manpower shortage had been serious at the beginning of 1917 and by the end it was much worse.[62] As regards morale, defensive warfare was no easy option and there is plenty of testimony that the Germans, even hard men like Jünger, found Third Ypres deeply dispiriting.[63] Yet the British army did not react as the French one had done, although in September a week-long revolt erupted in the staging camp at Etaples, led by Australasian and Scottish troops, against the severity of the military police and the training regime imposed on men during leave from the line. Eventually a detachment of officer cadets restored order, the camp commandant was replaced, and the regime relaxed. The revolt was not an anti-war protest,[64] but the postal censorship for the first time revealed evidence (some of which reached the cabinet) of despondency in the army and loss of confidence in victory.[65] In summary, Third Ypres was a wasteful failure, even if it remains uncertain how the British army could have been better employed. It has been persuasively argued that the best alternative was neither Italy nor Palestine but the 'Pétain method'. Short, limited offensives backed by massive firepower on the model of La Malmaison and Messines might have taken as much ground for fewer casualties, even though they would have damaged the Germans less. This option, however, did not enter the debate.[66] At times doing something may be worse than doing nothing.

The puzzle remains of why the cabinet failed to act on its resolution to prevent a repetition of the Somme. As in 1916, it failed to monitor Haig's progress. Lloyd George and Bonar Law privately sensed the horror of the troops' experiences, and the cabinet received reasonably accurate British casualty figures (though exaggerated German ones). It did not seem unduly disturbed, perhaps because so many were killed and wounded in the salient every month anyway. After all it was reasonable to give the military time, and Robertson supplied the cabinet with misleadingly optimistic reports while Haig was confident and urged that operations should continue. Most of the cabinet remained reluctant to second-guess them and it never reviewed the purposes of the campaign in relation to the losses. Instead its debates remained focused on alternatives in Italy and Palestine. During August ministers were preoccupied with peace initiatives and the Gothas; and Lloyd George, close to nervous exhaustion, spent much of September in Wales. In the same month Haig finally agreed to Pétain's transferring 100 guns to Italy, but Cadorna curtailed the eleventh battle of the Isonzo before using them. Although in the end it was Haig who called a halt, by November he was transferring units away from Flanders for yet another new attack.

The battle of Cambrai (20 November–7 December) is remembered for tanks as Messines is for mines, but in fact artillery was probably again the leading source of initial success.[67] Gunnery advances had reached the point where surprise attacks were again becoming possible through 'silent registration': better maps, closer analysis of meteorological data (wind speed and direction could modify a shell's flight), and calibration of individual guns were making it possible to deliver an accurate supporting barrage and counter-battery fire as soon as the infantry went over the top, without preliminary ranging shots. The idea for a surprise attack seems to have emanated from Brigadier-General H. H. Tudor, an artillery commander in the Third Army, in whose sector the battlefield lay. The concept was expanded after consultation with Lieutenant-Colonel Hugh Elles, the commander of the Tank Corps. While some tanks flattened the wire, others would drop 'fascines' or bundles of sticks into the enemy trenches to allow the attackers to cross them. As finally approved, what began as a proposal for a large raid became an offensive along a six-mile front with five infantry divisions and 476 tanks (216 in the initial assault), mostly of the new Mark IV model, which was better armoured and more reliable than the Mark I used on the Somme. Although Haig's belated approval gave the Third Army only four weeks to prepare, its groundwork was meticulous and it made great efforts to preserve concealment, the tanks being hidden in woods and overflying aircraft obscuring their engine noise. Cavalry were held in readiness (though too far back), and as the terrain had previously been undisturbed they might be able to operate. Although prisoners warned the Germans two days before the attack on 20 November the latter failed to realize what would hit them: a surprise bombardment by nearly 1,000 guns followed by an air strike and an infantry and tank advance behind a creeping barrage. By 9 a.m. the breach in their first line was five miles wide.[68]

Yet Cambrai ended as another Allied failure, or at best a draw, with 44,000 British and 51,000 German casualties and with a final position lying in places behind the start line. The tanks remained slow, unreliable, and vulnerable to artillery fire; 179 were lost (seventy-one due to mechanical failure and sixty-five to enemy action),[69] and after the first day they had much less impact. On the 20th the British advanced up to six miles, capturing over 4,000 prisoners and 100 guns, but the short November daylight left them little time to consolidate and Ludendorff sent up seven extra divisions in twenty-four hours. After two days the advance was halted and the government, determined to limit the action, warned that it would send no reinforcements. As usual Haig ordered further attacks, aimed at the higher ground round Bourlon Wood. Unlike earlier battles, however, Cambrai ended with a devastating counter-attack, launched on 30 November with twenty divisions and constituting the biggest German offensive against British troops since 1915. It achieved complete surprise, coming when the British supposed that operations had finished and were reducing the garrison of the newly created salient.* Although the Third Army escaped to a more defensible line, the outcome was desperately disappointing to the government, which for the first time in the war had ordered the celebratory ringing of church bells. Tanks, air superiority, and silent registration had restored the possibility of surprise, but the speed of the Germans' reinforcement still prevented open campaigning and the counter-attack showed they could achieve surprise too – although the British post mortem on the battle missed the significance of this development.[70]

Even at this late season, the British undertook one more campaign, in the shape of the Palestine offensive by the Egyptian Expeditionary Force (EEF) under Sir Edmund Allenby. On 31 October his troops began the third battle of Gaza, pushing the Turks back from the Gaza–Beersheba defence line, and on 9 December, after difficult fighting in the Judaean hills, they entered Jerusalem. British casualties in the advance were some 18,000 against Turkish losses of 25,000:[71] small compared with Ypres or Gallipoli, though very high compared with Victorian colonial operations. As the Palestine theatre lay in a narrow strip between the Mediterranean and the arid interior, it reproduced the high force-to-space ratios of Belgium and France. Allenby's success was to some extent a triumph of imaginative leadership, though it also owed much to the reinforcement of the EEF since he had replaced Murray after the earlier unsuccessful Gaza attacks.† He moved his headquarters closer to the front and made his presence unusually visible to his men. Despite fits of irascibility he was open to ideas from his subordinates, who suggested the successful plan of outflanking the Turks by seizing Beersheba, which the Australians captured by a surprise infantry charge, without a bombardment, before the defenders could destroy its vital wells. Ironically, the British had become so much stronger by October that another direct assault on Gaza, supported by the coastal water pipeline and railway constructed by the EEF, might have better inhibited their enemies' fighting retreat and destroyed more of their army. Allenby attacked with seven infantry and three cavalry divisions and a numerical superiority of at least two to one. He resisted political pressure to start prematurely, and received most of the reinforcements he asked for, including infantry from Salonika, heavy guns, and modern aircraft, with which he established air superiority and concealed his preparations.[72] He had backing from Lloyd George, who told him to capture Jerusalem by Christmas, both as a morale booster and in order to occupy territory the British wanted to control permanently. Robertson,

---

for his part, was less hostile to a Palestine diversion from the Western Front than to an Italian one. As CIGS he was responsible for defending the empire, and he took a broader view than Haig. Both he and the cabinet were worried by the formation under Falkenhayn's command of a new Turkish-German force known as Yilderim ('Lightning'), intended at first for Mesopotamia but subsequently for Palestine. To protect Egypt, Allenby needed to be reinforced: and Robertson seems to have shared the politicians' hopes that if the Turks were beaten they would sue for peace.[73] In fact Yilderim was formidable mainly in name. None of its three German battalions had reached Palestine by October, and only two of its nine Turkish divisions. Just one incomplete 1,275-mile railway linked the front to Constantinople, and it alternated between standard and narrow gauge, consignments sent along it having to be on- and off-loaded five times. By 1917 both the Ottomans' economy and their army were under great pressure, some 300,000 deserters roaming at large behind the front.[74] Yet increasingly, as Russia also disintegrated, the northern frontier was again becoming Constantinople's central concern. There was little chance that defeating second-rank Turkish forces in a peripheral theatre such as Palestine would make the Ottomans surrender while in the Caucasus long coveted territorial prospects beckoned to them.

By 1917 then, neither side seemed likely to win quickly. After the spring Russia and France could no longer mount major offensives and the Austrians could do so only with German support. Cadorna persevered on the Isonzo, but Austro-Hungarian reinforcements from Russia made a breakthrough even less probable. Only the German and British armies were strong and cohesive enough to achieve decisive results. But the former was stretched thin, and the Hindenburg Programme's shortfalls inhibited it from compensating for manpower shortages with *matériel*. During Third Ypres the Germans fired one-sixth as many shells as their enemies.[75] New artillery and infantry tactics succeeded in Galicia, at Riga, and at Cambrai, but Ludendorff deliberately restricted these operations. For bigger results he looked first to the U-boats and then to an offensive in 1918. On the Allied side the key difference from 1916, apart from exhaustion, was lack of mutual support. In 1916 Brusilov had taken the pressure off the Trentino, and the Somme had done the same for Verdun. In 1917 the Kerensky offensive coincided with neither Tenth nor Eleventh Isonzo, and Pétain's Verdun and Malmaison attacks were uncoordinated with the fighting in Flanders. The British army, despite its improvement since the Somme, could not break through the German line unaided. Uncertainty remains over whether a British operation started in May with tactics and forces comparable to those at Cambrai could have achieved more than did Third Ypres; the answer is probably yes, but against a determined and rapidly reinforced German army with defence-in-depth tactics it is unlikely that it would have been decisive. Command errors exacerbated the Allies' difficulties but did not alter the fundamentals.

If the war could not be ended by military breakthrough, on the home fronts too, the forces sustaining the 1915–16 escalation had weakened. The expansion of the armaments labour force was near its limits, and blockade and U-boat warfare forced harsh choices between economic priorities. Britain could no longer finance

Allied imports without American assistance, and sales of war bonds weakened, compelling more inflationary finance. The pro-war political truces were increasingly strained, and the ideological configurations that dominated inter-war Europe were emerging. The Austro-Hungarian nationalities reached out for self-rule; German opinion polarized between the centre-left and the extreme right; Britain, France, and Italy were divided between reconstructed centre-right governments and a liberal or socialist opposition. In Russia in November a political party that wanted to end the war at almost any cost seized power, but this case remained unique. Elsewhere the commitment to victory, though more fiercely contested, survived. The two sides reconsidered their war aims, but reduced them surprisingly little. They remained far apart, and their inflexible and incompatible objectives obstructed the peace feelers that proliferated during these months. The latter went through two main phases. In the spring and summer the weaker partners in the opposing coalitions – first Austria-Hungary and then Russia – sounded out their enemies while urging their partners to talk peace. Both failed, but in the autumn contacts opened between the stronger powers, Germany testing out Britain and France. Yet these initiatives too led nowhere. Hindenburg and Ludendorff insisted that decisive victory remained possible and that the peace settlement for this war must position Germany favourably for the next one, while the Allied leaders gambled that with American aid they could achieve a better outcome in the future than negotiation offered now. Neither side had abandoned hope of winning, or of attaining political objectives that might make winning worth the effort.

During 1917 war aims and peace diplomacy became so integral to the politics of the home fronts that these themes must be treated together. Thus in Austria-Hungary Karl's new course entailed both internal liberalization and intensified peace efforts. Though impetuous and inexperienced and lacking Franz Joseph's powers of application, Karl meant to be master of his own ship. He clipped the AOK's wings, moving it from Teschen to Baden (close to Vienna)[76] and appointing the comparatively unknown Arz von Straussenburg as CGS while demoting Conrad to command the Habsburg forces in the Tyrol. In addition he partly dismantled the coercive structure that the AOK had established in the Austrian lands. Prisoners were released, censorship was eased, and in May he reconvened the Reichsrat. After Tisza resigned rather than submit to pressure to broaden the franchise in Hungary,[77] a similar relaxation began there.[78] Yet these well-intentioned gestures intensified Karl's domestic difficulties. The 1915–16 repression had so alienated the nationalist parties that whereas before the war they had confined their demands to more self-government and linguistic rights, now (at least in the cases of the Czechs, Poles, and South Slavs) they wanted virtual independence. Nor were economic circumstances reassuring. Living standards in Vienna fell more drastically than in Paris or London and approached the desperate circumstances in Petrograd. By 1916–17 real wages in the city fell to 64 per cent of 1913–14 levels, and by 1917–18 to 37 per cent.[79] Before 1914 the Austrian half of the Monarchy imported 32 per cent of its cereals (65 per cent of this from Hungary), but by 1917 the Austrian harvest was 40 per cent of the pre-war level and imports from Hungary were only 2.4 per cent.[80] During 1917 industry contracted sharply, the poorly maintained railways running down and coal supplies reduced to 40 per cent of pre-war quantities.

Blast furnaces closed and even arms production suffered, output of shells falling from 50,000 to 18,000 a day between March and August[81] and that of machine gun bullets dropping by three quarters. In these dismal circumstances the Austrian SPD and the social democratic trade unions faced a grass roots challenge to their support for the war, especially after the February Revolution and the spectacular trial in May of Stürgkh's assassin, Friedrich Adler, who denounced the party's policy. In what now became a pattern across Europe, the months before the harvest became the season of greatest unrest. In May 42,000 metalworkers in the Vienna basin went on strike, calling for elected shop stewards, committees to distribute food, and peace. The socialist leaders appealed successfully for a return to work, but from July the authorities placed all industrial plants under military law (though also introducing rent control and a factory complaints commission). In the longer term, however, the May strikes moved the social democrats back to a more oppositional line, and they held on to their following more successfully than the moderates in Russia. Vienna became the centre of an impressive working-class peace movement, but it was to be national separatism rather than socialist insurrection that would bring the Habsburgs down.[82]

Karl had good reason to fear that time was running out, and he appointed as his foreign minister Count Ottokar Czernin, who shared his impatience and was willing to try unorthodox methods rather than let things drift.[83] By implication this meant questioning Franz Joseph's rocklike solidarity with the Germans, to whom Karl said nothing about his major new peace feeler through Prince Sixtus of Bourbon-Parma. But nor did Karl brief even Czernin fully about this episode, which he handled as an exercise in personal diplomacy. All the powers used unofficial intermediaries (who could more easily be repudiated) to conduct such initiatives, and Sixtus was unusually well placed to command confidence in both Vienna and Paris, the capitals he shuttled between (via Switzerland) in the spring of 1917. A scion of the Bourbon-Parma family, he was serving in the Belgian army, and he was also the brother of Karl's wife Zita. Through Sixtus, Karl suggested that if Serbia suppressed its anti-Habsburg subversive organizations it could regain its independence. In a signed letter offering to support Belgium's full restoration and France's 'just claims' in Alsace-Lorraine, he created the impression that he might break with Berlin. This message electrified the French, as it did Lloyd George when they consulted him. But neither France nor Britain had issues of direct contention with Austria-Hungary. Italy did, and when Ribot (the French premier) and Lloyd George met the Italian foreign minister in a railway carriage at St-Jean de Maurienne on 19 April, Sonnino insisted on the territorial pledges made to Italy in 1915. The promise of a sphere of influence in Asia Minor made him no more tractable. Lloyd George and Ribot, though exasperated, did not feel they could disregard Sonnino. To violate the Treaty of London would undermine their protestations that they were fighting to uphold international undertakings, and might also invalidate their own claims. Moreover, the military circumstances were unfavourable. Lloyd George failed to carry through his scheme to help Cadorna reach Trieste, and Karl refused to hand to Italy what it had failed to conquer. Nor, it turned out, were the Austrians willing to make a separate peace. Quite apart from the question of honour, they needed Germany's subsidies, and German generals commanded much of their army. Even if Karl had considered breaking away, doing so would have courted German retaliation and repudiation by his ministers, and might have cost him his throne. In any case Allied loyalty to Italy gave the emperor little encouragement to take the risk, and in summer 1917 Sixtus abandoned his quest.[84]

At the same time as Karl approached the French, Czernin tried to lower the barriers to peace by softening up the Germans. The circumstances seemed auspicious. For the first two years few cracks had opened in the German home front, but in the 'turnip winter' of 1916–17 German civilians suffered their worst privations of the war.* After the potato harvest failed, the arctic weather froze up the railways and waterways, preventing coal from reaching factories and homes. Millions in the cities endured cold and hunger unknown since pre-industrial times. The subsistence crisis helped to focus attention on the inequalities of wealth and power underpinned by the Prussian three-class franchise, and in April more than 200,000 metal, munitions, and other workers (at least half of them women) staged a protest strike against the mismanagement of food supplies.[85] At this time the Petrograd revolution had galvanized the socialists, and removed the threat from the tsarist autocracy that had previously motivated them to back the war. After the USPD broke away in April, many SPD and trade union loyalists feared being undercut and felt they were being used to police their members. Bethmann accepted that concessions were needed and decided to grasp the nettle. He had become disillusioned with the conservatives since clashing with them over war aims and submarines, and he needed working-class co-operation to fulfil the Hindenburg Programme. Without consulting Hindenburg and Ludendorff he agreed with Wilhelm on an 'Easter Message' from the sovereign, which promised franchise reform. It was still too little. The Centre Party, whose adhesion to the U-boat lobby had undermined the chancellor in 1916, now moved back to the left, forming a bloc in the Reichstag with the SPD, the Progressives, and the previously annexationist National Liberals. Between them these four groups commanded a majority, and they pressed for democratization and more moderate war aims.[86]

Against this background Czernin tried to scale down German objectives. He warned Bethmann in April that Austria-Hungary was exhausted, and if the war continued the 'tide of revolution' could sweep westwards from Petrograd. But the chancellor doubted revolution was close in either Germany or the Dual Monarchy. Moreover, rather than settling for the 1914 *status quo*, Czernin still hoped for territorial gains. In fact it suited Bethmann to steer Czernin towards the Balkans as the chancellor saw the Provisional Government in Petrograd as the weakest link in the Allied chain and he wanted a free hand to negotiate with it.[87] But he had to contend not only with Czernin and the Reichstag but also with Hindenburg and Ludendorff, whom the Easter Message outraged.[88] Of middle-class background, driven, insecure, Ludendorff was in many ways an outsider in the German officer corps. In strategic matters he was relatively flexible, but politically he saw victory as essential to consolidate the domestic political order. A promise of democratization would be seized on by the Allies as a sign of weakness and would encourage them to keep going. He did not want to reduce Germany's goals but to expand them and set them

---

*See ch. 11.

in concrete. The result was a sweeping new war aims statement, the secret Kreuznach Programme of 23 April. It envisaged that Germany would annex Courland and Lithuania as well as large parts of Poland, the rest of which it would dominate by indirect methods. It would demand a Central African colonial empire and a chain of overseas naval bases. In the west it would annex Longwy-Briey and Luxemburg, hold Liège and the Flanders coast for at least a century, and run Belgium's railways. Both Wilhelm and OHL endorsed the programme and although Bethmann initialled it under protest he accepted it as a guideline in the event of Germany's being able to dictate peace.[89] Hence an opposing and stronger force blocked Czernin. Faced with a refusal of concessions over war aims he attempted briefly to subvert Bethmann by 'paradiplomacy', liaising with the Bavarian government and with Matthias Erzberger, the leader of the left wing of the Centre Party, to whom he supplied secret information;[90] but after an Austro-German summit on 17–18 May (also held at Kreuznach) Czernin called off his pressure tactics. The rejection of the Sixtus peace feeler was probably one reason, as well as a temporary economic upturn and growing evidence that Russia was beaten. Despite his efforts, OHL's influence on German policy had if anything grown. Rebuffed by the Allies, Vienna acquiesced once more in German leadership.

If the Austrian search for peace dominated the spring, during the summer Russia took centre stage. Here too a change of leadership started the process, notably the restructuring of the Provisional Government in May. Whereas Miliukov, who had been foreign minister in Prince Lvov's first cabinet, assured the Allies that Russia would abide by the secret war aims treaties and reiterated the tsarist claim to Constantinople and the Straits, the Petrograd Soviet, while accepting that the war should continue (not least in order to defend the revolution against German aggression), wanted to modify its objectives. It called on the peoples of the world to bind their governments to the 'Petrograd formula': no annexations or indemnities and a peace settlement based on self-determination. The Soviet's position became increasingly popular among the soldiers' committees in the army, and conflict between it and the government over war aims led to constant friction. Matters came to a head on 20 April/3 May after the Provisional Government forwarded a memorandum on war aims to the Allies with a covering letter by Miliukov insisting on 'guarantees and sanctions'. Crowds of demonstrators demanded his resignation and he found himself virtually isolated. When the cabinet was broadened to include Mensheviks and SRs from the Soviet he resigned rather than accept its new foreign policy platform.[91]

The May crisis temporarily restored political harmony by uniting the cabinet and the Soviet in a programme of 'revolutionary defencism', which meant inter-Allied solidarity on the basis of non-imperialist war aims. The new government proclaimed that Russia must not let Germany defeat the Western Allies, as the Central Powers would then concentrate their forces against the revolution, but it accepted the formula of no annexations and indemnities and promised to take it up with Russia's partners. For practical purposes it abandoned the claim to Constantinople and it proposed that Poland should become independent, though in a 'free military alliance' with Russia and incorporating Germany and Austria-Hungary's Polish-inhabited areas. Hence it did not abandon all thought of weakening Russia's enemies, and clear blue water still ran between Russia's war aims and those of the Central Powers, as several contacts between March and June demonstrated. The most significant were conversations in Stockholm between Erzberger (acting with Bethmann's approval) and a Russian official, Kolyschko. Ludendorff, furious at not initially being consulted, intervened to toughen the German line, insisting that the Russians must abandon Poland and that Germany must expand along the Baltic coast. Similar terms were communicated when the Russian General Dragomirov made contact with German commanders at the front. The Provisional Government now knew the price of peace would be Poland becoming a German rather than a Russian buffer state, and concessions in the Baltic that might endanger Petrograd. It pursued the possibility no further.[92]

The Russians occupied an analogous position in the Allied camp to Karl's among the Central Powers. They were willing to investigate a separate peace, but their enemies gave them little encouragement to break ranks. Nor could they achieve a general peace by moderating their partners' objectives. While Czernin lobbied Bethmann, Tereshchenko (an ally of Kerensky who replaced Miliukov as foreign minister) forwarded the 'Petrograd formula' to Russia's allies and suggested a conference to revise the coalition's war aims. He received evasive replies and after the failure of the Kerensky offensive he withdrew the proposal.[93] But simultaneously – mirroring Czernin's 'paradiplomacy' – the Russians adopted less conventional methods, foremost among them being a campaign for a meeting at Stockholm between representatives of the socialist parties in the neutral and belligerent countries. The Stockholm conference project originated with the International Socialist Bureau (ISB), the secretariat of the old Second International, now led by the Scandinavians and the Dutch. In May the Petrograd Soviet took up the idea and launched a parallel appeal, and in July the neutral and Russian socialists issued a joint invitation.[94] Yet the conference never met, essentially because the Allies vetoed it. Although they placed the 'Petrograd formula' centrally in European politics, the Russians failed to build up a sufficient head of steam for war aims revision.

The international socialist movement had become divided not only between the two sides but also ideologically. The left consisted mainly of the Bolsheviks and smaller groups elsewhere, and was uncompromisingly hostile to the war. The right, which included the SFIO and SPD leaderships, some Italian socialists, and most of the British Labour Party, voted war credits, entered government when invited, and sometimes approved imperialist war aims. Except in Russia the big development of 1917 was less the growth of the left than the weakening of the right relative to the centre, which comprised the SFIO *minoritaires*, the German USPD, most of the Italian and American socialists, and the Labour dissentients in Britain. The views of the Mensheviks and SRs in the Petrograd Soviet were similar. These groups accepted the legitimacy of self-defence, but they opposed war credits and participation in government, demanded peace negotiations on the basis of no annexations or indemnities, and hoped to restore the Second International. Unsurprisingly they welcomed the Stockholm initiative, but it was a sign of the times that after initial wariness most of the right did likewise and joined the call for reconsideration of war aims. Hence Stockholm challenged not only diplomacy of the belligerent governments, but also their domestic political management. Yet the Central Powers' response was remarkably debonair. Czernin wanted a negotiated peace, and was willing to let the Austrian socialists attend. Bethmann was less enthusiastic but took the same line, thinking it might help keep the SPD on board; and to prevent the latter from appearing as stooges he was willing to let the USPD go too.[95] In contrast Woodrow Wilson unhesitatingly barred attendance by the American Socialist Party[96] just as the Italian government barred the PSI, but both these parties were thoroughly anti-war already. In France and Britain, large and previously moderate working-class movements changed direction over Stockholm, and in both countries the issue brought them into confrontation with their governments.

Across much of Europe during 1917 the labour and socialist movements tilted leftwards and non-socialist opposition to the war revived. In addition, grass roots protest movements gathered impetus, to some extent directed against the more patriotic socialist and trade union establishment. In France in 1915–16 living standards had stabilized, but in spring 1917 food prices surged.[97] Growing labour unrest reached its climax in May and June, when 100,000 went on strike in the Paris region alone, perhaps three quarters of them female: another sign of the radicalization of women workers. In the first instance their demands were for a five-and-a-half-day week and cost-of-living increases. The employers, encouraged by the interior ministry to settle quickly, conceded most of them, and work soon resumed. Since the February Revolution political activity had quickened. The traditional May Day demonstration, feeble in 1915 and 1916, now attracted large numbers, and some strikers unfurled red flags and called for peace. Moreover, after the disaster of the spring offensive and the mutinies (even though the press kept quiet about them) evidence was abundant for a mood of deep public depression. Hopes of a breakthrough had been shattered once too often, and an interior ministry survey of the provincial departments in June found that in only about half did the local authorities judge morale adequate. Nivelle's failure, the evil influence of soldiers on leave, and to a lesser extent the collapse of Russia were blamed.[98] The pessimism in the country was echoed by infighting and a loss of confidence among the elite. Briand's government, reshuffled in December 1916, resigned in March; that of Alexandre Ribot survived from March to September; and that of Paul Painlevé only from September to November, becoming the first French wartime administration to resign after a parliamentary defeat. These cabinets rested on a narrower parliamentary base than the coalitions of 1914–16, and the most obvious sign of fraying consensus was socialist alienation. By early 1917 the *minoritaire* movement was close to becoming the SFIO majority. Even so, the party leaders at first rejected the ISB invitation to Stockholm, but they reconsidered after the Russians associated themselves with it, especially when two hitherto pro-government deputies, Marcel Cachin and Marius Moutet, returned from a visit to Petrograd with information about the secret Doumergue Agreement.* It now seemed that the party had been duped into supporting a war of aggrandisement, and in May its National Council voted to attend Stockholm. Ribot considered granting passports but decided against when confronted simultaneously with a cabinet revolt, strikes in Paris, and a warning from Pétain (at the height of the

*See ch. 5.

mutinies) that if the socialists went to Sweden he would not answer for discipline in the army. On the other hand the premier was forced to clarify the government's war aims, and during three days of secret parliamentary debate he distanced himself from the Doumergue Agreement – but not from the Cambon letter, upholding claims to Alsace-Lorraine, the Saar coalfield, and a Rhineland buffer state. At the end of the session the Chamber passed the Dumont resolution of 6 June, an ambiguous declaration that appeared to confine French territorial demands to Alsace-Lorraine but left the door open for security 'guarantees' beyond that, and Ribot told the more conservative Senate that safeguards in the Rhineland were still his objective. Though he also supported the principle of a League of Nations, it was difficult to reconcile his programme with the Petrograd formula of no annexations or indemnities. The SFIO split over the Dumont resolution and when Painlevé took over in September they left the government. It was unsurprising that Painlevé's decision to keep on Ribot as foreign minister was the sticking point that provoked their resignation.[99]

In Britain Lloyd George had a stronger parliamentary base than Ribot and the BEF escaped mutiny, while lobbying for expansionist war aims occurred discreetly in the cabinet rather than coming (as in Germany) from chauvinist pressure groups or the high command. After the Easter Rising southern Ireland was virtually lost to the war effort (at least as a source of manpower), but in the rest of the United Kingdom the main challenge to the government came from the left. Engineering strikes between March and May involved some 200,000 workers across the English industrial districts. Most of them were against plans to extend dilution from state factories into privately contracted work and to abolish the 'trade card', a scheme under which trade unions could designate which men could be exempted from conscription.[100] The strikes were locally organized and (as in Germany) were led by shop stewards against the policies of the trade union national leaderships. Although the government at first refused to talk to the organizers, in the end it negotiated with them and with the unions simultaneously and postponed implementation of both its proposed measures, despite the pressing need to reallocate manpower to shipbuilding and the army. In fact the strikes set the limit to the militarization of the British home front, skilled workers rebelling against further threats to their position. Ministers were deeply impressed and set up regional commissions to investigate the causes; their reports emphasized food prices and profiteering, as well as conscription and the 'leaving certificates' needed when employment was changed. Winston Churchill, the new munitions minister, decided to scrap the certificates and abandon further dilution, fearing revolutionary unrest. In July the cabinet overrode Treasury opposition and voted for a bread subsidy, agreeing that 'for the vigorous prosecution of the war a contented working class is indispensable'. Men were no longer to be taken from agriculture; on the contrary the army had to release soldiers to help with harvesting. The cabinet was well aware that civilian morale depended on sustaining living standards, and henceforth was more constrained than ever in responding to the general staff's demands for munitions and men.[101]

The engineering strikes were mainly an economic protest, though one with major political implications. But in addition the UDC was expanding its membership and increasingly winning a hearing from the trade unions for its opposition to imperialist war aims.[102] In Glasgow 100,000 demonstrated against the granting of the freedom of the city to Lloyd George, and a further demonstration demanded the release from prison of the socialist leader John MacLean.[103] In June the Leeds Convention of left-wingers, permitted by the government with some trepidation, called for British soviets on the Russian model, though the appeal was largely ignored.[104] However, the situation was tense enough for the cabinet to be preoccupied by the risk of forfeiting Labour Party support over the Stockholm conference, and Lloyd George was even more concerned about the proposal's international implications. At first he inclined towards letting Labour attend, both to conciliate the Russians and to forestall an encounter between Russian and German socialists with no Allied ones present. At this stage the Labour leaders (in contrast to MacDonald and the Labour opposition) did not wish to participate. In August, however, the party reversed its decision and at a special conference voted three to one in favour of going after Arthur Henderson, the Labour member of the war cabinet (who like Cachin and Moutet had been swayed by visiting Petrograd), supported attendance. Henderson believed the conference would buttress the Provisional Government against the Bolsheviks (whom he detested) and had re-enthused himself in favour of more socialist war aims.[105] By this stage, however, the cabinet too had reconsidered, partly because of unanimous hostility to Stockholm from Britain's allies but also because the Russian government itself had grown cooler about Stockholm and because after the defeat of the Kerensky offensive there was less need to humour it anyway. Henderson's colleagues believed he had misled them, and his position in the cabinet became untenable, but after he resigned a new Labour representative replaced him and most of the working-class movement continued to oppose a compromise peace. Although the schism proved less serious than Lloyd George feared, the cabinet's decision to oppose Stockholm ended any lingering prospect of its going ahead.[106]

The implications for Russia were grave. By joining the government in May and endorsing 'revolutionary defencism' the Mensheviks and the SRs had exposed themselves to outflanking from the left, and it is unlikely that the Bolsheviks could have taken power had it not been for the war's destructive consequences and their opponents' fateful commitment to staying in it. Among the earliest of those consequences was Lenin's return from exile by courtesy of the Germans, who (although he was no puppet of Berlin) saw that he could serve their interests and so provided the notorious 'sealed train' across their territory that transported him from Zurich towards Finland. Once back in Petrograd in April he hectored a lukewarm Bolshevik leadership into an intransigently anti-war stance. Hence the Bolsheviks stayed out of the May coalition, Lenin contending in his *April Theses* that Russian workers had no interest in an Allied victory and that the conflict should become an international civil war between proletariat and bourgeoisie. Socialist revolution in Russia could come quickly, without a long preliminary phase of bourgeois rule, and although Lenin did not press for an immediate revolution, he urged that agitation for one should start at once.[107] The ground was fertile. The economic crisis that had precipitated the February Revolution worsened: monetary growth and inflation accelerated, and strikes disrupted the railways. Food supplies to the cities further dwindled.[108] Strikes to maintain living standards continued in much of industry, including the armaments plants. Above all, the Provisional Government failed to deliver an early ceasefire and the Kerensky offensive weakened its authority over the troops. Indeed, even while the offensive was in progress the government sparked another explosion, in the shape of the 'July Days', when it ordered to the front the First Machine Gun Regiment, a unit of 10,000 men that was garrisoned on the Vyborg side and seemed a permanent threat to it. The regiment resolved to stage an uprising unless the order was rescinded, and the Bolshevik military organization supported it, though the party's Central Committee believed the timing premature and urged restraint. None the less the insurrection went ahead on 3/16 July, a crowd of soldiers and Red Guards (workers' militias) surrounding Soviet and government representatives in the Tauride Palace. But although the Bolsheviks could probably have taken control of Petrograd at this juncture, their leaders still hesitated. The crowds dispersed, loyal troops arrived, and Lenin fled back to Finland. Yet although the government had survived, the combination of the uprising with the failure of the offensive spelled the end of the project embarked on in May. Russia had lost its remaining diplomatic leverage and Tereshchenko ceased to press the Allies over war aims, indeed encouraging the British to kill off the Stockholm initiative. The war remained the great albatross round the Provisional Government's neck and it no longer had a strategy to remove it.[109]

After the July Days the authorities made an abortive effort to recover their grip. Lvov felt he was not the man for repression and handed over the premiership to Kerensky, who restricted public gatherings and replaced Brusilov by Lavr Kornilov, a tough if naïve soldier who had contacts with business and the right. The new team reinstated the death penalty and introduced field courts, some of which pronounced death sentences on mutineers (a few of which were implemented). Thousands of deserters were rounded up and returned to the front, rebellious units were disbanded, and Bolsheviks were arrested and their organizations broken up. The repression had some success, but in August Russian politics reached another turning point. Kornilov hoped not only to restore military discipline but also to install an authoritarian regime, preferably in conjunction with Kerensky and the Provisional Government but if necessary against them. His relations with Kerensky broke down, the CGS apparently believing he had the premier's approval to stage a coup and sending troops under General Krymov to overthrow both the Provisional Government and the Soviet. The insurgency collapsed when railwaymen blocked the tracks and troops loyal to the revolution fraternized with Krymov's forces. Kerensky denounced Kornilov and reinstated Alekseyev in his stead. But the 'Kornilov affair' spread another shock wave through the army, and suggested that Kerensky could not be trusted. He lost most of his remaining credit, and the troops were unlikely to defend him again.[110] In an atmosphere of mounting chaos, the fortunes of the left revived. During the summer and autumn peasant seizures of gentry land, often violent, gathered pace in Russia's central provinces, strikers demanded control of industry through factory committees, Petrograd lost control over the provincial administrations, and Finland and the Ukraine declared their independence. After the Kornilov affair the Bolsheviks regained their freedom to organize, and between July and October their membership grew from 200,000 to 350,000, their support increased in Petrograd and Moscow city elections (where they won 33 per cent and 51 per cent of the vote respectively), and in September they gained control of the Petrograd Soviet.[111] At least in the major cities it seemed that Lenin's message of immediate peace and socialist revolution was what the people wanted to hear. Meanwhile, although most of the troops still remained at the front, the resolutions passed in the soldiers' committees indicated complete disillusionment with the Provisional Government, and the Bolsheviks increasingly took over these bodies too. Above all, as the nights grew chillier, officers' reports all noted that in no circumstances would the men endure another winter away from their homes.[112]

If Austrian pressure could not moderate German war aims, nor could Russian pressure moderate those of Britain and France. If peace was to come in 1917, the prerequisite was agreement between Paris, London, and Berlin. So far Austria-Hungary and Russia had taken the lead, but in the third phase of diplomatic soundings the initiative came from Germany, following a major political crisis in July and a change of chancellor. Since the spring Bethmann had been caught between pressure from the new Reichstag majority for democratization and reduced war aims, and OHL's resistance. The vagueness of the Easter Message had failed to satisfy either side. But at least during the spring the submarine offensive had bolstered German public opinion, and at one level the July political crisis resulted from the bankruptcy of the U-boat strategy. Holtzendorff still insisted it would succeed but offered no date, distancing himself from the earlier five-month prediction.[113] In a sensational speech in the Reichstag main committee on 6 July Erzberger documented how the campaign was falling short of its target.[114] Not only was he aware (via Czernin) of Austria-Hungary's desperation, he knew the navy had not delivered and he feared the SPD would desert to the anti-war camp. After his *démarche*, the parties of the new majority decided to pass a resolution stressing Germany's willingness for peace, and to seek a chancellor strong enough to act on it. Hindenburg and Ludendorff, on the other hand, inferred that Bethmann could no longer manage the legislature. In an unprecedented act of assertiveness, they warned Wilhelm that unless he sacked the chancellor they would resign. Colonel Bauer, of Ludendorff's staff, presented declarations of no confidence in Bethmann from the party leaders, and the emperor (who respected Bethmann despite his impatience with him) reluctantly decided to let him go. In fact Bethmann had resolved to resign unless he could introduce political reform at once,[115] so that Wilhelm faced a straight choice. By backing his chancellor he would have opted for the path of peace negotiations and controlled democratization that Germany embarked on from a much less favourable starting-point in October 1918. He declined, acquiescing instead in a flagrant infringement on his prerogatives. Yet Hindenburg and Ludendorff preferred to exercise a power of veto rather than take over the government themselves, and to describe their Germany as a military dictatorship would be an exaggeration. They had considered and rejected the possibility of Ludendorff's becoming chancellor, and they removed Bethmann without lining up an alternative. His successor was Georg Michaelis, a relatively obscure Prussian official who had been serving as food controller for Berlin. Hindenburg and Ludendorff consented to the appointment and appear to have supposed he would be pliable. He proved more independent than they would have liked, but he lacked the abilities required for the position. Nobody in Germany – emperor, commander-in-chief, or chancellor – could or would provide political leadership.[116]

As the power of emperor and chancellor ebbed away, that of both OHL and the legislature increased. Bethmann resigned on 13 July; six days later the Reichstag passed the Peace Resolution by 212 votes to 126. It called for 'a peace of understanding and international reconciliation' and repudiated 'forced acquisitions of territory and political, economic, and financial violations',[117] but this wording paid lip service to the Petrograd formula rather than genuinely repudiating expansion. Annexations had never bulked large in German war aims, and Erzberger and his colleagues remained willing to see nominally independent buffer states established.[118] In 1918 most of them voted for the draconian Brest-Litovsk treaty with Russia. The resolution, in other words, meant less than it seemed to, even for the sponsoring parties, and it failed to produce substantive change. Before touching off the crisis, Erzberger (like Bethmann when conspiring against Falkenhayn) seems to have miscalculated that a pact with Hindenburg and Ludendorff could lead Germany out of the war. Instead OHL removed a man whom they considered soft on war aims, while Erzberger had hoped for a chancellor who would pursue general negotiations but ended up with a much more cautious figure. For example, Michaelis declared he accepted the resolution only 'as I understand it', which, he commented privately, meant Germany could still make any peace it liked.[119] In practice he tacked like Bethmann between pressure from Austria-Hungary to reduce German objectives and from OHL to stand firm. Knowing little about foreign policy, he took up position in a series of consultations with OHL and Czernin during August. He supported his new foreign minister, Richard von Kühlmann, an experienced diplomat who had served in the London embassy before the war and who, like Bethmann, was willing to compromise over war aims in order to split the Allies, the difference being that Kühlmann saw Britain as the most promising prospect. Meanwhile Germany's economic war aims had considerably abated: the *Mitteleuropa* plans for a Central European customs union now had a low priority and the business community's main concern was to ensure that the Allied blockade did not continue after the peace.[120] Michaelis was willing to support Kühlmann by renouncing the annexation of the Briey basin in return for guaranteed access to its iron ore, but the new chancellor also expanded Germany's objectives by adding plans for a huge new buffer state in the Ukraine.[121] Berlin therefore reorientated its ambitions from west to east without abandoning the basic aim of continental dominance. Similarly, although Michaelis was willing to consider placing Poland under nominal Austrian sovereignty, the quid pro quo was permanent German control over Romania's grain exports and oil wells. Hopes for veiled expansion through economic domination remained very much alive.

This was the situation when a peace note from Pope Benedict XV started a new round of contacts. Before going public on 1 August the Vatican had consulted the Germans, but neither the Austrians nor the Allies.[122] Taking account of a warning that Germany could not accept French and British predominance in Belgium, the note called for the country to regain full independence and be guaranteed 'against any power whatsoever'. Essentially, however, it envisaged returning to the pre-1914 European boundaries without annexations or indemnities, a solution that cut across the objectives of both sides. Hence the Germans and Austrians tried to kill the initiative by delaying their response. Woodrow Wilson rejected a return to the pre-war *status quo*, and France (where many Catholics deplored the note) and Italy were scarcely less hostile. Only Britain was more willing to explore the possibilities. The Lloyd George cabinet, perhaps because of evidence that Haig's Flanders offensive was making little headway and certainly now viewing the Allies' war aims note to Wilson of 10 January 1917 as 'grasping', decided to test the Germans out. The British representative at the Vatican pointed out that the Central Powers had failed to say how they would make good the damage done to Belgium and restore its sovereignty. This was an invitation to Germany and Austria-Hungary to spell out their intentions, and the Vatican passed it on to Kühlmann. It arrived when the latter had just been startled to learn of a new Austro-French communication channel in Switzerland, the Armand-Revertera conversations. Armand, representing the French War Minister, Painlevé, had offered Austria-Hungary the whole of Poland (as well as Silesia and Bavaria from Germany) in return for a separate peace, and Czernin told Kühlmann that he wished to meet Painlevé. In fact Armand had probably misrepresented his superior, and it is unlikely that the French government would have allowed Painlevé to go. But Kühlmann was thoroughly alarmed, and felt he must counter this attempt to drive a wedge between Berlin and Vienna by inserting a wedge of his own between Paris and London. He and Michaelis agreed that an 'ocean of hate' separated Germany from France, and that Germany could cede little in Alsace-Lorraine. But if Britain could be satisfied over Belgium, Paris might be isolated. At the Bellevue Crown Council on 11 September Kühlmann won grudging support for such a plan. Michaelis, Hindenburg, and Ludendorff agreed that Germany should retain Liège and military guarantees in Belgium, at least until the latter had been tied irrevocably to Germany by economic bonds. OHL still wanted strategic control over the country, both as a shield for the Ruhr and as a springboard from which to threaten the Channel ports and Paris, and deter Britain and France from future aggression.[123] But the navy had to suspend its demand for permanent bases on the Flanders coast, and Wilhelm told Kühlmann that he had a free hand to get a settlement by Christmas.[124] Kühlmann then contacted the Marquis de Villalobar, the Spanish representative in the Low Countries, who notified London through the Spanish foreign minister that 'a very exalted personage' in Germany wished to make 'a communication relative to peace'.

Kühlmann was correct in sensing that British strength of purpose was wavering. Whereas Balfour, the Foreign Secretary, wished to inform all Britain's partners of the news at once, the cabinet decided to await the outcome of a meeting between Lloyd George and Painlevé (who had now replaced Ribot as French premier) at Boulogne. Lloyd George was tempted by a peace at Russia's expense that would allow Germany to expand in Eastern Europe in return for renunciation in the west, but Balfour feared that if the Russians found that Britain had negotiated behind their backs they would leave the alliance. Moreover, while the British deliberated, the French were discussing a separate approach. The 'Briand–Lancken affair' began with a sounding through Belgian intermediaries to Briand (now out

of office) from Baron von der Lancken, head of the German occupation administration in Brussels. Briand was keen to take up Lancken's offer of a meeting in
Switzerland, and the intermediaries assured him that Alsace-Lorraine might be
available. In reality Kühlmann had no intention of offering more than small frontier changes in Alsace, and viewed the feeler as secondary to the one to Britain.
Briand's errand would probably have been fruitless even if Ribot (now Painlevé's
foreign minister) had allowed it to go ahead. But Ribot condemned the proposal
as a trap, hinted to the Allies that it was an attempt to negotiate separately from
them, and used their disapproval to kill it. When Lloyd George met Painlevé at
Boulogne on 25 September he found the latter reluctant to approve the Lancken
meeting, not only from fear that the German terms would be so generous that the
French public would insist on accepting them,[125] but also from a suspicion that
the Germans intended to publicize the meeting in order to divide France from its
allies. The British attitude to the Villalobar 'kite' was similar. When Lloyd
George returned from Boulogne he was still attracted by peace negotiations that
by-passed the Russians, but most of the cabinet disagreed and it authorized Balfour to notify all the Allied ambassadors of the German approach. The ambassadors approved a reply that Britain would listen to any proposal but must
consult its partners: in other words that it too would not negotiate separately.
The Germans never responded, and in October Kühlmann burned his bridges by
telling the Reichstag that Germany would 'never' cede Alsace-Lorraine. Lloyd
George retaliated by declaring that Britain would fight on until France recovered
the lost provinces. Effectively this exchange closed the door on the possibility of
peace in the west.

The feelers had raised unrealistic hopes. One reason was that the go-betweens
exaggerated to each side the other's willingness to compromise: as the Belgian intermediaries did with Briand, Armand did to Revertera, and Sixtus with both the
French and the Austrians. And it was true that there was greater willingness for accommodation: Michaelis scaled down Germany's western objectives, and the
British and French were now at least willing to consider suggestions. Yet Alsace-
Lorraine remained a fundamental point of issue between France and Germany, as
did Belgium between Germany and Britain, to say nothing of Britain's desire for
all Germany's colonies and France's for a Rhineland buffer zone. Although individuals such as Lloyd George and Briand might waver, neither the British nor the
French leaderships collectively were willing at this stage to entertain a separate
peace. The military situation, for all the disappointments both sides had suffered,
did not yet seem to either side to render major concessions imperative. OHL was
convinced that Germany could still win.[126] The day after meeting Painlevé at
Boulogne, Lloyd George consulted Haig, who as usual exuded optimism,[127]
though this probably influenced the premier less than did his own appraisal that
the Allies would do better to hang on.[128] Certainly such a calculation weighed
heavily with Ribot, who was crucial in preventing the Briand–Lancken meeting
when many French politicians were wavering.[129] The peace feelers owed their failure not only to continuing military stalemate but also to the survival of a pro-war
consensus in the main belligerents and the new factor of American intervention.
These remaining elements in the equation must now be considered.

A common feature of domestic politics in the late summer and autumn was a counter-offensive against the moderating forces that had emerged since the spring, though in each belligerent it took a different form.*[130] In Austria-Hungary Karl and Czernin reverted to a 'German course' of closer co-operation with Berlin.[130] In Germany the lead came from OHL, which interpreted its sphere of interest ever more widely. Thus after displacing Bethmann, in August Hindenburg and Ludendorff removed another official: Wilhelm Groener, head of the *Kriegsamt*, which had been created in 1916 to supervise the DCGs' economic policies. Groener had co-operated with the trade unions in settling industrial disputes and OHL felt he had failed to prevent strikes from interrupting war production. Further, they suspected that he wanted to increase taxes on their allies in heavy industry, and his removal presaged greater resistance to working-class economic demands as well as political ones.[131] However, they also saw the need for more positive steps. In the first half of the war governments had largely relied on the mass media and on unofficial initiatives to justify the war at home. By 1917 they were entering the fray themselves. Ludendorff contributed to this trend by introducing 'patriotic instruction', or *Vaterländische Unterricht*, among the troops in July. The aim was to counter Allied propaganda and left-wing subversion by insisting that soldiers must obey their commanders, that Germany had to win, and that it must show unity and determination in order to dishearten its enemies. 'Directors of propaganda' were attached to each unit to provide compulsory lectures at least twice a week, backed up by films and mobile pamphlet libraries. A parallel initiative was the launching in September of the Fatherland Party, led by Tirpitz and by Wolfgang Kapp, with encouragement from the army and with funding from business. It grew rapidly, claiming 2,500 branches and 1.25 million members by July 1918.[132] Though professing to be non-political, it was a direct response to the peace resolution: it opposed any domestic reform until after the war, and it pressed for a 'Hindenburg victory' and big annexations. Authoritarian and anti-Semitic, it has rightly been seen as a precursor of National Socialism. Yet both these examples confirm that the new state-inspired propaganda was responding to the erosion of consensus rather than a move to help preserve it. It is doubtful whether 'patriotic instruction' achieved much,[133] and the Fatherland Party even exacerbated political polarization. Despite the propagandists' best efforts, the seventh war loan campaign in October was again disappointing. Nor did Michaelis stay long in office. In September he mismanaged the Reichstag discussion of the mutinies in the fleet, falsely accusing the USPD of complicity. He lost not only the legislature's confidence but also OHL's, because of his failure to defeat a bill for franchise reform. He was replaced by Count Georg von Hertling, and this time the Reichstag parties were consulted and some of their members entered the new administration.[134] Hertling was a septuagenarian southern Catholic who had been Bethmann's preferred successor. OHL did not particularly like him, and he defended the prerogatives of his office, disagreed with the soldiers about war aims, and supported Kühlmann's diplomacy. Despite continuing civil-military friction, however, and the deepening alienation of part of the workforce, the German elite remained united in its fundamental commitment to expansion.

---

*See ch. 15.

On the Allied side, Britain was the country most resistant to the Russian disease and Italy the most susceptible, with France falling somewhere between. Although Lloyd George was tempted by a peace at Russia's expense, when the peace feelers reached their climax the advocates of fighting on kept the upper hand. The measures taken against the U-boat menace and in response to the engineering strikes helped to prevent a subsistence crisis, although by the end of the year serious food shortages emerged for the first time. The cabinet was obliged to pay more attention to civilian living standards and also to public morale (always a key concern for Lloyd George personally), which was badly shaken during the year. Among the consequences were the attempts at Cambrai and in Palestine to deliver a victory for Christmas, and the formation in August of the National War Aims Committee to orchestrate domestic propaganda.* As in Germany, only when 'self-mobilization' proved inadequate did the state step in. However, Britain escaped relatively lightly from the Stockholm conference controversy, whose most lasting political legacy was the reunification of Labour while the Liberals remained divided. After leaving the government Henderson rebuilt his bridges with MacDonald and began realigning the Labour Party on a programme of progressive reform at home and rejection of imperialist war aims. He never, however, opposed the war as such, and he intended to construct a progressive alternative that would deny Bolshevism any British foothold.[135]

Italy was more vulnerable because its entry into the war had always been contested, and in 1917 the opponents of intervention resurfaced at the same time as the socialists became more radical, the PSI adopting the slogan, 'Out of the trenches before next winter'. The Pope's peace note deplored the 'useless slaughter', and Giolitti followed it up by returning to the political stage with a speech at Cuneo, saying foreign policy changes would be needed after the war. Cadorna's autocratic ways were crystallizing opposition in Italy as Joffre's had done in France, and Giolitti's followers (still numbering over 100 deputies) demanded more parliamentary control over the army. Elite disunity was accompanied by social unrest, as inflation followed the general tendency to accelerate. In the small towns and the countryside hundreds of disturbances occurred, the rural areas being where conscription had bitten most deeply and where women, often inadequately supported by separation allowances, were left to cope alone.[136] But order broke down most spectacularly with the Turin riots in August, whose resemblance to events in Russia was striking. Anti-war feeling had always been strong in the city, which had mushroomed on account of its war-related enterprises, notably Fiat. As in Petrograd, migrant workers crowded into inadequate housing and worked punishing hours (up to seventy-five per week)[137] under strict discipline. Local officials had warned an explosion was imminent and once again the spark was a bread shortage, occurring just after a visit by a Petrograd Soviet delegation. Beginning as a protest by women, the movement brought in workers, despite the local socialist leaders' efforts to pacify the crowds, and after the police opened fire barricades went up. At this point, however, the analogy with the February Revolution ends. The army obeyed orders and used machine guns and armoured cars to end the disturbances after five days of disorder during which thirty-five protesters

---

*On the NWAC, see further in ch. 16.

lost their lives.[138] The rioting failed to spread to Rome, and the authorities could contain the scattered rural outbreaks. Nor did revived political controversy seriously challenge either Italy's annexationist war aims or the government's determination to keep fighting. It is true that by the autumn the Boselli ministry was widely condemned as inadequate, and demonstrations called for its replacement. The Golittians wanted it to rein in the military, whereas the interventionists and the high command demanded tougher discipline. A combination of the two extremes overthrew Boselli by 314 to 96 votes on 27 October, but his replacement was a more effective coalition headed by the former interior minister, Vittorio Orlando. The vote coincided with a massive enemy offensive, which ended months of agonizing and did more than anything else to establish national unity.

A similar crisis occurred in France. Here the SFIO went further than the Labour Party and refused to participate in the Painlevé government, even though it continued to support the war. Probably more serious, the will to victory was faltering even among non-socialists, despite the work of a government-backed agency founded in March to oppose enemy peace feelers, the Union des grandes associations contre la propagande ennemie.* The most prominent example was Briand, who when premier had insisted on holding Verdun and had approved the Cambon letter and the Doumergue Agreement, but once out of office remained in touch with Lancken even after the government vetoed a meeting with the Baron. Painlevé similarly may have been in secret contact with the Austrians, offering them a compromise peace based on trading Alsace-Lorraine for French colonies. However, the politician most widely suspected of intelligence with the enemy was Joseph Caillaux, who was strongly believed to want a compromise peace despite his declaration that France must regain Alsace-Lorraine. Most other leading politicians shunned him, but he had a body of supporters in parliament.[139] Another major figure who became tarnished was the interior minister, Louis Malvy, whom the right thought too indulgent towards the socialists. He had indeed recommended not applying 'Carnet B' in 1914 and had tried to co-operate with the SFIO and the unions.[140] But though not a traitor he was tardy in responding to German-backed subversion, and in the summer and autumn of 1917 a series of scandals surfaced. The most notorious concerned the *Bonnet Rouge*, a left-wing journal subsidized at first by the interior ministry and later by the Germans. In 1917 one of its staff was caught with a cheque from Switzerland, and the newspaper's owner, Almereyda, was arrested and later found dead in prison. Clemenceau, the chairman of the Senate Army Commission, brutally attacked Malvy, implying that his laxness had caused the mutinies, and the minister resigned. Further scandals followed, such as that of the deputy Turmel, who had taken German bribes, and the businessman, Bolo Pasha, who had received enemy funds to assist the purchase of a leading Paris daily, *Le Journal*.[141] In several of these cases the police had acted slowly, suggesting complicity not only by Malvy but even Painlevé himself.[142] In November Poincaré noted in his diary that one third of the deputies wanted peace, although they dared not admit it.[143] Yet by now Pétain's measures were rehabilitating the army and the prefects' surveys suggested that civilian spirits were also recovering. Most leading politicians remained loyal to peace through victory and solidarity with

---

*On the UGACPE, see further in ch. 16.

the Allies. Finally, after the Painlevé government collapsed in November Poincaré faced what many commentators regarded as a choice between Caillaux and Clemenceau.[144] Despite Clemenceau's fierce animosity against the president, Poincaré opted for him, and the new government moved swiftly to check the spread of defeatism. This was a crucial decision, comparable with Wilhelm's selection of Michaelis and Hertling to succeed Bethmann rather than a chancellor committed to negotiation. The new ministry, formed largely from the Radical Party, apolitical technicians, and the prime minister's cronies, did not pretend to be a coalition, but it governed the more effectively because it ceased to be inclusive. French politics would henceforward be more divisive, a large left-wing minority moving into vociferous opposition, but the commitment to victory would survive.

Crucial in Britain, Italy, and France was the perception by political leaders that even without Russia they could still win. The United States was essential to this perception, and American policy the final element in the 1917 impasse. Before he intervened, Wilson had portrayed a 'peace without victory' as the most favourable outcome for future international stability; afterwards his goal became peace *through* victory, Germany's defeat becoming essential for a successful settlement. He used his influence against attempts at compromise, and gave enough assistance to see the Allies through their hour of crisis. Yet he remained suspicious of his partners and rationed his aid to them – aid of which anyway he had little to give, as America's economic and military build-up did not come to fruition until well into 1918. Hence American entry at first reinforced the stalemate, encouraging the Allies to persist while not yet convincing the Central Powers that their cause was hopeless.

America entered the war not completely unprepared but at a much lower level of readiness than the continental European powers in 1914. Initially its contribution was primarily maritime, financial, and diplomatic. Its shipping policy revealed a streak of economic nationalism: unlike the British the Americans did not concentrate their merchantmen on the Atlantic sea lanes at the expense of more profitable trade elsewhere, and the authorities requisitioned all ships under construction, even those ordered by their partners.[145] Similarly, the US navy – which was large and modern with some 300 vessels, including seventy destroyers – had a tradition of rivalry with the British. None the less, American assistance was of major importance both in persuading the Royal Navy that convoying was feasible, and in enabling the escort system to operate. Further, the American navy altered its building schedule in the light of the new priorities, suspending its 1916 programme for an expansion in capital ships and concentrating instead on launching destroyers and 'subchasers', small wooden vessels equipped with hydrophones and depth charges.[146] Although the Atlantic convoys were up and running before the Americans fully participated, by September half the American destroyers had been transferred to Ireland for escort duty and Jellicoe commented in retrospect that only US entry made it possible to adopt the convoy system in 1917.[147] The ability to ship goods and men safely across the ocean was crucial to the entire Allied effort.

The Allies also needed to be able to pay for the goods, and finance was the second area where American entry had an early impact. The US Treasury began lending direct to the Allied governments, starting with a loan to the British for $200 million at 3 per cent interest, or two points less than they had been paying for private finance.[148] Admittedly the loans were tied to the purchase of American products (whereas Britain's loans to its partners were not necessarily tied to purchases in Britain).[149] The British hoped that Washington would finance all Allied orders in the United States, but such a concession would have pushed Treasury Secretary McAdoo to the limits of what Congress had allowed him to borrow. This would have mattered less if American government credits had been dependably forthcoming, but they were not. McAdoo was Wilson's son-in-law and an ambitious man with presidential aspirations: he wished to avoid a quarrel with Congress, disliked J. P. Morgan for its partners' Republican sympathies, and hoped to see the dollar replace the pound as the world standard of value and New York overtake London as the global financial capital.[150] These resentments came to a head over the British government's overdraft with Morgan's, which he refused to service.[151] Nor was he keen to uphold the value of sterling against the dollar, which the British were attempting to sustain at \$4–76:£1.00. In the period from June to August they were nearly forced to let the rate fall, although doing so would make every Allied purchase from America more expensive. In the end their urging of this point seems to have persuaded McAdoo to support the rate, while rejecting British appeals to guarantee it. Yet although the Allies got less money than they wanted, they still received cheap credit without having to borrow privately and they used it for essential purchases (the French for example buying wheat and steel).[152] As in the naval sphere, American aid provided the margin for survival, if not much more.

The pattern was repeated in the sphere of diplomacy. America's declaration of war brought the Allies big advantages, of which the first was many further such declarations. After April 1917 ten Latin American countries broke off relations or declared war against Germany, and the enemy ships that had taken refuge in their ports became available to the Allies. In Brazil alone this meant forty-two vessels.[153] Coming on top of the German ships confiscated in the United States, the upshot was that the Allies and Americans now controlled five sixths of world merchant tonnage. American intervention also contributed directly to China's entry into the war in August. Britain and France had wanted this for some time, hoping to use Chinese labourers; in addition, the U-boat campaign made it a matter of urgency to seize the German merchantmen in Chinese harbours. The Japanese opposed Chinese entry, as they did not want Beijing at the peace conference, until in spring 1917 the European Allies secretly promised to back Japan's claims to Germany's territories in Shandong province.* When Washington broke off relations with Germany it invited other neutrals to do likewise, and China obliged.[154] The Americans did not want China to become a belligerent, but at this point Chinese internal politics intervened, in the shape of a struggle between President Li Yuan-hung, supported by the nationalist movement known as the Guomindang, and prime minister Tuan Chi-jui, supported by the northern military governors. Tuan favoured going to war in the hope of securing Allied finance that would assist him in the internal struggle; he and his supporters took Beijing in May and issued the declaration of war while the Guomindang set up a rival government at Canton. Intervention accelerated China's descent

---

*See ch. 5.

into chaos that would last for the next decade.[155] Nevertheless, Chinese and Latin American intervention, following on that of Greece, meant that by the end of 1917 most of the world had at least nominally joined the muster against the Central Powers. Moreover, American entry forced the remaining neutrals to comply more fully with the Allied blockade. Whereas fear of America had previously inhibited Allied policy towards the Dutch and the Scandinavians, Washington now insisted on the northern European neutrals being more severely rationed and receiving supplies only if the Allies could use their merchant shipping.[156] With the diplomatic obstacles to the blockade weakened, it could grip ever tighter.

Wilson also assisted Allied diplomacy by opposing a compromise peace. The Americans denied their socialists passports for Stockholm, and advised Balfour against discussing the Villalobar 'kite' until a definite proposal was made.[157] Wilson rejected the Pope's peace note, after Lansing had counselled that the military situation favoured the Central Powers and peace must be rejected until the United States had exerted its strength.[158] The president's bellicosity dismayed some of his European sympathizers, to whom the administration privately sent reassuring signals, House advising British radicals that 'when the time comes for action, they will find him [Wilson] on the right side'.[159] Wilson certainly wanted Germany beaten, and his reply to the Pope called implicitly for revolution in Berlin. But his alignment with the European Allies was tactical, and he foresaw a later confrontation with them. Thus he welcomed Britain's and France's growing financial dependence so that he could 'force them to our way of thinking' when the time was right; but that time had not arrived and he rejected a proposal from McAdoo to make loans conditional on war aims being moderated.[160] Similarly, he authorized House to establish 'The Inquiry', a team of experts to study the likely issues at the peace conference, so that America could take up an informed position and 'gather the influence we can use'.[161] It did not suit him to make peace yet, and he played a waiting game. America retained the status of an 'Associated Power', not signing the Pact of London and reserving the right to make a separate peace. It declared war against Austria-Hungary only in December, and never did so against Bulgaria and Turkey. Although not seconding Tereshchenko's demand for a conference to revise war aims, it distanced itself from what it learned of its partners' objectives. When Balfour visited Washington in April, he brought details of many of the secret treaties, including Sykes–Picot and the Treaty of London with Italy. House told him such arrangements were 'all bad' and 'a breeding ground for future war', and America must keep out of them.[162] Similarly, Wilson's reply to the Pope, published without consulting his partners, condemned plans for 'punitive damages, the dismemberment of empires, the establishment of selfish and exclusive economic leagues'.[163] Privately he warned the British that Americans felt themselves to be 'arbitrators rather than collaborators'.[164]

The Allied response was twofold. One tack was to seek American support for existing objectives. The Italians never broached the Treaty of London with Wilson, though they checked that Britain and France remained committed to it. The French did try to win America over, but made little headway. Wilson avoided a pledge to transfer Alsace-Lorraine to France, which he doubted was what the inhabitants wanted. He rejected French suggestions for a follow-up meeting to the Paris economic conference of 1916. The Americans were similarly evasive over a proposal from Clémentel that the Allies should maintain controls over world trade in foodstuffs and raw materials after the war, so that France could get what it needed for reconstruction and Germany would face strangulation if it misbehaved.[165] The one Allied power that did reach an accommodation with Washington was Japan, in the Lansing–Ishii Agreement of November 1917. This understanding followed on from China's intervention, and was negotiated to avert an American–Japanese confrontation. Both America and Japan had prospered from the conflict and both had increased their influence in East Asia, where the Europeans now counted for little. When the Americans entered the war they concentrated their fleet in the Atlantic but stopped supplying steel to Japan (hence impeding Japanese shipbuilding), claiming that they needed it at home. In June 1917 the Japanese asserted that they had 'paramount interests' in China, but Washington dissented. However, Lansing and Baron Ishii arrived at a *modus vivendi*, which was basically an agreement to disagree. The Tokyo government's advice from its experts was that it would lose a war with America, and it did not want direct control over China anyway. Wilson thought the Japanese threat a remote one and was willing for concessions to be made. The Lansing–Ishii Agreement recognised Japan's 'special interests' in China but insisted that Chinese 'territorial sovereignty . . . remains unimpaired'. Beijing was not consulted over the understanding, and refused to recognize it. It marked a temporary American retreat, as the Japanese continued to expand their economic interests and political influence on the Asian mainland. None the less, as in Europe, the Americans intended to reopen the issue at a more opportune time.[166]

The Allies' second response to the American diplomatic challenge was to modify at least the appearance of their war aims to take account of Wilson's rhetoric, as well as of demands from the European left. The most obvious instance was the League of Nations, approved in the French Chamber's resolution of 6 June and incorporated into the public objectives of France and Britain despite their leaders' private reservations. However, if this was meant to humour Wilson it probably failed, as he was unready for detailed discussions of the League and resisted Allied attempts to start them. The celebrated 'Balfour Declaration', issued on 2 November, can also be interpreted as an attempt to adjust British war aims to the new conditions. In an open letter from the Foreign Secretary to Lord Rothschild the British government pledged support for 'a national home for the Jewish people' in Palestine, without prejudice to the rights of non-Jews living there or those of Jews in other countries. It was issued as Allenby's advance on Jerusalem gave the British the power to implement it. During the summer they had sounded out Turkey about a separate peace, but France's and Italy's commitment to the Sykes–Picot and St-Jean de Maurienne agreements (and Turkish ambitions against Russia) left little scope for a deal. If peace with the Turks was unlikely, a public pledge to strip them of Palestine risked little. The imperialists in the cabinet – including Lloyd George himself – wanted to revise Sykes–Picot and place the Holy Land under British rather than international control, not least to create a barrier between the Suez Canal and the French in Syria. They believed that Jewish settlers in Palestine would be pro-British, and they feared that unless they endorsed the Zionist aspiration to a national homeland Germany would beat them to it. In addition they hoped for sympathy from Jewish communities worldwide. The Zionist movement was rapidly increasing its influence among both Russian and American Jews, as it was in Britain itself. Although Wilson was publicly circumspect, the Supreme Court justice and leading American Zionist Louis Brandeis seems to have converted the president to the cause and to favouring a British protectorate. Knowledge of the American attitude helped tip the London cabinet in favour of the Declaration after weeks of debate. Lloyd George and Balfour welcomed the principle of a Jewish state and seem to have expected that one would eventually result, but they issued the Declaration to serve their strategic interests in the Middle East and to win American goodwill.[167]

US intervention therefore brought the Allies major naval, economic, and diplomatic benefits, but the American contribution was carefully hedged. Wilson and his advisers kept in mind American national interests, whether the issue was shipping, loans, or war aims. Their assistance tided Britain over the financial and submarine crises and helped the Allied governments resist the challenge from the left. Without it, the European Allies would probably have been forced into negotiations. But it was little above the minimum necessary to keep them in the war, for reasons stemming partly from American unpreparedness but also from deliberate policy, and much the same can be said of the fourth category of American assistance, the American Expeditionary Force (AEF). Nivelle had envisaged the Americans would send only some 90,000 transport and medical specialists, as he assumed that the Allies could still win largely unassisted. But after the Chemin des Dames disaster Pétain made a big American army essential to his strategy.[168] Conversely, Wilson decided to encourage the French by sending troops quickly, authorizing a Franco-American framework agreement in May.[169] Thus the Americans expanded their commitment as the British had done before them, but the AEF also served Wilson's own objectives. The War Department (under Secretary Newton D. Baker) and the general staff considered France the decisive theatre. The president probably agreed, but to make sure (apparently in the light of Lloyd George's doubts about the Western Front) his military advisers gave him a memorandum in October that systematically rejected all alternatives. Unlike the British, the Americans opposed a 'sideshow' strategy, as they would again in the Second World War. It was quickly agreed that the AEF would go to Lorraine, which by 1917 was a quiet sector. The choice suited the French, who did not want foreign troops guarding the immediate approaches to their capital and supposed that if the Americans were sandwiched between French units in the east they would be less likely to develop close relations with the British. But it also suited the AEF commander, Pershing, because it would allow him to control an independent rail network running south of Paris to his supply ports on the Atlantic coast, and could serve as the springboard for a thrust into the Saar and German Lorraine.[170]

America's strategy was therefore ambitious. That Pershing wanted such an independent role reflected both his and Wilson's political standpoints. The commander was instructed to keep the AEF 'a separate and distinct component', and he believed that 'when the war ends our position will be stronger if our army acting as such will have played a distinct and definite part'.[171] Like the French and British, the American leaders believed their contribution to defeating Germany would shape their influence at the peace conference. They were determined to keep the AEF institutionally separate, even at the cost of clashes with France and Britain and delays before the force was ready. The French and British both doubted whether the tiny American officer corps could supply enough competent commanders and staff officers to direct independent AEF divisions and armies, and the British wanted to insert American troops into British-led units.[172] But the Americans refused, although they did agree to the French training their recruits, which the French mistakenly supposed would give them influence.[173] Americans were not to be sent to Europe simply to become cannon fodder, and even if the AEF built gradually, it would build soundly to serve the president's goals.

Only 77,000 Americans had reached France by November 1917.[174] Their tardy arrival caused dismay in Europe after the euphoria when the first 'doughboys' had landed in the summer, even though the United States in 1917–18 achieved a faster build-up than Britain in 1914–16. But as a land military power, America was starting virtually from scratch. During the neutrality period Allied contracts had expanded American munitions capacity, and the Council of National Defense, created by the 1916 National Defense Act, had drawn up an industrial mobilization plan. During the neutrality period some 16,000 young men (mainly college students) were trained in summer camps by voluntary initiative as potential officers, the army's budget was more than doubled, and it was set ambitious recruitment targets (although it failed to meet them). In April 1917 it numbered only 5,791 officers and 121,797 men, to whom should be added 181,620 in the National Guard. General staff officers numbered fewer than twenty. The army had performed poorly in Mexico, it had fewer than 1,500 machine guns, its rifles were outdated, its field guns were defective, and it had negligible numbers of aircraft.[175]

Wilson learned from the British experience in that he quickly overcame his hostility to conscription, the Selective Service Act coming into effect in May. Volunteering was weaker than it had been in Britain, and the act was partly intended to compensate. It was also meant to forestall the political embarrassment of a volunteer division recruited and headed by Theodore Roosevelt,[176] and to prevent the war economy from being disrupted by skilled men joining up: some 0.8 million agricultural and industrial workers were granted deferments.[177] Local boards registered nearly 10 million men in June, though all with dependants were exempted and some boards also exempted most married men. Conscientious objection was permitted, on religious and later also on secular grounds, although the 20,000 certified objectors were sent to training camps and more than 16,000 decided to serve after all as an alternative.[178] A total of 2,758,000 men were inducted and the army had no particular shortage of soldiers.[179] What it did lack (apart from transport ships) was training camps (built rapidly and expensively but often unready when the recruits arrived), officers (who were being trained in parallel with their men), and weapons.

The federal government tried to manage the war economy without resorting to nationalization or to compulsory powers. It decided to respect the Allies' existing war contracts, so that orders for the AEF would be additional. In consequence most of the AEF's weaponry was supplied by Allied industry, the army buying 10 million tons of supplies and equipment in Europe during the war and only 7 million in the United States.[180] Buying aeroplanes and field guns from France and Britain alleviated the pressure on America's own capacity, but the War Department exacerbated the overload by going on a spending spree, ordering in the first six months most of what the AEF received down to November 1918.[181] Often it by-passed the War Industries

Board (set up to supervise the procurement process) and dealt direct with individual companies. The outcome was that in the 1917–18 winter America ran into a production crisis.* None the less, industrial reconversion proceeded in the United States as elsewhere once enough money was thrown at the problem. Indeed the country financed its war effort relatively easily, although mainly by borrowing. Wilson's War Message had said the cost should be covered as far as possible by taxation, and McAdoo set a target of 50 per cent. As elsewhere, however, income tax (introduced as recently as 1916) was politically controversial, and an excess profits tax still more so. Congress stalled over tax increases but authorized McAdoo to launch a $2 billion bond issue, the first 'Liberty Loan', at a low but tax-free interest rate. The issue was oversubscribed, and McAdoo found it easiest to cover his costs through borrowing, the low interest enabling him to contain the burden of debt service.[182] But to sell the bonds (even though banks rather than individuals were the main purchasers) he needed to mobilize public patriotism, and he did so through saturation publicity. The authorities hoped to rely on patriotic 'self-mobilization', which the American public did eventually deliver, albeit more slowly than in Europe. But to achieve it the government used a surprising degree of coercion and manipulation, in a society whose cohesion had been challenged by a tremendous immigrant influx in recent decades and that had been further divided over the decision to intervene, which the largely immigrant-led American Socialist Party continued to oppose. The June 1917 Espionage Act empowered the postmaster-general to ban socialist publications from the interstate mails, and Washington entered the propaganda business. The Committee on Public Information (CPI), headed by a progressive newspaper editor and longstanding Wilson supporter, George Creel, launched a massive multilingual programme, its tone becoming increasingly proselytizing rather than 'factual' as it set itself the mission of 'Americanizing' recent immigrants.†[184] A process was beginning that would culminate later in a vehement reaction against progressivism.

During 1917 American spending power produced neither a large trained army nor a capable war industry. Although mistakes can be identified in the management of the home front, the basic reason was that creating these things needed time. The resources available to help the Allies were therefore restricted, and Wilson and his advisers' policy preferences made them more restricted still. Hence American intervention, offset by Russia's paralysis, reinforced the stalemate of 1917; stalemate at a lower level of violence than in 1916, but stalemate none the less. Despite changing tactics and technology on land and at sea, a military breakthrough remained remote; despite frenetic diplomatic activity, a negotiated compromise was equally elusive. The collapse of pro-war consensus in Russia failed to transfer to the west, and in America war fever was gathering intensity. The struggle would not end quietly. We must now examine the decisions that brought about its culmination.

---

*See further in ch. 16
†See further in ch. 16.

CHAPTER 15

THE CENTRAL POWERS'
LAST THROW, AUTUMN 1917–
SUMMER 1918

IN AUTUMN 1917 the Central Powers regained the initiative. Their counter-attack against the Kerensky offensive initiated a reversal of fortunes comparable to those marked by Gorlice-Tarnow in spring 1915 and the Brusilov offensive in summer 1916. It also signalled a partial return to a war of movement. Although the Allied attacks on the Isonzo, in Flanders, and in Palestine continued until the autumn, from that point on the Germans swept all before them. After expelling the Russians from Galicia in July, they captured Riga in September, and at Caporetto in October they inflicted on Italy one of the most spectacular defeats of the war. The Bolshevik Revolution in November enabled them to conclude a ceasefire on the Eastern Front and to impose peace treaties on Russia and Romania in spring 1918, before carving out a vast zone of satellite states from the Arctic Circle to the Caucasus. Finally on the Western Front, where the Cambrai counterstroke had already pushed back the British, five great German attacks from 21 March to 15 July 1918 confronted the Allies with their most dangerous crisis since 1914. With the defeat of these offensives, however, yet another turn in military fortunes restored the Allies' advantage, and this time definitively.

The Central Powers could seize their opportunity because their enemies faltered. By summer 1917 three years of slaughter had driven Russia into revolution and France into mutiny. America gave carefully rationed naval and financial aid, but was still converting to war production and as yet had placed no units in the line. Yet Germany and Austria-Hungary were also nearing exhaustion, even if a revolution in tactics gave them an operational advantage. Russia's withdrawal strengthened OHL's commitment to a massive western offensive as Germany's final bid for victory. Turning their backs on peace by negotiation – which it is true the Allies had also rejected – Berlin and Vienna opted once again for military breakthrough as the best exit from their impasse. By doing so they gambled away most of their remaining assets and left themselves exposed to a decisive counterstroke.

As in previous war winters, the Germans opted for a spring offensive in the belief that time was against them. The danger signals were indeed at red. Among their allies Bulgaria, which was still led by King Ferdinand and prime minister Radoslavov, had fended off the Allies in Macedonia, but internal opposition was growing.[1] Austria-Hungary, after its waywardness since Karl's accession, now snapped back into line, but its so-called 'German course' proved a mixed blessing. The new solidarity between Berlin and Vienna reflected the change in military fortunes: with the Russians out of Galicia and the Italians routed, Austrian soil was cleared of invaders. Paradoxically, in many ways Austria-Hungary's war was won, if not by its own efforts. Moreover, after Bolshevik Russia published the inter-Allied secret treaties, the extent of Italy's territorial appetite became public knowledge, and experience had demonstrated that the other Allies would not break with Rome. Nor were Karl and Czernin willing to risk a separate peace that might endanger their regime's survival, especially if Germany retaliated by invading the Dual Monarchy in order to maintain its communications to Constantinople and sided with the Austrian Germans against their rulers. A separate peace, said Czernin, would resemble suicide for fear of death.[2] In December 1917 he proclaimed that Austria-Hungary was fighting to defend Alsace-Lorraine and was as strongly committed to holding Strasbourg as to holding Trieste. He instructed his diplomats in neutral capitals to stress that Vienna would stand by the alliance.[3] Yet he also opposed domestic reform, advising that to appease one nationality would only antagonize others. The Dual Monarchy found itself trapped, unable to break with the German alliance, yet by that same alliance antagonizing all but its German and Magyar subjects, whose leaders would rather see the empire liquidated than share power equally with the other nationalities. Thus even after Tisza resigned as Hungarian premier, his party still dominated the Budapest parliament and blocked franchise reform. In January 1918 a new Hungarian government under Wekerle demanded a separate army.[4] Even the two core nationalities were drifting apart.

Economically the Central Powers were on a downhill slide. Bulgaria's railways were seizing up[5] and Turkey was lurching towards hyper-inflation. Reliable budgetary figures are lacking, but Ottoman government expenditure may have quadrupled during the war while revenue rose barely 20 per cent. The authorities could not cover the deficit by borrowing, and the paper currency introduced in 1915 rapidly depreciated. Retail prices in Constantinople had quadrupled by January 1917 and rose nearly twenty-fold by the end of the war.[6] The Young Turks' administration, on paper increasingly centralized, was losing control of the provinces. Parts of the Ottoman Empire, facing the collapse of trade, disruption of agriculture by conscription, and huge refugee movements, neared famine.[7] As for Austria-Hungary, its war economy was most successful from mid-1915 to early 1917,[8] though this meant success in supplying the army rather than feeding civilians. Of 3.6 million tons of steel produced in 1916, for example, 3.1 million went to the army, which in the 1917 Isonzo defensive battles had more munitions than it could use. Austria-Hungary took part in the Hindenburg Programme, and allocated 454 million crowns for the purpose.[9] But as in Germany the war ministry set over-ambitious targets for the programme at a moment when production was about to fall sharply. Inadequate powder production was the main bottleneck, though shortages of other materials such as copper also contributed. During the autumn and winter of 1917–18 the Monarchy's heavy industries began to shut down. Deterioration on the railways was central to a series of vicious circles. Too few wagons meant too little movement of coal, which meant more trains were halted and impeded steel production, forcing a choice between munitions and rolling stock. In the last year of the war, coal output halved; many steel firms had to close during the winter, and in early 1918 steel shortages forced all but the biggest arms firms to cut production.[10] Machine gun output fell from 1,900 to 350 pieces per month between October 1917 and February 1918. The army was fortunate that fighting on the Russian and Balkan fronts had virtually ceased, leaving only the Italian one active. Even so, it estimated its units were at two thirds of regulation strength. Over 70 per cent of draft-eligible men had been conscripted and most of the remainder worked in the war industries.[11] In real terms Austria-Hungary spent less on the war in 1917–18 than it had in 1914–15.[12] As Ludendorff recognized, the Habsburg army could now do little more than wait passively for the larger conflict to end.[13]

The German economy too had entered a downward spiral. In order to meet the Hindenburg Programme it had to rein back its profitable exports to neutrals. The Reichsbank sustained the mark's exchange value only by confiscating foreign securities held by Germans and selling them or using them as collateral for overseas borrowing, hence amassing external debts. At home, war loan sales failed to mop up the liquidity created by issuing treasury bills, or to close the widening budget deficit. Periodic levies on excess profits were one-off measures that produced no continuous income stream. As monetary policy loosened output contracted: the index of industrial production fell from 98 in 1913 to 81 in 1914, 66 in 1915, 63 in 1916, 61 in 1917, and 56 in 1918. The wholesale price index had jumped from 105 in 1914 to 142 in 1915, but then rose more slowly to 152 in 1916. Now, however, it jumped again, to 179 in 1917 and 217 in 1918. Male workers in war industries held their real wages in 1917 at 78.8 per cent of the pre-war level, but those in civilian industries were reduced to 52.7 per cent.[14] The combination of falling output and monetary depreciation created a war of all against all for what remained of the cake, but no social group maintained its living standards. Professional and small-business groups suffered most and inclined to support the new Fatherland Party, while Berlin metalworkers provided the core support for the USPD. Although the high command judged the situation at home to have improved since the crisis of the summer,[15] the outlook remained gloomy.

Germany's economic difficulties extended from the civilian into the military sector. The Allied blockade tightened further after American entry, and restricted supplies of petroleum, agricultural fertilizer, and a long list of raw materials needed for armaments, including non-ferrous metals, cotton, rubber, sulphur, and glycerine.[16] Partly for this reason, by September Hindenburg was lamenting that even though the Hindenburg Programme's goals had twice been reduced, industry had still not reached them.[17] Powder production of 9,200 tons in July 1917 lagged well

behind the target of 12,000 set for May,[18] and railway wagon shortages held back
steel production.[19] As in Austria-Hungary, not enough coal was transported to
where it was needed, so that too little steel was available to replace railway track
and rolling stock. In October the powder plants had to suspend production for
lack of fuel, and in December, at OHL's request, the navy lowered its buffer stocks
of coal. It was fortunate that during 1917 new defensive tactics, the Hindenburg
Line, and the Russian Revolution enabled Germany to fend off the Allies without
big increases in numbers or firepower. None the less, the Hindenburg Programme
did belatedly achieve results. Germany accumulated massive munitions stocks before its 1918 offensives, and neither shells nor infantry and artillery weapons were
short until the final stages of the war. By the winter of 1917–18 Hindenburg and
Ludendorff faced a situation (about which they were kept well informed) where
the general economy was rapidly deteriorating but arms and munitions were at
last becoming available in greater quantities.[20] To an extent these circumstances
make their strategic choices seem more rational.

Hindenburg and Ludendorff led an army that was tired but still solid. The 'Patriotic Instruction' introduced in 1917 appears to have been ineffective, and (unlike Pétain) OHL did little else to raise morale. By the autumn the army in
Flanders was exhausted and increasingly resentful of its officers; in the east it was
touched by the Russian ferment and up to 10 per cent of the men transported back
to the west tried to desert *en route*.[21] Hindenburg feared subversion in the army,
though he saw it as a danger for the future. But troop numbers were a serious
problem already: he complained in September 1917 that the lack of trained soldiers was severely impeding 'operational freedom'.[22] So far from the 1916 Auxiliary Service law having released more recruits for the front, the numbers of
exempted workers rose from 1.2 to 1.9 million between September 1916 and July
1917,[23] and the army relinquished 100,000 men for the Hindenburg Programme
and U-boat building.[24] Hindenburg wanted labour mobility restricted, but the interior ministry and the Kriegsamt opposed changes in the law, and the government ignored an OHL plea for all males aged fifteen to sixty to be liable for
military service. As of January 1918, 2.3 million workers in the war economy remained protected – a striking indication of the limits to OHL's 'dictatorship'.[25]
Hindenburg and Ludendorff were exasperated by Hertling's failure, as they saw
it, to take the drastic action necessary to raise production, husband manpower,
and combat pacifist agitation. The soldiers made available by Russia's collapse
came not a moment too soon.

OHL could profit with new vigour from that collapse because of a revolution
in tactics that was fundamental to the Central Powers' new run of success. It grew
out of separate lines of development in the artillery and infantry, which – although
its essence was to combine them – should here be treated in turn. As regards artillery, the week-long British bombardments before the Somme and Third Ypres
had never been the preferred German model. Before Gorlice-Tarnow the preliminary barrage lasted only four hours; before Verdun eight. On the Eastern Front in
1916–17 Lieut.-Colonel Georg Bruchmüller, an officer on the retired list before
the war who first came to notice for his role at the battle of Lake Narocz, took artillery tactics a further stage. He developed predicted shooting, i.e., bombardments

that dispensed with prior 'registration' or ranging shots, thereby facilitating surprise. The technique required aerial reconnaissance and photography for careful plotting of the target,[26] given that the guns would be aiming at map co-ordinates. During 1917, the artillery enhanced its capacities for predicted shooting by adopting the 'Pulkowski method', developed by a captain of that name, which entailed laboriously testing each gun on firing ranges to check how its range varied with wind speed and weight of shot. Besides rigorous preparation the new tactics required a centralized fire control scheme (in contrast to devolved British practice)[27] in order to disable the enemy positions. The essence of Bruchmüller's system was not to destroy the defence but to 'neutralize' or incapacitate it by a sudden hurricane bombardment that targeted it in depth. The enemy would be unable to move up reserves and his front-line troops would have to stay under cover until the assault forces were upon them, the advancing infantry being protected by a creeping barrage and by 'box barrages' screening the flanks of the attack sector.[28] By relying on gas shells to douse the opposing gun batteries and command posts the bombardment would economize on high explosive and be less likely to chew up the terrain. Resistance would be paralysed by an onslaught in three dimensions extending deep behind enemy lines, arguably anticipating Blitzkrieg and Desert Storm.[29] The attack on Riga on 1 September 1917 saw the largest test yet of Bruchmüller's artillery planning, which supported an assault by thirteen divisions of General Oskar von Hutier's Eighth Army across the river Dvina upstream of the city. Trench mortars were used against the Russian first lines, a 'box' sealed off the attack zone, and high explosives and gas descended on the enemy communication trenches and guns. The Germans concealed their build-up and unleashed the bombardment without registration at 4 a.m., the boat crossing following at 9:10 behind a rolling barrage. The Russian positions south of the city were less intensely bombarded and resisted long enough for the city garrison to escape, with the result that the operation achieved less than had been hoped for. None the less, for light casualties the Germans crossed the river and took Riga, and OHL now moved both Hutier and Bruchmüller to the west for larger tasks.[30]

Bruchmüller's methods were not wholly revolutionary, and resembled developments in the Allied camp, but they took on their full significance when conjoined with new infantry tactics. Although Riga was largely an artillery success, the infantry making little use of innovative methods, since 1915 the Germans had been experimenting with what came to be known as 'stormtroop tactics'. In December 1916 assault battalions were approved for each army on the Western Front and each army group in the east. The principle was one of attack by a thin and open skirmishing line supported by specially trained squads carrying not just rifles but also heavier weaponry – trench mortars, flamethrowers, and light and even heavy machine-guns. Squad leaders were set general objectives, or 'combat missions' (*Gefechtsaufträge*), but were left considerable discretion as to how to achieve them, and in general were to push as far and fast as possible through the enemy lines, bypassing and isolating strongpoints to be dealt with later. The counter-attack at Cambrai employed stormtroop tactics even though the units concerned had not been trained in them. General Georg von der Marwitz's Second Army attacked without ostentatious preparations and after a short Riga-style bombardment, achieving surprise against poorly consolidated British positions. The advance against the south of the British salient advanced up to five miles in a few hours, the assault groups infiltrating the enemy positions with flamethrowers and light machine-guns, even moving up field guns as they went, and being supported by aircraft and a pinpointed barrage. 'Assault blocs' followed up against the points of resistance. Despite the counter-offensive against the north of the salient being less successful (it used traditional bigger formations and failed to achieve surprise), the operation helped to convince Ludendorff that the new tactics could succeed in Western Front conditions. Early in 1918 he decided to disseminate them throughout the army.[31]

The biggest of the Central Powers' successes in autumn 1917 employed both the new artillery and the new infantry tactics. The battle of Caporetto was the only occasion on which the Germans intervened in strength in the Italian theatre. It was decided on at short notice as a fire-fighting operation in response to an Austrian plea for assistance. Ludendorff would have preferred after Riga to finish off the Romanians, who still hung on in what was left of their country and who after the defeat of the Kerensky offensive had fended off an Austro-German attack in August.[32] But the Austrians were hard pressed during the eleventh Isonzo battle in August–September when fifty-one Italian divisions with 5,200 guns attacked nineteen defending ones.[33] Like their German counterparts in Flanders, they were demoralized by endless defensive fighting, and Krafft von Delmensingen, a German mountain warfare expert who visited the front in the summer, reported to OHL that they could not withstand a twelfth such engagement.[34] On 26 August Karl informed Wilhelm that Austria-Hungary wanted to launch an offensive and he asked for German troops to replace Austrian ones in Russia so that he could move heavy artillery to Italy. Wilhelm ordered Ludendorff to examine the problem, but the latter doubted that the Habsburg troops, unschooled in the new tactics, could stage a successful offensive and he feared an Austro-Italian separate peace if they did. On the other hand, after Riga OHL had troops available for an Italian operation before the winter. It planned a temporary deployment with aims limited, in the first instance, to propping up the Austrians by driving the Italians back to the river Tagliamento, depriving the latter of their expensively won conquests. The battle would consist simply of a push forward from the Isonzo rather than a more ambitious pincer attack from both the Isonzo and the Tyrol, for which Ludendorff judged he had too few men. In short, the concept resembled Falkenhayn's for Gorlice-Tarnow two years before.[35]

From September onwards the Germans moved seven divisions to the Italian theatre (from both the Eastern and the Western Fronts, though Plumer's Ypres attacks caused a delay), incorporating them in a new Austro-German Fourteenth Army under German leadership. Otto von Below was the commander and Krafft von Delmensingen his CGS. Austria-Hungary moved five divisions to the Isonzo from the Eastern Front and the Tyrol.[36] On 24 October the Caporetto offensive was launched and quickly achieved overwhelming success, capturing or routing a large part of the Italian army and advancing more than fifty miles. In the theatre as a whole the Germans and Austrians had thirty-three divisions against the Italians' forty-one, but in the northern Isonzo attack sector they concentrated fifteen against six. They took pains to achieve surprise, camouflaging their artillery and moving up the assault infantry by night.[37] Bruchmüller did not direct the artillery, but it employed the usual techniques. Although there was some prior registration, it failed to alert the Italians to the scale of what was planned. The bombardment used 1,000 gas-projectors,[38] and more than twice as many artillery pieces as at Riga, the guns in one sector being only 4.4 metres apart. It opened at 2 a.m. and continued until the assault six hours later, fog and rain making it difficult for the Italians to locate the guns and hit back. Much of it was counter-battery fire to disable the enemy artillery, while phosgene gas shells (against which the Italians' masks were ineffective) were fired against the front lines, prior to a very accurate high explosive bombardment and a creeping barrage. The infantry attack was concentrated along two valley bottoms at Plezzo and Tolmino, some twenty-five kilometres apart. Because the Austrians still held bridgeheads west of the Isonzo, the Germans could break out without having to cross the river. The Italians had followed staff college practice and garrisoned the heights above, enabling the German forward commanders to drive forward at their own rapid pace until the valleys converged, not waiting for the artillery to follow them but by-passing the enemy positions.[39] The German infantry were equipped with the new Maxim 08/15 light machine-gun, and the *Jäger* (Alpine troops) additionally carried mortars and mountain guns. Many had already experienced mountain warfare in the Carpathians and the Vosges; others were given time beforehand to train and to acclimatize to the thinner air. Advancing ten to fifteen miles on the first day, by 27 October they were out of the mountains altogether and advancing across the Veneto plain.

The Italian army was ill prepared to meet this onslaught. Its commanders had failed to reinforce it in the crucial sectors, and Cadorna seems to have been complacent. After suspending the eleventh battle of the Isonzo he envisaged renewing it in the spring, discounting intelligence warnings of German intervention. Even after enemy ranging shots and interrogation of deserters had disclosed the location and date of the attack he had doubted it would come and been confident that if it did he could deal with it. He had been determined to hang on to his summer gains and the Italians had remained in their conquered positions, too many of them crammed too far forward and their reserves kept too far behind. He had ordered the line to be organized for defence in depth, but General Capello, who commanded the Second Army in the threatened sector, had ignored the instruction, apparently hoping to deal with the offensive by a flank attack.[40] Yet on his left Capello had placed recently conscripted munitions workers involved in the August uprising in Turin. When the blow fell, his army proved highly vulnerable to the bombardment, and the Germans easily infiltrated it.

Although it is possible to explain the breakthrough in operational terms, Cadorna described Caporetto as 'a kind of military strike' and blamed it on 'subversive propaganda'.[41] He so advised Orlando, accusing the Second Army of failing to fight.[42] It suited Cadorna and Capello to disseminate this view, which gained wide currency. It indeed had some basis, although Cadorna's aggressive strategy and indifference to his soldiers' welfare bore much of the blame for their mood. On 24 October and during the retreat several units did fight: in a few days the Second Army suffered 11,690 dead and 21,950 wounded, and by the time the attackers halted on the river Piave the Germans and Austrians had sustained 65–70,000 casualties.[43] Yet these figures were dwarfed by the capture in four weeks of 294,000 Italian prisoners (from an army of around 2 million), to say nothing of 3,136 guns (about half the Italian total) and huge quantities of munitions and stores.[44] The shock of the bombardment and the speed of the breakthrough left masses of soldiers cut off and leaderless. But German accounts make clear that many Italians gave up quickly and without resistance, abandoned their rifles and uniforms, and cheered the victors, while others abused units moving up. The surrenders began at once, the German Twelfth Division for example taking 15,000 prisoners on day one. Cadorna had no contingency plans for a withdrawal and was slow to authorize one; nor could the Italians manage what became an unprecedented traffic jam. Once the retreat began it snowballed out of control and the troops streamed south-eastwards alongside 400,000 civilian refugees, looting abandoned farms. In all about 300,000 'disbanded' soldiers (*sbandati*) were put in cages and reallocated to new units.[45]

None the less, the situation was contained, and the Piave line was held. This was not France in 1940 or South Vietnam in 1975, albeit in part because of the victors' self-limitation. Ludendorff had originally intended to pull out German troops after reaching the Tagliamento, although when Below decided to continue beyond it he acquiesced. But on 3 November he refused an Austrian request for reinforcements, possibly because of the continuing British pressure at Passchendaele, and insisted the Piave must be the final objective. The attackers were hampered by logistical factors – they lacked bridging equipment, their supporting railways were inadequate, they had few draught animals, and their steel-tyred lorries rutted the mountain roads. Hence they could advance their artillery only slowly, and kept going partly by capturing thousands of horses and armoured cars. After 28 October rain began, the troops (many of whom stopped to pillage) grew weary, and supply from their distant railheads was increasingly difficult. Conrad belatedly launched a subsidiary attack from the Tyrol, but never came close to enveloping the Italians. When in November Ludendorff decided after all to launch an Austro-German offensive from the Trentino, the best opportunity had passed.[46]

The halting of the advance did not result, however, simply from the Central Powers' difficulties. The Italians called on their allies for aid, and strengthened their own resistance. On 28 October Britain and France decided to send troops. By 10 November the soldiers were at the front, and in total five British and six French divisions, as well as air squadrons, were deployed. British and French fighters outmatched the Germans and impeded daylight bombing raids, whereas the Italian air force had been almost driven from the skies. Allied pressure was also instrumental in the (long overdue) dismissal on 7 November of Cadorna and his replacement by Armando Diaz. Before his removal Cadorna had, however, decided to stand on the Piave, a position he had been preparing since 1916. To fall back further would expose Venice, whose loss would be symbolically disastrous and oblige the Italian navy to retreat 500 miles down the Adriatic coast to its next base at Brindisi. Furthermore the Piave line (which extended along the river and through the heights of the Monte Grappa massif and the Asiago plateau) was only seventy-five miles long, compared with a front of 180 miles before Caporetto. This abridgement would also save Austrian manpower, but by increasing the force to space ratio (which had been lower than on the Western Front) it favoured the defenders. This was just as well, as to begin with the Italians were heavily outnumbered, though as they called up their 1899 conscript class and reintegrated the *sbandati* the balance began to equalize. Fierce fighting continued for much of November, but by the end of the month the Austrians (who were now deprived of German help) were making no headway, while the Italians (with British assistance) staged local counter-attacks. In December the AOK slowed down and promised to assist the projected German spring offensive in the west, agreeing to launch no further big Italian operations without OHL's consent.[47]

A barrier was thus established behind which Italy could recover. But the campaign had alleviated the pressure on Austria-Hungary sufficiently for Ludendorff to concentrate his forces elsewhere. During December he therefore moved the German divisions from the Italian to the Western Front, whither most of the Anglo-French ones later followed. Nevertheless, the Italian theatre was now tied in more closely with the war as a whole. One indication was Italy's inclusion in the Supreme War Council established by the Allies at the Rapallo conference in November, a direct response to the need (highlighted by the defeat) for strategic coordination. The SWC was just one of a series of new inter-Allied institutions, into which Italy became embedded.* A second indication was America's declaration of war on Austria-Hungary in December, intended mainly to encourage the Italians, although Wilson avoided calling for the break-up of the Habsburg Monarchy and distanced himself from Italy's annexationist objectives. Admittedly, the Italian government itself seemed willing to reduce the latter when in March 1918 it asked the Vatican to extend a secret feeler to Austria-Hungary.[48] But as Rome became more willing to compromise, Vienna, flushed by victory, grew less so. The confrontation in the Veneto would not end yet.

The fortunes of the Central Powers were already reviving when the Bolshevik Revolution tilted the balance even more heavily in their favour. They had partly created their own good fortune through OHL's decision to facilitate Lenin's return home. If he had stayed in Switzerland the Provisional Government might still have collapsed, but more likely in favour of a moderate socialist regime that rejected an immediate peace. Against fierce resistance from within his own party, Lenin steered the Bolsheviks into opposition to the government and distanced them from the Mensheviks and the SRs, thus enabling them to capitalize on the surge of anti-war feeling after the Kerensky offensive and to pose as the one reliable bulwark against reaction after the Kornilov coup. The Bolsheviks did not come to power by democratic processes, which Lenin despised anyway, except if they suited his tactical purposes. None the less, between the two revolutions their popular support had increased spectacularly, as shown by their expanding membership, their successes in municipal elections, and their growing popularity in the soldiers' committees and the soviets.[49]

---

*On the SWC, see further below.

If Lenin was no 'bourgeois' democrat, neither was he a pacifist. Marx and Engels had judged wars by their class character and whether they were historically progressive, and Lenin subjected the First World War to a similar analysis in his 1916 essay on *Imperialism, the Highest Stage of Capitalism*. His 'Letters from Afar', written after the February Revolution, argued that only a seizure of power by a working-class government could achieve peace. The new regime should publish the inter-Allied secret treaties and call for an immediate ceasefire and a revolutionary war against governments that refused a peace based on self-determination for oppressed nations within Europe and for colonies overseas.[50] He was emboldened by the unrest spreading across Europe, and above all by the strikes and naval mutinies in Germany, which all the Bolsheviks recognized as the crucial domino. He claimed the chances of insurrection spreading from Russia were '99 to 100', though probably he was privately willing to sign a separate peace if these prognoses proved wrong. This was not because the Germans had assisted his return and were probably subsidizing his party,[51] but because if he had to choose, his priority would be destroying class enemies in Russia over spreading socialism worldwide.

By autumn the Bolsheviks were strong enough to claim power in the name of the Petrograd Soviet. On 25 September (O.S.) the Bolsheviks gained a majority on its executive committee, and Leon Trotsky, who had recently joined the party, becoming its chairman. Lenin now planned to stage a coup, ostensibly in the name of the soviets but in practice on behalf of his party, before the meeting of the All-Russian Congress of Soviets scheduled for late October (O.S.) and to present it with a *fait accompli*. He foresaw that civil war might be the consequence, and accepted it in the belief that his side would win. He also argued that the international situation was propitious, and that the party should act before the Provisional Government abandoned Petrograd to the Central Powers; in this sense the fall of Riga did indeed help to destabilize Russia as OHL had intended it should.[52] On 10 October (O.S.) the Bolshevik Central Committee voted by ten to two in favour of an insurrection, though without setting a date.[53] Preparations centred on the Petrograd Soviet's Military Revolutionary Committee (MRC), with Trotsky as its guiding spirit. Kerensky shared the Bolsheviks' willingness for a showdown, underestimating the depths of his unpopularity and believing that if his enemies staged an uprising he could crush them as he had in July. After the dispute between Lenin and his Bolshevik opponents about whether to launch a coup went public in the party press, Kerensky ordered the bungled preventive measures that brought matters to a head. His government announced plans to transfer the Petrograd garrison to the front, with the consequence that most of the troops transferred their allegiance to the MRC (23 October O.S.). On the 24th, he ordered the closure of two Bolshevik newspapers, and the MRC began implementing its defence plan. The railway termini, central bank, post and telegraph offices, and telephone exchange soon fell into its hands, and Lenin now insisted on the attack on the Provisional Government's headquarters in the Winter Palace that took place on the following day. Almost no troops were willing to defend the ministers, and Kerensky had already left the city. The October Revolution therefore witnessed less mass mobilization than occurred in February and fewer casualties, though the fighting in Moscow was much heavier. With backing from the left SRs Lenin won the Congress of Soviets' endorsement, although the Mensheviks and the right SRs walked out in protest. Support from the soviets was the new regime's sole claim to legitimacy.[54]

The Council of Peoples' Commissars, which Lenin chaired and which ruled increasingly by decree, was totally lacking in governmental experience, of war and diplomacy as well as of domestic administration. Trotsky, the People's Commissar for Foreign Affairs, found that his ministry officials walked out *en masse*; Krylenko, the People's Commissar for War, found that the acting commander-in-chief, General Dukhonin, refused his orders. Undeterred, the Bolsheviks began by following their predetermined path. Their Decree on Peace denounced secret diplomacy and proposed immediate negotiations for a 'just and democratic' settlement, without annexations or indemnities. Next, Trotsky published the secret treaties, including the Turkish partition arrangements, the Treaty of London with Italy, and the Doumergue agreement. To the embarrassment of the Allied governments, all this material entered the public domain; in Britain, for example, it was published in the *Manchester Guardian*.[55] The Allies refused to recognize the new government or to join it in peace negotiations (though they did establish unofficial contacts with the revolutionary regime). After the peace decree proved fruitless, the Bolsheviks sought an armistice. When Dukhonin disobeyed the order to discuss one, Krylenko took over from him and the general was murdered by his troops. The new government permitted army commanders to negotiate local truces, which covered much of the front even before a general armistice with the Central Powers was agreed on 4/15 December. Nothing did more to win the Bolsheviks' support among the army, and by the end of the year they controlled most of the soldiers' committees. After the ceasefire, however, the bulk of the remaining troops departed en masse to return to their homes and to take part in the agrarian revolution. Having on the whole hung together through the upheavals since March, the army finally disintegrated.[56]

The armistice was a simple document, effective for a month in the first instance.[57] The two sides would remain in their existing positions. The Russians wanted fraternization between the armies, which was permitted on a restricted basis. They also (possibly because of unofficial advice from the Americans) stipulated that neither side should make strategic troop movements unless these were already in progress. This insertion was intended to prevent the Germans moving troops away from the Eastern Front, but as OHL had already issued orders to most of the units concerned and the Russians could not police the ban it meant little.[58] The impact on the balance of forces in the west was therefore disastrous, and this, followed by legislation in January repudiating the tsarist government's debts to its partners and sequestrating their investments, fuelled the anti-Bolshevism of the Allies and their resistance to a general peace process. When Trotsky invited them to participate in the armistice negotiations, they ignored him. With little evidence yet of revolution in Germany or of concessions from Russia's former partners, the Bolsheviks opened separate peace negotiations with the Central Powers at Brest-Litovsk on 20 December (N.S.). Trotsky still hoped to play for time until revolution spread or the peace negotiations became general. When neither of these eventualities materialized, in February the Central Powers imposed their terms at OHL's insistence.

To begin with, however, the differences between the two sides were veiled. The Germans and Austrians played the Russians along in order to widen the rift between the latter and their allies. But the Bolsheviks' motives for entering negotiations were in good measure propagandist. They insisted on the meetings being open, and at once published every word of their stenographers' transcripts. Lenin instructed his chief representative, Adolf Joffe, to demand a peace without annexations or indemnities and based on national self-determination. In the first session Joffe duly set out six principles that included evacuation and no annexation of territories taken during the war, no indemnities or unequal trade treaties, independence to be restored for nationalities deprived of it since 1914, and nationalities deprived of their independence before that date to be able to decide their future by referendum.[59] As the legatees of a multinational empire the Bolsheviks had attempted to apply these principles in their own domains. Their Declaration of the Rights of the Peoples of Russia called for 'a voluntary and honourable union' between the empire's nationalities. Lenin was willing to permit secession by Finland, which he hoped would inspire revolutionary movements elsewhere, and he conceded independence to a conservative government in Helsinki. Poland, which the Central Powers controlled and to which the Provisional Government had promised independence, was another special case. Lenin hoped, however, that the remaining nationalities would choose a continuing union with Russia. The critical case was the Ukraine, where the Rada, or assembly, announced after the Bolshevik coup that it was assuming power. At first Lenin offered it a federation, but in December an ultimatum was sent to Kiev and the Ukraine Bolsheviks set up a rival government in Kharkov. Nor were plebiscites held elsewhere in Soviet-occupied territory.[60] On nationality policy, as in other areas, the Bolsheviks quickly departed from their previously declared principles. They were on precarious ground in standing on the self-determination principle at Brest-Litovsk, and shortly they would be hoist with their own petard.

For peace to happen it was necessary not only for the Russians to ask for it but also for the Central Powers to concede it. The issue was complicated by disagreements between Vienna and Berlin and between OHL and the German civilians. During 1917 it had seemed that Austria-Hungary and Germany might finally be reaching consensus over their eastern war aims. As foreign minister, Kühlmann attached high priority to the alliance with Vienna and reinvigorated the *Mitteleuropa* negotiations.[61] In October he and Czernin agreed in principle that Poland should come under Austrian sovereignty but be in military and customs union with Germany, while Austria-Hungary and Germany would agree to a mutual assistance pact, a military convention, and tariff cuts. Vienna was also to accept German predominance in Romania, whose wealth in oil and grain had fired Wilhelm II's imagination.[62] However, whereas Kühlmann was impressed by the pro-German turn in Austrian policy, Hindenburg and Ludendorff saw the Habsburg Monarchy as a potential enemy. They would accept Austrian sovereignty over Poland only if Germany annexed a broad frontier strip, including some 2 million Poles, to protect the Upper Silesian industrial area and the communications between East Prussia and the rest of Germany. Kühlmann and Hertling, on the other hand, opposed incorporating large numbers of non-Germans, and the Austrians rejected sovereignty over Poland on these conditions. More fundamentally, Kühlmann and Hertling hoped not to estrange the new Russia permanently but to turn both it and Austria-Hungary into dependent German partners. Hence Kühlmann resisted OHL's plans to annex the coastal provinces of Lithuania and Courland, in order to protect the German minorities there, secure access to food production, and (as Hindenburg characteristically put it) control them as a manoeuvring ground for his left flank in the next war. Kühlmann was willing to return the Baltic coast to Russia if Germany ceded nothing in the west. He successfully evaded commitment over the region, and went into the Brest-Litovsk negotiations without clear instructions about either the Baltic or Poland. Indeed he told the Reichstag that he would adhere to the July 1917 peace resolution formula of no annexations or indemnities, although this wording still permitted more subtle forms of aggrandisement.[63]

Because of Czernin and Kühlmann's negotiating strategy, such vagueness did not initially matter. The two men set the guidelines for all four Central Powers. Czernin judged that even if the Bolshevik regime proved ephemeral (as most observers expected) a ceasefire would detach Petrograd from the Allies and enable the Russian soldiers to drift back home, thus preventing any resumption of fighting. By repudiating annexations and indemnities, the Central Powers could draw the Bolsheviks into a separate peace, but they would keep a free hand in the territories they had occupied (none of which were ethnically Russian) by stage-managing declarations of independence.[64] Kühlmann agreed with the conception. Germany's position was already safeguarded by a 'Council of Regency' in Poland, while in Courland a nominally representative body had appealed for the Kaiser's 'protection'. Self-determination could therefore be manipulated in order to push back Russia's borders and create a belt of ostensibly independent buffer states. On this basis, Czernin and Kühlmann were able to score a propaganda triumph with their 'Christmas Declaration' on 25 December 1917, offering to negotiate a general peace without annexations and indemnities if the Allies would do likewise. They reassured the nervous Turks and Bulgarians that as the Allies were hardly likely to accept, the Central Powers would not be risking anything. Indeed the Allies failed to respond to the declaration within the time limit, whereupon Kühlmann declared it void.[65] All the same, it had grave repercussions. In Austria-Hungary some of the Czechs and Slovaks and South Slavs issued an 'Epiphany Declaration' on 6 January, committing themselves for the first time to sever all links with the Monarchy.[66] In Germany, OHL had not been consulted beforehand, and Hindenburg and Ludendorff were predictably incensed. Hertling backed his foreign minister, insisting that the politicians were constitutionally responsible for peace negotiations, but Hindenburg and Ludendorff insisted on their duty before their consciences, history, and the German nation for the shape of the peace. Eventually Wilhelm, for once asserting his rights as an arbiter, endorsed a statement by Hertling that the Christmas Declaration was a legitimate 'move in the political game', that annexations in the east should be minimized, and that co-operation with Austria-Hungary was of cardinal importance.[67]

When the peace negotiations resumed (with Trotsky now leading the Bolshevik delegation) the Central Powers dropped the mask. They rejected demands to evacuate the occupied territories before plebiscites were held, maintaining that the inhabitants had already stated their wishes. They stipulated that Russia's frontier should run from Brest-Litovsk to the Gulf of Riga – in other words depriving it of most of Poland, Lithuania, and western Latvia. Moreover, south of this line lay the Ukraine, whose grain reserves both sides coveted and which itself became the crucial test of self-determination. In January representatives arrived at the peace conference from the Rada, or parliament, in Kiev, whose forces were now at war with the rival Bolshevik regime at Kharkov. The Rada had voted for Ukrainian independence and for a separate peace with the Central Powers, which would deprive Russia of much of the economic base for its claim to great-power status. While Trotsky tried to spin out the negotiations, OHL wanted 'clarity' in the east and was losing patience – as was Czernin, who desperately needed Ukrainian cereals in order to head off what he feared were quasi-revolutionary conditions in Austria's cities.[68] Yet the food crisis weakened his bargaining position relative to Germany, whose military strength would be vital to defend the Ukraine if the Bolsheviks attempted to overrun it. It also weakened him in relation to the Rada, which demanded the cession of the Cholm district in Russian Poland, where it claimed there was a Ukrainian majority. This issue was crucial, as the Habsburgs' ability to govern by consent in the Austrian half of the Monarchy depended on the Polish parties in the Reichsrat. But conceding the Ukrainian demands might deprive the Monarchy of this final basis of support, and so indeed it proved. On 9 February the Central Powers signed the peace treaty with the Ukraine, which promised to deliver more than a million metric tons of grain by 1 August. Austria-Hungary promised to grant autonomy to its Ruthenian (i.e. Ukrainian) minority, and the Ukraine was promised Cholm. Mass demonstrations followed in the Polish cities, and the Polish auxiliaries serving with the Habsburg forces mutinied. The Poles in the Reichsrat went into opposition, and declared themselves in favour of independence. Short of massive repression (from which Karl recoiled), little chance now remained of holding Austria-Hungary together.[69] The Ukrainian treaty also brought to a head the confrontation between the Central Powers and the Bolsheviks. Trotsky refused to recognize it and on 10 February walked out of the conference, declaring a condition of 'no war, no peace'. Russia would not accept annexationist peace terms, but it was unilaterally demobilizing its forces. Germany and Austria-Hungary now had to decide whether this was enough.

By this stage it was becoming evident that no revolutions in Vienna and Berlin would save the Bolsheviks. True, during January not only were the Dual Monarchy's nationalities radicalizing their demands, but an anti-war protest erupted. On the 14th the Austrian government announced a severe cut in bread and flour rations, provoking a general strike for peace that started at the Daimler works in Wiener Neustadt and spread through most of the Vienna region, some 750,000 people taking part. The strikers wanted better rations and an end to military discipline in the factories, but also a speedy peace at Brest-Litovsk, without negotiations being stymied by excessive demands. The Social Democrats supported the movement but they also channelled it by calling on the strikers to form workers' councils and formulate a four-point programme. Once the authorities agreed to meet the Vienna workers' council the party called for a return to work, and the strike ended after ten days.[70] It crumbled in the face of government concessions and socialist intercession, although it helped to push Czernin into conceding the

Ukrainians' demands. It was not dealt with primarily by repression, which was just as well because the armed forces were also restless. Over 400,000 returnees from Russian captivity were reintegrated into the army in spring 1918, but (like much else arising from the ceasefire with Russia) they proved a mixed blessing and contributed to a wave of revolts over the next few months. In early February 4,000 sailors mutinied at Cattaro, protesting against inadequate rations, excessive discipline, and officers' privileges, but also demanding national self-determination and a peace without annexations. However, this movement collapsed without a struggle and forty mutineers were court-martialled (of whom four were executed), the socialists co-operating in keeping the incident secret.[71] Even if the Monarchy was losing control of its nationalities, it was just about able to keep its workers and its armed forces in line.

The same was true in Germany, though here more coercion was used. The German pot came to the boil just after the Austrian one, and in part because of its example. On Monday 28 January 200,000 went on strike in Berlin, and by the end of the week the figure had reached 500,000 in the capital and many more elsewhere. This was a more politicized movement than in Vienna and the strikers did not make wage claims. It was prepared and led at plant level by the radical shop stewards' movement led by Richard Müller; the socialist trade unions opposed it and stayed neutral. The USPD supported it after it began, mainly because the party suspected excessive demands were stalling the Brest-Litovsk negotiations. More reluctantly, the SPD did so too, though probably more in protest against the recent obstruction of a franchise equalization bill in the Prussian parliament. Both parties joined a workers' council elected by the strikers, which called for a general peace without annexations or reparations, democratization of the Prussian franchise, better food, an amnesty for political prisoners, and an end to the army's special powers. This was not a revolutionary socialist programme, but it was a democratic one, and in contrast to Vienna the authorities refused to negotiate, breaking up meetings, suspending the SPD newspaper *Vorwärts*, arresting leaders, placing factories under military direction, and conscripting 50,000 strikers into the army. The military chiefs saw the SPD as revolutionaries and did not – or would not – acknowledge the party's role in moderating the unrest.[72] They wanted the strike suppressed and moved up troops towards Berlin. After a week the movement collapsed with nothing achieved. Its defeat silenced the German working-class movement until the autumn (unlike the aftermath in Vienna, where there was another strike in May), and killed any hopes that the Allies and Bolsheviks had placed in it. Resistance from within the Central Powers would prevent neither the Brest-Litovsk peace treaty nor Ludendorff's March offensive.[73]

The Bolsheviks' hopes of drawing in the Allies bore little more fruit. The Western leaders shunned both the armistice and the peace negotiations. All the same, after the Decree on Peace, the publication of the secret treaties, and the Christmas Declaration they could hardly simply stay aloof without courting a public relations disaster. Winter was always the most testing season for civilian morale, and now more than ever after the dispiriting campaigning of 1917, the Russian Revolution, and the first serious food shortages in London and Paris. Clemenceau's response was to silence the advocates of compromise, pursue defeatists, and to deflect all discussion of war aims. The Lloyd George cabinet, however, decided that British war aims needed repackaging. Its information was that trade union support for the war was ebbing and discontent among the troops was growing. The officially supported propaganda campaign by the National War Aims Committee was making little headway. On 29 November Lord Lansdowne, a leading Unionist and former foreign secretary, had a letter published in the *Daily Telegraph*, calling for Britain to confine itself to minimum aims and for a new joint definition of Allied objectives. Lloyd George believed the letter made a 'profound impression'.[74] The Labour Party's 'Memorandum on War Aims', approved by a special conference on 28 December, supported non-annexationist objectives. But in addition to the need to rally public opinion for a struggle that the cabinet now expected to continue into 1919,[75] an initiative was needed to split the enemy. Despite Czernin's turn towards the Germans, Austria-Hungary still seemed the best prospect, and a meeting took place in Switzerland in December between Smuts (who had joined Lloyd George's war cabinet) and the former Austrian ambassador to London, Count Mensdorff. The conversations ran into the usual deadlock, Mensdorff ruling out an Austro-Hungarian separate peace and offering mediation between the Allies and Germany, which Smuts rejected. Mensdorff did, however, call for Allied war aims to be reformulated, and a representative of the Turkish opposition signalled to Smuts that such a reformulation might weaken the Ottoman government. When Lloyd George delivered his Caxton Hall speech on war aims on 5 January the premier therefore had in mind a foreign as well as a domestic audience, though winning trade union support for new manpower plans was his immediate concern. Privately he denied the speech was a binding commitment, but it had cabinet approval and he had discussed it with the Liberal and Labour leaders as well as the Dominions before making it. It proposed that, outside Europe, the Ottoman Empire should be confined to ethnically Turkish regions, and the German colonies disposed of on a basis acceptable to their inhabitants – which was expected to mean that Germany would lose them. However, Lloyd George dropped a reference to the principle of self-determination when Hankey pointed out to him 'what a lot of trouble it would give the British Empire'.[76] Within Europe, Lloyd George gave only guarded support to Italy's territorial claims and even to France over Alsace-Lorraine. Austria-Hungary (provided it gave autonomy to its subject nationalities) should not be broken up, but unless Russia resisted 'enslavement' the Western Allies must abandon it to its fate. While Britain remained committed, then, to depriving Germany of Belgium and the Turks of Mesopotamia and Palestine, its support for Italy and France was qualified, and it seemed willing to abandon Russia to German domination. Compared to the statement of Allied war aims of 10 January 1917, Caxton Hall marked a retreat that left room for negotiations with Vienna and that would enable Germany to escape largely unscathed except for the loss of its colonies – a remarkable measure of the cabinet's pessimism.[77]

Caxton Hall was soon overshadowed by the address on 8 January in which Woodrow Wilson unveiled his Fourteen Points. This was much more directly a response to the Russian events. Within America, Wilson wanted to reaffirm his appeal to his traditional supporters on the progressive left, but his main intended audiences were overseas: the Bolsheviks (in order to keep them in the war), the opposition in the Central Powers, and socialists and progressives in Britain, France, and Italy. In addition he was serving notice on his allies to amend their war aims.[78] The Decree on Peace and the publication of the secret treaties placed him in an invidious position, given the discrepancy between the revelations about his partners' objectives and the principles laid down in his speeches. Initially he tried to address the problem by consultation, sending Colonel House to an important inter-Allied conference that met in Paris from 29 November to 3 December. Following on the founding of the SWC, this meeting wove a larger fabric of inter-Allied agencies, notably the Allied Maritime Transport Council (AMTC) to allocate shipping and the Inter-Allied Council on War Purchases and Finance to co-ordinate purchases in the United States. But attempts at diplomatic co-ordination were less successful. House wanted the Allies to refute charges of imperialism by denying they were fighting for the purpose of aggression or indemnity. Wilson telegraphed to him that the American people would not fight for the 'selfish aims' of any belligerent. The Colonel found Britain 'passively . . . willing' to support his declaration but France 'indifferently against it' and Italy 'actively so'. All that was agreed was that the Allies might reconsider war aims when Russia acquired a 'stable government'. The compromising disclosures from the Bolsheviks therefore remained unanswered, and in the face of this failure to reach a collective position Wilson acted unilaterally, consulting none of his partners before his Fourteen Points were unveiled. Nor did he consult his cabinet (though he took some advice from Lansing), House being his sole influential confidant.[79]

The president's speech differed considerably from Lloyd George's, notably in its call for Russia to be evacuated and left to develop freely. Points I–IV and XIV reaffirmed general principles that Wilson had stated already: open diplomacy, freedom of navigation on the seas in peace and war, the removal of economic barriers, the reduction of armaments 'to the lowest point consistent with domestic safety', and the creation of a League of Nations. The freedom of the seas was qualified by the possibility of internationally agreed blockades to implement international agreements and the third point meant not free trade (the United States itself being highly protectionist) but lower and non-discriminatory tariffs. But what made the speech innovative was its qualified commitment to Allied territorial aims. Belgium 'must' be evacuated and restored (Point VII), and there 'should' be an independent Poland with secure access to the sea (point XIII). But Point IX challenged the Treaty of London by specifying that Italy's frontier should follow 'clearly recognizable lines of nationality' and Point VIII was silent about French ambitions in the Rhineland and deliberately left some ambiguity about Alsace-Lorraine ('the wrong done to France by Prussia in 1871 . . . should be righted'). Like Lloyd George, however, Wilson did not mention national self-determination and was cautious about applying it. Thus there would be an 'impartial adjustment of all colonial claims' but only for Germany's colonies, the Allies' empires remaining intact. Points X and XII envisaged autonomy, not independence, for the subject peoples of Austria-Hungary and the Ottoman Empire (thus challenging the Turkish partition agreements). In short, the Fourteen Points would leave the Central Powers largely intact, obliged to 'restore' invaded territories but not otherwise suffering financial penalties or even being disarmed. While not denouncing the inter-Allied secret treaties explicitly, Wilson was strictly limiting what he would support, and as most of the points were prefaced with a 'should' he was not pledging the United States to fight on unconditionally. He offered a truncated and sanitized version of coalition objectives.[80]

The Fourteen Points later took on historic importance as the basis on which Germany agreed to a ceasefire, but their immediate impact was disappointing. Lloyd George and Clemenceau gave a non-committal welcome but no Allied government revised its war aims as a consequence or felt bound by the American programme, the British and French continuing to stand by the Turkish partition agreements and the Italians by the London Treaty. The Western European left welcomed the Fourteen Points more enthusiastically, but Brest-Litovsk and the German offensives did more than Wilson to reintegrate the labour and socialist movements into the pro-war consensus. As for the Bolsheviks, they placarded the speech on the walls of Petrograd, but it made Lenin no keener to continue fighting. Wilson's oratory seemed to have most effect on the Central Powers, for even if the January–February strike wave collapsed, the points re-inserted a wedge between Berlin and Vienna. Hertling grudgingly accepted the Fourteen Points in general but offered no concessions on specific ones, whereas Czernin was friendlier and appealed to Wilson to initiate general peace negotiations. In a follow-up speech on 11 February Wilson condemned Hertling and praised Czernin while announcing, in his 'Four Principles', a carefully qualified commitment to self-determination: that territorial settlements should be in the interests of the populations concerned and 'all well defined national aspirations' should be satisfied as far as was possible without generating international conflict. These provisos left room for discussion, and during February and March envoys from Karl again met British, French, and American representatives. But once more Czernin insisted that Vienna could make no separate peace. Finally during February Karl and Wilson exchanged correspondence directly through King Alfonso XIII of Spain, but the dialogue led nowhere. Wilson sought clarification of what autonomy the Austrians would offer their national groups; Vienna still refused to accommodate both Italy's claims on Austria-Hungary or France's on Germany.[81] In fact Czernin and Karl had probably decided to gamble on the outcome of the German spring offensive as the best hope of emerging from the war intact.[82] As ever, peace was on offer only if the Dual Monarchy would break with Germany and satisfy the Allies' demands. Once more it refused, and this was its final opportunity.

By the end of February the turmoil caused by the Bolshevik Revolution was subsiding and a new political landscape was visible. The Allies would not be drawn into the Brest-Litovsk negotiations; Vienna would not break with Berlin; revolution would not spread to the Central Powers; the Christmas Declaration was a subterfuge. Germany and Austria-Hungary planned to use a cloak of national self-determination to create a screen of eastern buffer states at Russia's expense. Trotsky's 'no war, no peace' gambit opened the way for crucial decisions on both sides: for the Germans to dictate a treaty, and for the Bolsheviks to submit to it. The German decision came at the Bad Homburg Crown Council on 13 February. Kühlmann argued for doing nothing and simply acquiescing in the Russian *fait accompli*, citing arguments that were plausible but turned out to be wrong: a new offensive would undermine political stability in Germany, and antagonize Vienna. Even if German troops reached Petrograd and the Bolsheviks signed, the latter might be overthrown, and blocking Russia's access to the Baltic would inhibit any later Russo-German rapprochement.[83] Ludendorff countered that resolving matters in the east would release divisions that were badly needed on the Western Front, whereas not doing so would risk abandoning Finland and the Ukraine to the Bolsheviks while Britain installed itself on the Baltic coast.[84] Victory in the east was possible, and Lenin's regime must be overthrown. This last consideration told with Wilhelm, who was infuriated by Trotsky's revolutionary agitation and favoured a 'police action' against Petrograd. Hertling was worried about the reaction within Germany and Austria-Hungary but gradually came round, safeguarding Ukrainian food supplies probably being the crucial consideration. Kühlmann was isolated and gave way. As all the participants recognized, Bad Homburg was a turning point that confirmed that peace would be imposed and a new German dominion carved out by force of arms. The goal of the advance was not – or at least not yet – to overthrow Lenin and Trotsky, but to compel the Bolsheviks to sign the peace.[85] But the terms would now be even harsher than those that Trotsky had rejected, and on 18 February the German columns moved forward.

They met no resistance, for since the armistice the old tsarist army had melted away. Lenin knew this, having been advised by delegates from the armed forces that they could neither resist the Germans nor defend Petrograd and he should make peace at any price. In his 'Twenty-One Theses' on 20 January (N.S.) he maintained it would be wrong to stake the survival of the revolution in Russia on the possibility of one in Germany, which was inevitable but not imminent. Without a German revolution a 'revolutionary war' was a 'romantic' policy that would lead to Russia's defeat, the overthrow of the Bolsheviks, and a new peace on worse terms. These inferences had the merit of realism, but most of the party leaders – and still more of the party organizations in the country – preferred resistance to accepting terms that Lenin acknowledged were scandalous. In the party's Central Committee on 8/21 January fifteen voted for a separate peace, but thirty-two for a revolutionary war and sixteen for Trotsky's middle course of 'no war, no peace', which rested on a wager that the Germans would do nothing and if it went wrong would at least make clear that there was no complicity between the Bolsheviks and the Central Powers. Assured by Trotsky that if the Germans called his bluff he would not support revolutionary war, Lenin decided to support the 'no war, no peace' position, calculating that it would mean the loss of more Baltic territory but the price was worth paying. Even so, he could not muster a majority for a separate peace until the Germans advanced, covering 150 miles in five days. When it appeared the Central Powers were no longer willing to make peace the Bolshevik leaders were prepared *in extremis* to seek assistance from the Allies, and the latter, for all their ideological distaste, would probably have given it; but as soon as the Germans communicated their terms the Russians accepted them, not bothering to negotiate in detail but preferring to swallow the medicine whole. Collaboration with the Allies, in other words, would have been conceivable only if the Central Powers had refused all compromise and had been determined to overthrow the regime. In the event, the aims of Ludendorff's operation *Faustschlag* or 'fist-blow' were more limited and on 3 March the Brest-Litovsk peace treaty was signed.[86]

Contrary to what Leninist analysis might have predicted, the treaty's economic terms were moderate.[87] The two sides reinstated their 1904 commercial treaty and Russia promised to stay out of any post-war Allied boycott of Germany. Russia would pay no reparations, though each side would reimburse the other for maintaining prisoners of war: an arrangement from which the Germans would emerge as big net beneficiaries. The territorial clauses were another matter. Russia signed away over a third of its population (some 55 million people, admittedly most of them ethnically non-Russian), much of its heavy industry and coal production, and its best agricultural land. It lost the Caucasus districts of Kars, Ardahan, and Batum to Turkey, and it recognized the Rada and evacuated the Ukraine. It also had to evacuate Finland and surrender sovereignty west of the Brest-Litovsk–Riga line, leaving Germany and Austria-Hungary to decide the fates of Poland and the Baltic provinces of Courland and Lithuania 'in agreement with their populations'. East of this line German troops would occupy Estonia and Livonia (further along the coast) until 'proper national institutions' had been established. As Lenin had foreseen, the price paid for going through the motions of 'no war, no peace' was the loss of two more Baltic provinces and allowing the enemy to move nearer to Petrograd.[88]

Brest-Litovsk therefore embodied the Kühlmann–Czernin concept of expanding the Central Powers' sphere of influence under the guise of self-determination. As the treaty contained no annexations or indemnities, the Reichstag ratified it easily, only the USPD voting against, while the SPD was divided and abstained. The other parties behind the 1917 peace resolution judged the treaty compatible with it, and voted in favour. Hence the collapse of resistance from the German parliamentary left followed on the collapse of the strike movement a month before. The Western powers, including Wilson, were disabused of any notion that they could appeal to the German opposition. Yet the crucial variable that ended the war in the east was the domestic change in Russia. Of the three elements (military, diplomatic, and political) in the post-1914 stalemate, the latter was the first to falter, giving the Central Powers the uncontested superiority needed to impose their demands. The Bolshevik regime sought an immediate general peace, but by signing the armistice it broke up its army, thus depriving itself of all bargaining leverage and being forced to conclude a separate settlement. Naturally, Lenin had no intention of abiding by it any longer than he had to; but nor had OHL, and Brest-Litovsk failed to halt military operations in the east. On the contrary, German expansion into former tsarist territory was only just beginning, while the treaty accelerated the drift of Russian internal conflict towards mass terror and civil war.

After his defeat at Bad Homburg Kühlmann put up less resistance to OHL, and Ludendorff was unwilling to restrain himself even though eastward expansion was starving his western army of desperately needed men. OHL lacked a grand general design, but aggrandisement continued via two main axes, along the Baltic and towards the Black Sea.[89] The Bad Homburg council agreed to occupy Estonia and Livonia, assemblies in the two provinces soon afterwards declaring independence from Russia and appealing for German protection. OHL wanted to protect the local German minorities and saw the region as an outlet for colonization as well as being strategically important for containing Russia and Poland. German hegemony in the Baltic threatened Petrograd, which Lenin evacuated in March, moving the Bolshevik capital to Moscow. Bad Homburg also (at OHL's behest and against foreign ministry wishes) approved intervention in the civil war that had broken out in Finland, on behalf of the Whites against the Bolshevik-backed Reds. Hindenburg and Ludendorff saw Finland as a source of nickel; Wilhelm hoped to place one of his sons on the Finnish throne. When 70,000 German troops were sent, the Reds were swiftly beaten. A friendship treaty bound Finland to make no alliance without German consent or raise tariffs against German imports, to accept German advisers, and to provide naval and military bases. Meanwhile the complementary German drive to the south-east began in the Ukraine, where Bolshevik troops menaced the Rada. With the Austrians in tow, the Germans moved in to restore the Rada to Kiev and to find food; in pursuit of coal to run the Ukrainian railways, they then occupied the Donets basin in the east of the country and overran the Black Sea ports. When the Rada defied them because their orders contradicted its land redistribution plan, they simply replaced it by General Pavel Skoropadsky. Under his authoritarian rule they obtained more horses and food, but never enough to do much more than feed the half a million troops tied down in the occupation, which faced increasing sabotage and peasant resistance. Even the Ukraine, however, was not the limit. In pursuit of the Russian Black Sea Fleet the Germans entered the Crimea, which had declared its independence and which Ludendorff (anticipating Hitler) saw as a terrain for German colonization. In May agreements with the newly independent state of Georgia gave Germany the right to use and occupy its ports and railways and to exploit its manganese. Russia's eclipse gave the Central Powers the opportunity to create a vast arc of satellite domains, extending hundreds of miles beyond the Brest-Litovsk boundary.[90]

The final element in the Central Powers' 'clarification' of the situation in the east was their peace treaty with Romania. After losing Bucharest and the south of the country, the Romanian government had moved to Jassy (Iasi) in the north. The Bolshevik Revolution and Russia's withdrawal isolated it from the other Allies, and when the Central Powers moved into the Ukraine they threatened it with encirclement. Moreover, Bratianu, who continued as premier after 1916, remembered the war of 1877, in which Romania under his father's leadership had joined the Russians against Turkey but at the peace had ceded Bessarabia to the tsar. After the Bolshevik Revolution he took advantage of an uprising by Romanian nationalists to reoccupy the province. In addition he feared (and with reason) that the Allies would renege on the promises made to him in the 1916 treaty, which was now an obstacle to their negotiating with Vienna. The Caxton Hall and Fourteen Points speeches, promising at most autonomy for the Habsburg subject peoples, seemed to contradict the Allies' earlier commitments and confirmed Bratianu's willingness to seek a separate peace. After signing an armistice in December 1917, he resigned in February and an all-party coalition under General Averescu began talks.

As it turned out the Central Powers allowed Romania both to keep Bessarabia and to cede relatively little territory elsewhere, largely because of disagreements among themselves. The Germans and Austrians wanted to restore their pre-1913 alliance with Romania, as a balance to a Bulgaria they distrusted. Hence Hungarian claims for a protective strip in the Carpathians were scaled back. The Bulgarians received the southern part of the province of Dobrudja, which had been promised to them in 1915, but wanted the northern part as well, which the Turks opposed unless the Bulgarians retroceded the land Turkey had given them as the condition for their entry into the war. In the end the northern Dobrudja was placed under a four-power condominium – an unstable arrangement that underlined how victory was exacerbating the divisions among the Central Powers. But if Romania got off lightly in terms of territory, in economic terms the Treaty of Bucharest in May 1918 was harsh. The Central Powers arrogated to themselves the right to purchase compulsorily Romania's harvest, as well as to fix its tariffs and control its central bank and foreign currency reserves. German-controlled companies would monopolize the pumping and marketing of its oil. Romania was the most striking instance of the Central Powers' indirect imperialism in action, an imperialism driven by the OHL's strategic concerns though also advancing the interests of the German banks, which had invested heavily in the country. Like Brest-Litovsk, the Bucharest treaty was a provisional document, but the two together demonstrate eastern Europe's likely future if the Central Powers had won.[91]

We now come to one of the most significant decisions of the war. Hindenburg and Ludendorff's all-out offensive in the west in spring 1918 opened the endgame. Its failure wrecked the German army and made possible an Allied victory that would otherwise have been delayed for at least another year and possibly might not have come at all. Yet from Berlin's perspective the alternative of a compromise settlement remained closed. The failure of Kühlmann's September 1917 feelers suggested that neither Britain nor France was willing to negotiate separately or give way over Belgium and Alsace-Lorraine; nor was Wilson prepared to talk until Germany had been democratized or at least had suffered a decisive defeat. Germany could have tried to unblock the diplomatic path by offering unilateral concessions. In particular, relinquishing Belgium would have given the British much of what they wanted and forced them to choose whether to fight on for Russia and for Alsace-Lorraine. Yet probably in such circumstances they would still have stood by their partners, and such a policy of renunciations (similar to that of Mikhail Gorbachev at the end of the Cold War) might have set off an uncontrollable process by demoralizing Germany's army, its home front, and its partners – as was indeed to happen in autumn 1918. But in any case Hindenburg and Ludendorff believed that a peace without tangible gains would undermine the Hohenzollern monarchy domestically and leave it vulnerable externally. Thus during the Brest-Litovsk negotiations Ludendorff exclaimed to Czernin, 'If Germany makes peace without profit, then Germany has lost the war!',[92] while Hindenburg warned Wilhelm that any peace must give Germany such powerful frontiers that its enemies would not start another conflict for years.[93] Similarly, in the west Belgium remained indispensable to OHL's security concept. Georg Wetzell (OHL chief of operations) wanted it as a permanent deployment base from which the German army could close off Calais as a British disembarkation point and could threaten to advance on Paris. Only thus could the Western Allies be deterred from attacking Germany, and defeated if deterrence failed.[94] On 11 December 1917 Hindenburg wrote to Hertling that as Kühlmann's feeler to Britain had failed and Germany's military situation had improved it should renew its claim to a 99-year lease on the Belgian coast and take the Liège area, keeping Belgium under military control until it was ready for an alliance with Germany.[95] Negotiation was now off the agenda.

So was the option of remaining on the defensive.[96] The U-boat gamble had brought America in while failing to knock Britain out. OHL paid close attention to U-boat building, but during 1917 and 1918 construction ran into difficulties despite receiving priority in labour and raw materials, and the submarine fleet failed to expand. Ludendorff and Colonel Bauer, head of the OHL economic section, doubted that the submarines would deliver decisive results in 1918 or stop US troops from being shipped *en masse* in the summer; indeed they may have overestimated the rate at which the Americans would arrive.[97] Once the US forces were in line, the outlook would at best be for a prolonged defensive, leading, as Hindenburg put it, to 'a gradual state of exhaustion'. Probably rightly, he and Ludendorff believed their soldiers dreaded more long defensive battles like Third Ypres. Reserves of men were running low, industrial productivity was waning, and even after the victories in Russia and Italy Germany's allies had less staying power than its enemies. If all hope of victory were lost, there would be no point in continuing the conflict. On the other hand they reasoned that even a failed offensive would encourage the army to try again in the next war,[98] and Ludendorff later told the Reichstag he was willing to lose a million men in the effort.[99]

Although OHL would probably have sought a western breakthrough even if Russia had stayed in the war, the Bolshevik Revolution made the chances seem unexpectedly bright. Germany could now look to a temporary superiority in manpower, in addition to its superior tactics and satisfactory equipment stocks. It had strengthened its eastern forces to deal with the Kerensky offensive, raising them to the highest level of the war. But from 1 November 1917 to 21 March 1918, according to the German official history, the Eastern Front divisions fell from eighty-five to forty-seven and those in the west rose from 147 to 191. Eight German divisions in Italy were also moved to the west, and smaller contingents from Macedonia, while a small Austro-Hungarian force arrived in France for the first time.[100] The highest-quality eastern units were transported, including guards divisions, and those left behind lost their men aged under thirty-five and fell well below strength, as well as sacrificing many of their horses. Also available to reinforce the western army was the 1899 conscript class, which came into the line early in 1918. As of 21 March the western army had 136,618 officers, 3,438,288 men, and 710,827 horses; the eastern army had respectively 40,095, 1,004,955, and 281,770.[101] Though mediocre, the latter remained numerically large, but fell further to 0.59 million personnel by July.[102] Despite Hindenburg and Ludendorff's pressure to resolve the Russian situation, in fact, most of the movement westwards preceded the Brest-Litovsk treaty, and afterwards it slowed down. On the other hand, Germany's political commitments in the east expanded. OHL stripped down its troop presence there, but not by enough.

As of 21 March, thirty of the eighty-one German divisions on the Western Front south of the river Oise had been moved from other theatres, as had eight of the thirty-three in Flanders.[103] The transfer from the east equalled more than half the size of the BEF at that date. By raising the German Western Front divisions to 191 against 178 Allied ones,[104] they gave the Germans numerical superiority for the first time since 1914. It is true that only one in six of the divisions that took part in the 21 March attack had been moved from other fronts,[105] but by holding quieter sectors the eastern forces freed up Ludendorff's best troops for the spring battles, much as the Americans later released British and French divisions. The figures illustrate, however, how OHL's hopes of breakthrough depended on the qualitative superiority of its existing Western Front armies rather than on quantitative reinforcement. Most of the best German divisions had always remained in the west, and by spring 1918 many had rested in quiet sectors for more than a year. Thus sixty-eight German Western Front divisions had missed the rigours of Third Ypres, against only nine British ones.[106] OHL counted on fresh but seasoned troops being schooled in the new tactics and achieving the breakthrough that had eluded their enemies.[107]

Ludendorff's choice of commanders showed the importance of the 1917 successes. Of the three armies that attacked on 21 March (from north to south, the Seventeenth, the Second, and the Eighteenth), the Seventeenth was commanded by Below, the victor at Caporetto, and the Eighteenth by Hutier, the victor at Riga, both men keeping their previous chiefs of staff. The Second came under Marwitz, the commander at Cambrai, whose new chief of staff had been involved in Galicia. Bruchmüller took charge of the Eighteenth Army's artillery and Behrendt (from Caporetto) of the Seventeenth's, but neither had overall authority, which proved unfortunate. OHL tried to distil the lessons from Caporetto, Cambrai, and Riga in its manual, *The Attack in Position Warfare,* published in January 1918 and distributed to every officer down to battalion commanders. It proposed to 'eat through' the Allied defences and regain manoeuvre, by keeping the enemy off balance, pressing the attack continuously, and reinforcing success. The artillery should strive for surprise, to neutralize and disrupt beforehand, and lay down a creeping barrage, but the infantry should set the pace of the advance, the lead units pressing forward without relief whatever the casualties (whereas British and French practice had been to relieve them during the action). The *Gruppe,* or section, of about nine riflemen and light machine-gunners under an NCO was to be the basic small unit, more specialized teams with flamethrowers and heavier weapons following on the advanced probe.[108] According to the newly revised *Training Manual for Foot Troops in War,* all soldiers should now be accustomed to assault squad methods. However, although Ludendorff took a close personal interest in training and tactics and intended to use the new methods on an unprecedented scale, he recognized that older men could not be recast as stormtroopers. He selected about a quarter of his infantry as 'attack divisions' formed of troops aged twenty-five to thirty-five, which were prioritized for food, new equipment, and instruction. The rest were designated 'positional divisions', which included a number of first-rate units but whose overall quality was poorer. Some fifty-six divisions were pulled out of the line in rotation for three weeks of intensive training, at first in old-fashioned drill (to restore discipline) and marksmanship, but progressing to fast long-distance marching, fighting on the move, and storming mock-ups of enemy trenches under live fire, while the artillery (often in conjunction) were trained in direct fire and rapid movement of their guns.[109]

The concomitant of the new tactics was new equipment. The army had no lack of the basics such as rifles and munitions. Pivotal for the assault divisions were the MG08/15 light machine-guns (for which production targets had not been met) and the MG08 heavy ones. Light mortars (*Minenwerfer*) were to be carried forward for use against determined resistance, and each division was to include a mortar company with medium weapons.[110] The 'Amerika Programme' for aircraft production had lagged behind schedule but now yielded increases in fighter strength. Total aircraft numbers had more than doubled from 1,200 in 1917 to 2,600, of which about 2,000 were available for active service in the west, new all-metal and single-wing models replaced earlier wooden types, and pilots were trained for ground attack as well as reconnaissance.[111] Yet although the army was well equipped to break into the Allied positions, for mobile warfare it was scarcely better placed than in 1914. It had 23,000 lorries but with the same steel tyres that had chewed up the roads at Caporetto: the Allies had 100,000 rubber-tyred vehicles.[112] Nor did the army have tanks (though even the fastest and lightest in 1918 were far from the weapons of 1940) apart from a handful captured from the Allies and its own prototype, the monstrously slow and unmanoeuvrable A7V. In his memoirs Ludendorff was unapologetic about tanks, expressing scepticism about their effectiveness and arguing that producing more would have meant sacrificing something else.[113] Yet they might have facilitated breakthrough operations with lower casualties, and manpower would soon become the Germans' most pressing concern.

OHL believed in its men – Hindenburg gave *Vertrauen* or trust, as his chief reason for confidence in victory[114] – but unlike at Riga or Caporetto they would face a first-class enemy and would enjoy no overwhelming advantage either in numbers or in *materiél*. Ludendorff considered he could mount only one attack at a time,[115] and he did not expect to finish the job at the first attempt, envisaging instead a succession of hammer blows. He told Wilhelm this would be the most colossal problem ever faced by any army: the offensive would begin at one point, continue at others, and last a long time.[116] None the less, since at least April 1917 he and Hindenburg had envisaged a great western offensive: the first (with the arguable exception of Verdun) since the Marne.[117] They and their advisers repeatedly described this operation as a 'last card': if it failed, said Ludendorff, 'Germany must go under'.[118] In October Wetzell had urged on Ludendorff an early spring attack in order to seek a decision in the west before the Americans arrived, even though at that stage he still expected Russia to remain a belligerent.[119] Ludendorff was already committed to the idea before the Mons conference of 11 November 1917, ironically held one year exactly before the end of the war. At Mons he and Wetzell conferred with the commanders of the two northern army groups on the Western Front, Crown Prince Rupprecht of Bavaria and Crown Prince Wilhelm of Prussia, and their chiefs of staff, Kuhl and Schulenburg. Ludendorff told the commanders (who were sceptical) that only the offensive could be decisive, that the troops wanted to go back onto the attack, and that Austria-Hungary and Turkey were nearing their limit. The meeting failed to agree on where the blow should fall, Kuhl wanting to strike the British in Flanders while Schulenburg preferred a new blow at Verdun.

Wetzell shared the latter view, considering the French army the larger and more dangerous antagonist yet also the one that held its front more thinly.[120] Ludendorff summed up by endorsing the principle of an offensive as early as possible, to give the maximum time before the Americans arrived. His preference was to attack the British, though not in Flanders but near St-Quentin, which was indeed what materialized. He believed he was not strong enough to defeat the French, especially as they had space to retreat, whereas the BEF was smaller and less skilful (which is not to say he treated it lightly). He ordered studies for a series of attacks, on Hazebrouck, Ypres, Arras, St-Quentin, Verdun, and the Vosges, but in January OHL settled on the St-Quentin operation (code-named 'Michael'), which on 10 March Hindenburg ordered for the 21st.[121]

Although Hertling and Wilhelm II approved the attack, they were consulted at a very late stage and appear not to have influenced the strategy, of which the political purpose was notably vague, Ludendorff saying the aim was to force Lloyd George and Clemenceau to negotiate before the Americans arrived in strength.[122] Nor were the operational objectives at St-Quentin particularly transparent. Ludendorff was preoccupied with the difficulty of the initial breakthrough and therefore selected the location largely on tactical grounds. Flanders was closer to the sea and to the Channel ports, but the terrain there was unlikely to dry out adequately until April, and he wanted to start sooner. Round Arras the British defences were formidable. Hence he opted for the less densely garrisoned southern section of the British line between Cambrai and St-Quentin and La Fère, where the land was relatively dry and flat. A breakthrough here would take no immediately important objectives, but it would enable him to pinch out at Flesquières the salient remaining from the Cambrai battle prior to a drive north-westwards that could separate the French and British armies and push the latter towards the sea. To some extent this conception mirrored that behind the battle of the Somme. Its danger, given Ludendorff's limited numerical superiority and his forces' lack of mobility, was that like Haig in 1916 he would deliver a blow into a void and then be halted in possession of ground that lacked strategic significance.[123]

None the less, Ludendorff was favoured – probably more than he realized – by the inadequacies of his opponents. The Americans were fewer than expected, the French and British were poorly co-ordinated, and (probably most important) the BEF's own defence measures were flawed. Between November 1917 and March 1918 the numbers of American troops in France rose from 78,000 to 220,000, though only 139,000 were combatants and of this potential of approximately six divisions, one at most was ready for action.[124] The reasons for this included the interval required to conscript and train the new divisions, as well as shipping shortages – although the Allies could have devoted more tonnage to troop transports, and after May they did. Moreover, the American commander, Pershing, backed by Wilson, still insisted on his forces developing into an independent army, and opposed even temporary amalgamation with the French or British because it might become permanent.[125] When in December 1917 Clemenceau complained that the AEF was unfit for battle and Pétain proposed that American regiments should be incorporated into French divisions for two months' training before they entered the line, Pershing still resisted, not only because yielding to the

French would set a precedent for the British, but also because he feared they would train his men only in 'trench warfare' techniques whereas he wanted them to learn 'open warfare' too. Eventually it was agreed the AEF's regiments would spend one month with French divisions until it had enough instructors of its own, but it would keep its operational independence.[126] Until May, Ludendorff's hammer blows would fall almost wholly upon the British and French.

During the 1917–18 winter the attempts of the Allies to reach agreement on a common strategic posture were largely abortive, and their failure contributed to a command crisis when Germany struck. The Supreme War Council established after Caporetto took the form of monthly meetings of the British, French, and Italian heads of government, while a committee of permanent military representatives (PMR) at Versailles acted as a secretariat, gathered information, and drew up plans for discussion. The PMR had advisory but no executive functions, and political rivalries complicated its work. Orlando nominated Cadorna to ease him out of his command role; Woodrow Wilson was reluctant to be committed politically, and although he appointed General Tasker H. Bliss as his military representative, he agreed only to an American diplomat acting as an observer at the heads of government meetings.[127] But the idea of the SWC had originated with the British, and specifically Sir Henry Wilson, who became the first British military representative, Lloyd George welcoming the opportunity for a more congenial source of advice than Robertson. From the beginning its decisions were contentious and hard to implement. When the heads of government asked the PMR to examine operations in 1918, the latter recommended staying on the defensive in France and Italy and attacking in Palestine and Mesopotamia only if no troops were diverted from the Western Front. Reflecting Henry Wilson's and Lloyd George's thinking, this recommendation was as much anathema to the French as it was to Haig and Robertson. However, Clemenceau reluctantly agreed to Middle Eastern offensives as long as Britain maintained its efforts in the west.[128] This debate had a bearing on Allied war aims (the Caxton Hall speech also underlining Britain's commitment to its Middle Eastern goals and its detachment from Europe) and also on two other issues discussed by the SWC. The first was the extension of the British sector. The BEF in May 1917 held 158 kilometres with sixty-five divisions and the French 580 with 109.[129] Although much of the French front was unlikely to be attacked, in Paris the disparity seemed excessive. The French wanted to release their older conscripts and Clemenceau hoped that making the British take on more line would hamper Lloyd George's activities in the Middle East, where France also had interests but lacked the strength to pursue them.[130] Lloyd George, in fact, welcomed the extension as a check on further offensives by Haig and he endorsed the principle. An agreement between Haig and Pétain therefore lengthened the British line by forty kilometres southwards to Barisis (just south of the Oise) in January 1918, but when the SWC asked for a further extension the British refused.

The most controversial proposal of all, however, was for an inter-Allied general reserve. On 2 February the governments approved a plan for the PMR under Foch's chairmanship to hold authority over a pool of thirty divisions as a reserve for the Western, Italian, and Macedonian Fronts. Henry Wilson was sympathetic, but Haig and Pétain were hostile, both because they rightly saw that it was linked to a rash scheme of Foch's for counter-offensives against the Germans, and also because they wished to control their reserves themselves. Clemenceau, apparently reluctant to ride roughshod over the two commanders, back-pedalled, but what killed the plan was civil–military infighting in Britain. The dismal outcome of Third Ypres and of Cambrai had dented GHQ's prestige, reducing its support from the Unionists and the press.[131] Indeed *The Times* was now openly critical. Moreover, Haig and Robertson had become estranged, Haig thinking Robertson not 'Western' enough. Haig's position became crucial when in February 1918 the High Tory *Morning Post* defied the censor by publishing an article denouncing the general reserve plan and condemning Lloyd George's 'incapacity to govern England in a great war'.[132] The incident brought civil–military tension to a head and Robertson was demoted. Wilson replaced him but only with the more restricted powers held by the CIGS before Robertson had taken up the post. In fact Wilson resembled Robertson in wanting to concentrate forces on the Western Front while also being sympathetic to imperial considerations, but he had better personal relations with Lloyd George and reasonable ones with Haig. The latter's price for not supporting Robertson was the destruction of the general reserve. He warned Lloyd George he would resign rather than assign troops to it, and once he refused Pétain did so too. In early March the SWC abandoned the scheme (over Foch's vehement protests but with Clemenceau's acquiescence) and approved a bilateral agreement between Haig and Pétain. If Haig's southernmost Fifth Army were attacked, the French would either take over a portion of its line or reinforce it with six divisions, Haig conversely undertaking to provide assistance if the French were the target.[133] It is doubtful if the general reserve scheme was much of a loss, and in the first phase of the German attack the bilateral arrangements worked quickly and effectively. All the same, Haig lived to regret them.

The most serious Allied weakness was not the collapse of the general reserve but the inadequacy of the British authorities' own preparations. Afterwards Haig and GHQ tried to blame this on factors outside their control, notably the extension of the British line and the government having starved them of troops.[134] They did so with some justice: in January the British sector was extended by about a quarter, the French appear to have handed over the line in mediocre condition, and the BEF received no compensating increase in its fighting strength, which was lower than a year before. The statistics became a political football, but – according to the War Office returns – although the total strength of the Expeditionary Force increased between the start of 1917 and the start of 1918 the number of combat troops fell from 1.07 million to 0.969 million, or by about 4 per cent.[135] Between January and November 1917 the BEF had suffered nearly 790,000 casualties, and in October the new Director of National Service, Auckland Geddes, said the home economy could spare no more men. Two debates followed. One was over whether Britain should adopt a more technology-intensive warfare, using tanks and other equipment to economize on manpower and save lives. Churchill, now munitions minister, led the advocates of 'new' tactics; Haig and GHQ were more conservative and reserved about the tanks' mechanical reliability and ability to substitute for infantry as a means of holding ground. The difference was partly one of nuance, and had more of a bearing on offensive than defensive operations. Churchill's advocacy won increasing support in the War Office but GHQ remained unpersuaded and actually tried (though unsuccessfully) in spring 1918 to reduce tank shipments to France.[136] The BEF experienced no big increase in weapons deliveries, but it lacked the personnel to use the equipment in any case, as a result of the second debate. On 26 November the war cabinet agreed that Britain must be able to continue fighting if necessary into 1919. It appointed a committee on manpower, which endorsed Lloyd George's emphasis on 'staying power' until more Americans arrived. The first manpower priority should be the navy, followed by shipbuilding, the air force, and naval aircraft production, then agriculture, timber felling, and building food stores, with the army at the bottom of the list. The military wanted 600,000 category 'A' men (the strongest and fittest) withdrawn from civilian life by November 1918; the manpower committee decided to allocate only 100,000.[137] More could have been provided, and in the emergency after the Germans attacked they were, so that in the event 372,330 category A men were made available by November. In addition to able-bodied civilians, around 175,000 trained soldiers were kept at home from January 1918, in part as a precaution against attempted invasion and internal unrest.[138] But until the German offensive the cabinet suspected that if it sent the men Haig would waste them in fruitless assaults, depriving Britain of the chance to contribute decisively in the final campaigns. Furthermore, partly because of Haig's advice, ministers underestimated how dangerous a German attack might be. In consequence not only was the BEF thinly stretched but also GHQ had to carry through a reorganization that the Germans and French had already implemented and the cabinet had long envisaged, namely of avoiding reducing the number of divisions by instead cutting the number of battalions in each division from twelve to nine. Excepting the Dominion divisions, between January and March forty-seven divisions lost three battalions each, a process carried out quickly and without warning. The reorganization probably disconcerted many men who were moved from their old units; it may also have exacerbated the stress of garrisoning the trenches. Because each division kept the same length of front, the first line would have to be garrisoned more weakly or the infantry rotated out of it less frequently.[139] Even allowing for the handicaps imposed on the BEF from outside, GHQ's new defensive dispositions probably made matters worse.

This is not to say that Haig got everything wrong. The government had insisted on GHQ being reshuffled after Cambrai, Lawrence replacing Kiggell as chief of staff and the very able Brigadier-General Cox replacing Charteris as head of intelligence and keeping Haig accurately informed about the movement of German divisions to the west. From December Haig expected a German attack in the New Year, and he ordered the BEF to construct a system of defence in depth. In February he correctly predicted a first attack in late March between Lens and the Oise, followed by a second one in April near Ypres. He was advised, following Riga, to expect a surprise bombardment followed by infiltration tactics.[140] Unfortunately the BEF was unused to defensive fighting and particularly to the system GHQ ordered, which rested on a misunderstanding of German defensive practice in 1917. The system comprised three zones: the forward zone, a 3,000-yard battle zone, and a rear zone four to eight miles behind it. The first zone, comprising 'outposts' rather than a continuous line of trenches, was to be held to the last man and in greater strength than by the Germans, and the battle zone was to be held rigidly. Counterattacks would be less speedy and automatic than under the German regime, fewer response troops being stationed in the rearward area to deliver them and less discretion being delegated to their commanders, in keeping with the BEF's more hierarchical practice.[141] In reality the Third and Fifth Armies hardly prepared the rear zone at all, and 84 per cent of the British battalions were within 3,000 yards of the front line (and therefore more exposed to bombardment) against a maximum of 50 per cent under the German system, while relatively few troops were available to relieve the 'redoubts' in the battle zone.[142] Gough's Fifth Army actually placed half its machine-guns in the forward zone, contrary to GHQ orders. This was the more serious because of a second weak point in the British scheme. The three most northerly British armies (the Second, First, and Third) all held their fronts more densely than the Fifth, and Haig's eight reserve divisions were in the north as well.[143] The Fifth Army held the newly acquired southern-most sector more thinly, and Haig had authorized Gough to conduct if necessary a fighting retreat towards the Somme, precisely because it was furthest from the coast and could yield ground most safely; it was also the army that Pétain would reinforce under the bilateral agreements. Haig may have planned, in fact, to hit the German advance in the flank, and he had been using the labour that was not preparing the battle zones to build lateral railways in the rear. If so, these dispositions were almost literally unhinged when Ludendorff's attack proved so strong that, as one historian has put it, it did not simply push on a revolving door but burst it out of its frame.[144]

Despite the retrospective apologias, Haig and his commanders were confident, even complacent, before the attack; indeed, on its very eve Haig approved special leave for 88,000 troops. The general staff in Whitehall held back the so-called 'mobile reserve' in Britain because of his assurances that he could withstand any attack for eighteen days.[145] On 7 January he reported optimistically to the war cabinet and on 2 March he told his army commanders (echoing Joffre before Verdun) that his only fear was that Germany would hesitate to strike.[146] Gough was similarly bullish, denying the Germans would break his line.[147] The Allies seem to have fallen victim to a deception campaign; Ludendorff launching raids and bombardments all along the front so as to obscure where the blow would fall.[148] The Germans also concealed the attack zone by moving up infantry at night, covering ammunition dumps, and battling to keep air superiority. The British found it difficult to take prisoners, and the prisoners knew nothing. None the less, from 9 March onwards a million soldiers were converging on the battle area and British overflights began to notice warning signs. By the 19th GHQ expected an attack within the next two days. On the eve GHQ and Haig himself had the locality and timing approximately right, but they foresaw initially a limited 'wearing-out' attack, similar to their own procedures, which would give them time to react.[149] What they got was the greatest onslaught since 1914.

The bombardment for the 'Michael' offensive began at 4:40 a.m. on 21 March and continued through seven successive phases until zero hour at 9:40 a.m. To a British machine-gunner 'It seemed as though the bowels of the earth had erupted, while beyond the ridge there was one long and continuous yellow flash. It was the suddenness of the thing that struck me most, there being no preliminary shelling but just one vast momentary upheaval.'[150] The Germans employed half their guns on the Western Front, some 6,473 in all (including 2,435 heavy pieces), plus 2,532 trench mortars, compared with the 1,822 guns at Caporetto and 680 at Riga, or the 1,437 British guns before the Somme. This was not, in fact, an enormous density along an attack front of some fifty miles, but the barrage was intense and accurate, firing off some 1.16 million shells in five hours, compared with 1.5 million fired by the British over seven days in June 1916.[151] It concentrated first on the artillery and command posts and later on the British first position before lifting to a rolling barrage when the infantry attacked, mixing high explosive with phosgene shells and a new lachrymatory gas designed to irritate men so intensely that they would tear off their masks. The infantry assault was equally prodigious, Ludendorff having assembled seventy-six of his 191 western divisions, thirty-two of them in the first wave with another twenty-eight to thirty-two following up. Despite the hunger in their stomachs, the German troops looked forward to success, to booty, and to finishing the war, and their commanders shared their confidence.[152] As Albrecht von Thaer put it, the attack had loomed before them like a 'dark curtain'.[153] The British Third and Fifth Armies opposing them comprised some twenty-six infantry divisions (twenty-one of which had fought at Third Ypres) and three cavalry divisions, whereas barely half the Germans had undergone a major battle in recent months. Between them the British armies had some 2,804 howitzers and guns.[154] The Germans' numerical advantage was probably proportionately less than the British had enjoyed at the start of Third Ypres,[155] but their achievements had no precedent since the start of trench warfare. They advanced up to eight miles and took 98.5 square miles of territory in one day, as much as the Allies had gained in 140 days on the Somme. German losses have been estimated at 39,929 (10,851 killed, 28,778 wounded and 300 prisoners of war), but they inflicted about equal losses on the defenders – 38,512 (7,512 killed, 10,000 wounded, and 21,000 prisoners of war) – as well as capturing some 500 British guns. These totals compare with British casualties on 1 July 1916 of 57,470 and German ones of 8,000.[156] The Germans everywhere overran the British forward zone, and along the southern quarter of the front they got through the battle zone too: a stunning contrast with the dismal Allied record since 1915. The Germans were lucky in the dense fog that lingered until noon and blinded the British defenders, who with some 6,000 machine-guns in the forward and battle zones (compared with the mere 200 with which the Germans had wrought such havoc on 1 July 1916) might otherwise have inflicted far greater damage.[157] But the paralysing deep bombardment and German infiltration tactics had their impact too, pulverizing the British front line and destroying the command stations behind it. Nor did the bombardment wreck the ground, which was flat, dry, and firm. The strongpoints in the forward zone were quickly by-passed and, although resisting more fiercely than the Italian ones at Caporetto, mostly surrendered once it was clear that they had little chance of being relieved. Many units simply disintegrating. The British artillery was in the dark, giving little support to the forward zone, and counter-attacks could not be ordered. The excellence of German tactics therefore underlined the inadequacy of the British defensive system and the mistakes of the BEF leaders. Byng, the Third Army commander, probably delayed too long before evacuating the Flesquières salient. Gough had left too many men too far forward, but once he ordered his subordinates to pull back they went further and faster than he had intended; this may have been just as well, as the territory relinquished was dispensable.[158]

The Germans still fell well short of Ludendorff's goal of breaking clean through on day one. None the less, on the evening of 21 March Gough ordered a general retreat behind the Somme and the Crozat canal. In contrast the Third Army, which was Ludendorff's real target, held better prepared defences more densely and with fewer men in the forward zone and it delayed the progress of the German Seventeenth and Second Armies, but gaps opened up between Byng and Gough and by the 23rd the Germans had broken a forty-mile wide hole into open country. The Allies now went through days of acute anxiety. At first the bilateral agreement seemed to work well. Haig's diary entries suggest that he and Pétain were agreed the two armies must hold together, and that Pétain was anxious to support him and was moving up reinforcements.[159] The French had accumulated a reserve of some forty divisions in contrast to Haig's eight, but Pétain's intelligence warned of a possible second German stroke in Champagne. However, he fulfilled and went beyond the agreement, offering three divisions on the 21st and three more on the 22nd, and on the 23rd promising another fourteen. On the latter day the first French troops arrived to help the British, and even if the general reserve had been created it is questionable whether assistance could have come faster.[160] Dramatic though the stormtroopers' initial progress had been, it took them three days to get through the defences, and this gave Haig and Pétain time to move up reinforcements. The 88,000 British troops on leave, as well as the mobile reserve, were rushed across the Channel. By the 23rd, however, Haig wanted twenty more French divisions to help cover Amiens, and this Pétain refused.[161] Both commanders now came to fear that co-operation would break down and their armies would be separated. Pétain issued orders on 24 March that his concern 'above all' was to keep the French army intact and only then to keep contact with the BEF. On the same day he told Haig that his instructions were to cover Paris at all costs, even if it meant leaving the BEF's right flank exposed. He feared – and with justification – that Haig envisaged retreating towards the Channel ports.[162] In fact the latter had decided to call for a mission from Britain and to accept subordination to a French generalissimo in order to get extra French divisions north of the Somme. Henry Wilson and Lord Milner, a member of the war cabinet, came over to confer with the commanders and Clemenceau. At Compiègne on 25 March and at Doullens on the 26th Pétain's pessimism made a bad impression on the politicians, in contrast with the insistence by Foch (who did not hold executive responsibility) that he would move in all available troops to keep the two armies together. At Doullens, Milner, Haig, and Wilson agreed with the French leaders to charge Foch with responsibility, acting in consultation with the national commanders, for 'the co-ordination of the action of the Allied armies on the Western Front'.[163]

Doullens was a moment of high symbolism, but not much more. Although Haig felt relieved, the war cabinet was infuriated over Doullens, Lloyd George telling Milner that a French commander in chief was impossible.[164] Foch had no staff and as a co-ordinator his function was ill defined. It is unclear what difference his appointment made. He told Gough to retreat no further, but the latter continued to do so. Haig, however, was dissuaded from contemplating a retreat to the Channel ports and Foch ordered Fayolle (who commanded the French reserve divisions) to retain contact with the BEF at all costs. Pétain cancelled his 24 March order and seven more French divisions were ordered up on the 26th, Pétain having apparently decided the German offensive was now so big that no danger could exist elsewhere. Moreover at a further conference at Beauvais on 3 April Foch gained responsibility for 'the strategic direction of military operations', and authority to order offensives, although Haig and Pétain remained responsible for 'the tactical conduct of their armies' and could appeal to their governments against him.[165] Events now seemed to have vindicated his appointment. But in fact, although the Allied leaders could not yet see it, by the time of Doullens the Germans were losing impetus anyway.

The German breakthrough forced critical decisions on both sides. Ludendorff's intention was to breach the defences and advance north-westwards. But the greatest success had come in the south, rather than between Cambrai and St-Quentin, and he decided to reinforce it by supplying Hutier's Eighteenth Army with six more divisions.[166] On 23 March he gave new orders to progress along three axes, the aim being to divide the French and British and drive the latter into the sea by advancing along both banks of the Somme. But on the 25th he further fragmented his plan, deciding instead of reinforcing Hutier to order an attack ('Mars') on the strong British positions round Arras, which took place on the 28th and was halted in a few hours. At this point he gave up hope of a general breakthrough with this offensive and authorized a new attempt in Flanders for early April, but in the meantime he concentrated on trying to sever the north–south trunk railway behind the British line. This meant pushing the Eighteenth Army through to Amiens, or at least capturing the high ground at Villers-Bretonneux from which the city could be bombarded.[167] After failing to do either, and given his determination to attack elsewhere rather than risk re-running a battle of attrition, on 4–5 April he called 'Michael' off. His constant telephone calls to his subordinates and his rapid changes of direction testified to his nervousness and uncertainty of purpose. Had he reinforced Hutier earlier, Amiens might have fallen; or by continuing north-westwards he could have threatened Arras. In the end the offensive conquered a huge new salient but no strategically significant objectives, and it weakened the Germans for their next attack. But, as always, at least as important as the actions of generals and politicians were those of soldiers and junior officers on the ground. Even when the Germans reached open country they faced more organized resistance than after Caporetto, the Allies improvising defence lines on woods and waterways as they fell back. After the first day, Ludendorff's men often abandoned infiltration for old-fashioned close-order attacks, presenting conspicuous targets and taking heavy casualties. The lifting of the fog assisted British machine-gunners while the RAF strafed the advancing enemy. The Germans became separated from their own artillery (one third of which was destroyed during the offensive), especially after they entered the wasteland of the 1916 Somme battlefield where it was difficult to construct roads and field railways. Like Moltke four years earlier Ludendorff was defeated partly by the difficulty of feeding and supplying his men once they had pushed more than forty kilometres beyond their railheads. The leading troops, who carried only two days' rations, were becoming exhausted, as they were expected to keep on the move and take casualties without relief for day after day. The army had disbanded much of its cavalry, it had too few horses and too little fodder, and its lorry fleet was far inferior to that of the Allies. Notoriously, German troops were distracted by the food and drink in British depots, but although this delayed the advance and exposed the junior officers' lack of control over their men it also highlighted deeper logistical weaknesses.[168] By the time of Doullens the Seventeenth and Second Armies were encountering increasingly stubborn resistance, and Hutier's army drove into a sack, Amiens remaining tantalizingly beyond its reach. Ludendorff might have done better with a more single-minded strategic purpose, but if the Allies maintained their resistance 'Michael' was always unlikely to prevail.

Nevertheless, by the time Ludendorff closed the operation he had done enormous damage, capturing 90,000 prisoners and 1,300 guns and killing or wounding some 212,000 Allied troops,[169] although his own dead and wounded numbered 239,000. His new line was not particularly favourable, but he held on to it in order to threaten Amiens.[170] By the end of the battle Haig had committed to it forty-eight of his fifty-six divisions, and the French a total of forty; by 3 April Haig was being left with just one division in reserve.[171] Hence the Allies faced a second emergency when after less than a week Ludendorff began a second offensive ('Georgette') on the river Lys. After another Bruchmüller bombardment, the German Fourth and Sixth Armies attacked on 9 and 10 April on a front of twenty miles rather than fifty, with twelve assault divisions out of a total of twenty-seven involved (in contrast with forty-seven assault divisions used for 'Michael').[172] They had 2,208 guns and 492 aircraft. Because of the cost of 'Michael', 'Georgette' was smaller than originally planned and used troops of lower quality. Further, although the Germans showed impressive logistical capacity in striking again so quickly, this time they marched by daylight and the Allies had more warning. All the same, Haig had expected a blow further south, and the British repeated some earlier mistakes. The best units in their First and Second Armies had been sent to the 'Michael' battle, and the attack sector was thinly held by six British divisions (five of which had been in the southern fighting) and two Portuguese ones. The bulk of the German assault hit a single Portuguese division holding six miles of front, which Horne, the First Army commander, had not relieved or reinforced despite intelligence warnings.[173] GHQ's guidance to commanders about the defence-in-depth system remained inadequate, and some units applied it but others did not. In fact a traditional use of machine-gun outposts and a trench line instead of a 'battle zone' halted the southern German attack, but further north the Portuguese broke and as they retreated the adjoining units had to do likewise, outposts being encircled and the command chain severed.

By the 12th the Germans were again able to break through on a front of thirty miles, forcing the British precipitately to evacuate their dearly won gains in the Ypres salient and fall back to the gates of the city. Haig issued what became a famous order, that 'with our backs to the wall we must fight it out to the end', which impressed the young VAD nurse Vera Brittain, though it seems simply to have caused more cynicism among the troops.[174] Yet once again, by the 18th reinforcements were moving up and the line was re-established. Ludendorff had judged that with the mild spring the ground was dry enough, but his troops still found the marshy Lys valley (bristling with machine-guns) difficult going and they ran ahead of their artillery. His senior commanders lost control of the battle and their subordinates again ordered costly mass attacks, although the troops were now refusing to undertake them and once more were distracted by supply dumps.[175] But Haig had hardly any reserves and found Foch more parsimonious with assistance than Pétain had been, the generalissimo fearing that the Lys was a diversion from a larger German operation planned elsewhere. Until 19 April Foch resisted sending reserves north, despite Haig exercising his right to appeal to his government, though in the end Foch sent twelve French divisions.[176] Even after they arrived, Mount Kemmel (one of the few dominating positions round Ypres) fell on the 25th. Yet despite British recriminations about the quality of the French reinforcements, the latter were crucial in repelling the final German assault on 29 April by firing off vast quantities of shells and machine-gun rounds. After this Ludendorff called 'Georgette' off, again without reaching the crucial targets. The Germans remained five miles from the railway junction of Hazebrouck, and failed to gain Cassel, from which their long-range guns could bombard Boulogne and Calais. They did, however, inch closer to Amiens in a second attack on Villers-Bretonneux, and the British marshalling yards behind the lines in Flanders were now more vulnerable to gunfire and air attack. The cost again was heavy: some 146,000 Allied killed and wounded and 109,000 Germans. But by the end of April both of Ludendorff's first onslaughts had stalled.

There was now a loaded pause. The interval was in itself a telling comment on the Germans' failing strength, given Hindenburg's strategic concept of 'so shaking the enemy building by closely sequenced partial blows that it . . . collapses'.[177] However, in May and June a more or less co-ordinated attack was unleashed by the Germans against the French and by the Austrians against the Italians. This time, however, the Allies finally got the measure of the new tactics. It is best to begin with the Austrians, and the road to the battle of the Piave, whose origins went back partly to the continuing struggle between Karl and Czernin. The eastern peace treaties appeared to vindicate Czernin's policy of co-operating with Berlin, although they brought little improvement in food supplies. But early in 1918 Karl multiplied his feelers to all the Allies, even while Czernin insisted that Austria-Hungary would never make a separate peace. A nervous man, divided in his loyalties, Czernin apparently hoped the Ludendorff offensives would chasten the Allies sufficiently to allow a general settlement. He decided to flush out the separate peace lobbyists round the emperor known as the 'Meinl Group'. In a speech on 2 April he attacked Clemenceau for wanting to annex Alsace-Lorraine, and alluded to the latest round of Austro-French contacts. Clemenceau felt he had to retaliate against the insinuation that he had initiated conversations after telling the French people he was committed to victory, and he did so by accusing Czernin of lying. He lifted the veil on the Sixtus affair, publishing the letter to the Prince of 31

March 1917 in which Karl had referred to French claims to Alsace-Lorraine. He scored a devastating propaganda victory.[178] Czernin obtained a signed statement from Karl (which both men knew was false) that he had never sent the letter, but the emperor then dismissed his minister, replacing him with Count Burián. The 'Czernin incident' further diminished Austria-Hungary's diplomatic independence. On 2 May Karl met the German leaders at Spa, and Kühlmann insisted he must accept the *Mitteleuropa* demands for an alliance, a military pact, and a trade convention. In addition the Germans obtained an agreement between Hindenburg and his Austrian counterpart, Arz von Straussenburg, that the two countries would mobilize every available man, co-ordinate training and deployment of troops, standardize weapons and munitions, exchange officers, and share war plans.[179] While Czernin's dismissal had alarmed the Austrian Germans and the Magyars, the other nationalities saw Spa as indicating total subservience to Berlin, a view shared by the Allies, who now doubted whether there was any point in letting Austria-Hungary survive. Karl could no longer clamber off the German locomotive before it hit the buffers.[180]

Before his fall Czernin had recommended a new offensive against Italy. Karl approved in principle and after the Czernin incident he probably hoped it would restore his stock in Germany.[181] Indeed the Germans insisted on it in return for food shipments, OHL welcoming the idea as a support for its Western Front attacks.[182] The Austrians hoped it would capture more supplies, make Rome negotiate, and guarantee for themselves some share in what they still expected to be a German victory.[183] Arz's officers had observed the Western Front offensives and he hoped to apply similar methods, as well as to synchronize the attack with the next German blow. The return of prisoners of war from Russia had restored the army to its regulation strength, and if it was going to attack it was better to do so before the Italians recovered any more.[184]

None the less, the Austrians laboured under many disadvantages. Karl compromised between the plans of Conrad, who wanted to launch the main offensive on the Asiago plateau, and Boroević, the commander on the Piave, who also wanted to deliver the principal blow. The emperor authorized offensives on both fronts, with the result that both were too weak. While Boroević tried to break the Piave line and advance on Venice, Conrad would attack the Monte Grappa massif. Austria-Hungary had sixty-five infantry divisions and twelve cavalry divisions in the Italian theatre, but this time it would have no German assistance, and it had only a bare superiority over the fifty-six Allied divisions, which still included a total of three British and French ones. The Allies had a more than twofold superiority in aircraft, and 7,000 guns and 2,400 mortars against 6,830 Austrian artillery pieces.[185] On paper Austria-Hungary had plenty of shells, but many were still in transit on the overstretched railway system when the battle began.[186] Some of the attacking soldiers had daily rations of only three ounces of meat and eight ounces of almost inedible bread: one incentive for them, like their German counterparts, was simply to lay their hands on food. In contrast, the Italian army had experienced an erratic but definite improvement in morale during the quiet spring months, and Allied front propaganda had more impact on the Austro-Hungarian army than the latter's had on the Italians.[187] Moreover, the Allies knew the 15 June starting date, thanks to interrogations of deserters and listening in on field telephone conversations. The assault began with a Bruchmüller-style bombardment that was relatively inaccurate because of a lack of aircraft and observation balloons, and ineffective because the Italians now had excellent British gas-masks. Nevertheless the Austrians established several bridgeheads and got 100,000 men across the Piave, but heavy rain and British bombers destroyed their pontoon bridges – another instance of airpower's growing versatility – and after an Italian counter-attack Boroević pulled his men back to the east bank. Conrad's attack in the Asiago and Grappa sectors was halted by the French and British and repelled by an Allied counterstroke. A week after the battle started it had ended with Austrian casualties and captured numbering 150,000 and Italian losses estimated at about 80,000.[188] In July Conrad was relieved of his command. An admittedly botched attempt to apply the new tactics for a second time on the Italian front had been halted in its tracks, and over the next three months disease and desertion reduced the Habsburg army by more than a third. Hindenburg and Ludendorff were dismayed, correctly recognizing that this would be the last time their ally would take the offensive.[189]

Meanwhile the German army plunged the Allies into one final emergency when between 27 May and 4 June it attacked in Champagne. During the Lys battle both OHL and the field commanders had observed that their troops' morale and effectiveness were dwindling rapidly. Thaer, who moved from Flanders to OHL in April, believed the infantry were 'more or less fought out': the best officers and men had been lost in the 'Michael' operation and the survivors were mortified that it had not ended the war.[190] The troops stationed in the Amiens salient found themselves in improvised and undermanned trenches.[191] Yet in May Thaer found Hindenburg and Ludendorff still confident and planning a long campaign, if only because the alternative was unthinkable – the Allies, said Ludendorff, were making no peace offers and he rejected a 'peace at any price'.[192] Flanders was still crucial, and Hindenburg hoped that by taking the coast he could close off the Channel and use long-range guns against the English south coast and even London.[193] But the French were supporting the British too strongly for either Amiens or the coast to be attainable, and in Wetzell's thinking it was time for a surprise attack against the French front, both for political impact and to draw off reserves before a renewed assault in Belgium.[194] Despite enormous casualties the German army was still well supplied with munitions. It was reincorporating prisoners of war from Russia and moving divisions from the east: some six in April and two in May.[195] After the Lys Ludendorff halted to allow rest, retraining, and re-equipment, and further refined the new tactics. The infantry received more light machine guns, rifle grenades, and anti-tank rifles, and were given machine guns to protect supply columns against aircraft.[196] All the same, the 27 May attack (codenamed 'Blücher') followed the usual basic formula. The selected sector was the Chemin des Dames ridge north of the river Aisne between Reims and Soissons, and the original intention was for a brief operation that would take the ridge and the Aisne before halting after twelve miles along the river Vesle.[197] Having rebuffed Nivelle's assault in April 1917 the Germans had abandoned the Chemin des Dames after Pétain's Malmaison offensive in October. They selected it now because retaking it would threaten Paris, and they knew it was weakly defended. Bruchmüller orchestrated his most intensive barrage yet, concentrating 5,263 guns against 1,422 British and French ones, the most favourable ratio the Germans ever enjoyed on the Western Front.[198] They fired 2 million shells in little more than four hours[199] before attacking with fifteen divisions and twenty-five more following on: a smaller force than 21 March but substantially larger than on the first day of 'Georgette'. Once again they struck in fog, and once again their enemies were unprepared.

The Germans faced sixteen Allied divisions: four French and three British ones in the first line, and seven French and two British in reserve.[200] The British, in the east of the sector, had been detached from the remainder of the BEF and sent there to rest. British intelligence had predicted an attack and local commanders had noted German registration, but the French Sixth Army chief, Duchêne, refused to believe an offensive was possible. Disregarding a directive from Pétain that the first line must be used to slow the enemy down, the bulk of the defenders being concentrated in the second position, Duchêne insisted on holding strongly his forward zone, north of the Aisne, with the result after the Germans broke through that the Allies' main battle zone was almost undefended. Pétain's defensive doctrine had met with scepticism from Clemenceau and Foch, who thought it too cautious and perhaps were reluctant to abandon French territory, and partly to avoid a clash with them Pétain had acquiesced in Duchêne's dispositions.[201] Hence in the face of Bruchmüller's bombardment and an assault by seasoned infantry the Allied defences melted away on the first morning.

The Germans crossed marshes, scaled a 300-foot ridge and traversed the Aisne, which was up to sixty yards wide, taking the bridges intact and pushing on through the second position into open country, advancing up to thirteen miles and reaching the target line in the afternoon. Even on 21 March they had achieved nothing like this. Ludendorff authorized them to continue and by the end of the third day they had moved forward up to thirty miles. Advancing against exhausted British troops who had lost much of their heavy equipment and had to resist with rifles and light machine-guns, the Germans did relatively little fighting, but carried mobile trench mortars, machine-guns, and field artillery in their first line behind an advance screen of scouts. Conversely, the Allied reserve divisions, which had slowed down 'Michael' and 'Georgette', were this time further away. During the May respite Foch had revived his plans for counter-offensives, despite objections from Pétain and Haig. Correctly divining Ludendorff's ultimate intentions, he kept most of the Allied reserves behind the British army. He did not foresee the Champagne offensive and at first dismissed it as a feint. On 27 and 28 May Pétain sent up the thirty divisions under his own control but Foch refused to release the French reserves in Flanders, and Clemenceau, though fearing that Paris was the Germans' objective, hesitated to press him. By the 29th the Germans were back on the Marne and by 3 June Paris was only fifty-six road miles and thirty-nine direct miles distant.[202]

The attackers had taken 50,000 prisoners and broken the trunk railway line from Paris to Nancy, for smaller losses than in the earlier offensives. And as they intended, their actions caused a loss of political nerve. On 5 June the British cabinet discussed evacuating the BEF.[203] Up to a million people fled from Paris, a city that during 1918 suffered not only from air raids but also from the Germans' 'Paris gun', which from March until the Germans were pushed out of range in August fired 283 shells against the city from fifty-five miles away and killed 256 people.[204] None the less, Clemenceau defended Foch and Pétain in an agitated Chamber of Deputies and shielded them against criticism from his allies at the SWC session in June. When the Germans reached the Marne Foch released more troops from Flanders, and French troops stabilized the river line with significant American assistance. By now the advance was losing impetus and once again Allied storage depots detained the invaders. Pétain's strategy was to hold the heights round Reims and Soissons as 'breakwaters'. Instead of feeding men in piecemeal he organized a ring defence with artillery support, following a line of natural barriers from the Villers-Cotterets forest to the Marne and Reims.[205] On 2 June twenty-five French and two US divisions counter-attacked, the Americans clearing out the Germans in a celebrated action at Belleau Wood.[206] The forward drive was halted.

Hindenburg and Ludendorff recognized in retrospect that they had let the advance run on too long.[207] Whereas in March Ludendorff had hesitated to reinforce Hutier's success, this time he sent in extra units and instead of contenting himself with a shallow salient on the Vesle he drove his men into a sack forty miles deep, serviced by only one railway near its western edge and vulnerable on both flanks. Yet he was reluctant to relinquish it, and an operation intended to divert French reserves from Flanders ended by distracting the Germans from what Ludendorff still considered the vital battleground. From May to July Champagne and the northern approaches to Paris remained the focal point of the fighting while Germany's margin of superiority ebbed away. Ludendorff knew that American forces were reaching Europe even faster than he had thought possible; the equivalent of fifteen divisions arrived between April and June.[208] During June, up to half a million German soldiers contracted influenza, this being the first of two great waves of 'Spanish flu' during 1918. Both sides suffered, but the undernourished Germans earlier and more severely. Stuck in the new salient, OHL was forced to postpone its planned renewal of the Flanders offensive (codenamed 'Hagen') and attempted instead to renew the threat to Paris and broaden out the salient by attacking near its northwestern corner. The result, from 9–11 June, was the fourth hammer-blow offensive, christened 'Gneisenau' by the Germans and by the French 'the battle of the Matz'.

The Matz followed on so quickly from the previous operation that the troops again had to move by day and French aviators detected the preparations. Georges Painvin, a codebreaker working for GQG, decrypted a German radio signal calling for accelerated munitions deliveries to the Eighteenth Army, which enabled the French to pinpoint the attack sector. Deserters reported the date would be 7 June, though in fact it was postponed for two days.[209] But this time the Germans would not benefit from surprise. Foch recalled French divisions from the British sector and obtained five American divisions that were training with the BEF. Haig still feared for Flanders and refused to send British divisions, appealing to his government for backing, but he did carry out a redeployment that enabled Pétain to gather reserves. The French Second Army had prepared – if incompletely – a defence in depth, and the Allies began a counter-bombardment fifteen minutes before the German attack.[210] Despite being preceded by another Bruchmüller barrage, and again being delivered in fog, the German assault used only nine under-strength divisions, whereas the defenders had seven in the front line, five in the second, and seven more close at hand. There was no rout, and the Germans were halted after six and a half miles. On 11 June French troops under General Charles Mangin counter-attacked from three sides and Ludendorff, surprised, abandoned the operation. German casualties were 25,000 and French 40,000.

The Matz was a limited battle: Ludendorff showed a greater willingness than before to cut his losses and Foch and Pétain halted the counter-offensive on 15 June in order to conserve men. Even so, it had a significance comparable to the Marne in 1914 (or Stalingrad and Alam Halfa in 1942) in that what seemed an irresistible offensive technique had been stopped, using superior intelligence, timely reinforcement under the aegis of an Allied generalissimo, and appropriate defensive tactics. Ludendorff had failed to reduce the vulnerability of the Champagne salient, and his strategic dilemma remained unresolved. He could neither abandon it nor hold it, and the same applied to his gains in the north. During the spring and summer the Germans captured ten times more territory than the Allies had done in 1917, and extended the length of the front between Verdun and the Belgian coast from 390 to 510 kilometres.[211] But their casualties were nearly a million, and although British and French losses were also enormous the Allies could count on American reinforcements. After the March offensive the Allies opened the floodgates, and over 200,000 Americans disembarked in every month between May and October. The total of American personnel in France rose from 284,000 on 30 March to 1,027,000 on 20 July and 1,872,000 on 2 November.[212] The new German salients threatened Allied communication nodes and Paris itself, but could be expanded no further. Mid-June 1918 marked the end of the run of military and political success for the Central Powers that had begun the previous autumn. As much of this success had rested on tactical superiority rather than greater resources, once that superiority was lost the balance would swing massively and the Allies' underlying advantages come fully into play against an enemy who in many ways had been weakened by triumph. It was time for the Allies to regain the initiative.

✦ CHAPTER 16 ✦

THE TURN OF THE TIDE, SUMMER–AUTUMN 1918

I N S U M M E R 1918 the long chain of Allied defeats and rearguard actions ended. Like the Central Powers in 1917, the Allies began their revival with counterattacks: on the Matz on 11 June and on the Marne on 18 July. But they went on to launch offensives, starting east of Amiens on 8 August and then through a succession of operations during August and September, including, in the St-Mihiel salient, the first big action by the American army. Finally on 26–28 September they launched converging assaults along much of the Western Front, from Flanders to the Argonne, an exercise attempted in September 1915 and April 1917 but now repeated on a vaster scale and much more successfully. Other offensives starting in Macedonia and in Palestine on 15 and 19 September routed the Bulgarians and the Turks, followed in October by an Austrian rout in Italy. At sea the U-boats were beaten back and in the air the Allies consolidated their superiority in all theatres. This transformation was sudden. Whereas in June Russia was lost, Paris endangered, and many Allied leaders feared defeat was imminent, at the end of September their enemies cracked, first Bulgaria and then the other Central Powers suing for a ceasefire. The nearest parallel to these events had been the co-ordinated offensives of summer 1916, but the strain imposed by that endeavour had plunged the Allies into months of crisis. This time, in contrast, the Central Powers sank without trace. Their eclipse resulted partly from their own over-extension. But it also confirmed the Allies' growing military effectiveness, which had developed since the middle of the war yet been obscured during the long months of Ludendorff's onslaughts. In analysing these developments it is necessary to begin with the Western Front, which was now more clearly than ever the decisive theatre, before considering what lay behind the startling Allied recovery.

The previous chapter took the story to the end of Ludendorff's fourth attack. It was over a month before he struck again, on 15 July, and by the time he did the numerical balance had turned against him. Yet in the meantime it seemed to be business as usual for the Germans. At the Spa Crown Council on 2 July, only four months before their defeat, Hindenburg, Ludendorff, and Hertling agreed on a new secret western European war aims programme similar to those of 1917, and rejected an 'Austrian solution' for Poland in favour of OHL's preference, the 'candidate solution': Poland would choose its sovereign but Germany would command its army and control its railways as well as annexing a wide frontier zone.[1] Absent from Spa was OHL's *bête noire*, foreign minister Kühlmann, who had intensified their distrust of him when at a conference held at The Hague in early June to discuss an exchange of prisoners of war he had authorized his representative to signal to the British that Germany would accept a *status quo* peace in the west. This initiative led nowhere, but it clashed with Ludendorff's continuing determination to keep Belgium under economic and political control,[2] and the breaking point came when Kühlmann told the Reichstag on 24 June that the war could not be resolved by military means alone. The Conservative and National Liberal party leaders condemned the comment as a sign of weakness, and Hindenburg and Ludendorff won another scalp by insisting with Wilhelm that unless the foreign minister went they themselves would go. Kühlmann's successor, Paul von Hintze, was not a career diplomat but a hard-bitten naval officer, whom Hindenburg trusted to sort out the foreign ministry,[3] and Ludendorff assured him that the next assault would be decisive.

If OHL held its ground over war aims, its strategy was increasingly contested. After the Matz, most of the army commanders wanted to wait before striking again, but Ludendorff rejected going over to the defensive, which he said would discourage Germany's allies and put an even greater strain on his troops. Instead he planned one more big attack at the tip of the Champagne salient formed in May, which would draw off Allied divisions by establishing bridgeheads across the Marne, threatening Paris, and cutting the Paris–Nancy railway. Two weeks later (and this expectation showed remarkable confidence in his logistical flexibility) the long delayed second Flanders blow against the British would finally force the Allies to submit.[4] Foch, on the other hand, had concluded from the Matz that the answer to German tactics comprised better intelligence (to avoid surprise), adequate forces in the first and second positions, and reserves to hold the two sides of any bulge formed and to counter-attack as soon as possible.[5] His problem during June was lack of information. He thought the next attack would come in the British sector, and asked Pétain to send artillery to Flanders, but the latter resisted and appealed to his government, though Clemenceau refused to back him.[6] Foch agreed, however, to recall French forces sent to the north of the front in return for Pétain restoring four British divisions to Haig. Additionally he asked Pétain to prepare a counter-offensive to capture the high ground west of Soissons, which would enable the Allies to bombard the main communication artery into the Champagne bulge. These measures gained in relevance when it became clear by early July that the next attack (which OHL did little to conceal) would come on the Marne, but that the Germans were also preparing an attack against the British sector. Hence, as before the battle of the Matz, the Allies had time to move up artillery, aircraft, and infantry. Pétain accumulated thirty-five French divisions in reserve; moreover, between April and July the numbers of the French army's fighter aircraft rose from 797 to 1,070 and it took delivery of over 500 Renault light tanks.[7] Hence the French planned both to meet the German attack head-on and to strike against its flank, their preparations for the second battle of the Marne echoing those for the first, four years previously.

When Ludendorff's *Friedenssturm* (or 'peace assault') began on 15 July, the French again surprised the Germans by delivering a counter-bombardment. The German attack was much bigger than the one on the Matz, being delivered with fifty-two divisions against thirty-four. Yet east of Reims, where the local comman-der, Gouraud, had followed Pétain's directions and adopted defence in depth, even an assault on this scale was halted on the first day: the French artillery fired 4 mil-lion 75mm shells during the battle and destroyed all twenty of the tanks (captured from the Allies) that the Germans used in support. West of Reims, however, where too many French troops were concentrated forward, the Germans crossed the Marne. Pétain committed all the manpower at his disposal and held them along the river by 17 July, but he wanted to cancel or postpone the planned counter-stroke. Foch, however, insisted that it went ahead. On 18 July, therefore, Mangin struck again with eighteen divisions (including the First and Second American Divisions) that had moved up secretly and hidden in the Villers-Cotterets forest. There was no prior registration and the troops advanced through open cornfields behind a creeping barrage and with over 300 tanks, the light Renault models prov-ing much superior to the St-Chamonds that had failed under Nivelle.[8] The Ger-mans held only shallow defences, and were outgunned, under-strength, and completely surprised, Ludendorff having already begun withdrawing artillery for his Flanders attack. To begin with, they put up almost no resistance, and the Americans advanced more than five miles. Subsequently, as the tanks broke down and machine gunners delayed Mangin's forces, Ludendorff suspended the troop movements to Flanders and his commanders organized a fighting retreat.

By the time the battle ended on 4 August, the Allies had captured 30,000 pris-oners and over 600 guns as well as re-establishing the transverse railway link be-tween Paris and Châlons-sur-Marne, although their casualties numbered 160,000 against 110,000 German ones.[9] They had not just halted but also thrown into re-verse an offensive launched with all the strength at OHL's command. The threat to Paris was much diminished, and Ludendorff's dilemma over the Champagne salient was settled by his troops being bundled out of it, leaving much of their equipment behind. Indeed, he was nonplussed by the Villers-Cotterets counter-stroke, reacting on 18 July with a furious and public row with Hindenburg. Ac-cording to his subordinates Ludendorff was nervous and agitated, losing self-control, blaming all around him, immersed in detail, and unable to take big de-cisions. Lossberg, the mastermind of Germany's defensive successes from Septem-ber 1915 to the Somme and Passchendaele, wanted to retreat to the Hindenburg Line and prepare a fallback position from Antwerp to the Meuse, but Ludendorff rejected this course as politically impossible because it would dishearten the army and public while buoying up the Allies. Despite abandoning the Champagne salient, he refused a more general withdrawal, though on 22 July he effectively called off the Flanders offensive by reassigning the troops concerned in order to strengthen his line elsewhere.[10] On 2 August he ordered his commanders to adopt the strategic defensive, and although he hoped soon to return to the attack he could not do so.[11] He never fully recovered from his quasi-breakdown, and two months later his symptoms returned with disastrous consequences. The Allies now had the edge in intelligence gathering, combined with artillery, tank, and aviation superiority and with American reinforcements, and they were at last positioned to make big territorial gains.

On 24 July Foch met Haig, Pétain, and Pershing at his headquarters. He circulated a memorandum (largely the work of his chief of staff, Maxime Weygand) that showed considerable prescience. The Allies, it said, had reached the 'turning point': they now had the advantage and should keep it. In the first instance this would mean a rapid sequence of limited blows to clear the transverse railways running eastwards from Paris towards Avricourt and northwards towards Amiens, as well as pinching out the St-Mihiel salient in Lorraine; other operations might push the Germans back from the Channel ports and advance towards the Briey iron ore basin and the Saar coalfield. The contrast with the Somme strategy and with Foch's earlier thinking was evident: the Allies should deliver sharp surprise attacks aimed at concrete objectives, and suspend them before the enemy fed in reserves and casualties mounted, although success in this initial phase might enable more ambitious operations later. Foch had toned down his doctrinal preference for the offensive at the moment when at last the realities were beginning to justify it.[12] He did not expect victory until at least 1919, but he believed that the sooner it came the better placed France would be to benefit, and he was therefore a man in a hurry; too much so for the national commanders, who thought the 24 July memorandum too adventurous, although they were won over.[13] Indeed, though Pétain doubted whether the French army could handle many more offensives, Haig had just submitted a proposal for what became the battle of Amiens of 8–12 August. If the Marne operations between 18 July and 4 August cleared the Paris–Avricourt line, this new battle would clear that from Paris to Amiens, and in the process would demolish Ludendorff's last hopes of victory.

Operation 'Michael' had created a German salient in dangerous proximity to the trunk railway that connected Paris to the Channel ports and served as one of the main transverse links behind the British front. The Germans had increased their threat to the junction at Amiens when a follow-up attack in April captured Villers-Bretonneux, and they were now less than four miles from the line.[14] However, raids and other intelligence gathering had revealed that Marwitz's German Second Army was under strength and its defences were sketchy. Haig asked Rawlinson, the commander at the Somme who had now taken over the Fourth Army (the successor to Gough's ill-starred Fifth), to begin planning. When Rawlinson submitted his proposals on 17 July, Haig insisted, as in 1916, on a more ambitious target (an advance of twenty-seven instead of seven miles) and – again as in 1916 – Foch obtained agreement to a French parallel attack before he gave the scheme his blessing.[15] Little else about the scheme, however, resembled the 1916 battle. Rawlinson and the Australian commander, Sir John Monash, learned from the French counterstroke at Villers-Cotterets on 18 July as well as from the British tradition of tactical innovation that had led up to the battle of Cambrai and to the battle of Hamel on 4 July

1918. The latter had been launched against a weak German sector south of the Somme and had ended within two hours, achieving all its objectives with 1,000 Allied casualties and twice that number on the German side, half of them prisoners. Like Cambrai it had begun with a surprise bombardment by some 600 guns, the German artillery being silenced by gas shells while a creeping barrage had protected the advance by Canadian and Australian infantry (heavily armed with Lewis guns and equipped with grenade-throwing rifles against machine-gun nests) and sixty Mark V tanks, which were somewhat faster, better armoured, and more reliable than their predecessors. A gas and high explosive barrage beyond the attack zone had provided a curtain against a counterstroke. The battle of Hamel helped convince Monash, a careful commander who believed in protecting his men, of the value of tanks in infantry support. Further, it was a laboratory for ideas that were repeated on a much larger scale in the Amiens attack.[16]

The battle of Amiens was a spectacular massed tank operation, even bigger than Cambrai and the largest of its kind during the war. Swinton and the intellectual authors of the new weapon had always intended it to be used in such a fashion, and Rawlinson was persuaded to commit the entire tank corps fleet of some 552 vehicles, including not only Mark Vs but also the new lighter Whippet tanks (capable of up to eight miles an hour) and armoured cars. As at Hamel, they were moved up secretly, aircraft flying overhead to drown out the engine noise. With a local superiority of four to one in aircraft (many German planes were still in Champagne) the British and French pilots could prevent overflights and ensure surprise, as well as supporting the ground advance. None the less, revitalized traditional arms formed the core of Allied strength. Like Bruchmüller, the British artillery now aimed to 'neutralize' the enemy and keep his head down rather than destroy his defences. The British had many more heavy guns than in 1916, their fire was more accurate, and they had more munitions than they needed. While the heavy artillery silenced the enemy batteries with phosgene and high explosive, the field guns shielded the infantry with a creeping barrage. Ten divisions would attack along a similar width of front to 1 July 1916, but so much had divisions shrunk since then that the assault force probably totalled 50,000 instead of 100,000. However, the paucity of men was offset by greater firepower, each battalion carrying thirty Lewis guns instead of four, eight trench mortars instead of one or two, and sixteen grenade-throwing rifles.[17] They faced dispirited German units that had recently arrived in the lines, knew their positions only poorly, and were outnumbered two to one.

When the attack began at 4:20 a.m. on 8 August, without a preliminary bombardment, across dry ground and under cover of mist, it achieved even more dramatic results than the French counterstroke in July. By mid-afternoon the Allies had advanced up to eight miles, suffering losses of 9,000 but inflicting three times that number on their enemies, and capturing 12,000 prisoners and over 400 guns. Even beyond the creeping barrage, the attackers could still move forward, suppressing machine-guns with tanks, although most of the latter broke down or were hit by artillery as the day went on. On 9 August, although the Canadians advanced another four miles, they had to operate with far fewer tanks, and the heavy guns could not be moved up to provide accurate counter-battery fire, while the

Germans reinforced their air and ground forces. Almost as significant as the attack itself, however, was its suspension, for on 11 August Rawlinson, aware like Monash and the Canadian commander, Currie, of the mounting difficulties, called a halt. Foch wanted to resume the assault within days, but Currie persuaded Rawlinson to protest, and Haig rejected Foch's demands. The Allies would no longer batter away along the same sector beyond the point of diminishing returns. The secret of success lay not only in new technology and good preparation, but also in a willingness to halt while the going was good before starting again elsewhere. Extravagance with transport and *matériel* brought economy in lives.[18]

The battle of Amiens broke up six German divisions and safeguarded the town and the railway line. Final British and French casualties were each around 22,000; German, around 75,000, of whom 50,000 were prisoners.[19] Yet this was a shorter, smaller action than the second battle of the Marne, and much of its significance lay in its impact on OHL. The German army's official history called it the worst defeat since the start of the war; Ludendorff, in a much-cited passage in his memoirs, said the days after 8 August were the worst he experienced until the final collapse.[20] He was caught unawares as much as were his men, and was shaken by the evidence of their mass surrender. Parts of the army resisted with the usual tenacity, but if the rest had lost the will to carry on, the game was up.[21] Abandoning hope of regaining the initiative, on 13 August Ludendorff told Hindenburg that the only course now was a defensive strategy with occasional limited attacks in order to wear down the Allies and gradually force them to terms.

This did not mean, however, that OHL had given up on a favourable, or at least drawn, outcome. Hindenburg and Ludendorff revealed their pessimism to their staff subordinates rather than to Hertling and Wilhelm, and the effect on German policy as a whole remained slight. Ludendorff advised the emperor that the war had become an unacceptable game of chance and must be ended, but a new summit meeting at Spa on 13/14 August decided merely to extend a peace feeler after the 'next . . . success in the west'.[22] Nor were the Germans yet prepared to write off Belgium, and Ludendorff still rejected advice to retreat to the Hindenburg Line and envisaged a stubborn foot-by-foot defence. But the recent battles had demonstrated that this approach too was no longer sustainable. By wagering all on the offensive option, Ludendorff had sacrificed the defensive one, as now became all too evident.

The next phase was one of piecemeal Allied advances until mid-September, which drove the Germans out of the remaining territory they had occupied since March. In 1916 such gains would have appeared exceptional feats of arms. Now the recaptures of historic towns and piercing of fortification complexes became weekly news items. Foch's dread – which he wanted to keep in contact with the Germans to prevent – was that the enemy would withdraw to a shorter line, regaining the troop densities needed to hold out until winter and reconstituting a reserve for a counterstroke.[23] Given Haig's refusal to persist at Amiens, Foch consented instead to British operations further to the north. On 21 August Byng's Third Army opened the battle of Albert: a smaller operation than 8 August with only one third the number of tanks. Two days later the Fourth Army attacked on both banks of the Somme, breaking the Germans' old 1916 fortifications and pushing them back to the 'Winter Line', which Ludendorff had planned to hold for the rest of the year. On the 26th the First Army and the Canadians started yet another attack further north and the Winter Line was outflanked. On 2 September the Canadians smashed one of the strongest German defences, the 'Drocourt-Quéant switch', and OHL reluctantly withdrew after all to the Hindenburg Line, their last major prepared position.[24] Although the British took the leading role during August, the French attacked south of the Somme towards the Oise, and Mangin renewed the advance halted on 4 August towards the Aisne. In Champagne too the Germans lost their 1918 gains and retreated to the line of hills from which they had defied all efforts to dislodge them since 1914. Indeed in the east they withdrew further as a result of the battle of St-Mihiel, the first big operation largely planned and executed by the newly constituted American First Army. The St-Mihiel salient was a 200 square-mile forested triangle, in which the Germans held the upper ground. Since the failure of a French attempt against it in 1915 it had been quiet. Foch had early marked it as a target, as had Pershing, who saw the Woëvre plain beyond as a suitable terrain for the war of manoeuvre he planned, threatening the main German lateral railway and the coal and steel of northern Lorraine. In late August, however, Foch asked the Americans to concentrate on the Meuse–Argonne sector. The St-Mihiel operation could proceed, but as a preliminary operation confined to pinching out the salient. As such, it proceeded smoothly and with an over-endowment of force. The southern side of the salient was assaulted on 12 September at 5 a.m. (following a four-hour bombardment with nearly 3,000 guns), and the western side three hours later. Pershing had 550,000 American and 110,000 French troops, 1,500 aircraft, and 267 French light tanks. The much smaller German forces had neglected their defences and were already removing their heavy artillery. They mounted little resistance. After the first morning the Germans ordered evacuation and most of their troops escaped, though with the loss of 17,000 men (mainly taken prisoner) and 450 guns, against 7,000 casualties on the American side.[25] However, once the salient had been eliminated the attack was closed down, which was almost certainly a mistake on Foch's part but one that mattered relatively little at this stage.

The unexpectedly rapid success of the limited offensives encouraged Foch to try an orchestrated assault in the west for the first time since April 1917. His aim now became 'rupture': to pierce the final German line of defences and enter open country, cutting off the Noyon bulge and driving towards the trunk railway between Cambrai, St-Quentin, Mézières, and Sedan.[26] Foch seems initially (like Pershing) to have envisaged the centrepiece of the operation as a rapid advance north-eastwards through St-Mihiel and the Woëvre towards the railway and the German border. Haig, on the other hand, proposed on 27 August a more concentric advance, the different thrusts converging rather than diverging (and therefore better supporting each other), and he won the Frenchman round. More clearly than Foch, Haig foresaw that the war could be ended that autumn, though this insight may simply have resulted from his habitual optimism and virtually nobody in London shared his confidence. Henry Wilson warned him on 31 August that the cabinet would become 'anxious' if he incurred heavy and futile losses against the Hindenburg Line,[27] or as Milner put it more bluntly, if Haig 'smashed up' this

British army he could not expect another. None the less, Rawlinson advised Haig that the Hindenburg Line could be forced, and a directive by Foch on 3 September envisaged undertaking a general attack at the end of the month. What materialized, after further consultations, was an American-led offensive in the Meuse–Argonne sector, starting on 26 September; an attack by the British First and Third Armies towards Cambrai on the 27th; one by the Belgians and the British in Flanders on the 28th; and an offensive by the British Fourth Army, with American and French support, towards Busigny on the 29th.[28] By now the Allies had some 217 divisions against the Germans' 197,[29] although by Allied estimates fewer than fifty of the latter were fully fit for action.[30] Collectively, the general offensive would be the largest – and decisive – battle of the war.

The fortunes of the converging arms were very varied. In particular, much smaller German forces brought the Meuse–Argonne operation to a standstill. The reasons went back to Foch's change of plan at Haig's suggestion. Pershing acknowledged the soundness in principle of a converging attack towards Mézières rather than a diverging one towards Metz, and was willing to undertake it if his army remained independent rather than under French command. Conversely, Foch's staff may have favoured the change of plan as a means of keeping more control over the Americans. They gave Pershing the option of cancelling St-Mihiel but he went ahead with it in order to protect his flank, and as a morale booster. They also let him choose to attack west or east of the Argonne, and he chose the latter option because supplying his troops would be easier although the terrain was harder. The Meuse–Argonne battlefield was indeed much more formidable than the Woëvre plain that lay beyond the St-Mihiel salient. The Americans would advance between the unfordable Meuse and the wooded Argonne eminences, through a broken country of forests and ravines. The Germans could enfilade them with artillery from both flanks and had built lines of defence in depth across their path, notably the Kriemhilde Stellung (part of the Hindenburg Line) on a ridge ten miles from the jumping off point. Pershing gambled on taking this position on the second day, before the Germans could reinforce it. But the sudden change of plan gave the First Army chief of staff, George C. Marshall, little time to prepare, and starting the attack barely two weeks after St-Mihiel proved too much. Only three rutted roads crossed the sixty miles between the two battlefields, over which 400,000 men had to be moved, all journeys taking place at night and against the sinister backdrop of the old Verdun killing grounds. In addition, and to save time, many poorly trained and completely inexperienced troops would participate. Pershing hoped to prevail by weight of numbers, and he enjoyed a superiority of nearly eight to one on the opening day; but although he committed 600,000 men they had fewer tanks than at St-Mihiel and half the numbers of aircraft. At first the Americans achieved surprise and had the advantage of fog, but they ran into increasing opposition from machine-guns and were unable to surmount the Montfaucon high ground that blocked their path. Supplies failed to reach the front-line soldiers, some of whom ran out of food. By 30 September the attack had halted, in good measure because of breakdowns in logistics and in the AEF command structure, though also on account of German reinforcements. Even after pausing to regroup, the Americans did not reach the Kriemhilde Stellung for another two weeks.[31] The eastern attack, in which Foch had placed such hopes, had proved strategically questionable and an operational fiasco.

Fortunately for the Allies, matters went better elsewhere, though the northern-most pincer in Flanders also ran into trouble. On the first day twenty-eight divisions took 10,000 prisoners and advanced eight miles across terrain that a year before had delayed the British for three months, including most of the ridge east of Ypres. But then the mud again encumbered transport and the operation was suspended for a fortnight.[32] In contrast, the attack unleashed on 27 September on a nine-mile front towards Cambrai had to overcome the formidable barrier represented by the Canal du Nord, which was 100 feet wide, fifteen feet deep, and heavily wired. The Canadians, fighting with the British First Army, implemented a risky plan to traverse a narrow dry section of the canal, getting artillery across on the first night and using it to repel counter-attacks. They preceded the operation with detailed reconnaissance, used tanks and smoke shells, and were helped by the German gunners' shortage of ammunition, the defence system being based on interlocking dug-outs that proved easy to isolate.[33] Yet casualties were heavy and on the following day the Canadians became bogged down in fighting round Cambrai, which did not fall until 9 October, the initial attack proving more successful than the follow-up. It was therefore the final assault by the British Fourth Army on 29 September that was the most damaging of the four, managing eventually to break right through the Hindenburg Line and its reserve positions.

The line in this section had been built as a continuous defence, easier to pierce than the pillbox systems of Passchendaele. Moreover, it had been neglected and was too large for its depleted garrison. During the battle of Amiens the Australians had captured detailed plans of the system. Its southern section centred on the St-Quentin canal, protected by wire and steep banks, while in the northern sector the canal ran through a tunnel, used by the Germans to shelter their men. In front of the canal lay a ridge, which the British captured in a preliminary attack, so that they overlooked the watercourse. As there was little prospect of achieving surprise, Monash (to whom Rawlinson again entrusted the preparations) adopted the more conventional approach of destroying as much as possible of the defences in a preliminary bombardment. The weight of this bombardment – some 750,000 shells fired over four days – was superficially comparable to that of June 1916, but by now few shells were duds and the fire against the enemy batteries was much more accurate (the British using mustard gas shells for the first time), and better at destroying wire. The crucial success came in the canal sector itself, where the Germans had not expected an attack and the British were aided by fog, as well as a bombardment that landed 126 field gun shells a minute for eight hours on every 500 yards of the German positions. After 29 September the advance was slowed in the usual fashion by more ragged tank and artillery support, not to mention heavy rain, but by 5 October the British were through the last defences and soon after they could advance, if still slowly, across unfortified ground.[34]

Even before these dramatic developments, Ludendorff had experienced a nervous breakdown on the evening of 28 September and had decided to press for an immediate armistice. He was responding not only to events in the west but also to the news that Bulgaria was suing for peace. In September 1918, in fact, a combination of Allied military success on the Western Front and elsewhere finally yielded breakthrough. Germany faced not only crisis in the west but also the collapse of its partners, and the Allied resurgence extended to every theatre of conflict. This included Russia, where Allied intervention in the Russian Civil War reconstituted an Eastern Front, directed not only against the Central Powers but also against the Bolsheviks as their *de facto* accomplices. Although by the summer German expansion into the former tsarist empire was slowing down, the Bolsheviks' survival was now in question. After seizing power in the capital they had extended their authority along the railways radiating out from the Petrograd–Moscow heartland. But the November 1917 elections to the Constituent Assembly indicated that their support was limited to barely a quarter of the electorate, and by dissolving the Assembly in January Lenin provoked a civil war with the other socialist parties. This struggle between 'Reds' (Bolsheviks) and 'Greens' was characteristic of 1918, although the better-known civil war between Reds and 'Whites' (non-socialists) soon subsumed it.[35] The Treaty of Brest-Litovsk itself was a second instigator of the conflict, as it broke the Bolshevik alliance with the left SRs, who had favoured resistance. In July they assassinated the German ambassador and attempted an uprising, after which the Bolsheviks [expelled them from the Soviets and Russia became effectively a one-party state.[36] The brutal murder of the ex-tsar and his family in the same month was a further sign of the regime's radicalization. Yet although Lenin's pro-German alignment intensified Russia's political polarization, civil war was something he had long anticipated and even welcomed. The Germans, in contrast, were wearying of the Bolshevik connection. Wilhelm wanted to suppress the revolutionary regime, Ludendorff favoured replacing it with the Whites if the latter would accept Brest-Litovsk, and OHL and the naval staff devised Operation 'Keystone', a plan to seize Petrograd and Kronstadt as bases for an advance towards the Barents Sea.[37] Lenin tried to protect himself against this danger by intensifying appeasement. He offered to the Germans an agreement that he hoped would fix Russia's frontiers, combined with economic concessions to mobilize the enemy capitalists in favour of a compromise. His aim was simply to win more breathing space, and he had no wish to abide by the terms any longer than necessary. On the German side Hintze, although appointed by Hindenburg and Ludendorff to pursue a tougher line than Kühlmann, continued to favour accommodation with the Bolsheviks. By keeping Russia in chaos, Hintze maintained, they served German interests better than would any conceivable alternative. Hence the 27 August supplementary agreements between Berlin and Moscow were signed in bad faith on both sides. The Bolsheviks accepted loss of sovereignty over Livonia, Estonia, and Georgia, and promised to hand over 6,000 million marks in reparation together with one-quarter of the Baku oilfield's production. The Germans promised to end support for separatist movements, and the Bolsheviks to expel Allied forces, failing which the Germans would do so – two provisions that implied military co-operation against the West.[38]

By the same token, Allied intervention in Russia had strongly anti-German overtones, although later it became more ideologically anti-Bolshevik. It was on a much smaller scale than the intervention by the Central Powers. Compared with the half million German and Austrian occupation forces, the biggest Allied contingent – the Japanese – numbered 70,000 in Eastern Siberia by November 1918, where they were accompanied by 9,000 Americans and 6,000 British and Canadians. British, French, and American forces in Archangel totalled about 13,000 at the same date, while about 1,000 British troops were deployed in Murmansk. Another 1,000 British Empire soldiers operated north of the Persian border at Ashkabad from September 1918, and 'Dunsterforce', a British detachment of about 1,400 under Major-General Dunsterville, occupied Baku between August and September. None the less, the Allied forces had an impact disproportionate to their size, and their presence helped intensify a Russian civil war whose eventual toll of between 7 and 10 million deaths through fighting and famine was almost as great as that of the World War itself.[39]

The Arctic and Siberia were the Allied–Soviet flashpoints. No Allied government considered the Bolsheviks a legitimate or representative authority, and in December 1917 the British and French secretly agreed to assist the anti-Bolshevik parties, though they would have been willing to co-operate with Lenin and Trotsky if the latter had stayed in the war. Indeed, when in spring 1918 it seemed possible that the Germans would crush the new regime rather than make peace with it, a panicky Trotsky authorized the Murmansk Soviet to seek Allied aid, British marines actually landing there in March. After signing at Brest-Litovsk Moscow wanted the marines expelled, but Murmansk refused as it wanted to keep them as suppliers of food and protectors of its fishing fleet, while the British wished to guard the munitions they had delivered to the port from falling into hostile hands.[40] Meanwhile, from early 1918 the British and French began to press for Japanese intervention in Siberia, as Japan, alone among the Allies, still had large trained reserves.[41] They hoped to maintain an Eastern Front, not only to tie down German and Austrian troops but also to prevent the Central Powers from circumventing the Allied blockade. By the summer, moreover, as the Germans drove towards the Caucasus, the British foresaw the creation of a hostile German–Soviet bloc that would menace their interests in the Middle East and India.[42] These concerns seemed more pressing than the risk of the Japanese establishing a dependency for themselves. In Tokyo, however, the Terauchi government was divided. The premier, foreign minister, and army chiefs feared the Bolshevik revolution would create a hostile power centre on the mainland, threatening their security and economic interests and challenging their efforts to dominate China. They wanted to establish a puppet regime in the Amur basin. More internationalist figures, including the elder statesman, Saionji, and the Seiyukai party leader, Hara, feared a confrontation with the West and would act only in agreement with the Americans. But Wilson was loath to respond to Anglo-French urgings. He had little sympathy for or understanding of the Bolsheviks, but he opposed intervention in a sovereign country on principle and also because of his disagreeable memories of involvement in Mexico. His advisers were much more worried than the British about the dangers of Japanese expansion, his strategic priority was Europe, and the American military opposed a Siberian commitment. Yet the president and Colonel House were reluctant to disappoint their partners at the height of the Ludendorff offensives, and Allied lobbying over the issue was insistent. By late spring Wilson's initial opposition to involvement in Russia was softening, but an uprising by the Czech Legion finally broke the logjam.[43]

The Legion was composed of former Austro-Hungarian soldiers who had deserted or been captured and had joined the Russian army. They numbered some 40,000 men. They had ample reason to avoid surrendering to the Central Powers, who might punish them for treason. In March the Bolsheviks decided to let them leave Russia via the Trans-Siberian Railway, but later they agreed to an Allied request for the westernmost Czechs to be evacuated through the Arctic ports. The Czechs found themselves beleaguered in the heart of a chaotic and hostile land mass, and rumours that they were to be divided brought tensions between them and the Reds to a head. On 14 May, when some of their comrades were arrested after a brawl they took over the Ural town of Cheliabinsk. Trotsky, now People's Commissar for War, over-reacted, ordering all armed Czechs to be shot. The Czechs' revolt seems not to have been co-ordinated with the Allies or the Bolsheviks' Russian opponents, but as the strongest local armed force they were able within a month to destroy Bolshevik authority along the entire length of the Trans-Siberian Railway. In July they supported the creation of an SR-dominated government, the Komuch, at Samara.[44] At a moment when the Allies had their backs to the wall and the Bolsheviks were moving ever closer to the Germans, the Eastern Front had providentially been reinstated, facilitating Japanese intervention and giving Wilson a plausible justification for getting involved. The president agreed that action was needed to help the Czechs at Vladivostok link up with those in the interior. He proposed a Japanese-American joint expedition, both governments pledging to respect Russian sovereignty. Despite this intended safeguard, however, the invitation gave the Japanese army the pretext it needed to intervene in strength. As a result of Wilson's invitation the Japanese occupied the Amur basin but made little effort to move inland or help the Czechs. None the less, the Allies' assistance to the Czech Legion brought them to the verge of hostilities with the Bolsheviks and made the Arctic situation critical too. Moscow demanded a British withdrawal from Murmansk, which was rejected. In August the Allies landed at Archangel, where a coup ousted the local Bolshevik authorities. The wasteland lying between Murmansk, Archangel, and Petrograd became a new theatre of war.[45]

A Russian civil war was always likely after the Bolshevik Revolution, given Lenin's incomplete control of the country and his contempt for his opponents. The Czech revolt both made it possible for the Allies to intervene and gave them a motive, as well as escalating the civil war to a bigger and more savage stage. Yet it is unlikely that Allied intervention drove the Bolsheviks into Berlin's arms: Lenin had already decided in May to negotiate with Berlin, calculating that he could better withstand a war against the Japanese than one against the Germans.[46] Similarly, even before the Czech revolt the Central Powers had moved into the Ukraine. But Allied intervention in Siberia created an additional reason for them to stay there, and fear of Allied involvement in the Arctic was a major reason for the German commitment in Finland.[47] The Russian quagmire sucked in hundreds of thousands of Austro-German troops who might have fought elsewhere.

Not only the Germans became victims of their success against Russia. So too did the Ottomans, who during 1918 advanced into Transcaucasia. Except in the Caspian oil city of Baku, the Bolsheviks were much weaker in the region than were national separatist groups and the Mensheviks. After the Bolshevik takeover in Petrograd the local parties established a fragile Transcaucasian Republic, linking Georgia, Armenia, and Azerbaijan.[48] It was not represented at the Brest-Litovsk negotiations, where the Turks reclaimed the Armenian districts of Batum, Ardahan, and Kars that they had lost to Russia in 1877–8. The Germans reluctantly supported the claim, the Bolsheviks washed their hands of the situation, and the Transcaucasians were left on their own. They were too weak to resist the Turks, who overran the three districts and annexed them in August, whereupon the Transcaucasian Republic broke up and its three components signed separate peace treaties with Constantinople. The Turks' ambitions, however, extended further. Enver Pasha hoped to dominate the Caucasus and establish a foothold on the Caspian Sea, controlling its oil and establishing buffer states against Russia.[49] By July the Turks had reached Baku, which they captured two months later, expelling the British 'Dunsterforce' from the city. Enver's Caucasus enterprise, however, embroiled him in a confrontation with the Germans, who also had designs on Transcaucasian oil and minerals, and supported Georgia with an assistance treaty and with troops.[50] They refused to recognise Turkey's peace treaties with the Transcaucasian states and threatened to withdraw their military aid. In a secret protocol to the August supplementary agreements with Lenin, they promised not to assist the Ottomans if the latter clashed with the Bolsheviks.[51] By now Berlin's pursuit of friendship with Moscow was undermining that with Constantinople, to the point where a scarcely disguised cold war was emerging between the two allies.

Another reason for German consternation about Transcaucasia was that by September the Ottomans had committed more than half their forces to the region. These units included some of their best divisions, which they had withdrawn from Europe after sending them there in 1916 to assist the Austrians in Romania and Galicia. The Turks had left themselves exposed against the British in Mesopotamia and Palestine, and arguably they missed an opportunity to retaliate while Allenby was vulnerable. After capturing Jerusalem in December 1917 Allenby had been halted by the winter rains and in February 1918 the Palestine front settled along a line from near Ramallah to Jericho.[52] The British cabinet wanted an offensive towards Damascus and Aleppo, but Allenby held back until he could set up new field intelligence networks and complete a double-tracked coastal railway. His caution proved fortunate, as the Ludendorff offensives in the west forced the War Office to strip him of troops. Six of his divisions lost nine of their twelve battalions, which were replaced by raw recruits from India.[53] While the new troops were being trained, Allenby authorized two large raids across the Jordan in March–April and April–May 1918, but both were ignominious failures. His basic aim was to sever the Hejaz railway, running east of his armies from Syria down to the Arabian Holy Places of Medina and Mecca. It was under guerrilla attack by the Northern Arab Army (NAA), led by Sharif Hussein's son Faisal, to which Colonel T. E. Lawrence acted as liaison officer, doing much to devise the strategy followed by the rebels and to win British support and assistance for it.[54] Aided with British equipment and a monthly subsidy, the Arabs held down some 25,000 Turks in Transjordan as well as besieging a garrison of 4,000 in Medina.[55] They were a cheap and useful ally to Allenby but were too weak to hold the railway permanently and the Turks repaired it fairly easily after their sabotage attempts. Allenby wanted to be able to supply them directly from Transjordan in the hope that the Arab revolt would spread into Syria, but the first Jordan raid was unable to get its artillery along rain-soaked roads to Amman, and retreated without taking the city. The second was recalled when a Turkish counter-attack threatened its line of retreat.[56] Hence Allenby had to spend the summer working towards an autumn offensive.

But while he did so, his enemy melted away. By summer 1918 over 500,000 Ottoman soldiers may have deserted since the start of the war, and as they were outlaws and could not return to their villages many joined armed bands that lived by robbery.[57] The Yilderim force was stripped of troops for the Caucasus. Aided by air superiority, the British built up a detailed photographic picture of the enemy positions, while concealing their own preparations. They learned that the railway tunnel to Palestine through the Taurus mountains would be closed for two weeks for repairs, and timed their attack accordingly. Moreover, by raiding the eastern end of the Turks' lines Allenby encouraged them in the delusion that as in 1917 he would try to outflank them by attacking in the interior. But in fact this time he intended to break through along the coast and funnel through cavalry to block the avenues of retreat, a secondary advance closing off the Jordan crossings. He attacked on 19 September with 57,000 infantry, 12,000 cavalry, and 550 guns against Turkish forces of 32,000, 2,000, and 400 respectively. After a hurricane bombardment a breach was quickly established and the cavalry swept through. The Turks, strafed by British aircraft, offered little resistance, and Allenby ordered an advance on Damascus, which fell on 1 October, followed a day later by Beirut. He took 75,000 prisoners (3,700 of them German and Austrian) for British casualties of 5,666.[58] This rout, usually referred to by the biblical title of the battle of Megiddo, ended the Palestine campaign but neither destroyed the Turks' main army nor threatened their Asia Minor heartland. It is doubtful whether it contributed significantly either to Ludendorff's or the Turks' decisions to seek an armistice. More influential in both cases were Germany's defeats on the Western Front and a further Allied September offensive: an assault in the Balkans.

Like Turkey, Bulgaria was an increasingly restless partner of the Central Powers by 1918, and it too was dissatisfied with the eastern peace treaties. The Bulgarian public had wanted the whole of the Dobrudja province from Romania, but the Turks claimed compensation for their previous assistance to the Bulgars. As an interim measure the northern Dobrudja remained under four-power occupation, though Ludendorff did not disguise his hostility to Bulgaria's claims.* Prime minister Radoslavov came under fire over the issue and King Ferdinand replaced him by the less Germanophile Molinov. Meanwhile the Bulgarian army was becoming dispirited on a largely quiet front, and many of its peasant soldiers were deserting: for three years they had been obliged to let their families gather in the harvest, they were not fighting on their home soil, they lacked food and clothing, and Allied and pacifist propaganda were gaining a hold.[59] OHL had scaled down its assistance, and by autumn 1918 only three German battalions were left there, alongside fourteen Bulgarian divisions and two Austro-Hungarian ones.[60] As against this, regular Greek forces had reinforced the Allies, whose unity of command benefited greatly when Clemenceau removed Sarrail, replacing him first by General Guillaumat and then in June by Franchet d'Espérey, one of the victors on the Marne in 1914.

---

*See ch. 15.

Clemenceau had criticized the Salonika campaign while in opposition, but once in government he resisted Lloyd George's efforts to pull the Allied troops out.[61] Franchet planned a major operation that would destroy the Bulgarian army and allow the Serbs to reconquer their homeland, but he had to undertake a lot of prior persuasion. The SWC military experts agreed on condition that no units were moved from the Western Front; Lloyd George would have preferred diplomacy against the Bulgars but eventually gave way.[62] The two sides' overall numbers in the theatre were about equal, but the French and the Serbs achieved a three to one superiority at the decisive point and Franchet accepted a bold proposal from the Serbs to attack across the mountains that separated them from Kosovo, hauling heavy artillery up to heights of nearly 8,000 feet. The operation was launched on 15 September and once it reached the Bulgarians' second line their army collapsed. By the 26th the Serbs were driving their enemies beyond the Vardar valley and had split them in two. Ludendorff ordered four divisions to move from the Eastern Front and Arz ordered two to move from the Piave, but before they could arrive the Bulgarians sued for an armistice. Their representatives met Franchet and signed a ceasefire in the Balkans on 29 September, which in a curious reversal of the chain of events in 1914 would lead on to a ceasefire in Europe as a whole.[63]

The Allies owed much to the disintegration of their enemies. The Turks in Palestine had fought hard in 1917, but when Allenby attacked in 1918 most surrendered at the first opportunity. The Bulgarian army had similarly decayed during months of inactivity while its supplies dried up and the Dobrudja dispute muddied the war's political objectives, and after the battle of the Piave the break-up of the Habsburg army accelerated. As for Germany, Ludendorff's offensives cost his army 1.1 million casualties between March and July (followed by another 430,000 dead and wounded and 340,000 prisoners between July and November). In the last months of the war the number of absentees, keeping away from the fighting fronts or refusing to join their units, has been estimated as being as high as 0.75 to 1 million.[64] The German army faced an insoluble crisis of effectives, and by the final months of the war it was also suffering for the first time since 1916 from weapons and munitions shortages. But above all, as Ludendorff was fully aware, its spirit was going. From July the numbers of German surrenders leapt up,[65] which partly resulted from warfare having become more mobile and the Allies being on the offensive (after all, thousands of British troops had surrendered on the first day of operation 'Michael'). But in addition much of the army was no longer fighting to the last, even if some units – notably machine gunners – resisted fiercely. The contrast between the tenacious defence of Passchendaele and the ease with which the Hindenburg Line fell a year later underlines that the Allies were no longer fighting the same army. German morale and discipline had shown signs of loosening since 1916, but the intense disappointment after the March–July offensives critically accelerated the process. Russia's collapse, daunting though its consequences appeared to the Allies, proved to be a poisoned chalice for the Central Powers. Reincorporated prisoners of war and sullen veterans from the east undermined the cohesion of the German and Austrian armies in other theatres, and arguments over the Russian and Romanian spoils divided the leaders of the Central Powers and unsettled their home fronts. German troops that were needed in the west were bogged down in the Ukraine (in far larger numbers than the Allied intervention forces in Russia) while the Turks became preoccupied with the Caucasus.[66] The Central Powers' outburst of energy between October 1917 and July 1918 contributed heavily to their subsequent downfall.

If it is true that in considerable measure the Central Powers manufactured to their own defeat, the Allies had indeed become more formidable. This development may be considered in its military, economic, and political aspects. The Allies' military superiority stemmed partly from their greater numbers, but also from their better equipment and the ability with which they used it.[67] By the end of the war they outnumbered their opponents on the Western Front, in Italy, and in Palestine, but this development was recent. Only in June and July did both sides on the Western Front recognize that the balance had shifted, though thereafter the Allied advantage widened rapidly. While German numbers dwindled from 5.2 to 4.1 million, the French called up the 1919 class (some 300,000 men) in April 1918 and conscripted another 120,000 men from their African colonies.[68] The British sent 351,824 men to France between 21 March and 13 July, scaling down their home army and sending out boys aged eighteen, convalescing men, and young industrial workers, although after the crisis eased they again gave their industrial needs priority.[69] Emergency legislation extended the age range for conscription and empowered the government to apply it in Ireland, though the attempt to do so caused another wave of protest and intensified the southern counties' drift towards Sinn Féin.[70] Among the Dominions, following New Zealand in 1916, Canada introduced conscription at the turn of 1917/18 to sustain its levels of recruitment.[71] All the same, in themselves these efforts would merely have permitted the Allied armies to shrink more slowly than Germany's. What allowed the armies to increase were the huge drafts from the United States.

AEF expansion was not achieved without a political struggle, on which the German offensives had a decisive impact. In June Lloyd George described the AEF as the 'worst disappointment' of the war,[72] but the Americans were faster than the British in training troops and shipping them to the Western Front. Further, the men's morale was high. Despite a vocal pacifist movement, there was little anti-romantic literature of disillusionment in America before April 1917. On the contrary, writers such as the Harvard poet Alan Seeger, who volunteered to join the French Foreign Legion and was killed on active service, purveyed a chivalric vision of the conflict, and his letters and diary became bestsellers. Politicians such as Theodore Roosevelt – though not Wilson himself – evoked traditional views of combat as a test of moral fibre and of manhood, and harked back to the American Civil War with surprising fondness.[73] For many who served in the AEF, their experience was indeed less alienating than that of the French and British. Black Americans, who constituted some 13 per cent of the draftees, may have been an exception. Only one in five of those sent to France saw action, and most served as dockers and labourers; the senior officers in the one all-black combat division (the 92nd) were white. Two regiments in the division fled on the first day at Meuse–Argonne, though the black American regiments under French command had a distinguished record.[74] Of the white Americans who served in the AEF, nearly 2 million went to France and 1.3 million came under fire, nearly all of them after July 1918. A total of 193,611 were wounded and 50,476 were killed, more than half of them at Meuse-Argonne (and another 57,000 died of influenza), but the great majority remained unscathed. Their combat experience was brief and took place in relatively unspoiled countryside, after long sea and rail journeys. Hence many soldiers' diaries were records of tourism as well as combat, and their idealism had little opportunity to become tarnished. Once they reached the battlefield, both German and Allied observers found them almost suicidally brave.[75]

None the less, for the first year after American entry into the war the AEF remained, from the European Allies' viewpoint, dishearteningly small. The cause lay partly in the 'amalgamation' imbroglio for which London and Paris shared the blame.* The British and French wanted American soldiers as cannon fodder to plug the gaps in their own armies: Pershing and Wilson wanted an independent force. Both sides saw the implications as political as well as operational. Pershing estimated that his allies could hold out until America fielded an independent army, the creation of which necessitated transporting equipment and administrators as well as front-line troops. The AEF's proportion of non-combatants actually rose from 20 to 32.5 per cent in the five months before Ludendorff's offensives.[76] However, 51 per cent of the Americans crossed in British or British-leased ships (as against 46 per cent in American ones)[77] and the March 1918 emergency enabled the British to close a bargain: they would make more ships available (at the expense of their own import needs) to convey 120,000 personnel a month, but on condition that the latter were infantrymen and machine-gunners. The Americans might well wonder why the ships had previously been unavailable, and the British indeed used them as a bargaining counter, but correctly suspected that the Americans were using their own merchant vessels to capture western hemisphere and Pacific trade rather than committing them to the common effort. After August both the availability of British ships and the size of the American contingents diminished, probably because once the peak of danger had passed both parties again put their narrower interests to the fore.[78] None the less, enough had been done to permit the dramatic increase in American strengths that followed April 1918:

TABLE 4.
American Troops Landing in France,
March–October 1918[79]

March	64,000
April	121,000
May	214,000
June	238,000
July	247,000
August	280,000
September	263,000
October	227,000

The crucial American contribution was indeed the sheer number of troops, which did much to convince Ludendorff and his soldiers that they could no longer

*See ch. 15.

win.[80] OHL's qualitative assessment, even before Meuse–Argonne, was that the Americans were brave but poorly trained and clumsily led. The earliest units learned quickly, but so many raw recruits flooded across after them that the average standard failed to improve.[81] The concessions to Britain and to France may also have handicapped the AEF. Bringing over extra front-line troops without non-combatant support possibly contributed to the logistical chaos at Meuse–Argonne, and the speed with which the battle was planned in order to meet the wishes of Foch and Haig certainly did. In addition, Pershing's operational concept may have been faulty. One reason he resisted amalgamation was that he feared his troops being schooled in cautious trench fighting techniques: an apostle of the offensive, he envisaged a decisive AEF breakthrough followed by open warfare. The huge size of the American divisions – approximately 28,000 men each or more than treble their German counterparts – was intended to economize on scarce officers but also to sustain the losses expected in the event of such an attack and still remain in the line. Pershing insisted on his men being trained to excel in marksmanship, though rifles rarely figured in trench fighting. The artillery was equipped with light and medium field guns rather than howitzers, and proved incompetent in laying down a creeping barrage.[82] By doctrine and weaponry the Americans were less well suited than the British and French to semi-open warfare.

What broke the Germans, apart from their own mistakes, was the combination of American numbers with Anglo-French combat effectiveness that both halted the March–July offensives with enormous losses and broke through every position after July, showing that not only the offensive battle was lost but also the defensive one. In this calculus the French army is often neglected, though during 1918 it captured 139,000 prisoners and 1,880 guns compared with the BEF's 188,700 and 2,840, the AEF's 43,300 and 1,421, and the Belgians' 14,500 and 474.[83] By November the BEF comprised roughly 1.75 million men, the Americans 2 million, and the French 2.5 million: the BEF held 18 per cent of the Western Front, the Americans 21 per cent, and the French 55 per cent.[84] French casualties between 1 July and 15 September were 279,000,[85] compared with BEF ones between 7 August and 11 November of 297,765.[86] Even after the Americans arrived in force the French and British still did most of the damage to the German army, and bore most of the cost.

The French seem to have used a similar combination of new technology and tactics to that employed by the British, although their role in 1918 has been less intensively studied.[87] Their counterstroke on the Marne was bigger than the battle of Amiens, even if in the climactic battle at the end of September they had a supporting role. Since 1917 their artillery had been re-equipped. By the armistice it had 13,000 pieces, two-thirds of them modernized, and during the summer it fired 280,000 75mm field gun shells every day.[88] Like the British and Germans the French had developed the use of short, intensive bombardments designed to neutralize the enemy and achieve surprise. In addition they had a large fleet of tanks: 467 heavy Schneider and St-Chamond models in March 1918, most of which were later knocked out. However, in replacement the army took delivery of 2,653 Renault light tanks during 1918, which spearheaded its 18 July counter-offensive. Finally, by the end of the war France had the biggest air force in the world. [89]

Pétain's GQG encouraged the army commanders to use defence in depth (which eventually they did, at least to some extent), and to try new methods of attack, centred on limited infantry advances in close liaison with artillery and tanks, constantly shifting to new baselines rather than pushing beyond the point of diminishing returns.[90] As in other armies a gap remained between doctrine and practice, but it seems the French participated fully in the transformation that restored mobility.

The history of the BEF during its 'Hundred Days' advance from August to November is now much better known. The first point to make is that it was not just a United Kingdom force. Of the sixty active BEF infantry divisions in the period, one came from New Zealand, four from Canada, and five from Australia, while South Africa provided a brigade. Their attacks had a higher average success rate than those by UK divisions, and they took the lead in operations such as the battles of Hamel and Amiens and the piercing of the Hindenburg Line.[91] They had largely been spared the defensive fighting of the spring; but in addition the Canadians were more heavily armed with weapons such as light machine-guns,[92] and unlike the divisions from the British Isles they had kept their twelve-battalion organization. By this stage of the war, moreover, they had much more independence. In June 1917 a Canadian professional officer, Lieut.-General Sir Arthur Currie, had taken over command of the Canadian Expeditionary Force (which had previously been British-led), and after Passchendaele he oversaw a successful reappraisal of offensive training and tactics.[93] The Australian divisions in France were grouped in 1917 as an Australian Corps, and from May 1918 they similarly came under an Australian commander, Sir John Monash. In addition to all these factors, however, as the British GHQ itself acknowledged, the individual officers and men of the Dominion forces simply displayed very high combat effectiveness.[94]

Both the British and Dominion forces applied a combination of technology and tactics that had greatly progressed since the Somme. The most conspicuous contrast between the battle of Amiens and the latter was the mass deployment of tanks, but these weapons were a valuable adjunct rather than the principal reason for success. It was true that Germany had none, thus weakening its capabilities for a counter-offensive. Ludendorff had previously given them a low supply priority because he had been unconvinced of their military value, but in August he belatedly ordered 900 for spring 1919. Tanks could crush enemy barbed wire without an artillery bombardment that pockmarked the ground, and could silence machine-gun nests, thus enabling advances beyond the range of the creeping barrage. In short, they saved lives, but they also needed infantry to keep pace with *them* for protection against hostile artillery. The new Mark V models still moved at little more than walking pace, had a maximum battle endurance of two to three hours, and were so hot and filled with carbon monoxide that their crews frequently passed out. They were easy targets, and German gunners hit several hundred Allied tanks during 1918. Although disabled machines could often be salvaged and refurbished (given that the Allies were advancing), spare parts were short and the repairs were slow to carry out. When tanks were used intensively their usable numbers therefore dwindled rapidly – for example, from 430 to 38 between 8 and 11 August[95] – but although 120 were lost permanently in the battle of Amiens, the numbers available to the British ranged around 200 to 300 for the rest of the war.[96] The BEF planned no further tank attack on the scale of 8 August (and neither did the French after 18 July), but they seem to have used tanks almost as much as their mechanical unreliability and other limitations permitted. 183 were committed to the battle of Albert on 21 August, and 181 to the 29 September assault on the Hindenburg Line.[97] But for the latter operation a surprise attack was less feasible than on 8 August as an advance bombardment was needed, while in the more open campaigning of the final month tanks were handicapped because they could not traverse long distances under their own power and had to be moved by lorries or trains. They could make an important contribution as part of a combination of weapons systems, but they were not war winning devices on their own.[98]

Much the same can be said about aircraft, although during 1918 the struggle to command battlefield airspace was unprecedentedly ferocious and both sides were experimenting with strategic bombing of targets deep behind the lines. German bomber raids against London continued until May (and against Paris until September, though the latter raids were lighter – it being harder to approach Paris undetected than it was to reach London over the North Sea). By the autumn Ludendorff had given up hope that city attacks could panic his enemies. Yet Allied strategic bombing was equally ineffective. Raids against Germany were largely a British effort, the French giving priority to liberating their territory and hesitating to court retaliation. The Lloyd George government, however, authorized a bombing offensive in reprisal for the Gotha raids, and (following a report by Smuts to the War Cabinet) created the Royal Air Force and the Air Ministry in April 1918 precisely with such an effort in mind, also establishing an 'Independent Force' with special responsibility for the mission.[99] DH4 and DH9 bombers were the mainstay of the campaign, which targeted Rhineland cities and industrial sites, mostly by day. It ran into fierce opposition from anti-aircraft guns, searchlights, and (by the end of the war) some 330 fighters, and 140 bombers were lost.[100] It did therefore divert German resources, probably more than the British devoted to the enterprise, as at the time of the armistice only 140 of the 1,799 RAF aircraft on the Western Front were assigned to it. In this as in other respects, it was a singular precursor of the Second World War, and if hostilities had lasted into 1919 it would have become much bigger, the four-engined Handley Page V-1500 (which could reach Berlin) becoming available after the armistice. But the iron and steel works attacked sustained only superficial harm, and the BASF works at Mannheim (the major chemical industry target) never had to halt production.[101] Strategic bombing killed 746 civilians in Germany during the war, compared with 1,414 in Britain.[102] It is doubtful if it did anything to shorten the conflict, and the crucial air battle came elsewhere.

Most of the RAF leaders were recruited from the RFC and accepted its doctrine that the principal function of airpower was support of the army. Sir Hugh Trenchard, who became the first commander of the Independent Force, was a leading advocate of this view, and devoted much of his effort against aerodromes and railways just behind the lines rather than more distant targets. By November 1918 Britain had 3,300 front-line aircraft and Germany 2,600, while the much smaller American force totalled about 740, most of it French-built.[103] Both sides had many more and much higher performance aircraft in 1918 than in previous years, fighting a mass battle of attrition in much bigger squadrons, and the losses were staggering.[104] The British had 1,232 aircraft on 21 March, but lost 1,302 by 29 April, and 2,692 more between 1 August and 11 November.[105] Industry just about delivered replacements, and remarkably the RAF found pilots: though it had little time to train them. The pressure on the Allies was greatest during the spring offensives, but the German air force remained large and dangerous until the end; for example, it took delivery by August of over 800 Fokker D7s, the best fighter of the war. Only in the final months did shortages of fuel and pilots begin to bite, but the qualitative superiority of the German aircraft always offset the Allies' numerical advantage. Hence the latter had little to spare for strategic bombing, and even their core functions stretched them. Armed with two machine-guns and able to carry a few hundred pounds of bombs, First World War aircraft had only limited scope for ground attack. Strafing helped delay the German advances in March and April, but Allied aircraft were less successful in assisting offensive operations. They wrecked the Marne bridges in July, but during the battle of Amiens, despite losing 243 aircraft in four days, they failed to destroy the Somme bridges over which the Germans were sending reinforcements.[106] Airpower's principal roles remained denying the enemy access to one's own airspace (before Megiddo as before Amiens) and gathering intelligence.

Photographic intelligence was reinforced by other information sources. During 1918 the British and the French gained the upper hand in signals intelligence. Whereas before Caporetto and the 'Michael' offensive the Germans used bogus wireless messages to confuse their antagonists by creating phantom armies, before the battle of Amiens the British misled the Germans into expecting a Flanders attack. By the summer the Allies were intercepting and decoding hundreds of German radio messages a week, including those that revealed the Matz attack. Conversely, the Allied offensives of 18 July and 8 August both came almost out of the blue, contributing powerfully not only to their success but also to breaking Ludendorff's nerve. Allenby's intelligence superiority before Megiddo was even more total.[107]

None the less, the most important single technological contributor to British success remained artillery. Many of the improvements in this arm's effectiveness during the war had emerged earlier, including the creeping barrage and firing without registration. By 1917 90 per cent of counter-battery observation already used aerial reconnaissance.[108] Nor, as Bruchmüller's career demonstrated, was the artillery revolution purely a British phenomenon. All the same, 1918 saw important new developments, not least in production. The Ministry of Munitions delivered 6,500 guns and howitzers in 1917, but 10,700 in 1918, the huge artillery losses in the spring offensives being quickly replaced from stocks.[109] British guns had more high explosive shells than they could fire, and many more gas shells were available. Although the gas clouds of Ypres and Loos remain the most notorious examples of 1914–18 chemical warfare, the quantity of gas employed increased in each year of the fighting. In 1915, 3,870 tons were used but this rose to 16,535 in 1916, 38,635 in 1917, and 65,160 in 1918.[110] Western Front gas casualties in 1915–17 numbered 129,000: in 1918 they were 367,000, of which 2.5 per cent were fatalities.[111] Gas was less lethal than high explosive, but the Western Front in 1918 was a chemical battlefield of a kind not seen again until the Persian Gulf in the 1980s, with many different types of gas available and several modes of delivery, although gas shells were predominant and accounted for up to 50 per cent of the munitions fired in British bombardments. Over 25,000, for example, were fired at Hamel, and gas was particularly effective for counter-battery work, sinking into gun pits that afforded cover from explosives and forcing the crews to don their masks.[112] In the more mobile warfare after September the use of gas diminished, in order not to contaminate the soil and atmosphere through which the infantry had to advance. Also crucial to neutralizing the enemy batteries, however, was British skill in locating them, through aerial photo-reconnaissance, flash spotting, and sound ranging (using microphones that located guns from the 'air ripples' generated when they were fired).[113] At Amiens, 95 per cent of German guns were identified before the battle began, and at the Canal du Nord on 27 September counter-battery fire was 80 per cent successful.[114]

Such results needed time and preparation, not least to pre-position the guns (and test and correct them for wear). Moreover, even though radio was beginning to be introduced during the Hundred Days, infantry-artillery communication during action remained difficult. Nevertheless the French and British had found the means to neutralize or destroy any German defence system by hurricane bombardments, following which well equipped infantry would overcome the remaining resistance with the aid of a creeping barrage, tanks, and aircraft. No one factor accounts for the dramatic increase in Allied success. Rather, it arose from a combination of new technologies and operational procedures, which had been maturing for some time but showed to their full advantage when applied to faltering opposition. Some credit is due to the men at the top. Pétain, notwithstanding his negativity in March 1918, had furthered innovation in his army despite resistance from subordinates and clashes with Foch and Clemenceau.[115] Haig and his GHQ, headed by new and more competent personnel, allowed greater scope to able commanders like Rawlinson, Currie, and Monash, and showed a new willingness to terminate attacks in good time. Further, Haig perceived in summer 1918 a chance to end the war quickly, at the cost of higher casualties in the short term but probably fewer in the long.[116] So did Foch, though probably both were at fault in diverting the American attack line from St-Mihiel to Meuse–Argonne. Foch's formal powers had been gradually extended and in June the French government deprived Pétain of the right to appeal against him. Even Pershing was surprisingly willing to defer to him. Haig was less so, refusing to reinforce the French before the battle of the Matz or to prolong the battle of Amiens. However, Foch (who in August was appointed a Marshal of France) viewed his role as resting on exhortation and consensus building rather than command power, and his control over the Allies' reserves mattered less after they passed to the offensive. He had mellowed and wisened, and his staff (minuscule in comparison with Eisenhower's in 1944–5) helped co-ordinate Allied strategy more effectively than would have been possible through bilateral arrangements, eventually delivering the first concerted general offensive for two years.[117]

Three preconditions for the mobile, technology-intensive pattern of Allied advance were flexible logistics, command of the seas, and a powerful industrial base. The BEF had reorganized its logistics in the winter of 1916–17, placing professional civilian railwaymen in charge, building more track, and shipping rolling stock across the Channel.[118] Tested in the chaos of the spring retreat, the system coped excellently: almost as many supply trains reached the front in April 1918 as during the five months of the Somme. During the Hundred Days advance from August to November the BEF remained adequately supplied, though with more difficulty as it moved ahead of its railheads across land devastated by the retreating enemy.[119] The French also kept their railways functioning, helped by rolling stock from Britain and the United States. Although strained, their railway system did not seize up as the Russian one had done and the Austrian and German systems were in the course of doing. As for the Americans, they improved the neglected lines leading from their Atlantic ports to Lorraine, though neither at St-Mihiel nor at the Meuse-Argonne did their supply arrangements run as smoothly as those of their partners.

The second precondition was command of the seas, so that men and armaments could reach the Atlantic and Channel ports (not to mention ports in Italy, Egypt, Greece, and Russia). Not only could the Allies draw in American troops but they also imported food, raw materials, and labour from all over the world. In addition to the Dominion troops, and the North and West Africans who plugged the French army's gaps, the French imported thousands of labourers from Indochina, and in 1917–18 around 95,000 Chinese came from Shandong province to labour for the BEF.[120] Whereas on the surface Britain's margin of superiority widened in 1914–16, in 1917–18 it diminished again, even with American assistance (five American dreadnoughts moved to Scotland in 1917–18, while the Americans provided 27 per cent of the Atlantic convoy protection forces).[121] Escort duty stripped the Royal Navy of its screen of cruisers and destroyers, and capital ships were seconded to protect the Scandinavian convoys. Although Britain's battleships and battlecruisers were concentrated together at Rosyth after April 1918, to some extent the U-boats achieved the Germans' longstanding objective of dispersing the Grand Fleet. In January the Admiralty approved a recommendation by Beatty (who after Jutland had replaced Jellicoe as commander in chief) that 'the correct strategy for the Grand Fleet is no longer to endeavour to bring the enemy to action at any cost, but rather to contain him in his bases until the general situation becomes more favourable to us'.[122] The new commander had learned Jutland's painful lessons almost too well. He believed his navy's shells remained inadequate and that only three of its battlecruisers were fit to fight in line against the enemy. Almost to the end the Admiralty was on edge, fearing that the Germans would capture the Russian Baltic Fleet or seize the Channel ports.[123] In the event the High Seas Fleet sallied out only once during 1918: on 22–25 April to attack a Scandinavian convoy, which it failed to find. By observing radio silence, however, the Germans had put to sea undetected, and although they broke it on their return (thus enabling the Grand Fleet belatedly to give chase) the episode showed that the British might not always receive any warning. If the Grand Fleet's strategy was one of containment rather than destruction, what did most to keep the Germans harmless was self-containment. Even after Jutland, the High Seas Fleet remained intimidated by its adversary.[124]

In the campaign against the submarines offensive measures still did less than convoying to keep the sea lanes open. It is true that U-boat losses totalled sixty-nine in 1918, compared with sixty-three in 1917 and forty-six in 1914–16. Fourteen were lost in May alone, a record for the war. However, twenty-two of the sixty-nine losses were due to mining, into which the Allies put much effort.[125] The Dover barrage, relaid as a new deep minefield in late 1917 with searchlights and trawlers carrying flares to force the U-boats to dive low at night, probably destroyed seven of them between December 1917 and April 1918. German destroyers damaged it in a night raid on 14–15 February and sank a trawler and seven drifters, but they never repeated the operation or attacked – as Beatty feared – with capital ships. Here again the High Seas Fleet sat passively by while Germany's time ran out. The Dover barrage did deter the passage of U-boats. Smaller submarines from the Flanders flotilla continued to run it, but after February all the High Seas Fleet boats used the much longer northern route; to bar this approach the Allies laid a minefield from Scotland to Norway between March and October 1918. The northern barrage was an American initiative, and was laid mainly by the US navy, using American mines of dubious reliability. The barrage sank six or seven U-boats but was no hermetic barrier and may not have justified the investment. A similar question mark hangs over another spectacular (and exceptionally courageous) operation, the British raid on Ostend and Zeebrugge on 23 April, which attempted to deny the Flanders U-boats' sea access by sinking blockships in the two exit channels, but failed in its objective despite incurring 635 casualties.[126]

Convoy remained the Allies' master card, and during 1918 it was extended to cover British coastal waters, where the submarines were now concentrating their attention. In the Mediterranean it was less effective because less complete and because the convoys had weaker escort forces, while attempts to pen in the German and Austrian U-boats by a barrage across the Straits of Otranto seem to have tied up Allied warships to negligible effect. For this reason the supply route to the Salonika and Palestine theatres remained precarious. In northern waters, however, new technology was bearing fruit: typically escort vessels might each carry thirty depth charges (as against four in 1917) and depth charges sank twenty-one U-boats compared with six in the previous year.[127] U-boats used radio frequently and Room 40 intercepted their messages, enabling the Admiralty to order convoys to avoid them.[128] Above all, Allied airpower made attacks on convoys more dangerous, not because the aircraft could sink submarines themselves but because they detected and reported them. During 1918 the RAF expanded its land-based aircraft committed to anti-submarine warfare from twenty-two to 223, and the American and French navies also deployed sizeable air services, whose pilots increasingly carried radios. Although the U-boats did not diminish in numbers, at least their growth was checked, the total in commission fluctuating between 128 in January and 125 in April, 112 in June, and 128 in September. The Germans assisted by lagging in their construction: of ninety-five U-boats ordered in June 1917, only five were ever delivered.[129] The autumn 1918 'Scheer Programme' belatedly envisaged a massive expansion to 333 submarines, but would probably not have been implemented for lack of resources even if the war had continued.[130] Moreover, even though numbers just held up, U-boat effectiveness declined. In March 1917 the High Seas Fleet boats were each destroying an average of 0.55 ships per day, but by June 1918 the figure was 0.07.[131] Allied counter-measures meant that U-boats had further to travel to their target zones, found fewer victims once they got there, and might well steer clear of convoys even if they located them. Bearing in mind the almost unimaginable circumstances inside a dying submarine, it is unsurprising that newer and younger crews or older and exhausted ones hesitated to take risks. Experienced and aggressive commanders became rarer, many of that 5 per cent who had previously accounted for 60 per cent of sinkings now being dead.[132] The upshot was that Allied shipping losses rose in the first three months of 1918 but fell in April and never again exceeded 300,000 tons per month (although as late as September they remained above 1915 levels). Further, after April new merchant ships coming into service exceeded those destroyed; and by the autumn, greatly so. After June, losses in the Mediterranean also fell sharply and permanently. Less dramatic than the Allied triumph in the battle of the Atlantic in May 1943, April and May 1918 still marked a turning point.

As on the surface, the Germans probably failed to make the most of their advantages. For example, the 'wolf pack' tactics of mass raids by surfaced submarines at night, which proved devastating in the Second World War, were attempted only once, when a dozen U-boats were concentrated in the western approaches in May 1918. Five merchant ships were sunk or damaged during the two weeks of the operation, but 293 were safely escorted through the danger zone, the U-boats lacking adequate radio communications to converge successfully and Room 40 detecting their whereabouts. Another possible missed opportunity was that of operating in American coastal waters with long-range boats, which was attempted after May 1918 but following cruiser rules. The U-boats sank ninety-three ships and perturbed the American public; New York City was blacked out for thirteen nights during June for fear of seaplanes. Although the Americans introduced coastal convoys, however, the Atlantic shipping lanes remained their priority and they did not pull back warships to home waters.[133] Wilhelm II insisted on restraint in these American operations, and the U-boat commanders doubted their value.[134] Finally, U-boats occasionally attacked the outward American troop convoys (most of which were under US naval escort), but more often the accompanying cargo ships rather than the troopships themselves, and usually the destroyers beat them off. One impounded German liner, the *Vaterland*, renamed *Leviathan*, carried 96,804 troops alone in ten voyages, steaming so fast that it often travelled without escorts. In all, three troopships were sunk on the return journey to America, and one British troopship went down in February with the loss of 166 soldiers and forty-four crew.[135] Yet despite Holtzendorff's prediction that no American troops would reach Europe, the U-boats continued to concentrate on the slower and more vulnerable cargo vessels.

Although the Allies thwarted the submarine menace, their tonnage losses remained high well into 1918 and the cumulative impact of the previous huge inroads on their shipping pool remained with them. The American troop transports exacerbated the resulting shortage, and it is unsurprising that the Allies had to ration their imports. Individually they had done so since at least 1916, but they now attempted to co-ordinate their efforts with the creation at the November–December 1917 Paris conference of the Allied Maritime Transport Council. Its members comprised the shipping ministers from Britain, France, and Italy, together with a US representative, and the Allied Maritime Transport Executive (the AMTC's permanent staff in

London) comprised senior officials from the ministers' departments. Under them came 'Programme Committees' for each commodity. Although the AMTC was not supranational, but operated by unanimity, and directly controlled only some 500,000 tons of chartered neutral ships, its deliberations had increasing influence. Among its concerns were finding space to ship food to France and Italy – coal for Italy being conveyed via the French railways in order to save tonnage – and supplying food relief to Belgium, as well as generally maximizing the use of shipping space and restraining imports.[136] This agenda is revealing of the coalition's priorities. In winter 1917–18 the crucial needs were for food and coal; by summer 1918 for American troops. Armaments might have moved up the list if the war had been prolonged, but in 1918 their claims were relegated.

From this there follows an important point. If the second condition for the Allies' success was command of the seas, the third was their industrial base. Their weapons came primarily from Britain and France, even though America had an essential supporting role. It might seem that with American entry the Allies would have no further worries. If measured by pre-war manufacturing output or by steel production, Britain, France, and the United States were about 2.5 times stronger than Germany and Austria-Hungary.[137] Yet America proved slower to turn its industrial potential into armaments than its young men into soldiers. Its GNP is estimated to have risen 20 per cent between 1914 and 1917 but fallen 4 per cent in 1917–18,[138] and its conversion from a civilian to a war economy was neither particularly quick nor particularly successful. The winter of 1917–18 saw a production crisis, due partly to harsh weather that froze up the east coast ports and crippled coal mining and rail transport. Britain and France had faced similar conversion pangs in 1915, and had handed control of procurement to armaments ministries with energetic civilian chiefs. In the United States, in contrast, procurement and control of contracts remained with the Navy and War Departments. The War Industries Board (founded in April 1917) lacked the powers needed to co-ordinate the process and during the winter crisis two of its chairmen resigned. It recovered under the leadership of Bernard Baruch, whom Wilson appointed in March 1918, a banker who used his influence to lower civilian automobile production. At the same time the War Department, led by General Peyton C. March at the general staff, reorganized its procurement arrangements and co-operated more closely with Baruch.[139] None the less, American production came on stream too late. In aviation, for example, Wilson authorized a secret investigation of an 'aircraft trust' because of the failure to meet targets. Only one fifth of the AEF's combat aircraft came from the United States. American industry copied Allied designs (notably the British DH4 bomber), but with deficient quality control. Its output of Liberty aero-engines rose from sixty-nine in January to 3,878 in October and might well have been huge by 1919, but during 1918 France with 44,563 engines remained the world leader.[140] Similarly, American output of 75mm field guns (following a French model) quadrupled between April and October, but without French industry the AEF would never have entered the field. At the armistice more than two thirds of its aircraft were French, as were all its field guns, all its tanks, and nearly all its shells.[141] French industry achieved this feat in addition to renewing France's own army and air force equipment under Pétain. But

Britain too, admittedly with larger manufacturing capacity and without having lost its chief industrial regions, supplied its army with all of and more than the shells and artillery needed, and delivered 30,671 aircraft in 1918 against 14,832 in 1917,[142] as well as maintaining a huge engineering complex for shipbuilding and naval repair. Italy's war production peaked in 1918, and by August had made good the massive equipment losses at Caporetto.[143] Its army received 3 million British gas masks and greater quantities of weapons of every kind, including tremendous numbers of shells. It fired off more munitions from January to October 1918 than in the whole of the period from 1915 to 1917: some 14 million projectiles, essentially in two battles.[144] In 1918 both Britain and France returned industrial workers to the front, in contrast with earlier decisions to prioritize manufacturing. The Western European allies were now profiting from investments in armaments infrastructure that America had still to accomplish.

Supply and finance, rather than finished weapons, were the areas where America made its biggest economic contribution. It was only because of American yards that the coalition built more ships than it lost in 1918, as Britain's merchant fleet continued to decline. The United States built over 3 million tons during the year, as much as the total annual world output before 1914.[145] It also made big commodity deliveries. In 1918 French steel purchases from the United States were at thirty times the 1913 level and petroleum purchases at ten times.[146] American food deliveries to France and Italy tided them over a subsistence crisis that greatly worried their governments in early 1918.[147] All this had to be paid for, and the European Allies had so run down their export industries that they could not do so themselves. But after a rocky start the British found the US Treasury reasonably accommodating, albeit under pressure from the State Department and the president. After the summer 1917 sterling crisis* McAdoo agreed to supply more or less regular monthly advances, allowing US credits to support the sterling exchange rate and even to repay the British government's overdraft with J. P. Morgan.[148] The French were not stinted for American purchases,[149] and inter-Allied co-operation propped up the franc until the armistice, while in July 1918 the United States and Britain promised more aid to uphold the Italian lira.[150] However, given Britain's pivotal position, as the purchaser in the United States on behalf of the alliance, the coalition's liquidity depended on Anglo-American financial relations, and London and Washington worked closely enough together to create an Allied currency bloc. Wilson and McAdoo did not for the moment make political demands in return, but they did insist on controlling the Allied purchasing commissions, so that after 1917 the Allies could buy almost nothing in the United States without the government's approval. Finally McAdoo required, and at the November–December 1917 Paris conference the Allies accepted, the creation of the Inter-Allied Council on War Purchases and Finance, to draw up an order of priority for their purchases.[151] They lost the power to play off different suppliers, and had to fit in with the demands on American industry that the War Industries Board was attempting to co-ordinate.

If America was not the 'arsenal of democracy' in the First World War, it did invaluably assist its partners by relieving their foreign exchange constraints and

*See ch. 14.

helping them feed their peoples while they concentrated on military production and manning their fighting services. With America in the war, moreover, the Allies could tighten the blockade. The Americans wanted it to be as watertight as possible, and applied extra leverage to the neutrals by announcing an export embargo, American exports to the Netherlands, Denmark, and Sweden in 1917–18 falling to less than 10 per cent of the 1915–16 figure.[152] Moreover, as Russia's collapse meant that the transit trade through Sweden no longer mattered, Stockholm lost a bargaining counter. The diplomacy was still slow, but in April 1918 the Allies and Americans reached a new agreement with Norway, in May with Sweden, and in September with Denmark, in each case further restricting supplies to Germany.[153] In March, Britain and America requisitioned some 130 Dutch ships lying at anchor in their ports. The Germans retaliated by demanding and obtaining the right to transport goods across Dutch territory, but during 1918 Dutch food deliveries to Germany almost halted.[154] By 1918 Germany's imports may have been only a fifth of the pre-war volume:[155] it was virtually sealed off from the outside world, and the lands it occupied were little compensation. The food supply prospect was the worst since the turnip winter of 1916–17.

The Allies, in contrast, maintained their civilians' and soldiers' food supplies and even improved them. Holtzendorff's predictions were invalidated not only by convoy but also by a range of other measures. By 1917 Britain's wood and timber imports were at a quarter of the pre-war level. Its food imports by tonnage in 1918 were 37 per cent less than in 1913; a big enough difference, it has been calculated, to enable the transport of 1.3 million American troops.[156] Yet despite importing less Britain maintained its munitions production, and its civilians' *per capita* calorific intake may have been little lower in 1918 than in 1914.[157] Government encouragement to farmers to plough up grassland probably contributed to restoring food production to pre-war levels by 1918 after a dip in 1916. However, it seems that the main credit for bolstering consumption levels came from 'food control': for example discarding less of the wheat when grinding flour and mixing in other cereals with it.[158] Rationing, which was introduced for some commodities in 1917–18, evened out food distribution rather than reducing the volume of consumption. Serious shortages occurred in London in early 1918, and working-class diets became less varied and attractive, but Britain's situation was far better than Germany's. That of France, with its smaller urban population and larger agriculture, was also favourable.[159]

The Allies also achieved greater financial stability and lower inflation levels than Germany and Austria-Hungary, thus reducing or at least postponing the danger of a Russian-style collapse. This accomplishment was easiest for the United States, even though once in the war it spent more on it per day than Britain, France, or Germany. Expenditure much exceeded McAdoo's estimates and his 1917 War Revenue Bill got stuck in Congress for six months while his 1918 bill was not approved until after the armistice.[160] Even so, the United States covered a higher proportion of its military spending by taxation than did any other belligerent (admittedly only 23 per cent), and it borrowed at a lower interest rate.[161] The proceeds of the 1917 and 1918 Liberty Loans enabled Wilson and McAdoo to be quite generous with America's partners, and a principal reason why inflationary pressures in the Allied countries were lower than in Germany was their greater ability to borrow abroad. A second reason, in Britain's case, was the capacity of the London discounting market, which absorbed Treasury bills that in Germany were held by the Reichsbank and which it could use to back the note issue.[162] But all the Allies remained cautious about raising taxes for fear of the political repercussions. Although the British lowered the income tax threshold, allowances introduced after 1916 meant that most skilled manual workers escaped liability.[163] However, the excess profits duty accounted for 36 per cent of central government revenue by 1918–19, and by the end of the war both business and the labour movement were becoming restive.[164] In Italy Orlando's finance minister, Francesco Nitti, cheapened food imports by arranging a revaluation of the lira and addressed a serious budget deficit by floating the fifth Italian war loan in spring 1918. This injected revenue into the government's coffers, but as the banks took up much of the issue it added to the danger of a post-war credit and inflation explosion. In France, similarly, Clemenceau's finance minister, Louis-Lucien Klotz, relaxed fiscal discipline and inflation gathered pace.[165] The Allies financed an ever more costly commitment without hyper-inflation or bankruptcy, but they found the task increasingly difficult.

Adequate food and gentle inflation in turn contributed to political stability. The basic pro-war consensus survived, and the enemy offensives reinvigorated it. The victors also benefited from superior leadership. Lloyd George, Clemenceau, and Wilson (and to a lesser extent Orlando) had exceptional abilities as figureheads, eloquently articulating a liberal and patriotic justification for fighting on. Lloyd George and Orlando were effective chairs of relatively broad coalitions of political heavyweights. Clemenceau's approach was the reverse; he excluded his cabinet from diplomacy and strategy, took the war ministry for himself, and assigned foreign affairs to a loyal subordinate, Stephen Pichon, thus directing the war in conjunction with a circle of intimates. Wilson's style was similar. Both models were effective, and both superior to arrangements in Germany, where neither Hertling nor Ludendorff communicated well with the public at large and Wilhelm failed to ensure concerted scrutiny of policy. Hence, prior discussion of the Ludendorff offensives seems to have been confined to the technicians, broader political considerations being even more marginalized than in July 1914 and before the unrestricted submarine warfare decision. Nor, until September 1918, did the Germans acknowledge that the war was lost. Possibly the politicians had deferred to OHL so long that they lacked the capacity for initiative, at least until Hintze became foreign minister. After the second battle of the Marne Berlin behaved as if paralysed, adopting neither a new strategic nor a new political course. The contrast with the forceful measures decided by the Allies to overcome their own emergency during the spring is striking.

Orlando, Clemenceau, and Lloyd George governed societies whose political unity was under challenge, and where the trade unions and the left were partially alienated. But the Austro-German offensives revived some of the mood of 1914. Orlando became premier just before Caporetto, and by replacing Cadorna eliminated a major source of political friction. Diaz established much better working relations with his subordinates and with the government. With Italian territory invaded the anti-interventionists were weakened; the clergy and the socialist moderates urged the duty of resistance and Giolitti gave the government cautious support. As the PSI mainstream leaders still opposed the war, however, the authorities imprisoned the party secretary and the editor of its newspaper *Avanti!*, and tried the Turin party leaders for causing the 1917 riots. Hence unity was based on repression as well as on rallying round the Orlando coalition and on Nitti's financial and economic stabilization measures. All these considerations, plus much lower casualty levels during 1918, helped to sustain Italy for the rest of the war.[166]

In France, Clemenceau led a more narrowly based ministry than his predecessors, from which political veterans such as Briand and Ribot, and the SFIO, were excluded. During the winter of 1917–18 he faced vociferous left-wing opposition to his Russian policy and to his ambiguity about war aims, but he had a secure majority and in economic matters he took power to rule by decree. As the Socialists were no longer in the government he no longer needed to conciliate them, and he ended the practice of holding secret parliamentary sessions, which had weakened his predecessors. At the same time, as war minister, he supervised Pétain closely and maintained a good working relationship with Foch until the armistice. His rule was constitutional but firm, and as in Italy it had a repressive component.[167] Thus he asked for Caillaux's parliamentary immunity to be suspended, and had him arrested and imprisoned. Anti-war activists such as Hélène Brion were tried; convicted traitors such as Bolo Pasha were executed. Clemenceau's actions reduced the parliamentary challenge to the government and broke up the defeatists, though pacifist and socialist opposition to the war continued and probably became more influential in the labour movement. May 1918 was a month of strikes in Paris and many provincial centres, including the steel and armaments plants of St-Etienne. The strikes were mostly occasioned by the call-up of workers, and their most frequent demand was for a negotiated peace (though not one at any price). Hence this was a political movement, though not a revolutionary one. It lacked support from much of the public, given the military emergency; the CGT disowned it, and the strikes quickly collapsed.[168] After the Allies overcame the crisis of the German breakthrough at the Chemin des Dames, Clemenceau's position in the country and in parliament was assured.

Under Lloyd George the British Empire was taking on some of the features of a coalition in its own right. He filled his cabinet and his Downing Street secretariat with visionary advocates of imperial expansion and closer ties between the mother country and its children. Whereas Asquith had avoided convening an Imperial War Conference, Lloyd George summoned one in March–April 1917, the premiers of the self-governing dominions coming to London and sitting in on specially enlarged sessions of the cabinet (renamed in this capacity the Imperial War Cabinet), of which Smuts became a permanent member. The Dominions were therefore somewhat better informed and consulted than previously (though the slaughter of their troops at Third Ypres provoked a furious backlash from their leaders against the British high command). Indeed, not only were Dominion war aims added to British objectives in Africa and the Pacific, but the Imperial War Conference also promised continuous consultation and a voice for the Dominions in imperial foreign policy after the war. This promise included India, whose British and princely rulers also attended the Conference; and the Montagu Declaration of August 1917 promised 'responsible government'. Although these offers of concessions in the future were intended to increase the Empire's present contribution, the war undoubtedly accelerated longer-term processes of decentralization and devolution.[169]

Concessions were needed because politics within the Dominions became more polarized in the second half of the conflict, with conscription as the catalysing issue. In Australia the ruling Labor Party split over it, and henceforward prime minister William Hughes led a 'National' coalition, confronting pacifist, working-class, Irish, and Catholic opponents. In Canada, Sir Robert Borden's government introduced compulsory service but with many exemptions, largely on account of wariness about confronting French Canada, where anti-recruiting riots broke out in Quebec City in 1918. Finally, in South Africa a republican and anti-imperial Afrikaner nationalist movement developed under the leadership of James Hertzog. While Hughes, Borden, and Smuts (and the New Zealand premier William Massey) were increasingly bound up in supporting the imperial war effort, old fault lines reopened at home.[170]

Within the British Isles this latter development was mirrored in southern Ireland. As a result of the spring 1918 emergency the government rushed through a Manpower Act that raised the conscription age from forty-one to fifty and made the Irish liable for the first time to compulsory (though non-combatant) service. The measure was never enforced – for fear of resistance when the army was already fully stretched – but it completed the ousting of moderate Irish nationalism by the harsher republican variant. Yet in the rest of the country Lloyd George generally had an easier political ride than Clemenceau, despite the BEF's near-collapse under Ludendorff's blows, which led to the most serious challenge to his ministry in parliament and could have been highly damaging. Major-General Sir Frederick Maurice, the Director of Military Operations until April 1918, alleged in the press that the government had kept the BEF undermanned and left troops in Palestine that could have been moved to France. The implication was that the government's statements were misleading and that it bore responsibility for the defeat. But in the 'Maurice debate' in the Commons on 9 May Asquith presented the issue poorly and Lloyd George extricated himself with evasions. He warned that if defeated he would resign and call an election, and a motion for a committee of inquiry was lost by 239 votes to 106.[171] The prime minister was fortunate not to face systematic opposition from Asquith, who had lost credit as a wartime leader and half of whose party supported the government. Lloyd George strengthened his position relative to the high command after Passchendaele, the removal of Robertson, and the crisis in March, which probably damaged the military leaders more than it did the government. Finally, industrial unrest was easing, on account of food rationing and wage increases for skilled workers, and possibly because of nervousness caused by the Bolsheviks' peace negotiations.[172] In Britain as in France the domestic regime became increasingly repressive in 1917–18, the authorities using censorship and the threat of conscription to silence dissent.[173] None the less, during the months of military emergency trade-union resistance to government policy virtually ceased, and strike activity revived only after the tide had turned. Even then, it was largely confined to economic grievances, and the authorities' monitoring of public opinion suggested (as in France) in autumn 1918 that it favoured carrying on until the Germans were decisively beaten.

Recent historical research has highlighted the 'remobilization' of political support for the war effort in the belligerents in 1917–18, following the initial patriotic upsurge of 1914–15.[174] In France the effort was spearheaded by the Union des grandes associations contre la propagande ennemie (UGACPE), founded in March 1917, and in Britain by the National War Aims Committee (NWAC), founded in August. Both were symptoms of a growing state concern to buttress civilian morale: the 'self-mobilization' of 1914–15 was no longer adequate. Moreover, the UGACPE was initially directed against German peace feelers; the NWAC was a response to the British strikes of May 1917. In contrast to earlier propaganda drives, they focused less on specific tasks such as recruitment and selling loans and more on maintaining general patriotic consciousness and support for the war. Thus both focused on the need for peace through victory and on rejecting compromise with a ruthlessly militaristic foe. Both had ministers on their governing committees and served official purposes, yet both professed to be independent. The UGACPE rested on local networks of schoolteachers and patriotic associations; the NWAC on the constituency organizations of the Conservative and Liberal Parties that in 1914–15 had led the parliamentary recruiting campaign. Each therefore represented a joint effort by the government and social elites, and their scale was imposing. The UGACPE represented 30,000 societies with over 11 million members:[175] it distributed 5 million tracts and organized over 3,000 meetings in 1917 and more in 1918; in 1918 the NWAC held 10,000 meetings.[176] Yet neither attracted much support from the left – an indication of the weakening of consensus. True, the NWAC held well-attended gatherings in working-class areas and had some success against pacifist agitation; but the UGACPE had little impact on workers' attitudes in France, where it seems the Ludendorff offensives did more than anything else to harden the public mood. In America the Committee on Public Information was even more ambitious: 75,000 lectures by 'four-minute men', 6,000 press releases, exhibitions visited by over ten million people, and 75 million copies distributed in several languages of over thirty pamphlets on the United States and the war.[177] Its director, George Creel, and the publicists he co-opted had an evangelistic fervour for communicating the justice of America's cause, but American ideological mobilization had a darker side. The Sedition Act, passed in May 1918, prohibited abusive or disloyal language about the constitution, flag, government, and army or navy uniform, Wilson endorsing it to head off something even more extreme. The American Protection League, a private organization with federal government funding, enrolled 250,000 citizens to spy on neighbours and work colleagues. It opened mail, intercepted telegrams, and carried out raids against suspected draft evaders, preparing the ground for the post-war 'red scare'.[178] The war became a disaster for the American progressive and pacifist movements, and by encouraging the growth of nationalist xenophobia (for example, in speeches condemning disloyal ethnic minorities) the president played sorcerer's apprentice, weakening the supporters of his diplomatic objectives. His home and foreign policies were poorly matched, and although he foresaw the danger his own actions magnified it. At the end of the war, when his ideals seemed to triumph abroad, he was politically humiliated at home.

Integral to rekindling support for the war effort was the issue of war aims. In response to war weariness, American pressure, the radicalization of the left, and the Russian Revolution, the Allied governments had begun revising their declared aims during 1917, as evidenced by the Dumont Resolution, the Balfour Declaration, and support for a League of Nations. Lloyd George's Caxton Hall speech and Wilson's Fourteen Points were the culmination of this process. In response to Brest-Litovsk and Ludendorff's hammer blows, the coalition achieved greater diplomatic solidarity and went over to the ideological offensive. Wilson had attempted with the Fourteen Points to appeal to the German and the Allied left against their governments, but he lost faith in the German socialists and his Baltimore speech on 6 April proclaimed that 'force, force to the utmost, must now decide the issue'.[179] He suspended his campaign against his partners' war aims, and the British showed greater support for France's claims to Alsace-Lorraine and its post-war economic objectives.

More dramatically, the Allies and Americans for the first time made Austria-Hungary's destruction in effect a public goal. Previously they had promised Habsburg territory to Italy, Serbia, and Romania and encouraged nationalist organizations as a source of manpower. Thus a Polish army was formed in France in June 1917, and later in the year the Western powers recognized the Polish National Committee as the official representative of the Poles abroad. Its counterpart, the Czechoslovak National Council, benefited from its authority over the Czech Legion in Russia, whereas the Yugoslav Committee (of South Slav exiles) was hampered by Italy's reluctance to allow it similar authority over Serbo-Croat prisoners of war.[180] Yet the Allies still hoped for a separate peace with Austria-Hungary, Lloyd George's and Wilson's January 1918 speeches envisaging only autonomy for its peoples, while Italy had no desire to see the Austrian threat replaced by one from a South Slav state. This situation changed after Brest-Litovsk, the Czernin incident, and the crisis caused by Ludendorff's attacks. Germany seemed to be building a vast and invulnerable dominion in Eastern Europe, and Austria-Hungary refused to break with it. Hence the Allies stepped up their support for the Habsburg nationalities as the only remaining card to play, rather than because they particularly desired the break-up of the Monarchy.

The French led the way, with the Americans and British not far behind. Polish claims received the strongest endorsement, an Allied declaration in June 1918 approving a united and independent Poland with free access to the sea. The Allies hoped to win over the Poles and undermine Germany and Austria, and could now ignore the traditional Russian obstacle to Polish aspirations.[181] The Italians could not be similarly ignored, but Caporetto weakened them and they were now less concerned that a Yugoslav state would mean a Russian naval base in the Adriatic. British intermediaries opened up a dialogue between the Orlando government and the Croat politicians in exile, and the Rome Congress of Oppressed Nationalities, held in April 1918, suggested that the Italians now viewed themselves and the South Slavs as fellow combatants against Habsburg tyranny and were willing to settle territorial differences by applying self-determination. In reality, they were following a dual policy, Sonnino remaining as foreign minister and still committed to the London Treaty promises of 1915. Nevertheless they loosened up enough to enable the Allies in June 1918 to express 'warm sympathy' for the Yugoslavs and Czechoslovaks in 'their struggle for liberty and the realization of their national aspirations'.[182] The latter was the crucial case, as an independent Czechoslovakia (which the Czech leaders were now demanding) would unambiguously signal not just the mutilation of the Dual Monarchy but its destruction. The Czech Legion's revolt in Russia increased the Czech lobbyists' influence, and an American statement on 28 June spelled out that 'all branches of the Slav race should be completely freed from German and Austrian rule',[183] implying that the autonomy envisaged in the Fourteen Points would no longer suffice. In any case, by this stage defeat at the battle of the Piave and the growth of separatism among the national leaders within the Dual Monarchy meant its break-up could scarcely be averted.

Such pronouncements, following the Allies' declarations in the winter of 1917–18, indicated that the war was becoming more aggressively ideological. It had always been defended as a struggle to defend democracy, law, and self-determination against oppressive and militaristic autocracies; increasingly it was becoming a crusade to destroy the regimes that had caused it. This reformulation – especially by Wilson, a figure who seemed remote from traditional imperialism – helped to reconcile the moderate left to supporting the Allied and American cause. It also had a bearing on the final topic to be considered here, that of troop morale. Under Diaz, a relatively humane commander who was anxious to improve morale and training, the Italian army underwent a recuperation process comparable to the French one under Pétain. Its rations improved, home leave almost doubled, and Cadorna's notorious summary executions virtually ceased.[184] On the Western Front, morale seems not to have been a problem among most of the Americans, even if discipline occasionally was: no AEF soldiers were executed for desertion, though thirty-three were executed for murder or rape.[185] As for the French army, although British and American observers noted its soldiers' caution, it suffered and inflicted heavy casualties during 1918 with no renewal of the mutinies. The same applied to the BEF, although GHQ removed the Australians from the line in October after serious unrest, provoked by their justified suspicion that they were being used too frequently as shock troops. None the less, the contrast with the routs of the Bulgarians and Turks in September and with the break-up of the German and Austro-Hungarian forces was evident.

Among the factors favouring the Allies were much better supplies of food and equipment, less oppressive discipline than earlier in the war, and confidence born of visible success and the approach of victory. In addition, however, the Allies embarked during 1918 on an aggressive propaganda drive against the enemy armies on the battlefronts. The AEF set up a 'front propaganda' agency in conjunction with the CPI, and American military intelligence distributed over 3 million leaflets into German lines by the armistice.[186] The European Allies' contribution was still more impressive. In March 1918 the French set up a new Centre d'action de propagande contre l'ennemi to step up propaganda against the German people and army,[187] and the British intensified their efforts at the same time. Their most significant overseas propaganda before 1917 had been in the United States, conducted discreetly through the agency of Wellington House. Such methods were not feasible in the Central Powers, and Lloyd George, an impatient man who knew similar men in Fleet Street, wanted something done. The outcome, after several reorganizations, was the appointment in March of Lord Northcliffe as Director of Propaganda in Enemy Countries and Lord Beaverbrook as Minister of Information.[188] Beaverbrook's responsibilities included the Ottoman Empire, but Austria-Hungary and Germany came under Northcliffe. His assignment was to act directly on public opinion through all the media available, and he concentrated first on the Dual Monarchy as the more vulnerable target. In February the cabinet authorized him to encourage the nationalities, on the condition of promising autonomy rather than independence.[189] For the purpose he brought in *The Times*'s foreign editor, Wickham Steed, and an academic specialist, R. W. Seton-Watson. The two men encouraged the Italians down the road that led to the Rome Congress, and helped to establish the Padua Commission, an inter-Allied propaganda agency attached to the Italian GHQ.[190] Following the battle of the Piave the beaten Austro-Hungarian troops were an easy prey. After May, however, Lloyd George asked Northcliffe to pay similar attention to the Germans.[191] Northcliffe and his agents had urged the Allies to commit themselves to self-determination as a weapon against Austria-Hungary, and now they wanted to use democratization against Germany. When the new civilian agencies were added to the longstanding efforts of French and British military intelligence, the effect was to deluge the German and Austro-Hungarian armies with propaganda, as the Central Powers had deluged the Russian army in 1917. Much of the material was dropped from balloons. Aircraft were also used against the Austrians, but not against the Germans, who threatened to try captured pilots. The French fired leaflets from shells, and they subsidized newspapers run by German dissidents in Switzerland and the Netherlands that were smuggled into the Reich. In spring 1918 British military intelligence was producing a million leaflets a month and up to 250,000 copies a week of a trench newspaper in German; between 1 and 2 million leaflets were fired at the Germans on 12 and 13 July, on the eve of their final offensive.[192] The themes included militarism, food shortages, tension between Prussia and the smaller states, and the charge that this was not the German people's war. Yet many factors caused the Central Powers' armies to collapse, and propaganda was only the icing on the cake. Although both Ludendorff and Hitler subsequently highlighted the contribution of Allied propaganda to Germany's collapse, they had their own reasons for exaggerating it,[193] and a modern study has questioned the effectiveness of propaganda even against Austria-Hungary.[194] Millions of leaflets could do their work only when accompanied by millions of shells.

All the same, the word 'propaganda' took on its modern connotation during the war.[195] Its rapid growth in the final months was another sign that the conflict was entering a new stage, taking on many characteristics shared by major wars ever since. In the summer and autumn of 1918 a tremendous outpouring of Allied energy fell on enfeebled enemies. The Allies created a new set of co-ordinating institutions: Foch's commandership, the SWC, the Inter-Allied Council on War Purchases and Finance, the AMTC, and the propaganda and blockade committees. They had become more cohesive, as a combination of democracies bound together by their command of the seas. They fed their populations better than did their enemies, and kept their currencies more stable. They comprehensively won the production battle for the key implements of the new warfare: light machine guns, heavy artillery, tanks, and aircraft. They combined veteran Anglo-French and Italian troops with fresh and rapidly transported Americans. Their logistical systems were resilient and they had evolved combinations of tactics to which the Central Powers had no answer. Their home fronts had partially recovered from the turmoil of 1917, and their political chiefs, for all their flaws, were effective rallying symbols and driving forces for their governments. Their war aims were better publicized and were linked to persuasive general principles. Their coalition held numerous inherent assets. Yet many of these assets came fully into play only because of the Central Powers' onslaught between Caporetto and the second battle of the Marne: it was this emergency that elicited the Fourteen Points, the huge increase in the flow of American troops, Foch's command, and the recovery of domestic political cohesion and diplomatic solidarity. As so often in such an evenly matched and hard fought struggle, one side's climacteric contained within it the seeds of its demise.

CHAPTER 17

CEASEFIRE

THE ALLIES HAD survived their 1917 crisis and the Central Powers had played their final card, bringing both sides to the watershed of summer 1918. Such shifts in the campaigning balance had occurred before, however, and in July and August hardly anyone in authority expected the fighting to end quickly. The 'short-war illusion' of 1914 had become a long-war illusion, so that when the cease-fire came it too was a surprise, and – or so many urged in retrospect – a premature one. The war's abrupt conclusion provides an object lesson in war termination gen-erally, partly because the conflict had been so intractable hitherto.[1] For despite the changes on the battlefields, the same underlying triple stalemate had remained in place: both sides thought victory possible, governments committed to it remained in office, and their war aims were too divergent for a negotiated settlement. It was true that hostilities on the Eastern Front had terminated and that for most of 1918 the Italian and Balkan Fronts were quiet. But this subsiding of violence in the lesser the-atres was overshadowed by the paroxysm in the west after Ludendorff began his of-fensives. Furthermore, for the bloodshed to stop *both* sides needed to agree they would no longer pursue the struggle between them by fighting. If the Central Powers had to request an armistice, the Allies and Americans had to concede one, at the moment when the tide was at last flowing their way. Like the decisions to start the war, those to stop it should be analysed as being in the first instance due to rational appraisal, despite there being evidence that both sides miscalculated. Given Luden-dorff's veto power over German policy the starting point could only be a reassess-ment by OHL, which led on 4 October to Berlin requesting a ceasefire and a settlement based on Wilson's peace programme. When the Germans published this appeal, however, Ludendorff hoped to get off lightly, or at least to win a breathing space. Only later did the Central Powers resolve to accept much harsher terms than they had initially envisaged. The first issue to consider here is therefore the armistice application, and the second the American and Allied response to it. The third is the Central Powers' acceptance of their enemies' conditions, not the least of the reasons being revolutions that overthrew Wilhelm II and broke Austria-Hungary into pieces.

After the second battle of the Marne Ludendorff still supposed he could wear out the Allies by a stubborn holding action with limited counter-attacks.[2] However, the battle of Amiens showed (as Hindenburg put it) that the army had failed in defensive as well as offensive mode.[3] But at the Spa conference on 13–14 August he and Ludendorff still envisaged that defensive operations might yet paralyse the Allies' will to fight and when Hertling pointed to civilian war weariness at home, Ludendorff said the answer was more discipline and repression. Hintze, the new foreign minister, doubted the Allies' resolve would falter, and warned that Austria-Hungary could not survive another winter and that the Turks were going their own way in the Caucasus. But it was agreed that Germany should seek peace after the next success in the west, rather than at once. When Karl arrived to plead for immediate peace conversations, he found the Germans still against them.[4] Hindenburg and Ludendorff told Arz von Straussenburg that by shortening the line and calling up reserves they hoped to equalize the contest, though they agreed with him that the Central Powers must keep their armies sufficiently intact to maintain internal order.[5] For the time being Germany remained committed to the Brest-Litovsk Treaty, and by the supplementary agreements of August it expanded its influence in Russia. Plans to tighten relations with Austria-Hungary also continued, resulting in October in an agreement to move towards freer trade.[6] As vice-chancellor Payer hinted in a speech on 10 September, the Germans hoped to maintain their predominance in Eastern and Central Europe in exchange for sacrificing their colonies and accepting the 1914 *status quo* in the west. But they still resisted ceding more than a fraction of Alsace-Lorraine or abandoning Belgium. The most Hintze could extract from OHL was agreement that Belgium could regain its independence on the guarantee that no other country would enjoy preferential status there over Germany.[7] The Allies were equally unbending, as the Austrians discovered when on 14 September, in defiance of Berlin's wishes, they publicly appealed for non-binding discussions between the two sides. After the battle of Amiens the Austrians had lost faith in German invincibility and were desperate for peace before the winter, but the Allied leaders flatly rejected their approach.[8] It seemed that the turn of military fortunes had failed to soften the Germans' war aims while hardening those of their enemies, and Vienna was ground between the two millstones.

The decisive change began at OHL (at this stage based at Spa in Belgium), where Ludendorff suffered something akin to a nervous breakdown. From mid-July, after two years of primary responsibility for his country's destiny, his tense, workaholic personality had shown signs of cracking. His temper was short, his relations with subordinates and with Hindenburg were strained, he could not sleep, and he drank to excess. The advice he had taken in early September from Dr. Hochheimer, a psychiatrist and an old friend, to go for walks and take more rest, had brought only temporary relief. On the evening of the 28th he collapsed, and decided Germany must at once seek a ceasefire.[9]

As in 1914, events in the Balkans started the avalanche. The news on 28 September that Bulgaria had requested an armistice overwhelmed Ludendorff even before he knew the final terms. As signed on the 29th, they required the Bulgarians to demobilize, evacuate Greece and Serbia, and allow the Allies to occupy their territory as a base for further operations.[10] An Allied advance could now undo the Central Powers' triumphs of 1915, cut overland communications with the Ottoman Empire, and revive the threat to Austria-Hungary's southern border. If the Allies entered Romania, the consequences would be still graver. Because of a disappointing harvest Romania had become less crucial as a grain supplier, but (so Ludendorff advised his government) the German army's aircraft depended entirely on Romanian oil and in its absence stocks would run out after two months. Half Germany's lorries and one third of the U-boats were equally dependent, and industry risked losing its principal source of high-grade lubricant.[11] This time, in contrast to the crisis caused by Romania's intervention in 1916, it was impossible to plug the Balkan dyke. Squabbling over the eastern peace treaties had fractured the Central Powers' solidarity, and they had fewer forces to spare. Bulgaria's surrender therefore mattered in its own right, and its impact on Ludendorff might seem to vindicate arguments that the Allies' efforts in 'sideshow' theatres counted more than those in France and Belgium. But in reality the Balkan offensive delivered the *coup de grâce* only because it was combined with unprecedented pressure in the main theatre. In late September OHL faced co-ordinated offensives all along the Western Front, backed by numerical superiority and massive artillery capacity. Ludendorff had known for days that the Bulgarians were on the run, and he may have used their ceasefire request as a pretext for an initiative that he had already decided was necessary. Although he told his close advisers that Bulgaria's defection meant the war was lost,[12] he was also extremely worried about the western battles. The Meuse–Argonne offensive had begun at dawn on the 26th, the British attack towards Cambrai on the 27th, and the British-Belgian attack in Flanders on the 28th itself, while on the same day the most intense bombardment of the war was in progress prior to the British Fourth Army's assault on the Hindenburg Line. One by one, the Allies were overcoming the Germans' best-prepared positions.[13] German unit strengths had fallen drastically because of battle casualties, desertion, capture, and illness, and Ludendorff and his staff had almost no reserve forces available.[14] Reports from the censors of German soldiers' correspondence made their despondency, especially in the rear areas, very clear to the army commands and to OHL.[15] Ludendorff was also well informed about the home front, where surveys had uncovered deepening civilian pessimism and anxiety since July,[16] and the food supply remained precarious.[17] None the less, what broke OHL was less the gradual deterioration of domestic circumstances than the emergency on the battlefronts.

On the morning of 28 September Ludendorff concluded that Germany must seek peace and form a parliamentary government for this purpose; by the evening he decided it must prove its seriousness by asking Wilson for an immediate armistice.[18] He found that Hindenburg shared his views, the two men agreeing that even if the Western Front held, the Balkan collapse meant the military situation could only worsen.[19] German troops everywhere still stood on enemy territory, but the key difference from earlier reappraisals was that no jokers remained to play. Even hopes of exhausting the enemy by a stubborn defensive were now unrealistic. Yet this was neither a simple technical judgement, nor a decision for a ceasefire on any terms. A key concern, as Ludendorff told his staff in an emotional conference afterwards, was that of protecting the army from a disorderly rout that would render it useless against revolution. Already it was being poisoned by socialist ideas, unreliable units were being pulled out of line, and '*no* confidence was possible in the troops'. The Allies were close to a 'wholesale' breakthrough, which must be avoided. He intended to bring into government the left-wing politicians whose conduct he blamed for the débâcle, so that they should sup on the broth they had cooked. He commented privately that accepting Wilson's programme might be harmless because the Fourteen Points were vague and open to interpretation: moreover, if the enemy demands proved excessive Germany could renew the fighting after having rested. This assumption was naive, not least because – despite warnings – Ludendorff underestimated the danger that appealing for an armistice might provoke the very collapse of discipline and order that he feared.[20]

OHL's change of tack had created an opening, but it was Hintze and the foreign ministry who saw most clearly how to exploit it. Hintze's significance was greater than his short tenure in office might suggest. He probably recognised earlier than Ludendorff that Germany needed to cut its losses. His diplomatic sources suggested that Berlin and Washington had common interests such as free trade and freedom of the seas and that it might be possible to play off America against Britain and France. Even if the Americans departed from their own programme, he foresaw that accepting it might provide a basis for revising the peace treaty later. His sources also suggested that Germany might get better terms if it changed its political system, and he believed the best way to muffle the political aftershock that followed defeat would be a stage-managed democratization: a 'revolution from above' to avert one from below.[21] In fact, even before Bulgaria collapsed, defeat and shortages had revived the restless political atmosphere of July 1917. Wilhelm was being publicly criticized, as was Hertling, whose franchise reform bill had been blocked in the Prussian upper chamber. Conditions were ripe for a change of ministry and for bringing in the socialists to share responsibility for defeat. However, the SPD would not enter government without constitutional amendments to allow ministers to be Reichstag deputies, which Hertling rejected.[22] Hintze now resolved to bypass the chancellor. On 28 September, independently of the events at OHL, a memorandum from his officials called for a broad national government formed in consultation with the Reichstag party leaders; 'at the opportune moment' it should secretly tell Wilson it accepted the Fourteen Points and ask him to arrange peace. On the same day Ludendorff's staff, without consulting their chief, invited Hintze to Spa. Hintze's plan did not envisage seeking an armistice or acting at once; Ludendorff feared that a change of government would cause delay. But with Hintze at Spa (and in Hertling's absence) the two conceptions could fuse. On the morning of the 29th Hindenburg and Ludendorff convinced Hintze of the urgency of the military situation; he won them over to his 'revolution from above' and the three men then brought round Wilhelm, probably convincing him that despite his distrust of Wilson this was the best way to save his throne. All concerned rejected the alternative of a dictatorship.[23] Hence, Imperial Germany would try simultaneously to democratize and to disengage from defeat. It embarked on its last and most perilous initiative on the basis of ill-founded expectations about America and of a failure to foresee that a public armistice appeal would shatter its alliances and what remained of its domestic cohesion.

Before the plan could be implemented the change of government caused delay. Hertling arrived in Spa that afternoon to find that critical decisions had been taken without him. As in 1914, Wilhelm was making policy impulsively in *ad hoc* conclaves rather than allowing collective deliberation. The chancellor resigned rather than accept constitutional change, and Hintze went too, claiming that for him to stay in the government would weaken the appearance of liberalization. On the 30th Prince Max of Baden was selected as Hertling's successor: a man acceptable to Ludendorff as the heir to the throne of the Grand Duchy but also a liberal with a reputation for moderation over war aims. Thus far politicians and emperor had simply accepted Ludendorff's programme without cross-questioning him about his military assessment. Max, in contrast, foresaw the risks of publicly admitting defeat and was not convinced the outlook was as bleak as OHL depicted it. He wanted more time to prepare a peace feeler. On 2 October, however, two fresh developments brought him round.[24] The first was a briefing of the party leaders by Major von dem Bussche on behalf of OHL. Bussche explained that the Bulgarian collapse threatened the Danube food supply route and contact with Turkey, while in the west Germany faced massive attacks supported by tanks and American troops and its manpower was nearly exhausted. It might soon have to abandon extensive territories and the weaker it grew the harsher would be the surrender terms. The report dumbfounded Bussche's listeners. Previously OHL had said a favourable outcome remained possible, but now it seemed the struggle was irretrievably lost.[25] The second development came that evening, when Wilhelm spelled out to Max that he had not been appointed to make difficulties for the high command. Max still feared an armistice request would exacerbate Allied jingoism and weaken Wilson, but faced with Ludendorff's continuing insistence the cabinet finally decided to send the note, which went off on the night of 4/5 October. It was short and simple, requesting Wilson to take in hand arrangements for an immediate armistice and for peace negotiations in which Germany would accept as a basis the Fourteen Points and the formulations in his subsequent speeches.[26]

The initiative appeared to emanate not from OHL but from a new government that represented the SPD, the Catholic Centre, and the Liberal parties who comprised the Reichstag majority, and was committed to democratic reform.[27] As Ludendorff intended, the parliamentary opposition could thus be saddled with responsibility for admitting defeat. In fact by now Ludendorff was taking a calmer view of conditions in the west and predicting an orderly withdrawal rather than a damburst, although he still believed that an armistice was urgent.[28] This new appreciation strengthens the evidence that on 28 September his nerves had failed, although he later denied it. But OHL had opened the way for the Hintze plan, Wilhelm agreeing to it with few questions and the new and inexperienced government soon falling into line. By autumn 1918 the Central Powers were going to be defeated in any event, but in the first instance their initiative determined the timing and the circumstances of the ending of the conflict. It could only do so, however, in conjunction with a response from the other side.

The Germans' request for an armistice was yet one more in a long line of efforts to divide their antagonists, admittedly this time by means of a general (if possibly temporary) ceasefire rather than a separate peace. It assumed that by appealing to the American president rather than the Allies collectively and by accepting in principle his peace programme, the Central Powers could protect themselves from more extreme demands. OHL made no close study of the Fourteen Points until 5 October,[29] Ludendorff casually assuming that they were subject to reinterpretation and that Berlin could disengage if the enemy conditions were too draconian.[30] The German politicians, however, had given the matter more careful attention. The co-ordinating committee of the Reichstag majority parties had agreed in February that the Fourteen Points offered a tolerable basis for peace provided Germany lost no territory (and Wilson had indeed left some leeway over Alsace-Lorraine).[31] Whereas Max himself wanted to hedge over the Points, Erzberger and Philip Scheidemann (the principal representatives of the Catholic Centre and the SPD in the new government) insisted on accepting them unequivocally.[32] Ever since the president had set out his terms, an appeal to him had been an obvious gambit, and in autumn 1918 he once again publicly distanced himself from his co-belligerents. House advised him to tie the hands of the 'reactionaries in authority' in the European Allied countries before military success made them less conciliatory,[33] and Wilson attempted to do so in his speech in New York on 27 September, in which he called for a peace based on impartial justice and condemned 'special, selfish economic combinations' outside the League of Nations – thus acknowledging German fears of being excluded from world markets after the war.[34] He was looking for a chance to bind his partners even before the German request arrived.

From 4 to 23 October the world therefore witnessed the spectacle of a public exchange of messages between Berlin and Washington while fighting continued and the European Allies were sidelined. Wilson sent three notes to Germany, on 8, 14, and 23 October, and Germany replied on the 12th, 20th, and 27th. The outcome was that Wilson undertook to seek an armistice and a peace based on the Fourteen Points, and having apparently reached a separate deal with Germany he turned to Britain, France, and Italy. He combined the roles of belligerent and arbiter. Yet his conduct was less impartial than this summary suggests, and in comparison with the Ludendorff/Hintze conception the Germans had to yield much ground. To begin with, however, Wilson was unsure how to respond and was feeling his way. He had little intelligence about Germany's intentions, his officials gave him conflicting advice,[35] and much of the press and Congress wanted him to reject the approach. None the less, he decided to take it further, probably because he sensed an opportunity to commit both sides to his terms. Without consulting his partners, he sent an exploratory reply on 8 October that tried to smoke the Germans out. Did they accept the principles in his speeches, he asked, and for whom did Max's government speak? The only military condition he mentioned was the evacuation of Allied territory, without stipulating a deadline, and his tentative language suggested to the Germans that they could withdraw to their frontiers at their own speed, not even abandoning Alsace-Lorraine.

In contrast Wilson's second note, on the 14th, effectively raised his conditions and opened the decisive phase. A contributory reason was the resurgence of the submarine issue after a U-boat torpedo sank a British liner, the *Leinster*, on 12 October, with the loss of 450 lives, including those of 135 women and children.[36] The timing could hardly have been worse, and the new note demanded an end to 'illegal and inhumane practices'. But other factors too converged to harden the president's line. The American mid-term elections were approaching and much of the Republican opposition was calling for unconditional surrender. In an intransigent Senate debate on 7 October even Democratic senators had urged going on to Berlin and the chairman of the Foreign Relations Commission had said it would be 'absolutely abhorrent' to stop now. Wilson was shocked by 'how war mad our people have become', and he accepted his advisers' recommendations against making peace with the men responsible for the war or giving Germany any strategic advantage. Further, when the Allied prime ministers warned that evacuating Allied territory was inadequate and that the armistice conditions must acknowledge the views of their military experts, he assured them that he agreed. Hence the 14 October note stipulated that the ceasefire must guarantee the Allies' 'present military superiority' and that the 'arbitrary power' governing Germany must be destroyed or rendered impotent. More than the first note this reflected Wilson's true position: he was willing for peace if the Germans accepted his conditions, but he would not let them use the armistice to gain military benefit and he wanted real constitutional change.

The German reply on 20 October apparently gave satisfaction on these points: it promised to stop torpedo attacks on passenger ships, insisted that future governments would be responsible to the Reichstag, and accepted that the Allied military advisers should decide the ceasefire terms. But now, in an episode recalling the Zimmermann telegram, the British disclosed to Wilson an intercepted cable from the German foreign ministry to its consulate in Georgia, envisaging stage-managed local appeals for the German garrison there to remain. Wilson saw this as further evidence of 'trickery and deceit', and his third note on 23 October agreed to forward Berlin's armistice request to his allies but reiterated that the ceasefire must render Germany unable to resist any eventual peace treaty and (if not in exactly these words) that he must demand an end to Wilhelm's control of policy. His minimum requirements were for a fully constitutional monarchy and parliamentary control over the high command. The president was privately willing for Wilhelm to stay in a purely titular capacity, and even saw him as a safeguard against Germany's becoming Bolshevik, but he remained wary and his Democratic Party election managers warned him not to expose himself to charges of being soft on the enemy. By this stage, however, most of his cabinet and the press had rallied to his support, and provided that an armistice contained adequate safeguards they were now willing to accept one.[37]

The Germans had submitted to American interference in their internal affairs, and accepted that the Allied military advisers would decide the armistice terms. This latter point was crucial as it meant the ceasefire would confirm the Allies' superiority and make it impossible to renew the war, and Berlin conceded it only after a civil–military crisis. Ludendorff had recovered from his panic, and on 9 October he told Max the army could defend the frontiers 'for a long time yet'. However, Wilson's first note suggested Germany could extricate itself by evacuating Allied soil (and not necessarily abandoning the east), and OHL wanted to preserve the army intact as an instrument of pressure in the peace negotiations.[38] In contrast the 14 October note ended the false sense of security, provoking demands from the right for a *levée en masse*: breaking off negotiations and calling up every available man on the model of the French Revolution. Yet Max and his ministers, aware of the longing for peace in Germany's cities, feared that if they failed to deliver it revolution would engulf them as it had the Russian liberals. They did not believe the war should continue, or would have popular support, over the issue of unrestricted submarine warfare.[39] Before the cabinet made up its mind, however, it reviewed all aspects of Germany's situation in a marathon session on 17 October: the decision to halt the war, in fact, was evaluated much more professionally than had been the decision to start it.

Ludendorff now advised that if they could get through the next few weeks, the pressure in the west would ease as winter drew in. An Allied breakthrough was 'possible' rather than 'probable'. Both he and (more emphatically) Scheer, his naval counterpart, believed that if Germany carried on into 1919 it could get better terms. Indeed, he said no worse conditions than the present ones were conceivable – to which Max rejoined that invasion and devastation would be worse, but Ludendorff denied things had come to that yet. Hintze's successor as foreign minister, Wilhelm Solf, commented that OHL had coerced Max into requesting the armistice, but as soon as difficult decisions were needed it said Germany could hold out after all. In fact there were genuine grounds for saying that with the campaigning season ending and the army retreating in good order Ludendorff had overestimated the danger and his new opinion was more realistic, though from his own testimony it was hard to see how matters could improve by the spring, in which case the original logic that it was better to stop before they further deteriorated continued to apply. The critical inference for the cabinet, however, was that Ludendorff was an opportunist whose appraisals were not delivered in good faith. Max had lost confidence in him and believed that within months Germany's position would become desperate, not least because of the loss of Romanian oil. The government resolved that negotiations must continue and that this meant concessions: it halted attacks on passenger ships, and (after the navy protested that it was impossible to operate cruiser rules) it secretly ordered U-boat operations to end completely. But this decision revived the old coalition of 1916, OHL supporting Scheer's insistence that unrestricted submarine warfare must continue, and that Germany should break off negotiations rather than submit. Probably Ludendorff was seizing a pretext to distance himself from a venture that had turned out differently from his expectations, but one of the Western Front army group commanders, Rupprecht of Bavaria, was warning the chancellor that the troops were exhausted and negotiations must be pursued. Hence Max decided to accept Wilson's conditions, bringing over Wilhelm (who opposed abandoning the submarine campaign) by threatening to resign. By so doing he drove a wedge between the Kaiser and the high command, though Wilhelm's relations with Ludendorff had always been strained and now reached breaking point.[40]

Wilson's third note completed the process. As before, the German cabinet feared that drafting working-class conscripts for last-ditch resistance would lead to revolution, and it perceived no need to break off the exchange; correctly, it did not see Wilson as insisting on Wilhelm's removal. Hindenburg and Ludendorff, in contrast, arrived in Berlin without permission and unilaterally issued an order to the army that the note was unacceptable. Max now had the flagrant insubordination that he needed to insist on a change in the high command, and Wilhelm was angry enough to overcome his fear of Ludendorff. After a furious confrontation with the sovereign on 26 October Ludendorff asked to be dismissed and Wilhelm agreed, while ordering that Hindenburg should stay and thus opening a lasting breach between the two generals. Ludendorff's successor, Wilhelm Groener, had been ousted in 1917 from his position as head of the Kriegsamt because Ludendorff thought him too sympathetic to working-class demands. He was much more supple and politically astute than his predecessor, and 26 October marked the end of OHL's veto over policy. Moreover, the new government was introducing legislation to allow ministers to sit in the Reichstag and to require that the chancellor enjoyed its confidence. In future the chancellor or the war minister (rather than Wilhelm's household) should appoint officers, and a declaration of war would need parliamentary approval. Together these changes would go far to subordinating the military and transforming Wilhelm into a constitutional monarch.[41] If Wilson was prepared to grant a peace based on the Fourteen Points, the German authorities were now willing and able to accept his conditions.

Thus far the negotiations had been largely a dialogue between Washington and Berlin. It remained to introduce the third element of the equation. Britain, France, and Italy had been in the war much longer and suffered much heavier losses than had the Americans, and they had borne the brunt of the fighting even in 1918. They now faced the risk of a *fait accompli* and of commitment by implication to a peace programme that their governments had never been consulted on and privately viewed with suspicion. Wilson had intended with the New York speech to bind them to his objectives and had handled the armistice correspondence with the same goal in mind, telling his cabinet on 20 October that he might have to coerce his partners if they made difficulties.[42] At the same meeting McAdoo warned about the financial implications of continuing into 1919, even for an economy as strong as that of the United States. It was probably more important for the president, however, that prolonging the conflict might undermine his political purpose by strengthening xenophobia and weakening support in America for a moderate peace programme, while too complete a victory would diminish his leverage over the European Allies.[43] On the other hand, France and Britain were willing to call a halt before the United States dominated the coalition even more completely, giving it the decisive voice at the peace conference. The differences among the victors explain the paradox that a weakening in Germany's war aims was not offset by a strengthening in Allied ones, and why enough common ground existed to restore peace.

The Allied leaders discussed the armistice conditions at two conferences in Paris, from 6 to 9 October and 29 October to 4 November. The first – at which the Americans were not represented – met to discuss the consequences of the Bulgarian armistice, but the news of Max's note of 4 October led the European Allied premiers to consider two sets of ceasefire conditions for Germany drafted by Foch and by the SWC permanent military representatives. They reached no conclusion, though they did successfully impress on Wilson that he should consult their military advisers. Angered though they were by American unilateralism, the Paris and

London governments were both willing to stop the war if the conditions were right, though they believed it would be impossible to renew the fighting and therefore needed guarantees now of everything they wanted.[44] Poincaré queried the principle of a ceasefire, but Clemenceau was furious at his interference and excluded him from further involvement. In contrast, neither Foch nor Pétain insisted on fighting on, but Foch advised that the government should occupy all the territory – including the left bank of the Rhine – that it might wish to control in the peace treaty, and Clemenceau accepted this recommendation. Furthermore, by late October the evidence reaching Paris was that Germany would accept practically any terms. The military clauses prepared by Foch in consultation with Clemenceau therefore envisaged that the Germans would evacuate and the Allies occupy not only the whole of France, Belgium, Alsace-Lorraine and the Saar, but also the left bank and three bridgeheads on the right bank of the Rhine, exposing the industrial concentrations round the Ruhr and Frankfurt and positioning Allied troops in all the areas on which France might have designs.[45]

In Britain the mood was more cautious. Ironically, Lloyd George questioned whether an armistice now might leave the Germans feeling they had not been beaten and encourage them to start again in twenty years' time,[46] but he did not insist and generally the British leaders were impressed by Germany's continuing resistance and the risk of losing an opportunity for peace by setting needlessly harsh conditions. As recently as the summer they had been expecting to go on well into 1919 or even 1920, and the sudden evidence of collapse caught them unprepared.[47] Haig believed the Germans could retreat to the Rhine and hold it through the winter, while his own army was handicapped by manpower shortages and growing logistical difficulties.[48] Henry Wilson estimated that by 1919 the BEF's divisions would fall from fifty-nine to forty-four or even thirty-nine, increasing the influence of the French army on the battlefield and the French government at the peace conference. If the war continued America too, the British feared, would be better placed to impose its views on freedom of the seas, trade, and German colonies. Britain, according to Smuts, was at its maximum strength and postponing a ceasefire into 1919 would mean an 'American peace', as well as threatening a Bolshevik takeover in Germany.[49] Ministers believed the Fourteen Points were acceptable if Britain could achieve its own interpretation of them, and British public opinion seemed mostly willing to settle now. The major exception was the navy, Beatty (unlike Haig) wanting to reject an armistice, or at any rate that Germany should surrender all its submarines and many of its surface ships. On 26 October the cabinet summed up by favouring 'a good peace if that is now attainable', leaving Lloyd George to attend the second Paris conference with a virtually free hand, its French counterpart extending similar latitude to Clemenceau.[50]

The Paris conference of 29 October to 4 November settled the German ceasefire terms and brought the European Allies into the Berlin-Washington consensus. Although the political and military conditions were negotiated in tandem, for the sake of clarity they will here be taken separately. The basis of the political agreement was that the European Allies accepted the Fourteen Points as the basis of the peace settlement but with important reservations, not all of which the Germans were informed of. The Americans acknowledged that the Points were ambiguous, and on 16 October Wilson explained to a British representative that France must regain Alsace-Lorraine and he would be happy for Britain to take over Germany's colonies, though preferably as a League of Nations trustee. Thus whereas the Germans supposed the Points might be stretched to their benefit they were in fact being interpreted in favour of the Allies. This process went further in the Cobb–Lippmann memorandum, a commentary on the Points that House had prepared soon after arriving in Paris as Wilson's representative, and to which the president lent his general endorsement. However, the memorandum also contained warnings for Wilson's partners. The use of blockade should be greatly restricted; France might gain Alsace-Lorraine but not the Saar; and Italy should receive only land with a population that was ethnically Italian.[51] Hence the conference's opening sessions were fraught. Lloyd George rejected the second Point (freedom of the seas), on the grounds that it would compromise Britain's right of blockade. House warned that America might make a separate peace, and Lloyd George retorted (with Clemenceau's backing) that in that case the Allies would fight on. House's threat was empty, as it was extremely unlikely that the American Congress would have permitted a separate peace (and the British sensed this), but Wilson could certainly curtail loans and troop shipments, and House advised him to do so. Yet before matters escalated, a deal was struck on 30 October. Lloyd George presented a note accepting the Fourteen Points but with an absolute reservation about the freedom of the seas and a clarification that the Allies could claim reparation for damage to their civilian populations and their property resulting from German aggression on land, at sea, and in the air. Although this draft was conceived from a British standpoint, Clemenceau fell in with it, leaving the Italians isolated. Wilson still wanted to insist on Point Two, but Lloyd George conceded merely that it might be discussed at the peace conference (in fact it was not) without accepting the principle. The British draft formed the basis of the 'Lansing Note', sent by the American Secretary of State to the Germans on 5 November, which reported that the Allies had agreed to the Fourteen Points subject to Lloyd George's two reservations. House presented this result to Wilson as a diplomatic triumph, although it was a rather theoretical one. In effect, the British had broken ranks before the European Allies had been able to form a united front. Both Lloyd George and Clemenceau understood the arguments for halting before American preponderance became greater and their countries suffered further loss; both believed the Points were flexible; and each was not only suspicious of the other but also had no intention of breaking with America for the sake of Italy.[52] House was pushing on an open door. But in addition the political aspects of the armistice agreement must be seen alongside the military ones, and the latter gave the Allies very substantial compensation for their lip service to Wilson's principles.

Whereas House gave the political agreement top priority and had an initial text in the shape of the Fourteen Points, over the technical clauses of the armistice neither circumstance applied. Wilson had conceded that the Allies' military advisers should draft the terms, and failed to prepare conditions of his own. He gave House minimal guidance, rashly sending him without written instructions 'because I feel you will know what to do'.[53] The cables he sent during the conference were often garbled in decryption, including a crucial message that too much security for the

Allies would complicate negotiations at the peace conference. This became interpreted as an instruction to support Foch's conditions.[54] Although Wilson advised that he opposed an Allied occupation of Alsace-Lorraine, the left bank of the Rhine, and right-bank bridgeheads, and wanted to confine the naval conditions to interning the U-boats in a neutral port,[55] the final terms proved far more severe and largely negated his views.

House dispensed with military advice, and in the technical negotiations he responded to Allied suggestions. Given the absence of an American alternative, British and French texts became the basis of the naval and military clauses. The British Admiralty led in drawing up the former, winning support from the other naval chiefs for demanding the surrender of 160 U-boats (which meant virtually all of them), two battleships, six battlecruisers, eight cruisers, and fifty destroyers (in other words, much of the High Seas Fleet). The First Sea Lord, Wester Wemyss, wanted to control the vessels so that Germany could not use them (as Wilhelm had long intended) as peace conference bargaining chips; the American Admiral William Benson (who shared Wilson's fears of Britain becoming too powerful) was isolated in favouring internment rather than surrender. Whether the Germans would accept was secondary for the admirals, though not for Foch, who was not prepared to prolong the war over the naval demands. Lloyd George was more moderate than his navy, but was under pressure from the Unionists in his government whom he was trying to persuade to continue the coalition after the armistice. Eventually the Allied leaders required that the surface ships the admirals had specified should be not surrendered but interned in a neutral port under Allied supervision. A last-minute insertion provided for them to go to the Allies if no obliging neutral could be found, and as Spain (the only one with a large enough harbour) refused, the ships went to Scapa Flow after all. Over the naval clauses, then, the Americans achieved some satisfaction, if largely in point of form. As all agreed that the U-boats must be surrendered and that the Allied blockade should continue after the armistice, the Germans gave up their strongest naval assets with no relaxation in the pressure on them.[56]

The land clauses conflicted still more strikingly with what Wilson had envisaged. The starting point here was Foch's draft. As presented to the Allied commanders at Senlis on 25 October it had envisaged not only the occupation of Alsace-Lorraine, the left bank, and bridgeheads on the right bank, but also a rapid evacuation that would force the Germans to jettison much of their heavy equipment. The terms proposed by Foch and Clemenceau entailed occupying the maximum territory for political motives that were unavowed but obvious enough to their British critics. At Senlis, Haig had expressed his pessimism about Allied exhaustion and his belief that Germany could still make an effective defensive stand. He believed that re-occupying the invaded territories and taking strongpoints in Alsace-Lorraine would suffice. But Pershing had been close to Foch's position – another example of the lack of American co-ordination – and Foch ignored Haig's views in his recommendations to the Paris conference, which provided for the Allies to occupy an area as extending to the Rhine bridgeheads at Mainz, Koblenz, and Cologne, and for a demilitarized strip forty kilometres wide to the east of the river. The Germans should surrender 5,000 artillery pieces, 36,000 machine-guns, and 2,000 aircraft, thus thoroughly disorganizing their army and destroying their power to resist. At Paris, Lloyd George challenged the need to go beyond Alsace-Lorraine on the grounds that the Allies should occupy only the territory they wanted (thus implying that Foch was willing to prolong the fighting for France's Rhineland objectives). But House failed to support Lloyd George's objections, and the latter gave way. Almost certainly Clemenceau obtained House's backing for the military clauses in return for French acquiescence in the Fourteen Points, thus forestalling an Anglo-American front against him on an issue he regarded as much more significant than Wilson's principles; while House, confused about the president's intentions, misjudged the significance of what he was doing. True, Clemenceau promised the troops would leave once the peace conditions were implemented, but that might take years. As the conference progressed, moreover, further military clauses were added. The French reserved their right to demand reparation for damage done and to make other financial claims: an issue that was rising up the political agenda as the retreating Germans flooded coal mines and despoiled farms and orchards. In addition the Allies reserved the right to insist on Germany withdrawing to its 1914 frontier in the east, meaning that some troops would stay to contain Bolshevism but essentially that the Brest-Litovsk and Bucharest treaties would collapse. Hence the armistice would destroy Germany's eastern *imperium,* begin the transfer of Alsace-Lorraine, and prepare for a prolonged Allied presence in the Rhineland. Germany would lose the ability to renew hostilities or resist the Allies' peace terms, and its fate would depend on Wilson's ability to hold his partners to the American peace programme. The terms were so stringent that Foch doubted Berlin would accept them, as did the British leaders. The Allies expected to win soon, but not that the bloodshed would end quite yet. None the less, all sides made concessions to reach an agreement, the outcome being a package that they delivered to Germany to take or leave. To the surprise of many of the victors, their recently so formidable enemies took it, and the war came to an end.[57]

The Central Powers accepted conditions that were far less favourable than Ludendorff and Hintze had had in mind. What had begun as a damage limitation exercise, intended to extricate Germany with at least some of its external gains and to cushion the impact on its political system, ended by protecting it neither from defeat nor revolution. Three developments after 4 October invalidated the initial calculations. In ascending order of importance the first was the continuing Allied advance in the west, the second the loss of Germany's allies, and the third an upheaval in Germany itself. The ceasefire request was not the primary cause of these developments, but it accelerated them all.

More than half a million soldiers were killed or wounded during the weeks of haggling over the armistice.[58] Most of them, including the English war poet, Wilfred Owen, fell on the Western Front. Yet events there influenced Germany's initial decision to seek an armistice more than its later decision actually to sign one. Ludendorff's greater optimism by mid-October was not entirely due to opportunism but also reflected his earlier overestimation of the danger. The co-ordinated Allied assault was bogged down at Meuse–Argonne and in Flanders; the Canadians were forced to pause after crossing the Canal du Nord; and although the British Fourth

Army pierced the main Hindenburg Line defences on 29 September it took an-other week to clear the rear sectors.[59] From here on, however, the BEF encoun-tered only improvised positions, which its artillery battered down. Against the line of the river Selle, where the Germans stood next, the British fired 127 million pounds of shell from 1,320 guns before pushing through on 17 October. On 23 and 24 October the Flanders advance resumed and the British crossed the Scheldt; on 4 November, after another enormous bombardment, they forded the Sambre and Oise Canal. From here on heavy fighting ceased on the British front and the Germans were in general retreat. Nevertheless, the BEF had to pick its way through a booby-trapped landscape without roads and track; by 5 November the Fourth Army was thirty miles beyond its railheads and needed to pause, but it had paused before during the Hundred Days campaign and thereafter the advance could probably have continued for as long as the weather permitted.[60] The French were also moving forward, and the only successful German resistance during Oc-tober was at Meuse–Argonne. There the Americans, whose first assault had stalled completely, did not take the Kriemhilde Stellung until the 14th, and they remained stuck there for another two weeks. All the same, they learned quickly, and they pushed north again on 1 November after thorough logistical preparation and with much more intense counter-battery fire and creeping barrages. During the Meuse–Argonne battle as a whole the AEF fired off a greater weight of ammu-nition than had the Union side during the entire American Civil War.[61] In the fi-nal days they progressed extremely rapidly against retreating enemies, capturing Sedan and menacing the main German lateral railway. By this stage the Germans could barely conduct even an orderly withdrawal. They had disbanded thirty-two divisions since April and had only one fresh division in reserve.[62] Their 'fully fit' divisions in the west fell from ninety-eight on 1 April to forty-seven on 1 Septem-ber, fourteen on 4 October, and four on 11 November, despite their calling up the 1919 conscript class.[63] That said, the Germans had decided to accept an armistice on virtually any terms after the crucial cabinet meeting on 17 October, at which stage a fighting retreat to new defences on the border had still seemed a plausible option. The accelerated Allied advance in early November probably reflected in part Groener's decision to pull back to the Antwerp–Meuse line. The situation re-mained one of rapid but controlled deterioration rather than rout, and the Ger-mans inflicted heavy casualties on their pursuers until the end.[64] There was no prospect of matters improving, but neither were they desperate enough to explain a decision to capitulate.

The second development in this period, and still more ominous, was the break-up of the Central Powers' coalition, leaving Germany alone. After the Bulgarian armistice, King Ferdinand abdicated. In the next month Allied forces advanced 500 miles, the Serbs liberating Belgrade before the front stabilized along the Danube.[65] The knock-on effect on Turkey was rapid. The Ottoman Empire's situation both on the military and on the home front was bad, but it was not critical enough to de-mand an immediate armistice until Bulgaria's collapse. Moreover, Turkey was expe-riencing a peculiar combination of success and overextension in the Caucasus with disaster everywhere else. Between 1.5 and 2.5 million Turks may have died because of the war, the majority being civilians or soldiers succumbing to famine and disease rather than to wounds.[66] The figures suggest losses comparable with those of France in a population half the size. By autumn 1918, despite having conscripted some 2.85 million men during the war, the army had only 560,000 left under arms, and no reserves to call on. But its best divisions, re-equipped with weaponry captured from Russia, were concentrated in the Caucasus for the drive to Baku, while Palestine and Mesopotamia were denied reinforcements. Four under-strength divisions guarded Constantinople and the Straits, and only a few battalions held the Bulgarian border. The Germans had warned the Ottomans of their danger, but Enver seems to have planned to use the Caucasus forces for a last-ditch defence in Turkey's Anatolian redoubt. He misled the cabinet about the precariousness of the position, and other ministers (notably Talat, who had been Grand Vizier since 1916) remained complacent and refused to consider a separate peace. Hence Bulgaria's surrender opened the road to Constantinople at the same time as Allenby rolled up the Ottomans' army in Palestine. The government recalled four divisions from the Caucasus, over a thousand miles away from Constantinople, but only one regiment had arrived by the time Turkey signed an armistice a month later. When news arrived of Germany's ceasefire appeal, the government (as in Berlin) resigned, hoping that domestic changes could secure more lenient treatment.[67]

In response to the Fourteen Points the Ottoman authorities had already indicated that they would accept autonomy for the non-Turkish parts of the empire; in summer 1918, probably to raise morale and hoping to demonstrate public support for their territorial claims, they lifted press censorship and allowed political exiles to return. Criticism of the Young Turks was growing, but it was the news from abroad that terminated their regime. Talat's cabinet stood down on 7 October and the new government of Izzet Pasha contained only a minority of CUP members, the party subsequently dissolving itself.[68] Izzet was a soldier and former war minister who had represented Turkey at the Brest-Litovsk negotiations; he had served the Young Turks but quickly distanced himself from them. His ministers' reading of the situation was that Constantinople was open to Allied attack, the treasury was bankrupt, much of the country was outside the government's control, and further resistance was impossible. To defend itself, Turkey needed money and armaments from Germany, but on 12 October Franchet d'Espérey's armies cut the rail link. Although Franchet's main advance was northwards towards Serbia, General Milne, commander of the British Salonika forces, was gathering seven divisions for a separate move on Constantinople. He would be unable to start for some weeks, and would have to cross difficult country with winter approaching, but the Allies began reinforcing their Dardanelles squadrons immediately. Hence on 16 October the Turks decided to seek a separate peace at once, and General Townshend, who had been captured with his soldiers at Kut (but had been treated far better than they) was selected as the intermediary to contact the offshore British warships. The Turks were willing to accept the Fourteen Points, to demobilize, and to open the Straits. Because of negotiating errors and their desperation for peace they eventually conceded much more.[69]

The Allies, for their part, had begun defining peace terms for the Ottoman Empire in their wartime secret treaties, although now these were difficult to reconcile with the promises made in the Caxton Hall and Fourteen Points speeches that even if the non-Turkish areas were detached the sovereignty of the Turkish-inhabited regions would be respected. They had not yet discussed armistice terms, partly because no one had expected the Middle Eastern war to end so quickly; and it was only after the Bulgarian ceasefire that the British government drafted conditions, which Lloyd George discussed in Paris on 6–8 October. The British were willing to be lenient in order to open the Straits and to release their forces for use elsewhere. But the French and Italians greatly extended the list, and this amplified set of conditions became the basis of the eventual agreement. The British proposed that they should occupy the Dardanelles forts, that the Turks should hand over their navy and make Constantinople available as a base, that the Allies should control Turkey's railways, and that Turkish troops should withdraw behind the 1914 borders, while those in the Arabian peninsula should surrender. To these demands the Paris conference added the Allied occupation of Baku and Batum, the surrender of the Turkish garrisons in Mesopotamia and Syria, and the demobilization of the rest of the Turkish army. In addition, Turkey should allow the Allies to occupy 'strategic points' – a provision inserted by the Italians to enable them to control the areas they claimed, and which allowed the Allies to take over almost any territory they wanted. Lloyd George's ministers were so anxious to finish with Turkey that they were willing to settle for much less, and so instructed their representative in the Aegean, Admiral Calthorpe, who negotiated the armistice with a delegation led by the new Turkish foreign minister, Rauf Bey. But by the time the Turks arrived on 27 October Austria-Hungary was collapsing and settling with Turkey was less urgent, while Rauf was prepared for concessions in order to settle quickly and because of a touching trust in British goodwill. Calthorpe read out the terms one by one, with the result that the Turks did not appreciate their collective import and lost the opportunity to trade one for another. Temporarily losing radio contact with their government, they signed on 30 October, obtaining as their one concession that only British and French (not Greek or Italian) troops would occupy the Straits forts. The terms prepared the way for the empire's dismemberment, much exceeding both what the Turkish government had initially envisaged and what the British regarded as a minimum. The main reasons on the Allied side for this harshness were the needs to satisfy France and Italy by making it possible to implement the secret treaties and the desire to acquire jumping off points for further operations against the Central Powers and Russia.[70] The armistice closed down a major portion of the war, and would have made more British naval and land forces available if fighting in Europe had continued into 1919. The news that Turkey was seeking peace, which reached Berlin on 18 October, was another heavy blow for Prince Max's government, and underlined how Ludendorff's decision to seek an armistice had helped to shatter the German-led coalition. Militarily and politically, however, it was less crucial than the final break-up of Austria-Hungary.

The Dual Monarchy was destroyed, as its leaders had long dreaded, by a combination of nationalist uprisings with pressure from outside. By the time it disintegrated neither its bureaucracy nor its army had the will or capacity to control the disaffected nationalities, and Karl preferred to lose his throne peacefully than to embark on a civil war. In fact the defeat and rout of his principal force at the battle of Vittorio Veneto at the end of October made military repression scarcely feasible anyway. Paradoxically by 1918 Austria-Hungary's war seemed virtually over and largely a success, albeit won mainly through German aid. Serbia, Montenegro, and Romania had been overwhelmed and Russia reduced to chaos. While Germany's casualties in 1918 were enormous, Austria-Hungary's were fewer than half those the Monarchy had sustained in 1914. As of 15 October, about 400,000 Austro-Hungarian fighting men were serving on the Italian front, 50,000 on the Balkan front, 150,000 in Russia and the Balkans as occupation troops, and 18,000 on the Western Front (i.e., some 600,000 in total), whereas over 1 million were at home or on sick leave.[71] However the forces in Italy had shrunk from 650,000 since 1 July, mainly due to illness (malaria, dysentery, and influenza) and desertion. Those who remained did not mutiny, but they lacked food, clothing, and munitions and were subjected to an intense propaganda campaign, playing on national grievances. In a final drive from September onwards, the Padua Commission produced 15 million leaflets, or thirty for every man in the dwindling Habsburg forces, though it is difficult to assess their impact when so much else – the battle of the Piave, Germany's defeats, the army's wretched material circumstances – all conspired to reinforce their message.[72] The army maintained a fighting front but it was rotting from within. Although the Italians also had a manpower shortage (and no AEF to compensate), when they finally attacked they outnumbered their enemies. Diaz still hesitated, but in October Orlando insisted on an offensive before the Italians' contribution lost any political value. After a massive preliminary bombardment, they moved forward on the 24th. For two days they encountered resistance, but revolts in some Habsburg units had started before the battle began. Within days up to 500,000 men surrendered to the Italians, for whom the campaign became a successful drive to occupy before the armistice the territories promised by the Treaty of London. As Diaz's intelligence had predicted, the Habsburg army had become a shell, which imploded once its crust was broken.[73]

The army's demise made it impossible for Karl to hold his empire together by force even if he had wanted to (and trains and coal to permit troop movements were lacking).[74] The final stage of its disintegration began before Vittorio Veneto. Though triggered by the armistice negotiations, it was accomplished by domestic insurgent movements that the authorities were unwilling – and unable – to suppress. The precondition for this process was the radicalization of the nationalist movements within Austria-Hungary, a development still poorly understood but for which the war was crucial. In 1914, virtually none of the Dual Monarchy's politicians were calling for independence. Princip's Young Bosnia movement was a minority phenomenon whose activities ceased after the conflict began. Instead the main foci of radical separatism in the first half of the war were the small groups of Polish, Czech, and South Slav exiles in the Allied countries and the United States, their counterparts at home remaining cautious. Only in 1917–18 did the latter become more intransigent, after Franz Joseph's death and the accession of Karl, who relaxed controls on political activity after two years of repression. But at the same time the government of the Austrian half appeared to be aligning itself with the Austrian Germans, and this, coupled with the Monarchy's loyalty to Berlin, weakened it as a rallying point for the non-German nationalities. By January 1918 the

Czech and South Slav leaders within the Monarchy supported independence, and after the peace treaty with the Ukraine the Poles followed suit.* The Austrian half of the empire could now be run as a dictatorship (for which Karl had no enthusiasm), or as a federal regime that was likely to fall apart, but the half-way house of dynastic rule based on consent was no longer viable. During 1918 in the Austrian half – and in the Croat lands of the Hungarian half – the independence movements organized themselves and attracted mass followings, while the authorities acquiesced and the ultimate sanction of the armed forces withered in their hands. By September deserters numbered 400,000, and in Croatia they formed armed bands in the countryside that the authorities were too weak to challenge.[75] Finally after Vittorio Veneto nearly all the remaining troops in the Italian theatre either gave themselves up or rebelled and went home.[76]

The nationalist movements constituted much the most important challenge to Habsburg rule. After the spring of 1918 the working-class strike movement that had so frightened the authorities subsided. The Austrian economy in 1918 displayed many of the symptoms of Russia in 1917 – railway paralysis, plummeting production, accelerating inflation, and a crisis in urban food supply (by June the daily ration was down to eight ounces of bread and three of meat)[77] – yet when the regime collapsed the revolutionary movements aimed primarily at political independence. Social protest played little part except in the German and Magyar areas, and even there the left was weaker than in Russia or Germany. It is therefore difficult to link the Dual Monarchy's economic crisis to the growth of the nationalist movements that destroyed it, although fear of being outflanked by Bolshevism encouraged the Czech leaders, for example, to make their move. In contrast, the European Allies and the United States certainly did assist the break-up of the Dual Monarchy through their ideological warfare, though this is not to imply that they could have prevented it. After summer 1918 they radicalized their position by calling not just for autonomy for the Monarchy's nationalities but also for independence,† and they probably helped the exiles (notably the Czechs) to persuade their counterparts within Austria-Hungary to reject any compromise with the dynasty.[78] Only a German victory could now save the regime.

After the German request for an armistice events moved quickly. Karl (who had not been consulted about it) followed the Germans' tactics of appealing to the Americans and pushing through domestic liberalization, but with even less success. While Wilson pursued his dialogue with Max of Baden, Austria-Hungary's application to him on 4 October for a ceasefire and a peace based on the Fourteen Points met with silence. On the 16th, attempting to comply with Wilson's Point Ten, Karl issued a manifesto establishing a federal state in the Austrian half, while the Hungarian government still rejected one in theirs. To the last, the Magyar leaders rejected democratization, and the end effectively came when Wilson finally responded in a note on 18 October, withdrawing the Tenth Point and saying it was up to the subject nationalities to decide their fate: a thinly disguised appeal for revolution.[79] The disruption of the Monarchy might not have been primarily

---

*See ch. 15.
†See ch. 16.

due to Allied diplomacy, but by this stage the Allies certainly wanted it. Indeed the Poles, so long a Habsburg mainstay, were already breaking away. On 10 October a national committee was formed in Cracow, representing most of the Polish parties; both they and the Poles represented in the German-created Regents' Council in Warsaw agreed to seek an independent Poland reunited from the country's three parts. On 24 October the Poles decided to withdraw from the Reichsrat and to take over the administration of the Polish-inhabited areas of Austria, which they had done by the end of the month.[80]

While Austria-Hungary could survive a Polish breakaway, it could not survive secession by the Czechs, and revolution in Prague was decisive. The government asked for help from the national committees emerging in the different parts of the empire in implementing its 16 October decree, but as the decree excluded the Hungarian half it would not facilitate Czech and Slovak unity and was therefore unacceptable to the Czech leaders, whose national committee was already preparing a peaceful takeover. Clutching at straws, a new government in Vienna (the last Karl ever appointed) decided to accept all of Wilson's conditions and request an immediate ceasefire, thus conceding the right of self-determination and breaking free of the German alliance. But when this note was published on 27 October it simply served as the signal for the Prague national committee to begin taking over the local administration, claiming it was implementing the 16 October manifesto, though in fact its aim was an independent Czechoslovak republic. The Habsburg officials did not resist, and the local army commander (who was losing control over his men) allowed the national committee to create volunteer forces, non-Czech troops being evacuated.[81] The transfer of power was orderly, bloodless, and rapid, and closely resembled events in Slovenia, which proclaimed independence on 1 November.

In the Kingdom of Hungary too, the Wekerle government was losing control over its periphery. The Romanian deputies withdrew from the Hungarian parliament, and in early November King Ferdinand of Romania appointed a pro-Allied government and re-entered the war, sending troops to occupy Transylvania while Czech forces moved into Slovakia. In Croatia Hungarian control had been ebbing for months, in the face of open nationalist agitation. The national council at Zagreb played a similar role to the Prague national committee, proclaiming on 24 October the independence of the Serbs, Croats, and Slovenes of Austria-Hungary and their intended union with Serbia and Montenegro. After forming a civic guard it took over Bosnia-Herzegovina, although the merger with Serbia and Montenegro into the Kingdom of the Serbs, Croats, and Slovenes (renamed Yugoslavia in 1929) came only in December. Here again, law, order, and continuity were the keynotes, the local military commanders liaising with the committee in order to ensure a smooth transition.[82]

The standard pattern was therefore for power to pass to committees of the local nationalist parties, accompanied by patriotic and anti-Habsburg demonstrations but not by widespread violence or disorder. Karl released his officers from their oath of allegiance and permitted them to join the armies of the new states, and many were prominent in the transition process.[83] Revolutions in Vienna and in Budapest confirmed the break, on a similar model though with a greater social

content. Even in Austria, however, the revolutionary movement was largely confined to Vienna and the provincial capitals, by-passing the conservative rural hinterland. The Socialist Party had not split like its German counterpart, and the
party leadership was closer to the trade unions and less challenged from the left.
Unlike the German SPD, it was not the biggest party, being outnumbered by the
Christian Socials, together with whom (as well as German nationalists) its Reichsrat representatives formed a Provisional National Assembly of an independent
German Austrian state on 21 October.[84] On the 30th, mass demonstrations for a
republic began in Vienna and Habsburg insignia were torn down (a common feature of the 1918 revolutions, as the removal of communist symbols would be
seventy-one years later). The provisional National Assembly took legislative powers and set up an executive state council, the imperial police and bureaucracy continued to serve the new government, law and order and food supply (such as it
was) were maintained, and the troops returning from Italy were quickly demobilized. The new Austrian German leaders, however, including the Social Democrats, had a wider national agenda. They claimed to represent all Germans in the
Monarchy, including those living in the Sudeten mountains (which had previously
been administratively part of Bohemia), but when Czech forces overran the Sudetenland they were powerless to retaliate. A majority of the Austrian-German leaders also wished for union with Germany itself, or *Anschluss*, and during October
both Wilhelm and Ludendorff were considering this project as a possible compensation for losing the war,[85] but the Germans dared not jeopardize the armistice negotiations by pursuing it. None the less, the demise of the Habsburgs in Austria
removed an obstacle to it, and the dynasty was about to lose Hungary too.

Crucial here was the break-up of the Hungarian army, whose South Slav units
began to rebel even before the battle of Vittorio Veneto. Officers in Budapest
demonstrated for peace and for a new ministry headed by the government's most
persistent critic, Michael Károlyi; the opposition parties formed a national council,
to which the city garrison pledged its loyalty. On the 31st the imperial authorities
appointed Károlyi prime minister, with socialist support; on the same day soldiers'
detachments took over public buildings. The old-guard politicians who had led
Hungary during the war were ousted, and Tisza himself was assassinated by a
band of marauding sailors who accused him of responsibility for the conflict. The
parties who had opposed the war (the Radicals, Independents, and Social Democrats), who had little following outside Budapest, took over with support from rebellious troops and with Karl's acquiescence. They hoped to maintain the unity of
the old Hungarian lands, but were speedily disabused, as the Romanians occupied
Transylvania, the Czechs overran Slovakia, and the South Slavs broke away.[86]
Even before Karl withdrew from the political arena on 11 November, Habsburg
authority had vanished throughout the former Dual Monarchy.

By the time of the ceasefires in Italy and the Balkans, then, the Allies were no
longer dealing with a single entity. They signed an armistice for the Italian front
on 3 November at the Villa Giusti near Padua, followed by a separate one with the
new Hungarian government (the Belgrade Convention) on 13 November.[87] The
Allies agreed to the terms of the Villa Giusti armistice at their conference in Paris
on 31 October. They required the Habsburg army to demobilize and hand over

half its artillery and equipment, and demanded the surrender of the major part of the fleet. German troops were to leave and the Allies to be free to occupy strategic points. House agreed (as with the occupation of the Rhineland) that the Italians could occupy up to the line promised to them by the 1915 Treaty of London, which they promptly did: another instance of his neglect of the political implications of military decisions. Despite South Slav protests, the Allies resolved not to recognize a Yugoslav state for the time being; and although they endorsed Karl's decision to transfer the fleet to the Croat national council, when the Italian navy seized the ships they accepted this *fait accompli*.[88] Politically, therefore, the armistice deprived the emerging Yugoslav state of a navy and of an ethnic frontier in the north. Militarily, it made possible an Allied advance to Germany's southern borders, creating a new theatre of war when the Germans were already stretched to the limit. Allied planners began work on a two-pronged invasion of Bavaria from Italy via Innsbruck in the south and along the Danube from Linz and Salzburg. With winter approaching and given the condition of the Austrian railways, it is doubtful if this operation could have been mounted quickly, but the Bavarians were alarmed and OHL redeployed its remaining forces to counter the threat.[89]

By early November the Germans had lost their allies and faced a new menace in the south, while the goal of upholding Austria-Hungary (for which they had gone to war in the first place) had been irretrievably defeated. It was now Germany's turn to face revolutionary unrest, which would oblige it to accept whatever terms were offered. Whereas the Austro-Hungarian revolutions had been led by pre-formed national committees, the German uprising surprised even the left-wing parties, resembling Russia's February Revolution rather than that of October. It originated from a mutiny in the fleet, provoked by secret plans for a naval offensive, or *Flottenvorstoss*, against Britain. Once more a misjudged military initiative made Germany's situation worse than if no action had been taken, and this time the damage was fatal.

The naval command structure had been reorganized in August, with the creation of a *Seekriegsleitung* (SKL) or Naval Warfare Directorate, modelled on OHL. Scheer headed it, his command of the High Seas Fleet being taken by Hipper, though the two men relied heavily on their respective chiefs of staff, Captain Magnus von Levetzow and Admiral von Trotha, both of whom had outspokenly conservative – not to say reactionary – political views. Although Wilhelm endorsed the change, its initiators intended it to reduce his powers of command.[90] It also divided the officer corps, antagonizing the supporters of Holtzendorff, whose post as chief of the Admiralty staff was abolished, and of Capelle, who lost his position as navy secretary. Following the reorganization almost half the captains and first officers of the navy's first-line squadrons were moved (some ships losing both officers simultaneously), after many of the best officers had already volunteered for secondment to the U-boats.[91] Indeed SKL accentuated the bias of naval policy towards the submarine arm. Its 'Scheer Programme', conceived on the analogy of the Hindenburg Programme, proposed raising U-boat production from the seven to twelve per month completed in late 1918 to thirty-six by October 1919, a glaring indication of the navy's lack of realism.[92] In SKL's opinion it did not need an armistice, and it ignored advice from OHL to avoid sinking passenger liners. However, when the

Leinster went down and Wilson insisted on submarine attacks being suspended, SKL mounted relatively little resistance, for it now envisaged an alternative.

SKL's proposal for a last-ditch assault against the Royal Navy originated as a reaction to the evidence that Germany had lost the war. Alongside its strategic rationale went a political and emotional one, arising from officers' forebodings for the future of their service if it surrendered to the British without once having been fully engaged in battle. Not only would this would be dishonourable, Trotha feared it would discourage Germany from rebuilding the navy in a post-defeat future (which, like Hintze and Ludendorff, he was now contemplating). He preferred a 'death struggle' – in other words, a massacre – to inaction. Levetzow agreed: for the navy's officers and men to lie 'in immortal fame at the bottom of the sea' would be better than the disgrace of internment. And Scheer, though he believed there was some chance of operational success, also described the question as one of 'honour and existence'.[93] Scheer and Levetzow therefore approved the principle of a surface attack if submarine warfare were suspended, but did so without consulting Max or Wilhelm (though they did brief Ludendorff). By so proceeding they were violating Wilhelm's instructions and probably acting unconstitutionally. Whether they hoped to sabotage the armistice negotiations is unproven (though it seems likely), but in any case they had no respect for the chancellor or for parliamentary government, and if they disclosed their intentions they might be overruled. Hipper's staff therefore secretly prepared an order for the High Seas Fleet to sortie into the Thames estuary while lighter vessels bombarded the Flanders coast and raided the Straits of Dover, the aim being to draw out the Royal Navy into a submarine ambush and naval battle off the island of Terschelling. On 27 October Scheer set the 30th as the start date.[94]

The plan's initiators had ignored the 80,000 sailors and stokers whose lives were to be gambled away. Yet the information reaching the high command was that the officers had been unsettled by the personnel changes, and among the men hostility to the war and willingness to act against it were growing. On 18 October Hipper warned that revolution might break out in the fleet at any moment, yet he and Trotha assumed their orders would not, ultimately, be defied. As far as the submarines and smaller surface ships were concerned this assumption was justified, but unrest in the First World War navies always centred on battleships. Here conditions approximated those in a large industrial plant, men carrying out taxing and repetitive routines with poor and monotonous food and being segregated from their officers, who were better fed than their subordinates and neither showed concern for them nor mixed with them – in contrast to submarine officers and infantry captains. These grievances had fuelled the August 1917 naval mutinies and had not been redressed, while memories of the suppression of those mutinies still rankled. The navy's management style, combined with months of inaction and regular contact with disillusioned civilians on shore, drove even patriotic seamen into a mood of rebellion. News of the armistice request, and the return of sailors and shipyard workers from the evacuated ports in Flanders, accentuated it.[95]

When in these circumstances the navy began to station ships in readiness and Hipper briefed his commanders, rumours quickly circulated that the fleet was destined for a suicide mission intended to subvert the government and wreck the armistice. From 27 October disobedience spread among the cruisers and capital ships, men refusing either to board their vessels or to weigh anchor and stoke the boilers, and extinguishing the ships' lights. Hipper received conflicting advice in favour of coercion and conciliation and the authorities opted for a disastrous combination of the two. On the 29th Hipper postponed his sailing orders, as despite mass arrests his subordinates could not move their vessels. He sent the Third Squadron of battleships to Kiel, in the hope that if the seamen rested and met their families their morale would improve. But when the Third Squadron arrived on 1 November its commander (reneging on earlier promises of an amnesty) arrested over 200 of his men and yet allowed the remainder on shore, where they set up a committee to demand the prisoners' release. Kiel was a radical centre that had supported the January 1918 strike, and demonstrations gathered impetus until on the evening of 3 November troops opened fire and killed several protestors. This was an analogous moment to Nicholas II's order in February 1917 to use force, and it provoked an analogous response. On 4 November ('Red Monday') seamen broke into the rifle stores and took over their ships, setting up a sailors' council; on land the protestors set up barricades and the Kiel garrison mutinied. The government had lost control of the town and the revolution had begun.[96]

Whereas in Russia revolution was sparked by bread shortages in the capital, in Germany it began in the provinces as a protest against futile further fighting. None the less, Germany's food situation was extremely threatening. Romanian supplies had helped in 1917 but were about to be cut off. Ukrainian deliveries were well below expectations and the other occupied regions had no more to yield.[97] Nor was there much chance of purchasing from the neutrals, given that the Allied blockade was now virtually hermetic. Serious shortages occurred between May and July, and the 1918 harvest was only a temporary respite. Though the wheat crop was better than in 1917, the potato crop was worse.[98] By 1917–18 the civilian death rate was well above pre-war levels and was still increasing: even leaving aside influenza victims, between 424,000 and 478,500 may have died (through tuberculosis and other diseases) as a result of the hardship caused by the war.[99] The press was remarkably free with details about food supply, concealing neither the rising death rate nor the dismal prospects.[100] All the same, according both to German internal reports and to Allied observers, the turn of military fortunes rather than the supply crisis most damaged public morale. Once there was no longer any chance of winning, continued hardship became intolerable, and fuelled impatience for peace.[101] Moreover, despite Max of Baden's constitutional reforms, little in Wilhelm's past record suggested he could function as a British-style monarch, and by late October his future was firmly on the political agenda. Wilson did not insist on abdication, but the third American note could be read as advocating it, and American diplomats in contact with the Germans in Switzerland and Denmark said that this was what the president wanted. Solf advised the chancellor that Wilhelm's departure could mean easier terms, and the SPD and its press took up the call. Most of the cabinet favoured the emperor's voluntary abdication, but Wilhelm – who on the 29th left without the government's approval for OHL at Spa – still resisted.[102] At this point the revolution intervened.

In the embittered climate of the Weimar Republic, the naval mutiny and the Kiel revolt became the centrepiece for right-wing accusations that a 'stab-in-the-back' had caused the defeat. They featured in the *Dolchstoss* trial at Munich in 1925 and were investigated for three years by the Reichstag commission of inquiry into Germany's collapse. Where left-wing testimony centred on the gulf between officers and men and the navy's abuses of authority, Levetzow and others blamed the mutinies on agitators. In fact, although USPD sympathies and anti-war feeling had been growing since 1917, the demands of the Third Squadron mutineers were confined initially to equal rations for officers and men and civil liberties for the latter. Those of the Kiel soldiers' and workers' council were similar: some elements of the sailors' movement wanted Wilhelm's abdication, immediate peace, and democratization of the franchise, but socialism – and still less Russian-style Bolshevism – did not figure.[103] Nor was the movement particularly violent: three naval officers were killed but the sailors' council agreed to pay compensation for damage to property. On the other hand, in early October an extreme left tendency had been formed within the socialist movement in the shape of the Spartakists, who were committed to soviet rule rather than parliamentarianism and to nationalizing land and property, but who remained a small and secret organization. The USPD was much bigger and wanted a socialist republic, but was divided in its attitudes to revolution and the Bolsheviks. Its trade-union allies, the 'revolutionary camarilla' of shop stewards centred on the Berlin metalworkers, were planning a revolutionary general strike, but the USPD counselled them to delay. The SPD chiefs, in contrast, though theoretically republican, were willing to work within a constitutional monarchy and stayed loyal for as long as they could to Max, though like him they wished to remove Wilhelm. The Kiel revolution, however, added a new dynamic to the situation, menacing the SPD with being outflanked. The party responded by sending out one of its leaders, Gustav Noske, who was welcomed, elected chairman of the sailors' council, and became governor of the city, with the consequence that he was quickly able to end the fighting. For a moment it seemed the revolution would be stifled through socialist agency.

Despite Noske's success, however, the movement spread in succeeding days as teams of mutineers fanned out. Lübeck and its garrison surrendered on 5 November when sailors arrived from Kiel; others reached Hamburg and joined with soldiers and workers to disarm officers, occupy the station and shipyards, and create a soviet. On 6 November a sailors' council was established in Wilhelmshaven, with even less resistance than at Kiel. While the coastal towns slipped out of the government's control, on 7 November sailors reached Cologne, establishing control within hours. The revolution spread rapidly across north Germany and into the Rhineland, meeting minimal resistance from the authorities and the local troops and being characterized by the councils' concern to avoid bloodshed and keep order. There was little plundering or violence, and officers were humiliated but not injured. The police fraternized with the rebels and the imperial bureaucracy remained intact. Once the insurgents controlled the Rhine bridges, however, it became harder for the field army to march home and suppress them. In contrast to Russia, sailors and soldiers spearheaded the uprising, though workers' councils were formed alongside the military ones.[104] The phenomenon of revolutionary soldiers in the homeland was crucial and has been little studied, though reports to the authorities suggested that the defeats had shaken the troops' confidence and they wanted an early peace, a republic, and full civil rights, with resentment of the officer corps being less of a force than in the navy.[105] Hence the soldiers' councils called for peace, democracy, and Wilhelm's removal. These generalizations mostly apply even to the most radical of the revolutions in the German provinces, that in Munich. Here the revolutionary situation resulted directly from Germany's armistice request and the invasion threat after Austria-Hungary collapsed. The local USPD leader, a Jewish intellectual and journalist from Berlin, Kurt Eisner, was planning an uprising and made contact with trade unionists and with soldiers' leaders before he acted on 7 November. He led his followers from a mass rally into a neighbouring barracks and seized control of the weapons, while the soldiers defected and the Bavarian king fled, allowing the insurgents to declare a republic in another bloodless coup. In contrast to the events in the north, however, the Munich revolt was planned and led by the Independent Socialists, even though the local SPD leader reluctantly joined the new government.[106]

Within days of the Kiel outbreak most of the provincial capitals were in revolutionary hands and the tide was lapping round Berlin. The denouement came with the signing of the armistice and the fall of the Hohenzollern dynasty. Crucial to both events was fear that without drastic action Germany would follow Russia's path, a prospect as abhorrent to the SPD leaders as it was to the middle-class parties and the army leadership. When the Allies drew up their armistice demands, however, they failed to realize that revolution in Germany was imminent. Wilson did not know about the naval mutinies until 6 November, and Lloyd George was not persuaded until the 8th that Germany had no choice but to sign.[107] The Germans, on the other hand, were disconcerted by the pause for Allied deliberations that followed their 27 October reply to Wilson, and were greatly relieved when the Lansing Note offered them an armistice on the basis of most of the Fourteen Points. On 6 November Max was advised by Groener, who had previously envisaged an orderly retreat to a shorter line, that Germany must seek a ceasefire at once, in view of the threat to the southern border and the events at Kiel; hence Max instructed the government's armistice delegation, headed by Erzberger, to seek a ceasefire on any terms. In this way the combination of Austria-Hungary's collapse with the outbreak of revolution finally broke German resistance. Erzberger and the commission were escorted through the French lines and on a surreal journey to a railway carriage in a forest clearing near Compiègne where Foch presented them with the Allied conditions, ostentatiously refusing to negotiate. However, Foch did take it upon himself to make a few concessions, evidently linked to counter-revolutionary concerns. As the German delegates wanted to maintain a disciplined force for use against Bolshevism, he reduced the numbers of lorries, aircraft, and machine-guns to be ceded, as well as lengthening the evacuation period from twenty-five to thirty-one days, narrowing the right-bank demilitarized zone to ten kilometres, and no longer requiring immediate withdrawal from Russia. Erzberger, who had accepted his task with great reluctance (it later earned him his assassination), considered these gains significant and advised Berlin to accept.[108]

By the time Erzberger's courier arrived, however, Max's government had fallen. The role of the SPD leaders was pivotal, and as the revolution spread they feared that unless they responded to it they would lose all control to the USPD. On 7 November they told Max that unless Wilhelm abdicated there would be social revolution: he must go and the constitution be fully democratized or they would leave the government. Max concluded that he had lost his Reichstag majority and offered his resignation, but Wilhelm refused to accept it or to renounce the throne. On the morning of 9 November, as the Social Democrats joined mass demonstrations in Berlin itself and the city's garrison began to defect, Max therefore announced on his own initiative that Wilhelm had abdicated, and handed over the chancellorship to a socialist-dominated government headed by Friedrich Ebert. In order to forestall a Spartakist proclamation of a soviet regime, another SPD leader, Scheidemann, declared from the Reichstag building that Germany was a republic.[109] Yet the SPD might still have failed to head off the extremists had Wilhelm not given way, and until the 8th, distanced from the capital at Spa, he insisted he would restore order at the head of his army. What finished him, as it had Nicholas II, was the desertion of his generals.

Of thirty-nine generals and regimental commanders on the Western Front contacted by OHL, only one thought the army could reconquer Germany, fifteen were doubtful, and twenty-three said the task was impossible; only eight believed the troops would fight even against Bolshevism. Hindenburg and Groener decided that with the big cities and railway junctions under rebel control, and with few dependable units, they could no longer suppress the revolutionary movement. When they confronted Wilhelm on the 9th, he – to his belated credit – refused to fight a civil war. Hindenburg advised his master that he could not guarantee his safety and recommended that he leave for Holland, which Wilhelm did on the 10th, the queen and cabinet there agreeing to grant him asylum.[110] His departure removed a first major obstacle to stabilizing the revolution; on the same day Ebert removed a second by agreeing to Foch's armistice conditions. The new government was in an uneasy constitutional position, being vested with its power by Max in his capacity as the last imperial chancellor but being shadowed by a newly formed executive council of the Berlin workers' and soldiers' soviets. Although the USPD joined the government Ebert intended from the start to rule only for an interim period until an elected constituent assembly established a parliamentary democracy. In the meantime he wanted to uphold public order, maintain the food supply, and leave the imperial bureaucracy intact. Therefore on 10 November he also opened secret conversations with Groener in which the government undertook to fight Bolshevism and to respect officers' rights of command (in contrast to Order No. 1's assault on military authority in Russia).[111] The November revolution was necessary for Wilhelm's removal, without which the prospects for successful democratization would have been even poorer; but from the beginning of the revolution the SPD leaders were determined to contain it and the auspices were favourable for their doing so, even though their success eventually opened the way to reaction.

That prospect, however, was still remote at 11 a.m. on 11 November when the guns along the Western Front – which continued firing until the very end – at last fell silent. It was an exceptional moment, if celebrated less rapturously by the Allied soldiers in the field than by the febrile crowds in Paris and London.[112] Yet two bringers of mass death were at work in 1918 and the second was at its peak of virulence. By late October the influenza pandemic was killing 7,000 people in Britain every week and in all it claimed over 500,000 American lives, exceeding US deaths in battle in the two World Wars, Korea, and Vietnam put together. Worldwide fatalities far exceeded combat deaths in the war and may have topped 30 million. There was no medical defence against the disease, and its victims died in pain and often in squalor. Its incidence was not directly linked to the conflict or to poor nutrition caused by blockade, though it disproportionately affected young adults and its spread was facilitated by the forced proximity of hundreds of thousands of servicemen in trenches, hospitals, trains, and passenger liners. It wrought some of its most concentrated depredations on the eastbound American troopships, a price that Wilson and his war department reluctantly accepted because of the imperative of rushing men to the Meuse-Argonne.[113] Yet the pandemic was overshadowed by the war at the time as it has been since, perhaps because it was a natural calamity rather than a man-made one, perhaps because most of the dead were not in the west, and perhaps because the world had grown callous. November 1918 was a strange, sad time, another moment of mass hysteria but quite different from that of July 1914. For the defeated, whatever crumbs of mitigation might be offered by the prospect of a Wilsonian peace, it was an occasion for foreboding. Still, at least on the Western and Italian fronts, in the Balkans and the Near East, and as far afield as East Africa, the killing would now stop, and that seemed reason enough to celebrate, as perhaps too was the sudden democratization of Central and Eastern Europe, raising hopes not seen since 1848 or again until 1989.

None the less, it soon came to be argued in the Allied countries that the armistice had come too early – and in Germany that it would have been unnecessary, had the armed forces not been stabbed in the back. Both these views were mistaken. The German revolution modified Groener's advice to the government and influenced Max's decision on 6 November to seek an armistice at once. But the naval mutiny that sparked it had been sparked in turn by the *Flottenvorstoss*, which was a reaction against the armistice negotiations. Groener's other key concern on 6 November – the threat to Germany's southern borders – arose from Austria-Hungary's disintegration, which was likewise precipitated by Germany's armistice appeal. The key to the entire process of collapse was Ludendorff's breakdown on 28 September, which was a response not to developments on the home front but to the combination of Bulgaria's surrender with the general Allied offensive, linked to the crippling of the German army by his attacks. The revolution was a consequence, not a cause, of Germany's defeat, and the SPD leaders did their best to moderate it. It is also true, however, that if Ludendorff had kept his nerve German resistance could have been prolonged until early 1919, although probably not much longer. His actions determined the manner rather than the fact of Allied victory.

Several American and Allied leaders questioned whether it was the right time to halt, including the Republicans in Congress, Pershing, Poincaré, and Lloyd George. Once the scale of Germany's débâcle became apparent, however, the

British premier accepted the decision had been right, and only when Germany began to challenge the Allies in the 1920s did doubts resurface. Lloyd George and Henry Wilson were relieved that their troops need not invade a Bolshevik-infested enemy heartland,[114] and no one advocated occupying territory much further east than the Rhine. Admittedly, Allied restraint meant that Ebert could welcome the German troops back to Berlin by pronouncing them unbeaten, nourishing the legend that they had somehow been cheated. Yet in 1870–71 a German siege and bombardment of Paris, followed by a victory march through the city, had still failed to eradicate French thoughts of vengeance. After 1945, it is true, the mindset of a completely defeated and devastated Germany really did change, but the transformation took years and its precondition was not just the conquest of Berlin but also continuing Soviet and Allied occupation and the agreement of the wartime victors, if on nothing else, that the country should never again become an independent first-class military power. Going on to Berlin in 1919 would probably not have helped the Allies much unless they had been willing to stay there, risking revolutionary instability in their own societies in the process. Even without their doing so, there was enough in the armistice to enable them to impose a severe and bitterly resented peace treaty eight months later, a treaty repressive enough to make it impossible for Germany to launch another major conflict, had the victors upheld it with the unity of purpose that had eventually won them the war. Lasting peace (or at least the absence of hostilities) was made possible for the North Atlantic area by the sacrifices of 1914–18, and to this extent there was genuine reason to celebrate in that grey November. The western world was not foredoomed to follow the disastrous trajectory that it pursued in the succeeding decades. Yet the very cost of victory, by undermining political and social stability, had stacked the odds against a peaceful future. No account of the impact and significance of the conflict can be complete without an assessment of its aftermath and its poisoned legacy.

Part Four

LEGACY

CHAPTER 18

PEACEMAKING, 1919–1920

T HE FIRST WORLD WAR was the greatest event of its time, not only for what happened during it but also for its subsequent impact. Its global reper- cussions extended down to 1945, and arguably to the collapse of Soviet Commu- nism and the end of the Cold War, not to say beyond. It has become customary to see it as the opening of an age of catastrophe, or as the beginning of a 'short twen- tieth century' that lasted until 1989, after which (and especially after 11 September 2001) the world entered a different era.[1] For individual combatants and their fami- lies, too, the war did not leave them in November 1918. Over half the troops of the British army on the Western Front in 1918 were less than nineteen years old:[2] the last participant in the November 1917 assault on Passchendaele died in 1998, and in 2003 thirty-seven BEF veterans were still living.* For many of them, the war remained vivid.

All the same, as the years have passed – and particularly since a second and even greater world war – that of 1914–18 has become a less dominating imagina- tive and political landmark. As the ripples from its impact have widened, their strength has diminished. The story of its legacy is one not only of the havoc its repercussions wreaked on western societies in the years that followed it, but also of the processes by which the wounds were healed and the pain assuaged. By the late 1920s these processes were well at work and a delayed but tangible recovery was in progress. It was a calamity that a German leader then took office who was com- mitted not to liquidating the war but to re-enacting it, unleashing a new conflict whose consequences overshadowed international history after 1945 as those of the first had dominated it after 1918. If it is true, however, that the Second World War would have been inconceivable without the First, the earlier war did not lead in- evitably to the later one. Events in the 1930s did not have to unfold as they did, and it is vital to distinguish between direct consequences of the 1914–18 war and

---

*BBC news report of Public Record Office reception (which nine veterans attended), 8 April 2003.

developments for which it was merely a precondition. In each successive decade after 1918, more events fell into the second category. To highlight how the war's shock-waves spread and then subsided, what follows will be organized in four chronological sections: first, the negotiation of the peace treaties in 1919–20; second, the abortive recovery of 1919–29; third the collapse of the post-war settlement, the rise of Nazism, and the approach of the Second World War; and fourth and finally the continuing influence of the memory of the war, largely in the cultural rather than the political domain, in the second half of the twentieth century and into the new millennium.

The peace treaties were the pre-eminent political legacy of the conflict. The struggle to enforce them was the essential issue in post-war international politics and almost equally fundamental to domestic developments. The eventual failure of the crucial treaty – that signed at Versailles with Germany – raised fundamental questions about the efficacy of using force in relations between states. Yet after fifty-two months of slaughter, costing the Western Allies alone some $130,000,000,000 and 3.6 million lives, their leaders considered they had the right and duty to legislate into existence a new body of public law, by which both they and their former enemies would be bound. As Foch had put the matter before the armistice, one made war in order to achieve results: if the victors were strong enough to impose their conditions, further bloodshed was needless. Unspectacular though the Allies' triumph might have been, it was indeed sufficient for this purpose. Although they began demobilizing after the armistice, they maintained the blockade machinery in place and kept substantial forces at the ready until they signed the peace treaty with Germany. The Austro-Hungarian army had broken up, and neither the Bulgarian nor the Ottoman armies could fight. Much of Europe was desperate for food supplies that only America and Britain could deliver. It was true that in Russia and in parts of Eastern Europe the victors had little influence, and they lost control over Asia Minor after Mustafa Kemal's Turkish nationalist movement emerged there during 1919. But in Germany, the Adriatic, the Balkans, and the Eastern Mediterranean – not to mention Africa and East Asia – if America and the European Allies could agree among themselves they could determine the shape of the settlement.

The Paris Peace Conference opened in January 1919 and continued until January 1920, after which a standing conference of Allied ambassadors replaced it.[3] It produced five peace treaties: with Germany at Versailles on 28 June 1919, with Austria at Saint-Germain-en-Laye on 10 September, with Belgium at Neuilly on 27 November, with Hungary at the Trianon on 4 June 1920, and with Turkey at Sèvres on 10 August 1920. The conference's travails were not simply due to administrative incoherence but also reflected deeper disagreements. Thus the European Allies remained reluctant to accept as binding the armistice political agreement and the Fourteen Points, with the result that the victors came to Paris without unanimity on their terms of reference. In addition the chaos afflicting much of Europe made peacemaking inherently intractable. Although the British and French foreign ministries commissioned studies of the 1814–15 Congress of Vienna, the political leaders paid these little attention. No precedent existed for the scale and complexity of the task ahead and the leaders improvised the Paris conference's procedures as they went along. Representatives of all the Allies attended the public plenary sessions, but to begin with the five great powers transacted business in the Council of Ten, comprising the American, British, French, Italian, and Japanese heads of government and foreign ministers or their delegates. Its sessions were rambling and inconclusive. In February 1919 Wilson and Lloyd George left for extended home visits and an assassination attempt temporarily disabled Clemenceau. From late March, therefore, with almost nothing yet decided except the Covenant (the founding document of the League of Nations), the three men started meeting daily with Orlando as the Council of Four, and settled the outlines of the German treaty in a month. They devolved much technical material to their officials, and all the delegations to the peace conference found co-ordination across its sprawling sub-committees difficult. In addition the Allied diplomats laboured under a misapprehension, in that they supposed they were drafting 'preliminary' terms that would be subject to renegotiation but which in fact became the definitive conditions. When the draft treaty was presented to the Germans on 7 May many in the British and American delegations were startled by its severity, but by then, after months of gruelling deliberations, their leaders preferred to impose the product in its entirety rather than revisit it. None the less, Wilson, Clemenceau, and Lloyd George were fully cognizant of the document's main terms, and to suggest that the powers stumbled into peace is as misleading as it is to claim that they had stumbled into war.

Perhaps the outstanding characteristic of the resulting settlement was fragility. The Sèvres treaty with Turkey was never implemented or even ratified, while the ink on the Versailles treaty was scarcely dry when the Germans began challenging it, and over the next two decades it was continually modified in their favour. Yet from the appearance at the end of 1919 of the bestseller by the British economist (and junior peace conference delegate) John Maynard Keynes, *The Economic Consequences of the Peace*, the tone of much contemporary commentary on the treaties – and soon on the war itself – was one of disillusionment. It became clear almost at once that the Germans would not voluntarily comply with the settlement, and that the Allies faced the prospect of continuing vigilance and confrontation at a time when most of their demobilized soldiers desperately wanted to return to normality and to their private lives. All the same, during the 1920s, although the post-war world was a turbulent place, at least there was little risk of another major armed conflict. By the 1930s even this was no longer true, and hopes that the sacrifices of 1914–18 could 'end war' – that they could eliminate the international insecurity that had caused the calamity – were cruelly disappointed. It was probably for this reason more than any other that many not only in the defeated countries but even in the victorious ones came to see the entire enterprise as having been futile, and this perception both modified the way in which the war was remembered and influenced Western politicians in favour of appeasement. Yet if it was not true that the terms of the armistice made a second war inevitable, nor did those of the peace treaty, and the peacemakers have had an undeservedly harsh press. Like the generals before them, they were feeling their way in unprecedented circumstances, but the settlement they constructed was more flexible than its critics acknowledged, and could either have accommodated a lasting reconciliation with the new republican regime in Germany or ensured that it remained militarily harmless. The real tragedy of the inter-war years was that it did neither, with the result that in 1939 Britain and France had to take up the task they had left off in 1918, and in much less favourable circumstances.

The main reason for this tragedy was not that the treaty terms were impracticable or unjust. Nor did the Allies lack adequate military strength. The more fundamental problem was their disunity, which was already evident during the peacemaking process and which disagreements over the treaty terms exacerbated. Russia, Japan, and Italy became more or less estranged from the Atlantic powers, and America, France, and Britain reached the limits of co-operation. A pattern of disunity emerged that contrasted sharply with the wartime cohesiveness of the anti-German coalition, and this disunity gave Hitler his opportunity.

Russia, Japan, and Italy should be considered first, as their relative detachment meant that America, France, and Britain dominated the peace process. The war's legacies in Russia included both the Bolshevik regime and Allied intervention. The latter began as an extension of the struggle against Berlin, but it continued long after the armistices and after Germany had evacuated the former tsarist territories. The victors stayed on in part because they still feared an alliance between Germany and Russia, although in fact the German revolutionary government rejected Moscow's advances, looking instead to Washington for food and for diplomatic assistance. However, other considerations also came into play. The Japanese army wanted to stay in control of eastern Siberia. Lloyd George wanted to pull out British forces, but was handicapped by his cabinet's anti-Bolshevism and by its sense of obligation to Lenin's opponents, the Whites. In addition the British hoped to weaken Russia permanently as a potential rival, by detaching its outlying provinces in Eastern Europe, the Baltic, and the Caucasus. Finally, Clemenceau, the most ideologically opposed of the Allied leaders to the Soviet regime, sent an expedition to Odessa in the hope of salvaging French investments in the Ukraine and replacing the Germans as the protecting power there. At this stage it was far from obvious that the Bolsheviks would win the Russian civil war, Red advances in winter campaigning being offset by White successes each summer. During the peace conference the Allies therefore tried half-heartedly to negotiate with Moscow but then placed their bets on a White victory, moving from an ostensibly impartial position to an explicitly anti-Bolshevik one.[4] In January 1919, they proposed a conference on Prinkipo Island in the Sea of Marmara between all the Russian factions. The Soviets agreed to participate, offering to service Russia's foreign debts and to refrain from subversion in the Allied countries, but the Whites, covertly encouraged by the French, rejected the invitation. In March the Bolsheviks again offered to negotiate if the Allies withdrew their forces and ended assistance to the Whites, but instead the Council of Four endorsed an American plan for a neutral commission under the Norwegian explorer Fridtjof Nansen, which would distribute food on condition that a ceasefire was observed and that America controlled the Russian railways; to which the Bolsheviks objected. Finally the Allied leaders gave conditional recognition in May to the White government of Admiral Kolchak, based in Omsk, promising to help him set up an all-Russian regime. Despite Russia's enormous contribution to defeating Germany, it would be excluded from the peace.

The impression of a missed opportunity should not be overstated. The Allied leaders would have faced enormous difficulties in winning parliamentary ratification for a peace treaty with the Bolshevik regime, which wide sections of their public opinion condemned for having signed the Brest-Litovsk treaty, expropriated foreign investments, trampled on civil liberties, and murdered the tsar. Further, Lenin's willingness to talk was purely tactical. He opposed a permanent ceasefire, and meant to settle accounts with the Whites. He saw the advantages of a 'second Brest' – a truce with the Allies while he won the civil war – but remained committed to world revolution. Until the mid-1920s the Bolsheviks saw exporting socialism into Central Europe as the best safeguard of their survival, and they wanted to establish communist parties in the Western countries and foment revolution in their colonies. It was never feasible to draw the Soviet leaders into a new encirclement of Germany. But nor was it feasible to overthrow them, although Sonnino, Foch, and Churchill, among others, advocated trying to do so. During 1919 the Red Army expanded to over 3 million men and the logistical and political obstacles to operations against it were immense. British troops at Folkestone mutinied against being sent to Russia, and after French sailors in the Black Sea Fleet likewise mutinied Clemenceau had to recall the Odessa expedition. Conscripts who had been willing to fight against Germany, and even to stay mobilized until peace was signed, had no intention of being despatched to a remote new theatre, and in any case the Allied governments were too stretched financially to send them. Hence the Allies confined themselves to sending Kolchak volunteers, trainers, and munitions, at the cost of deepening their estrangement from Moscow. Finally, in the winter of 1919–20, at which point the civil war had moved decisively in Lenin's favour, the Allies wrote off the Whites and restricted their aid to the newly independent states on Russia's fringes. The Soviets reconquered the Caucasus and most of the Ukraine, but the Baltic states and Finland maintained their independence, as did Poland, which with French assistance repelled invasion and seized extensive former Russian territories in the Soviet-Polish war of 1919–21. Meanwhile Romania held on to the Russian province of Bessarabia. With the Soviets pushed back in Europe but having elsewhere regained the pre-1914 tsarist territories, their frontiers were established for the rest of the inter-war years. The Soviet Union remained a dissatisfied power, no longer sharing a border with Germany; instead the new state of Poland lay between the two countries, and hostility towards it united them.

The peace conference's decisions also impeded co-operation between the Western countries and Tokyo. Perhaps even more than America, Japan gained from entering the war. It ran a balance of payments surplus and became a net international creditor. It had captured Germany's North Pacific islands and the base at Qingdao in Shandong province, and while the Europeans were preoccupied it strengthened its position in China. At the beginning of the peace conference it received equal representation as a great power. It was not included in the Council of Four, however, and its influence was confined to the Asian and Pacific settlement. Admittedly the Japanese government aspired to little more. It saw its primary interest as consolidating its regional predominance, and it instructed its delegates to take the initiative only in matters directly bearing on Japan's interests.[5]

To this generalization there was one exception, in the shape of Japan's proposal for a so-called 'racial equality clause' in the League of Nations Covenant: a non-discrimination provision that approved 'the principle of equality of nations and just treatment of their nationals'. In fact the Japanese were asking only for a general declaration rather than concrete measures. Even so, in the conference's League of Nations commission, eleven out of sixteen countries represented voted for the amendment, but Britain and America abstained and Wilson, as chairman, ruled that in the absence of unanimity it was lost. The most vocal objections came from the Australian premier, Hughes, but both Lloyd George and Wilson let him take the lead, because British imperial unity might be threatened unless Australia and New Zealand maintained the right to exclude Japanese immigrants, and because the American Senate might reject the Covenant if the Pacific coast states were forbidden to discriminate against them. The episode created the impression that Japan was good enough to be asked for help yet not good enough to be recognized as an equal. Moreover, although it was allowed to keep control of Germany's North Pacific islands, it did so as a League 'mandatory', acting under nominal international supervision and being forbidden to fortify them. Japan's ostensible partners evidently looked to contain it.

The biggest row with Tokyo at the conference, however, concerned Shandong. The Japanese wanted Germany's rights in Shandong unconditionally transferred to them, saying they intended to restore them to China, but through bilateral negotiations (in which they would have much the stronger position). The Chinese wanted to regain complete sovereignty in the province immediately. The British, French, and Italians had endorsed Japan's claims in secret agreements concluded in 1917, and Wilson found himself alone in opposing them. When the issue came to a head in April 1919 he judged that the Japanese would walk out rather than give way. Economic pressure on them would be ineffective, and he judged – correctly – that American opinion would not support a war. Lloyd George opposed a general renunciation of all foreign spheres of interest in China, so this alternative was closed off. In order to keep the Japanese at the peace conference and in the League, Wilson agreed with much heart-searching to a compromise that essentially gave them what they wanted, transferring Germany's rights to them on the understanding that they would return the leased territory to China at a time of their choosing. The American press denounced the arrangement, which eventually became one reason why the Senate later refused to ratify the Versailles treaty and America stayed out of the League. Nor was it much of a success for Japan: the Chinese also refused to approve it, and when the terms of the deal were published in China they triggered off the 'May Fourth Movement' of student-led protest demonstrations and a boycott of Japanese goods. Resentment reinvigorated the national pride of the Chinese, who during the 1920s fiercely resisted imperialist encroachments. Yet initially the effect of the war in East Asia was to consolidate Japan's position and to leave it in still less need of allies.

The parallels between Japan's situation and Italy's were recognized at the time.[6] One reason for Wilson's conciliatory attitude towards Tokyo was that in April 1919 he simultaneously faced confrontation with Rome. Like the Japanese, the

Italians ended the war in a stronger regional position, the militarily superior Austria-Hungary of over 50 million people being replaced on their northern border by a residual German Austria of 7 million and by the ravaged and internally divided South Slav kingdom of 12 million. The war had eliminated their old security nightmare more permanently than it disabled the German menace on France's eastern border and the Russian menace on Germany's. Also like the Japanese, the Italians had British and French support for their demands (in the 1915 London treaty), and although they still needed economic assistance they were no longer militarily dependent on their partners. All the same, Orlando mismanaged what should have been a favourable negotiating position, essentially by trying to straddle too wide a range of domestic views. When his ministers discussed their claims before the peace conference assembled, Sonnino wished to stand by the 1915 treaty. He saw the South Slavs as the principal threat, France coming second. In contrast Diaz was willing to drop the claim to Dalmatia, which he regarded as an indefensible liability, but the navy still insisted on it. Meanwhile, the city council of the Istrian coastal town of Fiume, which had a small Italian majority (though not if its suburbs were included), had voted for union with Italy. The London treaty had not assigned Fiume to Italy, but support for annexing it united Italian opinion from progressives to anti-Slav nationalists. Orlando was determined to keep his government intact and to avoid making unilateral renunciations, with the result that at the peace conference the Italians claimed Fiume in addition to the Treaty of London line in the Trentino, Istria, and Dalmatia, thereby including not only 230,000 German-speaking Austrians but an even greater number of Slovenes and Croats. By basing their demands on an inconsistent combination of self-determination, security needs, and treaty rights the Italians needlessly created a united front against themselves.

The British and French accepted that they were bound by the Treaty of London. When Orlando demanded Fiume as well, however, Lloyd George and Clemenceau aligned themselves with Wilson. In the Fourteen Points Wilson had said the Italians should receive only ethnically Italian territory. He was willing to compromise by accepting their claim on strategic grounds to a northern frontier on the Brenner Pass. He was also willing to demilitarize Dalmatia, internationalize Fiume, and offer them a pact of guarantee. But he had never signed the London treaty and he would not cede Fiume outright, while although Orlando could consider concessions over Dalmatia he risked (or so he said) revolution if he returned home without Fiume. As Lloyd George later commented, it was absurd that the town should have caused so bitter a dispute, but Wilson saw it as a test case for self-determination. The Italians' justification was poor, they were diplomatically isolated, he could discourage American loans to them, and his information was that Italian public opinion did not support the government. Hence he issued a public manifesto on 23 April and the Italians, who felt they were being picked on, left Paris for home. But although their reception back in Rome was rapturous, the gesture achieved nothing and it harmed their negotiating interests. In their absence, they were excluded from a share of Germany's colonies and the Allies allowed Greece to occupy the Smyrna (Izmir) district of Asia Minor that the St-Jean de Maurienne agreement of 1917 had assigned to Italy. In May Orlando returned, but the deadlock persisted. In September a private army under the poet and nationalist agitator, Gabriele d'Annunzio, occupied Fiume, and stayed there for a year. Eventually, under two treaties signed with the new Kingdom of the South Slavs in 1920 and 1924, Italy annexed the town while the rest of Istria was partitioned more or less along the border laid down in the Treaty of London. Yet the uproar over Fiume obscured Italy's very real achievements in completing its national unification and consolidating its strategic security, and gave currency to the complaint that its victory had, in d'Annunzio's phrase, been 'mutilated'. Although it would be excessive to say the dispute brought Benito Mussolini to office in 1922, it certainly assisted him, and it reinforced Italian perceptions of France and Britain as potential enemies. Even under Mussolini Italy was not lost as a partner in containing Germany and enforcing the Versailles treaty, but it was neither a consistent nor a reliable one.

Soviet Russia was excluded from the Allies' councils, Japan mostly confined itself to its regional interests, and Italy did likewise, as well as absenting itself at a crucial moment. The Versailles settlement with Germany in Europe was therefore a French, British, and American product. Although relations between Clemenceau, Lloyd George, and Wilson came close to breaking-point during the peace conference, the three statesmen felt impelled to maintain unity even at the price of painful concessions. Almost as soon as the treaty was signed, however, their countries drifted apart. Its terms were assailed in Germany and in the Anglo-Saxon countries as being too harsh and in France as being too lenient. It was indeed an accommodation between profoundly opposing conceptions. Scope for controversy existed not only because of Paris, London, and Washington's contrasting historical experiences and geographical locations but also because of the unpredictability of political conditions across Europe and not least in Germany itself. Temporarily, at least, the country was prostrate. Its army was mostly demobilized by January[7] and it handed over vast quantities of equipment, while much of .he navy – following the armistice provision that it would go to an Allied anchorage if no neutral one could be found – was in custody at Scapa Flow. The blockade was maintained strictly until March and more leniently until July, leading to perhaps a quarter of a million civilian deaths. Allied troops held the Rhine bridgeheads, and Frankfurt and the Ruhr lay defenceless. Yet the 1918 revolution had stopped halfway, removing Ludendorff and Wilhelm II but leaving Imperial Germany's officer corps, bureaucracy, judiciary, and academic and business elites intact. While the SPD-dominated government feared an extremist takeover like that in Russia, the far left wanted the revolution to be radicalized. In January elections returned a constituent assembly, which drafted the constitution of what became the Weimar Republic, but in the same month government-recruited paramilitary forces, the Freikorps, crushed a left-wing uprising in Berlin, and in March a communist government briefly took over in Munich. Both a return to authoritarian militarist rule and a pro-Bolshevik seizure of power seemed possible, while separatist stirrings in Bavaria and the Rhineland placed a question mark over German national unity. Hence while Clemenceau insisted that Germany remained a potential threat despite the creation of a republican regime, Lloyd George warned that excessive severity might drive it into red revolution.

The fundamental judgement for the peacemakers was what balance to strike between coercion and conciliation. Yet both Wilson and Lloyd George implied that the peace treaty should not simply address the 'German Question' but also achieve 'justice' in a more universal sense. It should deliver restitution and compensation for enemy war crimes, and limit the victors' gains to what progressive and humanitarian opinion deemed reasonable. To frame the debate in this way was to open Pandora's Box, and to expose the treaty to an onslaught from the Germans and from Anglo-American liberals from which its reputation never recovered. Between the wars commentators such as Keynes and Harold Nicolson in Britain and Ray Stannard Baker (probably Wilson's closest confidant at Paris) in the United States depicted the peace conference as a cosmic struggle between the cynical traditions of European power politics and the promise of a more enlightened international order. According to this reasoning, Wilson's defeat in the negotiations was the principal reason for the Versailles treaty's defects, and the Germans likewise contended that the Fourteen Points and the 'armistice contract' had been betrayed.[8]

It is certainly true that Wilson compromised over his peace programme, though whether this weakened the treaty is questionable. The political agreement that accompanied the armistice had been a tremendous success for him, but he was poorly placed to follow it through, in part because of his vulnerability at home. He fought a needlessly partisan campaign in mid-term elections in the autumn of 1918, which far from endorsing his leadership (as he requested) resulted in a Senate majority for his Republican opponents. Henry Cabot Lodge, an inveterate critic of the president, took over the chairmanship of the Senate Foreign Relations Committee and therefore became responsible for supervising Congressional scrutiny of the peace treaties. Wilson knew that American opinion was becoming more nationalistic, but he was willing to challenge the prevailing mood and to argue that America's interest lay in securing a more peaceful world through active diplomatic engagement and League of Nations membership. Yet he underestimated the obstacles facing him at home, as he underestimated those at the peace conference. In fact, during Wilson's voyage to Europe, his companions realized that he had only a hazy idea of what he wanted. Certainly the League of Nations was paramount: he insisted on it being dealt with first and embedded in the treaty with Germany, in order to deter the Senate (which had never failed to ratify a peace settlement) from rejecting it. Once the League was agreed he hoped the sense of insecurity in Europe would diminish, enabling territorial disputes to be discussed dispassionately. But even as concerned the League Covenant his proposals were contradictory and vague, and in the remaining questions at the conference he imagined that America's role as 'the most disinterested nation' would be to sit in judgement on others' pretensions. By implication he would rely heavily on the academic and financial experts he brought with him, aspiring to a 'scientific' peace based on 'facts'.[9] To be sure, the president had his speeches as a road map, but they could help him little over details. In economic matters he envisaged a quick abandonment of governmental controls on international commerce and a European reconstruction based primarily on private enterprise; as for Germany, of whose democratic credentials he was sceptical, he looked to a penitential interval of restraints on its behaviour to test its good faith before it could re-enter the world community. It would not at first be eligible to enter the League.[10] His approach was tentative and he envisaged later treaty readjustments under League auspices. He was clear, however, in wishing to maintain his distance from the European Allied governments, who, he told his experts, did not represent their peoples. If necessary he would appeal to their public opinion and apply economic pressure in order to bend them to his will.

This being said, the American president was arguably most successful in the first phase of the conference, when he formed a partnership with Britain to establish the League.[11] Although Wilson distrusted the British as much as he did the other Allies, Lloyd George and most of the British cabinet favoured working with the Americans rather than with the French, in the hope that by co-operating over the League of Nations Britain would get its way over other matters. Thus the British agreed that the League should head the conference agenda, and they supported Wilson against the Japanese racial equality clause and against French proposals for a League that would *de facto* continue the wartime alliance, equipped with machinery to police German disarmament and a general staffs' committee to draw up military plans. The Covenant that resulted (and which was embodied in the opening articles of each peace treaty) incorporated one key Wilsonian principle in Article X: a general guarantee of all members' independence and integrity. But from the British Empire delegation at the conference (principally Jan-Christian Smuts and Lord Robert Cecil) Wilson borrowed the League's structure of an assembly, a council (dominated by the great powers), and a secretariat; the idea that the Allies would administer former enemy colonies as League 'mandates'; and the League's procedures for the peaceful settlement of disputes. Under Articles XII–XVI of the Covenant members in dispute would accept a cooling-off period, submit their differences to arbitration, a judicial settlement, or investigation by the Council, and not go to war until three months after the judgement or recommendation was known. If all parties on the Council (other than a disputant) were unanimous, members could not start hostilities; if a party ignored these procedures the Council could require all members to apply economic sanctions and if necessary recommend them to use force. The underlying assumption, borrowed by Wilson and the British League enthusiasts from the wartime thinking of internationalist groups, was that public opinion could restrain governments from going to war – and if rapid and secret attack were outlawed war would be possible only in circumstances that made it very unlikely a power would embark on it. Yet this assumption was difficult to reconcile with the evidence (acknowledged elsewhere in the Versailles treaty) that the 1914 war had been due to the Central Powers' deliberate aggression. It placed much faith in democracy and in economic sanctions, and in states accepting willingly a period of reflection. Moreover, the Covenant embodied a potential conflict between the British concern to reinforce the pre-1914 Concert of Europe's dispute resolution procedures (which allowed for non-violent change) and Wilson's insistence on a general guarantee of the *status quo*, a *status quo* that the conference was modifying to the Allies' advantage. The League may appear in retrospect as one of the war's most striking legacies, but its founders had conflicting ideas about how it would operate, and its purpose was in part merely instrumental:

Wilson hoped it would create a constructive climate for negotiation and the British exploited it in the hope of manipulating him.[12]

The British government also needed the League in order to satisfy public clamour for such an institution. All the main political parties and most of the press supported the idea, as did the main internationalist pressure group, the League of Nations Union. Yet in other respects domestic pressure on Lloyd George was far less idealistic. Before the general election of December 1918 the prime minister and the Liberal MPs who supported him agreed with the Unionists to campaign on a common platform, thus enabling the coalition government to continue under his leadership and leaving the Asquith Liberals out in the cold. The agreement deepened the Liberal split but the coalition won a massive majority, Labour becoming the largest opposition force. Against Lloyd George's wishes, however, but stoked by the Northcliffe press, the campaign became the most xenophobic in British political history, the principal foreign policy issues being not the League but extracting reparations and punishing war criminals. Back in office with a strengthened Unionist party alongside him, Lloyd George had to tread warily over these aspects of the German settlement, though he had more leeway in dealing with territorial and security issues.

In fact the armistice had already satisfied many crucial British goals: Germany was expelled from Belgium; much of the High Seas Fleet and all the U-boats were interned; most of Germany's colonies, Palestine, and Mesopotamia were under British occupation. Although at the time of the armistice Wilson had reserved the right to reopen his challenge to Britain's right of blockade, in fact he dropped the matter. Moreover, permanent Allied control of Germany's ex-colonies was assured early in the Paris negotiations, under the Covenant's mandate provisions. The territories concerned would be ruled directly by the mandatories, subject only to periodic reports to the League, to restrictions on militarization (conscription being allowed only for defence), and to other countries enjoying equal access to trade. An implementation agreement confirmed the wartime understandings that Germany's North Pacific islands would go as mandates to Japan and the South Pacific ones to Australia and New Zealand. German South-West Africa went to South Africa; German East Africa was partitioned between Britain and Belgium (the latter taking the mandate of Ruanda-Urundi); and Britain and France divided Togo and the Cameroons. Wilson wanted Germany to lose its colonies, and though he forbade their formal annexation by the Allies he settled for something very similar.[13] Among the remaining points of contention between Britain and America, two were settled in April. By this stage Wilson had come back from his February visit to Washington, where he had encountered mounting opposition. A 'Round Robin' signed by thirty-nine Senators (enough to exercise a veto) had declared the draft Covenant unacceptable. To mollify them, Wilson won British support for an amendment to the Covenant, specifying that the League would respect the United States' traditional exclusion of other powers from Latin America under the nineteenth-century Monroe Doctrine. Explicitly or implicitly in return for this, the president made two concessions. One was over trying war criminals, on which Lloyd George and Clemenceau were insistent but which the Americans had so far dragged their feet, partly because they hesitated to set a legal precedent for such an intrusion on sovereignty. Finally, however, Wilson agreed to what became Articles 227 to 230 of the treaty, providing for suspects to be tried before military tribunals and for Wilhelm himself to be arraigned before a panel of Allied judges if the Dutch would release him.[14] Second, Wilson consented to a naval agreement, abandoning a new building programme he had submitted to Congress in 1918. However, Congress was unlikely to vote the money for it anyway, and the administration intended to proceed in full with its earlier 1916 programme, thus giving America a fleet of comparable quality and size to Britain's. This was a sign that the Anglo-American rivalry that had persisted even in wartime was now returning to the fore.[15] Wilson got on poorly with Lloyd George on a personal level, and after the Covenant was finalized the two delegations no longer co-ordinated tactics. Their disunity allowed Clemenceau to take the lead.

Over the treaty's financial clauses, indeed, the British found themselves closer to the French than to the Americans. No section of the treaty would be more controversial and more criticized than its chapter on reparations. Yet arguably it was most remarkable for its omissions and for its open-endedness. Article 231, which became notorious as the 'war-guilt clause', affirmed the Central Powers' responsibility for the entire loss and damage caused by their aggression against America and the Allies. Article 232, however, immediately qualified it, accepting that they could not pay the whole cost of the entire war and effectively limiting their liability to reparation for damage to property and reimbursement of war pensions. Germany was to pay in the interim the equivalent of 20,000 million gold marks (in 1914 values) in cash and kind, but neither the total liability nor the distribution ratios between the Allies were yet specified, these being left for determination before 1 May 1921 by an inter-Allied Reparation Commission.[16]

The driving forces behind the reparations clauses were emotional as well as financial. Precedents existed for imposing payments on defeated countries (notably the indemnity paid by France to Germany after 1871), but never before had the sums been so great. France and Britain, the principal claimants, ended the war with enormous budget deficits and loan repayment liabilities, both to their own citizens and overseas. They also faced ongoing war pension costs and (in France's case) daunting bills for reconstruction. As they took for granted that these costs had been imposed by enemy aggression, the issue was not only one of avoiding drastic tax increases or public expenditure cuts; it was also simple justice that Germany should pay for the damage it had done. Indeed, according to British thinking reparations (like trying war criminals) would deter such adventures in future. Without reparations, moreover, Germany might enjoy an unfair advantage. As the British Empire conference delegation was told in Paris, Germany *must* pay or what would become of France? These considerations notwithstanding, during the war the British Board of Trade and the French commerce ministry had envisaged making moderate demands. British officials wished to protect Germany as a trading partner; Clémentel and his advisers foresaw that large cash transfers could fuel inflation and make French products uncompetitive. After the armistice, however, the heated atmosphere of the December election drove Lloyd George to a harsher position, as did pressure from the Dominions (and particularly from Hughes) for extravagant claims in order to ensure they received a substantial sum. In addition, both Britain and France had hoped that the Americans would write off their wartime Treasury loans. But Wilson and his advisers (though agreeable to a repayment moratorium) ruled out cancellation, because of concerns that Congress would object and because of America's own fiscal burdens.[17] They also insisted on dismantling the wartime controls on inter-Allied shipping and on commodity exports, much to the chagrin of the French, who had hoped through this machinery to keep Germany on a leash and to secure cheap raw materials for reconstruction. Hence Clemenceau authorized his finance minister, Louis-Lucien Klotz, to demand not only reparations but also full war costs, and even reimbursement with interest of the 1871 indemnity. This was a bargaining position designed to impress the Americans rather than being seriously meant. But even if Washington had been more conciliatory France and Britain would still have claimed reparations. There was no issue – not even military security – that put Lloyd George and Clemenceau under greater pressure from their home fronts.

In contrast Wilson's economic advisers (who included Wall Street lawyers and financiers) wanted Germany to pay a modest lump sum that would be determined promptly and stated in the treaty. They took this line not only because America's own reparation claims were small, but also because they envisaged a European reconstruction financed by American private lending, which was impracticable while Germany's (and therefore the Allies') liabilities remained uncertain. Wilson's wartime speeches had condemned 'indemnities', and the armistice agreement had limited reparations to physical damage in the invaded territories. Hence the Americans believed they had sound moral, legal, and practical grounds for resisting demands that Germany should repay Allied war costs. As the French and British probably knew that such demands were unrealistic they quickly dropped them in the compromise embodied in Articles 231 and 232, which asserted the principle of Germany's total liability but immediately qualified it. Although the Allied leaders were convinced that Germany had been guilty of aggression they did not intend this assertion to be provocative; it became contentious only when the draft treaty was handed over and the Germans challenged it head on. Apart from this success over war costs, however, the Americans made little headway. In expert discussions of Germany's payment capacity the French were closer to the Americans than to the British, whose representatives, Lords Sumner and Cunliffe, demanded far more than Lloyd George believed feasible. But the prime minister, though rebuffing extremists in the House of Commons and giving the impression of being moderate, increased Germany's liability to approximately double that envisaged in the Fourteen Points by insisting on including war pensions – to which Wilson consented, against his experts' advice and in one of his most glaring departures from the armistice agreement. Not only this, but Colonel House (when deputizing for his ailing chief) conceded that there would be no time limit on reparations payments, and that unanimity on the Reparation Commission would be needed to reduce Germany's liability. Thus the issue might drag on for a generation. Lloyd George probably lobbied to add pensions in order to increase Britain's share of whatever was eventually paid; Clemenceau, on the other hand, had realized that a large and unspecified reparation liability might become the pretext for a prolonged Rhineland occupation. Through this mechanism, the financial, security, and territorial provisions of the settlement could become interconnected.

The principal security provisions in the Versailles treaty, apart from the League Covenant, were clauses permanently limiting Germany's armaments and demilitarizing the Rhineland, and temporarily allowing the Allies to occupy the left (western) bank and bridgeheads east of the river. Separate guarantee treaties, in which Britain and America undertook to assist France immediately against unprovoked aggression, supplemented these safeguards. Under the treaty's territorial clauses Germany restored Alsace-Lorraine to France and ceded Eupen, Malmédy, and part of Moresnet to Belgium. France would occupy the Saar coalfield, own and run the mines there, and incorporate it in the French monetary and customs zone, but under League supervision and pending a plebiscite after fifteen years to settle its future. Austria was forbidden to unite with Germany, and the German-speakers of the Sudetenland, previously part of Austria, were incorporated into the new state of Czechoslovakia. A territorial 'corridor' was created to give Poland access to the Baltic, dividing East Prussia from the rest of Germany, though plebiscites reduced the area that Germany ceded to Poland, as did a further plebiscite held in 1921 in Upper Silesia, as a result of which most of this coalfield region remained German. On the Baltic coast the formerly German port of Danzig became a free city under the League, but Poland controlled its docks and railways; Germany ceded Memel to Lithuania, and, after another plebiscite, lost northern Schleswig to Denmark. In all, Germany lost about 13 per cent of its area and 10 per cent of its population in Europe[18] (though most of those transferred were not ethnically German), in addition to all its overseas possessions.

The security and territorial clauses rested on a compromise between the Americans, British, and French, but the latter mostly took the negotiating initiative.[19] Wilson's thinking had not got much beyond the Fourteen Points, as clarified by the Cobb-Lippmann memorandum of October 1918.* As America lacked claims of its own in Europe he envisaged his role as arbitrating between others. In London the Foreign Office shared some of Wilson's idealism about self-determination and recognized that a peace satisfying national claims was more likely to endure. It looked to a settlement that would encourage neither xenophobia nor communist-inspired unrest, assure a stable framework for trade, and obviate the need for British military and diplomatic security commitments on the continent. As Lloyd George put it, he did not want to create new sources of grievance like Alsace-Lorraine.[20] But once Belgium had been liberated and Germany eliminated as a colonial and naval rival, the British delegation, like the American, had no agreed negotiating programme for the European territorial settlement. Wartime discussions in London about Germany's future had been inconclusive, and tinged by suspicion of Britain's allies. Now with Russia in chaos and Germany beaten, traditional Anglo-French animosity quickly resurfaced as a pervasive – and pernicious – influence on British policy. Not only were the French seen as colonial rivals but in Europe too, much of the British delegation from Lloyd George downwards suspected them of imperialist ambitions that would undermine a stable peace and might threaten Britain directly. These considerations set Britain against much of the French territorial and security programme. Yet Clemenceau

*See ch. 17.

for his part was determined to maintain the wartime alliance, though he presented demands similar to (and probably influenced by) the Briand government's war aims as expressed in the Cambon letter and Doumergue agreement of spring 1917. The main domestic pressure on him came from the centre and right, and the public demanded reparation and security rather than vengeance. If he failed he risked a clash with Foch and Poincaré. Yet his personal prestige and his parliamentary backing were so strong that he enjoyed considerable discretion, and he had general support from the political elite for his opening demands.

André Tardieu, the wartime high commissioner in Washington, pulled the French peace programme together. The French did not call for Germany to be broken up. They did ask, however, for its disarmament and for the whole of the left bank of the Rhine to be separated off as independent buffer states, under Allied occupation and in customs union with France. A permanent military presence on the Rhine would protect Paris and the Low Countries against surprise attack. The French also wanted to regain Alsace-Lorraine with expanded frontiers that included the southern part of the Saar coalfield, the remainder of which would become another small French satellite state. In addition, France proposed that Belgium, Holland, Denmark, and especially Poland should gain further German territory. Seen in conjunction with France's commercial, financial, and colonial demands, the programme represented a concerted effort to weaken Germany and redress the balance of power in Western Europe. Even so, just as the French would have moderated their reparation demands if the Americans had been more forthcoming over war debts, so in security matters Clemenceau's key objective was to keep in being the wartime alliance. When he presented his demands to the press conference he had no assurance of Anglo-American support except the Covenant, which had no teeth. He faced the prospect of continuing confrontation, deprived of the tsarist Russian alliance, with a Germany that he expected to remain aggressive and which outweighed France in population and industrial production. Of course he and his advisers relished the retribution for 1870, and they hoped to expand French territory and influence, but their demands arose from economic and security needs whose legitimacy Wilson and Lloyd George acknowledged. Nevertheless, neither leader could agree to everything Clemenceau asked. French demands went well beyond the provisions of the Fourteen Points. Lloyd George feared they would make France uncomfortably strong, generate constant unrest and tension, and encourage Germany to go Bolshevik. He set out some of these concerns in his 'Fontainebleau Memorandum' in March, a document that Tardieu easily rebutted with the justified comment that it proposed concessions at everybody's but Britain's expense. Lloyd George and Wilson needed an agreement with Clemenceau (in order to incorporate France into the League and to take home a peace treaty) almost as much as he needed one, but the process of accommodation was arduous.

The basis of the eventual compromise was a permanent and drastic series of restrictions on German sovereignty. Nineteenth-century precedents existed in the treatment of China and the Ottoman Empire, but Germany was a European great power. All the victors agreed on limiting Germany's armaments. At the behest of the British, Germany would be forbidden to build submarines or possess more than six battleships; the French specified that it should have no general staff, air force, poison gas, or tanks, and that its army should be limited to a conscript force of 200,000. Lloyd George and Wilson agreed instead to a volunteer force of 100,000, which would mean that the militarily trained population would gradually die out, while an inter-Allied disarmament commission would monitor compliance.[21] Nor was there much dispute about Alsace-Lorraine, whose restoration – which the French insisted should be without a plebiscite – would give France over a million extra citizens, in addition to iron ore, steel mills, and a partial frontier on the Rhine. Lorraine's northern border was where contention began. Wilson treated the Saarland as another test case of his resistance to claims that exceeded the Fourteen Points and violated self-determination. In early April he threatened to leave the conference rather than submit to them. But Lloyd George was less unyielding and by moderating their demands the French drove a wedge between the two men. Wilson acknowledged the justice of Clemenceau's claim to coal, in view of the Germans' sabotage of France's northern mines, and he reluctantly agreed to French control of the Saar under League of Nations supervision. He insisted on the Saar remaining nominally in Germany, but Clemenceau and his advisers believed they had gained enough leverage to be able to win a plebiscite there in fifteen years' time.

Regarding the remainder of the left bank of the Rhine, in contrast, Lloyd George was as emphatic as Wilson in resisting French proposals for independent buffer states, and more emphatic in resisting a permanent occupation. Demilitarizing the Rhineland (the Germans being forbidden to garrison it, fortify it, or conscript the inhabitants) was not problematic for him, but separating it from Germany was. Wilson and Lloyd George therefore countered on 14 March with their historic offer of a guarantee of France, whereupon Clemenceau dropped the buffer-state demand. Wilson did not regard the guarantee particularly seriously, however, and Lloyd George saw it as a stratagem to break the deadlock.[22] Clemenceau was rightly suspicious of it, and continued to pursue additional safeguards. By working on Wilson and isolating the British premier, he obtained agreement on a fifteen-year Rhineland occupation, with evacuation after five-year intervals from the northern, central, and southern zones in turn if Germany complied with the treaty, but subject to a right to prolong it and even to re-occupy if Germany resisted compliance or French security was inadequately protected. This was the provision that linked the security to the financial clauses, as Clemenceau confided to his cabinet that the Germans would fail to meet its reparation obligations and France could stay indefinitely, perhaps persuading the Rhinelanders to unite with it. Already the French military authorities were sealing the occupied areas off from the rest of Germany and making contact with the Rhineland autonomist movement. Clemenceau therefore had a hidden agenda when he traded off his buffer-state project for a temporary occupation and an Anglo-American guarantee, but he correctly foresaw that the US Congress might not ratify the guarantee, and for this reason he obtained the right to a longer occupation. Given the geographical remoteness and slow mobilization speed of the Anglo-American forces, he insisted, and the possibility of Germany's evading the disarmament clauses, France must have forward protection against attack, as well as the psychological reassurance needed to restore its nerve and confidence. Although all three parties gave ground in the bargaining over Germany's western borders, the absence of an Anglo-American common front permitted Clemenceau to secure much of what he wanted.

The French similarly took the lead over Germany's other frontiers. Britain and America rejected Tardieu's proposals to give Holland German territory in return for ceding land to Belgium, but they were willing to prohibit an Austro-German union, even though the German and Austrian governments both favoured one. This was one of the peacemakers' clearest violations of self-determination, but yielding would have encircled Czechoslovakia and enlarged Germany by some 7 million people. The Treaty allowed for the League Council to reconsider the ban, but this meant that France would retain a veto. As for the Sudetenland, all the Allies recognized its strategic and economic indispensability to Czechoslovakia and none wanted to award it to Germany, while the Germans themselves felt less strongly about German-speakers who had not been part of Germany before 1914. In this respect the Czechoslovak settlement contrasted with the Polish one, which outraged German opinion more than any other territorial change. Whereas the French supported big Polish gains, Lloyd George feared future difficulties and wanted to transfer as few German-speakers as possible, but Wilson was more sympathetic than Lloyd George to the Poles and again Clemenceau divided the opposition. The Allies initially assigned the Upper Silesian coalfield to Poland and agreed to a Polish corridor (which Lloyd George managed to narrow). Danzig, the port at the mouth of the river Vistula and ethnically overwhelmingly German, did not go to Poland but was placed under the League. The Allies knew these arrangements would create a fount of German resentment, but they had promised Poland access to the sea and Clemenceau contended that resentment was inevitable whatever they did.[23]

The treaty package achieved with such difficulty was presented to the Germans on 7 May, and signed, after weeks of tension, on 28 June. The Germans were allowed to present their case in writing, but there was no round-table discussion and they were not admitted as equals. The Germans protested against this 'dictation' (particularly as they had met round the table with the Russians at Brest-Litovsk), but there would have been no point in the Allies' victory if they had followed it by a freely negotiated settlement, and they would have reopened their divisions for their enemy to exploit. In fact the German delegation did not demand a simple return to 1914 and was willing to accept disarmament, but it contended that other terms were impossible to execute and contravened the armistice agreement. It called for plebiscites in Alsace-Lorraine, Austria, and the Sudetenland, and it wanted Germany to keep the Polish corridor, Danzig, and Upper Silesia, and to regain its overseas colonies. In return, the Germans offered 20,000 million gold marks in reparations by 1926 and up to another 80,000 million later. However, they also wanted immediate League of Nations membership, and a Rhineland occupation lasting only six months. Under these proposals Germany would have probably still lost Alsace-Lorraine, but by gaining Austria it would have emerged larger than in 1914. The Allies themselves would have paid for most of their reconstruction and French security would have been protected only by German disarmament, while the headline figure of 100,000 million in reparations meant considerably less than it seemed. None of the victors saw this response as adequate. Even so, it provoked a British revolt against the draft peace terms, and Lloyd George threatened that unless they were moderated Britain would not co-operate in using force to implement them. Both Clemenceau and Wilson resisted, however, partly because Lloyd George again envisaged that France and Poland should make sacrifices rather than Britain. The only big concession eventually made to Germany was a plebiscite in Upper Silesia, plus a civilian inter-Allied commission to oversee the Rhineland occupation. The German conference delegation recommended rejection and the German government resigned, but its successor won parliamentary approval for signing everything except the war guilt clause and the trial of Wilhelm II. Warned by Groener that military resistance was impossible, and facing imminent invasion, it finally acquiesced in these points too. Yet although it was the British who broke ranks, the German strategy at the peace conference had been to count on the Americans, capitalizing on the November 1918 revolution in order to distance the new Weimar Republic from responsibility for its predecessor's actions, even though Germany had given no such indulgence to the Bolsheviks. Wilson, however, was unconvinced that German democratization was permanent, and he believed a 'generation of thoughtfulness' was in order before the country could be rehabilitated. After his clashes with Japan, Italy, and France, moreover, he was determined to preserve inter-Allied unity as a basis for the work of the League. Hence this time the Germans' expectations of America were unfulfilled. Their endeavours – since appealing for the armistice – to salvage their great-power status by cultivating Washington had ultimately proved fruitless.[24]

The peacemakers had to contend not only with the collapse of the Romanov and Hohenzollern empires but also with the break-up of the Habsburg and Ottoman domains. In fact with the Versailles treaty the Allied leaders generated a standardized model that to a large extent they simply reproduced in dealing with the other Central Powers. Moreover, the lesser treaties were worked out after Wilson and Lloyd George left Paris, and as the American president's health faded and he became embroiled in the struggle for Senate ratification of the German settlement, he lost influence over the peace process. In so far as the victors could impose their views, Britain, France, and Italy had the greatest influence in south-eastern Europe. Despite their differences – the Italians were hostile to the South Slavs and the Greeks, and therefore more sympathetic to Hungary and Bulgaria – substantial agreement existed between them. Austria-Hungary's disintegration was the crucial development in the region, and the Allies had encouraged and were willing to accept it, but it was not the result of the peace treaties and the criticism that the peacemakers caused chaos by destroying the Dual Monarchy is misconceived. Nor could they put Humpty Dumpty together again, even if they had wanted to, given their very limited local troop strength (except for Italy in the Adriatic). All the same, they did exert some influence over the drawing of new borders, most of which would prove remarkably stable. Regarding Austria, the Council of Four's basic decision was that it should remain independent. It would pay reparations and its army would be limited to 30,000 men. Its frontier with Hungary in the

Burgenland was altered in its favour, and a plebiscite in 1920 confirmed that it would keep the Klagenfurt basin, which the South Slavs had occupied. Bulgaria was treated more harshly. Its army would be smaller, it ceded territory to the new South Slav kingdom, and it lost its outlet on the Aegean to Greece. Finally, Hungary's future was complicated when in March 1919 a socialist–communist ministry under Béla Kun took over from Michael Károlyi's more moderate republican government in Budapest. The precipitant was an Allied order that Hungary should allow Romania to occupy much of Transylvania, and Kun declared that he would defend the border by force. The Allies' response resembled their treatment of the Bolsheviks: they sent Smuts on a mission to present their demands, but refused either to negotiate with Kun or to send in troops, instead blockading Hungary and supplying the Romanians, who in August overthrew the communist regime. Because of the Kun affair Hungary lost more territory, the Treaty of Trianon amputating two thirds of the pre-1914 Hungarian kingdom, as well as exacting reparations and limiting the size of the army. Although Magyar-speakers did not inhabit most of the lost territory, more than 3 million of them were transferred to South Slav, Czechoslovak, and especially to Romanian rule. Romanians now governed Magyars in Transylvania instead of the other way round.[25]

In the Middle East inter-Allied rivalries were much sharper, but there was no lack of military back-up. Besides possessing naval supremacy, the British Empire had fielded over a million men in the region by the time of armistice. Its troops had borne the brunt of the fighting, they had overrun Mesopotamia and Palestine, and in October 1918 they entered Syria. In contrast, the Americans had never declared war on Turkey and had little claim to influence. Hence, although the Allies agreed to hold their Arab territories as League of Nations 'A' mandates, which were supposed to be allocated in accordance with the population's wishes, the report of the King–Crane Commission (composed of two Americans who sounded out local opinion) was disregarded. King and Crane advised that Syria should become a constitutional monarchy under Sharif Hussein's son Faisal, with the United States or Britain as the mandatory power; and that Arab opinion opposed Jewish immigration into Palestine. Yet Syria ended up under French rule, and over the next two decades the number of Jews in Palestine multiplied by a factor of nine.

In the absence of American involvement, the key decisions lay with Britain. Lloyd George had long been dissatisfied with the Sykes–Picot Agreement and after the Turkish surrender he was well placed to change it. In an informal bargain with him in December 1918 Clemenceau agreed to transfer Mosul to the British zone of Mesopotamia, and to place Palestine under British rather than international control. In return Clemenceau probably expected British support over the Rhineland at the peace conference, and was furious when it failed to materialize. Worse, after occupying Damascus the British established an Arab administration there under Faisal, thus challenging France's claims to Syria. Lloyd George and his ministers felt that Britain should gain spoils proportionate to its contribution to victory, and feared that if France took Syria a confrontation with Arab nationalism would ensue that might endanger Western interests more generally. Yet Clemenceau faced agitation from French colonialist groups who wanted Syria, and though unsympathetic to them he felt he had been double-crossed. No issue caused greater unpleasantness between him and Lloyd George. By September 1919, however, London had reconsidered. Here too with demobilization British forces were becoming overstretched, and the general staff saw the priorities as India, Mesopotamia, Egypt, Ireland, and potential unrest at home. By this time, Lloyd George feared permanent damage to relations with France, whose friendship he still needed, and he decided to withdraw from Syria after all, leaving Faisal to settle with Clemenceau. This meant a *de facto* French protectorate, and after a revolt in 1920 France invaded and took over the country. Simultaneously the British crushed a rebellion in Mesopotamia, which they incorporated with Mosul into a new kingdom of Iraq, appointing Faisal the first sovereign. T. E. Lawrence, who had hoped to oust the French from Syria and felt the Arabs had been betrayed, nevertheless helped persuade Faisal to accept this consolation prize.[26] While Syria and the Lebanon became French mandates, therefore, Iraq and Palestine became British ones, the latter being divided between the Holy Land itself, which was open to Jewish immigration, and another new kingdom, Transjordan (ruled by Faisal's brother Abdullah), which was not. By the end of 1923 the post-war settlement was more or less complete. Through the creation of Iraq – which had never formed an administrative unit under the Ottomans and which comprised an unstable combination of Kurds in the north with Sunni and Shia Muslims in the centre and south – and by facilitating Zionist objectives, it set off repercussions that would last for decades.[27]

In Asia Minor, the victors had much less say. Although they signed a peace treaty with the Turkish Sultan at Sèvres in August 1920, limiting the Ottoman army to 50,700 men and placing government finances completely under Allied control, it was never ratified or implemented, in good measure because of the Council of Four's decision in May 1919 to authorize the Greeks to occupy Smyrna.[28] The Greek-speaking inhabitants of the Smyrna region approximately equalled the Turkish-speakers in number, but the decision was not based primarily on grounds of self-determination. The British wanted Greece as an Eastern Mediterranean ally, and aimed to strengthen the Venizelos government in Athens against its less Anglophile opponents. The French and Americans feared that Italy would seize Smyrna unless such a move was pre-empted. The decision was hasty and poorly calculated, and had far-reaching consequences. Before the Smyrna landing Turkish disarmament had been proceeding with little opposition, but soon afterwards a new nationalist resistance movement led by Mustafa Kemal emerged in the Anatolian heartland. Although he was prepared to co-operate with Soviet Russia, Kemal's real objective was a new settlement with the west, provided he could establish a fully independent modern nation state. He was willing to abandon the Arab lands (and even Kurdistan), but insisted that over its own territories Turkey must have absolute sovereignty, untrammelled by outside interference. By the time the Allies began seriously discussing Turkey's future, in the winter of 1919–20, Kemal controlled much of Anatolia and their armies had mostly returned home.

The British had most at stake and found adjustment hardest. Their leaders were contemptuous of the Turks and remembered the latter's wartime atrocities, including those against British prisoners. Their sacrifices at Gallipoli made it all the harder for them to abandon their traditional Near Eastern concerns. Yet by now their army was mostly demobilized, and they feared that military action would drive Kemal into Lenin's arms. For similar reasons, neither the French nor the Italians would fight alongside Britain to impose the Sèvres treaty. Instead, the Allies authorized a Greek advance out of Smyrna in order to force the Turks to submit. Once the Kemalists beat back the invaders, the game was up. Kemal expelled the Greeks from Smyrna in 1922 and after a stand-off between Turkish and British forces near the Straits at Chanak, negotiations in Switzerland led to the July 1923 Lausanne treaty. In this instance alone, negotiation between approximate equals consolidated the settlement. Greece and Turkey exchanged populations wholesale; the Straits were opened to all shipping in peacetime, and would remain open in a war if Turkey stayed neutral; but otherwise Turkey regained full independence and Allied controls were abolished. Apart from a further modification of the Straits regime by the Treaty of Montreux in 1936, the new arrangements would prove remarkably enduring.

A stable accommodation was possible with Kemal, whose aims were consistent and modest, given that the Allies' primary Middle Eastern interests were in the Arab rather than the Turkish lands anyway. Lausanne did not, however, necessarily offer a superior model for dealing with Germany, as in Europe the two sides were still much further apart and the stakes had been far higher. All the same, the Germans struck a chord with many in Britain and America when they charged that the Versailles treaty was a hypocritical *Diktat*: a dictated peace, imposed by threat of force, violating the armistice agreement, and applying Wilson's principles one-sidedly. Germany was disarmed, but the Allies were not (although they promised to consider disarmament). Germany lost its colonies, but the Allies kept theirs, and added former German and Ottoman possessions. Self-determination was applied where it would damage Germany, but ignored where it might not. Versailles considerably exceeded a strict reading of the Fourteen Points (for example in the Saar and Rhineland and over war pensions), and the Allies gave Germany little if any credit for the removal of Wilhelm II's autocracy. However, these points do not establish that the treaty was unjust. France withdrew its buffer-state plans, and Germany lost little territory inhabited by ethnic Germans before 1914. The Austrian Germans and Danzig were not united with Germany, but neither were they placed under foreign sovereignty. Those living in the Polish corridor were, but Polish access to the sea was included in the Fourteen Points, and the corridor could not be drawn without some rough justice, which the Allies softened by allowing plebiscites and by requiring the Poles to sign a minority rights treaty. Furthermore, the Germans acknowledged the Allies' right to substantial reparations, although they were probably on their strongest ground in challenging the practical wisdom of such a large and lengthy financial transfer. The disarmament, war-guilt, and war-crime clauses rested on the facts of German aggression and atrocities, and the Allies had good grounds for their scepticism as to how far the November revolution marked a change of heart. As for the Rhineland occupation, despite Lloyd George's justified suspicion that the French had unacknowledged pro-separatist motives, Clemenceau was quite right to see it as crucial to treaty enforcement. The basic problem was that if accorded parity of treatment the Germans would obtain *de facto* superiority.[29] In view of their larger population and economic capacity, if they could not restrain themselves they would continue to endanger their neighbours unless they were restrained from outside. The French premier was probably correct in his gloomy prognosis that unless Germany changed much more radically the treaty would never win voluntary compliance, and any terms lenient enough to encourage such compliance would make the Allies' sacrifices pointless.

Yet the Versailles treaty did not make another war inevitable. On the contrary, disarmament and the Rhineland occupation made it impossible for the Germans to fight one. Although during the 1920s they tried to circumvent these clauses, when Hitler came to power defence spending remained less than 1 per cent of Germany's national income,[30] rendering its armed forces unable to take on even Poland, let alone Russia, Britain, or France. The treaty could have stopped another bloodbath if it had been upheld. More difficult is the question of whether it sealed the fate of German democracy and ensured the return of a militarist regime. On the one hand, the democratization of the country was incomplete even before the treaty was signed and the elites inherited from before the German revolution had not abandoned their struggle against the Allies. On the other, however, although the treaty certainly inflamed German nationalism, it contained deliberately inserted provisions to allow for relaxation and reconciliation if Germany's behaviour changed. The discriminatory commercial clauses (which unilaterally granted the Allies most-favoured nation status) would end after five years. The Rhineland occupation and France's presence in the Saar might likewise be temporary. The League of Nations could review the Austrian issue, and Germany was not indefinitely excluded from League membership. In short, although the Germans were entitled to protest against a breach of faith, the terms protected legitimate Allied economic and security needs, they did not predetermine a second round of conflict, and they left a variety of futures open. 'The treaty', Clemenceau told French parliamentarians, 'will be what you make of it.'[31]

CHAPTER 19

REBUILDING, 1920–1929

T HE WAR'S GLOBAL impact was at its strongest in the first post-1918 decade. Foremost among the consequences of the Allies' victory were the peace treaties, which set the agenda for international relations. But while statesmen attended to the conflict's political aftermath, their societies had to mourn the dead and to care for the survivors. They had also to rebuild the ruins, and to pay the bill. After an initial period of great turbulence, the world appeared by the mid- and later 1920s to be recovering from trauma and regaining equilibrium, as international tension diminished and internal pressures from the extremes of left and right subsided. The spectres of the trenches would not so easily be banished, however, and the new stability proved fleeting.

International developments make the best starting point, although they became inextricably interlinked with domestic ones. In Europe the leading theme of international politics became the continuation of the wartime struggle by other means, and the most serious long-term threats to peace came from the Germans' determination to challenge the Versailles settlement and the victors' failure to maintain a united front in support of it. As after the Second World War, military triumph removed the incentive for co-operation between a brittle coalition whose members had long histories of mutual antagonism before a common enemy had forced them together, and their victory paradoxically contained the seeds of its own dissolution. In some ways, indeed, the Allies' enforced co-operation had deepened their fear and dislike of each other. Cracks in their unity had already become visible during the peace conference, and afterwards the fissures widened. Whereas before 1914 and during the war the coalition encircling Germany had been impressive for its solidarity, after 1918 it was remarkable for the speed with which it fell apart.

Part of the explanation was that the victors had excluded Soviet Russia from the making of the post-war settlement, and Italy and Japan to an extent excluded themselves. The struggle over the peace treaties did not at first involve the whole of the world and several powers remained semi-detached. France, Britain, and Italy did not recognize the new Russian regime until 1924, and the United States

not for a further decade. The Western powers had claims against Berlin for reparations and against Moscow for compensation for repudiated loans and expropriated assets. It was therefore unsurprising that Germany and Russia embarked on
secret military co-operation and that in the Treaty of Rapallo in 1922 they renounced financial claims on each other. The Soviet regime denounced the Versailles treaty as imperialist, and would give no assistance in implementing it.[1]
Similarly, during Mussolini's first decade after taking power in Italy in 1922, he remained hostile to the Yugoslavs and to the new status quo in the Balkans. He also
had ambitions, if the opportunity arose, to take the offensive against Britain and
France and to control the Mediterranean. As for Japan, its most likely potential
enemy now seemed to be the United States. After the clashes at the peace conference, the American Senate refused to approve Wilson's compromise over Shandong, and Tokyo and Washington stood poised on the verge of an arms race in
the Pacific. It is true that the Washington conference of the winter of 1921–2 temporarily defused the situation and set general restrictions on the powers' warship
building. America, Britain, Japan, France, and Italy accepted a freeze on new capital ships, and adopted naval tonnage ratios of 5, 5, 3, 1.75, and 1.75 respectively.
They also promised (though without enforcement provisions) to respect China's
independence and integrity, the Japanese abandoning their rights in Shandong and
evacuating Siberia. Threatened by a recession at home and a naval building competition that it could not win, Japan reined back on its expansion and accepted ratios that built in its inferiority (though it would remain the strongest naval power
in its regional waters). On the other hand, largely because of American pressure,
Japan's alliance with Britain was replaced by a looser arrangement whereby
Britain, America, France, and Japan undertook to respect each other's possessions
and to settle disputes peacefully. The strongest diplomatic tie between Tokyo and
its wartime partners had been broken. At the time this mattered little, as during
the 1920s civilian politicians seeking co-operation with the West dominated
Tokyo's foreign relations, but the Versailles-Washington treaty settlement fed the
growth of nationalism in the Japanese armed forces and increased the risk that in
the longer run Japan would go it alone.[2]

   The most arresting evidence for disunity among the victors, however, was
America's failure to ratify the Versailles treaty. Wilson's Republican opponents in
the Senate mostly supported the treaty provisions regarding Europe. Their concerns centred on Article X of the Covenant, which they feared entailed an unlimited commitment to overseas intervention, although Wilson assured them that
Congress would retain its constitutional right to decide case by case on whether to
involve American forces. The Republicans wanted to add 'reservations' to the ratification document, which he rejected on the grounds that they would oblige him
to renegotiate the treaty. The Senate proved unable to muster the requisite two-
thirds majority for ratification either with the reservations or without them; and
while campaigning for the treaty, Wilson drove his health beyond the point of collapse. In the 1920 election, the Republican Warren Harding was swept into office,
and he concluded separate peace treaties with Germany, Austria, and Hungary,
while staying out of the League. In fact, the League's powers were so limited that
America's absence from it was probably of minor importance for world peace, but

the loss of the guarantee to France was more serious. Lloyd George used American non-ratification of the guarantee as a pretext to pull Britain out of the arrangement as well, leaving Paris high and dry, and the upshot was that Clemenceau had made his peace conference concessions without receiving a quid pro quo and his country remained unprotected by a powerful ally. Moreover, America withdrew its Rhineland occupation force in 1923, and its protectionist Fordney-McCumber tariff and new legislation restricting immigration were still further indications that it was pulling up the drawbridge. The Republicans remained willing to use American financial influence, even in Europe, but after the crusading interventionism of 1917–19 they retreated from global engagement.

The task of treaty enforcement would therefore fall mainly on Britain and France. But their co-operation too had rested primarily on fear of Germany, and while in France this fear soon became acute once again, in Britain it rapidly subsided. As early as 1920, Lloyd George and his advisers saw German economic revival as necessary to haul Britain's export industries out of depression, and they viewed France as a potential enemy.[3] At the Washington conference, they wanted to cap French battleship strength, while the French tried to exempt submarines from the naval tonnage limits because of their value as a threat to Britain's command of the seas.[4] In 1922, the British government approved a bomber construction programme as a deterrent against a French air threat to London.[5] After the breakdown of the Anglo-American guarantee of France, successive British governments refused any new security pledge.[6] Nor would they renew even the guarantee of Belgium, which they deemed to have lapsed in 1914.[7] The four-year sojourn in Flanders and France by millions of British personnel had done little to assuage historic animosities: on the contrary, memoirs by BEF veterans were shot through with antipathy to their allies. Not only Washington but also London reverted to isolationism.

These conditions undermined the peace treaties from the start, and the victors were fortunate that Germany's former allies could do little against them. Austria had to accept an international financial rescue plan under League auspices in 1922, as a result of which it pledged itself anew to preserve its independence from Germany. Against Hungary, where Karl tried to return to the throne in 1921, a united front was established. In 1920–1, Czechoslovakia and Yugoslavia signed a defensive alliance against it, and Romania joined them. The French supported this 'Little Entente' by signing pacts with its members. Yet this demonstration of solidarity was exceptional. As regarded Turkey, far from supporting Britain in enforcing the Sèvres treaty France and Italy made separate peace agreements with Ankara in 1921, thus setting a precedent for Britain to break ranks with them in Europe. In these circumstances the French, who had taken the largest part in the design of the German settlement, were burdened with the primary responsibility for executing it, unable to count for certain on any other power.[8] Against Germany, disunity among the victors impeded the success of both coercion and conciliation. Broadly speaking 1919–23 was an era of confrontation and of efforts to enforce Versailles, culminating in the occupation of the Ruhr by France and Belgium. In contrast 1924–29 was a period of negotiated dismantling of the treaty. Yet although Franco-German relations evolved from Cold War into *détente*, the key theme running throughout the decade was that neither Paris nor Berlin felt the struggle between them had ended.

Germany had accepted the peace treaty under protest and only when threatened with military action. This did not mean that the Allies had been wrong to halt the war in 1918, but it did mean that they needed to show continuing solidarity and firmness. In fact they only intermittently displayed either, and because they depended for treaty implementation on the German government's voluntary co-operation their enforcement efforts almost immediately ran into trouble. The moderate German political parties that signed at Versailles did poorly in the 1920 Reichstag elections, and their attempt to comply with the treaty provoked an abortive right-wing coup (with military acquiescence), the Kapp Putsch. It was not long before the newly trimmed German army, the Reichswehr, tried to circumvent the disarmament clauses. Conflict also took place over the interim reparation payments to be made before 1921, and notably over coal deliveries, which Germany again failed to comply with. The British, sensitive to their own economic needs, counselled moderation, and the quotas were revised downwards. Meanwhile German steel firms diversified from the Lorraine iron ore field (now returned to France) to sources in Spain and in Sweden and used more scrap, while inflation helped them to liquidate their debts and construct new plants. By 1923, partly owing to coal shortages, the French steel industry was operating at one third of capacity but its German counterpart was booming. In the battle between heavy industries France was losing.[9] Finally, when early in 1920 the Allies published a list of hundreds of wanted war criminals, including Hindenburg, Ludendorff, and Bethmann Hollweg, the outcry in Germany was such that the British and French feared either a communist or a nationalist takeover there. In the end, they settled for a compromise whereby the Germans' own supreme court at Leipzig would try the accused, although in fact it handed down only a very few extremely light sentences[10].

Possibly an even more disquieting development was the sustained campaign conducted by the German foreign ministry against the 'war guilt' accusation and the peace treaty's legitimacy.[11] Forty volumes of tendentiously edited diplomatic documents on the origins of the war were published as *Die Grosse Politik der Europäischen Kabinette 1871–1914* (J. Lepsius et al., [eds.], Berlin, 1922–27), in the hope of inciting the Allies to publish their own documents and of proving that they shared responsibility for the conflict. The ministry's *Kriegsschuldreferat* ('War Guilt Department') set up an ostensibly independent study institute and liaised with businesses and other organizations, arranging for speakers, rallies, pamphlets, and press articles. The 'war-guilt' campaign was taken seriously by most German school and university teachers, who fully co-operated with it, and it also spread abroad, notably to the United States, where work by 'revisionist' (anti-Versailles) historians such as Harry Elmer Barnes and Sidney Bradshaw Fay was subsidized and translated at German expense. However, the main following for revisionism was in Germany itself. Weimar politicians hoped the protest movement would consolidate the republic, but they entrusted it to bureaucrats mostly kept on from Wilhelm's era and its effect was probably to undermine the new regime.[12] It was the clearest of indications that many Germans resisted moral as well as military disarmament, and maintained, as they had done during the war, that they had committed neither aggression not atrocities and that Allied charges against them were hypocritical and groundless.

The assault on the 'war-guilt lie' was in itself a second-order issue for German diplomats. They professed to want an international commission of inquiry (which the victors rejected), but it is doubtful whether they were sincere, as full disclosure about the events of 1914 might have embarrassed both sides.[13] But the treaty's war-guilt clause was also the legal basis for the Allies' reparation claims, which were the most controversial Versailles provision in the confrontation that led up to the Ruhr occupation crisis. As the peace treaty had laid down, in May 1921 the Allies fixed the total reparation liability and agreed on an instalment scheme, the London Schedule of Payments, which the Germans again accepted at the point of a gun after Allied troops occupied Düsseldorf, Duisburg, and Ruhrort. The Schedule set the Central Powers' total liability at 132,000 million gold marks; but the only portion for which it specified a timetable was the first 50,000 million, to be paid over thirty-six years. This latter sum was moderate compared with the totals discussed at the peace conference, though the Allies reserved the right to ask for more. In fact the Germans paid nothing after summer 1921, pleading incapacity to do so; and in reality it seems probable that they deliberately let inflation accelerate rather than raise taxes to pay reparations.[14] At the same time the question of war debt – another piece of unfinished business left over from the hostilities – also became more acute, the new Republican-dominated Congress in Washington establishing a foreign debt commission and insisting on repayment schedules being negotiated, thereby tightening the squeeze on Paris. In a series of complex international conferences, the British tried in vain to mediate. Finally Poincaré, who had returned to the French premiership and was determined to see the peace treaty implemented, sent troops into the Ruhr in January 1923, using the pretext of German defaults on timber deliveries.[15] Although the Belgians joined him, the British and Italians stayed aloof, highlighting the former coalition's disarray. The Ruhr miners went on strike and their government subsidized them (a tactic known as 'passive resistance'). This bloodless confrontation became a new Franco-German showdown: a Verdun in reverse.

The occupation crisis was a turning point. Poincaré's aims were initially modest and centred on renewing reparation payments. As the crisis intensified, however, the strain on government finances drove Germany into hyperinflation and the French became more ambitious. The economic chaos encouraged an abortive coup attempt by Ludendorff and Adolf Hitler in Munich, as well as communist uprisings and a revival of Rhineland separatism. By the autumn Poincaré had won a technical victory in that the Ruhr firms agreed to supply France with coal and a new German government under Gustav Stresemann called off passive resistance. But by backing an unsuccessful separatist movement in the Rhineland the French premier overreached himself. Moreover, he turned down an offer from Stresemann of bilateral negotiations, and agreed instead to an American proposal for an international committee of experts to report on the reparation question, chaired by the Chicago banker, Charles Dawes. While it deliberated, France lost the initiative. In the winter and spring of 1923–4 Stresemann introduced a stable new German currency, the Rentenmark. There was a run on the franc (stabilized by a J. P. Morgan loan), and in new French elections Poincaré lost office to a left-wing coalition headed by the inexperienced Edouard Herriot, who was outmanoeuvred when the London conference of July–August 1924 accepted an arrangement based on the expert committee's recommendations, the Dawes Plan. The German government received an international loan, mainly from private American sources, and resumed cash payments on a more moderate provisional schedule. The French lost the power to use the Reparation Commission to declare Germany in default, and they agreed to evacuate the Ruhr. From now on, under Aristide Briand as foreign minister from 1925 to 1932 and with British and American encouragement, they embarked on a policy of conciliation, for the first time negotiating with their enemies as equal partners.[16]

The real issue in the Ruhr crisis was whether the peace treaty would be enforced and the restrictions and sanctions that the Allies had fought the war to impose on Germany would be upheld. Essentially the outcome demonstrated – as had been shown repeatedly since 1919 – that faced with non-compliance the Allies would compromise. Reparations was a difficult issue over which to fight the enforcement battle, as the victors' economic interests were at variance: the British wished to see German economic recovery and the Americans had no significant compensation claims of their own. The lesson the French drew, however, was that unilateral action would not succeed, and they later stuck to this principle even when faced with more radical challenges. But in the meantime they pursued a policy of co-operation, symbolized by an uneasy friendship between Briand and Stresemann, his German opposite number from 1923 to 1929. Briand had been the prime minister who had approved the Cambon letter and Doumergue agreement in 1917 (and Stresemann had likewise supported annexationist war aims), but now he preached goodwill and oversaw a rapprochement, though one intended to protect French interests. The centrepiece of the policy was the 1925 Rhineland Pact, agreed at Locarno in Switzerland. France, Germany, and Belgium undertook to respect each other's borders and submit disputes to arbitration, which meant that the French secured a non-invasion pledge, although because the pledge was reciprocal it also made it almost impossible for them to invade Germany again. Italy and Britain committed themselves to uphold the arrangements, but by a guarantee that was far from automatic and could easily be evaded. Moreover, further concessions to the Germans followed. These included the evacuation in 1927 of the international commission monitoring German disarmament, and an Allied agreement (at the Hague Conference in 1929) to withdraw completely from the Rhineland five years early (in 1930), in return for a new reparations schedule known as the Young Plan. Together these arrangements were optimistically billed as 'The Final Liquidation of the War'. In fact, abandoning the Rhineland made it almost impossible to react promptly to any future German military challenge, and went a long way towards completion of the process whereby the peace of Europe became dependent on German goodwill.

Two spectacular initiatives marked the culmination of the rapprochement, and both in their separate ways highlighted the changes the war had brought in the language and symbolism – if not the substance – of European politics. The first was the Kellogg-Briand Pact of 1928, a Franco-American initiative whereby all the main powers undertook not to go to war except in self-defence. Before 1914 such a gesture would have been inconceivable, though it was poor consolation for Briand, who had hoped for some more concrete American commitment. The second was Briand's proposal in 1929–30 for a 'European Union', based on a permanent consultative assembly, a continent-wide network of Locarno-style arbitration treaties, and a common market. Before 1914, isolated individuals had urged the need for European institutions, but there had been no continuously organized movement in favour of them. In the early 1920s such a movement emerged, several groups lobbying for a European customs union, and the 'Pan-Europa' organization led by Count Richard Coudenhove-Kalergi – of which Briand became an honorary president – calling for greater political unity. For this development too, the First World War can be seen as an essential precondition, persuading politicians, businessmen, and intellectuals in central and western Europe (though few in Britain) that the continent needed closer integration in order to fend off the American economic and cultural challenge and to reduce the dangers of revolution and war. Yet Briand was attracted to the notion as a means of inhibiting Germany from resorting again to violence at a moment when France's military advantage was in decay; and the Germans torpedoed his initiative precisely because they feared it would restrict their freedom of action and they wanted no extra reinforcement for their borders with Poland and Czechoslovakia in the east.[17] The failure of the 'Briand Plan' for a European Union therefore underlined that the relaxation of tension in the late 1920s was deceptive. It was true that American private loans were flowing into Germany, facilitating reparation payments, while at Locarno Britain encouraged Franco-German reconciliation by means of a reciprocal guarantee on both sides. With Washington and London returning to limited involvement in continental Europe, and both pressing for the Versailles treaty to be moderated, Franco-German relations became less of a zero-sum game. Yet the French opted for rapprochement only because they had tried coercion and found its results wanting, while the Germans remained too weak to obtain treaty revision except by co-operating. Once Paris could concede no more without jeopardizing vital interests, the *détente* process would run out of road. It might be possible to justify it, however, if it strengthened the moderates in Berlin and marginalized the extremists, and signs existed on both sides in the later 1920s of a cultural demobilization and a retreat from wartime hatreds. Tragically these changes ran only skin deep. Fundamentally, the war was still continuing by other means, and the international politics of the period cannot be understood in isolation from domestic developments.

During the war, the home fronts on both sides had many common features, not least because neither side knew which would win. After 1918, domestic circumstances in the victors and vanquished differed much more significantly. In the course of the 1920s all the former belligerents regained a measure of internal stability, but the process rested on much more solid foundations in the Allied countries than it did in Germany. The upheaval caused by four years of fighting presented two fundamental issues: first, the discrediting of established authority structures and the rise of radical challenges to them during the second half of the war; and second, the need to evolve new collective coping mechanisms in the face of mass disablement and bereavement. These themes will be examined first with reference to Britain, France, and the United States.

As of late 1918, it seemed that the conflict had strengthened radical and democratic forces. The left had taken power in Russia and Germany, Austria-Hungary and the Ottoman Empire had disintegrated, and trade unions and socialist parties worldwide found a new appeal and militancy. Yet outside Russia left-wing successes proved limited, and by the mid-1920s politics in the western world was being consolidated on conservative bases.[18] In the longer term the war probably benefited the right. The progressive movements in the major powers had been too weak or patriotic to prevent it from breaking out, or to force reductions in war aims and negotiations for a compromise peace. After 1918 they remained unable or unwilling to bring fundamental change to the international political system. The war had been a test of authority, and of established racial, class, and gender hierarchies, as belligerent governments had drawn heavily on contributions from their overseas possessions, from the working class, and from women. Yet the permanent consequences were surprisingly small.

As Lenin had pointed out, at one level the world war was a struggle for imperial redistribution.[19] The Germans and the Turks lost their colonial possessions, mainly to Britain, France, and Japan. Those most concerned had little voice. The French faced greatest opposition in Syria, where in 1925-7 they had to repress a rebellion. The Indochinese who had laboured for them in 1914-18 (and the Africans who had fought for them) received scarce compensation. The colonial minister Albert Sarraut introduced advisory councils into France's overseas territories in 1919-20, but their remit was purely economic, and the representatives of the indigenous population who served on them were neither elected nor in a majority.[20] Although within France the war had made the colonies an object of mass enthusiasm as never before, the nature of French rule showed much continuity with what had gone previously.[21]

In the British Empire, in contrast, four major developments can be seen as direct results of the conflict. The first was the Anglo-Irish war of 1919-21, following Sinn Féin's capture of the leadership of the nationalist movement after the 1916 Easter Rising and the 1918 conscription crisis, which was confirmed when it swept the board in Ireland's southern and western counties in the general election of December 1918. Lloyd George's government was unable to suppress the IRA's guerrilla campaign, but it did force the Sinn Féin leaders to accept considerably less than full independence in the December 1921 Anglo-Irish Agreement. Ireland was partitioned, and the British kept three treaty ports on the west coast of the new Irish Free State, which for the time being remained within the empire as a Dominion; but in this capacity the Irish added to the pressure that led to the second major change, which was the concession to the British Dominions of *de facto* control of their foreign policy. Automatically involved in war in 1914 by a decision in London, the Dominions were promised greater representation and consultation by the 1917 Imperial War Conference. They were separately represented (as part of the British Empire delegation) at the Paris Peace Conference, signed the peace treaties in their own names (as well as that of the Maharajah of Bikaner for the Indian princely states), and along with India they received separate seats in the League of Nations, an imperial conference in 1926 and the 1931 Statute of West-minster confirming that in future they would make their own decisions on matters of war and peace. Already in 1922, when Lloyd George had appealed for aid in his confrontation with the Turks at Chanak, Canada and South Africa had stalled, and in the appeasement crises of the 1930s their bitter experiences in the war impelled the Dominions to urge caution.[22]

The third major development came in Egypt (which Britain had administered since 1882 but had declared a protectorate after the outbreak of war), where a violent revolt broke out in 1919. Its cause was partly the burden of shortages, requisitioning, and inflation caused by Egypt's role as a military base, though the decision to exile the nationalist leader Saad Zaghlul was the last straw. General Allenby restored order but he recommended the end of the protectorate, the British in 1922 conceding to Egypt a severely curtailed independence that maintained their control over the country's foreign policy, their right to station troops there, and their control over the Suez Canal.[23] Finally, India also witnessed nationwide unrest in 1919–21. It had experienced similar economic pressures to Egypt during the war, and in 1917 London had promised progress by stages to responsible government. However, the 1919 Government of India Act introduced only elected local government and some autonomy for the provinces, the British administration retaining key functions (as it had reserved crucial powers in Ireland and Egypt). Disappointment with the measure (and with new curtailments of civil liberties) led to protests that culminated in the notorious Amritsar massacre in April 1919, in which troops opened fire and killed 379 demonstrators, lending impetus to Mohandas Gandhi's first national civil disobedience campaign. Although the British contained the opposition, from now on their authority depended increasingly on the Indian National Congress's tacit compliance. Moreover, the war pushed the government of the British Raj into a dangerous financial crisis and London promised that in future if Indian troops were used overseas the Indian taxpayer would not have to foot the bill, while Delhi was permitted to impose tariffs on Lancashire cotton imports.[24] The British hung on, though the Indian bulwark of their empire was of diminishing economic and strategic value to them.[25] Indeed, they faced a global challenge to their interests in the early postwar period, as Iraq too rebelled in 1920, and it cost more than all of Britain's wartime operations in the Middle East to put the revolt down. None the less, by the mid-1920s the British had beaten off the most pressing challenges to their global position, and the other Allied empires were much less stretched. In general, European colonial predominance over much of the rest of the world remained intact.

Similar conclusions can be reached about the impact of the war on the social structure of the metropolitan countries. In Britain, it probably caused a minor redistribution of income, mainly due to progressive taxation but also because flat-rate pay increases for manual workers narrowed some pay disparities.[26] After 1921 the inequalities widened again, but not to pre-war levels, and post-war social investigators found that in families when the wage-earner was employed, the incidence of poverty had notably diminished. Most manual working-class wages kept pace with inflation and in 1919–20 working hours were cut substantially, whereas income tax and supertax took nearly half the highest incomes in 1925, against one twelfth in 1914.[27] Even for those out of work, unemployment insurance was extended to cover two thirds of the male labour force in 1920. Between 1914 and 1921 trade-union membership doubled and between 1918 and 1924 Labour displaced the Liberals as the largest anti-Conservative party, as a consequence of the Asquith–Lloyd George split, the widening of the franchise in 1918, and the heightened class consciousness of British workers – all factors that could be attributed to the war. Yet in the longer term the shift to the left was less impressive. Trade-union membership collapsed again with the onset of depression in 1920, and unemployment remained at 10 per cent or more of the workforce for two decades. State control over the pits and railways ended within three years of the armistice, as did price controls and rationing, and the formidable miners' union, the MFGB, was beaten in two prolonged lockouts in 1921–2 and 1926.[28] In office in 1924 and from 1929 to 1931, Labour did little to help its supporters beyond raising unemployment benefit. Despite the strides made by the working-class movement, its principal achievement was better wages and shorter hours for those in jobs, possibly at the expense of more unemployed.

In the United States the picture was similar. Although in 1919 one in five American workers went on strike, the trade unions' hopes of winning collective bargaining rights and recognition and of organizing in the new mass-production industries were dashed when a national steel stoppage failed. Wartime state control over the railways ended, no significant pro-labour legislation was enacted, and wage cuts were imposed. 6,000 suspected communist-sympathizers were arrested on New Year's Day 1920 alone. Another sign of the times was the reaction against black Americans, of whom over 300,000 moved from the southern to the northern states in the years 1916 to 1920. The Ku Klux Klan was re-established – and now on a national basis rather than just in the South – and the incidence of southern lynchings more than doubled in the period 1917 to 1919, while in the summer of 1919 race riots erupted in Chicago and other northern cities. Wilson, who was of Southern provenance, was unsympathetic to black Americans' demands and did nothing to help them; simultaneously his administration encouraged the anti-communist hysteria of the period by raiding the Soviet offices in New York and by deporting workers of Russian origin.[29] If during the war the American labour movement had benefited, after the armistice there was a backlash.

Finally, France too underwent inflation and an upsurge of industrial action after the war, culminating in an unsuccessful national railway strike in 1919. Yet the governments that followed Clemenceau's departure at the end of that year quickly dismantled controls on prices and production, and the labour movement gained shorter working hours but not much else. In 1920 the SFIO and the CGT split into separate socialist and communist wings, forcing the socialists to refuse to take part in government for fear of losing their supporters. Right-wing governments therefore predominated for most of the 1920s, Herriot's *Cartel des Gauches* or 'left bloc' of 1924 (a Radical ministry with socialist backing though not participation) lasting little longer than the first Labour government in Britain. After its collapse Briand conducted his rapprochement policies with the backing of a centre-right coalition, and between 1926 and 1929 with Poincaré again as prime minister. Across the western world the wartime and post-war upsurge in class-conscious activism was beaten back, raising doubts in many minds about what the struggle had been fought for.

This discussion has stressed the limits of the gains made by the working-class and labour movements, and a similar emphasis is necessary in considering the advances made by women irrespective of their class position. It is true that they made some lasting political gains. During the war more practical clothing and the reduction of conventions such as chaperoning increased their freedom in daily life, and at the end of it they gained the vote in American federal elections, Wilson having supported the reform as 'vital to the winning of the war'.[30] Similarly in Britain the 1918 electoral reform act extended the franchise to women over thirty (the authors of the measure not wishing women to constitute a majority of the electorate),[31] but in France where the Chamber of Deputies approved a bill to emancipate French women, the Senate – fearing clerical influence on female voters – rejected it, and reform had to wait another generation.[32] In addition, middle-class and professional women permanently increased their presence in the workforce. In Britain, white-collar employment opportunities for them were greater after the war,[33] and they benefited from the 1919 Sex Disqualification (Removal) Act, which opened professions such as law and architecture, as well as parliament itself.[34] In France too, women's employment in finance, commerce, and the professions jumped during the war and continued to grow afterwards.[35] But with these exceptions the increase in women's economic power that characterized the war years was temporary and after 1918 they were bundled unceremoniously out of the labour market.

Although some writers have argued that war work constituted a form of female emancipation, others have questioned whether toiling for long hours and unequal pay in unsafe factories (against a background of queues and shortages and in the absence of loved ones) really deserves the label.[36] Yet many women in Britain, at least, found war work fulfilling and would have liked to continue in comparable employment after the armistice.[37] They were denied the choice. The Restitution of Pre-War Practices Act, passed during the war, obliged British women in manufacturing jobs to give them up once it ended. Labour and most of the trade unions accepted the government's view that men returning from military service (who were seen as the normal family breadwinners) must take priority. Women were laid off *en masse*, and by May 1919 they constituted three quarters of the unemployed. They received a six-month 'out of work donation' (of smaller value than that for men) and could apply for training only in traditional 'women's trades' such as textiles. After 1922 all married women were automatically excluded from unemployment benefit, on the assumption that it was their husbands' responsibility to keep them. Many were forced back into domestic service, from which they had hoped to escape, or out of the job market altogether, while the press, which had praised them during the war, now condemned them for denying jobs to ex-soldiers. By 1921 the percentage of women 'gainfully employed' was back to a lower figure (30.8 per cent) than in 1911 (32.3 per cent). Apart from the intangibles of companionship and self-confidence, for most women war work provided few lasting benefits.[38] In the United States about a million women had taken up war work, despite fierce trade-union hostility; most were single and came from less well-paid jobs, to which they now returned. By 1920 women made up a smaller per centage of the labour force than in 1910.[39] France differed in that a higher proportion of women (especially married women) was employed than in Britain before the war, but here again the conflict's lasting impact was slight. In metallurgy, 5.5 per cent of the workforce in 1911 was female, and in 1918 it was 25 per cent, but by 1921 it was 9.5 per cent, where for the rest of the inter-war years it stayed. Family allowances and new legislation against contraception and abortion were designed to encourage a return to domesticity and revive the country's flagging birth rate, which was now more urgent than ever.[40] Although middle-class women had more opportunity to remain in the workforce, the general contrast between their fortunes and those of working-class women and men encapsulated the broader restoration of traditional pre-war hierarchies.

By the late 1920s the war appeared to be losing its potency not only as a source of international conflict, but also as a source of challenge to the social order. Moreover, the establishment of a pervasive cult of war commemoration had the potential to act as a conservative, patriotic, integrative force, and governments deliberately encouraged it with this intention. The phenomenon of 'remembrance' was one of the most striking novelties of the decade, and it carried a special emotional charge because of the conflict's human balance sheet.

TABLE 5:
War Dead[41]

United Kingdom	723,000
British Empire (excluding UK)	198,000
France	1,398,000
Russia	1,811,000
Italy	578,000
USA	114,000
Other Allies	599,000
Total Allies and US	*5,421,000*
Germany	2,037,000
Austria-Hungary	1,100,000
Bulgaria and Turkey	892,000
Total Central Powers	*4,029,000*
Grand Total	**9,450,000**

Civilian deaths are harder to estimate than military ones, but those killed by war-related disease and famine or by bombardment and invasion may have reached 0.5 million in Germany and even higher figures in Austria-Hungary and Italy, while in Serbia and Montenegro the losses relative to total population were worst of all. Including estimates of babies never conceived because their fathers were mobilized (possibly 3.6 million in Austria-Hungary, over 3 million in Germany, 1.5 million each in France and Italy, and over 0.7 million in Britain), as well as those who died in Russia's civil war and in the influenza pandemic, the total population deficit in Europe between 1914 and 1921 may have exceeded 60 million.[42] The nearest precedent in European history was the 3.1 million deaths in the Napoleonic Wars (at least half of them French), but these were inflicted over fifteen years of intermittent campaigns. More recent casualty lists, such as the 190,000 dead in the Franco-Prussian War, had hinted at the losses that modern firepower might inflict, but in no previous conflict except the American Civil War had Western societies fought each other with mass armies and modern weaponry for much more than a year. Given the concentration of the dead among young men aged from twenty to thirty, by 1918 few families in the European belligerents would have been unaffected. In Britain alone, some 3 million people lost a close relative.[43] Post-war Europe was overshadowed by what Stephen Graham called 'the challenge of the dead'.

The first part of this challenge was to recover the bodies, identify, and inter them. It was clear to contemporaries from the opening campaigns that this war was the greatest in history and they believed its memory must be kept alive, not only to honour the fallen but also to prevent them from becoming a matter of indifference to later generations who might never understand what this one had endured. The names of the lost must be preserved,[44] and already during the war the belligerents prepared to commemorate them. Lawrence Binyon's elegy, 'To the Fallen', whose refrain 'We will remember them' became a fixture of British Armistice Day rituals, was written in September 1914. The Western European belligerents quickly established that all dead soldiers of whatever rank would be buried in special cemeteries. American legislation during the Civil War provided a precedent, but there was little in Europe, where the Napoleonic war dead had been shovelled into mass graves (and their remains even re-used as agricultural fertilizer). During the nineteenth century, however, tremendous romantic and humanitarian changes had suffused the attitudes of Western societies towards death, and democratic citizen armies, whether volunteer or conscript, evoked different feelings from the mercenary forces of earlier conflicts.

The French passed legislation in 1914 creating military cemeteries; by the end of 1915 they were gathering their dead for reburial,[45] and the war ministry issued regulations for the permanent care of the graves. In 1916–17 proposals emerged for a national mausoleum at Verdun.[46] Other countries followed this lead. In Britain a remarkable individual, Fabian Ware, began the work of recording the dead: the subsequent Graves Registration Commission was renamed the Imperial War Graves Commission (IWGC) in 1917. Street shrines had appeared in the East End of London in the previous year, listing the deaths in each neighbourhood;[47] the Civic Arts Association held a widely reported conference on memorial design and the Royal Academy of Arts set up a committee of architects and sculptors. Before the war ended the IWGC had already appointed the men – Sir Edwin Lutyens, Sir Herbert Baker, and Sir Reginald Blomfield – who would design the principal monuments in France and Belgium, and had determined the characteristics of the British Empire cemeteries. Uniform headstones would mark the graves, undifferentiated by rank. Families could add their own inscriptions, but could not build private memorials. Each cemetery would include a Stone of Remembrance, designed by Lutyens, with biblical inscription, 'Their Name Liveth for Evermore', chosen by Rudyard Kipling, and the more explicitly Christian 'Cross of Sacrifice'.

Their design represented a compromise between conventional religious imagery and more abstract elements.[48]

Once the guns fell silent, the first tasks on the battlefields were to remove the detritus of combat, explode the mines and shells, reclaim the soil, and reconstruct towns and villages. Along the Western Front these tasks were mostly accomplished within five years, but monuments such as the cathedral and cloth hall at Ypres were lovingly reconstructed and were not completed until 1930–34. Of the corpses, many of which had been buried (if at all) in mass or unmarked graves, tens of thousands were condemned to remain anonymous. The American government shipped back home all the identifiable bodies that their families wanted returned: eventually about half the total.[49] The 30,000 that remained were gathered into eight military cemeteries (the largest on the Meuse-Argonne slopes at Romagne), which set high standards of design and maintenance for other countries to emulate. The British government buried the dead close to where they fell, partly for reasons of cost but also for equity between those who had and had not been identified. The decision made visiting loved ones' resting places, difficult enough for most people in Britain, prohibitive for families from the Dominions. Finally, the French authorities also ruled initially that soldiers' corpses should stay on or near the spot, but after many were privately exhumed they relented. The remains of some 300,000 of the 700,000 identified French dead eventually returned home.[50]

Although official searches for BEF bodies ended in 1921, by 1939 another 38,000 had been uncovered. By the early 1930s the IWGC had completed some 918 cemeteries on the Western Front with 580,000 named and 180,000 unidentified British graves; there were further cemeteries in Italy and the Balkans, at Gallipoli, and in Iraq and Palestine. The climax of its work was the unveiling of the great arches listing the missing: Blomfield's Menin Gate at Ypres, with 54,896 names, completed in 1927 (another 34,888 being inscribed on the walls of Tyne Cot cemetery at Passchendaele); and Lutyens's Thiepval Arch completed in 1932, carrying the names of 75,357 killed on the Somme and with no known grave. Both architects used modified versions of traditional forms: the victory arch and gate dated back through Early Modern Europe to classical times, although these new structures honoured the sacrifice of ordinary soldiers rather than the triumphs of generals and emperors, an innovation that in Britain, for example, dated only from the South African War.[51] The Dominion architects who added their separate memorials (against the preferences of the imperial government) were more daring, particularly in the case of the Canadian National War Memorial on Vimy Ridge, which with its two obelisk-shaped pillars and symbolic figures was unveiled as late as 1936.[52] The even bigger French cemetery-building effort was mostly a state enterprise, though its most dramatic component – four ossuaries with the status of national memorials at Douaumont (Verdun), Dormans, Notre-Dame-de-Lorette, and Hartmannsweilerkopf – were built by private initiatives in which the church was heavily involved.[53] For this reason all were chapels as well as repositories for thousands of unnamed bones. The ossuary at Douaumont, opened in 1932, was by its size and associations the most significant, containing an estimated 32,000 French bodies. Whereas Notre-Dame-de-Lorette took the overtly Catholic form of a Romanesque basilica, however, Douaumont was a more modernist, not to say bleakly industrial edifice, resting on a base like a fortress wall but surmounted by a giant plinth on which a cross was inscribed.[54]

The battlefield monuments represented only a portion of the construction effort. The memorials in the home countries left an architectural imprint throughout the Western world. Some 54,000 were built in the British Isles, 38,000 in France, and at least 1,500 in Australia – one for every forty soldiers killed and for every 3,000 of the population.[55] In New Zealand there were over 500.[56] Most went up in the early 1920s, but some as late as a decade later. In France the government provided a small subsidy, but there was no obligation to build and the initiative came, as in the British Empire, from local communities. For this reason more variety was possible than in the official cemeteries, and the memorials revealed more about the response of ordinary towns and villages to mass bereavement. What in Anglo-Saxon countries were normally called war memorials became in France 'monuments to the dead' (*monuments aux morts*). Their central function in France or Britain was to list the dead; in Australia, which had rejected conscription, they had the more potentially divisive purpose of recording all volunteers, whether they died or returned. The French were described as having 'died for France', whereas most English memorials were less overtly patriotic. French monuments were rarely explicitly religious, and most commonly took the form of obelisks, funerary urns, or statues of infantrymen.[57] In Britain soldiers were depicted more rarely, Celtic crosses rivalled columns and obelisks, and Christian redemptive themes were common in the statuary and inscriptions.[58] In the United States, such memorials were fewer and more likely to take on utilitarian forms such as libraries or meeting halls. In general, local monuments were conservative in treatment, deliberately eschewed artistic modernism, and drew on the familiar and evocative imagery of classical, biblical, and romantic tradition to express the grief of their communities and to construct some meaning for their sacrifice.

The design of national war memorials served state rather than family and community purposes and was more liable to be contested. Thus although an Irish national memorial was completed in 1938, it was located well outside Dublin in order to avoid giving it political prominence.[59] In Britain plans for a new London boulevard and an immense hall of memory led nowhere, though the Imperial War Museum was established with official backing in 1917.[60] A museum, too, was the centrepiece of the Australian War Memorial at Canberra, which was not completed until 1941.[61] A South African memorial was constructed at Delville Wood on the Somme, using a statue of Castor and Pollux clasping hands to symbolize the collaboration of white South Africans of Boer and British descent.* The names of the 64,449 Indian war dead were inscribed on the arch of India Gate in New Delhi, and another monument to them, in distinctive style, was built on the battlefield of Neuve Chapelle, the site of their costliest Western Front action. The most characteristic creations of the period, however (and another innovation), were the tombs of the Unknown Soldiers. To some extent a forerunner of the idea in Britain

---

*608 black South African members of the South African Native Labour Contingent who drowned when the SS *Mendi* sank in the English Channel are annually commemorated at Altridgeville, near Pretoria. I am grateful to J. L. Keene for this information.

was the Cenotaph, literally an empty tomb, which Lutyens designed as a temporary feature for the Whitehall victory parade that celebrated the peace treaty. It
proved so popular that a permanent replacement was unveiled on 11 November
1920 when the Unknown Warrior (to give the correct title) was buried at West-
minster Abbey. The idea for such a tomb seems to have originated separately in
France and in Britain. It had a special significance after a conflict that had simply
obliterated without trace huge numbers of combatants. In Paris a warrior was
buried on the same day under the Arc de Triomphe in the midst of elaborate – not
to say macabre – ritual, and others were interred in Brussels and the United
States.[62] Having poured forth unprecedented resources on the war, the new industrial civilization now did likewise to commemorate it, creating a memorial architecture unparalleled since ancient Egypt. Yet the monuments were not simply
static representations: they became the focal points for public acts of mourning,
and here too patterns of ritual were pioneered that have since become familiar calendar fixtures.

In Britain the starting point was a silence. In Cape Town a daily silence had
been observed during the war, and the former High Commissioner in South Africa
brought the idea to Lloyd George's cabinet, with the aim, he wrote, not of mourning but saluting the dead and providing a reminder for later generations. Announced by maroons, gunfire, and bellringing, the impact of the two minutes'
pause in the middle of a working day at 11 a.m. on 11 November 1919 was unexpectedly overwhelming, and demands began at once for it to be an annual event.
Shops stopped serving, men removed their hats and stood bowed in market
squares, Lancashire cotton mills and the London stock exchange suspended work,
and trains halted on the tracks. In November 1920 the Silence (it was customarily
capitalized) accompanied the dedication of the Cenotaph and the burial of the Unknown Warrior. Up to a million visitors paid homage at the latter's tomb within a
week, 100,000 wreaths were deposited at the Cenotaph, and days afterwards there
was still a seven-mile queue to lay flowers. In later years the war memorials (frequently unveiled on 11 November) became the scene of local rituals to echo those
in the capital. On Remembrance Sunday, the nearest Sunday to Armistice Day, the
main British religious denominations held special services, normally incorporating
a procession to the memorial with veterans prominently in attendance. The sale of
poppies for the Haig Fund for the disabled began in 1921 and again elicited a massive and unexpected response: wearing poppies soon became almost universal. The
addition of the British Legion Festival of Remembrance at the Albert Hall in 1927,
centred on community singing of wartime songs and the fluttering of a million poppies from the ceiling to commemorate those now habitually referred to as the 'million dead', virtually completed the complex of remembrance. From the late 1920s
'pilgrimages' to the battlefields began, organized by the St Barnabas Society and the
British Legion, and from this time on the Last Post was sounded nightly at the
Menin Gate. By the 1930s the Cenotaph service on Armistice Day was broadcast
nationally and the Festival of Remembrance throughout the empire. In Australia,
however, the 'Anzac Day' anniversary of the Gallipoli landings on 25 April 1915
developed even during the war into a bigger occasion than the November remembrance, and among Northern Irish Protestants the date of 1 July – when the Ulster

Division, on the anniversary of the 1690 battle of the Boyne, had attacked on the Somme and lost one third of its strength – carried exceptional significance.[63]

The closest parallel to these developments in the British Empire occurred in France. There, the November ceremonies were not state occasions as in Britain but were organized by the veterans' associations, which in 1922 sponsored a law making 11 November a public holiday. The Douaumont ossuary served as an alternative focus to Paris; from 1927 onwards it witnessed an annual vigil and placing of flowers to commemorate the start of the Verdun battle in February 1916 as well as a victory celebration on the anniversary of the last German attack in June. Although the clergy participated and the Armistice Day commemoration (which occurred close to the festival of the dead on All Saints' Day) owed much to catholic liturgy, the veterans and their banners were its most prominent feature.[64] As in Britain, however, observing silence was the focus.

With the passage of time it becomes harder to recapture what these ceremonies meant. The two minutes' silence (one minute in France), the burying of the unknown soldiers, the building of the cemeteries: these resulted from official acts, whose intentions can be reconstructed from cabinet minutes and parliamentary debates. What the Armistice, Anzac, and Verdun rituals signified inwardly to the hundreds of thousands who participated is more elusive. In Britain 'victory balls', at which each November veterans celebrated their survival, were criticized by the press and clergy as unseemly, and were eventually discontinued. Speeches and sermons took on a note of earnestness, not to say imprecation: the bereaved should feel pride, the sacrifice had not been futile, the dead had fallen for a just and noble cause and to establish lasting peace, and England's destiny was to serve humanity.[65] The tone was patriotic but hardly jingoistic. Similarly, 11 November ceremonies in France included flags, bugles, and the playing of the Marseillaise, but they were less celebratory than the government would have liked. Moreover, the veterans' associations rejected the religious connotations of holding the occasion on the nearest Sunday, and to avoid the taint of militarism they refused to march in step.[66] The heart of the ceremony was the reading out of names and the laying of wreaths; the accompanying homilies mentioned neither revenge for 1870 nor Alsace-Lorraine, but stressed that France had fought for right and freedom and had repelled aggression. The effort had not been in vain, but victory was referred to only in conjunction with its horror and cost.[67]

As the war itself had been an apprenticeship in modern conflict, so in its aftermath Western countries evolved new modes of mourning, but they drew heavily on established civic and religious motifs. The British Unknown Warrior was buried with a crusader sword to denote the chivalry of his cause. In societies that were only partly dechristianized such symbols had an evocative and reassuring potential that abstract and modernist alternatives lacked.[68] However, the organizers of the Armistice Day rituals also wanted to communicate a message for the present: the British government hoped to distract attention from post-war social conflict, and in France veterans' speeches urged the need for national unity. The commemoration rituals may indeed have helped to serve these purposes, but only because Britain and France were relatively homogeneous societies with uncontested national identities. In Australia the Anzac Day commemorations unavoidably celebrated those who had volunteered over those who had not, and by extension the Protestant and Anglo-Saxon over the Catholic and Irish elements of the country's population.[69] War commemoration might not consolidate but be in fact subversive.

The wounded societies of the years after 1918 had not only to bury their dead but also to care for the living – disabled and able-bodied veterans, widows and orphans. Metropolitan France had mobilized 7,893,000 men, of whom 6,492,000 survived. Of every 100 men aged over twenty in 1930, forty-five were veterans. In the 1930s the government was paying nearly 1.1 million pensions to those who had suffered from wounds or disease during the war.[70] In Britain some half-million soldiers had been seriously disabled, of whom over 240,000 were major amputees, 60,000 had shell shock, and 10,000 were blinded.[71] The obligation was long-term: just before the Second World War 222,000 officers and over 419,000 other ranks were still receiving disability pensions.[72] In 1942 over half the 68,000 men being cared for in American veterans' hospitals were psychiatric casualties of the First able bodied World War.[73] The reintegration of the able-bodied was potentially as great a problem as care for the bereaved and the disabled. During the war anxiety mounted about the millions of young men who had spent years away from family and workplace, and who had been armed and trained to kill. Instead of thankfully readjusting to the long littleness of peacetime life they might linger on its margins, drifting into violence and extremism.[74] As it proved, the great majority of returning servicemen probably wanted precisely to return to civilian routine,[75] but a significant minority failed to readjust. Post-war governments risked bankruptcy if they were generous to the survivors, and civil unrest if they were frugal. Every country faced a challenge during demobilization, but the longer-term problem of veterans' loyalty to the *status quo* reached its climax in the 1930s. A basic distinction existed between Britain, France, and the United States, all of which coped relatively successfully with the problem, and Italy and Germany, which did not.

Two further legacies of the war were, therefore, a new apparatus of welfare provision in the former belligerent countries and a network of veterans' associations. Britain had traditionally assigned care for its ex-servicemen largely to private charities, and had to make a bigger adjustment than on the continent. However, the wartime separation allowances set a precedent for widows' and orphans' pensions, a ministry of pensions (which was essentially a ministry of war pensions) being established in 1916–17.[76] In 1915, at which stage the likely numbers remained small, legislation provided for retraining the disabled, and the government announced that all returning servicemen would receive free unemployment insurance for twelve months.[77] The Treasury's reluctance to sign a blank cheque set limits on these preparations, and discontent was strong enough to create a veterans' movement that threatened for a while to become embittered and alienated. While the war continued released soldiers were able to find unskilled work, but they demanded more training and their pensions fell behind inflation. In 1916 the Blackburn Association (later the National Association of Discharged Soldiers and Sailors – NADSS) was set up in protest against the way many were treated; and legislation which in 1917 implied that wounded and discharged men could be recalled to fight caused great anger and led to the emergence of the National Federation of Discharged and Demobilized Soldiers and Sailors (NFDDSS). As both these bodies were politically left-wing, Lord Derby (the architect of the Derby scheme) created a more deferential rival, the Comrades of the Great War (CGW). By 1919 the NADSS had about 50,000 members, the NFDDSS perhaps 100,000, and the CGW more than either.[78]

Derby's success notwithstanding, 1919 was a year of great unrest, at a time of acute industrial conflict and protest among the police and serving troops, and the veterans' groups came under Special Branch surveillance. A new organization, the Soldiers', Sailors', and Seamen's Union, tried to organize among serving troops; an NFDDSS demonstration in Hyde Park ended in clashes with police; veterans rioted in Luton and burned down the town hall. War memorials consumed resources that might have helped the survivors, as protests in November 1920 pointed out. During the 1919–20 boom unemployment was less of an issue, but the servicemen's representatives wanted higher disability pensions, more sensitive processing of applications, better rehabilitation and training, and 'justice, not charity'. To some extent, the authorities bought the movement off by meeting its most acute grievances. Reforms at the end of 1919 established a right to state training and preference for ex-servicemen in the employment exchanges. The War Pensions Act similarly established that pensions were no longer a royal bounty but a statutory right, with provision for appeals over entitlement, and payment scales were increased.[79] The government used veterans in 1919–21 as Auxiliaries and 'Black and Tans' against the republican guerrilla campaign in Ireland,[80] where some of them earned an evil reputation, but the ex-servicemen's associations failed to emerge as an independent political force. They fielded twenty-nine candidates in the December 1918 election but only one was returned. Moreover, although retraining was cut and ex-servicemen were hard hit when mass unemployment arrived after 1920, their organizations moved to the centre, the NFDDSS, the NADSS, and the CGW merging with the Officers' Association to form the British Legion in 1921. This was the pre-eminent veterans' body from now on, and a notably moderate one, voting for Haig (with some dissent) as its first president and Jellicoe as its second. It fought tenaciously, and with considerable success, for veterans' employment rights and pension benefits. In addition it integrated veterans into the remembrance ceremonies, through the poppy appeal, the Festival of Remembrance, and pilgrimages to the battlefields. If an opportunity had ever existed for either the far left or the right to harness ex-servicemen behind radical political change, it had now passed by.

The French veterans' movement followed a similar trajectory, also appearing during the war and being at first fragmented and polarized. By the early 1930s it was the largest of all such movements, with some 3 million members or almost half the country's surviving combatants.[81] A first wave of organizations appeared in 1915–17 to champion the rights of the discharged disabled to better pensions and job opportunities. The Union fédérale (UF) emerged in this period and became the biggest single body. A second wave came after the armistice, 1919 marking the peak of discontent in France as in Britain. Many soldiers had to remain under arms for months until Germany signed the peace treaty. Often they were demobilized in demeaning circumstances, being ferried back in goods wagons to find the army had lost the belongings they had handed over in 1914 and that all they received to re-sume civilian life was a cheap regulation suit. Their former jobs were supposed to be reserved for them, but they had to apply within the short time-span of fourteen days or risk unemployment. As in Britain, however, the government responded to veterans' demonstrations with concessions, exempting poorer soldiers from back-dated tax liabilities and providing cash sums and monthly subsidies. In addition, the Union nationale des combattants (UNC) was created, as an approximate coun-terpart of the CGW: it had support from Clemenceau, the army, and the church, and was funded by business, with which it co-operated in defeating the 1919 rail-way strike. Yet it grew very rapidly to rival the UF, the more revolutionary and pacifist organizations always failing to attract many members. Despite their differ-ent origins the UF and the UNC co-operated in campaigning for (and obtaining) pension increases in the 1924 elections, and from 1927 both were affiliated to a con-federation, the Conférence internationale des associations des mutilés et d'anciens combattants (CIAMAC). Henceforth the French movement settled down under leaders from the centre-left and centre-right as a patriotic (though not nationalist or fascist) supporter of the Third Republic, as long as the dead were honoured and the survivors' material needs were adequately met.[82]

Developments in the United States were comparable, although the American Legion was bigger and more vociferous than the British one. Founded in 1919 with high command encouragement, it had 1.153 million members by 1931 (about one in four of those mobilized). In 1927, 25,000 Legionaries and their fam-ilies sailed in fifteen liners on a 'sacred pilgrimage' to France. As well as being a social, mutual aid, and commemorative organization, with an elaborate cult of the flag, it was a formidable lobbyist. In 1924 Congress passed (over President Coolidge's veto) a 'bonus' bill to indemnify veterans for the difference between their service pay and what they might have earned as wartime civilian workers; by 1932, expenditure on American veterans exceeded that in Britain, France, and Germany combined. In addition, the Legion took up an overtly politicized posi-tion. Its ideology was 'Americanism', on which it published a manual. It cam-paigned against immigration and identified a set of anti-American influences: pre-eminently Bolshevism, but also radicalism, socialism, and pacifism. It was par-ticularly concerned to protect young people from such influences, establishing a large youth movement and monitoring teachers. Created during the 1919 'red scare', it remained marked by the circumstances of its birth.[83] Broadly speaking, in all the big three Atlantic democracies, the main veterans' organizations neverthe-less supported the political *status quo* rather than the revolutionary right and left.

The argument to this point has been that the stabilization of international politics in the later 1920s was paralleled by domestic stabilization within the former belliger-ents. The war had encouraged both radical socialism and radical nationalism, but by the mid-1920s moderate conservatives held office in Britain, France, and Amer-ica, and challenges to traditional class and gender hierarchies had been beaten back, while massive investments in memorial architecture and in welfare systems helped to reassure society that the war had been for a valuable purpose, that its sac-rifices would be solemnized, and that the survivors would be cared for. If this was one model for how the belligerent countries could cope with the aftermath of war, however, it was far from the only one, and the major powers involved in the conflict displayed an array of different responses. In Japan, for example, there was also a post-war move to the left, and in 1919 the first Japanese cabinet that predominantly comprised party politicians, rather than unelected officials, took office. A decade of parliamentary government ensued until the return of military and bureaucratic rule in 1932. But the war, in which Japan suffered less than 2,000 dead (commemorated at the nationalist focal point of the Yasukuni shrine in Tokyo), was far more peripheral in its impact than in Europe, and 11 November never became a national holiday.[84] In Soviet Russia, in contrast, where the war against the Central Powers had been devastating but was overshadowed by the even more terrible experience of the civil war and was anathematized by the Bolsheviks, no national monument was built, veterans' organizations were outlawed, and citizens had to come to terms with the experience in isolated and fragmentary fashion, without a public framework of commemoration.[85] Yet across the border in Latvia, which had belonged to the former tsarist empire and had been the scene of heavy fighting in 1916, the normal panoply of monuments and museums was established.

Much of the rest of continental Europe participated in a broader pattern of radical upsurge in 1919–20 and a right-wing counter-offensive in 1921–3, followed by stabilization, although on widely varying political bases, in the mid-1920s. To some extent the war synchronized the political cycle from California to Bavaria and Lombardy, though divergences later resurfaced. It also introduced the new factor of the Bolshevik Revolution, and Lenin's continuing efforts to spread it, symbolized by the founding in 1919 of the Third International (or Comintern) for the newly forming communist parties, while the socialists remained loyal to the Second International. In Britain and America, however, communist party membership was tiny, though in Germany and Italy (as well as France) competition with the socialists was keener. On balance the spread of communism outside Russia weakened the rest of the left, first by strengthening the reactionary right and governments' willingness to tolerate extra-constitutional procedures, and second, by dividing the progressive camp. Everywhere, in fact, the war seemed to weaken the liberal centre to the benefit of extremism, and in many countries it contributed to a new and ugly paramilitary political style.

Italy and Germany differed profoundly from the three Atlantic democracies in that in Italy the wartime victory was disdained as 'mutilated' and in Germany there had been no victory at all (though many Germans questioned the reality of the defeat). Despite the peace conference controversies, the Italian Liberal government interred its own Unknown Soldier (at the foot of the grandiose Risorgimento monument in Rome) and began the construction of immense memorials in the mountains, the most impressive being that to the Third Army at Redipuglia, the site of over 100,000 graves. The Redipuglia monument was started by veterans' associations in 1920–23 and in restrained classical style, but by the time the Fascist regime completed the work in the 1930s, the emphasis was on the soldiers' heroic status.[86] The difference symbolized a larger point. The majority of Italian veterans seem to have been as moderate as were veterans elsewhere, and the largest organization (the Associazione nazionale di combattenti) was reformist in outlook and strongest among peasant rankers and junior officers from the south and the Mediterranean islands, where its local committees challenged the landowners. Italy's post-war crisis, however, created a special opportunity for a militant minority. The rise of Italian Fascism was the first of a succession of inter-war disasters that it is difficult to imagine happening without the events of 1914–18. The conflict contributed to the Fascist triumph on at least four major counts, the first of which was the conversion of Mussolini himself from a radical socialist to an interventionist who did front-line service. The second was the stimulus to xenophobic nationalism provided by the controversy over Italian intervention and by disappointment with the peace settlement. Third, the Fascist movement's breakthrough came with the nationwide social unrest of 1919–21, which had pre-war precedents but had never occurred on such a scale. In the 1919 elections the traditional Liberal governing factions lost their parliamentary majority and in the midst of a delicate transition to mass democracy Italy had to cope both with the economic distortions caused by the war and with the fears caused by the spectre of Bolshevism, which the uncompromising rhetoric of the PSI did nothing to alleviate. In autumn 1920 socialist-controlled local authorities supported urban factory occupations and agricultural workers' strikes and protests in the Po valley, heightening the apparent resemblance to conditions in Russia. The fourth and final development was the formation of the Fascist 'squads', or Fasci di combattimento. They were centred on the towns of the north, pre-eminently Milan. Veterans often led and trained them, and their early supporters included the Italian equivalents of the German army's stormtroopers, the Arditi (who supplied Mussolini with his bodyguard), and also futurist painters, pro-war socialists, and university and school students who had not fought at the Front.[87] Though they claimed to embody the war generation they actually represented only a portion of it, and they were a radical political movement organized on paramilitary lines rather than a genuine channel for veterans' concerns. Italy's national interests and its claims at the peace conference were among the issues that galvanized them, but their hostility to socialism was the main cause of their explosive growth (with bourgeois support) as a violently repressive and strike-breaking force. Once they had closed down the socialist press and municipalities and taken control at local level, Mussolini was able to launch the 'March on Rome' in 1922 that intimidated the Liberals and the king into accepting him as premier, before in 1925 he completed the establishment of authoritarian rule. Even so, his control of Italy was always incomplete, and he could take neither Victor Emmanuel, nor the church, nor the army for granted, which helps to explain his initially cautious approach to foreign affairs.

Germany seemed at first sight closer to the democratic European norm, as the 1918–19 revolution moved quickly back to the centre. Thus German women got the vote under the Weimar Republic while at the same time being ruthlessly ousted from the workforce. Bosch at Stuttgart, for example, employed 580 women in 1914 and 5,245 at the armistice, of whom it promptly sacked 3,500.[88] However, their departure eased the re-absorption of the demobilized troops, whose potential for discontent worried the authorities far more. Those women who continued to work were forced back into sectors such as domestic service and agriculture, while others left the workplace altogether, as both the marriage and the birth rate (as in other European countries) rose temporarily at the end of the conflict.[89] But from the moment Ebert and the SPD took over the new leaders intended to avoid Kerensky's fate. While the government promised to Groener that it would respect army discipline and suppress disorder,* the trade unions concluded the Stinnes–Legien Agreement with the employers, settling for collective bargaining rights and an eight-hour day. The USPD resigned from the interim government in December 1918, and the workers' and soldiers' councils created during the revolution disappeared within months. Finally, after doing poorly in the 1920 elections (and losing ground to the communists), the SPD itself withdrew from government until 1928, joining the British Labour Party and the French SFIO in opposition. By the early 1920s the working-class gains from the revolution, apart from the Stinnes–Legien agreement, were workplace councils and not much else. While Stresemann from 1923 until his death while still in post as foreign minister in 1929 pursued his foreign policy of revising the peace treaties through co-operation with Germany's former enemies, his domestic support normally rested on an uneasy coalition between centrist and right-wing parties, many committed in principle neither to reconciliation abroad nor to democracy at home. Even in the period when the Weimar Republic seemed most secure, Hindenburg was elected president of the Republic in 1925 (partly because of divisions on the left) – another indication of the extent to which much of the German public had neither forgotten nor condemned the memory of the war.

Weimar Germany faced exceptional difficulties in using a cult of war memory to consolidate democratic institutions, both because the war had been lost and because as late as the summer of 1918 it had seemed so near to being won, thus lending support to right-wing insinuations that a stab in the back by domestic enemies had humbled an undefeated army. It also faced more practical problems. On much of the former Eastern Front the Germans had no access to the battlegrounds, and even in the west the French provided facilities grudgingly and the invaders were obliged to leave their dead where they lay. Nor could the governments of the former Central Powers spare much for memorial construction, and their soldiers' graves were tended by private organizations: the Volksbund deutscher Kriegsgräberfürsorger (VDK) in Germany and the Black Cross in Austria. Like the French and British, the Germans used uniform markers and Christian symbolism, though their graves were marked by stone or iron crosses, and no individual inscriptions were permitted – making their cemeteries appear more regimented and austere than their Allied counterparts. As for memorials – known significantly as 'warrior memorials' (*Kriegerdenkmäler*)[90] rather than as memorials to the war or to the dead as in England and France, fierce controversies over their design and installation testified to the continuing debates that had opened up since 1917 about the meaning and value of the war effort. Distinctively German was the *Heldenheim* or 'heroes' grove' comprising a copse centred on an oak, and strewn with boulders as a symbol of the primeval strength (*Urkraft*) of a nation that still lived. [91] So too was the *Totenburg* or citadel of the dead. A massive one was inaugurated at Tannenberg in 1927 round the graves of twenty unknown soldiers from the Eastern Front and

*See ch. 17.

surrounded by fortress-like walls, Hindenburg using the ceremony to deliver a bellicose oration.[92] But although a national memorial was planned it was never built
because of regional rivalries over where it should be located, the continuing Allied
occupation of the Rhineland being cited to justify postponement. Nor did a national tomb of the Unknown Soldier exist until in 1931 the Prussian state government (rather than the Reich government) dedicated one in the guardhouse of the
Neue Wache in Berlin. Unlike its Western counterparts, this vault remained empty.

In the embittered political landscape of Weimar Germany, commemoration of
the war was still more divisive. The VDK introduced a national day of mourning,
but at a government-organized service for the war dead in Berlin in 1924 the silence was shattered when rival sections of the crowd sang the 'Internationale' and
'The Watch on the Rhine'.[93] A rival patriotic cult to that sponsored by the authorities centred on the battle of Langemarck, supposedly an assault by student volunteers singing patriotic hymns during the first battle of Ypres. Actually almost
everything about this story was fabricated: the action (which was a disastrous failure) was not at Langemarck, the troops were mostly conscripts, and even the
singing was unconfirmed. But the German national student organization celebrated
an annual Langemarck Day every 10 November from 1919. In 1928–32 it supervised the building of a cemetery outside Langemarck, and a Nazi sympathizer
spoke at the inauguration ceremony. A widely distributed tract of 1928 contrasted
the ideals of Langemarck with those of Weimar and the Western democracies.[94]

As well as building memorials and devising remembrance ceremonies, Germany, like the victors, had to deal with the survivors. Here again its difficulties
were exceptional. It had the highest wartime casualty total and the largest problem
in the aftermath. Six million Germans were either disabled veterans, their family
members, or dependent survivors of the dead: 2.7 million had some permanent
disability, 533,000 were widows, and 1,192,000 were orphans. The pensions element of the national budget rose eight times between 1919 and 1922, and between
1924 and 1928 some 30 per cent of Reich expenditure (after deducting reparations
payments and transfers to the state governments) went under this head. Indeed, in
the later 1920s expenditure on war pensions as a per centage of the national budget was more than double that in Britain. Yet despite this generosity – which did
much to tip the country into fiscal crisis after 1929 – Weimar ended up with a disaffected veteran population.[95]

Germany already had a huge ex-servicemen's organization, the Kyffhäuserbund
der deutschen Landeskriegerverbände (KDL), which before the war had co-
operated with the army in recruitment and training and had campaigned against
the SPD, refusing to admit socialists as members. It lifted this ban in 1915, although subsequently it excluded communists. After 1918 Hindenburg became its
honorary president and it campaigned aggressively for a 'war of rectification', condemning France and Poland for the theft of German territory. It remained very
large (with 2.2 million members in 1922), and the authorities tolerated its nationalist stance but suspected its monarchist leanings, which encouraged the emergence
of numerous competitors.[96] Moreover it had a tradition of being highly politicized
while professing to be non-partisan, which was carried forward by the new bodies
that came into being in 1916–19, the younger veterans wanting different organiza-

tions from those of their grandfathers. As in the Allied countries, campaigners wanted generous pensions for the disabled and guaranteed employment for the able-bodied, but in the divisive atmosphere of 1917–19 they also developed more ambitious political views. The biggest new group was the Reichsband der Kriegs-beschädigten und ehemaligen Kriegsteilnehmer (RKK), founded in 1917. Led by socialists, it wanted better widows' and disabled pensions paid from war profits, de-mocratization of the franchise, and a 'peace of understanding'. In December 1918 it organized a rally of 10,000 disabled and bereaved in Berlin, a sombre spectacle that deeply impressed several Weimar artists. By 1924 some 1.4 million (something over half) of the disabled were organized: 640,000 in the RKK, 255,000 in the KDL, and 209,000 in the liberal-oriented Einheitsbund. In response to the discontent the government issued decrees to ensure places for the disabled in public employment, and accepted national responsibility for their welfare. Meanwhile legislation in 1920 created a single system of pensions, employment advice, and job training under the labour ministry. The measure was rushed and in Germany's difficult economic cir-cumstances it was administered ungenerously. But as the veterans saw it, the ad-ministration was slow to process their claims (as late as 1925, thousands did not know what their pensions would be), it set meagre rates to start with and failed to adjust them for inflation, and cuts in 1923 excluded hundreds of thousands of slightly disabled altogether. Although the RKK supported the Weimar Republic it could not defend the pensions administration, and in comparison with France, Britain, and America the divided German organizations were less effective lobbyists and less successful in alleviating veterans' discontents.[97]

Germany differed from the Allies in that it had less room for fiscal manoeuvre and in its veterans' inability to co-operate. In addition, many of its ex-servicemen joined mass paramilitary organizations. Like Italy's Fascist squads, these were in-tended to act as right-wing political strike forces rather than simply to defend veter-ans' interests, and several of the organizations were open to non-veterans. The first of them were the notorious Freikorps, employed against the left-wing uprisings of 1919.[98] Like the Fasci di combattimento, the Freikorps included many veterans but also right-wing civilians, notably students, and they totalled some 2–400,000 men by the spring of 1919, organized in local brigades under ex-officer leadership. The part-time Einwohnerwehren ('civic guard'), which predated 1914, had an older and more varied membership, but represented middle-class Germans alarmed by the manifes-tation of working-class power in the revolution of November 1918. Political violence and assassination (which had been extremely rare in Germany before 1914) became regular features of Weimar life, and if they came from the right the courts condoned them. Having first approved of these bodies the government lost control of them and in 1920 banned them, under pressure from the Allies and its own supporters. But clandestine organizations continued, and in the mid-1920s Germany saw the re-emergence of legal and open paramilitary leagues (Wehrverbände), composed of wartime veterans and of youths who had served in the post-war organizations. The new groups called for an authoritarian government and a war of liberation against France after 'internal' enemies had been dealt with. The best example of such a body is the Stahlhelm ('steel helmet'), whose founder, Franz Seldter, had lost an arm on the Somme. The Stahlhelm excluded Jews and left-wingers and probably had about 400,000 members in the mid-1920s, though it was overtaken by the Nazi SA (the brownshirts or party militia) at the end of the decade. Yet the largest of the 'political combat leagues was the Reichsbanner, created in 1924 as a republican answer to the Stahlhelm, and recruiting up to a million active members. The SPD, the DDP, the Catholic Centre, and the trade unions supported the veterans who led it, and it was open to all who shared its aim of defending the Republic, by means that included wearing uniform, marching, and undergoing military training. (The smaller Communist organization, the Rote Frontkämpferbund, with 100,000 members, was considerably more violent.) Even in Germany, the Reichsbanner as one of the largest veterans' organizations advocated neither an authoritarian government nor a war of revenge, though many others did.[99]

The pernicious influence of the war on Weimar Germany is essential to understanding the politics of this period. In international diplomacy, both the Briand Plan and the Kellogg-Briand Pact can be seen as responses to the memory of 1914–18, and before the war neither would have been conceivable as official policy rather than as the visions of idealists. The revelation of what modern war could mean spurred efforts to outlaw it and to transcend the old states system. After five years of Franco-German rapprochement since 1924, coupled with economic recovery and diminishing political extremism, it might seem that wartime hostilities were losing their sting. Powerful forces were at work to heal the wounds. Cemeteries, memorials, and a cycle of ritual comforted the bereaved and created an opportunity to consider the meaning of the sacrifice: welfare programmes catered for the victims, and the new veterans' associations provided companionship and mutual aid. European control over the colonial empires had been reasserted; women were mostly pushed back into their former occupations, though in many countries they were given political concessions; workers received some benefits such as the eight-hour day, but the trade unions were beaten down and even when socialist or labour parties attained office they made few changes. Stabilization on the domestic and the international planes proceeded in conjunction. Yet the Western countries had gambled after 1924 that by relaxing the Versailles treaty constraints they could conciliate and moderate Germany, whereas in fact the evidence suggested that although Germany was divided many of its population and its leaders had neither forgotten their military traditions nor reconciled themselves to defeat. The power of wartime myths and memories to stimulate nationalist feeling remained dangerously relevant. Further, the economic recovery that helped to tranquillize Europe in the late 1920s had shaky foundations, which would prove to be a fatal flaw of the entire stabilization edifice. Superficially, a decade after the war most of the Versailles treaty remained intact, Germany still being confined to the frontiers and levels of military force set in 1919, and between 1924 and 1931 paying reparations according to schedule. But since 1923 France's capability to enforce the settlement had atrophied, and this became brutally clear when the international climate again changed for the worse.

CHAPTER 20

DEMOLITION, 1929–1945

AFTER 1929 THREE developments command attention: the great depression, the rise of the Nazis, and the appeasement of the Third Reich. Between them these events brought to power a leader committed to another major war and meant that the former Allies would be unlikely to stop him before he could wage it. By this time the First World War was already a decade or more away. Yet although it did not make the catastrophes of the 1930s inevitable, it was once again their indispensable precondition and it immensely complicated the task of Western statesmen in responding to the challenges that confronted them.

The first point to consider is the Great War's economic impact. The war wrecked not only lives but also property, to an extent almost impossible to estimate. In 1930 the British statistician A. L. Bowley assessed the physical destruction at £2,000 million in pre-war prices, compared with an aggregate capital of £55,000 million for all European countries including Russia. He inferred that the world's capital stock in 1919 had regressed to the level of 1911, and had in addition suffered from a decade of neglect.[1] The worst destruction occurred in Belgium, France, Poland, Romania, Serbia, and Italy, although the static character of much of the fighting made the devastation less widespread than in 1945. Belgium lost 6 per cent of its housing, two thirds of its railway stock, and half its steel mills. France lost less as a proportion of its wealth, though more in absolute terms. Poland lost much of its livestock and railway infrastructure, and Britain nearly 8 million tons of shipping, but most of the maritime sinkings and the battle zone destruction were made good within a few years. The more lasting consequences of the war were less tangible, and they centred on trade and finance.

At first sight economic recovery was quite rapid. Industrial production in most neutral countries and in Britain and Italy was back to the 1913 level by 1920; after a slump in 1921 it grew further and in Britain, Italy, Belgium, and France was well above the pre-war level by 1924. But in Germany and Austria it remained below the pre-war figure at this date, and did not exceed it until the end of the decade. Broadly the neutrals suffered least and the Central Powers most, with the Allies in the middle.[2] The United States exceeded the European average growth rate in the 1920s, and Japan about equalled it, but in all these countries agriculture revived more slowly than industry. Overall, economic growth in capitalist Europe was slower between the World Wars than at any other time in the twentieth century. In 1913–50 Gross Domestic Product *per capita* in fifteen countries of Western and Central Europe grew on average by a mere 0.9 per cent a year, compared with 1.4 per cent in 1890–1914 and 4.0 per cent in 1950–73.[3] Living standards rose only slowly despite technical change continuing to be rapid (and in areas such as vehicles, aircraft, and chemicals having been accelerated by military requirements). Europe's economy was growing by less than its capacity would have permitted, and high unemployment and idle equipment were painfully visible in several countries well before the 1929 slump. And if the growth of output was disappointing, that of trade was even more so. During the war the world had taken many steps back from the open, rapidly integrating pre-1914 global economy, and in the 1920s the drive for self-sufficiency was only partially reversed before the great depression intensified it.

There were several reasons for the slow growth of international commerce, from which countries exporting a high proportion of their output (such as Britain and Germany) especially suffered. One of the most commonly cited is the creation of new nation states. Between 1914 and the 1919–20 peace treaties the number of independent states in Europe rose from twenty-six to thirty-eight, and the total length of political frontiers by 12,500 miles.[4] Under Habsburg rule South-Eastern Europe had formed a customs union, but now it was criss-crossed by tariff barriers, and even in Western Europe tariffs rose by some 50 per cent.[5] Soviet Russia was virtually debarred from foreign trade until the mid-1920s by its internal disorder and by other governments' refusal to extend diplomatic recognition to it. Until 1924 Germany likewise was too much of a political maelstrom to resume its pre-war prominence.

Trading recovery was further handicapped by the surplus productive capacity generated during the war. The post-armistice transition might have been smoother if wartime state intervention had continued longer, but the Allied agencies controlling shipping, wheat, and other commodities mostly ceased to function during 1919. This may help to explain the violent alternation between a global inflationary boom in 1919–20 and a precipitous slump in 1921–22. World shipbuilding capacity had almost doubled since 1914, and iron and steel capacity in the United Kingdom and in Central Europe was 50 per cent higher in the mid-1920s than it had been before the war. In order to emancipate themselves from importing German artificial dyes the Allies had enlarged their output of chemicals, with the result that between 1914 and 1924 Germany's share of the market halved.[6] Japan and India had increased their cotton textile output, partly because of non-supply from Britain, and now they were her competitors in meeting Asian demand. Rubber and tin production, stimulated in Malaya and Bolivia by military orders, slumped when call for them lapsed. As for foodstuffs, the United States, Canada, Australia, and Argentina between them raised their wheat output by nearly 50 per cent between 1909/13 and the mid-1920s, leading to huge unsold stocks, falling world market prices, and increased protective tariffs in Europe. Similarly for sugar, Cuba and Java expanded their cane output when European beet production fell due to the war, with the result that prices tumbled in 1924–5 and bounties and subsidies were introduced.[7]

In addition to the new political boundaries and to production surpluses, the reasons for the stagnation of international trade were primarily financial. The monetary cost of the conflict is little easier to assess than the physical damage it caused, and estimates vary considerably, though frequently cited totals are $61,500 million in current prices for the Central Powers and $147,000 million for their enemies, making a grand total of $208,500 million. In constant (1913) prices the respective totals were $24,700 million, $57,700 million, and $82,400 million.[8] The important question for the future was how these expenditures were paid for.* During the war most of the European belligerents suspended their link to the gold standard and ran up enormous budget deficits, taxation everywhere covering only a small proportion of government outgoings. Long-term borrowing (through bond issues at home or abroad) filled most of the gap, and treasury bills or unsecured central bank loans covered the remainder. None the less, the money stock grew more than output, thus creating a potential inflationary 'overhang', as retail prices had risen less than the amount of money in circulation. This problem too was a direct legacy of the conflict, and it was complicated by the end of inter-Allied financial co-operation, sterling and the French franc being devalued in 1919 after the United States ceased supporting them. Several responses were possible. Britain maintained low interest rates ('cheap money') during 1919, to secure a high level of economic activity until demobilization was completed. Then the authorities sharply raised the cost of borrowing, contributing to a severe recession and high unemployment but also bringing down prices. Events in the United States were similar. In France and Germany, in contrast, budgetary stabilization encountered more resistance, especially after 1921 when it became entangled with the reparations dispute. Like the British, the French faced an increased burden of expenditure on reconstruction, on pensions, and on servicing the swollen national debt, but Clemenceau's finance minister, Klotz, promised not to raise taxes until it was clear how much Germany would pay, and the authorities delayed increases until 1924. They failed to reduce the money in circulation, and inflationary pressure persisted. Whereas Britain in 1925 temporarily restored sterling to its pre-war parity of £1=$4.86 (another notably symbolic attempt to recapture a world now lost), for the franc this was impossible and French investors accepted a permanent devaluation of their pre-war financial holdings.[9] Conversely in Germany attempts to cut expenditure or raise taxes to balance the budget were open to attack as being designed to pay off its enemies. Germany's post-war fiscal problems were more acute than those of the Allied countries anyway, but as in France the reparations issue strengthened the opponents of stabilization.[10] Financial volatility became inextricably intertwined with the political struggles within and between the former belligerents that followed the war.

None the less, by the late 1920s it seemed that economically as well as politically Europe had turned the corner. The devastated areas had been rebuilt, production (though not trade) had regained and exceeded pre-war levels, and currencies were fixed. Following the mark in 1924 and sterling in 1925, the franc, the lira, and the

---

*See ch. 9.

yen were pegged to gold and the dollar. Although Europe's share of global exports had slipped during the conflict, by 1929 it had made good much of the lost ground. But the new depression that now set in was more than just a cyclical downturn like that of 1920: it caused lasting damage. Opened by a Europe-wide financial crisis in 1931, a general rise in tariffs, and a renewed breakdown of currency stability, the 1930s were a decade of terrible setbacks. Politically as well as economically the slump began what one historian has called 'The Age of Demolition'.[11]

The slump did not come from nowhere. At the time of the October 1929 American stock market crash that began the crisis, the problems created by the war had been alleviated rather than resolved. Commodities were falling in price and the countries exporting them were in difficulties. Sterling had been overvalued by some 10 per cent since being restored to the gold standard, and chronic unemployment persisted in Britain's export trades. Germany's post-1924 recovery had levelled out and its output was stagnating. The downturn in America intensified these problems, first because a collapse in US demand (exacerbated by the ferocious Hawley–Smoot import tariff of 1930) made it even harder for the rest of the world to sell there and to earn dollars, and second because it halted American capital exports. During the 1920s the United States had overtaken Britain as the greatest international investor. After the loan that floated the Dawes Plan American private money flowed to Germany in much larger amounts than the Germans were paying in reparations, or than the Allies were transferring to the United States to settle war debts.[12] Indeed, in the late 1920s the French received some of what they had sought at the peace conference: American finance (albeit supplied to Germany rather than to France) facilitated European recovery, and the British provided a qualified security guarantee at Locarno. Anglo-American involvement created a climate in which the French could make concessions to Germany with more confidence. But the American loans made Germany dangerously dependent. As the great 1920s Wall Street bull market reached its climax, American foreign lending dried up, and after the crash outstanding credits were recalled. Partly as a result, in 1931 a succession of defaults spread across Europe. The largest Austrian bank, the Creditanstalt, failed in May; after a German banking crisis in July the Weimar authorities effectively abandoned the gold standard; and in September Britain did likewise. The British introduced tariffs on most imports by the 1932 Import Duties Act, and one of Franklin Roosevelt's first actions as American president in 1933 was unilaterally to devalue the dollar. By now exchange and trade controls were operating across much of the world.

The key questions for this analysis concern the connections between the war and the depression and between the depression and Nazism. On the first point, the legacy of the war was not relevant to the American origins of the slump but it did facilitate its transmission to Europe. The war helps explain why the downturn had such drastic repercussions and why recovery was so difficult. In particular, it was partly responsible for the over-capacity in primary producing countries (including Eastern Europe) that left them vulnerable when the American and Western European markets contracted and capital outflows dried up. Second, the war was the source of the reparations controversy, and it was partly in order to alleviate this that the US authorities had encouraged the 1924 loan that began the outflow of American money to Germany. Third, it contributed to the 1931 financial crisis. In 1930, for reasons to be discussed below, German foreign policy became more assertively nationalist, and in the spring of 1931 the government of Heinrich Brüning announced it planned a customs union with Austria and would no longer meet the reparation payments scheduled in the Young Plan. The 'final liquidation of the war' proclaimed in 1929 had lasted less than two years. France retaliated by exploiting the Creditanstalt crisis, making assistance to Austria conditional on the latter's referring the customs union project to the international court at The Hague (which ruled against it). The French then stalled on a proposal by the American president Herbert Hoover for a moratorium on war debts and reparations payments. The legacy of the war – as embodied in Franco-German rivalry and in the Versailles treaty's Austrian clauses – inhibited co-operation against an economic blizzard that menaced all the western democratic regimes.[13] Moreover, government budgets were still encumbered not just by reparations and by overseas war debts but also by the burden of servicing the internal borrowing incurred in 1914–18. This problem was probably most acute in Britain, because its inflation had been less severe and its war loans had kept their value. But war pensions were also a huge charge on the German government, which early in 1929 ran out of money to fund them. Hence both Britain and Germany went into the crisis heavily indebted and with less scope to counter the downturn by running a budget deficit; and in France, as soon as the recession bit, the government found itself in deficit too. Nor did the repercussions end there. In Britain and the United States devaluations and interest rate cuts helped eventually to turn the corner. After the mark came off gold in 1931, in contrast, Brüning persisted with policies of retrenchment and deflation, apparently to show once and for all that Germany could not afford the reparations bill.[14]

There were therefore many links between the war and the depression, and at first sight the link between the depression and Nazism seems even more obvious. Hitler's party first gained wide support (though only in the south of Germany) during the 1923 hyperinflation crisis. In the 1928 Reichstag elections – fought after four years of prosperity – its following had dwindled away. Yet its performance revived at a local level in 1929, and at national level in the 1930 Reichstag elections (when it became the second largest party) and still more in the Reichstag and presidential elections of 1932. It seemed that as the queues of jobless lengthened the Nazi vote grew. In reality, although some of the unemployed voted for Hitler and joined the brownshirts of the SA, working-class voters were more likely to switch from the socialists to the communists, whose votes also rose as the depression tightened its grip. To explain the Nazi success, we therefore need to incorporate non-economic factors. The party's breakthrough after 1929 came among middle-class voters in the Protestant north and east, and especially in the rural areas, small towns, and suburbs. It took place not only among young first-time voters but also among traditional supporters of the conservative (DNVP) and liberal (DVP and DDP) parties, whose popularity withered in consequence.[15] Certainly Hitler offered solutions to an economic crisis that threatened farmers and shopkeepers with bankruptcy and white-collar workers with proletarianization, and the SA seemed a bulwark against revolution from the left. But he also benefited from (and contributed to) a cultural shift, central to which was a change in attitudes to the war.

Pacifism in Weimar Germany was stronger than before 1914, but it never had much political influence. The great painters of the Weimar era, such as Otto Dix, Georg Grosz, and Max Beckmann, were unsparing in their depiction of the war and its aftermath (if also fascinated by the phenomenon),[16] and it is true that in 1918 much of the German army wanted only to return home.[17] In the early and mid-1920s German publishers found only a limited popular market for books about the conflict, and the cinema avoided the topic. But even in this period the war-guilt and the stab-in-the-back controversies about the events of 1914 and 1918 showed that many Germans had neither abandoned their wartime attitudes nor reconciled themselves to defeat, as did political developments such as the founding of the Stahlhelm and Hindenburg's election to the presidency. As early as 1928, at the height of economic prosperity, the radical right renewed its offensive against the republic. The Stahlhelm leaders avowed their hatred for a regime that prevented Germany from rearming, and Hitler decided to seek power through the electoral process, joining with the Stahlhelm and the DNVP to campaign against the Young Plan in a referendum held in 1929. Although they lost, the size of their vote surprised contemporaries, and it marked the start of the Nazis' comeback at the ballot box at the same time as the SA started the phenomenal rise that allowed it to overtake the Stahlhelm as the largest right-wing paramilitary organization, growing from 50,000 members in 1929 to over 500,000 by January 1933.[18] Political and cultural trends were moving in parallel, as 1929–30 were also the years of the 'war books' boom. Central to this phenomenon was the runaway success of Erich Maria Remarque's *Im Westen Nichts Neues* (*All Quiet on the Western Front*), given saturation billing as the greatest novel about the war, and proving the biggest publishing success yet known. Within a year of its appearance in January 1929 it sold nearly a million copies in Germany and a million more abroad, where in 1930 it became the basis of an equally successful Hollywood film. Yet Remarque's tone of elegiac pathos was atypical of the German war books.[19] Individually he outsold the nationalist writers who competed with him, but their readerships too were big. Foremost among the latter was Ernst Jünger, and they also included Jünger's brother, Friedrich, as well as others such as Franz Schauwecker and Ernst von Salomon. Unlike Remarque they glorified combat as the noblest of the arts and as part of the natural order, Jünger likening the war to 'the crucifixion paintings of the old masters . . . a grand idea overwhelming sight and blood'.[20] Writing originally in the Stahlhelm's journal, they demanded a leadership of front-line soldiers, hardened by the trenches, to unseat the democratic politicians and prepare Germany for renewed expansion. Books published in Germany about the war rose in number from 200 in 1926 to over 400 in 1930, and over 500 after Hitler took power in 1933.[21] If Remarque's was the outstanding success of 1929, thereafter the nationalist authors took his place, and a similar trend was evident in the cinema, where the American film of *All Quiet* was banned, ostensibly because it harmed Germany's reputation but actually because internal order was threatened after the Nazis disrupted its Berlin screening.[22]

The changing domestic mood helped to radicalize German foreign policy well before Hitler came to office, and it began a vicious circle. In October 1929 Stresemann died, and in 1930 a new government headed by Heinrich Brüning of the

Catholic Centre Party took over. A veteran himself, he supported the ban on the film version of *All Quiet*, and presented his government as a 'cabinet of front-line soldiers'. It rejected the Briand Plan as too constrictive on German ambitions,[23] and after the French evacuated the Rhineland on 3 June it issued a celebratory nationalist declaration. After the Nazis' triumph in the September 1930 elections, Brüning moved even further onto the foreign policy offensive in order to try to head off their growth, suspending reparation payments and launching his attempted customs union with Austria. By the early 1930s, indeed, Allied concessions over the Versailles terms seemed to have done nothing to check the progress of the German extremists. Although reparations were ended in all but name at the Lausanne conference of 1932, and the former Allies conceded the principle of parity in armaments at the Geneva conference of 1931–3, support for the Nazis continued to expand, driving the last Weimar governments into authoritarianism at home and assertiveness abroad. The army leaders had secretly resumed strategic planning after 1924, and in 1932 Brüning's successor, Franz von Papen, adopted a big rearmament programme. The growth of nationalism not only among the public but also among the country's leadership is essential to an explanation of why Hitler was appointed chancellor, at Hindenburg's invitation and with the army's approval, in January 1933.[24]

In short, the war was essential to the Nazi takeover not only through its contribution to the economic crisis but also through its role in reawakening German nationalism as the memory of 1914–18 was re-evaluated. This does not mean that veterans were the main component of Nazi support. After Brüning imposed cuts in war veterans' allowances in 1930 the Nazis launched a campaign to win over the disabled,[25] but how many voted for them is difficult to determine. As for the stormtroopers, most of them were simply too young, the SA's 'active' members being generally under twenty-five. Although the SA recruited among former army and Freikorps officers, taking on some Freikorps units *en bloc* and later poaching from the Stahlhelm, probably well under a quarter of the entrants who flocked into the brownshirt movement between 1929 and 1933 were ex-servicemen.[26] Hence caution is needed in seeing the memory of the war experience as an independent causal variable. In Germany as elsewhere there had been many war experiences, and many views existed about the significance of the conflict. But ten years after its end changes in the country's internal and external circumstances created a new receptivity for the message from the radical right. Although Hitler was muted in his public comments about foreign policy and did not openly advocate a new war, he did denounce Versailles and the 'criminals' who had betrayed Germany in November 1918, and he offered a total and redemptive transformation of the country, rather than simply a solution to its material problems.[27] Further – and a crucial point – the vicious anti-semitism characteristic of the Nazi leaders had become much more pervasive among the German right in 1917–18, and especially among the radical expansionists of the Pan-German League and the Fatherland Party who in many ways were Hitler's precursors. After 1916 Jews were no longer given commissions in the Prussian army, following groundless allegations that disproportionately few of them were serving at the Front. Food shortages, the Russian Revolution, and military disaster all contributed to a strange and virulent atmosphere in which racist agitation gained a footing that it never lost.[28] This was one more reason why for the Nazi leaders, most of whom had served in the war, its influence was fundamental. According to Rudolf Hess, 'the Third Reich comes from the trenches', and Hitler described the years 1914–18 as 'the greatest and most unforgettable time of my earthly experience'.[29] Like Brüning – and Mussolini – they presented themselves as the Front generation in power, and they were generous to veterans. The new regime celebrated the annual heroes' memorial day with characteristic pageantry and initiated a new day of commemoration for the supposed upsurge of national unity in July 1914.[30] However, Hitler's real concerns lay elsewhere. His *Mein Kampf,* written in 1924, offered a blueprint for avoiding Wilhelm II's mistakes. Next time, it argued, Germany must avoid encirclement, and – by cultivating Italy and Britain and concentrating on a 'reckoning' with France to be followed by a drive into the Ukraine – it might be able to do so. Within days of coming to office Hitler told his generals that after gaining control at home his first priority would be rearmament with a view to 'the conquest of living space in the east and its ruthless Germanization'.[31] Although a Western Front veteran, what he really wished to re-enact was the war that Germany had won: that against Russia.

The world's only chance of containing Hitler without terrible bloodshed was to act before he rearmed and while the remaining Versailles constraints were in place. But in the political atmosphere of the early and mid-1930s he had little difficulty in heading off renewed encirclement. Victory had divided the 1914–18 Allies, and during the depression their divisions intensified.[32] Planners in the Tokyo general staff had concluded from Germany's defeat in 1918 that Japan must be self-sufficient, and the depression, leading to the collapse of the silk export trade to America and poverty in the northern rural areas from which the Japanese army traditionally recruited, underlined the message.[33] In pursuit of greater economic independence junior officers organized the Manchurian 'Incident' of 1931–3, in the course of which Manchuria became a satellite under military control and Japan itself began its evolution into an authoritarian regime. By 1936 Japan was beginning diplomatic co-operation with Hitler in the Anti-Comintern Pact. Mussolini too became more radical during the depression. He exploited Germany's revival to pursue a more aggressive foreign policy and in 1935–6 he launched his conquest of Abyssinia; by the end of the operation he had burned his bridges with the Western Powers and gravitated into an alignment with Hitler that he would probably have preferred to avoid. On the other hand, the Soviet Union reacted to Hitler's takeover by showing new interest (at least as a fallback option) in co-operation with the West, entering the League of Nations in 1934 and signing security pacts with France and Czechoslovakia in 1935, while the Comintern suspended its revolutionary line. But tragically, it was now – arguably more than in the 1920s – that the memory of the First World War influenced the foreign policies of the Atlantic democracies most potently. France, America, and Britain will be taken in turn.

France was the power most immediately threatened by Hitler, and because of its large armed forces and its location on Germany's border its consent was essential for any preventive move. The end of the 1920s seems to have marked less of a change in attitudes here than in Germany and Britain, though there was a quickening of interest in the war experience. Remarque sold well in translation; books about Verdun proliferated; the Douaumont ossuary was inaugurated partially in 1927, definitively in 1932, and regular vigils were initiated there.[34] Some of the most lasting French novels about the war appeared in the 1930s, and the French veterans' organizations reached their maximum influence early in the decade, when their membership exceeded 3 million and represented nearly a quarter of the electorate.[35] The secretary-general of the CIAMAC was pensions minister from 1933 to 1935, and held to 3 per cent the cuts in payments to France's nearly 1.1 million war pensioners at a time of acute fiscal crisis. More spectacularly, in riots in Paris on 6 February 1934 UNC members and right-wing paramilitaries clashed with the police, and a left-wing government resigned in favour of a more conservative one under Gaston Doumergue, the signatory of the 1917 war aims agreement with Nicholas II. The riots helped convince many on the left of a fascist threat to French democracy, and promoted the formation of the socialist-communist-radical alliance known as the Popular Front that in the next elections, held in 1936, was able to win a majority.

There was some basis for left-wing suspicions. The Croix de Feu, founded in 1928, bore resemblances to the Stahlhelm. Originally non-political and confined to ex-servicemen, under a new leader (Colonel de la Rocque) after 1931 it denounced the political system as corrupt, and 6–7,000 of its members took part in the February 1934 demonstrations.[36] Yet most of the veterans' organizations supported more moderate changes designed to strengthen governmental stability without destroying the democratic system, and they all supported the Popular Front government's social reforms.[37] Although the Croix de Feu was brought under de la Rocque's command and its members marched and wore uniform, the mainstream organizations were neither regimented nor bellicose. They elected their leaders, who were rarely regular officers, and they still blamed the 1914–18 high command for causing needless casualties, tenaciously pursuing the rehabilitation of the victims of wartime courts-martial and achieving a revised code of military justice. Nor did the main veterans' organizations glorify war, and they reacted vehemently when others, such as Mussolini, did so. They opposed unilateral disarmament, but during the 1920s they endorsed the League of Nations and Briand's rapprochement policies. In the 1930s, though not sympathizing with Hitler, they supported appeasement, the UNC and the UF coming close to wanting peace at any price. Many veterans felt that fighting achieved nothing, and as the philosopher and veteran Alain argued, that to surrender to the belief that war was inevitable would really make it so.[38] They participated in international demonstrations and in federations that included Italian and German veterans; in 1934 over 400 went to meet Mussolini and in the same year the head of the UF, Pichat, met Hitler. Pichat also attended the Munich conference in 1938 and after it he issued a supportive statement. However, the movement was not united in this view, and by spring 1939 the veterans' organizations favoured rearmament, in this reflecting the trend of French public opinion as a whole.[39] None the less, the relative unity and firmness with which France entered the Second World War was swiftly eroded during the months of waiting that preceded Germany's attack of

May 1940, and the speed of the subsequent collapse strengthens the impression that the wounds left by the crisis in morale in 1917 had never really healed.[40]

The influence of war memory on French public opinion was thus to move it in favour of appeasement at precisely the time when Hitler might have been halted at relatively little cost. But other war-related factors were operating in the same way, and probably more powerfully. The manpower available to French planners diminished from 1935 onwards as a result of the 1914–18 decline in the birth rate. France had to pay most of its reconstruction costs (only a small proportion of Germany's reparations liability ever being collected), and much of its budget was committed to repaying war loans and supporting the bereaved and disabled. Unlike Germany, it also repaid war debts to the United States, until it defaulted on them. All these factors reduced the sums available for prompt rearmament. But in any case much of the money available went not on tanks and aircraft but on the steel and concrete of the Maginot Line. Embarked on in 1929 (and bearing the name of a disabled veteran who served as war minister), the Maginot Line was designed to protect the border industrial areas against a new invasion. Fearing that another precipitate opening offensive would squander precious lives, French military chiefs favoured a waiting strategy and a long haul, which in turn underlined Britain's indispensability to them, in order to blockade Germany and supply finance, shipping, and raw materials.[41] In French official strategy and diplomacy the 'lessons' of 1914–18 had been all too thoroughly learned. Many of these developments came to a head in the Rhineland crisis of March 1936, when Hitler reoccupied the demilitarized zone at a moment when a weak caretaker ministry held power in Paris during the run up to elections, the franc was vulnerable, and the government had just contracted a British Treasury loan. The army faced a manpower shortage and had yet to begin serious rearmament. Although French military intelligence accurately appraised Hitler's intentions, it overestimated his strength and supposed a retaliatory strike would lead to another long war of attrition.[42] Hence support from the British seemed essential, but London preferred to accept the German *fait accompli*. From this point on, French governments were obliged to follow a British lead, (thereby forfeiting any military advantage they held at the beginning of the decade), and until 1939 this lead was in favour of conciliation.

Part of the reason for Britain's position was that the country's policy was decided in a global rather than purely European context, and much importance attached to America. Despite rejecting the Versailles treaty, during the 1920s the United States had intervened a good deal in Europe, using its financial leverage to encourage treaty revision in Germany's favour. In the depression years, it became more introverted. It too geared its policy towards avoiding the mistakes of the past, which meant attempting through the so-called Neutrality Acts to prevent any possible repetition of the 1914–17 path to belligerency. The process began in the late 1920s when the United States experienced its equivalent of the literary reevaluations of the war that occurred in Europe. Writers such as John Dos Passos, e.e. cummings, and Ernest Hemingway painted a disillusioned picture of the conflict, driven by scepticism about authority and distrust of the ideals of an older generation. Yet these writers were radical rather than pacifist, their views were probably atypical of those of the AEF veterans, and conventionally patriotic literature continued to be published. A survey of Americans who had volunteered to serve as ambulance drivers found most still convinced of the validity and necessity of their conduct.[43] More politically significant was the developing debate about America's neutrality. From the early 1930s international lawyers and historians as well as the US peace societies argued that future policy should be directed less to preventing wars than to staying out of them.[44]

Senator Gerald Nye of North Dakota capitalized on this mood. A progressive from America's landlocked heartland, he distrusted the east coast establishment and blamed the war on bankers and munitions manufacturers. In 1934 a rash of books appeared about the arms trade and Nye seized the opportunity to secure approval for a special Senate committee of investigation under his chairmanship. It used subpoena powers to comb the arms companies' files, and its hearings illuminated their lobbying activities, their connections with the War and Navy Departments, and their enormous wartime profits. At the same time, huge pacifist demonstrations took place among college students, and Walter Millis's *Road to War: America, 1914–1917* (Boston, 1934) implied that intervention had been against America's national interest and exports to the Allies had been a major cause of it: the book sold over 20,000 copies. President Roosevelt testified in the Nye committee hearings that he believed Bryan had been right to favour non-involvement in 1915, and he asked the committee to prepare legislation. Though believing in a more activist foreign policy than did Nye, Roosevelt welcomed measures that would prevent the United States from being drawn into another war over what he considered the secondary issue of neutral rights. Hence he went along with the Neutrality Acts of 1935, 1936, and 1937, although they were to tie his hands more than he might have wished. The culminating 1937 Act specified that in a war or civil war endangering the peace of the United States the president must prohibit arms and munitions sales and loans to belligerents, as well as banning travel by US citizens in belligerent ships. He gained discretion to impose 'cash-and-carry' conditions on purchases of goods other than arms: i.e., that purchasers must pay for the goods and transport them in their own vessels, which in practice would benefit Britain and France over Germany. It is difficult not to see this legislation as a most remarkable attempt to slam the stable door and to avoid the supposed mistakes of twenty years previously. In 1937 Gallup polls showed overwhelming public support for staying out of a European conflict.[45] The depression, the Manchurian crisis, and the growing European tension may all have contributed to this state of mind, from which Roosevelt himself – who during the First World War had been Assistant Secretary of the Navy but was now in many ways a disillusioned Wilsonian – was not immune.

American isolationism had its counterpart in Britain, where a critical countercurrent had existed even during the war, and it continued after the armistice. Thus men such as Paul Nash, C. R. W. Nevinson, and Sir William Orpen painted protest canvases in 1918–19, despite being officially commissioned as war artists. Keynes's *Economic Consequences of the Peace* focused on the peace treaty rather than the war, but questioned the value of the Allied victory and the sincerity of its motives, and C. E. Montague's *Disenchantment* (1922), by a *Manchester Guardian* journalist who had volunteered in 1914, also condemned the treaty and compared a stable pre-war world with a hollow and apathetic present.[46] In contrast the leading representatives of the modernist movement in literature neither participated in the fighting nor addressed the war directly, but a shell-shocked officer committed suicide in Virginia Woolf's *Mrs Dalloway* (1925) and the sombre imagery of T. S. Eliot's *The Wasteland* (1922) unmistakably alluded to the conflict. Even so, given high modernism's obliqueness and its limited dissemination, its broader influence is questionable, and the more widely read 'middlebrow' novels of the period tended to be anti-German and patriotic.[47] Rupert Brooke, whose *1914 and Other Poems* had reached a sale of 300,000 copies by 1930,[48] remained the best-known war poet, while much war-related publishing took the form of official histories and of the memoirs of politicians and generals. During the 1920s, Armistice Day sermons and speeches insisted that the defeat of Germany, despite its cost, had been neither unnecessary nor in vain.[49] Only at the end of the decade did a fundamental change in attitudes towards the war become discernible, and here again its direction was towards abhorrence and disengagement.

It became a commonplace among critics in 1914–18 that the great art of the war would come later. In fact the most lasting literary commemorations came after a decade, and from able though not first-rank writers. Thus in Britain too there was a 'war books' boom from about 1928 to 1931. It began earlier and continued later than in Germany, and it embraced poetry and drama as well as novels and autobiographies. As a Western Front correspondent for the *Daily Chronicle*, Philip Gibbs had written consistently optimistic dispatches. In 1928, however, his *The Politics of War* (published in the United States as *Now It Can Be Told*) was an embittered attack on the patriots and profiteers of the home front and on the secret diplomacy of old men that had caused young men to be massacred. In January 1929, R. C. Sherriff's *Journey's End* opened at the Savoy Theatre. London's West End had previously shied away from war themes, but this play was the most successful yet produced there, running for 593 performances and probably seen by half a million people, while the text sold over 175,000 copies and made the name of the Gollancz publishing house. Although not articulating an anti-war message, it did depict British soldiers contending with drunkenness and cowardice on the eve of the March 1918 German attack, and many veterans vouched for its authenticity.[50] Almost equally striking was the appearance in translation in March of Remarque's *All Quiet on the Western Front*, which sold 25,000 copies in a fortnight.[51] In fact the boom in autobiography had begun in Britain with the appearance in 1927 of T. E. Lawrence's *Revolt in the Desert* (later *Seven Pillars of Wisdom*) and in 1928 of Edmund Blunden's *Undertones of War* and Siegfried Sassoon's *Memoirs of a Fox-Hunting Man*; these were followed in 1929 by Robert Graves's *Goodbye to All That* (which did well enough to enable Graves to retire to Majorca), Richard Aldington's *Death of a Hero*, and Charles Carrington's *A Subaltern's War*. In 1930 it continued with Sassoon's *Memoirs of an Infantry Officer* and Frederick Manning's *Her Privates We*, and in 1933 with Vera Brittain's *Testament of Youth*. Reviewing the war books in 1930, the critic H. M. Tomlinson referred to the conflict as 'the greatest disturbance of mankind since the glaciers pushed our hunting forefathers down to the south'.[52] The middlebrow war novels of 1929–30, unlike those of ten years earlier, preached international brotherhood and denounced war as a waste.[53]

Lloyd George's *War Memoirs,* another bestseller that appeared in 1933–6, blamed the war on accident rather than on German aggression and mounted a sustained polemic against Haig.[54] In *The Real War* (1934) the ex-prime minister's military adviser, Sir Basil Liddell Hart, amplified the case with an indictment of the Western Front strategy and the high command, contending that the primary factor in the eventual victory had been the blockade.[55] The phenomenon extended to the cinema—the American version of *All Quiet* was a huge success in London and was followed by a cinematic representation of *Journey's End.* These films broke with the celebratory tone of the war documentaries produced (sometimes with government help) in the 1920s, and probably reached more people than all the other manifestations of the war boom put together.[56]

Many of the leading war books emerged from a group of officers (few were written by private soldiers) who knew each other during the conflict. Graves helped post Sassoon to the Craiglockhart hospital for the shell-shocked in 1917 after the latter had called for an end to the war in a letter to *The Times*: at Craiglockhart, Sassoon met Wilfred Owen and introduced him to Barbusse's *Under Fire,* which much impressed both men. Blunden, one of the principal memoirists himself, published in 1931 the first full edition of Wilfred Owen's verse (though during the 1930s Owen's work still sold slowly). The new British literature (like that of Barbusse, Remarque, and Hemingway) concentrated on depicting individual war experience. As a genre these works were not without precedent, but nineteenth-century wars had generated fewer examples. Their vantage point disregarded the high politics of strategy and diplomacy and spotlighted episodes of horror, pathos, confusion and farce,[57] as in Graves's shocking description of the Loos gas attack. This is not to say that the war books authors were pacifists. After Sassoon's gesture of protest, he had rejoined his regiment. Owen juxtaposed suffering at the Front with complacency and jingoism at home, but the fundamental contention in his famous 'Preface' was about the appropriate language for describing war, which should spurn romanticism and bombast. None the less, the autobiographers were painfully aware of what war cost the combatants, and they commanded the authority that came from personal witness. In addition they wrote self-consciously as part of an international movement – one of the leading comments in reviews of Remarque, for example, noting his demonstration of the shared traits between German and Allied soldiers' experience.[58] A commonplace of the memoirs was the bond between soldiers of all nations created by reminiscences incommunicable except between themselves, and the chasm that separated them from others. Yet the new writers now tried to bridge this chasm, and they did so with considerable effect.

Graves and Sassoon observed that a long interval was needed before they could write with sufficient detachment, given that a major part of their purpose was self-therapy. The comparison with the similar hiatus that preceded artistic explorations of America's later military involvement in Vietnam is obvious, though telling. It was not simply the writers, however, who preferred to wait. The earlier booms in memorial-building and in commemorative rituals had testified to the constant public interest in the war, and the Menin Gate and Thiepval Arch were completed during the war books boom: 100,000 people signed the Menin Gate visitors' book in

1930 in a period of only three months.[59] Yet paradoxically before the late 1920s publishers had found little market for disillusioned personal testimonials and film-makers had played safe with adventurous and patriotic themes. The end of the decade saw a change in attitudes and a different approach. The General Strike of 1926 has been seen as one reason. Its conflictual language and disruption of ordi-nary life resurrected something of the wartime mood: the trade unions' defeat may have symbolized the end of the post-war transition and the start of something new.[60] By 1929 the election of a Labour government, headed by wartime pacifists (including Ramsay MacDonald as premier), the beginnings of the slump, and the revival of German nationalism may have contributed to the impression that the war had been fought for nothing and Europe was moving into another pre-conflict period.[61] The view developed, which was not a commonplace before the 1930s but has become one since, that the sacrifices of 1914–18 had been futile. In Britain as in Germany, the memory of the war both shaped the inter-war years and yet was also re-evaluated in the light of subsequent experience. Indeed the more or less simulta-neous cultural shifts that occurred in the two countries at the end of the 1920s pro-pelled one in a belligerently nationalist and the other in a pacifist direction.

Unlike in Germany, there was little patriotic reaction in Britain against the new literary trend, although some army officers and older literary critics were sharply critical, and commentaries in 1930 in works by two historians, D. Jerrold's *The Lie about the War* and Cyril Falls's *War Books*, stressed the war's high motives and in-sisted on its achievements. Neither, however, romanticized armed conflict as a fulfil-ment of the individual and a purification of society in the way that Jünger did. Moreover, there were signs in the late 1920s and early 1930s of a political as well as a cultural reappraisal of Britain's role, and the war books boom must be seen as part of something larger. The Labour government was in some ways a breath of fresh air, for example responding positively to a longstanding campaign to abolish 'Field Punishment No. 1', which entailed disciplining soldiers by tying them to an artillery wheel. In 1929 there were calls in the House of Commons to end Armistice Day, but Labour decided to continue the ceremony, though with a re-duced military presence. On the occasion of the 11 November commemorations in the 1930s speeches and press commentaries, even from the right, stressed more strongly than before that 1914–18 must be a war to end war, and that there should never be another conflagration like it.[62] Similarly, the British Legion supported the League of Nations and disarmament and during the 1938 Czechoslovak crisis its president, Frederick Maurice, flew to Germany to meet Hitler.[63] As in America, however, while older groups like the Legion, the League of Nations Union, and the UDC supported collective security, from the early 1930s a more radical and unilat-eral pacifist movement came to the fore. The members of the Peace Pledge Union, founded in 1935 by the Reverend Dick Sheppard, pledged themselves in no cir-cumstances to fight in another war (by 1939, 150,000 had made this commitment), and in 1933 the Women's Co-operative Guild began selling white poppies on Armistice Day to commemorate the dead of the Central Powers as well as those of the Allies. In the same year the students of the Oxford Union Society voted in favour of a resolution never to fight for King and Country and the Labour Party's Hastings conference supported a general strike in the event of war. Although

Britain had no Nye committee, it too saw agitation against the arms trade and a Royal Commission reported on the manufacture and sale of armaments, the Labour Party in parliament voting against the defence estimates until 1937.

The British public, like the American, was therefore at its most isolationist at precisely the moment when rapid preventive action was needed if Hitler were to be halted before he could launch a major war. The window of opportunity was brief, as he began secret rearmament in 1933, announced the reintroduction of conscription and an air force in 1935, and reoccupied the Rhineland in 1936. All the same, some notes of caution should be sounded before attributing British passivity simply to the memory of the 1914–18 conflict. Many other factors encouraged disengagement from the continent, including the collapse of world trade and new unrest in the empire. By the 1930s the horror of war was epitomized not only by the Somme and Passchendaele but also by new nightmares, particularly that of air attack. Moreover, politicians exaggerated the extent to which the new public mood tied their hands. A good example is the 1933 East Fulham by-election, in which a Labour candidate defeated the candidate of the ruling national coalition: later the prime minister cited the result as a reason for delay in embarking on rearmament. In fact the Labour candidate was a decorated veteran who supported collective security and the League, and the main campaign issue was housing.[64] When all allowances are made, however, it is difficult not to see public revulsion against 1914–18 (and Dominion hostility to any re-enactment) as powerful factors in favour of appeasement until at least 1938. Indeed, politicians and officials shared the popular mood, and a leading feature of their policy and strategy was concern to avoid what were seen as earlier errors. Thus they resisted secret staff conversations with the French, which took place for the first time after Hitler reoccupied the Rhineland, and even then only for two days. Further joint planning had to wait until the spring of 1939. In the 1930s the BEF was smaller and had more old-fashioned equipment than in 1914, and until 1937 it was training primarily to defend Egypt (as well as being increasingly preoccupied with holding the ring in Palestine, where an Arab revolt had erupted against Jewish immigration), while the Treasury, mindful of Britain's financial straits in 1917 and of the American Neutrality Acts, warned against premature rearmament and of the dubious prospects in a long conflict. All the same, in the end the tide turned. The Spanish Civil War weakened pacifist feeling on the left, and by the time of the 1938 Munich crisis opinion polls suggested that opinion was divided and a substantial minority sympathized with Czechoslovakia and was critical of Neville Chamberlain's appeasement policies.[65] Finally by August 1939 a majority of 76 per cent over 19 per cent said they were willing to fight Germany if it attacked Poland or Danzig.[66] However awful the memory of the First World War might be, it did not stop the British public, in the end, from accepting a second round.

This conclusion reinforces the fundamental point. There was no one single or uniform memory of the war experience, and the phenomenon cannot be reduced to a unified determining force. On the contrary, there were many memories, varying within and between countries as well as over time. In both Germany and the West the meaning of the war was interpreted differently in the 1930s from the 1920s, and the defeated and the victors drew contrasting conclusions. With the outbreak of the

CATACLYSM

Second World War in Europe in 1939, moreover, and its expansion into a global war in 1941, memories of the previous conflict lost much of their political significance. For most participants, the impact of the new conflict in casualties and in disruption of ordinary life was vastly greater. Even in Britain, where arguably the impact was less, Armistice Day was cancelled in the years 1939 to 1945, although poppy sales continued and Remembrance Sunday was still honoured.[67] At the level of generalship and statecraft, however, the 'lessons' of the previous conflict still had a perceptible influence on the Second World War leaders, many of whom had served their apprenticeships in it and this time wanted to manage things better. The first war was not only an essential precondition for the second but also shaped the way it was fought – and not fought. To a large extent this generalization applies to both the Axis and the Allies.

The 1914–18 precedent was least relevant for the Japanese and Italians, who were fighting against their former partners, in different theatres and in very different conditions. In 1940 Mussolini probably tried to replicate Salandra's and Sonnino's gambit of 1915, hoping for a quick and easy operation that would strengthen him domestically and protect Italy's independence by assuring it a share of the spoils of victory. He miscalculated even more seriously than they had done, not only about the war's length and cost but also about who would win it, and once again such miscalculations brought down an Italian regime. In Germany, in contrast, both the army and the newly recreated air force in the 1930s paid great attention to the tactical lessons of the First World War, including (in the army's case) the importance of soldiers and junior officers acting on their own responsibility, and (in the case of the Luftwaffe) the need to concentrate forces and obtain air superiority in support of army operations.[68] When war broke out the navy urged immediate recourse to unrestricted submarine warfare and active employment of the surface warships to prevent demoralization of their crews.[69] At the level of strategy, the army during the Weimar Republic (when Groener was defence minister) reverted to Schlieffen's principles: that it must use modern technology to secure surprise, encirclement, and decisive victories, eschewing another war of attrition.[70] (Notwithstanding these considerations, the planning for the May 1940 offensive in the west was not initially for a rerun of 1914 but for a strike into the Low Countries directed against the British.[71]) At the highest level, Hitler himself, who mused extensively on how he would have fought the first war differently (and constantly reminisced about it during the second), similarly intended to progress – at least in the first instance – by swift, sudden blows against isolated victims and by keeping his potential enemies divided. If the 1914 war had begun because of an incident in the Balkans and in what Hitler considered to be the wrong year, future wars would be started at times and in circumstances of his choosing, if necessary by stage-managing assassinations as pretexts.[72] Wilhelmine Germany, he believed, had erred in trying to do everything by halves, and had needlessly antagonized Britain. Hence his hope, at least to begin with, of enlisting London's favour by abstaining from naval and colonial expansion, with the priority being rather to recreate the domination of Eastern Europe that had been established in 1918. After the 1940 armistice with France was signed (on Hitler's orders) in the same railway carriage as that of 1918, he was gripped by the sensation of revenge and Goebbels spoke of 'a feeling of being born again', while Wilhelm from his Dutch exile telegraphed congratulations on the achievement in a few weeks of what had previously proved impossible in four years. Again, Hitler selected the anniversary of the 1918 armistice for the complete occupation of France on 11 November 1942.[73] On the other hand, he recognized the importance of preventing a new 'stab in the back' by maintaining high civilian living standards.[74] Food and raw material stocks were higher in 1939 than in 1914, and wage and price controls restrained inflation more successfully. Partly because Germany could ransack the rest of Europe and exploit forced labour, its living standards were better protected than in the first conflict, although repression was much harsher both in the army and at home.[75] Indeed the fear of new stab-in-the back accusations inhibited the conservative leaders of the opposition to Hitler.[76] The Führer also drew still more sinister lessons from the previous conflict, blaming the Jews for the demoralization of the German home front and commenting in *Mein Kampf* that if 12–15,000 of them had been eliminated the sacrifices at the Front might not have been in vain.[77] On the other hand, his attribution of the 1918 débâcle to domestic weakness went with a consistent underestimation of the US contribution and of the Americans' military potential, which encouraged him to make light of declaring war against them in 1941.[78] He may also simply have paid less attention to previous lessons as the Second World War developed its own distinctive character and he himself became more impatient. Thus when Britain failed after the fall of France to respond to his peace overtures, he launched his drive into Russia regardless of the dangers of a conflict on two fronts. At first intending to avoid Wilhelm's megalomania, he developed far worse delusions of his own.

On the Allied side, the influence of the First World War complex was probably even greater. Of the major leaders, we know least about Stalin, although his reluctance to take precautions against an attack in 1941 may have been influenced by concern that the 1914 Russian mobilization had needlessly precipitated conflict. Nor were the 1918 Allied intervention and the 1919–21 Polish–Soviet war ever far from his mind, even if he had many other reasons to distrust the West and the Poles. In a moment of banter with Churchill he conceded that his war aims (which included a Polish buffer state, freer passage through the Straits, and territorial gains from Turkey) had much in common with those of the tsars. About Stalin's Atlantic partners, however, we know much more. Britain and France began extremely cautiously, advising Poland in the 1939 crisis to avoid premature mobilization for fear of starting a chain reaction and a war by accident, though also signing an alliance with Warsaw in August in the hope of avoiding a repeat of the uncertainty about London's position that was thought to have encouraged German brinkmanship in July 1914.[79] During the phoney war period they refrained from massive opening offensives on the 1914 model, and indeed from doing very much at all. Perhaps influenced by Liddell Hart's contentions, they put much of their trust in blockade and a possible collapse in the German war economy or even an anti-Nazi revolution; indeed, unwarranted confidence in such possibilities had underpinned their willingness to risk war in the first place and implied a serious misreading of what had happened in 1918.[80] More positive lessons were also drawn from the previous conflict, for example in devising French plans for economic mobilization[81] and in Britain's prompt re-institution of convoy (indeed the Royal Navy was complacent about the U-boats),[82] but the overriding concern was not to risk strategic disaster and ruin civilian morale by repeating battles like the Somme. Unless the Allies' wishful thinking about Germany's weaknesses proved justified, however, this doctrine left it unclear how they could win before running out of funds.

After the 1940 campaign and France's exit under the leadership of Pétain – the hero of Verdun but a man who knew the true cost of war and had revealed his defeatist tendencies in March 1918 – leadership in the western camp passed first to London but increasingly to Washington. Roosevelt had been sympathetic to the Neutrality Acts in so far as they prevented him from staking national prestige on defending neutral rights. He did not rule out intervention, but only on behalf of fundamental national interests. Indeed, he did not believe that it was necessary to declare a state of war at all, preferring to act flexibly and at his discretion. The Neutrality Acts were revised in 1939 to allow cash sales of weapons to belligerents (which meant in practice to the Allies), but even so Britain ran out of foreign exchange in the winter of 1940–41, and thereafter once again kept fighting only with American aid, this time dispensed, however, not through loans but through the agency of the March 1941 Lease-Lend Act. Once the United States was brought into the war, the reaction against First World War diplomacy continued. There were no new Fourteen Points, among other reasons being that Roosevelt wished to deny Hitler any chance to snatch at negotiations before being defeated: a stance confirmed in the 'Unconditional Surrender' doctrine that he and Churchill announced at Casablanca in 1943.[83] The enemy must be beaten thoroughly, and in looking to the post-war settlement Roosevelt saw as the principal danger that disunity among the victors would again allow their enemies to recover. Hence his 'Four Policemen' concept of a US-British-Soviet-Chinese policing of the post-war world. This principle would be embodied in the primary responsibility for international peace and security invested in the Security Council of the United Nations, which was intended, despite superficial resemblances, to function very differently from the League.[84] Roosevelt was also determined, in contrast to Wilson, to maintain bipartisan support in Congress (for example by including Republicans in the American delegation to the UN founding conference at San Francisco). Nor would the United States insist (as after 1918) on the repayment of war loans, Lend-Lease aid being mostly written off. It would seek to re-establish and maintain an open world economy through its founder membership of the World Bank and the International Monetary Fund, and later of the General Agreement on Tariffs and Trade. It would maintain powerful military forces, and a worldwide chain of bases and overflight rights. In short, its external policy would be active and interventionist, though this time with bipartisan support.

Yet to an extent American objectives were contradictory. Roosevelt wanted no inter-Allied secret treaties anticipating the post-war settlement, and he stopped a British–Soviet treaty in 1942 that would have guaranteed Stalin his 1941 frontiers. A further major obstacle to an understanding with Stalin was Western delay in organizing a 'second front' in north-western Europe, but a major reason for that delay was British hesitation, caused partly by Churchill's fear of British casualties like those of 1916–18.[85] By agreeing to a Mediterranean strategy and delaying a second front until 1944 Roosevelt essentially made co-operation with London take precedence over that with Moscow. His policy even towards Germany itself was schizophrenic. On the one hand he inclined to much greater harshness than after the First World War, as shown by his support in 1944 for the 'Morgenthau Plan', devised by his treasury secretary, for partitioning Germany and pastoralizing its economy. On the other hand the State Department planners looked forward to a prosperous and democratized Germany that could eventually be reintegrated into the Atlantic community. These approaches drew divergent lessons from the 1914–18 and inter-war experiences, and in the end a combination based on both of them would be implemented.

To some extent wartime planning was followed through after 1945. The United States provided relief to Germany and to occupied Europe more generously than after 1919. Germany and Japan were occupied, demilitarized, and democratized from above, and their economies held down while their future was decided. From 1947–8 onwards, however, with the launching of the Marshall Plan in Europe and its counterpart, the 'Reverse Course', in Japan, the primary concern of American diplomacy became the stresses within the second wartime alliance, and the defeated Axis enemies were contained largely by arrangements within the Western camp rather than through collaboration with Moscow. The Soviet-American Cold War escalated to an extent unparalleled by the Franco-British-American tensions of the 1920s, and international politics entered a new era, in which the lessons of 1919 became less relevant – though a Soviet-German rapprochement on Rapallo lines remained a Western bugbear for years to come. None the less, as the new post-war settlement evolved along unforeseen lines in a world reshaped by an even more devastating conflict, the legacy and memories of 1914–18 seemed finally to recede from the forefront of contemporary events.

CHAPTER 21

CONCLUSION:
THE WAR BECOMES HISTORY

B Y THE MID-TWENTIETH century the world had completed a second cycle through the onset, course, and liquidation of a great world war. With the
end of the Second World War and post-war reconstruction, the First World War's
significance as a precedent dwindled. In new crises such as those over Korea and
Suez, Western leaders looked for lessons to the experience of the 1930s from
Manchuria to the Rhineland and Munich. In the 1962 Cuban missile crisis, President Kennedy is reported to have been influenced by his reading of Barbara Tuchman's bestselling account of the 1914 crisis, *The Guns of August*, but the analogies he
discussed with the Executive Committee of his National Security Council were Munich, Pearl Harbor, Suez, and Hungary, and as the crisis developed they dispensed
with historical parallels altogether.[1] In so far as the superpower leaders contemplated military operations, the lessons of Stalingrad, Normandy, and Hiroshima
seemed far more relevant than those of Tannenberg or Ypres. Inter-war flashpoints
such as reparations no longer mattered; population transfers more or less settled
Germany's eastern borders; Alsace-Lorraine (reincorporated by Hitler in 1940) returned definitively to France; and the Saar (after a decade of sometimes acrimo-
nious dispute) to West Germany. It is true that elsewhere the imperial redistribution
after 1918 had created a series of time bombs, several of which took decades to detonate. Czechoslovakia and Yugoslavia disintegrated in the 1990s: the former peacefully, the latter not. Other entities created after the First World War were racked by
inter-communal violence, including Ruanda (formed out of the colonial territory
transferred from German East Africa to Belgium); the Lebanon (broadened by the
French in 1920 to incorporate more Muslims and containing only a bare Maronite
Christian majority); and Northern Ireland, established after the Anglo-Irish Treaty
of 1921. Still others were held together by authoritarian rule, notably Iraq, which
the British cobbled together out of three Ottoman provinces, comprising an unstable combination of Kurds in the north and Sunni and Shia Muslims in the centre

and south, where colonial administrators drew an arbitrary frontier with Kuwait. Finally in Palestine, where the British mandate was confirmed in 1920, and where Jewish immigration soared because of depression and anti-Semitic persecution in the 1930s, a new ethnic conflict emerged whose consequences would reverberate even more powerfully. Yet many of the dragons' teeth sown during the war remained buried until much later. By breaking up the Austro-Hungarian, German, and Ottoman empires, it created possibilities for a string of succession disputes across their former territories, but the links were far less direct than those connecting the Great War to Fascism and Nazism, the 1929 depression, and the origins of the Second World War.

Henceforth the legacies of 1914–18 slipped off the international political agenda. The war's battlefields retained a symbolic potency as backdrops for gestures of reconciliation, as when Charles de Gaulle and Konrad Adenauer visited the Chemin des Dames before signing the 1963 Franco-German friendship treaty or when in 1984 François Mitterand and Helmut Kohl clasped hands at Verdun. For private individuals its impact remained all too real. Nearly 3,000 limbless British survivors were still being cared for in the 1970s.[2] Yet in Britain the lighter total losses incurred in the Second World War – even though proportionate casualties in the 1944 battle of Normandy, for example, were worse than at Third Ypres[3] – may have anaesthetized the wound to the collective memory inflicted by the earlier conflict. Although after 1945 the ritual cycle of commemoration resumed, the Silence on 11 November was replaced by Armistice Sunday, and lost a good deal of its emotional charge. In the Soviet Union, conversely, the sacrifice exacted in the second war was far, far heavier, and the monumental and ceremonial infrastructure created in the west in the 1920s was now imitated in Russia on an even more massive scale. In most other participant countries too the Second World War was more traumatic and destructive than the First, and it might well seem to those who had not been personally involved that the latter could now in every sense be consigned to history.

The historicization of the war had begun much earlier; indeed plans to write official histories were launched while it was in progress, for example in Britain by the historical section of the cabinet's Committee of Imperial Defence. Much of the interwar work on the conflict took the form of personal testimony in autobiographies and memoirs, but more general histories also appeared, and these were frequently written by participants. Moreover, enormous quantities of source material entered the public domain remarkably early. A first provider of information was the multinational series on the war's economic and social dimension published by the Carnegie Endowment for International Peace in the 1920s and 1930s. A second was the mountain of pre-1914 diplomatic documents published because of the warguilt controversy,* although wartime diplomacy and the peace conference remained *terra incognita* for much longer. A third was the official histories of military and naval operations produced (among others) by Austria-Hungary, Britain, the Dominions, France, Germany, Italy, and Turkey. To some extent they bore the marks of their provenance. The main author of the British official history of the Western Front, Sir

---

*See ch. 19.

James Edmonds, envisaged an account that could be used in military academies. He cross-checked his drafts with comments from surviving commanders, suppressed his private reservations about GHQ and, especially after the broadside against Haig fired in Lloyd George's memoirs, attempted to rehabilitate the commander-in-chief's posthumous reputation.[4] The official history of the blockade, in contrast, was thought so revealing that it remained closed until 1961.[5] In Germany, on the other hand, the ex-officers responsible for the official history of land operations sought to salvage the GGS's reputation by arguing that the Schlieffen Plan had been a 'victory recipe' that the younger Moltke had adulterated and misapplied.[6] Such drawbacks notwithstanding, the inter-war official publications furnished later writers with an invaluable quarry for raw material and a framework for interpretation and debate.

They did so only after a pause. During the Second World War and – more surprisingly – for a decade afterwards, little of note was published about its predecessor. Even among academic historians, the First World War seemed overshadowed and neglected. Only from around 1960 did a second wave of work begin, which arguably has maintained its momentum ever since. If the inter-war documentary editions constituted a first evidence revolution, the opening of the major Western archives (those in Britain from 1968, those in Austria and France soon afterwards), marked a second and even more significant expansion in the raw material available. However, the quickening of interest in the war preceded the availability of the files, which sustained a phenomenon that had already begun. The late 1950s and early 1960s witnessed a rediscovery of the war in some ways replicating that of thirty years earlier, and again Germany and Britain were its focal points, both countries witnessing new controversies that reverberated outside the scholarly community. In both, moreover, what purported to be discussions of 1914–18 owed something of their keenness to being implicitly about the Second World War and Cold War too.[7]

The German debate centred, once again, on war guilt. It overturned a new consensus that appeared to have superseded the 1920s polemics. After 1945 most West German historians still denied Berlin's primary responsibility in 1914, blaming systemic factors and asserting that none of the powers had wanted war. In 1950 (the year of the Schuman Plan for a Western European coal and steel pool), a meeting of leading French and German historians pronounced that 'the documents do not permit attributing [*sic*] a premeditated desire for European war on the part of any government or people in 1914', and school textbooks in both countries were to be revised accordingly.[8] This agreement suited the needs of the time for West German integration into the Atlantic alliance and the emerging European communities. Once again the war (or at least its origins) was being reinterpreted in the light of current imperatives. And yet a very different picture emerged from the three-volume account of *The Origins of the War of 1914* by the Italian liberal journalist (and 1915 interventionist) Luigi Albertini, which remains the fullest examination of the war's diplomatic antecedents ever written. Though comparatively unknown when first published in Italian during the Second World War, it appeared in English translation in 1952–57. Its conclusions emphasized not only miscalculation but also Germany's responsibility, and resembled the analysis of the July crisis later expounded in Fritz Fischer's *Griff nach der Weltmacht: die Kriegszielpolitik des kaiserlichen Deutschland 1914/18* ('Grasp for World Power: the War Aims Policy of Imperial Germany'), whose appearance caused a furore in the Federal Republic in 1961 and itself became a historic event. In 1914, it argued, the Berlin leaders not only willed a local Balkan war but also deliberately risked a continental one, which had been no accident or a by-product of an anarchic international system for which no country bore sole blame. This assertion gathered its full import from Fischer's documentation of German war aims on the basis of intensive research in the surviving files, many of them (including Bethmann Hollweg's September Programme) located in East Germany and therefore closed to other western scholars. He claimed that both imperial Germany's military and its civilian leaders, supported by the country's business and intellectual elites, had endorsed aggressive objectives whose purpose was not only to consolidate the regime at home but also to establish a global power position by dominating the continent and expanding overseas. These goals, he suggested, lay in a line of continuity extending back to *Weltpolitik* in the 1890s and forward to Nazi racist imperialism. Writing in the year of the construction of the Berlin Wall, he implied that Germany had been responsible not only for the 1939 war (which many German historians blamed readily enough on Hitler and treated as an aberration from national traditions) but also for that of 1914, in which case the country's neighbours might claim every justification for keeping it divided.[9]

Despite *Griff nach der Weltmacht*'s appearance as a forbiddingly scholarly tome, Fischer well understood its implications. He wished to force his nation to confront its past. His book was fiercely attacked in the German historical profession, with covert government encouragement, and became a cause célèbre. As the storm grew his theses became harsher, and in 1969 his second major study, *Krieg der Illusionen: die Deutsche Politik von 1911 bis 1914* ('War of Illusions: German Policy from 1911 to 1914'), identified a design for war dating back to the 'War Council' of 8 December 1912. This contention was not sustainable in its most extreme form, and Fischer himself later retracted it.[10] Even though his first book has better withstood criticism, it overstated the unanimity within the Berlin elite and understated the resemblances between Germany's war aims and those of the Allies. None the less, most German historians came round to its more nuanced assessment of Germany's role in the July crisis, and (despite some important qualifications by subsequent writers) much of its analysis of the scope of German wartime ambitions has survived unchallenged.* The 'Fischer controversy' broke up the earlier 'revisionist' consensus and no single orthodoxy supplanted it. Instead German historians split up into several schools, of which Fischer and his disciples were only one. The consequence, as he pointed out retrospectively, was to promote intellectual pluralism in West Germany's universities and arguably in society more broadly, in this way helping to normalize the country and make it easier to win its neighbours' acquiescence in its reunification when the opportunity came.[11]

Fischer's work was part of a broader phenomenon. During the 1960s radical writers challenged existing interpretations of a series of major topics in the history of international relations, including pre-1914 imperialism,[12] appeasement,[13] and the origins of the Cold War.[14] In the USA, which appeared to have set aside the acrimony of the 1930s and accommodated itself to an interventionist foreign pol-

---

*See ch. 5.

icy, they revisited the Wilson presidency, portraying the Fourteen Points and the Paris Peace Conference as early attempts at anti-Soviet containment.[15] Whereas most previous studies of the origins of the war had concentrated on the diplomatic interplay between all the powers, Fischer exploited the new archival sources to highlight the connections between foreign and domestic policy in one country. He inspired a succession of comparable studies of pre-1914 foreign policy and of war aims in the other powers. Hence during the 1970s and 1980s the diplomatic history of the war's origins, course, and aftermath was substantially rewritten, while the intensification of the superpower arms race in the era of Euromissiles and the Strategic Defense Initiative stimulated interest among political scientists in 1914 analogies.[16] The new research uncovered more evidence of pre-war contingency planning for a European conflict, but little for any premeditated decision to launch one, and it suggested that war aims in the Allied countries were more tentative, defensive, and detached from domestic conflicts than they were in Germany. None the less, all the belligerent governments paid close attention to their political objectives, and examination of the other powers reinforced Fischer's essential insight that the killing was begun and prolonged through deliberate political will.

In Britain, the second focus of the 1960s renaissance, controversy focused less on the politics of the war than on its strategy. If Fischer can be seen as riding the crest of a global reaction against Cold War conservatism, in Britain similarly the early 1960s, leading up to the fiftieth anniversary of Sarajevo in 1964, was a time of ferment, prompted by economic stagnation, decolonization, uncertainty about the country's future international role, and the sordid decay of the Macmillan government, as well as to forebodings (most notably articulated by the Campaign for Nuclear Disarmament) about a possible Third World War. Crises over Berlin and Cuba, and the escalation of American involvement in Vietnam encouraged contemporaries to look beyond the 'good' war of 1939–45 and rediscover the earlier bad one.[17] In this climate a counterpart to the West End debut of *Journey's End* in 1929 was provided by the satire *Oh! What a Lovely War* (1963: film version 1969); to the 'war books' by new studies of the campaigning, such as Leon Wolff's *In Flanders Fields* (1958) and Alan Clark's *The Donkeys* (1961); to the film of *All Quiet on the Western Front* by the BBC television harrowing documentary series in twenty-six parts on *The Great War*, seen by an average of 8 million people in 1964–5;[18] and to Liddell Hart's *The Real War* by A. J. P Taylor's *The First World War: an Illustrated History* (1963), which Liddell Hart advised on and which became the most influential single-volume account of the conflict, selling a quarter of a million copies by 1989. Wilfred Owen's poetry, partly because of its use in Benjamin Britten's *War Requiem* (1961) and its seemingly prophetic qualities, became celebrated as never before, and a mainstay of the secondary school syllabus. Much of the new British output was therefore politically radical in its inspiration. In contrast to Fischer, however, rather than targeting Lloyd George and the political direction of the war, it focused on a callous and incompetent officer class, with Haig at its apex. Its implicit agenda was to indict a privileged elite that after its rehabilitation in 1940–45 was now once again failing. Even Taylor's presentation – though in contrast to *Oh! What a Lovely War* fully acknowledging the politicians' importance – differed from Fischer's by portraying the history of the conflict as one of miscalculation and blunders, culminating in a blind, meaningless slaughter. Writing as a founder member (though later a disenchanted one) of CND, he implied that if the deterrent had failed to deter in 1914, similar miscalculations might cause catastrophe in the nuclear age. Yet the 1960s saw the beginnings of divergence not only between Taylorite interpretations and new research into the politics and diplomacy of the conflict, but also between popular understandings of the military history of the war and new investigations into its strategy. This dichotomy was already evident in the BBC series, which owed its memorable artistic impact to its combination of disturbing images, plangent music, and sombre narration, but whose script, much of it written by John Terraine and Correlli Barnett, tried to convey that the struggle had been necessary, that the Western Front concentration had been unavoidable, and that British generalship had risen to the challenge of intimidating circumstances. Similar themes appeared in Terraine's *Douglas Haig: the Educated Soldier* (1963), and in a succession of later works by the same author, which at the time went against the grain of much writing on the war, but grew in influence in the 1980s and 1990s when a later generation of researchers drew on the newly opened War Office and cabinet archives and private papers.[19] Some of their work still criticized the British high command, on occasion severely, but it depicted the BEF and the Dominion forces as learning from their mistakes, increasing their effectiveness, and playing a major role – perhaps the major role – in breaking the German army. Despite its national focus, it lent essential insights into the operational history of the war as a whole, which were paralleled by more isolated studies of command and strategy in the continental countries.

By the 1990s, however, some of the most innovative research into the history of the war was taking a different direction. By this stage there were signs of yet another popular rediscovery of interest in the struggle, following those of the 1930s and 1960s. The revival has been plausibly linked to a generational turnover, the grandchildren and great grandchildren of the ever fewer remaining veterans reaching maturity and revisiting their elders' sufferings and achievements as the sons and daughters had done in earlier years.[20] Perhaps, as the 1930s rediscovery owed something to revived fears of global conflict, and that of the 1960s to nuclear weapons and Vietnam, so that of the 1990s was linked to post-Cold War insecurities and the renewed spectacle (not least in Sarajevo itself) of campaigning and atrocities on European soil. Perhaps too the fiftieth anniversary of 1945 and the increasing distance even of the Second World War revived interest in the conflicts in the first half of the twentieth century as a general phenomenon. In Britain, the testimony of survivors was recorded for posterity in oral history archives and in paperback editions and, as a result of tabloid newspaper campaigning, the two minutes' silence on 11 November was unofficially reinstated. In France an anthology of soldiers' letters became the most successful bestseller of its kind since the 1930s. New study groups made their appearance, often including many Second World War veterans, such as the Western Front Association (1980) in Britain and the Great War Society (1987) in the United States, as well as new museums, notably the Historial de la Grande Guerre (1992) at Péronne. As the last eyewitnesses disappeared and the war grew still more remote – and trench archaeology developed as a new branch of investigation – its memory had rarely been more sedulously cultivated.[21]

While academic research into the history of the war resulted in an avalanche of new titles (and revived after 1991, for example, in Russia), the most significant new intellectual trend in this period was interest in its cultural history. French and American writers did much to launch the new boom, but others in Britain, Germany, and Italy soon followed, and like the earlier revival of diplomatic history it became a genuinely international phenomenon. It too reflected broader trends, paralleled in other fields of history and social science, as the end of the Cold War and the collapse of the Soviet Union encouraged studies of collective memory, nationalism, and ethnicity. Yet no one writer dominated this new approach as Fischer had done earlier (though Paul Fussell was probably the most widely acknowledged pioneer), and neither was it characterized by an overriding 'thesis': on the contrary its leading protagonists were often divided.[22] Further, the discourse between them became confused, not least because of the range of association and versatility of significance of the term 'culture' itself, one of the most complex in the English language.[23] None the less, three main sets of findings from the new literature may be singled out.

In the first place, the new research clarified the connection between the war and the rise of the most characteristic twentieth-century artistic movement, that of 'modernism' – an iconoclastic revolt against conventional narrative form in the novel, representational 'realism' in painting, nineteenth-century historicism in architecture, and romanticism in music. In fact among the European avant-garde the modernist revolution was already well under way before the war, as evidenced by the emergence from around 1908 of Cubism, Futurism, and Expressionism in painting, Stravinsky's 1913 ballet score 'The Rite of Spring', and the functionality of Adolph Loos's 'House without Eyebrows' (1910) on the Michaelerplatz in Vienna. The war added little further impetus to these developments: the one important new departure during it was the emergence of the Dadaist movement in Switzerland and Germany after 1916. In some ways it may have caused a reaction, as painters such as Picasso, for example, reverted to more traditional forms, in part for patriotic reasons.[24] Overwhelmingly the art and architecture of war commemoration evoked themes from classical, romantic, and Christian sources, and even 'anti-war' painters and writers such as Nevinson and Owen used relatively traditional techniques, possibly in order to communicate more effectively.[25] As the 1920s progressed modernist trends in literature and painting re-emerged vigorously, but the war's influence on them was minimal. Secondly, in contrast, its impact on broader Western cultural attitudes towards armed conflict was much more profound, though it differed from society to society and from decade to decade. Thus during the war itself, and even in the years of monument building and creation of ritual in the 1920s, it was still acceptable in Britain and France to use sentimental, archaic, and euphemistic words and imagery about the conflict and its cost.[26] The reaction against such practices surfaced most strongly in the 1930s, but it did not lead to universal and unconditional pacifism. On the contrary, the second war was eventually accepted almost as dutifully as the first, and after 1945 its relatively benign memory encouraged support for military preparedness and an assertive foreign policy in Britain, America, and even in Gaullist France, whereas the memory of the first had had the contrary effect. What changed for good, however, was the tone of the language used about bloodshed. As Barbusse had put it, 'The act of slaughter is always ignoble: sometimes necessary, but always ignoble.'[27] Yet – third and finally – if much of the new cultural history centred on how the war was represented and remembered, it also illuminated soldiers' and civilians' motives at the time for accepting it, and the devices used by governments to mobilize and remobilize consent. Foremost among the resulting insights was the extent to which a conflict normally perceived as less ideological than the Second World War or the Cold War was rationalized by contemporaries as a clash of civilizations and of moral absolutes: in Germany as a struggle to the death against western materialism and benighted Slavic despotism; in the West as a crusade to banish autocracy, atrocities, and militarism.[28] It seems likely that it is in the borderlands between cultural and political history that the most important insights into the mainsprings of the conflict will continue to be found.

Since the 1960s successive waves of investigation have profoundly modified our understanding of the war's political, operational, and cultural faces; only its economic history remains comparatively under-explored.[29] What light has this immense labour shed on the questions with which this book began? Central to the entire story were developments in Germany: a 'sublime but glaucous sea', in de Gaulle's encapsulation, 'where the fisherman's net hauls up monsters and treasures'. To an extent, as the inter-war revisionists argued, the war was indeed the child of fear and insecurity, born of an international system based on armed and sovereign states, in which the developing nineteenth-century forces of democratization and economic integration failed to eclipse the balance of power system. All the European powers contributed to the growth of tension in the pre-1914 decade. None the less, the fundamental contention of the Versailles 'war-guilt' article was justified, and the work of writers such as Albertini and Fischer has confirmed it. The rulers of Austria–Hungary and Germany did not predetermine before 1914 their decision to resort to force, but in the July–August crisis they made a decision to start a Balkan war and to accept the risk that it would escalate into a European one. Certainly both governments felt threatened, but for neither was this much of a mitigating circumstance. Although the Austrians were exasperated with Serbia, they greatly overestimated the threat it posed to them, and to have accepted its qualified acquiescence in their ultimatum would have been a more than adequate response to the challenge that the Sarajevo assassinations undoubtedly posed. As for the Germans, though they were diplomatically isolated and made potentially vulnerable by the evolution of the land arms race, no evidence exists that Russia, France, or Britain intended to attack them, even if the military balance moved still further in favour of the Entente. Provided the Germans maintained adequate land and naval defence forces, there was no risk to their territory, and alternatives to war as a solution to their predicament had not been exhausted. But the quality of decision-making in Berlin was execrable: the Schlieffen-Moltke Plan appeared to offer a possible technical solution to the Reich's political problems, and the memory of 1870, still nurtured through annual commemorations and the cult of Bismarck, had addicted the German leaders to sabre rattling and to military gambles, which had paid off before and might do so again. In this way the war of 1870 contributed to causing that of 1914, as the 1914 war did that of 1939; and if Germany had again won quickly (as it probably would have done if Britain had stayed out) the temptation for further gambles would have been stronger than ever. The most likely consequence would have been a German-dominated Western Europe engaged in constant friction with

Britain and, sooner or later, a hot war between the two powers. Almost certainly the British leaders were right about the threat that a German victory would pose to them, and in believing that this time they could not afford to remain aloof – even if they massively underestimated the price of intervention.

At the root of everything that followed was Germany's decision to march 2 million men westwards across industrial and rural landscapes that had known decades of peace. The shock it caused to other countries was scarcely less than such an event might cause today. By the time the Schlieffen–Moltke plan had failed, hundreds of thousands of young men had been killed or wounded and the German forces had implanted themselves in formidably well-fortified positions on French and Belgian soil. To expel them the Allies possessed neither smart bombs nor cruise missiles, but only citizen armies unprotected by armour and supported by light field artillery firing almost blind with few and unsuitable shells. By the end of 1915 the Central Powers had driven even deeper into Russia, and to the atrocities linked with invasion had added others – gas, submarines, zeppelins – that had convinced their neighbours that no stable peace settlement was possible unless the Germans were brought to defeat. By 1917, following a decision to gamble on unrestricted submarine warfare that reproduced many of the features of that of 1914, they had brought the American government to the same point of view. Yet having once occupied Western and Eastern European territory at such cost Berlin had no intention of relinquishing control (even if it rejected annexation), and a compromise peace was unacceptable both because of the domestic impact on the Hohenzollerns' autocratic system and because of the risks to Germany's external security in an international environment that its own actions had made ever more menacing.

Three other factors were crucial in the escalation phase of the war. On the level of grand strategy the Allies failed to translate their superiority in resources into comparable battlefield effectiveness, at least until 1916; on the tactical level neither side yet possessed the technology (notably in the spheres of mechanization and airpower) that would enable much faster decisions in future conflicts; and governments on both sides were able to prevail on their soldiers and civilians not just to accept the war but actively to support and participate in it. If the Allies were unable to bring overwhelming strength to bear against Germany and Austria-Hungary, so conversely were the Germans unable, despite concentrating against Russia in 1915, and against France in 1916, and against Britain in 1917, to sunder the bonds that held their opponents together. The middle phase from winter 1914 to spring 1917 was a terrible apprenticeship in modern conflict, being both an international and a general struggle (as the American Civil War, the Franco-Prussian War, and the Russo-Japanese War had not been) between two highly industrialized coalitions of comparable strength. Nothing like it had been seen before, as contemporaries knew only too well, and by the time of the immense attrition battles of 1916 it had plumbed unimagined depths of horror and destruction. It was also true that no one was in overall control, in Clausewitz's basic sense that neither side could dictate the responses of the other and both played wild cards. Yet if it is misleading to view the war as accidental or unintended in its origins, so it is mistaken to see its prolongation and escalation as a phenomenon independent of human agency. On the contrary, the campaigns and battles that claimed so many lives were set in motion by the deliberate decisions of commanders who mostly enjoyed political consent; and the alternative of negotiated peace was repeatedly rejected by both sides. It is at best a half-truth to say that neither the Allies nor the Central Powers 'wanted' war in 1914 and that neither wanted it to continue thereafter. Certainly neither relished hostilities but both were willing to accept them in preference to the alternatives. Each winter new strategic assessments were undertaken, and each summer new peace feelers were rejected; and as the casualty tolls mounted so it became harder to liquidate the conflict without commensurate gains to show for the sacrifice. As a contemporary caricaturist pointed out, the opposing leaders found themselves like so many Macbeths, 'in blood stept in so far that should I wade no more, returning were as tedious as go o'er'.

In 1917, however, with the Russian Revolution and American intervention, the war passed into a third phase, though its character was not fully transformed until 1918. Strategically, the Western and Italian Fronts became a single, central theatre; politically the struggle became more polarized; operationally, a series of tactical and technological revolutions came to fruition. It has been convincingly argued that the key to the Central Powers' defeat was the crumbling of the German army,[30] but that crumbling was linked to a combination of antecedent factors, including OHL's own mistakes. Second only to the Germans' folly in starting the war in the first place was the blunder of unrestricted submarine warfare, without which they could almost certainly have disengaged on much more favourable terms; but the Ludendorff offensives, too, condemned them to worse conditions than might have been achieved by an offer to the Allies of a return to the *status quo ante* in autumn 1917. The failure of the offensives did more than anything else to break the German army's spirit (and to plunge it into an insurmountable crisis of manpower), and for all the undoubted gain in Allied fighting prowess a German defeat could otherwise have been postponed for at least another year. Yet both the submarine decision and the 'Michael' attack were responses to the Allies' slow strategic squeeze – and particularly in the first case to the coordinated offensives of the summer of 1916 and in the second to the impending prospect of massive American intervention. In the end attrition from earlier campaigning, AEF troop shipments, British and French military successes, blockade, and the breakthrough against Bulgaria all contributed to the breakdown of German morale and discipline, and to Ludendorff's fit of panic that brought the house crashing down. However, military and political factors must be woven together to understand the cause and timing of the Central Powers' collapse. America's intervention as an 'associated power' made it easier to overcome the impasse between the two sides' war aims, both by appearing to scale down Allied objectives and by offering the Germans a golden bridge for their exit from the conflict, even if their hopes of using Washington to cut their losses were eventually to be disappointed.

As for the final question of the war's longer-term legacy, this was most obvious in the first decade after 1918. It is hard now to appreciate how overwhelming an event and how crushing in its aftermath the conflict must have seemed. Not only did the struggle over the peace treaties dominate European politics and diplomacy for two decades, but the war – and the ensuing Franco-German cold war – led to financial and monetary chaos and to massive disruption of trade, output, and employment.

On a more general level, victors and vanquished alike emerged with wounded societies, weighed down by hundreds of thousands of maimed and bereaved and by ruinous commitments to reconstruction and rehabilitation. Even so, the post-war decade eventually bore impressive witness to Europe's recuperative powers, until in the early 1930s a tragic concatenation of circumstances brought on a new crisis, as economic catastrophe and the rise of the Nazi movement coincided with the retreat of the former victors into deepening disunity, isolationism, and pacifism. Hence they missed the chance to act in the brief interval when Hitler might have been contained without a major war, before belatedly standing firm against him. None of this means that the First World War was a complete and sufficient cause of the Second as opposed to being a necessary precondition, but its repercussions stacked the dice against a lasting peace, and a combination of good fortune with exceptional statesmanship was needed to secure one. Neither condition materialized.

The 1914–18 conflict has long possessed a sombre reputation for horror and futility, matched in the West only by the American intervention in Vietnam. In fact, despite imperialist accretions the Allies' central cause was neither trivial nor unworthy. The expulsion of German forces was a genuine liberation for the occupied territories, and the destruction of Wilhelm II's autocracy created an opportunity, albeit fleeting, for a more firmly rooted peace than had existed before 1914. Moreover, by the end the victors had accomplished, if painfully slowly, many of the indispensable ingredients – industrial mobilization, strategic co-ordination, command of the sea and air – that would bring them success in later conflicts. Although these were not minor achievements, in retrospect they seemed overshadowed by the cost, especially when the war to end wars proved not to have eliminated international insecurity after all. Yet now that decades of historical research have stripped away the encrustations of hindsight and better enabled us to see the struggle as it appeared to the contemporaries who waged it, the governments seem more purposive, the armed forces more adaptive, and the ordinary soldiers and civilians more willing and informed participants than once was thought. These changes of perspective have made it easier to understand both how the massacre could happen and why it was so difficult to stop. Their danger is they may obscure the deeper insight that the war was still a tragedy, a vast and avoidable waste that Woodrow Wilson, for all his limitations, rightly condemned as an indictment of the political structures that had produced it. Even so, it may seem now that the decades-long cycle of confrontation and violence that the conflict initiated has finally drawn to an end. The struggles between mass citizen armies that ran from the later nineteenth to the later twentieth centuries and of which the First World War was a supreme example have almost certainly become a thing of the past. In another decade, when we approach the centenary of these events, they will be as remote from us as – in 1914 – were the Napoleonic battles whose centenaries had just been commemorated.[31] Yet since the end of the Soviet-American Cold War the spectacle of real, shooting, hot war has become not less but much more frequent and familiar, forcing the present generation to revisit age-old arguments about the legitimacy of using force in international politics. It might seem easiest to adopt the absolute pacifist position – that in no circumstances can force ever be justified – were it not for the evidence that inaction may lead to even greater evils. Yet any decision for war must confront the historical evidence that it is a fearfully blunt instrument, the repercussions of whose use cannot reliably be predicted and which may make matters even worse. Intrinsic to all military undertakings, however legitimate their motives, is the risk that they will violate the principle of proportionality between ends and means, and that they too will lead to a bad war and a bad peace. The 1914–18 conflict and the settlement that followed it remain archetypes of both, and the insights to be gained from studying them have a universal applicability, if only as a distant but a forceful warning. It is too soon yet for us to lose the catch in the throat or the shiver in the spine at the sound of Wilfred Owen's bugles calling from sad shires or in the resonance at twilight by the Menin Gate.

BIBLIOGRAPHY

This bibliography has no pretensions to be comprehensive. For reasons of space, its main purpose is to specify the sources referred in the endnotes, although a few other standard works have been included. References are therefore to the edition consulted rather than the first edition. For works in languages other than English, where an English translation exists it has normally been cited in preference to the original.

Acton, E., *Rethinking the Russian Revolution* (London 1990).

Adams, R. J. Q., *Arms and the Wizard: Lloyd George and the Ministry of Munitions, 1915–1916* (London, 1978).

Adams, R. J. Q., and Poirier, P., *The Conscription Controversy in Great Britain, 1900–1918* (Basingstoke and London, 1987).

Afflerbach, H., *Falkenhayn: Politisches Denken und Handeln im Kaiserreich* (Munich, 1996).

_____ 'Planning Total War? Falkenhayn and the Battle of Verdun', in Chickering and Förster (eds.), *Great War, Total War*.

Albert, A., *Latin America and the First World War: the Impact of the War on Brazil, Argentina, Peru, and Chile* (Cambridge, 1988).

Albertini, L., *The Origins of the War of 1914* (3 vols., London, 1952–7).

Albrecht-Carrié, R., *Italy at the Paris Peace Conference* (New York, 1938).

Aldcroft, D. H., *From Versailles to Wall Street, 1919–1929* (London, 1977).

Allain, J.-C., *Agadir 1911: une crise impérialiste en Europe pour la conquête du Maroc* (Paris, 1976).

_____ *Joseph Caillaux* (Vol. 2, Paris, 1981).

Andrew, C. M., *Secret Service: the Making of the British Intelligence Community* (London, 1985).

Andrew, C. M., and Kanya-Forstner, A. S., 'France, Africa, and the First World War', *Journal of African History* (1978).

Andrew, C. M., and Kanya-Forstner, A. S., *France Overseas: the Great War and the Climax of French Imperial Expansion* (London, 1981).

Andrews, E. M., *The Anzac Illusion: Anglo-Australian Relations during World War I* (Cambridge, 1993).

Angell, N., *The Great Illusion: a Study of the Relation of Military Power in Nations to their Economic and Social Advantage* (London, 1914).

Artaud, D., 'Le Gouvernement américain et la question des dettes de guerre au lendemain de l'armistice de Rethondes (1919–1920)', *Revue d'histoire moderne et contemporaine* (1973).

Ashton, N. J., 'Hanging the Kaiser: Anglo-Dutch Relations and the Fate of Wilhelm II, 1918–1920', *Diplomacy and Statecraft* (2000).

Ashworth, T., *Trench Warfare, 1914–1918: the Live and Let Live System* (London and Basingstoke, 1980).

Aspinall-Oglander, C. F., *Military Operations: Gallipoli* (Vol. 2, London, 1937).

Asprey, R., *The German High Command at War: Hindenburg and Ludendorff and the First World War* (London, 1994).

Asquith, H. H., *Memories and Reflections, 1852–1927* (2 vols., London, 1928).

Audouin-Rouzeau, S., '"Bourrage de crâne" et information en France en 1914–18', in Becker and Audouin-Rouzeau (eds.), *Les sociétés européennes*.

_____ *Men at War, 1914–1918: National Sentiment and Trench Journalism in France during the First World War* (Providence, RI, and Oxford, 1992).

_____ *La Guerre des enfants, 1914–1918* (Paris, 1993).

_____ 'Children and the Primary Schools of France, 1914–1918', in Horne (ed.), *State, Society, and Mobilization.*

Audouin-Rouzeau, S., and Becker, A., *14–18, Retrouver la guerre* (Paris, 2000).

Babington, A., *Shell-Shock: A History of the Changing Attitudes towards War Neurosis* (London, 1997).

Bailey, J., 'The First World War and the Birth of the Modern Style of Warfare' (Occasional Paper, Camberley, 1996).

Bailey, S., 'The Berlin Strike of January 1918', *Central European History* (1980).

Baker, R. S., *Woodrow Wilson and World Settlement* (3 vols., London, 1923).

Balderston, T., 'War Finance and Inflation in Britain and Germany, 1914–1918', *Economic History Review* (1989).

Barbeau, A., and Florette, H., *The Unknown Soldiers: Black American Troops in World War I* (Philadelphia, 1974).

Barbusse, H. *Under Fire* (London, 1965).

Barker, A. J., *The Neglected War: Mesopotamia, 1914–1918* (London, 1967).

Barnett, C., *The Swordbearers: Supreme Command in the First World War* (London, 2000).

Barnhart, M. A., *Japan and the World since 1868* (London, 1995).

Barraclough, G., *From Agadir to Armageddon: Anatomy of a Crisis* (London, 1982).

Barral, P., 'La paysannerie française à l'arrière', in Becker and Audouin-Rouzeau (eds.), *Les sociétés européennes.*

Bauer, M., *Der Grosse Krieg im Feld und Heimat: Erinnerungen und Betrachtungen* (Tübingen, 1921).

Baumgart, W., *Deutsche Ostpolitik, 1918: Von Brest-Litovsk bis zum Ende des Ersten Weltkrieges* (Vienna and Munich, 1966).

Baumgart, W., and Repgen, K. (eds.), *Brest-Litovsk* (Göttingen, 1969).

Becker, A., *War and Faith: the Religious Imagination in France, 1914–1930* (Oxford and New York, 1998).

Becker, J.-J., *1914: Comment les Français sont entrés dans la guerre* (Paris, 1977).

_____ 'Union sacrée et idéologie bourgeoise', *Revue historique* (1980).

_____ *The Great War and the French People* (Leamington Spa, Heidelberg, and Dover, NH, 1985).

Becker, J.-J., and Audouin-Rouzeau, S. (eds.), *Les Sociétés européennes et la guerre de 1914–1918* (Paris, 1990).

Beckett, I. F. W., 'The Real Unknown Army: British Conscripts, 1916–1919', in Becker and Audouin-Rouzeau (eds.), *Les Sociétés européennes.*

_____ 'Operational Command: the Plans and the Conduct of Battle', in Liddle (ed.), *Passchendaele in Perspective.*

_____ *The Great War, 1914–1918* (Harlow, 2001).

Beesly, P., *Room 40: British Naval Intelligence, 1914–18* (London, 1982).

Bell, A. C., *A History of the Blockade of Germany and of the Countries Associated with Her in the Great War, Austria-Hungary, Bulgaria, and Turkey* (London, 1937: published 1961).

Beller, S., 'The Tragic Carnival: Austrian Culture in the First World War' in Roshwald and Stites (eds.), *European Culture.*

Ben-Moshe, T., 'Churchill's Strategic Conception during the First World War', *Journal of Strategic Studies* (1989).

Berghahn, V. R., *Germany and the Approach of War in 1914* (Basingstoke, 1995).

Bernède, A., 'Third Ypres and the Restoration of Confidence in the Ranks of the French Army', in Liddle (ed.), *Passchendaele in Perspective.*

Berov, L., 'The Bulgarian Economy during World War I', in Király and Dreisziger (eds.), *East Central European Society.*

Berti, G., and del Negra, P. (eds.), *Al di qua e al di là del Piave: l'Ultimo Anno della Grande Guerra* (Milan, 2001).

Bésier, G., 'Les Églises protestantes en Allemagne, en Grande-Bretagne, en France, et le front intérieur (1914–1918)' in Becker and Audouin-Rouzeau (eds.), *Les sociétés européennes.*

Beskrovnyi, L. G., *Armiya i Flot Rossii v Nachale XX V: Ocherki Voenno-Ekonomicheskovo Potentsiala* (Moscow, 1986).

Bessell, R., *Germany after the First World War* (Oxford, 1993).

_____ 'Mobilization and Demobilization in Germany', in Horne (ed.), *State, Society, and Mobilization.*

Best, G. F. A., *Humanity in Warfare: The Modern History of the International Law of Armed Conflicts* (London, 1980).

Bethmann Hollweg, T. von, *Betrachtungen zum Weltkriege* (2 vols., Berlin, 1919).

Bidwell, S., and Graham, D., *Fire-Power: British Army Weapons and Theories of War, 1904–1945* (London, 1982).

Birnbaum, K. E., *Peace Moves and U-Boat Warfare: A Study of Imperial Germany's Policy towards the United States, April 18 1916–January 9 1917* (Uppsala, 1958).

Bliss, M., 'War Business as Usual: Canadian Munitions Production, 1914–1918' in Dreisziger (ed.), *Mobilization for Total War.*

Bloch, I., *The Future of War in its Technical, Economic, and Political Relations* (Boston, 1899).

Blunden, E., *Undertones of War* (London, 1982).

Bobroff, R., 'Devolution in Wartime: Sergei D. Sazonov and the Future of Poland, 1910–1916', *International History Review* (2000).

Boemeke, M., *et al.* (eds.), *The Treaty of Versailles: a Reassessment after 75 Years* (Washington and Cambridge, 1998).

Bogacz, T., '"A Tyranny of Words": Language, Poetry, and Antimodernism in England in the First World War', *Journal of Modern History* (1986).

_____ 'War Neurosis and Cultural Change in England: the Work of the War Office Committee of Enquiry into "Shell-Shock"', *Journal of Contemporary History* (1989).

Boll, F., 'Le Problème ouvrier et les grèves: l'Allemagene, 1914–1918', in Becker and Audouin-Rouzeau (eds.), *Les sociétés européennes*.

Bond, B. (ed.), *The First World War and British Military History* (Oxford, 1991).

_____ 'Passchendaele: Verdicts Past and Present', in Liddle (ed.), *Passchendaele in Perspective*.

_____ *The Unquiet Western Front: Britain's Role in Literature and History* (Cambridge, 2002).

Bond, B., and Cave, N. (eds.), *Haig: a Reappraisal 70 Years On* (Barnsley, 1999).

Bonwetsch, B., *Kriegsallianz und Wirtschaftsinteressen: Russland in den Wirstschaftsplänen Englands und Frankreichs, 1914–1917* (Düsseldorf, 1973).

Bonzon, T., 'The Labour Market and Industrialization', in Winter and Robert (eds.), *Capital Cities at War*.

_____ 'Transfer Payments and Social Policy', in Winter and Robert (eds.), *Capital Cities at War*.

Bonzon, T., and Davis, B., 'Feeding the Cities', in Winter and Robert (eds.), *Capital Cities at War*.

Borg, A., *War Memorials: from Antiquity to the Present* (London, 1991).

Bosanquet, N., 'Health Systems in Khaki: the British and American Medical Experience', in Cecil and Liddle (eds.), *Facing Armageddon*.

Boswell, J., and Johns, B., 'Patriots or Profiteers? British Businessmen and the First World War', *Journal of European Economic History* (1992).

Bosworth, R. J. B., *Italy the Least of the Great Powers: Italian Foreign Policy before the First World War* (Cambridge, 1979).

Bourbon, S. de, *L'Offre de paix séparée de l'Autriche (5 décembre 1916–12 octobre 1917)* (Paris, 1920).

Bourke, J., *Dismembering the Male: Men's Bodies, Britain, and the Great War* (London, 1996).

_____ *An Intimate History of Killing: Face-to-Face Killing in Twentieth-Century Warfare* (London, 1999).

Bourne, J. M., *Britain and the Great War, 1914–1918* (London, 1989).

_____ 'The British Working Men in Arms', in Cecil and Liddle (eds.), *Facing Armageddon*.

Bowley, A. L., *Some Economic Consequences of the Great War* (London, 1930).

Bracco, R. M., *Merchants of Hope: British Middlebrow Writers and the First World War, 1919–1939* (Providence, RI, and Oxford 1993).

Bradley, J., *Allied Intervention in Russia* (London, 1968).

Braybon, G., *Women Workers in the First World War: the British Experience* (London, 1981).

Bridge, F. R., *From Sadowa to Sarajevo: the Foreign Policy of Austria-Hungary, 1866–1914* (London, 1972).

_____ *The Habsburg Monarchy among the Great Powers, 1815–1918* (Leamington Spa, 1990).

Brittain, V., *Testament of Youth: an Autobiographical Study of the Years 1900–1925* (London, 1978).

Brock, M. and E. (eds.), *H. H. Asquith: Letters to Venetia Stanley* (Oxford, 1985).

Brose, E. D., *The Kaiser's Army: the Politics of Military Technology in Germany during the Machine Age, 1870–1918* (Oxford, 2001).

Brown, I. M., 'Not Glamorous but Effective: the Canadian Corps and the Set-Piece Attack, 1917–1918', *Journal of Military History* (1994).

_____ *British Logistics on the Western Front, 1914–1919* (Westport, CT, and London, 1998).

Brown, J. M., and Louis, W. R. (eds.), *The Oxford History of the British Empire*. Vol. IV: *The Twentieth Century* (Oxford and New York, 1999).

Brown, M., and Seaton, S., *Christmas Truce: the Western Front, December 1914* (London, 1999).

Bruntz, G. G., *Allied Propaganda and the Collapse of the German Empire in 1918* (Stanford, 1938).

Brusilov, A. A., *Mémoires du Général Brusilov: Guerre 1914–1918* (Paris, 1929).

Bucholz, A., *Moltke, Schlieffen, and Prussian War Planning* (New York, 1991).

Buitenhuis, P., *The Great War of Words: Literature as Propaganda 1914–18 and After* (London, 1989).

Bunselmeyer, R. E., *The Cost of the War, 1914–1919: British Economic War Aims and the Origins of Reparation* (Hamden, CT, 1975).

Burchardt, L., 'The Impact of the War Economy on the Civilian Population of Germany during the First and Second World Wars', in Deist (ed.), *German Military*.

Burgwyn, J. H., *The Legend of the Mutilated Victory: Italy, the Great War, and the Paris Peace Conference, 1915–1919* (Chapel Hill, 1976).

Burk, K., 'J. M. Keynes and the Exchange Rate Crisis of July 1917', *Economic History Review* (1979).

_____ 'The Mobilization of Anglo-American Finance during World War I' in Dreisziger (ed.), *Mobilization for Total War*.

_____ (ed.), *War and the State: the Transformation of British Government, 1914–1919* (London, 1982).

_____ 'The Treasury: from Impotence to Power', in Burk (ed.), *War and the State*.

_____ *Britain, America, and the Sinews of War, 1914–1918* (Boston, London, and Sydney, 1985).

Burke, E., 'Moroccan Resistance, Pan-Islam, and German War Strategy, 1914–1918', *Francia* (1975).

Burkhardt, J., *et al.* (eds.), *Lange und Kurze Wege in den Ersten Weltkrieg* (Munich, 1996).

Burnett, P. M., *Reparation at the Paris Peace Conference (from the Standpoint of the American Delegation)* (2 vols., New York, 1940).

Buse, D. K., 'Domestic Intelligence and German Military Leaders, 1914–18', *Intelligence and National Security* (2000).

Bushaway, B., 'Name upon Name: the Great War and Remembrance', in Porter (ed.), *Myths of the English* (Cambridge, 1992).

Calder, K. J., *Britain and the Origins of the New Europe, 1914–1918* (Cambridge, 1976).

Campbell, N. J. M., *Jutland: an Analysis of the Fighting* (Annapolis, 1986).

Carsten, F. L., *Revolution in Central Europe, 1918–1919* (London, 1972).

Cassar, G. H., *The French and the Dardanelles: a Study of Failure in the Conduct of War* (London, 1971).

_____ *The Tragedy of Sir John French* (Newark, NJ, 1985).

Ceadel, M., *Pacifism in Britain, 1914–1945: the Defining of a Faith* (Oxford, 1980).

Cecco, M. de, *Money and Empire: the International Gold Standard* (London, 1984).

Cecil, H., and Liddle, P. H. (eds.), *Facing Armageddon: The First World War Experienced* (London, 1996).

_____ (eds.), *At the Eleventh Hour: Reflections, Hopes, and Anxieties at the Closing of the Great War, 1918* (Barnsley, 1998).

Chapman, G., *A Passionate Prodigality: Fragments of Autobiography* (Greenwich, CT 1967).

Charmley, J., *Splendid Isolation? Britain, the Balance of Power, and the Origins of the First World War* (London, 1999).

Chi, M., *China Diplomacy, 1914–1918* (Cambridge, MA, 1970).

Chickering, R., *Imperial Germany and the Great War, 1914–1918* (Cambridge, 1998).

Chickering, R., and Förster, S. (eds.), *Great War, Total War: Combat and Mobilization on the Western Front, 1914–1918* (Cambridge, 2000).

Childs, D. J., *A Peripheral Weapon? The Production and Employment of British Tanks in the First World War* (Westport, CT, and London, 1999).

Churchill, W. S. L., *The World Crisis* (6 vols., London, 1923–31).

Clark, A., *The Donkeys* (London, 1991).

Clark, C., *Kaiser Wilhelm II* (Harlow, 2000).

Clarke, I. F., *Voices Prophesying War, 1763–1984* (London, 1966).

Clausewitz, C. von, *On War*, (eds.) M. E. Howard and P. Paret (Princeton, NJ, 1976).

Cochet, A., 'Les Soldats français', in Becker and Audouin-Rouzeau (eds.), *Les Sociétés européennes*.

Coetzee, F., and Shevin-Coetzee, M. (eds.), *Authority, Identity, and the Social History of the Great War* (Providence, RI, and Oxford, 1995).

Coffman, E. M., *The War to End All Wars: the American Military Experience in World War I* (Lexington, KY, 1998).

Cohen, D., *The War Come Home: Disabled Veterans in Britain and Germany, 1914–1939* (Berkeley, Los Angeles, and London, 2001).

Cohen, S. A., 'The Genesis of the British Campaign in Mesopotamia, 1914', *Middle Eastern Studies* (1976).

Consett, M. W. P., *The Triumph of Unarmed Forces (1914–1918)* (London, 1923).

Contarmine, H., *La Victoire de la Marne: 9 septembre 1914* (Paris, 1970).

Coogan, J. W., *The End of Neutrality: the United States, Britain, and Maritime Rights, 1899–1915* (Ithaca, NY, and London, 1981).

Coogan, J. W. and P. F., 'The British Cabinet and the Anglo-French Staff Talks, 1905–1914: Who Knew What and When did He Know It?', *Journal of British Studies* (1985).

Cooper, J. M., Jr., *The Vanity of Power: American Isolationism and the First World War, 1914–1917* (Westport, CT, 1969).

_____ 'The Command of Gold Reversed: American Loans to Britain, 1915–1917', *Pacific Historical Review* (1976).

_____ *The Warrior and the Priest: Woodrow Wilson and Theodore Roosevelt* (Cambridge, MA, and London, 1983).

Cooper, M., *The Birth of Independent Air Power: British Air Policy in the First World War* (London, Boston, and Sydney, 1986).

Cornwall, M. (ed.), *The Last Years of Austria-Hungary: Essays in Political and Military History, 1908–1918* (Exeter, 1990).

_____ 'The Dissolution of Austria-Hungary' in Cornwall (ed.), *Last Years*.

_____ 'News, Rumour, and the Control of Information in Austria-Hungary, 1914–1918', *History* (1992).

_____ *The Undermining of Austria-Hungary: the Battle for Hearts and Minds* (Basingstoke, 2000).

Craig, G. A., *Germany, 1866–1945* (Oxford, 1978).

Craig, L. A., and Fisher, D. F., *The Integration of the European Economy, 1850–1913* (New York, 1996).

Crampton, R. J., *The Hollow Détente: Anglo-German Relations in the Balkans, 1911–1914* (London, 1979).

_____ *Bulgaria, 1878–1918: a History* (New York, 1983).

Crosby, A. W., Jr., *Epidemic and Peace, 1918* (Westport, CT, and London, 1976).

Cruickshank, J., *Variations on Catastrophe: Some French Responses to the Great War* (Oxford, 1982).

Cruttwell, C. R. M. F., *A History of the Great War, 1914–1918* (London, 1982).

Curami, A., 'L'Industria bellica italiana dopo Caporetto', in Berti and del Negra (eds.), *Piave*.

Curry, R. W., *Woodrow Wilson and Far Eastern Policy, 1913–1921* (New York, 1968).

Czernin, O., *In the World War* (London, 1919).

Dalisson, R., 'La Célébration du 11 novembre ou l'enjeu de la mémoire combattante dans l'entre-deux-guerres (1918–1939)', *Guerres mondiales et conflits contemporains* (1998).

Dallin, A., *et al.*, *Russian Diplomacy and Eastern Europe, 1914–1917* (New York, 1963).

Daniel, U., 'Women's Work in Industry and Family: Germany, 1914–1918', in Wall and Winter (eds.), *The Upheaval of War.*

_____ *The War from Within: German Working-Class Women in the First World War* (Oxford and New York, 1997).

Daunton, M., 'How to Pay for the War: State, Society, and Taxation in Britain, 1917–1929', *English Historical Review* (1996).

Davidian, I., 'The Russian Soldier's Morale from the Evidence of Military Censorship', in Cecil and Liddle (eds.), *Facing Armageddon.*

Davis, B., 'Food Scarcity and the Empowerment of the Female Consumer in World War I Berlin', in de Grazia and Furlough (eds.), *The Sex of Things: Gender and Consumption in Historical Perspective* (Berkeley, Los Angeles, and London, 1996).

_____ *Home Fires Burning: Food, Politics and Everyday Life in World War One Berlin* (Chapel Hill, 2000).

Dawn, C. Ernest, 'The Influence of T. E. Lawrence on the Middle East', in Meyers (ed.), *T. E. Lawrence.*

Dawson, G., 'Preventing 'a great moral evil': Jean de Bloch's *The Future of War* as Anti-Revolutionary Pacifism', *Journal of Contemporary History* (2002).

Dayer, R. A., 'Strange Bedfellows: J. P. Morgan & Co., Whitehall, and the Wilson Administration during World War I', *Business History Review* (1976).

Deák, I., 'The Habsburg Army in the First and Last Days of World War I: a Comparative Analysis', in Király and Dreisziger (eds.), *East Central European Society.*

Deakin, W., 'Imperial Germany and the "Holy War" in Africa, 1914–1918', Leeds University pamphlet (n.d.).

Debo, R. K., *Revolution and Survival: the Foreign Policy of Soviet Russia, 1917–1918* (Toronto, 1979).

Dedijer, V., *The Road to Sarajevo* (New York, 1966).

Deist, W. (ed.), *The German Military in the Age of Total War* (Leamington Spa and Dover, NH, 1985).

_____ 'Die Politik der Seekriegsleitung und die Rebellion der Flotte Ende Oktober 1918', *Vierteljahrshefte für Zeitgeschichte* (1966).

_____ 'Censorship and Propaganda in Germany during the First World War' in Becker and Audouin-Rouzeau (eds.), *Les Sociétés européennes.*

_____ 'The Military Collapse of the German Empire', *War in History* (1996).

Devlin, P. A., *Too Proud to Fight: Woodrow Wilson's Neutrality* (London, 1974).

Dewey P. E., 'Food Production and Policy in the United Kingdom, 1914–1918', *Transactions of the Royal Historical Society* (1980).

_____ 'Military Recruiting and the British Labour Force during the First World War', *Historical Journal* (1984).

Dickinson, F. R., *War and National Reinvention: Japan in the Great War* (Cambridge, MA, 1999).

Diehl, J. M., 'Victors or Victims? Disabled Veterans in the Third Reich', *Journal of Modern History* (1987).

Divine, R. A., *The Illusion of Neutrality* (Chicago and London, 1962).

Djordjević, D., 'Vojvoda Putnik, the Serbian High Command, and Strategy in 1914', in Király and Dreisziger (eds.), *East Central European Society.*

Dockrill, M. L., and French, D. (eds.)., *Strategy and Intelligence: British Policy during the First World War* (London and Rio Grande, OH, 1996).

Dockrill, M. L., and Goold, D. J., *Peace Without Promise: Britain and the Peace Conferences, 1919–1923* (London, 1981).

Doerries, R. R., 'Promoting Kaiser and Reich: Imperial German Propaganda in the United States during World War I', in Schroeder (ed.), *Confrontation and Cooperation.*

Dogliani, M., 'Les Monuments aux morts de la Grande guerre en Italie', *Guerres mondiales et conflits contemporains* (1992).

Doise, J., and Vaïsse, M., *Diplomatie et outil militaire* (Paris, 1987).

Doyle, P., and Bennett, M. R., 'Military Geography: Terrain Evaluation and the British Western Front, 1914–1918', *Geographical Journal* (1997).

Doyle, P., and Bennett, M. R., 'Military Geography: the Influence of Terrain in the Outcome of the Gallipoli Campaign, 1915', *Geographical Journal* (1999).

Dreisziger, N. F., *Mobilization for Total War: the Canadian, American, and British Experience, 1914–1918, 1939–1945* (Waterloo, Ontario, 1981).

Düllfer, J., *Regeln gegen den Krieg? Die Haager Friedenskonferenzen von 1899 und 1907 in der internationalen Politik* (Frankfurt, 1981).

Düllfer, J., and Holl, K. (eds.), *Bereit zum Krieg: Kriegsmentalität in Wilhelmischen Deutschland, 1890–1914* (Göttingen, 1986).

Düllfer, J., *et al.* (ed.), *Vermiedene Kriege: Deeskalation von Konflikten der Grossmächte zwischen Krimkrieg und Erstem Weltkrieg (1856–1914)* (Munich, 1997).

Dülmen, R. von, 'Der Deutsche Katholizismus und der Erste Weltkrieg', *Francia* (1974).

Duppler, J., and Gross, G. P. (eds.), *Kriegsende 1918: Ereignis, Wirkung, Nachwirkung* (Munich, 1994).

Duroselle, J.-B., *La France et les Français, 1914–1920* (Paris, 1972).

_____ *La Grande Guerre des français, 1914–1918: l'incompréhensible* (Paris, 1994).

Dutton, D., 'Paul Painlevé and the End of the Sacred Union in Wartime France', *Journal of Strategic Studies* (1981).

_____ *The Politics of Diplomacy: Britain and France in the Balkans in the First World War* (London and New York, 1998).

Dyer, C., *The Missing of the Somme* (London, 1994).

Dyer, G., 'The Turkish Armistice of 1918', *Middle Eastern Studies* (1972).

_____ 'Turkish "Falsifiers" and Armenian "Deceivers": the Historiography of the Armenian Massacres', *Middle Eastern Studies* (1976).

Eberle, M., *World War I and the Weimar Artists: Dix, Grosz, Beckman, Schlemmer* (New Haven, 1985).

Eckart, W. U., '"The Most Extensive Experiment That the Imagination Can Conceive": War, Emotional Stress, and German Medicine, 1914–1918', in Chickering and Förster (eds.), *Great War, Total War*.

Eckart, W. U., and Gradmann, C. (eds.), *Die Medizin und der Erste Weltkrieg* (Pfaffenweiler, 1996).

Egerton, G. W., *Great Britain and the Creation of the League of Nations: Strategy, Politics, and International Organization, 1914–1919* (Chapel Hill, 1978).

Eichengreen, B., *Golden Fetters: the Gold Standard and the Great Depression, 1919–1939* (New York and Oxford, 1992).

Eichengreen, B., and Flandreau, M. (eds.), *The Gold Standard in Theory and History* (New York, 1997).

Eksteins, M., *Rites of Spring: The Great War and the Birth of the Modern Age* (London, 1990).

Ellinwood, D. C., and Pradham, S. D. (eds.), *India and World War I* (New Delhi, 1978).

Elliott, C. J., 'The *Kriegervereine* and the Weimar Republic', *Journal of Contemporary History* (1975).

Emin, A., *Turkey in the World War* (New Haven and London, 1930).

Engel, B. A., 'Not by Bread Alone: Subsistence Riots in Russia during World War I', *Journal of Modern History* (1997).

Englander, D., 'Die Demobilmachung in Grossbritannien nach dem Ersten Weltkrieg', *Geschichte und Gesellschaft* (1983).

_____ 'The French Soldier, 1914–1918' *French History* (1987).

Englander, D., and Osborne, J., 'Jack, Tommy, and Henry Dubb', *Historical Journal* (1978).

Epkenhans, M., *Die Wilhelminischen Flottenrüstung, 1908–1914: Weltmachtstreben, industrieller Fortschritt, soziale Integration* (Munich, 1991).

Epstein, K., *Matthias Erzberger and the Dilemma of German Democracy* (Princeton, NJ, 1959).

Evans, R. J. W., and Pogge von Strandman, H. (eds.), *The Coming of the First World War* (Oxford, 1986).

Falkenhayn, E. von, *General Headquarters 1914–16 and its Critical Decisions* (London, 1919).

Falls, C., *The First World War* (London, 1960).

_____ *Caporetto 1917* (London, 1965).

Farr, M., 'A Compelling Case for Voluntarism: Britain's Alternative Strategy, 1915–1916', *War in History* (2001).

Farrar, L. L., Jr., *The Short-War Illusion: German Policy, Strategy, and Domestic Affairs, August–December 1914* (Santa Barbara, CA, 1973).

_____ 'Opening to the West: German Efforts to Conclude a Separate Peace with England, July 1917–March 1918', *Canadian Journal of History* (1975).

_____ *Divide and Conquer: German Efforts to Conclude a Separate Peace, 1914–1918* (New York, 1978).

_____ 'Nationalism in Wartime: Critiquing the Conventional Wisdom' in Coetzee and Shevin-Coetzee (eds.), *Authority, Identity, and the Social History of the Great War*.

Farrar, M. M., *Conflict and Compromise: the Strategy, Politics, and Diplomacy of the French Blockade, 1914–1918* (The Hague, 1974).

Farwell, B., *The Great War in Africa, 1914–1918* (London, 1987).

Feinstein, C. H, Temin, P., and Toniolo, G., *The European Economy between the Wars* (Oxford, 1997).

Feldman, G. D., *Army, Industry, and Labour in Germany, 1914–1918* (Princeton, NJ, 1966).

_____ *German Imperialism, 1914–1918: the Development of a Historical Debate* (New York, 1972).

_____ *The Great Disorder: Politics, Economy, and Society in the German Inflation, 1914–1924* (New York and Oxford, 1993).

Ferguson, N., 'Public Finance and National Security: the Domestic Origins of the First World War Revisited', *Past & Present* (1994).

_____ *Paper and Iron: Hamburg Business and German Politics in the Era of Inflation, 1897–1927* (Cambridge, 1995).

_____ 'Constraints and Room for Manoeuvre in the German Inflation of the Early 1920s', *Economic History Review* (1996).

_____ *The Pity of War* (London, 1998).

_____ *Empire: How Britain Made the Modern World* (London, 2003).

Ferris, J. (ed.), *The British Army and Signals Intelligence during the First World War* (Stroud, 1992).
_____ 'Airbandit: C^{3}I and Strategic Air Defence during the First Battle of Britain, 1915–18', in Dockrill and French (eds.), *Strategy and Intelligence*.
Ferro, M., 'Le Soldat russe en 1917: indiscipline, patriotisme, pacifisme et révolution', *Annales* (1971).
_____ *The Great War, 1914–1918* (London, 1973).
Fiebig von Hase, R., 'Der Anfang vom Ende des Krieges: Deutschland, die USA, und die Hintergründe des Amerikanischen Kriegseintritts am 6. April 1917', in Michalka (ed.), *Erste Weltkrieg*.
Fieldhouse, D. K., *Economics and Empire, 1830–1914* (London, 1973).
Fifield, R. H., *Woodrow Wilson and the Far East: the Diplomacy of the Shantung Question* (New York, 1952).
Figes, O., *A People's Tragedy: the Russian Revolution, 1891–1924* (London, 1997).
Fischer, C., *Stormtroopers: A Social, Economic and Ideological Analysis, 1919–35* (London, 1983).
Fischer, F., *Germany's Aims in the First World War* (London, 1967).
_____ *War of Illusions: German Policies from 1911 to 1914* (London, 1975).
_____ 'Twenty-Five Years Later: Looking Back at the "Fischer Controversy" and its Consequences', *Central European History* (1988).
Flood, P. J., *France, 1914–1918: Public Opinion and the War Effort* (Basingstoke, 1990).
Floto, I., *Colonel House in Paris: a Study of American Policy at the Paris Peace Conference, 1919* (Aarhus, 1973).
Foch, F., *Mémoires pour servir à l'histoire de la guerre de 1914–1918* (Vol. 2, Paris, 1931).
Foley, R., 'East or West? Erich von Falkenhayn and German Strategy, 1914–15' in Hughes and Seligman (eds.), *Leadership in Conflict*.
_____ 'The Origins of the Schlieffen Plan', *War in History* (2003).
Fong, G., 'The Movement of German Divisions to the Western Front, Winter 1917–1918' *War in History* (2000).
Förster, J., 'Der deutsche Generalstab und die Illusion des kurzen Krieges, 1871–1914: Metakritik eines Mythos', *Militärgeschichtliche Mitteilungen* (1995).
Förster, S., *Der Doppelte Militarismus: die Deutsche Heeresrüstung zwischen Status-Quo-Sicherung und Aggression, 1890–1913* (Stuttgart, 1985).
_____ 'Facing "People's War": Moltke the Elder and Germany's Military Options after 1871', *Journal of Strategic Studies* (1987).
Forsyth, D. J., *The Crisis of Liberal Italy: Monetary and Financial Policy, 1914–1922* (Cambridge, 1993).
Foster, J., 'Working-Class Mobilization on the Clyde, 1917–1920', in Wrigley (ed.), *Challenges of Labour*.
Fowler, W. B., *British-American Relations, 1917/1918: the Role of Sir William Wiseman* (Princeton, NJ, 1969).
Fraser, T. G., 'Germany and Indian Revolution, 1914–18', *Journal of Contemporary History* (1977).
French, D., 'Spy Fever in Britain, 1900–1915', *Historical Journal* (1978).
_____ 'The Military Background to the "Shell Crisis" of May 1915', *Journal of Strategic Studies* (1979).
_____ 'The Origins of the Dardanelles Campaign Reconsidered', *History* (1983).
_____ *British Strategy and War Aims, 1914–1916* (London, 1986).
_____ 'The Dardanelles, Mecca, and Kut: Prestige as a Factor in British Eastern Strategy, 1914–1916', *War and Society* (1987).
_____ 'The Meaning of Attrition, 1914–1916', *English Historical Review* (1988).
_____ 'Watching the Allies: British Intelligence and the French Mutinies of 1917', *Intelligence and National Security* (1991).
_____ *The Strategy of the Lloyd George Coalition, 1916–1918* (Oxford, 1995).
_____ 'Failures of Intelligence: the Retreat to the Hindenburg Line and the March 1918 Offensive', in Dockrill and French (eds.), *Strategy and Intelligence*.
_____ '"Had We Known How Bad Things Were in Germany, We Might Have Got Stiffer Terms"': Great Britain and the Armistice', in Boemeke *et al.* (eds.), *Treaty of Versailles*.
Frey, M., 'Bullying the Neutrals: the Case of the Netherlands', in Chickering and Förster (eds.), *Great War, Total War*.
Fridenson, P. (ed.), *The French Home Front, 1914–1918* (Providence, RI, and Oxford, 1992).
Friedman, I., *The Question of Palestine, 1914–1918: British-Jewish-Arab Relations* (London, 1973).
_____ *Palestine: a Twice-Promised Land? The British, the Arabs, and Zionism, 1915–1920* (New Brunswick, NJ, and London, 2000).
Fuller, J. G., *Troop Morale and Popular Culture in the British and Dominion Armies, 1914–1918* (Oxford, 1990).
Fuller, W. C., *Civil-Military Conflict in Imperial Russia, 1881–1914* (Princeton, NJ, 1985).
_____ 'The Eastern Front', in Winter, Parker, and Habeck (eds.), *Great War*.
Fussell, P., *The Great War and Modern Memory* (New York and London, 1975).
Gabriel, R. A., and Metz, K. S., *A History of Military Medicine* (2 vols., Westport, CT, and London, 1992).
Galántai, J., *Hungary in the First World War* (Budapest, 1989).
Galbraith, J. S., 'No Man's Child: the Campaign in Mesopotamia, 1914–1918', *International History Review* (1984).
Garson, N. G., 'South Africa and World War One', *Journal of Imperial and Commonwealth History* (1979).
Gatrell, P., *Government, Industry, and Rearmament in Russia, 1900–1914: the Last Argument of Tsarism* (Cambridge, 1994).

_____ *A Whole Empire Walking: Refugees in Russia during World War I* (Bloomington and Indianopolis, IN, 1999).

Gatzke, H. W., *Germany's Drive to the West: A Study of Western War Aims during the First World War* (Baltimore, 1950).

Geiss, I., *Der Polnische Grenzstreifen, 1914–1918: ein Beitrag zur Deutschen Kriegszielpolitik im Ersten Weltkrieg* (Lübeck and Hamburg, 1960).

_____ (ed.), *July 1914: the Outbreak of the First World War* (London, 1967).

Gelfand, L. E., *The Inquiry: American Preparations for Peace, 1917–1919* (New Haven, 1963).

Gemzell, C.-A., *Organization, Conflict, and Innovation: a Study of German Naval Strategic Planning, 1880–1940* (Lund, 1973).

Geyer, D., *Russian Imperialism: the Interaction of Domestic and Foreign Policy, 1860–1914* (Leamington Spa, 1987).

Geyer, M., *Deutsche Rüstungspolitik, 1866–1980* (Frankfurt, 1984).

Gilbert, B. B., 'Pacifist to Interventionist: David Lloyd George in 1911 and 1914. Was Belgium an Issue?', *Historical Journal* (1985).

Gilbert, C., *American Financing of World War I* (Westport, CT, 1970).

Gilbert, M., *The First World War* (London, 1995).

Gill, D., and Dallas, G., 'Mutiny at Etaples Base in 1917', *Past & Present* (1975).

Gill, D., and Dallas, G., *The Unknown Army: Mutinies in the British Army in World War I* (London, 1985).

Glover, J., and Silkin, J. (eds.), *The Penguin Book of First World War Prose* (Harmondsworth, 1990).

Godfrey, J. D., *Capitalism at War: Industrial Policy and Bureaucracy in France, 1914–1918* (Leamington Spa, Hamburg, and New York, 1987).

Goemans, H. E., *War and Punishment: The Causes of War Termination and the First World War* (Princeton, NJ, 2000).

Goldberg, J., 'The Origins of British-Saudi Relations: the 1915 Anglo-Saudi Treaty Revisited', *Historical Journal* (1985).

Goldrick, J., *The King's Ships Were at Sea: the War in the North Sea, August 1914–February 1915* (Annapolis, 1984).

Goldstein, E., and Maurer, J. (eds.), *The Washington Conference, 1921–22: Naval Rivalry, East Asian Stability, and the Road to Pearl Harbor* (London and Portland, OR, 1994).

Gooch, J., 'The Maurice Debate, 1918', *Journal of Contemporary History* (1968).

_____ *The Prospect of War: Studies in British Defence Policy, 1847–1942* (London, 1981).

_____ 'Italy in the First World War', in Millett and Murray (eds.), *Military Effectiveness*.

_____ 'Morale and Discipline in the Italian Army, 1915–1918', in Cecil and Liddle (eds.), *Facing Armageddon*.

Goold, D. J., 'Lord Hardinge and the Mesopotamian Expedition and Inquiry, 1914–1917', *Historical Journal* (1976).

Gorce, P.-M. de la, *La République et son armée* (Paris, 1963).

Gordon, A., *The Rules of the Game: Jutland and British Naval Command* (London, 1996).

Gorman, L., 'The Anciens Combattants and Appeasement: from Munich to War', *War and Society* (1992).

Gottlieb, W. W., *Studies in Secret Diplomacy during the First World War* (London, 1957).

Grant, R. M., *U-Boats Destroyed: The Effects of Anti-Submarine Warfare, 1914–1918* (London, 1964).

Graves, R., *Goodbye to All That* (London, 1960).

Gregory, A., *The Silence of Memory: Armistice Day, 1919–1946* (Providence, RI, and Oxford, 1994).

Greenhalgh, E., 'Why the British were on the Somme in 1916', *War in History* (1999).

_____ 'Flames over the Somme: a Retort to William Philpott', *War in History* (2003).

Grieves, K., *The Politics of Manpower, 1914–1918* (Manchester, 1988).

_____ 'C. E. Montague and the Making of Disenchantment, 1914–1921', *War and History* (1997).

Griffith, P., *Battle Tactics of the Western Front: the British Army's Art of Attack, 1916–18* (New Haven and London, 1994).

_____ (ed.), *British Fighting Methods in the Great War* (London and Portland, OR, 1996).

Grigg, J., *Lloyd George: War Leader* (London, 2001).

Groh, D., 'The "Unpatriotic Socialists" and the State', *Journal of Contemporary History* (1966).

Groot, G. de, *Douglas Haig, 1868–1928* (London, 1980).

_____ *The First World War* (New York, 2001).

Gudmundsson, B. I., *Stormtroop Tactics: Innovation in the German Army, 1914–1918* (Westport, CT, and London, 1989).

Guinard, P., Devos, J.-C., and Nicot, J., *Inventaire sommaire des Archives de la Guerre, Série N: 1872–1919*, Vol. 1 (Troyes, 1975).

Guinn, P., *British Strategy and Politics, 1914–1918* (Oxford, 1965).

Gullace, N., 'Sexual Violence and Family Honour: British Propaganda and International Law during the First World War', *American Historical Review* (1997).

_____ 'White Feathers and Wounded Men: Female Patriotism and the Memory of the Great War', *Journal of British Studies* (1997).

Haber, L. F., *The Poisonous Cloud: Chemical Warfare in the First World War* (Oxford, 1986).

Hall, R. C., *The Balkan Wars, 1912–1913: Prelude to the First World War* (London, 2000).

Halpern, P. G., *A Naval History of World War I* (London, 1994).

Hamard, B., 'Quand la victoire s'est gagnée aux Balkans: l'assaut de l'armée alliée d'orient de septembre à novembre 1918', *Guerres mondiales et conflits contemporains* (1996).

Hamilton, I., *Gallipoli Diary* (2 vols., London, 1920).

Hamilton, R. F., and Herwig, H. H., (eds.), *The Origins of World War I* (Cambridge, 2003).

Hammer, K., 'Der Deutsche Protestantismus und der Erste Weltkrieg', *Francia* (1974).

Hanak, H., 'The Union of Democratic Control during the First World War', *Bulletin of the Institute of Historical Research* (1963).

Hankey, M. P. A. H., *The Supreme Command, 1914–1918* (2 vols., London, 1961).

Hanna, M., *The Mobilization of Intellect: French Scholars and Writers during the Great War* (Cambridge, MA, 1996).

Hardach, G., *The First World War, 1914–1918* (London, 1977).

_____ 'Industrial Mobilization in 1914–1918: Production, Planning, and Ideology', in Fridenson (ed.), *French Home Front.*

Harris, J. P., *Men, Ideas, and Tanks: British Military Thought and Armed Forces, 1903–1939* (Manchester and New York, 1995).

Harris, J. P., and Barr, N., *Amiens to the Armistice: the BEF in the Hundred Days' Campaign, 8 August–11 November 1918* (London and Washington, 1998).

Harris, R., 'The "Child of the Barbarian": Rape, Race, and Nationalism in France during the First World War', *Past & Present* (1993).

Harrison, M., 'The Fight against Disease in the Mesopotamian Campaign', in Cecil and Liddle (eds.), *Facing Armageddon.*

_____ (ed.), *The Economics of World War II: Six Great Powers in International Comparison* (Cambridge, 1998).

Hartcup, G., *The War of Invention: Scientific Developments, 1914–18* (London, 1988).

Harvey, A. D., *A Muse of Fire: Literature, Art, and War* (London and Rio Grande, OH, 1998).

Hasegawa, T., *The February Revolution: Petrograd 1917* (Seattle and London, 1981).

Haupt, G., *Socialism and the Great War: the Collapse of the Second International* (Oxford, 1972).

Hautmann, H., 'Vienna: a City in the Years of Radical Change, 1917–20', in Wrigley (ed.), *Challenges of Labour.*

Hayne, M. B., *The French Foreign Office and the Origins of the First World War, 1898–1914* (Oxford, 1993).

Hazelhurst, C., *Politicians at War, July 1914 to May 1915: a Prologue to the Triumph of Lloyd George* (London, 1971).

Heinemann, U., *Die Verdrängte Niederlage: Politische Öffentlichkeit und Kriegsschuldfrage in der Weimarer Republik* (Göttingen, 1983).

Heller, J., 'Sir Louis Mallet and the Ottoman Empire: the Road to War', *Middle Eastern Studies* (1976).

Helmreich, E. C., *The Diplomacy of the Balkan Wars, 1912–1913* (New York, 1969).

Helmreich, J. E., *Belgium and Europe: a Study in Small Power Diplomacy* (The Hague, 1976).

Helmreich, P. C., *From Paris to Sèvres: the Partition of the Ottoman Empire at the Peace Conference of 1919–1920* (Columbus, OH, 1974).

Henniker, A. M., *Transportation on the Western Front, 1914–1918* (London, 1937).

Herrmann, D. G., *The Arming of Europe and the Making of the First World War* (Princeton, NJ, 1996).

Herwig, H. H., 'German Policy in the Eastern Baltic Sea in 1918: Expansion or Anti-Bolshevik Crusade?', *Slavic Review* (1973).

_____ 'The Dynamics of Necessity: German Military Policy during the First World War', in Millett and Murray, (eds.), *Military Effectiveness.*

_____ *The First World War: Germany and Austria-Hungary, 1914–1918* (London and New York, 1997).

_____ 'Clio Deceived: Patriotic Self-Censorship in Germany after the First World War', in Wilson (ed.), *Forging the Collective Memory.*

_____ 'Total Rhetoric, Limited War: Germany's U-Boat Campaign, 1917–1918', in Chickering and Förster (eds.), *Great War, Total War.*

Herwig, H. H., and Trask, D. F., 'The Failure of Imperial Germany's Undersea Offensive against World Shipping, February 1917–October 1918', *The Historian* (1970–1971).

Heuser, B., *Reading Clausewitz* (London, 2002).

Hewitson, M., 'Germany and France before the First World War: a Reassessment of German Foreign Policy', *English Historical Review* (2000).

Hiley, N., 'The News Media and British Propaganda, 1914–18', in Becker and Audouin-Rouzeau (eds.), *Les sociétés européennes.*

Hindenburg, P. von, *Aus Meinem Leben* (Leipzig, 1920)/*Out of My Life* (London, 1933).

Hinsley, F. H., *Power and the Pursuit of Peace: Theory and Practice in the History of Relations between States* (Cambridge, 1963).

Hoag, J., 'Students at the University of Vienna in the First World War', *Central European History* (1984).

Hobsbawm, E. J., *Age of Extremes: the Short Twentieth Century, 1914–1991* (London, 1995).

Holland, R., 'The British Empire and the Great War, 1914–1918', in Brown and Louis (eds.), *The Oxford History of the British Empire.* Vol. IV: *The Twentieth Century* (Oxford and New York, 1999).

Holmes, R., *The Little Field Marshal: Sir John French* (London, 1981).

_____ 'The Last Hurrah: Cavalry on the Western Front, August–September 1914', in Cecil and Liddle (eds.), *Facing Armageddon*.

Holmes, T., 'The Reluctant March on Paris', *War in History* (2001).

Hoover, A. J., *God, Germany, and Britain in the Great War: a Study in Clerical Nationalism* (Westport, CT, and London, 1989).

Hopkin, D., 'Domestic Censorship in the First World War', *Journal of Contemporary History* (1970).

Hopwood, R. F., 'Czernin and the Fall of Bethmann Hollweg', *Canadian Journal of History* (1967).

Horn, D. (ed.), *War, Mutiny, and Revolution in the German Navy: the World War I Diary of Seaman Richard Stumpf* (New Brunswick, NJ, 1967).

_____ *Mutiny on the High Seas: the Imperial German Naval Mutinies of World War I* (London, 1973).

Horn, M., 'The Concept of Total War: National Effort and Taxation in Britain and France during the First World War', *War and Society* (2000).

_____ *Britain, France, and the Financing of the First World War* (Montreal and Kingston, Ont., 2002).

Horne, A., *The Price of Glory: Verdun, 1916* (Harmondsworth, 1978).

Horne, J., 'L'Impôt du sang: Republican Rhetoric and Industrial Warfare in France, 1914–18', *Social History* (1989).

_____ *Labour at War: France and Britain, 1914–1918* (Oxford, 1991).

_____ 'The State and the Challenge of Labour in France, 1917–20', in Wrigley (ed.), *Challenges of Labour*.

_____ 'Soldiers, Civilians, and the Warfare of Attrition: Representations of Combat in France, 1914–1918', in Coetzee and Shevin-Coetzee (eds.), *Authority, Identity, and the Social History of the Great War*

_____ *State, Society, and Mobilization in Europe during the First World War* (Cambridge, 1997).

Horne, J., and Kramer, A., 'German "Atrocities" and Franco-German Opinion, 1914: the Evidence of German Soldiers' Diaries', *Journal of Modern History* (1994).

_____ *German Atrocities, 1914: A History of Denial* (New Haven and London, 2001).

Houston, D. F., *Eight Years with Wilson's Cabinet (1913–1920)* (2 vols., London 1926).

Hovanissian, R. G., *Armenia on the Road to Independence, 1918* (Berkeley and Los Angeles, 1967).

_____ (ed.), *The Armenian Genocide: History, Politics, Ethics* (Basingstoke and London, 1992).

Howard, M. E., 'Men against Fire: Expectations of War in 1914', *International Security* (1984).

_____ *The Invention of Peace: Reflections on War and International Order* (London, 2001).

_____ *The First World War* (Oxford, 2002).

Howorth, J., 'French Workers and German Workers: the Impossibility of Internationalism, 1900–1914', *European History Quarterly* (1985).

Hughes, J., 'The Battle for the Hindenburg Line', *War and Society* (1999).

Hughes, M., *Nationalism and Society: Germany, 1800–1945* (London, 1988).

_____ *Allenby and British Strategy in the Middle East, 1917–1919* (London and Portland, OR, 1999).

Hughes, M., and Seligman, M. (eds.), *Leadership in Conflict, 1914–1918* (Barnsley, 2000).

Hüppauf, B., 'Langemarck, Verdun, and the Myth of a New Man in Germany after the First World War', *War and Society* (1988).

Hurewitz, J. C. (ed.), *Diplomacy in the Near and Middle East: a Documentary Record* (2 vols., Princeton, NJ, 1956).

Hürter, H., 'Die Katholische Kirche im Ersten Weltkrieg', in Michalka (ed.), *Erste Weltkrieg*.

Hürter, J., *Paul von Hintze: Marineoffizier, Diplomat, Staatssekretär. Dokumente einer Karriere zwischen Militär und Politik, 1903–1918* (Munich, 1998).

Hussey, J., 'The Movement of German Divisions to the Western Front, Winter 1917–1918', *War in History* (1997).

_____ 'The Flanders Battleground and the Weather in 1917', in Liddle (ed.), *Passchendaele in Perspective*.

Hynes, S., *A War Remembered: the First World War and English Culture* (London, 1990).

_____ *The Soldier's Tale: Bearing Witness to Modern War* (London, 1998).

Inglis, K. S., 'War Memorials: Ten Questions for Historians', *Guerres mondiales et conflits contemporains* (1992).

_____ 'World War One Memorials in Australia', *Guerres mondiales et conflits contemporains*.

Jaffe, L. S., *The Decision to Disarm Germany: British Policy towards Post-war German Disarmament, 1914–1919* (London, 1985).

Jahn, H. F., *Patriotic Culture in Russia during World War I* (Ithaca, NY, and London, 1995).

Jansen, M. B., *The Japanese and Sun Yat-sen* (Cambridge, MA, 1954).

Janssen, K. H., 'Der Wechsel in der Obersten Heeresleitung 1916', *Vierteljahrshefte für Zeitgeschichte* (1959).

_____ *Macht und Verblendung: Kriegszielpolitik der deutschen Bundesstaaten, 1914/18* (Göttingen, 1963).

_____ *Der Kanzler und der General. Die Führungskrise um Bethmann und Falkenhayn (1914–1916)* (Göttingen, 1967).

Jarausch, K. H., *The Enigmatic Chancellor: Bethmann Hollweg and the Hubris of Imperial Germany* (New Haven, 1973).

Jäschke, G., 'Zum Problem der Marne-Schlacht von 1914', *Historische Zeitschrift* (1960).

Jeffery, K., *Ireland and the Great War* (Cambridge, 2000).

Jelavich, B., *Russia's Balkan Entanglements, 1806–1914* (Cambridge, 1991).

Joffre, J-J. C., *Mémoires du Maréchal Joffre, 1910–1917* (2 vols., Paris, 1932).

Joll, J., *The Second International, 1889–1914* (London, 1955).

_____ *The Origins of the First World War* (London, 1984).

Joly, B., 'La France et la revanche (1870–1914)', *Revue d'histoire moderne et contemporaine* (1999).

Jones, D. R., 'Imperial Russia's Forces at War', in Millett and Murray (eds.), *Military Effectiveness*.

Jones, N., *The Origins of Strategic Bombing: a Study of the Development of British Air Strategic Thought and Practice up to 1918* (London, 1973).

Jones, S., 'Antonio Salandra and the Politics of Italian Intervention in the First World War', *European History Quarterly* (1985).

Judah, T., *The Serbs: History, Myth, and the Destruction of Yugoslavia* (New Haven and London, 1997).

Judd, J., *Empire: the British Imperial Experience, 1765 to the Present* (London, 1996).

Jünger, E., *Storm of Steel* (New York, 1985).

Kahn, D., *The Codebreakers: the Story of Secret Writing* (London, 1966).

Kaiser, D. E., 'Germany and the Origins of the First World War', *Journal of Modern History* (1983).

Kajima, M., *The Diplomacy of Japan, 1894–1922* (Vol. 3, Tokyo, 1980).

Kann, R. A., Király, B. K., and Fichtner, P. S. (eds.), *The Habsburg Empire in World War I: Essays on the Intellectual, Military, Political, and Economic Aspects of the Habsburg War Effort* (New York, 1977).

Kanya-Forstner, A. S., 'The War, Imperialism, and Decolonization', in Winter, Parker, and Habeck (eds.), *Great War*.

Karsh, E. and I., 'Myth in the Desert, or Not the Great Arab Revolt', *Middle Eastern Studies* (1997).

Kaspi, A., *Le Temps des Américains: le concours américain à la France en 1917–1918* (Paris, 1976).

Katz, F., *The Secret War in Mexico: Europe, the United States, and the Mexican Revolution* (Chicago and London, 1981).

Kavanagh, G., 'Museum as Memorial: the Origins of the Imperial War Museum', *Journal of Contemporary History* (1988).

Kazamzadeh, F., *The Struggle for Transcaucasia (1917–1921)* (New York and Oxford, 1951).

Kedourie, E., *In the Anglo-Arab Labyrinth: the McMahon–Husayn Correspondence and its Interpretations, 1914–1939* (Cambridge, 1976).

Keegan, J., *The Price of Admiralty* (London, 1988).

_____ 'Jutland', *MHQ: the Quarterly Journal of Military History* (1989).

_____ *The Face of Battle: a Study of Agincourt, Waterloo, and the Somme* (London, 1991).

_____ *The First World War* (London, 1998).

Keene, J. D., *The United States and the First World War* (Harlow, 2000).

Keiger, J. F. V., *France and the Origins of the First World War* (London, 1983).

_____ 'Britain's "Union sacrée" in 1914', in Becker and Audouin-Rouzeau (eds.), *Les Sociétés européennes*.

_____ *Raymond Poincaré* (Cambridge, 1997).

Kenez, P., 'Changes in the Social Composition of the Officer Corps during World War I', *Russian Review* (1972).

Kennedy, D. M., *Over Here: the First World War and American Society* (New York and Oxford, 1980).

Kennedy, G. C., 'Strategy and Supply in the North Atlantic Triangle, 1914–1918' in McKercher and Aronson (eds.), *The North Atlantic Triangle in a Changing World: Anglo-American Relations, 1902–1956* (Toronto, 1996).

_____ (ed.), *The Merchant Marine in International Affairs, 1850–1950* (London, and Portland, OR, 2000).

Kennedy, P. M. (ed.), *The War Plans of the Great Powers* (London, 1979).

_____ *The Rise of the Anglo-German Antagonism, 1860–1914* (London, 1982).

_____ 'Britain in the First World War', in Millett and Murray (eds.), *Military Effectiveness*.

_____ 'Military Effectiveness in the First World War', in Millett and Murray (eds.), *Military Effectiveness*.

_____ *The Rise and Fall of the Great Powers: Economic Change and Military Conflict from 1500 to 2000* (London, 1989).

_____ *The Rise and Fall of British Naval Mastery* (London, 1991).

Kennedy, T. C., 'Public Opinion and the Conscientious Objector, 1915–1919', *The Journal of British Studies* (1973).

Kent, B., *The Spoils of War: the Politics, Economics, and Diplomacy of Reparations, 1918–1932* (Oxford, 1989).

Kent, M. (ed.), *The Great Powers and the End of the Ottoman Empire* (London, 1984).

Kent, S. K., 'Love and Death: War and Gender in Britain, 1914–1918', in Coetzee and Shevin-Coetzee (eds.), *Authority, Identity, and the Social History of the Great War*.

Kenwood, A. G., and Lougheed, A. L., *The Growth of the International Economy, 1820–2000* (London, 1999).

Kernek, S. J., 'The British Government's Reaction to President Wilson's "Peace Note" of December 1916', *Historical Journal* (1970).

Kerner, R. J., 'Russia, the Straits, and Constantinople, 1914–1915', *Journal of Modern History* (1929).

Kershaw, I., *Hitler* (2 vols., Vol. 1. *1889–1936: Hubris*; Vol. 2. *1936–1945: Nemesis*, London, 1998 and 2000).

Keynes, J. M., *The Economic Consequences of the Peace* (London, 1920).

King, J. C., *Generals and Politicians: Conflict between France's Command, Parliament, and Government, 1914–1918* (Berkeley and Los Angeles, 1951).

Király, B. K., and Dreisziger, N. F. (eds.), *East Central European Society in World War I* (New York, 1985).

Kirby, D., 'International Socialism and the Question of Peace: the Stockholm Conference of 1917', *Historical Journal* (1967).

_____ *War, Peace, and Revolution: International Socialism at the Crossroads, 1914–1918* (London, 1986).

Kitchen, M., *The Silent Dictatorship: The Politics of the German High Command under Hindenburg and Ludendorff* (London, 1976).

Kluge, U., *Die Deutsche Revolution 1918/1919: Staat, Politik, und Gesellschaft zwischen Weltkrieg und Kapp-Putsch* (Frankfurt, 1985).

Knock, T. J., *To End All Wars: Woodrow Wilson and the Quest for a New World Order* (New York and Oxford, 1992).

Koch, H. W. (ed.), *The Origins of the First World War* (London, 1972).

Kocka, J., *Facing Total War: German Society, 1914–1918* (Leamington Spa, 1984).

Koenker, D. P., and Rosenberg, W. G., *Strikes and Revolution in Russia, 1917* (Princeton, NJ, 1989).

Komjáthy, M. (ed.), *Protokolle des Gemeinsamen Ministerrates der Österreichischen-Ungarischen Monarchie (1914–1918)* (Budapest, 1966).

Koralka, J., 'Germany's Attitude to the National Disintegration of Cisleithania (April-October, 1918)', *Journal of Contemporary History* (1969).

Koszyk, K., *Deutsche Presse, 1914–1945* (Berlin, 1972).

Kriegel, A., *Aux Origines du Communisme français, 1914–1920* (Paris and The Hague, 1964).

Krizmann, B., 'Austro-Hungarian Diplomacy before the Collapse of the Empire', *Journal of Contemporary History* (1969).

Krumeich, G., 'Le Soldat allemand sur la Somme' in Becker and Audouin-Rouzeau (eds.), *Les Sociétés européennes.*

_____ "Saigner la France"? Mythes et réalité de la stratégie allemande de la bataille de Verdun', *Guerres mondiales et conflits contemporains* (1996).

Kitchen, M., *The Silent Dictatorship: the Politics of the German High Command under Hindenburg and Ludendorff* (London, 1976).

Kühlmann, R. von, *Erinnerungen* (Heidelberg, 1948).

Kurat, Y. T., 'How Turkey Drifted into World War I' in Bourne and Cameron Watt (eds.), *Studies in International History* (London, 1967).

Kuznets, S., 'Quantitative Aspects of the Growth of Nations', *Economic Development and Cultural Change* (1967).

La Fargue, T. E., *China and the World War* (Stanford, 1937).

Lambert, N., *Sir John Fisher's Naval Revolution* (Columbia, SC, 1999).

Lambi, I. N., *The Navy and German Power Politics, 1862–1914* (Boston, 1984).

Langdon, J. W., *July 1914: the Long Debate, 1914–1990* (New York and Oxford, 1991).

Lange, K., *Marneschlacht und Deutsche Öffentlichkeit, 1914–1939: eine verdrängte Niederlage und ihre Folgen* (Düsseldorf, 1974).

Langhorne, R. T. B., *The Collapse of the Concert of Europe: International Politics, 1890–1914* (London, 1981).

The Lansing Papers, 1914–1920 (2 vols., Washington, 1939).

Lasch, C., 'American Intervention in Siberia: a Reinterpretation', *Political Science Quarterly* (1962).

Lasswell, H. D., *Propaganda Technique in the World War* (London and New York, 1927).

Lautenschläger, K., 'Technology and the Evolution of Naval Warfare', *International Security* (1983).

Laux, J. M., "Gnôme et Rhône" – an Aviation Engine Firm in the First World War', in Fridenson, (ed.), *The French Home Front.*

Lawrence, J., 'Material Pressures on the Middle Classes', in Winter and Robert (eds.), *Capital Cities at War.*

Lawrence, J., Dean, M., and Robert, J.-L., 'The Outbreak of War and the Urban Economy: Paris, Berlin, and London in 1914', *Economic History Review* (1992).

Lebow, R. N., 'Agency versus Structure in A. J. P. Taylor's Origins of the First World War', *International History Review* (2001).

Lederer, I. J., *Yugoslavia at the Paris Peace Conference: a Study in Frontier-Making* (New Haven and London, 1963).

Lee, D. E. (ed.), *The Outbreak of the First World War: Who Was Responsible?* (Boston, 1966).

Lee, J., 'Administrators and Agriculture: Aspects of German Agricultural Policy in the First World War', in Winter (ed.), *War and Economic Development.*

Leed, E. J., *No Man's Land: Combat and Identity in World War I* (Cambridge, 1979).

Leese, P., 'Problems Returning Home: The British Psychological Casualties of the Great War', *Historical Journal* (1997).

Lenin, V. I., *Imperialism the Highest Stage of Capitalism* (Beijing, 1975).

Lentin, A., 'The Treaty that Never Was: Lloyd George and the Abortive Anglo-French Alliance of 1919', in Loades (ed.), *The Life and Times of David Lloyd George* (Bangor, 1991).

Lentin, A., 'Several Types of Ambiguity: Lloyd George at the Paris Peace Conference', *Diplomacy and Statecraft* (1995).

Leslie, J., 'The Antecedents of Austria-Hungary's War Aims: Policies and Policy-Makers in Vienna and Budapest before and during 1914', *Wiener Beiträge zur Geschichte der Neuzeit* (1993).

Levin, N. G., Jr., *Woodrow Wilson and World Politics: America's Response to War and Revolution* (New York, 1968).

Levy, J., 'Preferences, Constraints, and Choices in July 1914', *International Security* (1990–91).

_____ 'The Causes of War and the Conditions of Peace', *Annual Review of Political Science* (1998).

Liddell Hart, B., *Foch: the Man of Orléans* (London, 1931).

_____ *History of the First World War* (London, 1972).

Liddle, P. H., *Men of Gallipoli: the Dardanelles and Gallipoli Experience, August 1914 to January 1916* (London, 1976).

_____ *The British Soldier on the Somme, 1916* (Strategic and Combat Studies Institute: Occasional Paper No. 23, 1996).

_____ (ed.), *Passchendaele in Perspective: the Third Battle of Ypres* (London, 1997).

Lieven, D. C. B., *Russia and the Origins of the First World War* (Basingstoke, 1983).

_____ *Nicholas II: Emperor of all the Russias* (London, 1993).

Lih, L. T., *Bread and Authority in Russia, 1914–1921* (Berkeley, Los Angeles, and Oxford, 1990).

Link, A. S, *Wilson: Campaigns for Progressivism and Peace, 1916–1917* (Princeton, NJ, 1965).

Linke, H. E., *Das Zarische Russland und der Erste Weltkrieg: Diplomatie und Kriegsziele, 1914–1917* (Munich, 1982).

Lipgens, W., 'Europäische Einigungsidee 1923–1930 und Briands Europaplan im Urteil der deutschen Akten', *Historische Zeitschrift* (1966).

Liulevicius, V. G., *War Land on the Eastern Front: Culture, National Identity, and German Occupation in World War I* (Cambridge, 2000).

Livesey, A., *The Viking Atlas of World War I* (New York, 1994).

Lloyd George, D., *War Memoirs* (2 vols., London, 1938).

Long, J. W., 'American Intervention in Russia: the North Russian Expedition, 1918–1919', *Diplomatic History* (1982).

Louis, W. R., *Great Britain and Germany's Lost Colonies, 1914–1919* (Oxford, 1967).

Low, A. D., 'The Soviet Hungarian Republic and the Paris Peace Conference', *Transactions of the American Philosophical Society* (1963).

Lowe, C. J., and Dockrill, M. L., *The Mirage of Power: British Foreign Policy, 1914–1922* (3 vols., London, 1972).

Lowe, C. J., and Marzari, F., *Italian Foreign Policy, 1870–1940* (London, 1975).

Lowe, P., *Great Britain and Japan, 1911–1915: a Study of British Far Eastern Policy* (London, 1969).

Lowry, B., *Armistice 1918* (Kent, OH, and London, 1996).

Luckau, A., *The German Delegation at the Paris Peace Conference* (New York, 1941).

Ludendorff, E., *My War Memories, 1914–1918* (2 vols., London, 1919)/*Meine Kriegserinnerungen, 1914–1918* (Berlin, 1919).

_____ *The General Staff and Its Problems* (2 vols., London, 1920).

Luebke, F. C., *Bonds of Loyalty: German-Americans and World War I* (DeKalb, IL, 1974).

Lundberg, P. K., 'The German Naval Critique of the U-Boat Campaign, 1915–1918', *Military Affairs* (1963).

Lundgreen-Nielsen, K., *The Polish Problem at the Paris Peace Conference: a Study of the Great Powers and the Poles* (Odense, 1979).

Lupfer, T. T., 'The Dynamics of Doctrine: the Changes in German Tactical Doctrine during the First World War' (Fort Leavenworth Paper, Fort Leavenworth, KS, 1981).

Lutz, R. H. (ed.), *The Causes of the German Collapse in 1918* (Stanford, 1934).

Lyle, C., 'Jutland, or a Second "Glorious First of June"', *The Mariner's Mirror* (1996).

Lynn, J. A. (ed.), *Feeding Mars: Logistics in Western Europe from the Middle Ages to the Present* (Boulder, San Francisco, and Oxford, 1993).

Lyon, M. B., 'A "Peasant Mob": the Serbian Army on the Eve of the Great War,' *Journal of Military History* (1997).

Lyons, F. S. L., *Internationalism in Europe, 1815–1914* (Leyden, 1963).

Macartney, C. A., *The Habsburg Empire, 1790–1918* (London, 1968).

MacDonald, L., *1914: the Days of Hope* (London, 1989).

_____ *Somme* (London, 1993).

_____ *They Called It Passchendaele: the Story of the Battle of Ypres and of the Men Who Fought in It* (London, 1993).

_____ *1915: the Death of Innocence* (London, 1997).

_____ *Spring 1918: to the Last Man* (London, 1999).

McDonald, D. M., *United Government and Foreign Policy in Russia, 1900–1914* (Cambridge, MA, 1992).

McDougall, W. A., *France's Rhineland Diplomacy, 1914–1924: the Last Bid for a Balance of Power in Europe* (Princeton, NJ, 1978).

McEwen, J. M., 'Brass-Hats" and the British Press during the First World War', *Canadian Journal of History* (1983).

MacFie, A. L., *The End of the Ottoman Empire, 1908–1923* (London and New York, 1998).

MacKenzie, S. P., 'Morale and the Cause: the Campaign to Change the Outlook of Soldiers in the British Expeditionary Force, 1914–1918', *Canadian Journal of History* (1990).

McLean, D., 'Popular Protest and Public Order: Red Clydeside, 1915–1919' in Quinault and Stevenson (eds.), *Popular Protest and Public Order: Six Studies in British History, 1790–1920* (London, 1974).

McLean, R. R., *Royalty and Diplomacy in Europe, 1890–1914* (Cambridge, 2001).

McMillan, J. F., *Housewife or Harlot? The Place of Women in French Society, 1870–1940* (Brighton, 1981).

_____ 'French Catholics: *Rumeurs infames* and the *Union sacrée*, 1914–1918' in Coetzee and Shevin-Coetzee (eds.), *Authority, Identity, and the Social History of the Great War*.

Maier, C. S., *Recasting Bourgeois Europe: Stabilization in France, Germany, and Italy in the Decade after World War I* (Princeton, NJ, 1988).

Major, R. H., *Fatal Partners: War and Disease* (Garden City, NY, 1941).

Malcolm, N., *Bosnia: a Short History* (London and Basingstoke, 1994).

Mamatey, V. S., *The United States and East Central Europe, 1914–1918: a Study in Wilsonian Diplomacy and Propaganda* (Princeton, NJ, 1957).

_____ 'The Union of Czech Political Parties in the Reichsrat, 1916–1918', in Kann, Király, and Fichtner (eds.), *Habsburg Empire*.

Manning, A., 'Wages and Purchasing Power', in Winter and Robert, (eds.), *Capital Cities at War*.

Marchand, A., *Les Chemins de fer de l'Est et la Guerre de 1914–1918* (Paris, 1924).

Marder, A. J., *From the Dreadnought to Scapa Flow: the Royal Navy in the Fisher Era, 1904–1919* (5 vols., London, 1961–70).

_____ 'The Dardanelles Reconsidered: Further Thoughts on the Naval Prelude', in *From the Dardanelles to Oran: Studies of the Royal Navy in War and Peace, 1915–1940* (London, 1974).

Marks, S., *The Ebbing of European Ascendancy: an International History of the World, 1914–1945* (London, 2002).

Marquis, A. G., 'Words as Weapons: Propaganda in Britain and Germany during the First World War', *Journal of Contemporary History* (1978).

Marsland, E., *The Nation's Cause: French, English, and German Poetry of the First World War* (London and New York, 1991).

Martin, G., 'German Strategy and Military Assessments of the American Expeditionary Force (AEF), 1917–8', *War in History* (1994).

Martin, L. W., *Peace Without Victory: Woodrow Wilson and the British Liberals* (New Haven, 1959).

Mawdsley, E., *The Russian Civil War* (Edinburgh, 2000).

Max of Baden, Prince, *Memoirs,* (2 vols., London, 1928).

May, E. R., *The World War and American Isolation, 1914–1917* (New Haven, 1959).

_____ (ed.), *Knowing One's Enemies: Intelligence Assessment before the Two World Wars* (Princeton, NJ, 1984).

Mayer, A. J., *Political Origins of the New Diplomacy, 1917–1918* (New Haven, 1959).

_____ 'Domestic Causes of the First World War', in L. Krieger and F. Stern (eds.), *The Responsibility of Power: Historical Essays in Honor of Hajo Holborn* (New York, 1967).

_____ *Politics and Diplomacy of Peacemaking. Containment and Counter-Revolution at Versailles, 1918–1919* (London, 1968).

_____ *The Persistence of the Old Regime: Europe to the Great War* (London, 1981).

Mayeur, J.-M., 'Le Catholicisme français et la première guerre mondiale', *Francia* (1974).

Meier, K., 'Evangelische Kirche und Erster Weltkrieg', in Michalka (ed.), *Erste Weltkrieg*.

Meigs, M., *Optimism at Armageddon: Voices of American Participants in the First World War* (Basingstoke, 1997).

Melograni, P., *Storia politica della Grande Guerra, 1915–1918* (Bari, 1969).

Merridale, C., *Night of Stone: Death and Memory in Russia* (London, 2000).

Meyer, H. C., *Mitteleuropa in German Thought and Action, 1815–1945* (The Hague, 1955).

Meyers, J. (ed.), *T. E. Lawrence: Soldier, Writer, Legend. New Essays* (Basingstoke and London, 1989).

Meynell, H., 'The Stockholm Conference of 1917', *International Review of Social History* (1960).

Michalka, W. (ed.), *Der Erste Weltkrieg: Wirkung, Wahrnehmung, Analyse* (Munich, 1994).

Michel, B., 'L'Autriche et l'entrée dans la guerre en 1914', *Guerres mondiales et conflits contemporains* (1995).

Michel, M., *L'Appel à l'Afrique: contributions et reactions à l'effort de guerre en A.O.F. (1914–1919)* (Paris, 1982).

_____ 'Mythes et réalités du concours colonial' in Becker and Audouin-Rouzeau, (eds.), *Les Sociétés européennes*.

Middlebrook, M., *The First Day on the Somme* (London, 1971).

_____ *The Kaiser's Battle* (London, 2000).

Miller, S. M., *et al.* (eds.), *Military Strategy and the Origins of the First World War* (Princeton, NJ, 1991).

Millett, A. R., and Murray, W. (eds.), *Military Effectiveness* (3 vols., Winchester, MA, 1988).

Millman, B., 'British Home Defence Planning and Civil Dissent, 1917–1918', *War in History* (1998).

_____ *Managing Domestic Dissent in First World War Britain* (London and Portland, OR, 2000).

_____ 'A Counsel of Despair: British Strategy and War Aims, 1917–18', *Journal of Contemporary History* (2001).

_____ *Pessimism and British War Policy, 1916–1918* (London and Portland, OR, 2001).

Milner, S., *The Dilemmas of Internationalism: French Syndicalism and the International Labour Movement, 1900–1914* (New York, Oxford, and Munich, 1990).

Miquel, P., *Le Chemin des Dames: Enquête sur la plus effroyable hécatombe de la Grande Guerre* (Paris, 1997).

Mitchell, A., *Revolution in Bavaria, 1918–1919: the Eisner Regime and the Soviet Republic* (Princeton, NJ, 1965).

Mitchell, B. R. (ed.), *International Historical Statistics: Europe, 1750–1993* (4th ed., London and Basingstoke, 1998).

Mombauer, A., *Helmuth von Moltke and the Origins of the First World War* (Cambridge, 2001).

_____ *The Origins of the First World War: Controversies and Consensus* (Harlow, 2002).

Mommsen, W. J., 'The Topos of Inevitable War in Germany before 1914', in Berghahn and Kitchen (eds.), *Germany in the Age of Total War* (London, 1981).

_____ 'German Artists, Writers, and Intellectuals and the Meaning of War, 1914–1918', in Horne (ed.), *State, Society, and Mobilization*.

Montant, J.-C., 'L'organisation centrale des services d'informations et de propagande du Quai d'Orsay pendant la Grande Guerre', in Becker and Audouin-Rouzeau (eds.), *Les Sociétés européennes*.

Monticone, A., *Gli Italiani in uniforme 1915/1918: intelletuali, borghesi, i desertori* (Bari, 1972).

Mór-O'Brien, A., 'Patriotism on Trial: the Strike of the South Wales Miners, July 1915', *Welsh History Review* (1984).

Moran, Lord, *The Anatomy of Courage* (London, 1945).

Morley, J. W., *The Japanese Thrust into Siberia, 1918* (New York, 1957).

Morrow, J. H., Jr., *German Air Power in World War I* (Lincoln, NE, and London, 1982).

_____ *The Great War in the Air: Military Aviation from 1909 to 1921* (Washington and London, 1993).

Morton, D., 'Junior but Sovereign Allies: the Transformation of the Canadian Expeditionary Force, 1914–1918', *Journal of Imperial and Commonwealth History* (1979).

Mosier, J., *The Myth of the Great War: a New Military History of World War One* (London, 2001).

Mosse, G. E., *Fallen Soldiers: Reshaping the Memory of the World Wars* (New York and Oxford, 1990).

Murray, W., *War in the Air, 1914–45* (London, 1999).

Nagler, J., 'German Imperial Propaganda and the American Homefront in World War I: a Response to Reinhard R Doerries', in Schroeder (ed.), *Confrontation and Cooperation*.

Neilson, K., 'Kitchener: a Reputation Refurbished?', *Canadian Journal of History* (1980).

_____ *Strategy and Supply: the Anglo-Russian Alliance, 1914–1917* (London, 1984).

_____ 'Reinforcements and Supplies from Overseas: British Strategic Sealift in the First World War', in Kennedy (ed.), *Merchant Marine*.

Nelson, H. I., *Land and Power: British and Allied Policy on Germany's Frontiers, 1916–1919* (London, 1963).

Nenninger, T. K., 'American Military Effectiveness in the First World War', in Millett and Murray (eds.), *Military Effectiveness*.

Nevakivi, J., *Britain, France, and the Arab Middle East, 1914–1920* (London, 1969).

Newell, J., 'Learning the Hard Way: Allenby in Egypt and Palestine, 1917–1919', *Journal of Strategic Studies* (1991).

Nicolson, H., *Peacemaking, 1919* (London, 1937).

Nish, I. H., *Alliance in Decline: a Study in Anglo-Japanese Relations, 1908–1923* (London, 1972).

_____ *Japanese Foreign Policy, 1869–1942: Kasumigaseki to Miyakezaku* (London, 1977).

Norton Cru, J., *Du Témoignage* (Paris, 1997).

Nowak, K. F. (ed.), *Die Aufzeichnungen des Generalmajors Max Hoffmann* (2 vols., Berlin, 1930).

Offer, A., *The First World War: an Agrarian Interpretation* (Oxford, 1989).

_____ 'Going to War in 1914: a Matter of Honour?', *Politics and Society* (1995).

Olson, M., Jr., *The Economics of the Wartime Shortage: a History of British Food Supplies in the Napoleonic Wars and in World Wars I and II* (Durham, NC, 1963).

Omissi, D., *The Sepoy and the Raj: the Indian Army, 1860–1940* (Basingstoke and London, 1994).

_____ (ed.), *Indian Voices of the Great War: Soldiers' Letters, 1914–18* (Basingstoke, 1999).

Oncken, E., *Panthersprung nach Agadir: die Deutsche Politik während der Zweiten Marokkokrise 1911* (Düsseldorf, 1981).

Overy, R. J., *Why the Allies Won* (London, 1995).

Page, M. E. (ed.), *Africa and the First World War* (Basingstoke, 1987).

Palazzo, A., *Seeking Victory on the Western Front: the British Army and Chemical Warfare in World War I* (Lincoln, NE, and London, 2000).

Papagannis, N., 'Collaboration and Pacifism in France during World War I', *Francia* (1977).

Parsons, E. B., 'Why the British Reduced the Flow of American Troops to Europe in August–October 1918', *Canadian Journal of History* (1977).

Paschall, R., *The Defeat of Imperial Germany, 1917–1918* (New York, 1994).

Patterson, A., Temple, *Jellicoe: a Biography* (London, 1969).

Pearson, R., *The Russian Moderates and the Crisis of Tsarism, 1914–1917* (London, 1977).

Pedersen, S., 'Gender, Welfare, and Citizenship in Britain during the Great War', *American Historical Review* (1990).

_____ *Family, Dependence, and the Origins of the Welfare State: Britain and France, 1914–1945* (Cambridge, 1993).

Pedroncini, G., *Les Mutineries de 1917* (Paris, 1967).

_____ *Les Négociations secrètes pendant la Grande Guerre* (Paris, 1969).

_____ *Pétain: Général en chef, 1917–1918* (Paris, 1974).

Perman, D., *The Shaping of the Czechoslovak State: Diplomatic History of the Boundaries of Czechoslovakia, 1914–1920* (Leiden, 1962).

Peschaud, M., *Politique et fonctionnement des transports par chemin de fer pendant la guerre* (Paris, 1926).

Pethybridge, R., *The Spread of the Russian Revolution: Essays on 1917* (London, 1972).

Petrovich, M. B., *A History of Modern Serbia, 1804–1918* (2 vols., New York and London, 1976).

Philpott, W., 'Britain and France go to War: Anglo-French Relations on the Western Front, 1914–1918', *War in History* (1995).

_____ *Anglo-French Relations and Strategy on the Western Front, 1914–1918* (London, 1996).

_____ 'Squaring the Circle: the Higher Co-ordination of the Entente in the Winter of 1915–16', *English Historical Review* (1999).

_____ 'Marshal Ferdinand Foch and Allied Victory', in Hughes and Seligman, (eds.), *Leadership in Conflict*.

_____ 'Why the British were Really on the Somme: a Reply to Elizabeth Greenhalgh', *War in History* (2001).

Picht, C., 'Zwischen Vaterland und Volk. Das Deutsche Judentum im Ersten Weltkrieg', in Michalka (ed.), *Erste Weltkrieg*.

Pick, D., *War Machine: the Rationalisation of Slaughter in the Modern Age* (New Haven, 1993).

Pierrefeu, J. de, *GQG Secteur I: trois ans au Grand Quartier Général; par le rédacteur du 'communiqué'* (2 vols., Paris, 1920).

Pipes, R., *The Russian Revolution, 1899–1919* (London, 1999).

Plaschke, R. G., 'The Army and Internal Conflict in the Austro-Hungarian Empire, 1918', in Király and Dreisziger (eds.), *East Central European Society*.

Poidevin, R., and Bariéty, J., *Les Relations franco-allemandes, 1815–1975* (Paris, 1977).

Poincaré, R. N. L., *Au Service de la France. Neuf années de souvenirs* (10 vols., Paris, 1926–33).

Pope, S., and Wheal, E.-A., *The Macmillan Dictionary of the First World War* (London and Basingstoke, 1995).

Porch, D., 'The Marne and After: a Reappraisal of French Strategy in the First World War', *Journal of Military History* (1989).

_____ 'The French Army in the First World War', in Millett and Murray (eds.), *Military Effectiveness*.

Porter, B., *The Lion's Share: a Short History of British Imperialism, 1850–1955* (London, 1996).

Prete, R. A., '*Imbroglio par excellence*: Mounting the Salonika Campaign, September–October 1915', *War and Society* (2001).

Prior, R., and Wilson, T., *Command on the Western Front: the Military Career of Sir Henry Rawlinson, 1914–1918* (Oxford, 1992).

Prior, R., and Wilson, T., *Passchendaele: the Untold Story* (New Haven and London, 1996).

Procacci, G., 'A "Latecomer" in War: the Case of Italy', in Coetzee and Shevin-Coetzee (eds.), *Authority, Identity, and the Social History of the Great War*.

Prost, A., *Les Anciens combattants et la société française, 1914–1939* (3 vols., Paris, 1977).

_____ 'Die Demobilmachung, der Staat, und die Kriegsteilnehmer in Frankreich', *Geschichte und Gesellschaft* (1983).

_____ 'Verdun', in Nora, P., (ed.), *Les Lieux de la mémoire*: Vol. 2 (Paris, 1986).

_____ *In the Wake of War: 'Les anciens combattants' and French Society, 1914–1939* (Providence, RI, and Oxford, 1992).

_____ 'Monuments to the Dead', in Kritzmann, L. de, *Realms of Memory: the Construction of the French Past*, Vol. 1 (New York, 1997).

Pugh, M., 'Politicians and the Woman's Vote, 1914–1918', *History* (1974).

_____ *The Making of Modern British Politics, 1867–1939* (Cambridge, MA, and Oxford, 1993).

Rachamimov, A., *POWs and the Great War: Captivity on the Eastern Front* (Oxford and New York, 2002).

Rae, J., *Conscience and Politics* (London, 1970).

Raithel, T., *Das 'Wunder' des inneren Einheit: Studien zur deutschen und französischen Öffentlichkeit bei Beginn des Ersten Weltkrieges* (Bonn, 1996).

Ranft, B., 'The Royal Navy and the War at Sea', in Turner (ed.), *Britain and the First World War*.

Rauchensteiner, M., *Der Tod des Doppeladlers: Österreich-Ungarn und der Erste Weltkrieg* (Graz, 1993).

Rawling, B., *Surviving Trench Warfare: Technology and the Canadian Corps, 1914–1918* (Toronto, Buffalo, and London, 1992).

Reeves, N., 'Film Propaganda and its Audience: the Example of Britain's Official Films during the First World War', *Journal of Contemporary History* (1983).

_____ *Official British Film Propaganda during the First World War* (London, 1986).

Reid, A., 'The Impact of the First World War on British Workers', in Wall and Winter (eds.), *The Upheaval of War*.

Rémond, R., 'Les Anciens combattants et la politique', *Revue française de science politique* (1955).

Remarque, E. M., *All Quiet on the Western Front* (London, 1996).

Renouvin, P., *The Forms of War Government in France* (New Haven, 1927).

_____ 'Le Gouvernement français et les tentatives de paix en 1917', *La Revue des Deux Mondes* (1964).

_____ *L'Armistice de Rethondes, 11 novembre 1918* (Paris 1968).

_____ *La Crise européenne et la première guerre mondiale (1904–1918)* (Paris, 1969).

Renzi, W. A., 'Who Composed Sazonov's "Thirteen Points"? A Re-examination of Russia's War Aims of 1914', *American Historical Review* (1983).

_____ *In the Shadow of the Sword: Italy's Neutrality and Entrance into the Great War, 1914–1915* (New York, 1987).

Reynolds, D. J., 'The Origins of the Two "World Wars": Historical Discourse and International Politics', *Journal of Contemporary History* (2003).

Rhodes James, R., *Gallipoli* (London, 1965).

Ribot, A. (ed.), *Journal d'Alexandre Ribot et correspondances inédites, 1914–1922* (Paris, 1936).

Riddell, Lord, *Intimate Diary of the Peace Conference and After, 1918–1925* (London, 1953).

Ringer, F. K., *The Decline of the German Mandarins: the German Academic Community, 1890–1933* (Cambridge, MA, 1969).

Ritter, G. A., *The Schlieffen Plan: Critique of a Myth* (London, 1958).

_____ *The Sword and the Sceptre: the Problem of Militarism in Germany* (4 vols., London, 1969–73).

Robb, G., *British Culture and the First World War* (Basingstoke and New York, 2002).

Robbins, K., 'British Diplomacy and Bulgaria, 1914–1915', *Slavonic and East European Review* (1971).

Robert, J.-L., 'Women and Work in France during the First World War', in Wall and Winter (eds.), *Upheaval of War*.

_____ 'The Image of the Profiteer', in Winter and Robert (eds.), *Capital Cities at War*.

Roberts, D. D., 'Croce and Beyond: Italian Intellectuals and the First World War', *International History Review* (1981).

Roberts, P., 'The Anglo-American Theme: American Visions of an Atlantic Alliance, 1914–1933', *Diplomatic History* (1997).

Robertson, W., *Soldiers and Statesmen, 1914–1918* (2 vols., London, 1926).

Robson, S., *The First World War* (London and New York, 1998).

Rochat, G., 'Il Comando supremo di Diaz' in Berti and del Negra (eds.), *Piave*.

Roeseler, K., *Die Finanzpolitik des Deutschen Reiches im Ersten Weltkrieg* (Berlin, 1967).

Rogger, H., 'Russia in 1914', *Journal of Contemporary History* (1966).

_____ *Russia in the Age of Modernization and Revolution, 1881–1917* (London and New York, 1983).

Röhl, J. C. G., 'Admiral von Müller and the Approach of War, 1911–1914', *Historical Journal* (1969).

_____ 'An der Schwelle zum Weltkrieg: eine Dokumentation über den "Kriegsrat" vom 8. Dezember 1912', *Militärgeschichtliche Mitteilungen* (1977).

_____ *Wilhelm II. Der Aufbau der Persönlichen Monarchie, 1888–1900* (Munich, 2001).

Roshwald, A., and Stites, R. (eds.), *European Culture and the Great War: the Arts, Entertainment, and Propaganda, 1914–1918* (Cambridge, 1999).

Rothenberg, G. E., *The Army of Francis Joseph* (West Lafayette, IN, 1976).

_____ 'The Austro-Hungarian Campaign against Serbia in 1914', *Journal of Military History* (1989).

_____ 'The Habsburg Army in the First World War, 1914–1918', in Kann *et al.* (eds.), *Habsburg Empire*.

Rothwell, V. H., *British War Aims and Peace Diplomacy, 1914–1918* (Oxford, 1971).

Rubin, G. R., *War, Law, and Labour: the Munitions Acts, State Regulation, and the Unions, 1915–1921* (Oxford, 1987).

Rudin, H., *Armistice 1918* (New Haven, 1944).

Ryder, A. J., *The German Revolution of 1918: a Study of German Socialism in War and Revolt* (Cambridge, 1967).

Safford, J. J., *Wilsonian Maritime Diplomacy, 1913–1921* (New Brunswick, NJ, 1978).

Saini, K. G., 'The Economic Aspects of India's Participation in the First World War', in Ellinwood and Pradhan (eds.), *India and World War I* (New Delhi, 1978).

Salandra, A., *Italy and the Great War* (London, 1932).

Salmon, P., *Scandinavia and the Great Powers, 1890–1940* (Cambridge, 1997).

Salter, A., *Allied Shipping Control: an Experiment in International Administration* (Oxford, 1921).

Samuels, M., *Command or Control? Command, Training, and Tactics in the British and German Armies, 1888–1918* (London, 1995).

Sanborn, J. 'The Mobilization of 1914 and the Question of the Russian Nation: a Reexamination', *Slavic Review* (2000).

Sarter, A., *Die Deutschen Eisenbahnen im Kriege* (Stuttgart, 1930).

Saunders, N. J., *Trench Art: A Brief History and Guide, 1914–1939* (Barnsley, 2001).

Sazonov, S., *Fateful Years, 1909–1916* (London, 1928).

Scarry, E., *The Body in Pain: the Making and Unmaking of the World* (New York, 1985).

Schaper, B. W., *Albert Thomas: trente ans de réformisme social* (Paris, c.1960).

Scherer, A., and Grünewald, J. (eds.), *L'Allemagne et les problèmes de la paix pendant la Première Guerre Mondiale* (4 vols., Paris, 1966–78).

Schindler, J. R., 'Disaster on the Drina: the Austro-Hungarian Army in Serbia, 1914', *War in History* (2001).

Schorske, C. E., *German Social Democracy, 1905–1917: the Development of the Great Schism* (Cambridge, MA, 1955).

Schroeder, H.-J. (ed.)., *Confrontation and Cooperation: Germany and the United States in the Era of World War I, 1900–1924* (Oxford, 1993).

Schuker, S. A., *The End of French Predominance in Europe: the Financial Crisis of 1924 and the Adoption of the Dawes Plan* (Chapel Hill, 1976).

Schwabe, K., *Woodrow Wilson, Revolutionary Germany, and Peacemaking, 1918–1919: Missionary Diplomacy and the Realities of Power* (Chapel Hill and London, 1985).

Schwarz, B., 'Divided Attention: Britain's Perception of a German Threat to Her Eastern Position in 1918', *Journal of Contemporary History* (1993).

Scott, J. B. (ed.), *Official Statements of War Aims and Peace Proposals, December 1916- November 1918* (Washington, 1921).

Service, R., *Lenin: A Political Life. Volume 2: Worlds in Collision* (Basingstoke, 1991).

Seton-Watson, C., *Italy from Liberalism to Fascism, 1870–1925* (London, 1967).

Seymour, C. M. (ed.), *The Intimate Papers of Colonel House* (4 vols., London, 1926–8).

Shaffey, Y., *British Military Intelligence in the Palestine Campaign, 1914–1918* (London and Portland, OR, 1998).

Shanafelt, G. W., *The Secret Enemy: Austria-Hungary and the German Alliance, 1914–1918* (New York, 1985).

Sharp, A., *The Versailles Settlement: Peacemaking in Paris, 1919* (London, 1991).

Sheffield, G. D., 'Officer–Man Relations, Discipline, and Morale in the British Army of the Great War', in Cecil and Liddle (eds.), *Facing Armageddon*.

_____ 'The Shadow of the Somme: the Influence of the First World War on British Soldiers' Perceptions and Behaviour in the Second World War', in Addison and Calder (eds.), *Time To Kill: the Soldier's Experience of War in the West, 1939–1945* (London, 1997).

_____ *Leadership in the Trenches: Officer–Man Relations, Morale, and Discipline in the British Army in the Era of the First World War* (Basingstoke, 2000).

_____ *Forgotten Victory. The First World War: Myths and Realities* (London, 2001).

_____ *The Somme* (London, 2003).

Sheffy, Y., *British Military Intelligence in the Palestine Campaign, 1914–1918* (London and Portland, OR, 1998).

Sherman, D. J., 'Bodies and Names: the Emergence of Commemoration in Inter-War France', *American Historical Review* (1998).

Showalter, D. E., 'Even Generals Wet their Pants: The First Three Weeks in East Prussia, 1914', *War and Society* (1984).

_____ *Tannenberg: Clash of Empires* (Hamden, CT, 1991).

Showalter, E., *The Female Malady: Women, Madness, and English Culture, 1830–1980* (New York, 1985).

Siegelbaum, L. H., *The Politics of Industrial Mobilization in Russia, 1914–17: a Study of the War-Industries Committees* (London and Basingstoke, 1983).

Silberstein, G. E., *The Troubled Alliance: German-Austrian Relations, 1914 to 1917* (Lexington, KY, 1970).

Silver, K. E., *Esprit de Corps: the Art of the Parisian Avant-Garde and the First World War, 1914–1925* (Princeton, NJ, 1989).

Simkins, P., *Kitchener's Army: the Raising of the New Armies, 1914–16* (Manchester and New York, 1988).

_____ 'Co-Stars or Supporting Cast? British Divisions in the "Hundred Days", 1918', in Griffith (ed.), *British Fighting Methods*.

Simpson, K., 'The British Soldier on the Western Front', in Liddle (ed.), *Home Fires and Foreign Fields: British Social and Military Experience in the First World War* (London, 1985).

Sims, R. L., *A Political History of Modern Japan, 1869–1952* (New Delhi, 1991).

Siney, M. C., *The Allied Blockade of Germany, 1914–1916* (Ann Arbor, 1957).

Singleton, J., 'Britain's Military Use of Horses, 1914–1918', *Past & Present* (1993).

Sixte de Bourbon, Prince, *L'Offre de paix séparée de l'Autriche (5 décembre 1916–12 octobre 1917)* (Paris, 1920).

Sked, A., *The Decline and Fall of the Habsburg Empire, 1815–1918* (London and New York, 1989).

Smith, C. J., *The Russian Struggle for Power, 1914–1917: a Study of Russian Foreign Policy during the First World War* (New York, 1956).

Smith, L. V., *Between Mutiny and Obedience: the Case of the Fifth French Infantry Division during World War I* (Princeton, NJ, 1994).

_____ 'Masculinity, Memory, and the French World War I Novel: Henri Barbusse and Roland Dorgelès', in Coetzee and Shevin-Coetzee (eds.), *Authority, Identity, and the Social History of the Great War*.

Smith, L. V., Audouin-Rouzeau, S., and Becker, A., *France and the Great War, 1914–1918* (Cambridge, 2003).

Smith, S. A., *Red Petrograd: Revolution in the Factories, 1917–1918* (Cambridge, 1983).

Snell, J. L., 'Wilson's Peace Programme and German Socialism, January-March 1918', *Mississippi Valley Historical Review* (1951).

_____ 'Wilson on Germany and the Fourteen Points', *Journal of Modern History* (1954).

Snyder, J., *The Ideology of the Offensive: Military Decision Making and the Disasters of 1914* (Ithaca, NY, 1984).

Soutou, G.-H., 'La France et les marches de l'est, 1914–1919', *Revue historique* (1978).

_____ *L'Or et le sang: les buts de guerre économiques de la Première Guerre mondiale* (Paris, 1989).

_____ 'Le Problème du social-impérialisme en Allemagne et en Angleterre pendant la Grande guerre', in Becker and Audouin-Rouzeau (eds.), *Les sociétés européennes*.

_____ 'Die Kriegsziele des Deutschen Reiches, Frankreichs, Grossbritanniens, und den Vereinigten Staaten während des Ersten Weltkrieges', in Michalka (ed.), *Erste Weltkrieg*.

Spears, E. L., *Liaison 1914: a Narrative of the Great Retreat* (London, 1930).

_____ E. L., *Prelude to Victory* (London, 1939).

Spector, S. D., *Rumania at the Paris Peace Conference: a Study in the Diplomacy of Ion I. C. Bratianu* (New York, 1962).

Spiers, E. M., *Haldane: an Army Reformer* (Edinburgh, 1980).

_____ *Chemical Warfare* (Basingstoke, 1986).

Stargardt, N., *The German Idea of Militarism: Radical and Socialist Critics* (Cambridge, 1994).

Stark, G., 'All Quiet on the Home Front: Popular Entertainments, Censorship, and Civilian Morale in Germany, 1914–1918', in Coetzee and Shevin-Coetzee (eds.), *Authority, Identity, and the Social History of the Great War*.

Stegemann, B., *Die Deutsche Marinepolitik, 1916–1918* (Berlin, 1970).

Steglich, W., *Die Friedenspolitik der Mittelmächte, 1917–1918* (Vol. 1, Wiesbaden, 1964).

Stein, L., *The Balfour Declaration* (London, 1961).

Steinberg, J., *Yesterday's Deterrent: Tirpitz and the Birth of the German Battle Fleet* (New York, 1965).

_____ 'Diplomatie als Wille und Vorstellung: die Berliner Mission Lord Haldanes im Februar 1912', in Schottelius and Deist (eds.), *Marine und Marinepolitik im Kaiserlichen Deutschland, 1871–1914* (Düsseldorf, 1972).

Steiner, Z. S., and Nielson, K., *Britain and the Origins of the First World War* (Basingstoke, 2003).

Stevenson, D., *French War Aims against Germany, 1914–1919* (Oxford, 1982).

_____ 'Belgium, Luxemburg, and the Defence of Western Europe, 1914–1920', *International History Review* (1982).

_____ *The First World War and International Politics* (Oxford, 1988).

_____ (ed.), *British Documents on Foreign Affairs: The First World War, 1914–1918* (12 vols., Frederick, MD, 1989).

_____ *Armaments and the Coming of War: Europe, 1904–1914* (Oxford, 1996).

_____ *The Outbreak of the First World War: 1914 in Perspective* (Basingstoke, 1997).

_____ 'War by Timetable? The Railway Race before 1914', *Past & Present* (1999).

_____ 'French Strategy on the Western Front, 1914–1918', in Chickering and Förster (eds.), *Great War, Total War*.

Stibbe, M., *German Anglophobia and the Great War, 1914–1918* (Cambridge, 2001).

Stites, R., 'Days and Nights in Wartime Russia: Cultural Life, 1914–1917', in Roshwald and Stites (eds.), *European Culture*.

Stone, N., 'Army and Society in the Habsburg Monarchy, 1900–1914', *Past & Present* (1966).

_____ 'Die Mobilmachung der Österreichisch-Ungarischen Armee 1914', *Militärgeschichtlichen Mitteilungen* (1974).

_____ *The Eastern Front 1914–1917* (London, 1975).

_____ 'Moltke and Conrad: Relations between the Austro-Hungarian and German General Staffs, 1909–1914', in Kennedy (ed.), *The War Plans*.

Strachan, H. F. A., 'The Morale of the German Army, 1917–18', in Cecil and Liddle (eds.), *Facing Armageddon*.

_____ (ed.), *The Oxford Illustrated History of the First World War* (Oxford, 1998).

_____ *The First World War*. Vol. 1: *To Arms* (Oxford, 2001).

Strikwerda, C., 'The Troubled Origins of European Economic Integration: International Iron and Steel and Labor Migration in the Era of World War I', *American Historical Review* (1993).

Struve, P. B., *Food Supply in Russia during the World War* (New Haven, 1930).

Sumida, J. T., *In Defence of Naval Supremacy: Finance, Technology, and British Naval Policy, 1889–1914* (Boston, 1989).

_____ 'Forging the Trident: British Naval Industrial Logistics, 1914–1918' in Lynn (ed.), *Feeding Mars*.

Summerskill, M., *China on the Western Front: Britain's Chinese Workforce in the First World War* (London, 1982).

Swain, G. R., *The Origins of the Russian Civil War* (London, 1996).

Swartz, M., *The Union of Democratic Control in British Politics during the First World War* (Oxford, 1971).

Sweet, P. R., 'Leaders and Policies: Germany in the Winter of 1914–15', *Journal of Central European Affairs* (1956).

Sweetman, J., 'The Smuts Report of 1917: Merely Political Window-Dressing?', *Journal of Strategic Studies* (1981).

Tanenbaum, J. K., *General Maurice Sarrail, 1856–1919: The French Army and Left-wing Politics* (Chapel Hill, 1974).

Tarrant, V. E., *Jutland: the German Perspective* (London, 1995).

Taylor, A. J. P., *The Troublemakers: Dissent over Foreign Policy, 1792–1939* (London, 1957).
_____ *The First World War: an Illustrated History* (Harmondsworth, 1966).
_____ *War by Timetable: How the First World War Began* (London, 1969).
Taylor, P. M., 'The Foreign Office and British Propaganda during the First World War', *Historical Journal* (1980).
Terraine, J., *Douglas Haig the Educated Soldier* (London, 1963).
_____ *Business in Great Waters: the U-Boat Wars, 1916–1945* (Ware, 1999).
Thaer, A. von, *Generalstabsdienst an der Front und in der OHL* (Göttingen, 1958).
Thom, D., 'Women and Work in Wartime Britain', in Wall and Winter (eds.), *Upheaval of War.*
_____ *Nice Girls and Rude Girls: Women Workers in World War I* (London and New York, 2000).
Thomas, D. H., *The Guarantee of Belgian Independence and Neutrality in European Diplomacy, 1830s–1930s* (Kingston, RI, 1983).
Thompson, J. A., 'Woodrow Wilson and World War I: a Reappraisal', *Journal of American Studies* (1985).
Thompson, J. L., *Politicians, the Press, and Propaganda: Lord Northcliffe and the Great War, 1914–1919* (Kent, OH, and London, 1999).
Thompson, J. M., *Russia, Bolshevism, and the Versailles Peace* (Princeton, NJ, 1966).
Thompson, W. C., 'The September Program: Reflections on the Evidence', *Central European History* (1978).
Tillman, S. P., *Anglo-American Relations at the Paris Peace Conference of 1919* (Princeton, NJ, 1961).
Tirpitz, A. von, *My Memoirs* (London, 1919).
Tobin, E. H., 'War and the Working Class: the Case of Düsseldorf, 1914–1918', *Central European History* (1985).
Tomassini, L., 'Industrial Mobilization and the Labour Market in Italy during the First World War', *Social History* (1991).
Torrey, G. E., 'Rumania and the Belligerents, 1914–1916', *Journal of Contemporary History* (1966).
_____ 'The Rumanian Campaign of 1916: its Impact on the Belligerents', *Slavic Review* (1980).
_____ 'The Redemption of an Army: the Romanian Campaign of 1917', *War And Society* (1994).
Trachtenberg, M., '"A New Economic Order": Etienne Clémentel and French Economic Diplomacy during the First World War', *French Historical Studies* (1977).
_____ *Reparation and World Politics: France and European Economic Diplomacy, 1916–1923* (New York, 1980).
_____ *History and Strategy* (Princeton, NJ, 1991).
Trask, D. F., *The United States in the Supreme War Council: American War Aims and Inter-Allied Strategy, 1917–1918* (Westport, CT, 1961).
Travers, T., 'A Particular Style of Command: Haig and GHQ, 1916–1918', *Journal of Strategic Studies* (1987).
_____ *The Killing Ground: The British Army, the Western Front, and the Emergence of Modern Warfare, 1900–1918* (London, 1987).
_____ 'Could the Tanks of 1918 Have Been War-Winners for the British Expeditionary Force?', *Journal of Contemporary History* (1992).
_____ *How the War Was Won: Command and Technology in the British Army on the Western Front, 1917–1918* (London and New York, 1992).
_____ 'Command and Leadership Styles in the British Army: The 1915 Gallipoli Model', *Journal of Contemporary History* (1994).
_____ 'Reply to John Hussey: The Movement of German Divisions to the Western Front, Winter 1917–1918', *War in History* (1998).
Travers, T., 'The Ottoman Crisis of May 1915 at Gallipoli', *War in History* (2001).
Travers, T., *Gallipoli, 1915* (Stroud, 2001).
Trebilcock, R. C., 'War and the Failure of Industrial Mobilization, 1899 and 1914', in Winter (ed.), *War and Economic Development.*
Trotsky, L., *My Life: the Rise and Fall of a Dictator* (London, 1930).
Trumpener, U., *Germany and the Ottoman Empire, 1914–1918* (Princeton, NJ, 1968).
_____ 'The Road to Ypres: the Beginnings of Gas Warfare in World War I', *Journal of Modern History* (1975).
_____ 'War Premeditated? German Intelligence Operations in July 1914', *Central European History* (1976).
Tuchman, B., *The Zimmermann Telegram* (New York, 1966).
Tucker, S., *The Great War, 1914–18* (London, 1998).
Turner, J. (ed.), *Britain and the First World War* (London, 1980).
_____ *British Politics and the Great War: Coalition and Conflict, 1915–1918* (New Haven and London, 1992).
Turner, L. C. F., *Origins of the First World War* (London, 1970).
Tyng, S., *The Campaign of the Marne 1914* (London, 1935).
Ullman, R. H., *Anglo-Soviet Relations, 1917–1921* (3 vols., Princeton, NJ, 1962–73).

Ullrich, B., and Ziemann, B. (eds.), *Frontalltag im Ersten Weltkrieg: Wahn und Wirklichkeit. Quellen und Dokumente* (Frankfurt, 1994).

Unruh, K., *Langemarck: Legende und Wirklichkeit* (Koblenz, 1986).

Unterberger, B. E., 'President Wilson and the Decision to Send American Troops to Siberia', *Pacific Historical Review* (1955).

Valiani, L., *The End of Austria-Hungary* (London, 1973).

Valone, S. J., '"There Must Be Some Misunderstanding": Sir Edward Grey's Diplomacy of August 1, 1914', *Journal of British Studies* (1988).

Van Creveld, M., *Supplying War: Logistics from Wallenstein to Patton* (Cambridge, 1977).

Verhey, J., *The Spirit of 1914: Militarism, Myth, and Mobilization in Germany* (Cambridge, 2000).

Vermes, G., 'Leap into the Dark: the Issue of Suffrage in Hungary during World War I', in Kann *et al.* (eds.), *Habsburg Empire.*

Vinogradov, V. N., 'Romania in the First World War: the Years of Neutrality, 1914–1916', *International History Review* (1992).

Vogel, J., *Nationen im Gleichschritt: der Kult der "Nation im Waffen" in Deutschland und Frankreich, 1871–1914* (Göttingen, 1997).

Wade, R. A., 'Why October? The Search for Peace in 1917', *Soviet Studies* (1968).

_____ *The Russian Search for Peace, February-October 1917* (Stanford, 1969).

Waites, B., 'The Effect of the First World War on Class and Status in England, 1910–1920', *Journal of Contemporary History* (1976).

Walker, C. J., 'World War I and the Armenian Genocide', in Hovanissian (ed.), *The Armenian People from Ancient to Modern Times* (2 vols., Basingstoke and London, 1997).

Wall, R. and Winter, J. M. (eds.), *The Upheaval of War: Family, Work, and Welfare in Europe, 1914–1918* (Cambridge, 1988).

Ward, S. R., 'Intelligence Surveillance of British Ex-Servicemen, 1918–1920', *Historical Journal* (1973).

Wargelin, C. F., 'A High Price for Bread: the First Treaty of Brest-Litovsk and the Break-up of Austria-Hungary, 1917–1918', *International History Review* (1997).

Watson, D. R., *Georges Clemenceau: a Political Biography* (London, 1974).

Watson, J. S. K., 'Khaki Girls, VADs, and Tommy's Sisters: Gender and Class in First World War Britain', *International History Review* (1997).

Wawro, G., 'Morale in the Austro-Hungarian Army: the Evidence of Habsburg Army Campaign Reports and Allied Intelligence Officers', in Cecil and Liddle (eds.), *Facing Armageddon.*

Wegs, R., *Die Österreichische Kriegswirtschaft, 1914–1918* (Vienna, 1979).

_____ 'Transportation: the Achilles Heel of the Habsburg War Effort', in Kann *et al.* (eds.), *Habsburg Empire.*

Weir, G. E., 'Tirpitz, Technology, and Building U-Boats, 1897–1916', *International History Review* (1984).

_____ *Rebuilding the Kaiser's Navy: the Imperial Navy and German Industry in the Tirpitz Era, 1890–1919* (Annapolis, 1992).

Welch, D. A., 'Cinema and Society in Imperial Germany, 1905–1918', *German History* (1990).

_____ *Germany, Propaganda, and Total War, 1914–1918* (London, 2000).

Werth, G., 'Flanders 1917 and the German Soldier', in Liddle (ed.), *Passchendaele in Perspective.*

Wette, W., 'From Kellogg to Hitler (1928–1933): German Public Opinion Concerning the Rejection or Glorification of War' in Deist (ed.), *German Military.*

_____ (ed.), *Der Krieg des Kleinen Mannes: eine Militärgeschichte von Unten* (Munich and Zurich, 1992).

Whalen, R., *Bitter Wounds: German Victims of the Great War, 1914–1939* (Ithaca, NY, and London, 1984).

Wheeler-Bennett, J. W., *Brest-Litovsk: the Forgotten Peace, March 1918* (London, 1938).

Whiting, R. C., 'Taxation and the Working Class, 1915–24', *Historical Journal* (1990).

Wildman, A. K., *The End of the Russian Imperial Army* (2 vols., Princeton, NJ, 1980, 1987).

Willan, B. P., 'The South African Native Labour Contingent, 1916–1918', *Journal of African History* (1978).

Williams, M. J., 'The Treatment of the German Losses on the Somme in the British Official History', *Journal of the Royal United Services Institution* (1966).

Williamson, J. G., *Karl Helfferich, 1872–1924: Economist, Financier, Politician* (Princeton, NJ, 1971).

Williamson, S. R., *The Politics of Grand Strategy: Britain and France Prepare for War, 1904–1914* (Cambridge, MA, 1969).

_____ *Austria-Hungary and the Origins of the First World War* (Basingstoke, 1991).

Willis, J. F., *Prologue to Nuremberg: the Politics and Diplomacy of Punishing War Criminals of the First World War* (Westport, CT, and London, 1982).

Wilson, K. M., 'Imperial Interests in the British Decision for War: the Defence of India in Central Asia', *Review of International Studies* (1984).

_____ *The Policy of the Entente: Essays on the Determinants of British Foreign Policy, 1904–1914* (Cambridge, 1985).

_____ (ed.), *Decisions for War, 1914* (London, 1995).

_____ (ed.), *Forging the Collective Memory: Government and International Historians through Two World Wars* (Providence, RI, and Oxford, 1996).

Wilson, T., 'Britain's "Moral Commitment" to France in August 1914', *History* (1979).
_____ 'Lord Bryce's Investigation into Alleged German Atrocities in Belgium, 1914–1915', *Journal of Contemporary History* (1979).
_____ *The Myriad Faces of War: Britain and the Great War, 1914–1918* (Cambridge, 1986).
Winter, D., *Death's Men: Soldiers of the Great War* (Harmondsworth, 1979).
_____ *Haig's Command: a Reassessment* (London, 1991).
Winter, J. M., 'Arthur Henderson, the Russian Revolution, and the Reconstruction of the Labour Party', *Historical Journal* (1972).
_____ (ed.), *War and Economic Development: Essays in Honour of David Joslin* (Cambridge, 1975).
_____ *The Great War and the British People* (Basingstoke, 1986).
_____ 'Some Paradoxes of the First World War', in Wall and Winter (eds.), *Upheaval of War.*
_____ *The Experience of World War I* (London, 1988).
_____ *Sites of Memory, Sites of Mourning: the Great War in European Cultural History* (Cambridge, 1995).
_____ 'Surviving the War: Life Expectation, Illness, and Mortality Rates in Paris, London, and Berlin, 1914–1919' in Winter and Robert (eds.), *Capital Cities at War.*
Winter, J. M., and Baggett, B., *1914–18: the Great War and the Shaping of the 20th Century* (London, 1996).
Winter, J. M., and Robert, J.-L. (eds.), *Capital Cities at War: London, Paris, Berlin, 1914–1919* (Cambridge, 1997).
Winter, J., Parker, G., and Habeck, M. R. (eds.), *The Great War and the Twentieth Century* (New Haven and London, 2000).
Wohl, R., *French Communism in the Making, 1914–1924* (Stanford, 1966).
Woodward, D. R., 'David Lloyd George, a Negotiated Peace with Germany, and the Kühlmann Peace Kite of September 1917', *Canadian Journal of History* (1971).
_____ *The Collapse of Power: Mutiny in the High Seas Fleet* (London, 1973).
_____ 'The British Government and Japanese Intervention in Russia during World War I', *Journal of Modern History* (1974).
_____ 'Britain in a Continental War', *Albion* (1980).
_____ *Lloyd George and the Generals* (Newark, NJ, and London, 1983).
_____ 'Did Lloyd George Starve the British Army of Men Prior to the German Offensive of 21 March 1918?', *Historical Journal* (1984).
Wootton, G., *The Politics of Influence: British Ex-Servicemen, Cabinet Decisions, and Cultural Change (1917–57)* (Cambridge, MA, 1963).
Wright, D. G., 'The Great War, Government Propaganda, and English "Men of Letters", 1914–1916', *Literature and History* (1978).
Wrigley, C., *David Lloyd George and the British Labour Movement: Peace and War* (Hassocks and New York, 1976).
_____ 'The Ministry of Munitions: an Innovatory Department' in Burk (ed.), *War and the State.*
_____ (ed.), *Challenges of Labour: Central and Western Europe, 1917–1920* (London and New York, 1993).
Wynne, G. C., *If Germany Attacks: the Battle in Depth in the West* (London, 1940).
Yapp, M. E., *The Making of the Modern Near East, 1792–1923* (London, 1987).
Young, H. F., 'The Misunderstanding of August 1, 1914', *Journal of Modern History* (1976).
Zabecki. D. T., *Steel Wind: Colonel Georg Bruchmüller and the Birth of Modern Artillery* (Westport, CT, 1994).
Zagorsky, S. O., *State Control of Industry in Russia during the War* (New Haven, 1928).
Zeidler, M., 'Die Deutsche Kriegsfinanzierung 1914 bis 1918', in Michalka (ed.), *Erste Weltkrieg.*
Zeman, Z. A. B., *The Break-Up of the Habsburg Empire, 1914–1918: a Study in National and Social Revolution* (London, New York, and Toronto, 1961).
Zieger, R. H., *America's Great War: World War I and the American Experience* (Lanham, MD, and Oxford, 2000).
Ziemann, B., 'Enttäuschte Erwartung und kollektive Erschöpfung: die Deutschen Soldaten an der Westfront 1918 auf dem Weg zur Revolution', in Duppler and Gross (eds.), *Kriegsende 1918.*
Živojinović , D., 'Robert Lansing's Comments on the Pontifical Peace Note of August 1, 1917', *Journal of American History* (1960).
Zuber, T., 'The Schlieffen Plan Reconsidered', *War in History* (1999).
_____ 'Terence Holmes Reinvents the Schlieffen Plan', *War in History* (2001).
_____ *Inventing the Schlieffen Plan: German War Planning, 1871–1914* (Oxford, 2002).
_____ 'Terence Holmes Reinvents the Schlieffen Plan – Again', *War in History* (2003).
Zuckerman, F., 'The Political Police, War, and Society in Russia, 1914–1917', in Coetzee and Shevin-Coetzee (eds.), *Authority, Identity, and the Social History of the Great War.*
Zürcher, E., 'Little Mehmet in the Desert: the Ottoman Soldier's Experience', in Cecil and Liddle (eds.), *Facing Armageddon.*

NOTES

Introduction

1. BBC TV *Horizon*, 8 January 1998; Crosby, *Epidemic and Peace*, p. 207.
2. Heuser, *Reading Clausewitz*, ch. 2.
3. Scarry, *Body in Pain*, ch. 2.
4. Howard and Paret (eds.), *Clausewitz: On War*, p. 75.
5. For Britain, see Middlebrook, *First Day*; *Kaiser's Battle*; MacDonald; *1914*; *1915*; *Somme*; *Passchendaele*; *Spring 1918*.

Chapter 1

1. In German 'der grosse Krieg' referred to the Thirty Years War: Liulevicius, *War Land*, p. 39.
2. Clarke, *Voices Prophesying War*; Pick, *War Machine*.
3. Hinsley, *Power and the Pursuit*; Howard, *Invention of Peace*.
4. Dülffer *et al.* (eds.), *Vermiedene Kriege*.
5. Hinsley, *Power and the Pursuit*; Langhorne, *Collapse of the Concert*; Dülffer, *Regeln*.
6. Best, *Humanity in Warfare*, ch. 3.
7. Kuznets, 'Quantitative Aspects', p. 19; Kenwood and Lougheed, *Growth of the International Economy*, ch. 2.
8. Offer, *First World War: Agrarian Interpretation*, Pt. 2.
9. Craig and Fisher, *Integration of the European Economy*.
10. Strikwerda, 'Troubled Origins'.
11. Lyons, *Internationalism*, Pt. I.
12. Eichengreen and Flandreau (eds.), *Gold Standard*; de Cecco, *Money and Empire*.
13. Ferguson, *Pity of War*, ch. 5.; cf. Angell, *Great Illusion*.
14. Fieldhouse, *Economics and Empire*, p. 3.
15. Berlin: Verhey, *Spirit of 1914*, p. 15; Serbia: Petrovich, *History of Modern Serbia*, Vol. 2, p. 586.
16. McLean, *Royalty and Diplomacy*, ch. 2; see generally Mayer, *Persistence*.
17. M. E. Brown *et al.* (eds.), *Debating the Democratic Peace* (Cambridge, Mass., 1996).
18. Lautenschläger, 'Technology', pp. 12–14.
19. Snyder, *Ideology of the Offensive*, ch. 1.
20. Dawson, 'Preventing'.
21. Howard, 'Men against Fire'.
22. Strachan, *First World War: To Arms*, pp. 1005–1014.
23. For the origins of the war, Albertini, *Origins*, and Joll, *Origins*. On Sarajevo, Dedijer, *Sarajevo*; Strachan, *To Arms*, chs. 1–2.
24. Judah, *The Serbs*, p. 31.
25. Petrovich, *Serbia*, Vol. 2, pp. 613–17.

26. On Serbia, see Cornwall in Wilson (ed.), *Decisions for War*, ch. 3; Petrovich, *History of Serbia*; Malcolm, *Bosnia*, ch. 11.

27. Judah, *The Serbs*, p. 155.

28. Petrovich, *Serbia*, Vol. 2, pp. 608–609.

29. Strachan, *To Arms*, p. 68.

30. Judah, *The Serbs*, p. 85.

31. Geiss (ed.), *July 1914*, docs. 9, 19.

32. On Austria-Hungary: Williamson, *Austria-Hungary*; Bridge, *Habsburg Monarchy*; Rauchensteiner, *Tod des Doppeladlers*.

33. Sked, *Decline and Fall*, p. 278.

34. Stone, 'Army and Society'.

35. Leslie, 'Antecedents'.

36. Geiss (ed.), *July 1914*, docs 6, 8.

37. Fischer, *Germany's Aims*; *War of Illusions*; Berghahn, *Germany and the Approach of War*.

38. Förster, 'Facing "People's War"'.

39. Clark, *Kaiser Wilhelm II*, and the multi-volume biography in progress by John Röhl.

40. Hughes, *Nationalism and Society*, pp. 154, 128–9.

41. On the constitution, Craig, *Germany, 1866–1945*, ch. 2.

42. Steinberg, *Yesterday's Deterrent*; Berghahn, *Germany and the Approach of War*.

43. Epkenhans, *Wilhelminischen Flottenrüstung*; Marder, *Dreadnought to Scapa Flow*, Vol. 1; Lambert, *Fisher's Naval Revolution*.

44. Kennedy, *Anglo-German Antagonism*, ch. 13; Charmley, *Splendid Isolation?*, ch. 17.

45. Joly, 'La France et la revanche'.

46. Steinberg, 'Diplomatie als Wille'.

47. Kaiser, 'Germany and the Origins'.

48. Ferguson, 'Domestic Origins'; Ferguson, *Pity of War*, chs. 4, 5. On armaments: Stevenson, *Armaments*; Herrmann, *Arming of Europe*; Förster, *Doppelte Militarismus*.

49. Stargardt, *German Idea of Militarism*.

50. Stevenson, *Armaments*, p. 6.

51. ibid.

52. Generally Kennedy (ed.), *War Plans*; Snyder, *Ideology of the Offensive*.

53. Ritter, *Schlieffen Plan*; Buchholz, *Moltke, Schlieffen, and War Planning*; Zuber, 'Schlieffen Plan'; W. Dieckmann, 'Der Schlieffenplan' (n.d.), BA-MA W–10/50220.

54. Fischer, in *War of Illusions,* pp. 177–89 saw Germany's 1913 army law as part of a premeditated preparation for war, but this view has not been generally accepted.

55. Generally on the crises, Albertini, *Origins*, vol. 1; Stevenson, *Armaments*.

56. Barraclough, *Agadir to Armageddon*; Allain, *Agadir 1911*; Oncken, *Panthersprung*.

57. Helmreich, *Diplomacy of Balkan Wars*; Hall, *Balkan Wars*.

58. Fischer, *War of Illusions*, ch. 9; Röhl, 'Admiral von Müller'; Röhl (ed.), 'An der Schwelle'.

59. Crampton, *Hollow Détente*, pp. 111, 117.

60. Förster, 'Der deutsche Generalstab', sections 4 and 5.

61. Offer, 'Going to War in 1914'.

62. On Russia, Geyer, *Russian Imperialism;* Lieven, *Russia*.

63. Lieven, *Russia*, pp. 77–83.

64. Gatrell, *Government, Industry, and Rearmament*, chs. 3, 4, 7.

65. For the context, McDonald, *United Government and Foreign Policy*.

66. Jelavich, *Russia's Balkan Entanglements*, pp. 241–48.

67. Albertini, *Origins*, Vol. 2, pp. 352–62.

68. ibid. But Cornwall on Serbia in Wilson (ed.), *Decisions for War*, pp. 76–81, gives a different view.

69. Geiss (ed.), *July 1914*, doc. 77.

70. Showalter, *Tannenberg*, ch. 1.

71. Trumpener, 'War Premeditated?'

72. Trachtenberg, *History and Strategy*, pp. 93–5.

73. Rogger, 'Russia in 1914', p. 109.

74. Mayer, 'Domestic Causes', p. 293.

75. Hayne, *French Foreign Office*, p. 294.

76. On France: Keiger, *France*; and Keiger, *Raymond Poincaré*.

77. Stevenson, *Armaments*, pp. 377–8.

78. Hewitson, 'Germany and France', p. 600.

79. Keiger, *France*, pp. 44, 55–6.

80. Groh, 'The "Unpatriotic Socialists"', pp. 178–79.

81. Young, 'Misunderstanding'; Valone, 'Misunderstanding', Trachtenberg, *History and Strategy*, pp. 58–9.

82. Strachan, *First World War: To Arms*, p. 95.

83. Generally, Steiner and Neilson, *Britain*.

84. On Belgium, Stengers, in Wilson (ed.), *Decisions for War*.

85. Brock (ed.), *Asquith: Letters to Venetia Stanley*, p. 150.

86. Brock, in Evans and Pogge von Strandmann (eds.), *Coming of the First World War*, pp. 150–60.

87. Thomas, *Belgian Independence*, pp. 511–13.

88. Kennedy, *Anglo-German Antagonism*, chs. 12–14.

89. Andrew, *Secret Service*, ch. 2; French, 'Spy Fever'.

90. Gooch, *Prospect of War*, pp. 9–14; Marder, *Dreadnought*, Vol. I, pp. 344–58 .

91. Wilson, *Policy of the Entente*; Ferguson, *Pity of War*; Charmley, *Splendid Isolation?*

92. Coogan, 'British Cabinet and Anglo-French Staff Talks'; Williamson, *Politics of Grand Strategy*.

93. Wilson, 'Britain's "Moral Commitment"'.

94. Wilson, 'Imperial Interests'.

95. Hazelhurst, *Politicians at War*; Gilbert, 'Pacifist to Interventionist'.

96. Offer, *First World War: Agrarian Interpretation*, ch. 21.

97. French, *Britain's Strategy and War Aims*, pp. 24–5.

98. Keiger, 'Britain's "Union sacrée" in 1914', in Becker and Audouin-Rouzeau (eds.), *Sociétés européennes*.

99. Joll, *Second International*; Haupt, *Socialism*.

100. Milner, *Dilemmas of Internationalism*; Howorth, 'French Workers'.

101. Becker, *1914*; Becker, 'Union sacrée et idéologie bourgeoise'.

102. Verhey, *Spirit of 1914*.

103. Becker, *1914*, p. 580; Flood, *France, 1914–1918,* ch. 1.

104. Raithel, 'Wunder', p. 500.

105. Michel, 'L'Autriche et l'entrée dans la guerre', pp. 6–10.

106. Sanborn, 'Mobilization of 1914'.

107. Ferguson, *Pity of War,* p. 182.

108. Strachan, *First World War: To Arms*, p. 156.

109. Gorce, *La France et son armée*, p. 131.

110. Strachan, *First World War: To Arms*, p. 158.

111. Sanborn, 'Mobilization of 1914'.

112. Mommsen, 'Topos'; Dülffer and Holl (eds.), *Bereit zum Kriege*.

113. Taylor, *War by Timetable*; Lebow, 'Agency versus Structure'.

114. Levy, 'Preferences, Constraints, and Choices'.

115. Joll, '1914: the Unspoken Assumptions', in Koch (ed.), *Origins*, p. 311.

116. Levy, 'Causes of War', p. 148.

117. Vogel, *Nationen im Gleichschritt,* p. 288.

Chapter 2

1. Renouvin, *Forms of War Government*, pp. 18–52.

2. Wilson, *Myriad Faces*, p. 154.

3. Chickering, *Imperial Germany*, p. 33.

4. Strachan, *First World War: To Arms*, p. 850.

5. Kennedy (ed.), *War Plans*; Snyder, *Ideology*; Buchholz, *Moltke, Schlieffen and Prussian War Planning*.

6. Ritter, *Schlieffen Plan*.

7. Zuber, 'Schlieffen Plan Reconsidered'.

8. Generally, Buchholz, *Moltke, Schlieffen and Prussian War Planning;* W. Dieckmann, 'Der Schlieffen Plan', BA-MA W-10 50220.

9. But see the controversy between Zuber, 'Schlieffen Plan Reconsidered' and 'Terence Holmes', Holmes, 'Reluctant March', and Foley 'Origins of the Schlieffen Plan'.

10. Stevenson, *Armaments*, p. 301.

11. Strachan, *First World War: To Arms*, p. 1005.

12. Ritter, *Schlieffen Plan*, p. 166.

13. Stevenson, *Armaments*, pp. 47, 50.

14. Samuels, *Command or Control?*, ch. 1; Mosier, *Myth*, ch. 2.

15. Stevenson, *Armaments*, pp. 41, 93.

16. Brose, in *The Kaiser's Army* stresses the army's inadequate modernization, partly due to lack of resources.

17. Livesey, *Viking Atlas*, p. 15.

18. Mosier, *Myth*, ch. 2.

19. Strachan, *First World War: To Arms*, pp. 207, 210; Wilson, *Myriad Faces*, p. 41.

20. Stevenson, *Armaments*, pp. 301, 299.

21. Helmreich, *Belgium and Europe*, pp. 153–66.

22. Williamson, *Grand Strategy*, pp. 181, 315.

23. Stevenson, *Armaments*, p. 6.

24. Holmes, *Little Field Marshal*, pp. 200–201.

25. Porch, 'The Marne and After', pp. 365–8.

26. Williamson, *Grand Strategy*, chs 1, 5.

27. May (ed.), *Knowing One's Enemies*, chs. 5, 6; undated memorandum by Greiner on German knowledge of French plans, 1885–1914, BA-MA W-10 50267.

28. Snyder, *Ideology*, ch. 3; Stevenson, *Armaments*, pp. 217–18.

29. Stevenson, *Armaments*, pp. 306–7, 330.

30. EMA 3rd Bureau, 'Plan XVII: Bases du Plan' (April 1913?) SHA 1.N.11.

31. Mosier, *Myth*, pp. 22–3.

32. Stevenson, 'War by Timetable?', pp. 167–9, 175–6.

33. Mosier, *Myth*, p. 45.

34. Guinard *et al.*, *Inventaire*, Vol. 1, pp. 58–60.

35. Holmes, 'The Last Hurrah', p. 280.

36. Glover and Silkin (eds.), *First World War Prose*, pp. 27, 93.

37. Horne and Kramer, *German Atrocities*, p. 13.

38. Mosier, *Myth*, p. 57.

39. ibid., ch. 3; Strachan, *First World War: To Arms*, pp. 211–12.

40. Renouvin, *Crise européenne*, pp. 238–9.

41. Barnett, *Swordbearers*, pp. 26–7.

42. Mosier, *Myth*, pp. 60–62.

43. Joffre, *Mémoires*, Vol. 1, p. 277.

44. Strachan, *First World War: To Arms*, p. 213; Keegan, *First World War*, p. 101.

45. Smith, *Between Mutiny and Obedience*, ch. 3.

46. Keegan, *First World War*, p. 107.

47. Strachan, *First World War: To Arms*, p. 230; Mosier, *Myth*, p. 80.

48. Joffre, *Mémoires*, Vol. 1, p. 299.

49. Barnett, *Swordbearers*, p. 59.

50. Mombauer, *Moltke*, p. 253.

51. Van Creveld, *Supplying War*, p. 126.

52. ibid, pp. 129–32; undated memorandum: 'Marnefeldzug und Eisenbahnen', BA-MA W-10 50799.

53. Van Creveld, *Supplying War*, pp. 124–5, 135.

54. Ferris (ed.), *British Army and Signals Intelligence*, p. 5.

55. Herwig, *First World War*, p. 98.

56. Memorandum, 'Marnefeldzug und Eisenbahnen', BA-MA W-10 50799; cf. Mombauer, *Moltke*, p. 243.

57. ibid., pp. 244–7; Barnett, *Swordbearers*, p. 52; Plessen diary, 25 August 1914, BA-MA W-10 50676.

58. Jäschke, 'Marne-Schlacht', p. 325.

59. Barnett, *Swordbearers*, pp. 63–70.

60. Cassar, *Tragedy of Sir John French*, pp. 120–23.

61. Strachan, *First World War: To Arms*, pp. 226–7.

62. Joffre, *Mémoires*, Vol. 1, p. 352–3; Joffre circular 25 August, GQG minute 30 August 1914, SHA 16.N. 1709.

63. Peschaud, *Politique et Fonctionnement*, p. 513.

64. Cassar, *Tragedy of Sir John French*, pp. 128–38; Holmes, *Little Field Marshal*, pp. 228–35.

65. Joffre, Mémoires, Vol. 2, pp. 312, 324.

66. Generally on the Marne, Strachan, *First World War: To Arms*, pp. 242–62, and Tyng, *Campaign of the Marne*.

67. Mosier, *Myth*, pp. 92–8.

68. Renouvin, *Crise européenne*, p. 247.

69. Jäschke, 'Marne-Schlacht', pp. 336–7; Strachan, *First World War: To Arms*, p. 994.

70. Brose, *Kaiser's Army*, p. 210.

71. Barnett, *Swordbearers*, p. 77.

72. Jäschke, 'Marne-Schlacht', p. 336.

73. Herwig, *First World War*, p. 102.

74. Hindenburg circular, 24 May 1917, BA-MA PH 3160; Hentsch to Hindenburg, 14 May 1917, BA-MA W-10 51062.

75. Jäschke, 'Marne-Schlacht', pp. 337–47.

76. Mombauer, *Moltke*, pp. 258, 265ff.

77. Keegan, *First World War*, p. 135; Herrmann, *Arming*, p. 90.

78. Cruttwell, *History of the Great War*, p. 36.

79. Joffre, *Mémoires*, Vol. 2, p. 424.

80. Contamine, *Victoire de la Marne*, p. 375.

81. Afflerbach, *Falkenhayn*, p. 190.

82. Contamine, *Victoire de la Marne*, p. 289.

83. Liulevicius, *War Land*, p. 14.
84. Stone, *Eastern Front*, pp. 57–8, 84.
85. Fuller, *Civil–Military Conflict*, pp. 52–3.
86. Jones, 'Imperial Russia's Forces', pp. 278–9.
87. Stone, *Eastern Front*, pp. 30–35; Stevenson, *Armaments*, pp. 155–6, 159.
88. Stone, *Eastern Front*, p. 32.
89. Jones, 'Imperial Russia's Forces', p. 262.
90. ibid., p. 281.
91. Keegan, *First World War*, p. 152.
92. Snyder, *Ideology*, ch. 7.
93. Stone, 'Army and Society', p. 107.
94. Herwig, *First World War*, p. 14.
95. Rothenberg, 'Austro-Hungarian Campaign', p. 129.
96. Stevenson, *Armaments*, p. 356.
97. Stone, 'Mobilmachung', pp. 68–77; Stone, 'Moltke and Conrad', pp. 225–30.
98. Stone, *Eastern Front*, p. 57.
99. Showalter, 'Even Generals', p. 67.
100. Stone, *Eastern Front*, p. 58.
101. ibid., p. 51.
102. Keegan, *First World War*, pp. 160–61.
103. ibid., p. 58.
104. Showalter, *Tannenberg*, pp. 172ff.
105. Asprey, *German High Command*, ch. 5.
106. Showalter, 'Even Generals', pp. 74–80.
107. Showalter, *Tannenberg*, p. 293; Mombauer, *Moltke*, p. 247.
108. Asprey, *German High Command*, p. 78.
109. Herwig, *First World War*, p. 86.
110. Showalter, *Tannenberg*, p. 378.
111. Stone, *Eastern Front*, pp. 67–9.
112. Stone, 'Moltke and Conrad', pp. 233–42.
113. Stone, 'Mobilmachung', p. 91.
114. Strachan, *First World War: To Arms*, pp. 347–51.
115. Herwig, *First World War*, pp. 89–90.
116. Stone, *Eastern Front*, pp. 83–90.
117. Herwig, *First World War*, pp. 94–5.
118. Rachamimov, *POWs*, ch. 1.
119. Keegan, *First World War*, p. 166.
120. Stevenson, *Armaments*, p. 354; Lyon, 'A "Peasant Mob"', p. 492.
121. Lyon, '"A Peasant Mob"', pp. 487–501; Rothenberg, 'Austro-Hungarian Campaign', pp. 134–5.
122. Herwig, *First World War*, pp. 87–8.
123. Djordjević, 'Vojvoda Putnik', pp. 576–9.
124. Afflerbach, *Falkenhayn*, pp. 190–91; Lange, *Marneschlacht,* pp. 45–9.
125. Mombauer, *Moltke*, pp. 165–70.
126. Falkenhayn, *General Headquarters*, p. 23; Afflerbach, *Falkenhayn*, pp. 190–93.
127. Mosier, *Myth*, pp. 104–15
128. Joffre, *Mémoires*, Vol. I, p. 148.
129. ibid., pp. 457–8; Cassar, *Tragedy of Sir John French*, pp. 154–5.
130. Strachan, *First World War: To Arms*, p. 993; Joffre, *Mémoires*, Vol. 1, pp. 429–30.
131. Joffre, *Mémoires*, Vol. 1, pp. 429–30;and Hardach, 'Industrial Mobilization', p. 59.
132. Strachan, *First World War: To Arms*, pp. 272–3.
133. Asprey, *German High Command*, p. 122.
134. Falkenhayn, *General Headquarters*, p. 29; Afflerbach, *Falkenhayn*, pp. 191ff.
135. Joffre, Mémoires, Vol. 1, pp. 467, 478.
136. Holmes, *Little Field Marshal*, p. 246; Cassar, *Tragedy of Sir John French*, p. 164.
137. Plessen diary, 18 November 1914, BA-MA W-10 50656.
138. Unruh, *Langemarck*; and Hüppauf, 'Langemarck, Verdun', pp. 71–85.
139. Falkenhayn, *General Headquarters*, pp 34 –7, 40–42.
140. GQG memo, 26 November 1914, SHA 16.N.1709; Joffre, *Mémoires*, Vol. 1, pp. 481–2.
141. Asprey, *German High Command*, p. 112.
142. Falkenhayn, *General Headquarters*, pp. 18, 21; Herwig, *First World War*, p. 106.
143. Stone, *Eastern Front*, p. 93.
144. Asprey, *German High Command*, p. 125.
145. Afflerbach, *Falkenhayn,* pp. 196–7; Falkenhayn, *General Headquarters*, pp. 25ff.
146. Keegan, *First World War*, pp. 180ff.

147. Rothenberg, 'Austro-Hungarian Campaign', pp. 141–3; Djordjević, 'Vojvoda Putnik', pp. 581–4; Schindler, 'Disaster on the Drina', p. 191.

148. Showalter, 'Even Generals', p. 69.

149. Strachan, *First World War: To Arms*, p. 448.

150. ibid., p. 454.

151. Halpern, *Naval History*, p. 69. This is the best survey of the war at sea.

152. Keegan, *First World War*, pp. 231ff.

153. Marder, *Dreadnought*, Vol. 2, pp. 101–17.

154. Halpern, *Naval History*, pp. 91–3.

155. Strachan, *First World War: To Arms*, pp. 476–8.

156. Sumida, *In Defence of Naval Supremacy*, ch. 2.

157. Halpern, *Naval History*, p. 84.

158. Strachan, *First World War: To Arms*, pp. 480; Cruttwell, *History of the Great War*, p. 75.

159. Marder, *Dreadnought*, Vol. 2, p. 1. Also on the naval war in Europe, Goldrick, *King's Ships*.

160. Lambi, *Navy and German Power Politics*, p. 405.

161. Gemzell, *Organization, Conflict, and Innovation*, pp. 176–7.

162. Tirpitz, *Memoirs*, Vol. 2, p. 366.

163. Keegan, *First World War*, p. 289.

164. Gemzell, *Organization, Conflict, and Innovation*, pp. 177–9, 138.

165. Marder, *Dreadnought*, Vol. 2, pp. 42–3; Halpern, *Naval History*, pp. 23, 27.

166. Halpern, *Naval History*,, pp. 6–9.

167. Tarrant, *Jutland*, pp. 16–19.

168. Strachan, *First World War: To Arms*, pp. 406–7.

169. Williamson, *Politics of Grand Strategy*, pp. 187–93.

170. Halpern, *Naval History*, pp. 23–4.

171. Barnett, *Swordbearers*, p. 116.

172. Halpern, *Naval History*, pp. 24–5; Marder, *Dreadnought*, Vol. 2, p. 1.

173. Offer, *First World War: Agrarian Interpretation*, chs. 16, 21.

174. Marder, *Dreadnought*, Vol. 1, pp. 60–61.

175. Cruttwell, *History of the Great War*, p. 67.

176. Barnett, *Swordbearers*, p. 110.

177. Halpern, *Naval History*, p. 17; Strachan (ed.), *Illustrated History*, pp. 109–110.

178. Halpern, *Naval History*, pp. 11–15, 59–60.

179. Marder, *Dreadnought*, Vol. 1, pp. 55, 66–75.

180. Patterson, *Jellicoe*, pp. 70–71.

181. Strachan, *First World War: To Arms*, pp. 435–6.

182. Eksteins, *Rites of Spring*, pp. 150–51.

183. Mosier, *Myth*, pp. 143–4.

184. Brown and Seaton, *Christmas Truce*.

185. Ashworth, *Trench Warfare*, pp. 24ff.

186. Guinard *et al.*, *Inventaire*, Vol. 1, p. 45.

187. Strachan, *First World War: To Arms*, p. 278.

188. Mosier, *Myth*, p. 121.

189. Wildman, *End of the Russian Imperial Army*, Vol. 1, p. 85.

190. Stone, *Eastern Front*, p. 122.

191. Foley, 'East or West?', p. 122. Mosier, *Myth*, p. 12.

192. Becker, *Great War and the French People*, p. 47.

193. Horne and Kramer, *German Atrocities*, p. 82.

194. Horne and Kramer, 'German "Atrocities"'; *German Atrocities*, pp. 43, 74–6.

195. Gullace, 'Sexual Violence', p. 735.

196. Stevenson, *French War Aims*, pp. 13–14.

197. Farrar, *Short-War Illusion*, pp. 118–19; Sweet, 'Leaders and Policies'.

198. Marder, *Dreadnought*, Vol. 1, p. 63.

199. Simkins, *Kitchener's Army*, ch. 3.

200. Becker, *Great War and the French People*, pp. 48–63; Hopkin, 'Domestic Censorship' pp. 153–5; Deist, 'Censorship and Propaganda', pp. 201–4.

201. Lawrence, Dean, and Robert, 'Outbreak of War'.

202. Guinard *et al.*, *Inventaire*, Vol. 1, p. 204.

203. Stone, *Eastern Front*, pp. 123, 216.

204. Ullrich, and Ziemann (eds.), *Frontalltag*, p. 114.

205. Afflerbach, *Falkenhayn*, p. 194.

206. Good discussion in Strachan, *First World War: To Arms*, ch. 12.

207. Simkins, *Kitchener's Army*, ch. 4; Dewey, 'Military Recruiting'.

Chapter 3

1. Ferguson, *Pity of War*, ch. 10; Kennedy, 'Military Effectiveness', p. 345.

2. Keegan, *Price of Admiralty*, p. 90.

3. On Verdun: Cruttwell, *History of the Great War*, p. 251; Gilbert, *First World War*, pp. 299–300. On the Somme: Winter, *Haig's Command*, p. 46.

4. Stevenson, *Armaments*, p. 6.

5. Harrison, *Economics of World War II*, p. 21.

6. Ferguson, *Pity of War*, p. 320.

Chapter 4

1. Reynolds, 'Origins of the Two "World Wars"', pp. 29–33.

2. Holland, British Empire', p. 118.

3. Andrews, *Anzac Illusion*, pp. xiv, 8,13, 40–41.

4. Brown and Louis (eds.), *Oxford History of the British Empire*, Vol. 4, p. 115; Ferguson, *Empire*, p. 303.

5. Renzi, *Shadow of the Sword*, p. 265.

6. Nish, *Japanese Foreign Policy*, p. 93.

7. ibid., pp. 83–97; Nish, *Alliance in Decline*, ch. 7; Lowe, *Great Britain and Japan*, chs. 6, 7.

8. Sims, *Political History of Modern Japan*, pp. 115–35; Barnhart, *Japan and the World*, ch. 4; Nish in Wilson (ed.), *Decisions for War*, ch. 8; Dickinson, *War and National Reinvention*.

9. In general: Strachan, *First World War: To Arms*, ch. 8; Gottlieb, *Studies in Secret Diplomacy*; Kent (ed.), *Great Powers and the End of the Ottoman Empire*; MacFie, *End of the Ottoman Empire*; Yapp, *Modern Near East*; Yasamee, in Wilson (ed.), *Decisions for War*, ch. 9.

10. Heller, 'Sir Louis Mallet'; Kurat, 'How Turkey Drifted'.

11. Kurat, *How Turkey Drifted*, and Trumpener, *Germany and the Ottoman Empire*.

12. Renzi, *Shadow of the Sword* is now the best account. See also Bosworth, *Italy the Least of the Great Powers*; Lowe and Marzari, *Italian Foreign Policy*; Salandra, *Italy and the Great War*; Gottlieb, *Studies in Secret Diplomacy*; Jones, 'Antonio Salandra'; Valiani, *End of Austria-Hungary*.

13. Beckett, *Great War*, pp. 85–6; Stevenson (ed.), *British Documents*, Vol. 2, docs. 273, 274.

14. Crampton, *Bulgaria*; Robbins, 'British Diplomacy'; Smith, *Russian Struggle for Power*, pp. 309–35; Silberstein, *Alliance*, ch. 7.

15. Vinogradov, 'Romania'; Torrey, 'Rumania'; Silberstein, *Troubled Alliance*, chs. 8–10; Spector, *Rumania*, pp. 5–39.

16. Yasamee, in Wilson (ed.), *Decisions for War*, p. 229.

17. Generally, Trumpener in Strachan (ed.), *Oxford Illustrated History*, ch. 6; Strachan, *First World War: To Arms*, pp. 680–93; Emin, *Turkey*, pp. 78ff.

18. Strachan, *First World War: To Arms*, pp. 712–29.

19. On Armenia: Hovanissian, *Armenia*, and Hovanissian (ed.), *Armenian Genocide*; Walker, 'Armenian Genocide'; Dyer, 'Turkish "Falsifiers"'.

20. On the Dardanelles see especially: Travers, 'Ottoman Crisis'; Travers, *Gallipoli, 1915*; Rhodes James, *Gallipoli*. For memoir accounts, see Hamilton, *Gallipoli Diary*; Churchill, *World Crisis*, Vol. 2.

21. Travers, *Gallipoli*, p. 229; Aspinall-Oglander, *Military Operations: Gallipoli 1915*, Vol. 2, p. 488.

22. Andrews, *Anzac Illusion*, pp. 51–63.

23. Ben-Moshe, 'Churchill's Strategic Conception'.

24. Cassar, *French and the Dardanelles*.

25. French, 'Origins of the Dardanelles Campaign'; French, *British Strategy and War Aims*, chs. 3–5.

26. Travers, *Gallipoli 1915*, p. 32 corrects earlier sources on this point; cf. also Marder, 'Dardanelles Reconsidered'.

27. French, 'Dardanelles, Mecca, and Kut'.

28. Doyle and Bennett, 'Military Geography. . . Gallipoli Campaign'.

29. For discussion, see Travers, *Gallipoli 1915*, pp. 163–76, 221–9; Liddle, *Men of Gallipoli*.

30. Hamilton, *Gallipoli Diary*, Vol. 1, pp. 62, 196, 204.

31. Travers, *Gallipoli 1915*, ch. 8.

32. Travers, 'Command and Leadership Styles', p. 433.

33. Cohen, 'Genesis of the British Campaign'.

34. Barker, *Neglected War: Mesopotamia*; Goold, 'Lord Hardinge'; Galbraith, 'No Man's Child'.

35. MacFie, *End of the Ottoman Empire*, pp. 149–50.

36. Kennedy, 'Britain in the First World War', p. 71.

37. Trumpener in Strachan (ed.), *Oxford Illustrated History*, p. 88.

38. Best account is in Strachan, *First World War: To Arms*, chs. 6, 7.

39. On Africa see also Farwell, *Great War in Africa*; Page (ed.), Africa; *Journal of African History*, Vol. 19, No. 1 (1978).

40. Strachan, *First World War: To Arms*, pp. 498–505.

41. Goldberg, 'Origins of British–Saudi Relations'.

42. Karsh, 'Myth in the Desert'.

43. French, 'Dardanelles, Mecca, and Kut', p. 45.

44. Porter, *Lion's Share*, p. 238; Ellinwood and Pradham (eds.), *India*, p. 26; Burke, 'Moroccan Resistance', p. 440.

45. On West Africa: Michel, *L'Appel à l'Afrique*, p. 469.

46. Omissi, *Sepoy and the Raj*, pp. 135, 137, 148.

47. Fraser, 'Germany and Indian Revolution'.

48. Burke, 'Moroccan Resistance'.

49. Deakin, 'Imperial Germany and the "Holy War"'; generally on German subversion, see Fischer, *Germany's Aims*, ch. 4; Strachan, *First World War: To Arms*, ch. 9.

Chapter 5

1. Stevenson, *French War Aims*, p. 95.

2. Goemans, *War and Punishment*, p. 16.

3. For general surveys of war aims, ibid.; also Stevenson, *First World War and International Politics*, ch. 3; and Soutou, *L'Or et le sang*.

4. Trumpener, *Germany and the Ottoman Empire*, pp. 131–4.

5. Komjáthy (ed.), *Protokolle*, pp. 352–72; Scherer and Grünewald (eds.), *L'Allemagne*, Vol. 1, docs. 86, 144, 151, 162, 164; Ritter, *Sword*, Vol. 3, pp. 83–9.

6. Fischer, *Germany's Aims*, p. 106.

7. ibid., pp. 103–5.

8. Soutou, 'Kriegsziele' pp. 29–30, Soutou, *L'Or et le sang*, ch. 2; Thompson, 'September Program'.

9. Farrar, *Short-War Illusion*, ch. 9; Scherer and Grünewald (eds.), *L'Allemagne*, Vol. 1, docs. 13, 14, 16, 20, 21.

10. Scherer and Grünewald (eds.), *L'Allemagne*, Vol.1, docs. 172, 183, 206; Fischer, *Germany's Aims*, pp. 215–24.

11. ibid., ch. 8.

12. Scherer and Grünewald (eds.), *L'Allemagne*, Vol. 1; docs. 52, 75; Linke, *Zarische Russland*, pp. 102–4.

13. Geiss, *Polnische Grenzstreifen*, p. 91.

14. Meyer, *Mitteleuropa*, ch. 9.

15. Afflerbach, *Falkenhayn*, pp. 321–22.

16. Generally on Poland: Scherer and Grünewald (eds.), *L'Allemagne*, Vol. 1, docs. 131, 140, 165, 167, 221, 227, 261, 296, 303–5; Fischer, *Germany's Aims*, pp. 236–44, 271–3.

17. Fischer, *Germany's Aims*, pp. 228–30; Scherer and Grünewald (eds.), *L'Allemagne*, Vol. 1, docs. 243, 255, 350, 384.

18. Soutou, *L'Or et le sang*, ch. 11.

19. Goemans, *War and Punishment*, p. 85.

20. Farrar, *Divide and Conquer*, p. 23.

21. Jarausch, *Enigmatic Chancellor*, pp. 200, 217.

22. On this topic, see Janssen, *Macht und Verblendung*.

23. Soutou, *L'Or et le sang*, ch. 2.

24. Jarausch, *Enigmatic Chancellor*, pp. 214–16; Fischer, *Germany's Aims*, pp. 193–4.

25. On Russia: Linke, *Zarische Russland*; Smith, *Russian Struggle*; Dallin (ed.), *Russian Diplomacy*.

26. Bobroff, 'Devolution', pp. 512–14.

27. Linke, *Zarische Russland*, pp. 131–2.

28. Bobroff, 'Devolution', pp. 522–7.

29. Smith, *Russian Struggle*, pp. 45–50, 97–108; Renzi, 'Sazonov's Thirteen Points'.

30. Renzi, 'Sazonov's Thirteen Points', p. 18; Dallin (ed.), *Russian Diplomacy*, ch. 2; Perman, *Shaping of the Czechoslovak State*, ch. 1.

31. Sazonov, *Fateful Years*, p. 252.

32. For the background, see Bodger on 'Russia', in Kent (ed.), *Great Powers and the End of the Ottoman Empire*, ch. 4.

33. Smith, *Russian Struggle*, pp. 185–238; Gottlieb, *Studies in Secret Diplomacy*, chs. 4–6; Kerner, 'Russia, the Straits, and Constantinople'.

34. Stevenson, *French War Aims*, p. 28; Dallin (ed.), *Russian Diplomacy*, p. 89.

35. Goemans, *War and Punishment*, pp. 128–32.

36. Smith, *Russian Struggle*, pp. 363–82, 418–24; Linke, *Zarische Russland*, pp. 54–60.

37. Stevenson, *French War Aims*, ch. 1.

38. ibid., pp. 17, 27.

39. Andrew and Kanya-Forstner, *France Overseas*, ch. 4; Nevakivi, *Britain, France*, pp. 36–44.

40. Soutou, *L'Or et le sang*, ch. 5.

41. Soutou, *L'Or et le sang*, ch. 7; Trachtenberg, '"New Economic Order": Clémentel'.

42. Stevenson, *French War Aims*, pp. 38–56.

43. Rothwell, *British War Aims*, Introduction. Generally on Britain, see ibid. and French, *British Strategy and War Aims*.

44. Louis, *Great Britain and Germany's Lost Colonies*, ch. 2.

45. Kent, 'Britain', in Kent (ed.), *Great Powers and the End of the Ottoman Empire*, ch. 7.

46. Generally, Kedourie, *Anglo-Arab Labyrinth*; Friedman, *Palestine: a Twice Promised Land?* ch. 5.

47. Hurewitz (ed.), *Diplomacy in the Near and Middle East*, Vol. 2, doc. 8.

48. Friedman, *Palestine: a Twice-Promised Land?*, chs. 1–2.

49. Rothwell, *British War Aims*, pp. 70–75.

50. Steiner and Neilson, *Britain and the Origins of the First World War*, p. 66.

51. Rothwell, *War Aims*, pp. 266ff.; Bunselmeyer, *Cost of the War*, chs. 2–5.

52. Stevenson, 'Belgium, Luxemburg, and the Defence of Western Europe'.

53. Rothwell, *British War Aims*, pp. 38–52.

54. Lloyd George, *War Memoirs*, vol. 1, pp. 1049–50.

55. French, *British Strategy and War Aims*, pp. 191–4, 210; Hankey MSS, CCAC, 1/1, Diary 14, 15, 21 March, 24 May 1916.

56. Scott (ed.), *War Aims and Peace Proposals*, pp. 26–9, 35–8; Kernek, 'British Government's Reaction'; Stevenson, *French War Aims*, pp. 45–7.

57. Asquith, *Memories and Reflections*, Vol. 2, pp. 138–47; Lowe and Dockrill, *Mirage of Power*, Vol. 2, pp. 244–5.

58. Lowe and Dockrill, *Mirage of Power*, Vol. 2, pp. 223–7; Seton-Watson, *Italy*, pp. 462–7.

59. Nish, *Alliance in Decline*, ch. 11; Halpern, *Naval History*, p. 393.

60. Jansen, *Japanese and Sun Yat-sen*, ch. 8; La Fargue, *China*, chs. 2–3; Nish, *Japanese Foreign Policy*, ch. 5; Lowe, *Great Britain and Japan*, ch. 8.

Chapter 6

1. Afflerbach, Falkenhayn, pp. 233–54; Foley, 'East or West?', pp. 123–30.

2. Rachamimov, *POWs*, p. 38.

3. Stone, *Eastern Front*, ch. 6; Rauchensteiner, *Tod des Doppeladlers*, pp. 199–211.

4. Herwig, *First World War*, pp. 130–34; Falkenhayn, *General Headquarters*, pp. 53–64; cf. ch. 5 above.

5. Afflerbach, 'Planning Total War?', p. 119.

6. Strachan, *First World War: To Arms*, p. 1037; Falkenhayn, *General Headquarters*, pp. 43–5.

7. Tucker, *Great War*, p. 76. Afflerbach, *Falkenhayn*, p. 312. Generally on this campaign, see Stone, *Eastern Front*, chs. 6, 8.

8. Falkenhayn, *General Headquarters*, pp. 114, 127–9, 145–51; Afflerbach, *Falkenhayn*, pp. 294–313.

9. Afflerbach, *Falkenhayn*, pp. 336–7; Falkenhayn, *General Headquarters,* pp. 159–62.

10. See generally French, *British Strategy and War Aims*, pp. ix-xiv.

11. Clark, *Donkeys*, chs. 3, 4; Prior and Wilson, *Command*, pp. 19ff.

12. French, *British Strategy and War Aims*, ch. 4; Neilson, 'Kitchener', pp. 207, 217, 225.

13. Mosier, *Myth*, ch. 8.

14. Guinard *et al.* (eds.), *Inventaire*, Vol. 1, p. 219.

15. Stevenson, 'French Strategy', pp. 305–6.

16. Mosier, *Myth*, pp. 125, 148, 181–2.

17. ibid., pp. 145, 149. Casualties, May–June: Germany 73,000; France 102,000; Britain 37,000 (Tucker, *Great War*, p. 65).

18. Paléologue report, 25 December 1914: SHA 6.N.34.

19. Laguiche report, 19 March 1915: SHA 6.N.34.

20. Mosier, *Myth*, pp. 148–52.

21. Gooch, 'Italy in the First World War', p. 162.

22. Millett and Murray (eds.), *Military Effectiveness*, Vol. 1, pp. 165–6.

23. Melograni, *Storia politica*, p. 44.

24. Poincaré, *Au Service de la France*, Vol. 7, pp. 36–7, 68–9; Stevenson (ed.), British Documents, Vol. 2, doc. 123.

25. Notes by Nudant and Operations Bureau, 18 and 20 June 1915: SHA 16.N.1709.

26. Poincaré, *Au Service de la France*, Vol. 7, pp. 36–8, 68–9.

27. Haig MSS, NLS, Box 96, diary 19 Aug. 1915.

28. French, *British Strategy and War Aims*, ch. 6.

29. Prior and Wilson, *Command on the Western Front*, pp. 100ff.; Wilson, *Myriad Faces*, pp. 254–8.

30. Champagne: France 144,000; Germany 85,000. Artois: Britain 62,000; France 48,000; Germany 51,000 (Tucker, *Great War*, pp. 51, 70).

31. See generally Dutton, *Politics of Diplomacy*.

32. Tanenbaum, *Maurice Sarrail*; King, *Generals and Politicians*, pp. 67–88.

33. Prete, '*Imbroglio par excellence*'.

34. Philpott, 'Squaring the Circle'; Conference conclusions, LHCMA Robertson MSS I/9.

35. Fuller, 'Eastern Front', p. 45.

36. French, 'Meaning of Attrition'.

37. British and French rebuttals, 16 and 27 December 1915, SHA 5.N.118.

38. Robertson, *Soldiers and Statesmen*, Vol. 1, pp. 184, 239–40, 253.

39. Horne, *Price of Glory*, p. 327; but cf. Mosier, *Myth*, pp. 225, 227.

40. Falkenhayn, *General Headquarters*, pp. 209–32; Afflerbach, *Falkenhayn*, pp. 351–69.

41. Afflerbach, 'Planning Total War?', pp. 121–3; Krumeich, '"Saigner la France"?', Sheffield, *Somme*, p. 15.

42. Horne, *Price of Glory*, p. 48.

43. King, *Generals and Politicians*, pp. 89–100.

44. Horne, *Price of Glory*, p. 299.

45. Krumeich, '"Saigner la France"?'

46. Stone, *Eastern Front*, pp. 227–9.

47. Herwig, *First World War*, pp. 204ff.

48. Keegan, *First World War*, p. 297; Brown, *British Logistics*, p. 112; Stone, *Eastern Front*, p. 212.

49. Reports by General Pau, 5 Mar., 9 April 1916, SHA 5.N.139.

50. Pau report, 9 March 1916, SHA 5.N.139.

51. Brusilov, *Mémoires*, pp. 184–8.

52. Report by de Laguiche, 3 June 1916, SHA 5.N.139.

53. Brusilov, *Mémoires*, pp. 187–202, 208.

54. Stone, *Eastern Front*, pp. 247–62, 270–73.

55. Sheffield, *Somme*, p. 151. The British Official History inflated German losses to over 600,000: Williams, 'Treatment of German Losses', pp. 69–74.

56. Winter, *Haig's Command*, p. 45.

57. ibid., pp. 49–63; Philpott, *Anglo-French Relations*, ch. 7; Greenhalgh, 'Why the British Were on the Somme'. See also the recent controversy: Philpott, 'Why the British Were Really on the Somme', Greenhalgh, 'Flames over the Somme'.

58. Foch, *Mémoires*, Vol. 2, pp. xv–xvii; GQG memo, 16 May 1916, SHA 16.N.1710.

59. French, *British Strategy and War Aims*, ch. 10; Chamberlain memo, 17 January 1916, AC 13/3/14.

60. Middlebrook, *First Day on the Somme*; Prior and Wilson, *Command on the Western Front*, chs. 15–17; Travers, *Killing Ground*, chs. 6, 7; Sheffield, *Somme*, pp. 41–68.

61. Sheffield, *Somme*, p. 88.

62. ibid., pp. 89–90, 94–6, 120; Andrews, *Anzac Illusion*, pp. 96–8.

63. Griffith, *Battle Tactics*, pp. 65ff.

64. Travers, *Killing Ground*, pp. 86, 127–8; Haig Diary, 1, 12, 22, August, 2, 5, 15 October, 3, 12 November 1916, Haig MSS, NLS, Box 97.

65. Greenhalgh, 'Why the British Were on the Somme', p. 148.

66. Afflerbach, *Falkenhayn*, pp. 417–20.

67. Krumeich, 'Le Soldat allemand', p. 168; Jünger, *Storm of Steel*, pp. 92–110.

68. Torrey, 'Rumanian Campaign'.

69. Janssen, 'Wechsel'; Janssen, *Der Kanzler und der General*, ch. 24; Afflerbach, *Falkenhayn*, ch, V.23.

70. Wynne, *If Germany Attacks*, pp. 128–30.

71. Herwig, *First World War*, p. 249.

72. Joffre, *Mémoires*, Vol. 2, pp. 346–7. GQG memoranda, 31 October, 10 December 1916, SHA 16.N. 1710.

73. Melograni, *Storia politica*, p. 238.

74. Gondrecourt report, 22 January 1917, SHA 5.N.144.

75. Reports by Janin, 18 January, and de Castelnau, 2 February 1917, SHA 5.N.140.

76. Meeting with Russian War Minister, 2 February 1917, SHA 5.N.140.

77. French, *Strategy of the Lloyd George Coalition*, ch. 2.

78. King, *Generals and Politicians*, pp. 135–9; Joffre, *Mémoires*, Vol. 2, ch. 6.

79. Mosier, *Myth*, p. 272.

80. Philpott, *Anglo-French Relations*, ch. 8; Winter, *Haig's Command*, ch. 5.

81. Stevenson, 'French Strategy', pp. 312–14; Miquel, *Chemin des Dames*, chs. 1–3; Nivelle's justification in SHA 5.N.255.

82. Wynne, *If Germany Attacks*, pp. 165–6, 170–84. Wilson, *Myriad Faces*, pp. 450–56.

83. Mosier, *Myth*, pp. 273–4.

84. For general accounts, see Spears, *Prelude to Victory* and Miquel, *Chemin des Dames*.

Chapter 7

1. Griffith, *Battle Tactics*, p. 30.

2. ibid.

3. Keegan, *First World War*, pp. 198–202.

4. Falkenhayn, *General Headquarters*, pp. 13, 40–41.

5. ibid., pp. 36–7; Wynne, *If Germany Attacks*, pp. 13–17.

6. Doyle and Bennett, 'Military Geography'.

7. Wynne, *If Germany Attacks*, pp. 100–103.

8. Keegan, *First World War*, pp. 197–98.

9. Ashworth, *Trench Warfare*, pp. 3–7; Fussell, *Great War*, ch. 2.

10. Keegan, *First World War*, p. 203; Henniker, *Transportation*, p. xxi.

11. Prior and Wilson, *Command on the Western Front*, pp. 64–5.

12. Sarter, *Deutschen Eisenbahnen*, p. 91; Marchand, *Chemins de fer*, p. 125.

13. Singleton, 'Britain's Military Use of Horses'.

14. Whalen, *Bitter Wounds*, p. 50.

15. Gudmundsson, *Stormtroop Tactics*, pp. 94–5.

16. Griffith, *Battle Tactics*, p. 38.

17. Wynne, *If Germany Attacks*, p. 76.

18. ibid., pp. 34, 54.

19. Travers, *Killing Ground*, pp. 155, 157.

20. Wynne, *If Germany Attacks*, pp. 91ff.

21. French, 'Military Background to the "Shell Crisis"', pp. 197–8; GQG memoranda, 30 May and 2 June 1915, SHA 16.N.1709.

22. Whalen, *Bitter Wounds*, p. 42.

23. Prior and Wilson, *Command on the Western Front*, pp. 36–41.

24. Mosier, *Myth*, p. 149.

25. Stevenson, 'French Strategy', pp. 306–307.

26. Prior and Wilson, *Command on the Western Front*, p. 166.

27. Keegan, *Face of Battle*, pp. 235–6.

28. Bidwell and Graham, *Fire-Power*, pp. 8–9.

29. Ibid, p. 141; Hartcup, *War of Invention*, pp. 76–8.

30. Prior and Wilson, *Command on the Western Front*, chs. 16, 17. French, "Shell Crisis", pp. 199–200.

31. Willan, B. P., 'South African Native Labour Contingent', p, 61; Robb, *British Culture*, p. 17.

32. Keegan, *Face of Battle*, p. 123; Prior and Wilson, *Command on the Western Front*, p. 156; Henniker, *Transportation*, p. 119; Brown, *British Logistics*, ch. 4.

33. Marchand, *Chemins de fer*, pp. 390, 406.

34. Gudmundsson, *Stormtroop Tactics*, pp. 27–35; Hartcup, *War of Invention*, pp. 62–6.

35. Gudmundsson, *Stormtroop Tactics*, pp. 44–5, 58, 64.

36. Generally on gas, Haber, *Poisonous Cloud*; Spiers, *Chemical Warfare*, ch. 2; Trumpener, 'Road to Ypres'.

37. Graves, *Goodbye to All That*, pp. 125ff.

38. Horne, *Price of Glory*, pp. 282–88.

39. Prior and Wilson, *Command on the Western Front*, pp. 234, 239.

40. Mosier, *Myth*, pp. 238–9.

41. Andrews, *Anzac Illusion*, p. 99.

42. Mosier, *Myth*, pp. 274–5.

43. Bidwell and Graham, *Firepower*, pp. 100–103.

44. Griffith, *Battle Tactics*, p. 136.

45. Ferris, 'Airbandit', pp. 36–41.

46. Wilson, *Myriad Faces*, pp. 87, 156–7, 389–93.

47. Murray, *War in the Air*, pp. 32–3.

48. Hartcup, *War of Invention*, pp. 145–7; Morrow, *German Air Power*, pp. 48–56.

49. Cooper, *Birth of Independent Air Power*, pp. 71–4.

50. Murray, *War in the Air*, p. 41.

51. ibid., pp. 74–80.

52. Griffith, *Battle Tactics*, p. 153; Hartcup, *War of Invention*, pp. 70–76.

53. Sheffield, *Somme*, p. 72.

54. Griffith, *Battle Tactics*, pp. 142–6.

55. Gudmundsson, *Stormtroop Tactics*, pp. 83–7; Herwig, *First World War*, p. 253.

56. Greenhalgh, 'Why the British', p. 157; Horne, *Price of Glory*, ch. 25.

57. Gudmundsson, *Stormtroop Tactics*, p. 88.

58. Lupfer, 'Dynamics', pp. 38–9; Pierrefeu, *GQG*, Vol. 1, p. 163.

59. Griffith, *Battle Tactics*, pp. 176–9.

60. On this, Wynne, *If Germany Attacks* is essential.

61. Cruttwell, *Great War*, p. 446.
62. De Gondrecourt to Joffre, 19 November 1915, SHA 7.N.735.
63. EMA 2nd Bureau, reports on Isonzo offensives of August-November 1916, SHA 7.N. 743.
64. Millett and Murray (eds.), *Military Effectiveness*, Vol. 1, pp. 171–2, 177.
65. Fuller, 'Eastern Front', pp. 61–2.
66. Stone, *Eastern Front*, pp. 93–4.
67. Stone, *Eastern Front*, p. 131; Gudmundsson, *Stormtroop Tactics*, pp. 108–11.
68. Brusilov, *Mémoires*, pp. 197–201, 208–9; Millett and Murray (eds.), *Military Effectiveness*, Vol. 1, pp. 310–12.
69. Ferguson, *Pity of War*, pp. 300–302.

Chapter 8

1. Whalen, *Bitter Wounds*, p. 39.
2. Millett and Murray (eds.), *Military Effectiveness*, Vol. 1, p. 278. Wildman, *End of the Russian Imperial Army*, Vol. 1, p. 96.
3. Guinard *et al.* (eds.), *Inventaire*, Vol. 1, p. 204.
4. Beckett, *First World War*, p. 399; Dewey, 'Military Recruiting', p. 199.
5. Jones, 'Imperial Russia', p. 278.
6. Guinard *et al.* (eds.), *Inventaire*, Vol. 1, p. 210.
7. ibid., p. 204.
8. Smith, *Between Mutiny and Obedience*, p. 126.
9. Guinard *et al.* (eds.), *Inventaire*, Vol. 1, p. 213.
10. ibid., p. 206.
11. Horne, 'L'Impôt du sang'.
12. Michel, 'Mythes et réalités du concours colonial', pp. 364–5; Michel, *L'Appel à l'Afrique*, pp. 404–8.
13. Wildman, *End of the Russian Imperial Army*, Vol. 1, pp. 85, 95.
14. Jones in Millett and Murray (eds.), *Military Effectiveness*, Vol. 1, pp. 279–80.
15. ibid., p. 281; Wildman, *End of the Russian Imperial Army*, Vol. 1, p. 98.
16. Stone, *Eastern Front*, p. 217.
17. Wildman, *End of the Russian Imperial Army*, Vol. 1, p. 99.
18. Stone, *Eastern Front*, p. 281; Kenez, 'Changes in Social Composition', p. 370.
19. Kenez, 'Changes in Social Composition', p. 373.
20. Wildman, *End of the Russian Imperial Army*, Vol. 1, p. 100.
21. Kenez, 'Changes in Social Composition', p. 369.
22. Robb, *British Culture*, pp. 16–17, 22–3; Judd, *Empire*, p. 245; Holland, 'British Empire', p. 117.
23. Bourne, 'British Working Men', p. 339.
24. Spiers, *Haldane*, p. 186.
25. Simkins, *Kitchener's Army*, pp. 49ff.
26. Beckett, *Great War*, p. 210.
27. Jeffery, *Ireland*, pp. 7, 35.
28. Dewey, 'Military Recruiting'.
29. Simkins, *Kitchener's Army*, ch. 6; Winter, *Death's Men*, pp. 32ff.
30. Omissi, *Sepoy and the Raj*, pp. 38–9; cf. Omissi (ed.), *Indian Voices*.
31. Holland, 'British Empire', p. 126.
32. ibid.; Andrews, *Anzac Illusion*, p. 45; Winter, *Death's Men*, p. 27.
33. Generally Adams and Poirier, *Conscription Controversy*, chs. 5–8; Simkins, *Kitchener's Army*, pp. 138ff. For the army's case, see Robertson memos, 12 January and 21 March 1916, AC 19/1/15a and 19/1/30.
34. Grieves, *Politics of Manpower*, p. 1.
35. Winter, *Death's Men*, p. 29.
36. Generally, Rae, *Conscience and Politics*; Kennedy, 'Public Opinion and the Conscientious Objector'.
37. Dewey, 'Military Recruiting', pp. 214–16.
38. Grieves, *Politics of Manpower*, p. 35.
39. Simpson, 'British Soldier', p. 136.
40. Melograni, *Storia politica*, p. 238.
41. GQG memo, 1 December 1915, LHCMA Robertson MSS 1/9/41a; Grieves, *Politics of Manpower*, p. 35.
42. French, 'Meaning of Attrition', p. 397; cf. Mosier, *Myth*, pp. 181–2.
43. Zürcher, ' Little Mehmet', p. 232.
44. Stone, *Eastern Front*, pp. 122–7.
45. Herwig, *First World War*, p. 139.
46. ibid., p. 234.

47. ibid., p. 168.

48. Whelan, *Bitter Wounds*, pp. 39–41; Bessell, 'Mobilization and Demobilization in Germany', p. 218.

49. Guinard *et al.* (eds.), *Inventaire*, Vol. 1, pp. 212–13.

50. Liulevicius, *War Land*, p. 22.

51. Bourke, *Intimate History of Killing*, p. 6.

52. Ashworth, *Trench Warfare*, pp. 56ff.

53. Whelan, *Bitter Wounds*, p. 61.

54. Eckart and Gradmann, (eds.), *Die Medizin*, p. 355.

55. Bosanquet, N., 'Health Systems', p. 462.

56. Harrison, 'Fight against Disease in the Mesopotamian Campaign', p. 475.

57. Zürcher, 'Little Mehmet'.

58. Major, *Fatal Partners*, p. 253.

59. Gabriel and Metz, *History of Military Medicine*, Vol. 2, p. 244.

60. Eckart and Gradmann (eds.), *Die Medizin*, p. 363.

61. ibid., p. 344.

62. Gabriel and Metz, *History of Military Medicine*, Vol. 2, p. 243.

63. ibid., p. 243; Bosanquet, 'Health Systems', p. 453.

64. Eckart and Gradmann (eds.), *Die Medizin*, p. 363.

65. Harrison, 'Fight against Disease in the Mesopotamian Campaign', p. 459.

66. Whelan, *Bitter Wounds*, p. 40.

67. Wildman, *End of the Russian Imperial Army*, Vol. 1, p. 95.

68. Omissi, *Sepoy and the Raj*, p. 118.

69. Beckett, *First World War*, p. 228.

70. Winter, *Death's Men*, p. 136.

71. On shell shock in the BEF, see generally Showalter, *Female Malady*, ch.7; Babington, *Shell-Shock*; Bourke, *Dismembering*, ch. 2; Bogacz, 'War Neurosis'. For international comparisons, see Eckart, '"Most Extensive Experiment"'; special issues of *Journal of Contemporary History* (2000) and *14/18*.

72. Zürcher, 'Little Mehmet', p. 234.

73. Stone, *Eastern Front*, p. 191.

74. Wildman, *End of the Russian Imperial Army*, Vol. 1, p. 91.

75. Wawro, 'Morale in the Austro-Hungarian Army', p. 402.

76. Ferguson, *Pity of War*, p. 369.

77. Wawro, 'Morale in the Austro-Hungarian Army, p. 404.

78. Ferguson, *Pity of War*, pp. 368–88.

79. Ashworth, *Trench Warfare*, pp. 204ff.

80. Fussell, *Great War and Modern Memory*, p. 96.

81. Prost, *Anciens Combattants*, Vol. 3, pp. 20–21.

82. Fuller, *Troop Morale*, ch. 8.

83. Fussell, *Great War and Modern Memory*, pp. 65–6.

84. Winter, *Death's Men*, pp. 164–5.

85. Audouin-Rouzeau, *Men at War*, ch. 5.

86. Remarque, *All Quiet*, pp. 113–32.

87. Englander and Osborne, 'Jack, Tommy, and Henry Dubb', p. 600.

88. Winter, *Death's Men*, pp. 102–3, 147–8.

89. Jünger, *Storm of Steel*, p. 2, 3.

90. Prost, *In the Wake of War*, pp. 3–9.

91. Moran, *Anatomy of Courage*, p. x.

92. Norton Cru, *Du témoignage*, pp. 55ff.

93. Wette, (ed.), *Krieg des Kleinen Mannes*, p. 130.

94. Keegan, *Face of Battle*, p. 277.

95. Englander and Osborne, 'Jack, Tommy, and Henry Dubb', p. 595.

96. Gooch, 'Morale and Discipline, p. 438; cf. Monticone, *Gli Italiani in uniforme*, ch. 6.

97. Englander, in Strachan (ed.), *Oxford Illustrated History*, p. 192.

98. Ullrich and Ziemann (eds.), *Frontalltag*, p. 24.

99. Hynes, *Soldier's Tale*, pp. 81–3.

100. Omissi (ed.), *Indian Voices*, p. 12.

101. Prost, *Les Anciens combattants*, Vol. 3, p. 17.

102. Englander, 'French Soldier', p. 55.

103. Sheffield, 'Officer–Man Relations', p. 417; Sheffield, *Leadership in the Trenches*; Keegan, *Face of Battle*, p. 272.

104. Stone, *Eastern Front*, pp. 125–6.

105. Kenez, 'Changes in Social Composition', p. 369.

106. Gooch, 'Morale and Discipline, pp. 436–7.

107. Fussell, *Great War and Modern Memory*, ch. 4; Winter, *Sites of Memory*, pp. 64–8.

108. Thomas, K., *Religion and the Decline of Magic: Studies in Popular Beliefs in Sixteenth- and Seventeenth-Century England* (Harmondsworth, 1973), ch. 22.

109. Audouin-Rouzeau, *Men at War*, pp. 85–90; Fuller, *Troop Morale*, pp 156–7.

110. Wawro, 'Morale in the Austro-Hungarian Army', p. 400; Stone, *Eastern Front*, pp. 126–7.

111. Rachamimov, *POWs*, pp. 31–44.

112. Wildman, *End of the Russian Imperial Army*, Vol. 1, p. 104.

113. Ullrich and Ziemann (eds.), *Frontalltag*, p. 22.

114. Audouin-Rouzeau, *Men at War*, chs. 5, 6; Cochet, 'Les Soldats français'.

115. Interviews with Turkish veterans, LC TU.01.

116. Liddle, 'British Soldier on the Somme'. pp. 9, 17, 21.

117. Fuller, *Troop Morale*, ch. 3; Winter, *Death's Men,* pp. 209–11, 229–33.

118. Wette (ed.), *Krieg des Kleinen Mannes*, pp. 110–25; Leed, *No Man's Land*, pp, 80ff.

119. Krumeich, 'Le Soldat allemand', pp. 368–72.

120. Ashworth, *Trench Warfare*, p. 55.

121. Some of this pride is conveyed in the memoirs of L. Kalepky and K. Lubinski, LC GE.09 and GE.13.

122. Cornwall, M., *Undermining of Austria-Hungary*, ch. 10.

123. Mackenzie, 'Morale and the Cause', p. 219.

124. Blunden, *Undertones of War*, chs, 11–13 conveys the changing mood.

125. Gooch,, 'Morale and Discipline', p 439.

126. Pedroncini, *Mutineries*, pp. 38–46.

127. Smith, *Between Mutiny and Obedience*, p. 172.

128. Davidian, I., 'Russian Soldier's Morale'.

129. Wildman, *End of the Russian Imperial Army*, Vol. 1, pp. 106–20.

Chapter 9

1. Hardach, *First World War*, p. 153.

2. Ferguson, *Pity of War*, p. 320.

3. Horn, 'Concept of Total War', pp. 6–7.

4. ibid., p. 323; Balderston, 'War Finance', p. 225.

5. Strachan, *First World War: To Arms*, pp. 815–816.

6. Forsyth, *Crisis of Liberal Italy*, p. 84; Tomassini, 'Industrial Mobilization', p. 82.

7. Williamson, *Helfferich*, pp. 126–7.

8. Whiting, 'Taxation', p. 897; Boswell and Johns, 'Patriots or Profiteers?', p. 427.

9. Balderston, 'War Finance', pp. 226–8; Williamson, *Helfferich*, pp. 122–6.

10. Robert, 'Image of the Profiteer'.

11. Strachan, *First World War: To Arms*, p. 883.

12. Forsyth, *Crisis of Liberal Italy*, p. 76.

13. Gatrell, *Government, Industry and Rearmament*, pp. 149–50.

14. Hardach, *First World War*, p. 171.

15. ibid., p. 172.

16. Ferguson, *Pity of War*, pp. 129–35.

17. Zeidler, 'Die deutsche Kriegsfinanzierung', p. 424; Feldman, *Great Disorder*, pp. 39–42; Strachan, *First World War: To Arms*, pp. 912–13.

18. Strachan, *First World War: to Arms*, pp. 914–19.

19. Duroselle, *Grande Guerre*, pp. 159–60. Horn, *Britain, France, and the Financing*, pp. 79–81.

20. Stone, *Eastern Front*, pp. 287–8.

21. Hardach, *First World War*, p. 153.

22. Wegs, *Österreichische Kriegswirtschaft*, pp. 41–3.

23. Strachan, *First World War: To Arms*, pp. 942–5.

24. Forsyth, *Crisis of Liberal Italy*, pp. 152, 162–7.

25. Burk, *Britain, America, and the Sinews of War*, pp. 45–6; Strachan, *First World War: To Arms*, p. 957.

26. Burk, 'The Treasury', pp. 90–91.

27. For what follows, see Burk, *Britain, America, and the Sinews of War*, pp. 61–80.

28. Strachan, *First World War: To Arms*, pp. 823–5.

29. French, *Strategy and War Aims*, pp. 191–4, 210; Farr, 'A Compelling Case for Voluntarism'.

30. Burk, *Britain, America, and the Sinews of War*, pp. 80–95; Cooper, 'Command of Gold Reversed', p. 227; Horn, *Britain, France, and the Financing*, pp. 163–5; cf., however, Ferguson, *Pity of War*, pp. 326–9.

31. The best general account of industrial mobilization is Strachan, *First World War: To Arms*, ch. 11.

32. Kennedy, *Rise and Fall of the Great Powers*, p. 333.

33. Ferguson, *Pity of War*, p. 250.

34. Bonzon, 'Labour Market and Industrial Mobilization', pp. 191, 193.

35. Godfrey, *Capitalism at War*, p. 257.

36. Joffre, *Mémoires*, Vol. 2, ch. 2.

37. Forsyth, *Crisis of Liberal Italy*, p. 80.

38. Hardach, 'Industrial Mobilization'; Horne, 'L'Impôt du sang', pp. 204–5; Robert, 'Women and Work in France', p. 255.

39. Summerskill, *China on the Western Front*.

40. Wilson, *Myriad Faces*, p. 218.

41. Duroselle, *Grande Guerre*, p. 174.

42. Tables in SHA 10.N.28; Review of Allied Munitions Programmes, 1918, in SHA 10.N.146; Laux, 'Gnôme et Rhône', p. 149.

43. War ministry meeting, 31 July 1915, SHA 10.N.29; GQG memo, 9 August 1916, SHA 16.N.1710.

44. Lloyd George, *War Memoirs*, Vol. 1, pp. 154, 159–61; Wrigley, 'Ministry of Munitions', p. 34.

45. Strachan, *First World War: To Arms*, pp. 1083–4.

46. Trebilcock, 'War and the Failure of Industrial Mobilization', pp. 154–6.

47. French, 'Military Background to the "Shell Crisis"', pp. 200–202; Prior and Wilson, *Command on the Western Front*, pp. 84–92.

48. Adams, *Arms and the Wizard*, pp. 241–5.

49. Strachan, *First World War: To Arms*, p. 1081.

50. Bliss, 'War Business as Usual'; Saini, 'Economic Aspects of India's Participation'; Strachan, *First World War: To Arms*, pp. 1086–9.

51. Adams, *Arms and the Wizard*, pp. 65–9.

52. Forsyth, *Crisis of Liberal Italy*, p. 78.

53. Wilson, *Myriad Faces*, p. 237.

54. Boswell and Johns, 'Patriots or Profiteers?', p. 430.

55. Wrigley, *Lloyd George and the British Labour Movement*; Rubin, *War, Law, and Labour*.

56. Adams, *Arms and the Wizard*, pp. 72, 74–5.

57. ibid., pp. 125–6; Thom, 'Women and Work', p. 306.

58. On Woolwich Arsenal: Thom, *Nice Girls*, ch. 7.

59. Adams, *Arms and the Wizard*, p. 84.

60. Forsyth, *Crisis of Liberal Italy*, pp. 64, 84.

61. François reports, 19 September 1915 and 20 January 1916, SHA 7.N.743 and 5.N.144.

62. Gooch, 'Italy in the First World War', p. 163; Review of Allied Munitions Programmes, 1918, in SHA 10.N.146.

63. Mitchell (ed.), *International Historical Statistics*, p. 467.

64. Forsyth, *Crisis of Liberal Italy*, pp. 74–86.

65. Gooch, 'Italy in the First World War', p. 163; Tomassini, 'Industrial Mobilization', p. 61.

66. Tomassini, 'Industrial Mobilization', pp. 63–72.

67. Zagorsky, *State Control*, pp. 32–7.

68. ibid., p. 76; Siegelbaum, *Politics of Industrial Mobilization*, pp. 30–31.

69. Stone, *Eastern Front*, p. 160.

70. Zagorsky, *State Control*, pp. 76–80.

71. Stone, *Eastern Front*, p. 152.

72. ibid., pp. 157–8.

73. ibid., p. 197; Siegelbaum, *Politics of Industrial Mobilization*, p. 70.

74. Stone, *Eastern Front*, p. 209.

75. Beskrovnyi, *Armiya, i Flot*, pp. 76, 86, 91, 94, 105.

76. Stone, *Eastern Front*, p. 211.

77. Wegs, *Österreichische Kriegswirtschaft*, p. 26.

78. Rauchensteiner, *Tod des Doppeladlers*, p. 160.

79. Compare Beskrovnyi, *Armiya i Flot*, pp. 76, 82 and Wegs, *Österreichische Kriegswirtschaft*, p. 119.

80. Rauchensteiner, *Tod des Doppeladlers*, pp. 139–41.

81. Strachan, *First World War: To Arms*, p. 1044.

82. Herwig, *First World War*, pp. 236–42.

83. Daniel, 'Women's Work', p. 273.

84. Ferguson, *Paper and Iron*, p. 107.

85. Chickering, *Imperial Germany*, pp. 169, 38.

86. Falkenhayn, *General Headquarters*, pp. 43–4.

87. Strachan, *First World War: To Arms*, pp. 1025–9, 1036–7.

88. Falkenhayn, *General Headquarters*, p. 46.

89. Feldman, *Army, Industry, and Labour*, p. 152.

90. Geyer, *Deutsche Rüstungspolitik*, pp. 101–4.

91. Hindenburg letters, 31 August, 14 September, 23 October, 1 November 1916, in Ludendorff, *The General Staff and Its Problems*, pp. 74–6, 81–3, 92–6; 98–101.

92. Bethmann letter, 30 September 1916, in Ludendorff, *The General Staff and Its Problems*, p. 88.

93. Feldman, *Army, Industry, and Labour*, pp. 533–41.

94. ibid., p. 301.

95. Wegs, *Österreichische Kriegswirtschaft*, pp. 123–4.

96. Feldman, *Army, Industry, and Labour*, pp. 385–6.

97. Sarter, *Deutschen Eisenbahnen*, pp. 115–19.

98. Chickering, *Imperial Germany*, p. 81; Feldman, *Army, Industry, and Labour*, p. 272; 'Hindenburg-Programm und Hilfsdienstgesetz', BA-MA W-10/50397.

99. Morrow, *German Air Power*, pp. 73–93.

Chapter 10

1. Weir, *Rebuilding the Kaiser's Navy*, p. 159.

2. Halpern, *Naval History*, p. 65.

3. ibid., p. 84.

4. Neilson, 'Reinforcements and Supplies', p. 47.

5. Robb, *British Culture*, p. 17.

6. Neilson, 'Reinforcements and Supplies', p. 47.

7. Gooch 'Italy in the First World War', p. 166.

8. Kennedy, *Rise and Fall of British Naval Mastery*, pp. 183–5, 196.

9. Zagorsky, *State Control*, p. 16.

10. Halpern, *Naval History*, p. 183.

11. ibid., p. 32; Siney, *Allied Blockade*, pp. 109.

12. Herwig, *First World War*, p. 288.

13. Halpern, *Naval History*, pp. 48–9.

14. Ranft, 'Royal Navy', p. 57.

15. Ferguson, *Pity of War*, p. 253.

16. Offer, *First World War: an Agrarian Interpretation*, p. 61.

17. Lee, 'Administrators and Agriculture', pp, 232, 234.

18. Herwig, *First World War*, pp. 274–7.

19. Stevenson (ed.), *British Documents on Foreign Affairs*, Vols. 9, 10: monthly reports by W. G. Max Müller.

20. Farrar, *Conflict and Compromise*, p. 2.

21. Britain's, however, was 11.6 percent. Ferguson, *Pity of War*, p. 253.

22. Coogan, *End of Neutrality*, ch. 6.

23. ibid., pp. 148ff.

24. Devlin, *Too Proud to Fight*, p. 199.

25. On Wilson and the blockade, May, *World War*, chs. 1, 3, 15; Devlin, *Too Proud to Fight*, chs. 5–7, 16; Coogan, *End of Neutrality*, *passim*.

26. Siney, *Allied Blockade*, p. 144.

27. Devlin, *Too Proud to Fight*, pp. 517–18.

28. Farrar, *Conflict and Compromise*, pp. 31–2.

29. ibid., pp. 135ff.

30. Consett, *Triumph of Unarmed Forces*, p. 129.

31. Consett, *Triumph of Unarmed Forces*, pp. 211–20; Siney, *Allied Blockade*, p. 261.

32. Farrar, *Conflict and Compromise*, p. 10.

33. Frey, 'Bullying the Neutrals', p. 108.

34. Siney, *Allied Blockade*, pp. 94ff.

35. Torrey, Rumanian Campaign', p. 29.

36. Farrar, *Conflict and Compromise*, p. 85.

37. Frey, 'Bullying the Neutrals', pp. 112–14.

38. Halpern, *Naval History*, p. 141.

39. ibid., p. 287.

40. Strachan, *First World War: To Arms*, p. 440.

41. Marder, *Dreadnought*, Vol. 2, p. 447.

42. Beesly, *Room 40*, Andrew, *Secret Service*, ch. 3.

43. Tarrant, *Jutland*, p. 37.

44. Halpern, *Naval History*, pp. 315–16.

45. Keegan, 'Jutland', p. 111.

46. Tirpitz, *Memoirs*, Vol. 2, p. 366n.

47. Weir, *Rebuilding the Kaiser's Navy*, pp. 157, 161, 214.

48. Sumida, 'Forging the Trident', pp. 227–8.

49. Tarrant, *Jutland*, p. 50.

50. On Jutland: Gordon, *Rules of the Game*; Marder, *Dreadnought*, Vol. 3; Campbell, *Jutland*, Tarrant, *Jutland*.

51. Tarrant, *Jutland*, p. 167.

52. Keegan, 'Jutland', p. 122.

53. Lyle, 'Jutland'.

54. Marder, *Dreadnought*, Vol. 3, p. 185.

55. ibid., p. 206; Tarrant, *Jutland*, p. 279.

56. Halpern, *Naval History*, p. 335.

57. Weir, *Rebuilding the Kaiser's Navy*; Weir, 'Tirpitz, Technology'.

58. Herwig, 'Total Rhetoric, Limited War', p. 205.

59. Terraine, *Business in Great Waters*, pp. xv-xvi, Stegemann, *Deutsche Marinepolitik*, pp. 26-7.

60. Gemzell, *Organization, Conflict, and Innovation*, pp. 141-4; Halpern, *Naval History*, pp. 287-95.

61. Terraine, *Business in Great Waters*, pp. 34, 772.

62. ibid., pp. 24-38; Halpern, *Naval History*, p. 303.

63. Devlin, *Too Proud to Fight*, ch. 10; May, *World War*, chs. 7, 8; Link, *Wilson*, Vol. 3, chs. 12, 13.

64. Gemzell, *Organization, Conflict, and Innovation*, pp. 186ff.

65. Afflerbach, *Falkenhayn*, ch. V.19.

66. Birnbaum, *Peace Moves*, pp. 75-90.

67. Bethmann Hollweg, *Betrachtungen*, Vol. 2, p. 260.

68. Chickering, *Imperial Germany*, pp. 141-2; Stevenson (ed.), *British Documents on Foreign Affairs*, Vol. 10, docs. 27, 28: reports by W. G. Max Müller for December 1916.

69. Birnbaum, *Peace Moves*, chs. 6-9.

70. Stegemann, *Deutsche Marinepolitik*, p. 27.

71. Admiralstab report, 15 October 1916, BA-MA RMS/905.

72. Terraine, *Business in Great Waters*, p. 768.

73. Herwig, 'Total Rhetoric, Limited War', pp. 193-7; Stegemann, *Deutsche Marinepolitik*, pp. 51-62.

74. Stegemann, *Deutsche Marinepolitik*, pp. 48, 75.

75. Goemans, *War and Punishment*, pp. 97-8; report by Württemberg attaché, 1 October 1916, HStA MS 1/2. 114

76. Birnbaum, *Peace Moves and U-Boat Warfare*, pp. 321-2.

77. Tuchman, *Zimmermann Telegram*, p. 138.

78. Jarausch, *Enigmatic Chancellor*, p. 301.

Chapter 11

1. See generally Becker, *Great War and the French People*; Flood, *France 1914-1918*; and Smith, Audouin-Rouzeau, and Becker, *France and the Great War*.

2. King, *Generals and Politicians*, pp. 135ff.

3. Horne, *Labour at War*, pp. 56-7.

4. Bésier, 'Les églises protestantes'; Mayeur, 'Le Catholicisme français'.

5. Horne and Kramer, *German Atrocities*, p. 230.

6. Harris, 'Child of the Barbarian'.

7. Montant, 'L'Organisation centrale'.

8. Audouin-Rouzeau, 'Children'; Audouin-Rouzeau, *La Guerre des enfants*.

9. Becker, *Great War and the French People*, p. 57.

10. ibid., pp. 96, 105, 194.

11. Horne, 'Soldiers, Civilians, and the Warfare of Attrition'.

12. Audouin-Rouzeau, 'Bourrage de crâne'.

13. Meyeur, 'Le Catholicisme français', pp. 380, 395.

14. Hanna, *Mobilization of Intellect*.

15. Becker, *War and Faith*, pp. 105-13.

16. Winter, 'Some Paradoxes', p. 20; Winter, 'Surviving the War'.

17. Lawrence, 'Material Pressures'; Manning, 'Wages and Purchasing Power', p. 272; Bonzon, 'Transfer Payments', p. 292.

18. Flood, *France 1914-1918*, chs. 3, 4; Barral, 'La Paysannerie française', p. 237.

19. Becker, *Great War and the French People*, p. 101.

20. Becker, 'Union sacrée'.

21. McMillan, 'French Catholics'.

22. Smith, 'Masculinity'.

23. Horne, *Labour at War*, pp. 67, 261ff.; Schaper, *Albert Thomas*.

24. Papagannis, 'Collaboration and Pacifism'. Generally Wohl, *French Communism*; Kriegel, *Aux Origines du Communisme*.

25. On Britain: Wilson, *Myriad Faces*; Bourne, *Britain and the Great War*; Turner (ed.), *Britain and the First World War*.

26. Bourne, *Britain and the Great War*, pp. 107–14; Wilson, *Myriad Faces*, ch. 19; Pugh, *Making of Modern British Politics*, pp. 165ff.

27. McEwen, "Brass-Hats" and the British Press'; Thompson, *Politicians, the Press, and Propaganda*.

28. Bourne, *Britain and the Great War*, pp. 120–31; Wilson, *Myriad Faces*, ch. 38; Turner, *British Politics*, ch. 3; revealing is Chamberlain to Chelmsford, 8 December 1916, AC 15/3/8.

29. Horne (ed.), *State, Society, and Mobilization*, p. 5.

30. Hiley, 'News Media', pp. 176–7.

31. Buitenhuis, *Great War of Words*, chs. 2, 4; Wright, 'Great War, Government Propaganda'.

32. Bogacz, 'Tyranny of Words'.

33. Marsland, *Nation's Cause*, ch. 1.

34. Bogacz, 'Tyranny of Words'; Fussell, *Great War and Modern Memory*, ch. 5.

35. Hoover, *God, Germany, and Britain*, p. 24.

36. Eksteins, *Rites of Spring*, pp. 183ff.

37. Wilson, 'Lord Bryce's Investigation'; Horne and Kramer, *German Atrocities*, pp. 231–7.

38. Gullace, 'Sexual Violence and Family Honour'.

39. Willis, *Prologue to Nuremberg*, ch. 2.

40. McEwen, '"Brass-Hats" and the British Press', p. 46.

41. Hopkin, 'Domestic Censorship', p. 154.

42. Marquis, 'Words as Weapons', pp. 472–4, 476–80.

43. Bourne, *Britain and the Great War*, p. 206.

44. Hiley, 'News Media', p. 477; Reeves, 'Film Propaganda', pp. 467–8, 471, 481.

45. Taylor, *First World War*, p. 140.

46. Ferguson, *Pity of War*, p. 199; cf. Jeffery, *Ireland and the Great War*, p. 6.

47. Pugh, 'Politicians and the Woman's Vote', pp. 359–60.

48. Kent, 'Love and Death'.

49. Gullace, 'White Feathers'.

50. Watson, 'Khaki Girls'.

51. Dewey, 'Military Recruiting', pp. 205, 220.

52. Ferguson, *Pity of War*, p. 275.

53. Mór-O'Brien, 'Patriotism on Trial'.

54. MacLean, 'Popular Protest and Public Order'.

55. Horne, *Labour at War*, pp. 46, 220.

56. Reid, 'Impact of the First World War'.

57. Pedersen, 'Gender, Welfare, and Citizenship', p. 984.

58. Winter, 'Some Paradoxes', p. 14; *Great War and the British People*, chs. 4, 7.

59. Rae, *Conscience and Politics*; Kennedy, 'Public Opinion'; Ceadel, *Pacifism in Britain*, pp. 31–63.

60. Taylor, *Troublemakers*, ch. 5; Hanak, 'Union of Democratic Control'; Swartz, *Union of Democratic Control*.

61. Deist, 'Censorship and Propaganda', p. 200; Koszyk, *Deutsche Presse*, pp. 14–15.

62. Koszyk, *Deutsche Presse*; Marquis, 'Words as Weapons', pp. 472, 474–5.

63. Ferguson, *Pity of War*, p. 245.

64. Marquis, 'Words as Weapons', pp. 480–84.

65. Chickering, *Imperial Germany*, p. 48.

66. Stark, 'All Quiet on the Home Front'.

67. Welch, 'Cinema and Society', pp. 28–9, 32–3, 39–40, 42.

68. Marquis, 'Words as Weapons', pp. 490–91.

69. Horne and Kramer, *German Atrocities*, pp. 237–47.

70. Hammer, 'Deutsche Protestantismus'.

71. On the Jewish community, see Picht, 'Zwischen Vaterland und Volk'.

72. Dülmen, 'Deutsche Katholizismus', p. 348.

73. Hammer, 'Deutsche Protestantismus', p. 399.

74. Hoover, *God, Germany, and Britain*, pp. 51ff.

75. Verhey, *Spirit of 1914*, pp. 126ff.

76. Meier, 'Evangelische Kirche', p. 693.

77. Ringer, *Decline of the German Mandarins*, pp. 180ff.

78. Mommsen, 'German Artists', pp. 30–31.

79. See Stibbe, *German Anglophobia*, for a general discussion.

80. Ferguson, *Pity of War*, p. 250.

81. Kocka, *Facing Total War*, p. 22.

82. Tobin, 'War and the Working Class', pp. 267–75.

83. Manning, 'Wages and Purchasing Power', p. 260.

84. Kocka, *Facing Total War*, p. 41.

85. Bonzon and Davis, 'Feeding the Cities'.

86. Chickering, *Imperial Germany*, p. 41.

87. Davis, 'Food Scarcity', pp. 297–9.

88. See monthly digests of DCG reports, (e.g., 3 January 1917) in BA-MA PH2/62.

89. Chickering, *Imperial Germany*, pp. 141–2.

90. Fischer, *Germany's Aims*, ch. 5; Soutou, 'Le Problème du social-impérialisme', p . 280.

91. May, *World War*, p. 259.

92. Janssen, 'Der Wechsel', pp. 339–40.

93. Boll, 'Le Problème ouvrier'.

94. Schorske, *German Social Democracy*, p. 308.

95. ibid., pp. 282–315.

96. Ringer, *Decline of the German Mandarins*, pp.190–92; Hürter, 'Die katholische Kirche', pp. 729–30.

97. Digests of reports, 3 January, 3 February, and 3 March 1917, BA-MA PH2/62.

98. Generally, Galántai, *Hungary in the First World War*; Cornwall (ed.), *Last Years*, ch. 4.

99. Beller, 'Tragic Carnival'.

100. Cornwall, 'News, Rumour', pp. 52–4.

101. Rauchensteiner, *Tod des Doppeladlers*, p. 150.

102. Hoag, 'Students at the University of Vienna', p. 303.

103. Beller, 'Tragic Carnival', p. 139.

104. ibid., p. 132.

105. Macartney, *Habsburg Empire*, pp. 811–12; Perman, 'Shaping of the Czechoslovak State', ch. 1; Cornwall, 'News, Rumour', pp. 56–8.

106. Rauchensteiner, *Tod des Doppeladlers*, p. 266.

107. Herwig, *First World War*, p. 274.

108. ibid., p. 275.

109. Macartney, *Habsburg Empire*, p. 817.

110. Galántai, *Hungary in the First World War*, pp. 103–4, 200.

111. Seton-Watson, *Italy from Liberalism to Fascism*, p. 471.

112. Roberts, 'Croce and Beyond'.

113. Seton-Watson, *Italy from Liberalism to Fascism*, pp. 454–60; Procacci, 'A "Latecomer" in War'.

114. Rogger, *Russia in 1914*, pp. 255–6.

115. Zuckerman, 'Political Police', p. 36.

116. Stites, 'Days and Nights', pp. 10, 12.

117. ibid., p. 9.

118. ibid. and Jahn, *Patriotic Culture*.

119. Gatrell, *A Whole Empire Walking*, p. 3.

120. Lieven, *Nicholas II*, pp. 210–17.

121. Jahn, *Patriotic Culture*, pp. 62, 134, 165.

122. Rogger, *Russia in 1914*, p. 265

123. Wildman, *End of the Russian Imperial Army*, Vol. 1, pp. 96–7.

124. Engel, 'Not by Bread Alone'.

125. Zuckerman, 'Political Police', p. 50.

126. Stone, *Eastern Front*, p. 288.

127. Soutou, 'Le Problème du social-impérialisme'.

128. Lieven, *Nicholas II*, pp. 227, 231.

129. Goemans, *War and Punishment*, pp. 107–15.

130. Ferguson, *Pity of War*, p. 247.

131. Farrar, 'Nationalism in Wartime' gives a useful critique.

Chapter 12

1. Gilbert, *First World War*, p. 378.

2. Kaspi, *Temps des Américains*, p. 170.

3. Falkenhayn, *General Headquarters*, pp. 43–4; Guinard *et al.* (eds.) *Inventaire*, Vol. 1, pp. 72, 123; Keegan, *First World War*, pp. 424–5.

4. Livesey, *Viking Atlas*, p. 134; cf. Falls, *First World War*, p. 265.

5. Tables in SHA 10.N.28.

6. Undated memorandum on the Hindenburg Programme, pp. 127ff., BA-MA W-10/50397.

7. Summary of DCG reports, 3 March 1918, BA-MA PH2/62.

8. Millman, *Pessimism and British War Policy*.

Chapter 13

1. Best account is Hasegawa, *February Revolution*; see also Pipes, *Russian Revolution*; Figes, *People's Tragedy*; and the commentary by Acton, *Rethinking*.

2. Figes, *People's Tragedy*, p. 307; Stone, *Eastern Front*, p. 296.

3. ibid., pp, 296–300; Pethybridge, *Spread of the Russian Revolution*, ch. 1.

4. Stone, *Eastern Front*, pp. 295–6.

5. Lih, *Bread and Authority*, pp. 22–55; cf. Struve, *Food Supply*.

6. Smith, *Red Petrograd*, p. 46.

7. ibid., pp. 9–10.

8. ibid., p. 13; Figes, *People's Tragedy*, p. 300.

9. Hasegawa, *February Revolution*, p. 570.

10. Koenker and Rosenberg, *Strikes and Revolution*, p. 25.

11. ibid., pp. 57, 66.

12. Wildman, *End of the Russian Imperial Army*, Vol. 1, p. 123.

13. Hasegawa, *February Revolution*, p 579.

14. Acton, *Rethinking*, ch. 5.

15. Wildman, *End of the Russian Imperial Army*, Vol. 1, pp. 129–54.

16. ibid., p. 124.

17. Pipes, *Russian Revolution*, pp. 278–80.

18. Davidian, 'Russian Soldier's Morale', pp. 429–32.

19. Stone, *Eastern Front*, p. 210.

20. Pipes, *Russian Revolution*, pp. 290–96.

21. Pipes, *Russian Revolution*, p. 228.

22. Pearson, *Russian Moderates and the Crisis of Tsarism*.

23. Hasegawa, *February Revolution*, p. xiv.

24. Pipes, *Russian Revolution*, pp. 287–9, 297–8.

25. Wildman, *End of the Russian Imperial Army*, Vol. 1, pp. 203–15; Pipes, *Russian Revolution*, pp. 309–13.

26. Pipes, *Russian Revolution*, pp. 304–306; Wildman, *End of the Russian Imperial Army*, Vol. 1, pp. 176–87.

27. Wildman, *End of the Russian Imperial Army*, Vol. 1, pp. 234–5.

28. Ferro, 'Le Soldat russe', pp. 17, 20.

29. Cooper, *Warrior and the Priest*, pp. 307–8.

30. Knock, *To End All Wars*, p. vii.

31. ibid.; Roberts, 'Anglo-American Theme', p. 334.

32. *Lansing Papers*, Vol. 1, pp. 470–71.

33. Devlin, *Too Proud to Fight*, ch. 18; Link, *Wilson*, ch. 5, Seymour (ed.), *Intimate Papers of Colonel House*, Vol. 1, ch. 13.

34. Devlin, *Too Proud to Fight*, ch. 19.

35. Seymour, *Intimate Papers of Colonel House*, Vol. 2, pp. 434–5.

36. Fiebig von Hase, 'Anfang vom Ende', pp. 151–2.

37. Link, *Wilson*, p. 296.

38. See Tuchman, *Zimmermann Telegram* for a general account; cf. Andrew, *Secret Service*, pp. 106–14. On Mexico, see Katz, *Secret War*, chs. 8, 9.

39. Link, *Wilson*, pp. 330–36.

40. Zimmermann in Reichstag Budget Commission, 3 March 1917, HStA E130a. 1213.

41. Katz, *Secret War*, p. 362.; Tuchman, *Zimmermann Telegram*, p. 182.

42. Stevenson, *First World War and International Politics*, p. 70.

43. Doerries, 'Promoting Kaiser and Reich'; Nagler, 'German Imperial Propaganda'.

44. Buitenhuis, *Great War of Words*, ch. 5.

45. Cooper, *Vanity of Power*, p. 21.

46. Luebke, *Bonds of Loyalty*, pp. 29–45.

47. Tuchman, *Zimmermann Telegram*, pp. 184–7; Link, *Wilson*, pp. 357–8;

48. Link, *Wilson*, pp. 296–309.

49. Cooper, *Warrior and the Priest*, p. 318.

50. Thompson, 'Woodrow Wilson', p. 339.

51. Link, *Wilson*, pp. ix, 410–15.

52. Devlin, *Too Proud to Fight*, ch. 20; Houston, *Eight Years*, p. 243.

53. Link, *Wilson*, pp. 378–82.

Chapter 14

1. Hindenburg, *Out of My Life*, p. 271; Wildman, *End of the Russian Imperial Army*, Vol. 1, p. 358.

2. Murray, *War in the Air*, pp. 69, 73–4.

3. Beckett, *Great War*, p. 192.

4. Robb, *British Culture*, p. 200; Ferris, 'Airbandit'.

5. Terraine, *Business in Great Waters*, p. 766.

6. ibid., pp. 41–3.

7. Wilson, *Myriad Faces*, p. 429.

8. Marder, *Dreadnought*, Vol. 4, p. 146.

9. Lundberg, 'German Naval Critique', p 113.

10. Halpern, *Naval History*, pp. 338–9, 341.

11. ibid., p. 336.

12. Lloyd George, *War Memoirs*, Vol. 1, pp. 683–93.

13. Halpern, *Naval History*, pp. 351–60.

14. Terraine, *Business in Great Waters*, p. 64.

15. ibid., p 90.

16. Marder, *Dreadnought*, Vol. 4, p. 280.

17. Terraine, *Business in Great Waters*, pp. 61, 65.

18. Herwig, 'Total Rhetoric, Limited War', pp. 200–204.

19. French, *Strategy of the Lloyd George Coalition*, pp. 76–81.

20. Marder, *Dreadnought*, Vol. 4, p. 278.

21. Wildman, *End of the Russian Imperial Army*, Vol. 2, pp. 5–6.

22. Figes, *People's Tragedy*, p. 408.

23. Cornwall, *Undermining of Austria-Hungary*, ch. 3.

24. Wade 'Why October?', pp. 37–43; Wildman, *End of the Russian Imperial Army*, Vol. 2, ch. 1.

25. Wildman, *End of the Russian Imperial Army*, Vol. 2, p. 43.

26. Cornwall, *Undermining of Austria-Hungary*, pp. 34–5.

27. Strachan, 'Morale of the German Army', pp. 388–9.

28. Herwig, *First World War*, pp. 376–7; Woodward, *Collapse of Power*, ch. 3; Horn (ed.), *War, Mutiny, and Revolution*.

29. Pedroncini, *Les Mutineries*, ch. 2, and pp. 308–9.

30. ibid., pp. 311–12, and Smith, *Between Mutiny and Obedience*, ch. 8.

31. Smith, *Between Mutiny and Obedience*, pp. 207–12.

32. Pedroncini, *Les Mutineries*, p. 254.

33. Pedroncini, *Pétain*, pp. 68–72.

34. ibid., pp. 90–91; Bernède, 'Third Ypres'.

35. Pedroncini, *Pétain*, pp. 100–108.

36. GQG 3rd Bureau memos, 17 September and 27 November 1917, SHA 16.N.1712 and 16.N.1690; Pedroncini, *Pétain*, p. 123, 133–4.

37. Melograni, *Storia politica*, pp. 287, 293–6, 305, 307.

38. Beckett, 'Real Unknown Army'.

39. French, *Strategy of the Lloyd George Coalition*, p. 78; Prior and Wilson, *Command on the Western Front*, p. 393.

40. Brown, *British Logistics*, ch. 5.

41. Murray, *War in the Air*, pp. 55–61.

42. Travers, *Killing Ground*, ch. 4; Haig diary, 1 May 1917, NLS.

43. Winter, *Haig's Command*, ch. 5.

44. Prior and Wilson, *Passchendaele*, p. 186.

45. Conference with army commanders, Haig diary, 4 June 1917 NLS.

46. Neilson, *Strategy and Supply*, p. 272.

47. ibid., p. 260; Robertson memo, 9 May 1917, LHCMA Robertson MSS 4/6/1; Haig diary, 9 June 1917, NLS.

48. Woodward, 'Britain in a Continental War', p, 56.

49. French, *Strategy of the Lloyd George Coalition*, ch. 4.

50. Prior and Wilson, *Passchendaele*, p. 37.

51. Dutton, *Politics of Diplomacy*, ch. 5.

52. French, 'Watching the Allies'.

53. French, *Strategy of the Lloyd George Coalition*, ch. 4; Prior and Wilson, *Passchendaele*, ch. 4.

54. Prior and Wilson, *Passchendaele*, ch. 6.

55. Wynne, *If Germany Attacks*, pp. 283–98.

56. Haber, *Poisonous Cloud*, p. 265.

57. Hussey, 'Flanders Battleground'; Prior and Wilson, *Passchendaele*, p. 97.

58. Haig diary, 26 October 1917, NLS.

59. Travers, *How the War Was Won*, p. 17.

60. Chapman, *A Passionate Prodigality*, p. 149.

61. Prior and Wilson, *Passchendaele*, p. 179.

62. Beckett, 'Operational Command', p. 112; Bond, 'Passchendaele: Verdicts', pp. 486–7.

63. Jünger, *Storm of Steel*, pp. 164ff.; and Werth, 'Flanders 1917'.

64. Gill and Dallas, 'Mutiny at Etaples Base'; Gill and Dallas, *Unknown Army*, chs. 6, 7.

65. MacKenzie, 'Morale and the Cause', pp. 220–25.

66. Prior and Wilson, *Passchendaele*, p. 198.

67. Harris, *Men, Ideas, and Tanks*, p. 109.
68. ibid.; Paschall, *Defeat of Imperial Germany*, pp. 104–11; Winter, *Haig's Command*, ch. 7.
69. Paschall, *Defeat of Imperial Germany*, p. 125.
70. Travers, *How the War Was Won*, p. 31.
71. Falls, *First World War*, p. 308.
72. Newell, 'Allenby'; Hughes, *Allenby*, ch. 3.
73. Robertson to Haig, 24 and 27 September 1917, LHCMA Robertson MSS, 7/7/53, 7/7/54.
74. Hughes, *Allenby*, p. 34.
75. Herwig, *First World War*, p. 332.
76. Rauchensteiner, *Tod des Doppeladlers*, p. 429.
77. ibid., p. 471.
78. Cornwall, 'News, Rumour', pp. 58–61.
79. Hautmann, 'Vienna', p. 89.
80. Wargelin, 'High Price', p. 76.
81. Rauchensteiner, *Tod des Doppeladlers*, p. 459.
82. Hautmann, 'Vienna', pp. 91–3; Herwig, *First World War*, p. 282.
83. Czernin, *In the World War*, pp. 146–50.
84. Sixte, *L'Offre*, pp. 35–105; Ribot, *Journal*, pp. 62–72, 103–25; Lloyd George, *War Memoirs*, Vol. 4, ch. 61.
85. Davis, *Home Fires Burning*, pp. 201–2.
86. Jarausch, *Enigmatic Chancellor*, pp. 329–34.
87. Scherer and Grünewald (eds.), *L'Allemagne*, Vol. 2, docs. 68, 104, 113.
88. Kitchen, *Silent Dictatorship*, pp. 127–30.
89. Fischer, *Germany's Aims*, pp. 346–51.
90. Hopwood, 'Czernin and the Fall of Bethmann Hollweg'.
91. Wade, *Russian Search for Peace*, ch. 3.
92. Epstein, *Matthias Erzberger*, pp. 168–79.
93. Wade, 'Why October?', pp. 41–3.
94. On Stockholm: Meynell, 'Stockholm Conference'; Kirby, 'International Socialism ... Stockholm Conference'; Kirby, *War, Peace, and Revolution*; Mayer, *Political Origins*.
95. Czernin, *In the World War*, p. 168; Scherer and Grünewald (eds.), *L'Allemagne*, Vol. 2, docs. 95, 102, 215.
96. *Lansing Papers*, Vol. 2, p. 17.
97. Becker, *Great War and the French People*, p. 207.
98. ibid., chs. 14, 15; SHA 7.N.1538.
99. Stevenson, *French War Aims*, pp. 67–71.
100. Wrigley, *David Lloyd George*, ch. 12.
101. ibid., pp. 203, 218; French, *Strategy of the Lloyd George Coalition*, pp. 84–92.
102. Hanak, 'Union of Democratic Control', pp. 179–80; Swartz, *Union of Democratic Control*, chs. 8, 9.
103. Foster, 'Working-Class Mobilization', p. 165.
104. Wrigley, *David Lloyd George*, p. 197.
105. Winter, 'Arthur Henderson'.
106. Wilson, *Myriad Faces*, pp. 523–5.
107. Figes, *People's Tragedy*, pp. 384–93.
108. Strachan, *First World War: To Arms*, pp. 920–21; Pethybridge, *Spread of the Russian Revolution*, chs. 1, 2.
109. Figes, *People's Tragedy*, pp. 421–37; Wildman, *End of the Russian Imperial Army*, Vol. 2, ch. 4.
110. Wildman, *End of the Russian Imperial Army*, Vol. 2, chs. 6, 7; Figes, *People's Tragedy*, pp. 442–54.
111. Figes, *People's Tragedy*, p. 457.
112. Wildman, *End of the Russian Imperial Army*, Vol. 2, pp. 225–7.
113. Stegemann, *Deutsche Marinepolitik*, pp. 82, 86–7.
114. Epstein, *Matthias Erzberger*, pp. 183–4.
115. Jarausch, *Enigmatic Chancellor*, pp. 343–5.
116. Kitchen, *Silent Dictatorship*, ch. 6; Epstein, *Matthias Erzberger*, pp. 193–201.
117. Text in Feldman (ed.), *German Imperialism*, doc. 12.
118. Epstein, *Matthias Erzberger*, pp. 202–4.
119. ibid., p. 206.
120. Soutou, *L'Or et le sang*, pp. 443–5.
121. Scherer and Grünewald (eds.), *L'Allemagne*, Vol. 2, doc. 207.
122. On the note and its aftermath: Stevenson, *International Politics*, pp. 162–9; Rothwell, *British War Aims*, pp. 102–9; Farrar, 'Opening to the West'; Woodward, 'David Lloyd George'; Renouvin, 'Le Gouvernement français'; Pedroncini, *Négociations secrètes*.
123. Wetzell memo, 30 September 1917, BA-MA PH 3/267.
124. Steglich, *Friedenspolitik*, Appendix.
125. Stevenson, *French War Aims*, pp. 88–92.
126. Ludendorff memo, 14 September 1917, Scherer and Grünewald (eds.), *L'Allemagne*, Vol. 2, doc. 251.

127. French, *Strategy of the Lloyd George Coalition*, p. 146.
128. Lloyd George, *War Memoirs*, Vol. 2, pp. 1242–6.
129. Stevenson, *French War Aims*, p. 80.
130. Shanafelt, *Secret Enemy*, ch. 7.
131. Feldman, *Army, Industry, and Labour*, pp. 373–99.
132. Welch, *Germany, Propaganda, and Total War*, p. 199.
133. ibid., p. 221.
134. Epstein, *Matthias Erzberger*, p. 232.
135. Winter, 'Arthur Henderson'.
136. Melograni, *Storia politica*, pp. 286, 331–2, 360.
137. Wrigley (ed.), *Challenges of Labour*, p. 109.
138. Melograni, *Storia politica*, pp. 337–342.
139. Duroselle, *France et les Français*, p. 295.
140. Horne, 'State and the Challenge of Labour', pp. 243–5.
141. Duroselle, *France et les Français*, pp. 303–4.
142. Dutton, 'Paul Painlevé', pp. 53–5.
143. Poincaré, *Au service de la France*, Vol. 9, p. 365.
144. Smith, Audouin-Rouzeau, and Becker, *France and the Great War*, pp. 141–3.
145. Parsons, 'Why the British', pp. 174–8; Kaspi, *Temps des Américains*, p. 67.
146. Nenninger, 'American Military Effectiveness', p. 129.
147. Coffman, *War to End All Wars*, p. 96.
148. Kennedy, *Over Here*, p. 100. Kennedy provides an excellent overview. For two new accounts, see Keene, *United States and the First World War*; Zieger, *America's Great War*.
149. Kaspi, *Temps des Américains*, p. 70.
150. Burk, 'J. M. Keynes and the Exchange Rate Crisis', pp. 408–9.
151. Dayer, 'Strange Bedfellows', pp. 134ff.
152. Kaspi, *Temps des Américains*, pp. 58–67.
153. Renouvin, *Crise mondiale*, pp. 456, 473.
154. Lansing, *War Memoirs*, p. 285.
155. La Fargue, *China and the World War*, ch. 4.
156. Renouvin, *Crise mondiale*, p. 456; Hardach, *First World War*, p. 29.
157. Fowler, *British–American Relations*, p. 93.
158. Živojinović, 'Robert Lansing's Comments', p. 571.
159. Martin, *Peace without Victory*, p. 139.
160. ibid., p. 141; Fowler, *British–American Relations*, p. 43–4.
161. Gelfand, *The Inquiry*, p. 26.
162. Seymour (ed.), *House*, Vol. 3, pp. 47–8.
163. Scott (ed.), *Official Statements*, pp. 133–5.
164. Martin, *Peace without Victory*, p. 141.
165. Stevenson, *French War Aims*, pp. 83–6; Trachtenberg, *Reparation and World Politics*, ch. 1.
166. On Lansing-Ishii: Curry, *Woodrow Wilson*, ch. 6; Chi, *China Diplomacy*.
167. On the Declaration: Stein, *Balfour Declaration*; Friedman, *Palestine*.
168. Kaspi, *Temps des Américains*, pp. 23, 29–30, 38–9.
169. Coffman, *War to End All Wars*, p. 42; Nenninger, 'American Military Effectiveness', p. 124; Kaspi, *Temps des Américains*, pp. 44–5.
170. Kaspi, *Temps des Américains*, pp. 91–102.
171. Nenninger, 'American Military Effectiveness', pp. 124, 126.
172. Coffman, *War to End All Wars*, p. 5.
173. Kaspi, *Temps des Américains*, pp. 106–15.
174. ibid., p. 193.
175. Coffman, *War to End All Wars*, pp. 14–18, 23, 38–41.
176. Kennedy, *Over Here*, p. 149.
177. Nenninger, 'American Military Effectiveness', p. 122.
178. Kennedy, *Over Here*, pp. 163ff.
179. Coffman, *War to End All Wars*, p 29.
180. Nenninger, 'American Military Effectiveness', p. 121.
181. ibid., p. 120.
182. Strachan, *First World War: To Arms*, pp. 935–41; Kennedy, *Over Here*, pp. 99ff.

Chapter 15

1. Ludendorff, *Kriegserinerungen*, pp. 432–33.
2. Czernin, *In the World War*, p. 217.

3. Shanafelt, *Secret Enemy*, pp. 149–51.
4. Vermes, 'Leap into the Dark', pp. 37–40.
5. Berov, 'Bulgarian Economy', p. 171.
6. Emin, *Turkey in the World War*, pp. 144–7.
7. MacFie, *End of the Ottoman Empire*, p. 150.
8. Wegs, 'Transportation', p. 101.
9. Wegs, *Österreichische Kriegswirtschaft*, pp. 60, 122–3.
10. ibid., pp. 62–4, 89, 110–13, 124–5.
11. Herwig, *First World War*, pp. 357, 359.
12. Strachan, *First World War: To Arms*, p. 899.
13. Ludendorff, *Meine Kriegserinnerungen*, p. 432.
14. Feldman, *Great Disorder*, pp. 44–6, 39–40, 77–83; Roeseler, *Finanzpolitik*, pp. 145–9.
15. Hindenburg memo, 10 September 1917, BA-MA W-10/50397.
16. Bauer, *Grosse Krieg*, p. 169.
17. Hindenburg memo, 10 September 1917, BA-MA W-10/50397.
18. Feldman, *Army, Industry, and Labour*, p. 272.
19. Oberkircher memo on Hindenburg Programme, p. 131, BA-MA W-10/50397.
20. Memo on 1917–1918 economic situation, BA-MA W-10 50400.
21. Deist, 'Military Collapse', pp. 194–5.
22. Hindenburg memo, 10 September 1917, BA-MA W-10/50397.
23. Feldman, *Army, Industry, and Labour*, p. 301.
24. Memo on 1917–1918 economic situation, p. 6, BA-MA W-10/50397.
25. Feldman, *Army, Industry, and Labour*, pp. 413–17.
26. Herwig, *First World War*, p. 207.
27. Bailey, 'Modern Style of Warfare', p. 16.
28. Zabecki, *Steel Wind*, passim.
29. Bailey, 'Modern Style of Warfare', pp. 3–5.
30. Gudmundsson, *Stormtroop Tactics*, pp. 114ff.
31. On Cambrai, ibid., ch. 9.
32. Torrey, 'Redemption of an Army'.
33. Seton-Watson, *Italy from Liberalism to Fascism*, p. 474.
34. Gudmundsson, *Stormtroop Tactics*, p. 126.
35. Falls, *Caporetto*, ch. 2.
36. Asprey, *German High Command*, p. 45.
37. Herwig, *First World War*, p. 339; Seton-Watson, *Italy from Liberalism to Fascism*, p. 477; Melograni, *Storia politica*, p. 404.
38. Gudmundsson, *Stormtroop Tactics*, pp. 131–2.
39. Melograni, *Storia politica*, pp. 404–412.
40. ibid., pp. 394–5; Cruttwell, *History of the Great War*, p. 458; Falls, *Caporetto*, p. 35.
41. Keegan, *First World War*, p. 375; Falls, *Caporetto*, p. 39.
42. Melograni, *Storia politica*, p. 435.
43. ibid., p. 423; Herwig, *First World War*, p. 394.
44. Melograni, *Storia politica*, p. 423.
45. ibid., p. 478.
46. Falls, *Caporetto*, pp. 72, 84.
47. ibid., p. 93; chs. 4–7.
48. Melograni, *Storia politica*, p. 403.
49. Figes, *People's Tragedy*, p. 457; Wildman, *End of the Russian Imperial Army*, Vol. 2, ch. 8.
50. Debo, *Revolution and Survival*, p. 9.
51. Service, *Lenin*, Vol. 2, pp. 241–51.
52. ibid., p. 252.
53. Figes, *People's Tragedy*, pp. 459–73.
54. ibid., pp. 475–92.
55. Seymour (ed.), *Intimate Papers of Colonel House*, Vol. 3, p. 326.
56. Wildman, *End of the Russian Imperial Army*, Vol. 2, p. 400.
57. Text in Ludendorff (ed.), *General Staff*, pp. 517–19; on the negotiations, Nowak, *Hoffmann*, pp. 190–92.
58. Nowak, *Hoffmann*, p. 192.
59. Wheeler-Bennett, *Brest-Litovsk*, pp. 117–18. Also on Brest-Litovsk, see Debo, *Revolution and Survival*, chs. 3–7.
60. Service, *Lenin*, Vol. 2, pp. 284–8.
61. Kühlmann, *Erinnerungen*, p. 526.
62. Scherer and Grünewald (eds.), *L'Allemagne*, Vol. 2, docs. 299, 300, 302.
63. ibid., Vol. 3, docs. 45, 62, 71; Wheeler-Bennett, *Brest-Litovsk*, pp. 107–10.
64. Czernin, *In the World War*, pp. 217–18.

65. Kühlmann, *Erinnerungen*, pp. 522–5; Fischer, *Germany's Aims*, ch. 17.

66. Mamatey, 'Union of Czech Political Parties', p. 63.

67. Ludendorff (ed.), *General Staff*, pp. 524–39.

68. Wargelin, 'High Price', p. 773.

69. ibid., pp. 784–5.

70. Hautmann, 'Vienna', pp. 93–4; Wegs, *Österreichische Kriegswirtschaft*, pp. 102–3; Plaschke, 'Army and Internal Conflict', pp. 340–3.

71. Plaschke, 'Army and Internal Conflict', pp. 345–7.

72. Buse, 'Domestic Intelligence', pp. 43–5.

73. Bailey, 'Berlin Strike'; Feldman, *Army, Industry, and Labour*, pp. 442–57.

74. French, *Strategy of the Lloyd George Coalition*, p. 200.

75. ibid., p. 183.

76. Hankey, *Supreme Command*, Vol. 2, p. 737.

77. Text of the speech in Scott (ed.), *Official Statements of War Aims*, pp. 225–33; see also, Rothwell, *War Aims*, pp. 145–53; French, *Strategy of the Lloyd George Coalition*, pp. 199–205; Lloyd George, *War Memoirs*, Vol. 2, ch. 70.

78. Martin, *Peace Without Victory*, p. 158; Seymour (ed.), *Intimate Papers of Colonel House*, Vol. 3, p. 330.

79. Kaspi, *Temps des Américains*, ch. 7; Trask, *Supreme War Council*, p. 47; Seymour (ed.), *Intimate Papers of Colonel House*, Vol. 3, pp. 284–91.

80. Text in Scott (ed.), *Official Statements of War Aims*, pp. 234–9; on the background, Mayer, *Political Origins*, pp. 329–67; Gelfand, *Inquiry*, ch. 5; Seymour (ed.), *Intimate Papers of Colonel House*, Vol. 3, ch. 11; Levin, *Woodrow Wilson*, ch. 2.

81. Text of the Principles in Scott (ed.), *Official Statements of War Aims*, pp. 265–71; see also Mamatey, *East Central Europe*, pp. 219–32; Snell, 'Wilson's Peace Programme'; Pedroncini, *Négociations secrètes*, pp. 77, 83–91.

82. Shanafelt, *Secret Enemy*, p. 181

83. Baumgart and Repgen (eds.), *Brest-Litovsk*, pp. 50–54.

84. Ludendorff (ed.), *General Staff*, pp. 548–50.

85. Baumgart and Repgen (eds.), *Brest-Litovsk*, pp. 57–62.

86. Wheeler-Bennett, *Brest-Litovsk*, chs. 5, 6; Debo, *Revolution and Survival*, chs. 4–6; Trotsky, *My Life*, ch. 32.

87. Soutou, *L'Or et le sang*, ch. 16.

88. Text in Wheeler-Bennett, *Brest-Litovsk*, Appendix V.

89. Baumgart, *Deutsche Ostpolitik*, pp. 375–7.

90. Generally see ibid., and Kitchen, *Silent Dictatorship*, chs. 9, 10.

91. On the Romanian treaty, Kitchen, *Silent Dictatorship*, ch. 8; Spector, *Rumania*, pp. 45–56; Fischer, *Germany's Aims*, pp. 515–23.

92. Shanafelt, *Secret Enemy*, p. 174.

93. Lutz (ed.), *Causes of the German Collapse*, p. 25.

94. Wetzell memo, 30 September 1917, BA-MA PH 3/267.

95. Lutz (ed.), *Causes of the German Collapse*, pp. 88–9.

96. Hindenburg, *Aus Meinem Leben*, p. 248.

97. Ludendorff, *Meine Kriegserinnerungen*, p. 430; Bauer, *Grosse Krieg*, p.175; Lutz (ed.), *Causes of the German Collapse*, pp. 60–64.

98. Hindenburg, *Aus Meinem Leben*, pp. 235, 249.

99. Cruttwell, *History of the First World War*, p. 486.

100. For a discussion, see Hussey, 'Movement'; Travers, 'Reply to John Hussey'; Fong, 'Movement'.

101. Lutz (ed.), *Causes of the German Collapse*, pp. 53–4.

102. Deist, 'Military Collapse', p. 190.

103. Fong, 'Movement', p. 232.

104. Keegan, *First World War*, p. 421. Middlebrook, in *Kaiser's Battle*, p. 20, gives 169 Allied divisions: French, 98; British, 57; US, 6; Belgians, 6; Portuguese, 2.

105. Travers, 'Reply to John Hussey', p. 369.

106. Middlebrook, *Kaiser's Battle*, p. 43.

107. Bauer, *Grosse Krieg*, p. 177.

108. Samuels, *Command or Control?*, pp. 244–6; Lupfer, *Dynamics*, pp. 41–4; Gudmundsson, *Stormtroop Tactics*, pp. 145–51.

109. Gudmundsson, *Stormtroop Tactics*, pp. 146–7, 151; Samuels, *Command or Control?*, pp. 246–7.

110. Ludendorff, *Meine Kriegserinnerungen*, p. 460.

111. Herwig, *First World War*, p. 397.

112. ibid., p. 401.

113. Ludendorff, *Meine Kriegserinnerungen*, p. 463.

114. Hindenburg, *Aus Meinem Leben*, p. 234.

115. Barnett, *Swordbearers*, p. 283.

116. Ludendorff (ed.), *General Staff*, p. 548.
117. Fong, 'Movement' p. 227.
118. Herwig, *First World War*, p. 392; Asprey, *German High Command*, p. 367.
119. Wetzell memo, 23 October 1917, BA-MA PH 3/27.
120. Wetzell memo, 5 November 1917, BA-MA PH 3/27.
121. Barnett, *Swordbearers*, pp. 283–5; Herwig, *First World War*, p. 394.
122. Ludendorff, *Meine Kriegserinnerungen*, pp. 476–7.
123. ibid., pp. 473–4.
124. Pedroncini, *Pétain*, p. 179.
125. ibid., p 180; Coffman, *War to End All Wars*, pp. 178–80.
126. Kaspi, *Temps des Américains*, pp. 169–80; Pedroncini, *Pétain*, pp. 180–82.
127. Trask, *Supreme War Council*, pp. 47, 174.
128. French, *Strategy of the Lloyd George Coalition*, pp. 188–92.
129. Pedroncini, *Pétain*, p. 141.
130. Watson, *Clemenceau*, pp. 293–7.
131. Guinn, *British Strategy and Politics*, pp. 269–74
132. ibid., pp. 290–300; French, *Strategy of the Lloyd George Coalition*, pp. 218–219.
133. Pedroncini, *Pétain*, pp. 271–5; French, *Strategy of the Lloyd George Coalition*, pp. 215–22.
134. 'Notes on the Operations on the Western Front' , NLS, Haig MSS, 213a; Travers, *How the War Was Won*, p. 50.
135. Travers, *How the War Was Won*, p. 36; Woodward, 'Did Lloyd George Starve the British Army?', p. 244.
136. Travers, *How the War was Won*, pp. 35–46.
137. Woodward, 'Did Lloyd George Starve the British Army?', p. 248.
138. Millman, 'British Home Defence Planning', p. 205.
139. Middlebrook, *Kaiser's Battle*, pp. 85–9.
140. Winter, *Haig's Command*, pp. 177–8.
141. Samuels, *Command or Control?*, ch. 7.
142. ibid., pp. 217–18; Travers, *How the War Was Won*, pp. 55–65.
143. Middlebrook, *Kaiser's Battle*, p. 71; French, 'Failures of Intelligence'.
144. Winter, *Haig's Command*, pp. 180–82.
145. Woodward, 'Did Lloyd George Starve the British Army?', p. 251.
146. French, *Strategy of the Lloyd George Coalition*, p. 223.
147. Middlebrook, *Kaiser's Battle*, p. 121.
148. French, *Strategy of the Lloyd George Coalition*, p. 222.
149. Travers, *How the War Was Won*, p. 54.
150. Middlebrook, *Kaiser's Battle*, p. 151.
151. ibid., p. 52.
152. ibid., p. 63; Bauer, *Grosse Krieg*, p. 177; Hutier diary, 20 March 1918 BA-MA W–10/50640.
153. Thaer, *Generalstabsdienst*, p. 163.
154. Middlebrook, *Kaiser's Battle*, p. 25.
155. Travers, *How the War Was Won*, p. 53.
156. Middlebrook, *Kaiser's Battle*, pp. 308–22.
157. ibid., pp. 330–31.
158. Travers, *How the War Was Won*, pp. 76–82.
159. Haig diary, 21, 22, 23 March 1918, NLS Haig MSS.
160. Pedroncini, *Pétain*, pp. 295–300.
161. French, *Strategy of the Lloyd George Coalition*, p. 225.
162. Pedroncini, *Pétain*, pp. 307–11; Travers, *How the War Was Won*, pp. 66–70; Winter, *Haig's Command*, p. 186.
163. King, *Generals and Politicians*, pp. 216–18.
164. Guinn, *British Strategy and Politics*, pp. 301ff.
165. Pedroncini, *Pétain*, pp. 319–35, 343.
166. Barnett, *Swordbearers*, p. 311.
167. ibid., pp. 315–18, 322, 327; Hindenburg, *Aus Meinem Leben*, p. 250.
168. Travers, *How the War Was Won*, pp. 86–9; Gudmundsson, *Stormtroop Tactics*, pp. 166–7.
169. Gudmundsson, *Stormtroop Tactics*, p. 168: though estimates, as usual, vary.
170. Ludendorff, *Meine Kriegserinnerungen*, p.483.
171. Paschall, *Defeat of Imperial Germany*, p. 146; Pedroncini, *Pétain*, p. 324; Falls, *First World War*, p. 320.
172. Barnett, *Swordbearers*, pp. 330–31.
173. Asprey, *German High Command*, p. 394.
174. Brittain, *Testament of Youth*, pp. 419–20. Taylor, *Illustrated History*, p. 223.
175. Paschall, *Defeat of Imperial Germany*, p. 148.
176. Pedroncini, *Pétain*, p. 351.

177. Hindenburg, *Aus Meinem Leben*, p. 256.
178. Scott (ed.), *Official Statements of War Aims*, pp. 298–322.
179. Herwig, *First World War*, p. 370.
180. Shanafelt, *Secret Enemy*, pp. 183–90.
181. ibid., p. 184; Herwig, *First World War*, p. 370.
182. Ludendorff, *Meine Kriegserinnerungen*, p. 497.
183. Shanafelt, *Secret Enemy*, p. 197.
184. Falls, *Caporetto*, pp. 140–52.
185. ibid., pp. 152–3.
186. Wegs, 'Transportation', p. 130.
187. Melograni, *Storia politica*, pp. 484, 500; Cornwall, *Undermining Austria-Hungary,* chs. 5, 6.
188. Tucker, *Great War*, p. 168.
189. Hindenburg, *Aus Meinem Leben*, p. 262.
190. Thaer, *Generalstabsdienst*, pp. 182, 187.
191. Hutier diary, 11 April 1918, BA-MA W-10/50640.
192. Thaer, *Generalstabsdienst*, pp. 194–8.
193. Hindenburg, *Aus Meinem Leben*, p. 256.
194. Wetzell memos, 19 and 28 April 1918, BA-MA W-10/50640.
195. Fong, 'Movement', p. 232.
196. Ludendorff, *Meine Kriegserinnerungen*, pp. 494–6.
197. Hindenburg, *Aus Meinem Leben*, pp. 257–8.
198. Robson, *First World War*, p. 167.
199. Keegan, *First World War*, p. 436.
200. Falls, *First World War*, p. 326.
201. Pedroncini, *Pétain*, pp. 215–25.
202. Asprey, *German High Command*, p. 419.
203. Winter, *Haig's Command*, p. 193.
204. Asprey, *German High Command*, p. 383; Beckett, *Great War*, p. 192.
205. Travers, *How the War Was Won*, p. 107; Barnett, *Swordbearers*, p. 335.
206. Coffman, *War to End All Wars*, pp. 217–21.
207. Hindenburg, *Aus Meinem Leben*, p. 260; Falls, *First World War*, p. 328.
208. Ludendorff, *Meine Kriegserinnerungen*, p. 512.
209. Kahn, *Codebreakers*, pp. 346–7.
210. Pedroncini, *Pétain*, pp. 380–82.
211. Paschall, *Defeat of Imperial Germany*, p. 160; Deist, 'Military Collapse', p. 199.
212. Kaspi, *Temps des Américains*, p. 238.

Chapter 16

1. Fischer, *Germany's Aims*, pp. 622–3.
2. Renouvin, *Crise européenne*, pp. 670–72.
3. Hürter (ed.), *Paul von Hintze*.
4. Barnett, *Swordbearers*, p. 336; Ludendorff, *Meine Kriegserinnerungen*, p. 518.
5. Foch, *Mémoires*, Vol. 2, p. 112.
6. ibid., pp. 115–18.
7. Pedroncini, *Pétain*, pp. 401–2.
8. Coffman, *War to End All Wars*, p. 239; Travers, in Strachan (ed.), *Oxford Illustrated History*, pp. 274–5.
9. Foch, *Mémoires*, pp. 145–60; Asprey, *German High Command*, p. 441.
10. Barnett, *Swordbearers*, pp. 349–57.
11. Asprey, *German High Command*, p. 443.
12. Liddell Hart, *Foch*, p. 343.
13. Foch, *Mémoires*, Vol. 2, pp. 162–9.
14. Falls, *First World War*, p. 354.
15. Prior and Wilson, *Command on the Western Front*, ch. 26.
16. ibid., pp. 295–300.
17. ibid., ch. 27.
18. ibid., chs. 28, 29.
19. Asprey, *German High Command*, p. 61.
20. Terraine, *Douglas Haig*, p. 458.
21. Ferguson, *Pity of War*, pp. 386–7.
22. Asprey, *German High Command*, p. 432.
23. Foch, *Mémoires*, Vol. 2, pp. 185–7.
24. Prior and Wilson, *Command on the Western Front*, ch. 30.

25. Coffman, *War to End All Wars*, pp. 273–82.

26. Foch, *Mémoires*, Vol. 2, pp. 205–15.

27. Wilson to Haig, 31 August 1918, NLS Haig MSS 213a (appendix).

28. Travers, *How the War Was Won*, p. 157.

29. Falls, *First World War*, p. 387.

30. Travers, *How the War Was Won*, p. 154.

31. Paschall, *Defeat of Imperial Germany*, pp. 181–4.

32. Falls, *First World War*, p. 378; Liddell Hart, *Foch*, p. 368.

33. Brown, 'Not Glamorous', pp. 437–40; Travers, *How the War Was Won*, pp. 160–64.

34. Travers, *How the War Was Won*, pp. 157–8, 166–9; Prior and Wilson, *Command on the Western Front*, chs 31–33.

35. See Swain, *Origins of the Russian Civil War*, and Mawdsley, *Russian Civil War*, for general accounts.

36. Mawdsley, *Russian Civil War*, pp. 40–41.

37. Herwig, 'German Policy in the Eastern Baltic Sea'.

38. Fischer, *Germany's Aims*, pp. 571–3; Debo, *Revolution and Survival*, ch. 12.

39. Ullman, *Anglo-Soviet Relations*, Vol. 1, pp. 152, 309, 320, 332, Vol. 2, pp. 20, 28; Mawdsley, *Russian Civil War*, pp. 285–7.

40. Debo, *Revolution and Survival*, pp. 154–5, 266–70.

41. Woodward, 'British Government and Japanese Intervention'.

42. Schwartz, 'Divided Attention'.

43. Morley, *Japanese Thrust*, passim; Dickinson, *War and National Reinvention*, ch. 5; Seymour (ed.), *Intimate Papers of Colonel House*, Vol. 3, pp. 398–408; Unterberger, 'President Wilson'; Lasch, 'American Intervention'.

44. Debo, *Revolution and Survival*, ch. 11; Bradley, *Allied Intervention*, ch. 4.

45. Long, 'American Intervention'; Morley, *Japanese Thrust*, pp. 260–89.

46. Debo, *Revolution and Survival*, p. 259.

47. Kitchen, *Silent Dictatorship*, pp. 223–6.

48. Kazamzadeh, *Struggle for Transcaucasia*, pp. 56–7.

49. ibid., pp. 81ff.; MacFie, *End of the Ottoman Empire*, pp. 154, 158.

50. Trumpener, *Germany and the Ottoman Empire*, ch. 6.

51. MacFie, *End of the Ottoman Empire*, p. 156.

52. Sheffy, *British Military Intelligence*, pp. 300, 346.

53. Hughes, *Allenby*, p. 69.

54. Dawn, 'Influence of T. E. Lawrence', pp. 71–9.

55. Falls, *First World War*, p. 376.

56. Hughes, *Allenby*, ch. 5.

57. Emin, *Turkey*, p. 262.

58. Falls, *First World War*, pp. 376–9; Renouvin, *Crise européenne*, p. 600.

59. Renouvin, *Crise européenne*, pp. 533–4, 605–6.

60. Hamard, 'Quand la victoire', p. 30.

61. Dutton, *Politics of Diplomacy*, pp. 167–76.

62. Renouvin, *Crise européenne*, p. 594.

63. ibid., p. 599; Hamard, 'Quand la victoire', p. 31.

64. Herwig, *First World War*, p. 425.

65. Ferguson, *Pity of War*, p. 370.

66. Travers, *How the War Was Won*, pp. 149–50.

67. Travers in Strachan (ed.), *Oxford Illustrated History*, pp. 288–90.

68. Herwig, *First World War*, p. 420; Guinard *et al.* (eds.), *Inventaire*, Vol. 1, p. 205; Andrew and Kanya-Forstner, 'France, Africa, and the First World War', pp. 15–16.

69. Grieves, *Politics of Manpower*, pp. 195–6.

70. Wilson, *Myriad Faces*, pp. 566, 645.

71. Kennedy, 'Strategy and Supply', p. 57.

72. ibid., p. 59.

73. Kennedy, *Over Here*, pp. 178–85; Meigs, *Optimism at Armageddon*, ch. 1.

74. Kennedy, *Over Here*, pp. 159–62; Coffman, *War to End All Wars*, pp. 231–3; Barbeau and Florette, *Unknown Soldiers*.

75. Meigs, *Optimism at Armageddon*, ch. 2; Martin, 'German Strategy', pp. 181, 189–90.

76. Kaspi, *Temps des Américains*, p. 193.

77. Halpern, *Naval History*, p. 435.

78. Parsons, 'Why the British'.

79. Kaspi, *Temps des Américains*, p. 237.

80. Ludendorff, *Meine Kriegserinnerungen*, pp. 512, 514.

81. Martin, 'German Strategy', pp. 181–92.

82. Kennedy, *Over Here*, pp. 173–4; Nenninger, 'American Military Effectiveness', p. 143.

83. Travers, in Strachan (ed.), *Oxford Illustrated History*, p. 290.

84. Harris and Barr, *Amiens to the Armistice*, pp. 191.

85. Travers, in Strachan (ed.), *Oxford Illustrated History*, p. 280.

86. Travers, *How the War Was Won*, p. 145.

87. Pedroncini, *Pétain*, pp. 199–230.

88. ibid., pp. 401–2; Travers, in Strachan (ed.), *Oxford Illustrated History*, p. 289.

89. Morrow, *Great War in the Air*, p. 282.

90. Suinard, *Inventaire*, Vol. 1, p. 129.

91. Simkins, 'Co-Stars or Supporting Cast?', p. 53.

92. Winter, *Haig's Command*, p. 148.

93. Morton, 'Junior but Sovereign Allies'; Brown, 'Not Glamorous', pp. 429–31; Rawling, *Surviving Trench Warfare*, p. 189.

94. Andrews, *Anzac Illusion*, pp. 147–8.

95. Harris, *Men, Ideas, and Tanks*, p. 179.

96. Travers, 'Tanks of 1918', p. 394.

97. Harris, *Men, Ideas, and Tanks*, pp. 182–3.

98. Childs, *A Peripheral Weapon?*

99. Cooper, *Birth of Independent Air Power*, ch. 10; Jones, *Origins of Strategic Bombing*, p. 178; Sweetman, 'Smuts Report of 1917'.

100. Sweetman, 'Smuts Report of 1917', p. 198.

101. Cooper, *Birth of Independent Air Power*, pp. 135–6.

102. Falls, *First World War*, pp. 348–9.

103. ibid., p. 353; Coffman, *War to End All Wars*, p. 210.

104. Morrow, in Strachan (ed.), *Oxford Illustrated History*, p. 272.

105. Morrow, *Great War in the Air*, pp. 311–12.

106. Cooper, *Birth of Independent Air Power*, p. 149.

107. Ferris (ed.), *British Army and Signals Intelligence*, pp. 19–21; Andrew, *Secret Service*, pp. 172–3; Shaffy, *British Military Intelligence*, pp. 315–19.

108. Bidwell and Graham, *Fire-Power*, p. 143.

109. Prior and Wilson, *Command on the Western Front*, p. 393.

110. Spiers, *Chemical Warfare*, p. 13.

111. Haber, *Poisonous Cloud*, pp. 241–2.

112. Palazzo, *Seeking Victory*, pp. 167–76.

113. Prior and Wilson, *Command on the Western Front*, pp. 293–5.

114. Travers, in Strachan (ed.), *Oxford Illustrated History*, pp. 281–4.

115. Pedroncini, *Pétain*; Porch, 'French Army', pp. 210–25.

116. Travers, *How the War Was Won*, pp. 176–8.

117. See Philpott, 'Foch', for a recent reappraisal.

118. Brown, *British Logistics*, ch. 5.

119. ibid., ch. 7.

120. Summerskill, *China on the Western Front*.

121. Herwig and Trask, 'Failure of Imperial Germany's Undersea Offensive', p. 634.

122. Halpern, *Naval History*, p. 404.

123. Marder, *Dreadnought*, Vol. 5, pp. 138, 158.

124. ibid., p. 334.

125. ibid., p. 120; Grant, *U-Boats Destroyed*.

126. Halpern, *Naval History*, ch. 13.

127. Marder, *Dreadnought*, Vol. 5, p. 119.

128. Terraine, *Business in Great Waters*, p. 120; ch.15.

129. Beesly, *Room 40*, p. 118; Halpern, *Naval History*, p. 424.

130. Halpern, *Naval History*, pp. 421–3.

131. Terraine, *Business in Great Waters*, p. 131.

132. Marder, *Dreadnought*, Vol. 5, p. 83.

133. Terraine, *Business in Great Waters*, pp. 120–23; Halpern, *Naval History*, pp. 430–35.

134. Herwig and Trask, 'Failure of Imperial Germany's Undersea Offensive', pp. 626–7.

135. Halpern, *Naval History*, pp. 435–7.

136. Salter, *Allied Shipping Control*; Safford, *Wilsonian Maritime Diplomacy*, p. 149.

137. Kennedy, *Rise and Fall of the Great Powers*, p. 350.

138. Gilbert, *American Financing of World War I*, p. 205.

139. Coffmann, *War to End All Wars*, pp. 162–5.

140. Morrow, *Great War in the Air*, pp. 342, 294.

141. Kaspi, *Temps des Américains*, pp. 244–5

142. Morrow, *Great War in the Air*, p. 329.

143. Curami, 'L'Industria bellica', p. 557; Rochat, 'Il Comando Supreme di Diaz', p. 265.

144. Seton-Watson, *Italy from Liberalism to Fascism*, p. 497.
145. Safford, *Wilsonian Maritime Diplomacy*, p. 153.
146. Kaspi, *Temps des Américains*, pp. 266–7.
147. Burk, *Britain, America, and the Sinews of War*, pp. 186–7.
148. ibid., pp. 203, 206, 220.
149. Kaspi, *Temps des Américains*, p. 333
150. Forsyth, *Crisis of Liberal Italy*, pp. 183, 186.
151. Burk, *Britain, America, and the Sinews of War*, pp. 137, 148–9.
152. Frey, 'Bullying the Neutrals', p. 238.
153. Salmon, *Scandinavia*, pp. 143–5.
154. Frey, 'Bullying the Neutrals', pp. 240–41.
155. Offer, *First World War: an Agrarian Interpretation*, p. 62.
156. Olson, *Economics of the Wartime Shortage*, pp. 109–111.
157. Dewey, 'Food Production', p. 72.
158. ibid., pp. 82–8.
159. Bonzon and Davis 'Feeding the Cities', pp. 309, 314, 326, 330.
160. Kennedy, *Over Here*, p. 112.
161. Gilbert, *American Financing of World War I*, pp. 221–4.
162. Balderston, 'War Finance', pp. 237ff.
163. Whiting, 'Taxation and the Working Class', pp. 898–9.
164. Daunton, 'How to Pay for the War', pp. 888ff.
165. Strachan, *First World War: To Arms*, p. 858.
166. Seton-Watson, *Italy from Liberalism to Fascism*, pp. 480–91.
167. Duroselle, *Grande Guerre des français*, ch. 15.
168. Becker, *Great War and the French People*, pp. 251ff.
169. Lloyd George, *War Memoirs*, Vol. 1, ch. 55; Holland, 'British Empire and the Great War'.
170. Holland, 'British Empire and the Great War'; Andrews, *Anzac Illusion*, ch. 5; Garson, 'South Africa'.
171. Gooch, 'Maurice Debate'; Wilson, *Myriad Faces*, pp. 573–5.
172. Wilson, *Myriad Faces*, pp. 654–5.
173. Millman, *Managing Domestic Dissent*, chs. 7, 10.
174. Horne (ed.), *State, Society and Mobilization*, p. 15.
175. Bruntz, *Allied Propaganda*, p. 13.
176. Horne (ed.), *State, Society, and Mobilization*, p. 207. On the NWAC, see also Millman, *Managing Domestic Dissent*, ch. 9.
177. Kennedy, *Over Here*, p. 61.
178. ibid., pp. 81–3.
179. Scott (ed.), *Official Statements of War Aims*, pp. 309–12.
180. Calder, *Britain and the Origins of the New Europe*, pp. 190–1.
181. Stevenson, *French War Aims*, pp. 106–7.
182. Calder, *Britain and the Origins of the New Europe*, pp. 190–91, 201–3; Mamatey, *East Central Europe*, pp. 239–45, 273–4, 314–15; Lederer, *Yugoslavia*, pp. 25–40.
183. Calder, *Britain and the Origins of the New Europe*, pp. 191–4, 204–11; Mamatey, *East Central Europe*, pp. 252–73, 300–311; Perman, *Shaping of the Czechoslovak State*, ch. 11.
184. Rochat, 'Il Comando Supreme di Diaz', pp. 266–7.
185. Meigs, *Optimism at Armageddon*, pp. 60, 232n.
186. Bruntz, *Allied Propaganda*, pp. 30–39.
187. ibid., p. 16ff.
188. Taylor, 'Foreign Office and British Propaganda', pp. 886–92.
189. Calder, *Britain and the Origins of the New Europe*, pp. 176–7.
190. Cornwall, *Undermining of Austria-Hungary*, pp. 176, 201–2.
191. Bruntz, *Allied Propaganda*, p. 26.
192. ibid., pp. 41–57.
193. Ferguson, *Pity of War*, pp. 212–13; Lasswell, *Propaganda Technique*, p. 3.
194. Cornwall, *Undermining of Austria-Hungary*, pp. 442–3.
195. Bruntz, *Allied Propaganda*, p. v.

Chapter 17

1. Goemans, *War and Punishment*, ch. 2.
2. Renouvin, *L'Armistice*, pp. 23–6.
3. Hindenburg, *Out of My Life*, p. 394.
4. Rudin, *Armistice*, pp. 21–7; Hürter, *Paul von Hintze*, p. 100.
5. Minutes of Spa meeting, 14 August 1918, BA-MA W-10/50290.

6. Meyer, *Mitteleuropa*, p. 285.

7. Rudin, *Armistice*, p. 28.

8. Shanafelt, *Secret Enemy*, pp. 202–3.

9. Asprey, *German High Command*, p. 404.

10. Lowry, *Armistice*, p. 7.

11. Ludendorff circular, 19 October 1918, BA-MA W-10/50400, app. 35.

12. Thaer, *Generalstabsdienst*, p. 233.

13. Hughes, 'Battle for the Hindenburg Line', p. 57.

14. Ludendorff memo, 18 June, and discussion 1 July 1918, BA-MA W-10/50287.

15. Ziemann, 'Enttäuschte Erwartung', pp. 175–6; reports from unit commanders, July–September 1918 in BA-MA W-10/51833.

16. Summary of DCG reports, 3 August 1918, BA-MA PH2/62.

17. Mehrens memo on food situation in 1918, BA-MA W-10/50434; Stevenson (ed.), *British Documents*, Vol. 12, p. 360.

18. Renouvin, *L'Armistice*, pp. 66–7.

19. Rudin, *Armistice*, p. 49.

20. Thaer, *Generalstabsdienst*, pp. 234–6.

21. ibid., p. 237; Hürter, *Paul von Hintze*, pp. 103–6; Schwabe, *Woodrow Wilson*, p. 31.

22. Rudin, *Armistice*, pp. 42–4.

23. ibid., pp. 50–52; Hürter, *Paul von Hintze*, p. 105; Ludendorff, *My War Memories*, Vol. 2, p. 722.

24. Max of Baden, *Memoirs*, Vol. 2, pp. 10–22.

25. Rudin, *Armistice*, pp. 66–72.

26. The armistice correspondence is in Scott (ed.), *Official Statements of War Aims*, pp. 415ff.

27. Epstein, *Matthias Erzberger*, pp. 262–3.

28. Rudin, *Armistice*, pp. 110–14.

29. Schwabe, *Woodrow Wilson*, p. 33.

30. Thaer, *Generalstabsdienst*, p. 236.

31. Schwabe, *Woodrow Wilson*, p. 23.

32. Epstein, *Matthias Erzberger*, p. 264.

33. Seymour (ed.), *Intimate Papers of Colonel House*, Vol. 4, pp. 67–73.

34. Scott (ed.), *Official Statements of War Aims*, pp. 399–405.

35. Schwabe, *Woodrow Wilson*, pp. 39–42.

36. Rudin, *Armistice*, p. 121.

37. Schwabe, *Woodrow Wilson*, pp. 50–55, 58–71; Renouvin, *L'Armistice*, pp. 133–6.

38. Max of Baden, *Memoirs*, Vol. 2, p. 67–70.

39. ibid., pp. 89–98.

40. Max of Baden, *Memoirs*, Vol. 2, pp. 99–157; Rudin, *Armistice*, pp. 141ff.

41. Max of Baden, *Memoirs*, Vol. 2, pp. 167–204; Ryder, *German Revolution*, p. 124; Asprey, *German High Command*, pp. 480–84.

42. Schwabe, *Woodrow Wilson*, p. 66.

43. Lowry, *Armistice*, p. 39.

44. ibid., pp, 17–24.

45. Stevenson, *French War Aims*, pp. 118–25.

46. French, 'Had We Known', p. 72.

47. Millman, 'Counsel of Despair', p. 259; French, *Lloyd George Coalition*, pp. 253–8.

48. French, 'Had We Known', pp. 72–3.

49. ibid., pp. 74–9.

50. Lowry, *Armistice*, pp. 57–8; Stevenson, *French War Aims*, p. 125.

51. Snell, 'Wilson on Germany', pp. 364–9; Seymour (ed.), *Intimate Papers of Colonel House*, Vol. 4, pp. 156–8, 198–209.

52. Floto, *Colonel House*, pp. 49–60; Lowry, *Armistice*, ch. 5.

53. Seymour (ed.), *Intimate Papers of Colonel House*, Vol. 4, p. 88.

54. Schwabe, *Woodrow Wilson*, p. 88.

55. Lowry, *Armistice*, p. 96.

56. ibid., pp. 53–4, 89–91, 135–7.

57. ibid, ch. 7; Stevenson, *French War Aims*, pp 125–8.

58. Cruttwell, *Great War*, pp. 577.

59. Travers, *How the War Was Won*, p. 164; Prior and Wilson, *Command on the Western Front*, p. 379

60. Harris, *Amiens to the Armistice*, pp. 287–91.

61. Crosby, *Epidemic and Peace*, p. 156.

62. Cruttwell, *Great War*, p. 583

63. Travers, *How the War Was Won*, p. 154.

64. ibid., p. 143; Ferguson, *Pity of War*, p. 300.

65. Hamard, 'Quand la victoire', p. 33.

66. Emin, *Turkey in the World War*, p. 253.

67. Dyer, 'Turkish Armistice', pp. 143–52.

68. Emin, *Turkey in the World War*, pp. 264–7.

69. Dyer, 'Turkish Armistice', pp. 152–69.

70. ibid., pp. 313–47; Rothwell, *British War Aims*, pp. 236–44.

71. Deák, 'Habsburg Army', p. 308.

72. Cornwall, *Undermining of Austria-Hungary*, pp. 406–7, 422.

73. Rochat, 'Il Comando Supremo di Diaz', pp. 270–2; Cruttwell, *Great War*, pp. 602–4.

74. Deák, 'Habsburg Army', p. 309.

75. Galántai, *Hungary in the First World War*, p. 299; Cornwall, 'Dissolution', p. 135.

76. Deák, 'Habsburg Army', p. 309.

77. Plaschke, 'Army and Internal Conflict', p. 341.

78. Zeman, *Break-Up of the Habsburg Empire*, p. 248.

79. Krizmann, 'Austro-Hungarian Diplomacy', pp. 100–109.

80. Zeman, *Break-Up of the Habsburg Empire*, pp. 237–40.

81. ibid., pp. 227–30; Carsten, *Revolution in Central Europe*, pp. 49–52.

82. Zeman, *Break-Up of the Habsburg Empire*, pp. 242–3; Spector, *Rumania*, pp. 62–3.

83. Rothenberg, 'Habsburg Army', p. 82; Plaschke, 'Army and Internal Conflict', p. 348.

84. Carsten, *Revolution in Central Europe*, pp. 21ff.

85. Koralka, 'Germany's Attitude', pp. 93–4.

86. Zeman, *Break-Up of the Habsburg Empire*, pp. 241–4.

87. Lederer, *Yugoslavia*, pp. 56–7.

88. ibid., p. 59; Lowry, *Armistice*, pp. 106–12.

89. Lowry, *Armistice*, pp. 113–14; Hamard, 'Quand la victoire', p. 41.

90. Deist, 'Politik der Seekriegsleitung', pp. 342–6.

91. Woodward, *Collapse of Power*, pp. 130–31.

92. Deist, 'Politik der Seekriegsleitung', p. 346.

93. ibid., pp. 352–5.

94. ibid., pp. 357–61; Woodward, *Collapse of Power*, p. 9.

95. Horn (ed.), *War, Mutiny and Revolution*, pp. 11–14; Deist, 'Politik der Seekriegsleitung', p. 363.

96. Rudin, *Armistice*, pp. 248–55.

97. Mehrens memo on food supply in 1918, BA-MA W-10/50434.

98. Stevenson (ed.), *British Documents*, Vol. 12, p. 375.

99. Offer, *First World War: Agrarian Interpretation*, p. 54; Winter, 'Surviving the War', p. 517.

100. Stevenson (ed.), *British Documents*, Vol. 12, pp. 360–61.

101. Summary of DCGS' reports on public opinion, 3 August 1918, BA-MA PH2/62.; Stevenson (ed.), *British Documents*, Vol. 12, pp. 316–17.

102. Schwabe, *Woodrow Wilson*, pp. 100, 104–6.

103. Horn, *Mutiny on the High Seas*, pp. 231–2, 251–2.

104. Kluge, *Die Deutsche Revolution*, p. 54.

105. Ziemann, 'Enttäuschte Erwartung', pp. 177–81.

106. Michell, *Revolution in Bavaria*, pp. 94–106.

107. Schwabe, *Woodrow Wilson*, p. 111; French, 'Had We Known', p. 85.

108. Rudin, *Armistice*, pp. 263–4, 321; Lowry, *Armistice*, pp. 156–60.

109. Ryder, *German Revolution*, pp. 149–53.

110. Rudin, *Armistice*, p. 362; Ashton, 'Hanging the Kaiser'.

111. Ryder, *German Revolution*, pp. 160–63.

112. Cecil and Liddle (eds.), *At the Eleventh Hour*.

113. Crosby, *Epidemic and Peace*, pp, 55–8, 124–5.

114. Lowry, *Armistice*, p. 160.

Chapter 18

1. Hobsbawm, *Age of Extremes*; pp. 4–6; Winter and Baggett, *1914–18*, p. 10.

2. Fussell, *Great War and Modern Memory*, p. 18.

3. Detailed notes will not be provided for this section, but for general accounts of the peace conference, see Sharp, *Versailles Settlement*; Boemeke *et al.* (eds.), *Treaty of Versailles*.

4. Fullest accounts of relations with the Bolsheviks are in Mayer, *Politics and Diplomacy*; Thompson, *Russia, Bolshevism, and the Versailles Peace*.

5. On Japan at the conference, see Fifield, *Woodrow Wilson and the Far East*; Kajima, *Diplomacy of Japan*; Nish, *Japanese Foreign Policy*; Dickinson, *War and National Reinvention*.

6. On Italy, see Albrecht-Carrié, *Italy*; Burgwyn, *Legend of the Mutilated Victory*.

7. Bessell, *Germany*, p. 228.

8. Keynes, *Economic Consequences*; Nicolson, *Peacemaking* ; Baker, *Woodrow Wilson*.

9. Seymour (ed.), *Intimate Papers of Colonel House*, Vol. 4, p. 291; Baker, *Woodrow Wilson*, Vol. 1, pp. 184–5.

10. Schulze, *Woodrow Wilson*, p. 398.

11. Tillman, *Anglo-American Relations*, for this section.

12. Egerton, *Great Britain and ... League of Nations*, chs. 5, 6.

13. Tillman, *Anglo-American Relations*, ch. 3; Louis, *Lost Colonies*, ch. 4.

14. Willis, *Prologue to Nuremberg*, ch. 5.

15. Marder, *Dreadnought*, Vol. 5, chs 9, 10.

16. On reparations, see Burnett (ed.), *Reparation*; Trachtenberg , *Reparation and World Politics*, ch. 2; Kent, *Spoils of War*, ch. 2; Marks, in Boemeke (ed.), *Treaty of Versailles*, ch. 14.

17. Artaud, 'Le Gouvernement américain'.

18. Marks, *Ebbing of European Ascendancy*, p. 94.

19. For more detail on the territorial negotiations, see Schuker, in Boemeke (ed.), *Treaty of Versailles*, ch. 12; Stevenson, *French War Aims*, ch. 6; McDougall, *France's Rhineland Diplomacy*, ch. 2; Nelson, *Land and Power*, pp 192–281.

20. Riddell, *Intimate Diary*, p. 43.

21. Jaffe, *Decision to Disarm Germany*.

22. Lentin, 'Treaty that Never Was'.

23. Perman, *Shaping of the Czechoslovak State*, chs. 6, 7; Lundgreen-Nielsen, *Polish Problem*.

24. On the Germans at the conference, see Luckau, *German Delegation*; Schwabe, *Woodrow Wilson*.

25. Low, 'Soviet Hungarian Republic', is the best account.

26. Dawn, 'Influence of T. E. Lawrence', pp. 83–5.

27. Andrew and Kanya-Forstner, *France Overseas*, ch. 8; Dockrill and Goold, *Peace without Promise*, ch. 4.

28. Generally, Dockrill and Goold, *Peace without Promise*, ch. 5, and Helmreich, *Paris to Sèvres*.

29. Taylor, *Origins of the Second World War*, p. 54.

30. Carroll, B. E. *Design for Total War: Arms and Economics in the Third Reich* (The Hague and Paris, 1968) p. 184.

31. Watson, *Clemenceau*, pp. 352, 361.

Chapter 19

1. 'Preliminary Draft of Theses on the National and Colonial Question', in J. E. Connor (ed.), *Lenin on Politics and Revolution* (Indianopolis and New York, 1968), p. 316.

2. Generally, Goldstein and Maurer (eds.), *Washington Conference*.

3. Trachtenberg, *Reparation and World Politics*, pp. 194–5.

4. Goldstein and Maurer (eds.), *Washington Conference*, ch. 6.

5. Howard, M. E. *The Continental Commitment: the Dilemmas of British Defence Policy in the Era of the Two World Wars* (London, 1972), pp. 182–5.

6. Orde, A. *Great Britain and International Security, 1920–1926* (London, 1978).

7. Stevenson, 'Belgium, Luxemburg, and the Defence of Western Europe'.

8. Generally on post-war French policy, see Adamthwaite, A. *Grandeur and Misery: France's Bid for Power in Europe, 1914–1940* (London, 1995).

9. Poidevin and Bariéty, *Les Relations franco-allemandes*, ch. 15.

10. Willis, *Prologue to Nuremberg*, chs. 7, 8.

11. For general accounts, see Heinemann, *Die Verdrängte Niederlage*; Herwig, 'Clio Deceived'.

12. Herwig, 'Clio Deceived', pp. 99–107, 120.

13. Heinemann, *Die Verdrängte Niederlage*, pp. 220–21.

14. Ferguson, *Pity of War*, p. 411; Marks, in Boemeke *et al.* (ed.), *Treaty of Versailles*, pp. 359–67.

15. For recent appraisals of French motives, see Keiger, *Raymond Poincaré*; Adamthwaite, *Grandeur and Misery*.

16. Schuker, *End of French Predominance*, provides the fullest account.

17. Pegg, C. H. *The Evolution of the European Idea, 1914–1932* (Chapel Hill and London, 1983); Lipgens, 'Europäische Einigungsidee'.

18. See Maier, *Recasting Bourgeois Europe*, for an overview.

19. Kanya-Forstner, 'War, Imperialism, and Decolonization', pp. 231ff.

20. Marks, *Ebbing of European Ascendancy*, p. 141.

21. Andrew and Kanya-Forstner, *France Overseas*, ch. 10.

22. Clayton in Brown and Louis (eds.), *Oxford History of the British Empire*, Vol. 4, pp. 281–6.

23. Darwin, J., *Britain, Egypt, and the Middle East: Imperial Policy in the Aftermath of War, 1918–1922* (London, 1981).

24. Tomlinson, 'India and the British Empire, 1880–1935', *Indian Economic and Social History Review* (1975).

25. In general on the post-war crisis, Porter, *Lion's Share*, pp. 247–57; Jeffery, K. *The British Army and the Crisis of Empire, 1918–1922* (Manchester, 1984).

26. Waites, 'Effect of the First World War'.

27. Bowley, *Some Economic Consequences*, ch. 6.

28. Tawney, R. H. 'The Abolition of Economic Controls, 1918–1921', *Economic History Review* (1943).

29. Kennedy, *Over Here*, pp. 270–83.

30. ibid, p. 284.

31. Pugh, 'Politicians and the Woman's Vote', p. 364.

32. Macmillan, *Housewife or Harlot?*, pp. 178–9.

33. Braybon, *Women Workers*, p. 221.

34. Hynes, *A War Remembered*, p. 361.

35. Robert, 'Women and Work in France', p. 264.

36. Daniel, *War from Within*, chs. 1, 6.

37. Thom, 'Women and Work', p. 315.

38. Braybon, *Women Workers*, ch. 7.

39. Kennedy, *Over Here*, pp. 284–7.

40. Pedersen, *Family, Dependence*, pp. 128–30.

41. Ferguson, *Pity of War*, p. 337.

42. Aldcroft, *From Versailles to Wall Street*, p. 17.

43. Gregory, *Silence of Memory*, p. 43.

44. Dyer, *Missing of the Somme*, p. 7; cf. Barbusse, *Under Fire*, pp. 328–9.

45. Mosse, *Fallen Soldiers*, p. 81.

46. Prost, 'Verdun', p. 123.

47. Bushaway, 'Name upon Name', p. 140.

48. Winter, *Sites of Memory*, p. 107.

49. Inglis, 'War Memorials', p. 9.

50. Winter, *Sites of Memory*, pp. 26–7.

51. Borg, *War Memorials*, ch. 7.

52. ibid., p. 89.

53. Sherman, 'Bodies and Names', pp. 748ff.

54. Inglis, 'World War One Memorials in Australia', p. 58.

55. For Australia: ibid, p. 55. For France, Prost, 'Monuments to the Dead', p. 307.

56. http://www/nzhistory.net.nz/Gallery/Anzac/memorial.

57. Prost, 'Monuments to the Dead', pp. 310–16.

58. Borg, *War Memorials*, ch. 6.

59. Jeffery, *Ireland and the Great War*, pp. 114–18.

60. Kavanagh, 'Museum as Memorial'.

61. http://www.awm.gov.au/aboutus/origins.htm.

62. Gregory, *Silence of Memory*, pp. 24–8; Mosse, *Fallen Soldiers*, pp. 95–6.

63. Andrews, *Anzac Illusion*, pp. 84–91; Jeffery, *Ireland and the Great War*, pp. 55–9.

64. Prost, 'Monuments to the Dead', pp. 317–25.

65. Gregory, *Silence of Memory*, pp. 34–7.

66. Dalisson, 'La Célébration du 11 novembre'.

67. Prost, 'Monuments to the Dead', pp. 325–30.

68. Winter, *Sites of Memory*, p. 115.

69. Inglis, 'World War One Memorials in Australia', p. 54.

70. Prost, *In the Wake of War*, pp. 43–4.

71. Gregory, *Silence of Memory*, p. 52.

72. Bourke, *Dismembering the Male*, p. 33.

73. Leed, *No Man's Land*, p. 183.

74. ibid, ch. 6; Ward, 'Intelligence Surveillance', p. 188.

75. Bessell, *Germany after the First World War*, p. 257; Bourke, *Dismembering the Male*, pp. 22–3; Englander, 'Demobilmachung', p. 209.

76. Leese, 'Problems Returning Home', p. 1055.

77. Englander, 'Demobilmachung', p. 196.

78. Ward, 'Intelligence Surveillance', pp. 180–81.

79. Wootton, *Politics of Influence*, p. 109.

80. Townshend, C. *The British Campaign in Ireland: the Development of Political and Military Policies* (Oxford, 1975), p. 46.

81. Prost, *In the Wake of War*, p. 43.

82. ibid, ch.2; Prost, 'Demobilmachung', pp. 178ff.

83. Kennedy, *Over Here*, p. 363; Rémond, 'Les Anciens Combattants', pp. 281–8.

84. Dickinson, *War and National Reinvention*, p. 1.

85. Merridale, *Night of Stone*, pp. 125–6.

86. Dogliani, 'Monuments aux morts'.

87. Morgan, P. *Italian Fascism, 1919–1945* (Basingstoke, 1995), pp. 13–16.

88. Bessell, *Germany after the First World War*, p. 141.

89. ibid, p. 229.

90. Inglis, 'War Memorials', p. 11.

91. Mosse, *Fallen Soldiers*, pp. 87–90.

92. ibid, p. 97; Showalter, *Tannenberg*, p. 348.

93. Mosse, *Fallen Soldiers*, p. 83; Whalen, *Bitter Wounds*, p. 32.

94. Hüppauf, 'Langemarck, Verdun', pp. 77–81.

95. Cohen, *War Come Home*, p. 194.

96. Elliott, '*Kriegervereine*'.

97. Whalen, *Bitter Wounds*, chs. 7–12.

98. Informative is Diehl, J. M. *Paramilitary Politics in Weimar Germany* (Bloomington, IN, and London, 1977).

99. ibid., and Berghahn, V. R., *Der Stahlhelm: Bund der Frontsoldaten, 1918–1935* (Düsseldorf, 1966).

Chapter 20

1. Bowley, *Some Economic Consequences*, p. 87.

2. Feinstein *et al.*, *European Economy*, p. 60.

3. ibid., pp, 9, 13.

4. Aldcroft, *From Versailles to Wall Street*, p. 22.

5. Strikwerda, 'Troubled Origins', p. 1110.

6. Aldcroft, *From Versailles to Wall Street*, pp. 47–9.

7. Feinstein *et al.*, *European Economy*, pp. 71–6.

8. Hardach, *First World War*, p. 153.

9. Schuker, *End of French Predominance*, chs. 2–4.

10. Ferguson, 'Constraints and Room for Manoeuvre'.

11. Thomson, D. *Europe since Napoleon* (London, 1966) p. 649.

12. Schuker, S. A. *American "Reparations" to Germany, 1919–33: Implications for the Third-World Debt Crisis* (Princeton, NJ, 1988).

13. Bennett, E. W. *Germany and the Diplomacy of the Financial Crisis, 1931* (Cambridge, MA, 1962).

14. On these points, see Eichengreen, *Golden Fetters*.

15. Childers, T. *The Nazi Voter: the Social Foundation of Nazism in Germany, 1919–1933* (Chapel Hill, 1983) .

16. Eberle, *World War I and the Weimar Artists*.

17. Bessell, *Germany after the First World War*, p. 228.

18. Fischer, *Stormtroopers,* p. 25.

19. Eksteins, *Rites of Spring*, ch. 9.

20. ibid., p. 410.

21. Wette, 'Kellogg to Hitler'.

22. Eksteins, *Rites of Spring*, p. 397.

23. Lipgens, 'Europäische Einigungsidee'.

24. Cf. Wette, 'Kellogg to Hitler'.

25. Diehl, 'Victors or Victims?', p. 700.

26. Fischer, *Stormtroopers*, pp. 49–54.

27. Kershaw, *Hitler*, Vol. 1, p. 331.

28. ibid., p. 100.

29. ibid., p. 87.

30. Diehl, 'Victors or Victims?', p. 726; Verhey, *Spirit of 1914*, pp. 223–8.

31. Adamthwaite, A. P. (ed.), *The Making of the Second World War* (London, 1979), doc. 4.

32. Boyce, R. and Robertson, E. M. (eds.), *Paths to War: New Essays on the Origins of the Second World War* (Basingstoke and London, 1989), ch. 2.

33. Barnhart, M. *Japan Prepares for Total War: the Search for Economic Security, 1919–1941* (Ithaca, NY, 1987).

34. Prost, 'Verdun', pp. 129–30.

35. Prost, *In the Wake of War*, ch. 2.

36. Rémond, 'Les Anciens Combattants', pp. 272–5.

37. Prost, *In the Wake of War*, p. 42.

38. ibid., pp. 75–6.

39. Gorman, 'Anciens Combattants and Appeasement'.

40. Becker, *Great War and the French People*, p. 327.

41. Young, R. J. *In Command of France: French Foreign Policy and Military Planning, 1933–1940* (Cambridge and London, 1978).

42. Schuker, S. A. 'France and the Remilitarization of the Rhineland, 1936', *French Historical Studies* (1986); Emmerson, J. T. *The Rhineland Crisis, 7 March 1936: a Study in Multilateral Diplomacy* (London, 1977).

43. Kennedy, *Over Here*, pp. 222–30.

44. Divine, *Illusion of Neutrality*, ch. 3.

45. ibid., p. 181.

46. Grieves, 'C. E. Montague'.

47. Bracco, *Merchants of Hope*, pp. 1, 12.

48. Beckett, *Great War*, p. 445.

49. Gregory, *Silence of Memory*, pp. 35–40.

50. Bracco, *Merchants of Hope*, ch. 5.

51. ibid., p. 145.

52. Cruickshank, *Variations on Catastrophe*, p. 40.

53. Bracco, *Merchants of Hope*, p. 15.

54. Bond, *Unquiet Western Front*, pp. 46–9.

55. Liddell Hart, *History of the First World War*, p. 460.

56. Hynes, *War Remembered*, pp. 446–8.

57. Fussell, *Great War and Modern Memory*, chs 6, 7.

58. Eksteins, *Rites of Spring*, pp. 394–5.

59. Dyer, *Missing of the Somme*, p. 104.

60. Hynes, *War Remembered*, ch. 20.

61. Gregory, *Silence of Memory*, pp. 118–19.

62. ibid., pp. 121–3.

63. Wootton, *Politics of Influence*, p. 119.

64. Stannage, C. T. 'The East Fulham By-election', *Historical Journal* (1971).

65. Adamthwaite, A. P. 'The British Government and the Media, 1938–9', *Journal of Contemporary History* (1983).

66. Thorne, C. *The Approach of War, 1938–1939* (London, 1967), p. 220.

67. Gregory, *Silence of Memory*, pp. 174–6.

68. Messerschmidt, M., in Millett and Murray (eds.), *Military Effectiveness*, Vol. 3, pp. 244–6.

69. Weinberg, G. L. *A World at Arms: a Global History of the Second World War* (Cambridge and New York, 1994), pp. 86, 235.

70. Messerschmidt, M. in Millett and Murray (eds.), *Military Effectiveness*, Vol. 3, p. 227.

71. Weinberg, G. L. *World at Arms*, pp. 108–9.

72. ibid., pp. 21–2.

73. Kershaw, *Hitler*, Vol. 2, pp. 298–9, 542.

74. ibid., p. 563.

75. Burchardt, 'Impact of the War Economy', pp. 59–62.

76. Kershaw, *Hitler*, Vol. 2, pp. 657–8.

77. ibid., Vol. 1, p. 244.

78. Weinberg, *World at Arms*, pp. 83, 153, 262.

79. ibid., pp. 41, 50.

80. ibid., pp. 66, 72.

81. Beckett, *Great War*, p. 279.

82. Weinberg, *World at Arms*, p. 70.

83. ibid., p. 439.

84. May, E. R. *"Lessons" of the Past: the Use and Misuse of History in American Foreign Policy* (London, 1973), ch. 1.

85. Weinberg, *World at Arms*, pp. 612, 660–61; Beckett, *Great War*, pp. 462–3.

Chapter 21

1. May, E. R. and Zelikow, P. (eds.), *The Kennedy Tapes: Inside the White House during the Cuban Missile Crisis* (Cambridge, MA, and London, 1997), p. 1; Turner, *Origins*, p. 118.

2. Bourke, *Dismembering the Male*, p. 33.

3. Sheffield, 'Shadow of the Sun', p. 35.

4. French, in Bond (ed.), *First World War and British Military History*, ch. 3.

5. Bell, *History of the Blockade*.

6. Zuber, 'Schlieffen Plan Reconsidered', pp. 262–7.

7. Bosworth, R. J. B., *Rethinking Auschwitz and Hiroshima: History Writing and the Second World War, 1945–1990* (London, 1993).

8. Lee (ed.), *Outbreak of the First World War*, p. 64.

9. For overviews of the Fischer debate, see Langdon, *July 1914*; Mombauer, *Origins of the First World War*.

10. Fischer, ' Twenty-Five Years Later', p. 24.

11. ibid., p. 223.

12. Gallagher, J. and Robinson, R. *Africa and the Victorians* (London and Basingstoke, 1961).

13. Taylor, A. J. P. *The Origins of the Second World War* (Harmondsworth, 1964).

14. Alperowitz, G. *Atomic Diplomacy: Hiroshima and Potsdam* (New York, 1965).

15. Mayer, *Political Origins*; *Politics and Diplomacy*; Levin, *Woodrow Wilson*.

16. Miller *et al.* (eds.), *Military Strategy*.

17. Bond, *Unquiet Western Front*, ch. 3.

18. ibid., p. 68.

19. Cf. Bond and Cave (eds.), *Haig: a Reappraisal*.

20. Audouin-Rouzeau and Becker, *14–18*, p. 11.; cf. Faulks, S., *Birdsong* (London, 1995).

21. On archaeology, see the special issue of *14/18*, No. 2 (1999); cf. Saunders, *Trench Art*.

22. Among the key works: Fussell, *Great War and Modern Memory*; Leed, *No Man's Land*; Eksteins, *Rites of Spring*; Mosse, *Fallen Soldiers*; Hynes, *War Remembered*; Winter, *Sites of Memory*.

23. Williams, R. *Keywords: a Vocabulary of Culture and Society* (London, 1976), p. 87.

24. Silver, *Esprit de Corps*. ch. 6.

25. Winter, *Sites of Memory*, ch. 4; Harvey, *Muse of Fire*, p. 172.

26. Bogacz, 'Tyranny of Words'; Winter, *Sites of Memory*, ch. 8.

27. Barbusse, *Under Fire*, pp. 340–41.

28. On Germany and the East, see Liulevicius, *War Land*, pp. 163–5.

29. Strachan, *First World War: To Arms*, chs 10, 11, and Ferguson, *Pity of War*, chs. 9, 11, are important recent exceptions.

30. Ferguson, *Pity of War*, ch. 13.

31. Of which they were well aware: Burkhardt, J., 'Kriegsgrund Geschichte? 1870, 1813, 1756 – Historische Argumente und Orientierungen bei Ausbruch des Ersten Weltkrieges', in Burkhardt, J. *et al.*, *Lange und Kurze Wege in den Ersten Weltkrieg* (Munich, 1996), pp. 36–53.

INDEX